Jonathan Fenby is a former editor of t̶̶̶̶̶̶̶̶̶̶̶̶
the *South China Morning Post* in Hong Kon̶
handover of the colony from Britain to China ̶i̶n̶ ̶1̶9̶9̶7̶.̶
for *The Economist*, the *Guardian*, the *Independent* and Reuters. His previous
books include *On the Brink: The Trouble With France*, *Generalissimo: Chiang
Kai-shek and the China He Lost* and *The Sinking of the Lancastria*. He lives
in London.

Further praise for *Alliance*

'Fenby, a superb researcher . . . tells a compelling story brilliantly well and
lets the most important facts shape his conclusions. We had leaders and
they led, didn't they? No, we had titans when we needed them, and they
found a way to tower over the smoking ruins the Nazis left behind'
Observer

'[A] quite brilliant narrative . . . Effectively this is a blow-by-blow reporter's
account of how three very different and remarkable war leaders led us to
one of history's most crucial victories – the defeat of Hitler's fascism . . .
Fenby combines the reporter's skill in narrative and flavour as well as
dedicated research in welding together in highly readable form a
formidable assembly of memoirs from the great and good of the Second
World War'
Tribune

'Fenby, a former editor of the *Observer* . . . has trawled through countless
records and reminiscences to make the conferences in Casablanca,
Potsdam and Yalta come vividly alive'
Catholic Herald

'*Alliance* is an engaging book and, particularly for readers wishing to
discover this rewarding subject, as comprehensive and entertaining a place
to start as any'
BBC History Magazine

ALLIANCE

The Inside Story of
How Roosevelt, Stalin and Churchill
Won One War and Began Another

JONATHAN FENBY

**POCKET
BOOKS**

LONDON • SYDNEY • NEW YORK • TORONTO

First published in Great Britain by Simon & Schuster UK Ltd, 2006
This edition first published by Pocket Books, 2008
An imprint of Simon & Schuster UK Ltd
A CBS COMPANY

Copyright © 2006 by Jonathan Fenby

Picture credits
The publishers have made every effort to contact those holding rights in material
reproduced in this work. Where this has not been possible the publishers will be happy to
hear from anyone who recognises their material.

Getty Images: 1, 2, 3, 5, 6, 8, 9, 11, 14, 17, 18, 19, 20, 21,
23, 24, 26, 28, 29, 31, 32, 33, 34, 37, 38, 39, 40, 41
Corbis: 7, 12, 25
Popperfoto: 10, 15
Clark Kerr journal, British Archives, Foreign
and Commonwealth Office: 13
Empics: 16
Imperial War Museum: 22

The right of Jonathan Fenby to be identified as author of this work
has been asserted in accordance with sections 77 and 78 of
the Copyright, Designs and Patents Act, 1988.

3 5 7 9 10 8 6 4

Simon & Schuster UK Ltd
Africa House
64–78 Kingsway
London WC2B 6AH

www.simonsays.co.uk

Simon & Schuster Australia
Sydney

A CIP catalogue record for this book is available
from the British Library.

ISBN: 978-1-4165-2282-9

Typeset in Baskerville by M Rules
Printed and bound in Great Britain by
Cox & Wyman Ltd, Reading, Berks

To Alice and Max
With love

CONTENTS

Acknowledgements   xi

Prologue
Dinner in Teheran, 29 November 1943   1

1   Buffalo, Bear and Donkey   5

2   The First Summit
    Placentia Bay, Newfoundland, 9–12 August 1941   31

3   Uncle Joe
    Moscow, September 1941   64

4   World War
    Washington, Chequers, Moscow, Chungking, Rome, Berlin,
    6–12 December 1941   77

5   Four Men Talking
    Moscow, Washington, London, 9 December 1941–14 January 1942   85

6   Undecided
    London, Washington, January–April 1942   103

7   The Commissar Calls
    Moscow, London, Washington, May–June 1942   117

8   Torch Song
    Hyde Park, Chungking, Washington, London, June–July 1942   126

9   Midnight in Moscow
    Moscow, August 1942   138

10 As Time Goes By
    North Africa, Moscow, Casablanca, October 1942–January 1943 158

11 Stormy Weather
    Washington, Moscow, London, Hyde Park, Quebec,
    January–August 1943   181

12 Russian Overture
    Moscow, October 1943   203

13 Pyramid
    Cairo, 21–26 November 1943   213

14 Over the Rainbow
    Teheran, 28 November–1 December 1943   226

15 Ill Wind
    Cairo, Tunis, Carthage, Washington, December 1943–May 1944 263

16 Triumph and Tragedy
    London, Washington, Normandy, Paris, Warsaw,
    June–September 1944   284

17 The Plan
    Washington, Quebec, 12–16 September 1944   302

18 Percentage Points
    Moscow, 9–18 October 1944   322

19 Red Blues
    London, Washington, Moscow, Athens, Paris, Chungking,
    November 1944–January 1945   336

20 Yalta
Malta, the Crimea, 30 January–15 February 1945   349

21 Death at the Springs
Suez Canal, Washington, London, Warm Springs,
13 February–12 April 1945   385

22 Journey's End
Potsdam, 17 July–2 August 1945   401

Source Notes   421
Bibliography   445
Index   453

ACKNOWLEDGEMENTS

The idea for this book came out of a lunchtime conversation at an Italian restaurant with Andrew Gordon and Christopher Sinclair-Stevenson. So my first thanks must be to them for that, and for nurturing the project in the following couple of years.

Among those who helped along the way I would like particularly to thank André Villeneuve who was a constant source of support, ideas and material, and who came up with many useful comments after reading the draft manuscript. He and Lisa were, once again, hospitable hosts during the writing, as were Annie Besnier, Peter Graham, Sarah and Andrew Burns, Brian Oatley and the Harthill group, including the style guru. Jim and Susan Verna showed generosity out of measure in New York while I was researching in American archives, as did Anne and David Cripps.

Luba Vinogradova came up with Soviet material. Warren Kimball offered advice from his great fund of knowledge at the start of the project, and David Carlton and Odd Arne Westad contributed most useful pointers. Allen Packwood guided me at the Churchill Archive in Cambridge, and provided Foreign Office documents. Rob Hale gave medical insights. I am extremely grateful to Robert Harvey for providing me with invaluable source material and for his stimulating observations. Michael Barratt Brown came up with an unknown story of Churchill as a penicillin guinea-pig.

As always, I am greatly indebted to the staffs of libraries and archives consulted, notably those at the Roosevelt Library in Hyde Park for the papers of both the President and Harry Hopkins, the Oral History Archives at the Truman Library and Columbia University, and, in Britain, the Public Record Office, the British Library, the London Library, the Imperial War Museum, the Foreign Office, the Churchill Archives in Cambridge and the Cabinet Rooms and Churchill Museum in London. The voluminous documents in the Foreign Relations of the United States (FRUS) collection were an invaluable source. I have also made much use of memoirs, diaries and other papers of participants in the wartime alliance, as recorded in the notes; as with previous books, I am only grateful that so many people kept such full, and often frank, private records.

Edwina Barstow was an excellent and cheerfully patient editor, Martin Bryant applied his eagle-eye to the copy, and Sue Gard polished the proofs. Sara Arguden was as helpful as ever, and Alexander urged me on from the other side of the world. My greatest debt, as always, is to Renée, whose support, editing, comments – and patience – make her the perfect partner in every way.

PROLOGUE

Dinner in Teheran

29 NOVEMBER 1943

'The only thing worse than allies is not having allies.'

WINSTON CHURCHILL[1]

IT WAS JOSEF STALIN who sparked the row. Throughout the lavish dinner the Soviet leader had been needling Winston Churchill. His tone was heavily jocular, his sniping relentless. 'Marshal Stalin lost no opportunity to get in a dig at Mr Churchill,' the official American account recorded. 'Almost every remark that he addressed to the Prime Minister contained some sharp edge.'[2]

The Prime Minister refused to be provoked even when Stalin referred to the long-standing British reservation about launching a frontal attack on Nazi forces in France as suggesting a secret affection for Germany – perhaps he even wanted to offer the enemy 'a soft peace'. Just because the Russians were simple people, the dictator said, it was a mistake to believe they were blind.

As the waiters brought hors d'oeuvres, borsch, fish, meat, salads, and fruit, wine, Russian champagne, vodka and brandy, Franklin Roosevelt said little, sitting in his wheelchair and confining himself to commonplaces and clichés. Later, he told his Cabinet he found Stalin's teasing of Churchill very amusing. His interpreter, Charles Bohlen, on the other hand, described the atmosphere as 'acrid'.

Neither the President nor the Prime Minister was well that evening as they dined in the Soviet Legation in Teheran, Iran, on the second day of their first tripartite summit meeting with Stalin. Both had made long journeys, by sea and air. An attack of acute indigestion had forced Roosevelt to leave a dinner he had hosted the previous night – according to Churchill, he turned green during the first course of the Soviet banquet. Though a closely guarded secret, Roosevelt's blood pressure was dangerously high, and he had both anaemia and signs of pulmonary disease; four months later, he would be diagnosed as having hypertension, hypertensive heart disease, congestive heart failure and chronic bronchitis. Churchill was suffering from a cold and a sore throat, but his main problem was that the pressure of the war was taking its toll on a man in his late sixties who, however indomitable, was highly unfit and overweight, drank too much and suffered from heart trouble; at times, he was simply 'too ill and too tired to think straight'.[3]

Since becoming Prime Minister in 1940, Churchill had banked everything on winning Roosevelt's friendship. The Anglo-American alliance was at the heart of his 'system'. On his way to Teheran, he had told his daughter, tears in his eyes: 'I love that man.' No man had studied his mistress more closely than he had studied the President, he once remarked.

But the object of his affections had come to the summit in Teheran with one prime aim – to win Stalin's confidence. To achieve this, Roosevelt was intent on not doing anything that could lead the super-suspicious dictator to think that he was siding with the British. If that meant snubbing the Prime Minister, so be it. He had ducked requests from London for preparatory meetings to discuss the Western agenda. In Teheran, he moved into quarters at the Soviet Legation and met Stalin bilaterally, while refusing even to lunch alone with Churchill. Naturally, this did not go down well with the representatives of the country which had stood alone against Hitler in 1940 when Moscow was allied with Berlin. At one point, Churchill recounted to his entourage the unlikely tale that Roosevelt's closest aide had described the President as 'inept'.

As Churchill began to drink brandy at the end of the dinner, Roosevelt's main aide, Harry Hopkins, raised a toast to the Soviet army. In his reply, Stalin got on to the subject of the German General Staff. At least fifty thousand senior officers should be summarily shot, he said, possibly a hundred thousand.

At that, Churchill snapped. Red in the face, he got to his feet to pace the room. The idea was contrary to the British sense of justice, he said. No one, Nazi or not, should be dealt with summarily by a firing squad. 'The British Parliament and public will never tolerate mass executions,' he thundered.

'Fifty thousand must be shot,' Stalin repeated, throwing in a fresh aside about the British leader's 'pro-German' sympathies.

'I would rather be taken out into the garden here and now and be shot myself than sully my own and my country's honour by such infamy,' Churchill fired back.

Stalin's eyes twinkled as the words were interpreted to him. He turned to ask Roosevelt, who had been suppressing a smile, what he thought. The President tried to use banter to calm things down. 'Perhaps we can say that, instead of summarily executing fifty thousand war criminals, we should settle on a smaller number,' he said. 'Perhaps, forty-nine thousand.'

The Americans and Russians round the table laughed. Anthony Eden, the British Foreign Secretary, signalled to Churchill that it was all a joke. But Stalin would not drop the matter and asked each of the guests for comments. Adopting a diplomatic approach, Eden said more study was needed. The Americans noted that victory in Europe was still some way off. Then came the turn of Roosevelt's son, Elliott, an air intelligence officer who accompanied his father to summits.

The young man, who may have been affected by the champagne poured out for him, said he hoped many hundreds of thousands of Nazis would be taken care of. Stalin walked over to fling an arm round his shoulder. When the dictator proposed a toast to Elliott's health, Churchill confronted the young American.

'Are you interested in damaging relations between the Allies?' he growled. 'Do you know what you are saying? How can you dare say such a thing?'*

---

* In his memoirs Churchill calls Elliott's version of the conversation 'highly coloured and extremely misleading'. Elliott, a controversial figure who was accused of trading on his father's name in later life, was anti-British and pro-Soviet. His memoirs contain a number of episodes which reflect poorly on Churchill. He says he based them on wartime logs, contemporary notes and memory. Though they have been criticised, there seems no objective reason to discount them – the leading historian Warren Kimball judges that his recollections of conversations with FDR, which will be cited later, 'captured the flavour of his father's arguments'. For his part, Churchill, as we will see, was prone to shape his version of history for his purposes. After the brush at Teheran, invitations to Elliott to visit Churchill's country home when in England dried up.

Then, Churchill stalked from the room. It was the first time for many years anybody had walked out on Stalin. Standing in the gloom of an adjoining chamber, the Prime Minister felt hands on his back. Turning, he saw Stalin and Vyacheslav Molotov, the Foreign Minister. Both grinned broadly. It was only play, they said. They had not been serious.

The British leader was not convinced; he could remember how, when allied with Hitler, the Soviets had slaughtered 22,000 Polish prisoners of war. He had little doubt about Stalin's ability to deliver on his threat. But he knew that any rupture with the Kremlin would be deeply damaging for the war effort. So he returned to the table, and recorded that the rest of the evening 'passed pleasantly'. According to Archibald Clark Kerr, British ambassador to Moscow, the two protagonists ended by standing with their hands on one another's shoulders, looking into each other's eyes.

Still, the portents were plain. Later that night, Harry Hopkins went to the British Embassy to urge Churchill not to delay the invasion of France, for which Stalin had been pressing since 1941. The Americans and Russians had made up their minds, the aide said. The British should fall into line. After he had left, Churchill talked mournfully to members of his delegation about future wars to come, and said that British bombers would be able to reach Moscow. On his return to London, he depicted himself as having been 'with the great Russian bear on one side of me, with paws outstretched, and on the other side was the great American buffalo, and between the two sat the poor little English donkey who was the only one . . . who knew the right way home.'[4]

As well as fighting the war on three continents, the three Allied leaders were framing the peace to follow at meetings such as the Teheran summit. Unlike the First World War, the second war did not conclude with a single peace conference to decide the future of the world. Rather, the process was drawn out over five years, marked by personal encounters, agreements and clashes, which brought out deep differences that had to be submerged to achieve victory, but would surface again as the new world approached. Six decades on, the story of how the Big Three made their alliance, managed it, and then found themselves unable to preserve it is a supreme object lesson in international politics at the highest level.

1

★ ★ ★

Buffalo, Bear and Donkey

'The structure of world peace . . . must be a peace which rests on
the cooperative effort of the whole world.'

FRANKLIN ROOSEVELT[1]

THE THREE MEN WHO WON the biggest conflict in human history and
shaped the globe for half a century thereafter knew from the start that they
could not afford to fail. Once total war had been forced on them by the
Axis powers, no compromise was possible. Victory over 'Hitler's gang' in
Europe and the Imperial Way in Asia had to be total. 'If they want a war of
extermination, they shall have one,' said Stalin.[2]

The conflict was more wide-ranging than the First World War, stretching
across the Atlantic and Pacific, through Europe and Asia, from the Arctic
to North Africa. More than 50 million people died in 2,174 days of fighting
between 1939 and 1945 – many others perished earlier in Japan's invasion
of China that began in 1931. Mass killing of civilians was taken for granted
on all sides – half the 36 million people who died in Europe were non-
combatants, and Chinese civilian casualties amounted to many millions.
Though there was bitter and bloody hand-to-hand fighting, death and
destruction was often inflicted by men who did not see those they killed
from the air or by artillery. Hiroshima and Nagasaki were logical extensions
of the London Blitz. As well as the cost in human lives, the conflict brought
enormous material destruction; North America escaped damage but much
of Germany and Japan was levelled while a quarter of the Soviet Union's
capital assets were destroyed.

Old continuities were broken for ever as two very different powers with competing philosophies came to dominate the globe, and Britain found itself on a path of decline in the twilight of European empires. Big government, already installed in the Soviet Union after the Bolshevik Revolution, became a fact of life in the other two Allied nations. In America, wartime spending enabled recovery from the Great Depression while Roosevelt crafted the imperial presidency; as Supreme Court Justice Robert Jackson noted, the strengthening of the executive was inevitable because 'the President is the only officer who represents the whole nation.'[3]

Mass mobilisation, mechanisation, state power and technology were exerted on a massive scale in all three Allied countries. Huge industrial programmes churned out tanks, guns, warships and planes – 50,000 people worked on the biggest single American project, the B-29 Superfortress, which cost a million dollars apiece. Though Britain had re-built its economy after the Great Slump, the draining of its resources once the conflict became global would show just how enormous the strain of total war was. Generals managed the deployment of unprecedented forces across the globe. As the historian Eric Hobsbawm notes, it 'was the largest enterprise hitherto known to man.'[4] From the conflict came the United Nations, the Bretton Woods financial system, the International Monetary Fund, the World Bank and a host of other institutions. The struggle for supremacy produced great technological leaps, whether it was the atom bomb, or the work done by code breakers that spurred on the computer.

Social and democratic conditions, including the employment of women, were altered for ever in some nations. Despite the mass murders by Stalin and Mao, which were greater numerically, Hitler's genocide of the Jews left the century with its most powerful symbol of man's inhumanity to man, and led to the creation of the state of Israel. Japan's sweeping victories in 1941–2 fatally undermined the status of the colonial powers in Asia while the trauma of the third German–French war acted as a powerful catalyst for the European Union.

To a far greater extent than in the 1914–18 conflict, the Second World War was a personal struggle between towering figures – Roosevelt, Stalin, Churchill, and Hitler, with a supporting cast that included Benito Mussolini, Chiang Kai-shek and Mao Zedong, General Tojo and Emperor Hirohito, Charles de Gaulle and European governments-in-exile in London. These men had a vital influence, not just on the course of the war but on the world which emerged from it. There was a constant stream of correspondence between the White House and Downing Street, and, to a lesser extent, with the Kremlin. In contrast with the previous conflict, during which European governments changed during the fighting, Stalin and the Democrats ruled throughout the war and Churchill was Prime Minister from May 1940 to the late summer of 1945.

Though Churchill liked to draw a parallel with the coalition led against France by his ancestor the Duke of Marlborough, the association of powers was hardly a classic alliance. The geometry of its meetings was variable. Roosevelt and Churchill had eleven bilateral conferences. Churchill crossed the Atlantic six times and went twice to Moscow. Roosevelt and Stalin never visited either of the other Allied nations. The three leaders gathered as a group only twice – at Teheran, close to the Soviet southern border, and then at Yalta in the Crimea, both locations chosen for the convenience of Stalin who hated flying.

American and British troops never fought in any major fashion alongside the Red Army. While the Western Allies waged a two-hemisphere war for three and a half years, Stalin maintained a non-aggression pact with Tokyo until the summer of 1945 to ward off the threat of Japan opening a second front in Siberia. Nor was there any meaningful joint staff planning between the Western Allies and Moscow. The Kremlin was extremely parsimonious with information, and suspicious of the West – Stalin thought warnings of Hitler's attack on the Soviet Union in 1941 were a plot to embroil him in war with Berlin. As the conflict went on, one of his main sources was the Soviet spy apparatus in London and Washington.[5]

Though Washington and London began detailed military discussions well before the United States went to war, meetings of the Combined Chiefs of Staff were marked by fundamental strategic differences. While the US Chiefs wanted a single hammer blow against the Germans in Northern France, the British favoured an indirect approach against the 'soft underbelly' of North Africa and Southern Europe. Arguments between the British and the American Chiefs became so violent at times that junior officers had to be asked to leave the room so as not to witness the verbal brawls. China was a particular source of discord. Roosevelt counted on it becoming one of the four post-war global policemen, but Churchill had no time for a country he dismissed as 'four hundred million pigtails', which could only divert much-needed aid from Britain – and he was sure Stalin shared his distaste for 'all this rot about China as a great power'.[6]

During 120 days of meetings Roosevelt and Churchill developed genuinely warm feelings for one another – if the President ever had genuinely warm feelings for anybody. Before Pearl Harbor, Roosevelt had manoeuvred his way towards giving aid to Britain while America was still technically neutral, seeing the island as a first line of defence. After Pearl Harbor, the Western alliance grew in scope and depth, giving Churchill hope for a post-war partnership of English-speaking peoples that would sustain his nation. But, by the summer of 1943, Roosevelt was seeking bilateral contacts with Stalin, specifically designed to cut out the British.[7]

This was symptomatic of an alliance which was far more complex and contradictory than it appeared, particularly from the gloss put on it by Churchill in his memoirs. The differences between the policies of the three countries was inescapable. While Washington refused to contemplate any territorial deals as the war was going on, Stalin had set out his stall at the end of 1941, with a demand for a deep security zone in which governments would follow Moscow's bidding. Three years later, Churchill proposed a mathematical division of interests in eastern and central Europe between Britain and the USSR.

Roosevelt wanted an end to colonies; Churchill declared that he had not been appointed to oversee the liquidation of the British Empire. Roosevelt pressed the Prime Minister to talk to Indian nationalists; at one point Churchill threatened to resign if the President did not let up. Washington linked the spread of democracy with free trade on American lines; the British clung to the preferential system of their imperial domain. The interpretation of high-sounding references to democracy and self-determination in summit statements were so far apart that discussion was usually pointless. As the war progressed, Churchill became increasingly concerned about Soviet power, especially since Roosevelt proposed to withdraw US troops from Europe two years after victory. But the American was confident of being able to handle Stalin, and foresaw the day when the US and Soviet systems would converge as accommodation on his part was met by accommodation from Moscow and a new world was born to parallel the New Deal at home.[8]

Above all, there was never any question in Roosevelt's mind of America confronting the USSR militarily. Always the acute domestic politician, he knew that, having won one war, the United States would not be in a mood to fight another for far-away countries. He had to present a rosy picture of the future to voters and looked to a new period in world history in which the United States, working through a global body, would be able to solve differences between the others because 'we're big, and we're strong, and we're self-sufficient', as Elliott recorded his father saying. 'The United States will have to lead. Lead and use our good offices always to conciliate . . . America is the only great power that can make peace in the world stick.'[9]

When their alliance came into being Churchill was sixty-seven, Stalin sixty-two and Roosevelt fifty-nine. All were men of long experience. Churchill first entered government in London in 1905, and went on to hold a string of senior posts before going into the political wilderness in the 1930s. Roosevelt had been Under Secretary for the Navy during the First World War; he had then served as Governor of New York and run as a vice-presidential candidate before winning the White House in 1932. Stalin's revolutionary career stretched back to the early part of the century, after which he had clawed his way to the top of the Soviet system, besting his rival Leon Trotsky, and consolidating his power with the great purges of the 1930s.

None of the three was physically imposing. Churchill and Stalin were short and stout. Despite his leonine head and erect bearing, Roosevelt was confined to a wheelchair by the polio he suffered in 1921, though his insistence on standing to deliver speeches and the discretion of the media meant that most Americans had no idea how badly he had been affected. But they became three of the greatest figures on earth, Churchill with V-signs and cigars, Roosevelt with his jaunty air, Stalin all implacable resolve. As believers in the 'great men theory' of history, all were masters at making themselves legends in their own lifetimes.

While economic and industrial strength were essential for victory, and two of them had to take account of their electorates, this was a time when the decisions of a tiny group of individuals made all the difference. The centre of power was wherever they were. As President, Roosevelt was Commander-in-Chief. After the German attack, Stalin became Commissar of Defence and Supreme Commander of Soviet Forces as well as General Secretary of the Central Committee of the Communist Party and Chairman of the Council of People's Commissars. Churchill insisted on being Minister of Defence as well as Prime Minister.

They were all adroit users of the media, knowing the importance of their personalities, and their relationship with their countries. Despite having a few trusted cronies, they were solitary figures. Roosevelt had a close confidant in Harry Hopkins, and worked through Averell Harriman, the multi-millionaire envoy to London and Moscow. Churchill had the mercurial Canadian imperialist Lord Beaverbrook, and Stalin could count on Molotov, his right-hand man in the purges and the mass repression of the peasantry. But, though Churchill recognised the authority of the War Cabinet, none of the three was able to share the enormous pressure.

Stalin treated ambassadors as lackeys. Personal summits and 1,700 written messages between Churchill and Roosevelt made envoys largely redundant. The President, who had always operated through his kitchen cabinet, took his Secretary of State to only one wartime conference, and told Churchill he could 'handle Stalin better than either your Foreign Office or my State Department. Stalin . . . he thinks he likes me better, and I hope he will continue to do so.' If he could dine with Stalin once a week, Churchill remarked in 1944, 'there would be no trouble at all.'[10]

The first of the Big Three to be at war with Hitler was the most outgoing and emotional of the trio, though he could show subtle skills in alliance politics. While making much of having had an American mother, the aristocratic Winston Leonard Spencer Churchill was a pure product of British tradition; he was, as has been said, half American but all British. His belief in the importance of the Empire and the genius of the Anglo-Saxon people was unrestrained – at a lunch in Washington in 1943, he told Vice President Henry Wallace simply: 'We are superior.'[11]

It is a commonplace to say that, had the war not brought Churchill to Downing Street in May 1940, he would have gone down in history as a political shooting star which had crashed to earth. What was extraordinary was how, having achieved the prime ministership, and despite his vagaries, he got so many things right. Aspects of his wartime performance have come in for robust criticism, but he usually had no choice, as in pursuing the relationship with the United States. Nor can his country's post-war global decline be laid at his door, while the notion that Britain could have withdrawn from the war and somehow preserved its imperial position is, at best, a fantasy that takes no account of the realities of the time.

Churchill's weakness was that he had little interest in social and economic matters. Invaluable as his personality was in rallying his country with defiant optimism in 1940, his traditional mindset consigned him to try to deny the looming future. In the words of the broadcaster Edward Murrow he 'mobilised the English language and sent it into battle', but, with it, went an anachronistic approach that was profoundly out of tune with the changes the war was bringing. He was, as he himself said, 'a child of the Victorian era', not a man for the new world after victory.[12]

In pursuit of his mission, he was brave to the point of recklessness, as if convinced that he was indestructible now that he had met his moment of destiny. His bodyguard reckoned that he had twenty brushes with death during his life including assassination attempts by an Indian nationalist, a German sniper team and a bomb-planting group of Greek Communists. During the war, he made hazardous flights over thousands of miles, and voyages across seas harbouring German submarines. On one occasion, flying to Moscow in a converted bomber, he dozed with a lighted cigar in his hand while oxygen hissed out round him. In London, he climbed to the roof in Whitehall to watch the Blitz, and, in 1944, it took a royal veto to prevent him witnessing the D-Day landing from a warship off France. 'There have been few cases in history where the courage of one man has been so important to the future of the world,' wrote his faithful military aide 'Pug' Ismay.[13]

Churchill was, as he put it himself, 'a war person'. His wife said she never thought of the time after the conflict because 'I think Winston will die when it is over.' He lived for action, a restless, constant font of invention, pushing subordinates to the limit as he fired off notes on everything from grand strategy to prison conditions. He would never give up. 'KBO' – Keep Buggering On – was his watchword. He had a hundred ideas a day, 'and about four of them are good', Roosevelt remarked. His obsessions and refusal to delegate drove those around him to distraction. His manner could become overbearing – in the summer of 1941, his wife warned him that a devoted member of his entourage had told her he risked being 'generally disliked by colleagues and subordinates'. She, too, had noticed that – 'you are not so kind as you used to be'.[14]

But nobody doubted that he was invaluable to the war effort. 'Energy, rather than wisdom, practical judgment or vision, was his supreme qualification,' recalled Deputy Prime Minister Clement Attlee. Throughout, he remained respectful of parliamentary democracy. He was 'able to impose his will upon his countrymen, and enjoy a Periclean reign, precisely because he appeared to them larger and nobler than life and lifted them to an abnormal height in a moment of crisis,' judged the philosopher Isaiah Berlin. 'It was Churchill's unique and unforgettable achievement that he created this necessary illusion within the framework of a free system without destroying it or even twisting it.'[15]

'I have known finer and greater characters, wiser philosophers, more understanding personalities, but no greater man,' Dwight Eisenhower wrote. Still, the conflicting emotions he aroused were well summed up in the diary of the Chief of the Imperial General Staff, Alan Brooke (ennobled as Lord Alanbrooke), who found the Prime Minister a 'public menace at playing at strategy', but also 'quite the most wonderful man I have ever met'. The world, the general added, 'should never know, and never suspect, the feet of clay of that otherwise superhuman being . . . Never have I admired and despised a man simultaneously to the same extent. Never have such opposite extremes been combined in the same human being.'[16]

Churchill had the longest political career of the Big Three, dating back to his election at the age of twenty-six in 1900 as a Conservative MP. Having switched to the Liberals, he became Under Secretary for the Colonies in 1905, and a full member of the Cabinet as President of the Board of Trade three years later. First Lord of the Admiralty in the First World War, he had to resign after the disastrous expedition to the Dardanelles, an example of the indirect strategic approach through daring ventures that would always appeal to him. After serving at the front in France, he returned to government as Minister for Munitions, and then switched back to the Conservatives to become Chancellor of the Exchequer after the war.[17]

Having teetered on the edge of bankruptcy in the 1929 crash, he spent much of the 1930s in the political wilderness, isolating himself by his vehemence over India, backing Edward VIII in the Abdication Crisis of 1936–7, and sounding warnings about the rise of Hitler's Germany. Regarded as unreliable by his fellow Conservatives and deeply reactionary by the Labour Party, his career was saved by the outbreak of war in 1939 when he was recalled to the Admiralty. But his future was still not assured, and the Americans had their doubts. Visiting Britain in 1940, Roosevelt's favourite diplomat, Under Secretary of State Sumner Welles, dismissed him as a third- or fourth-rater and 'a drunken sot'. Though the President wrote to Churchill in 1939 to propose that they should start a personal correspondence, he told the American ambassador that he retained a dislike for the British politician. He also recalled that, at their only meeting at the end of the First World War, Churchill had struck him as 'a stinker', 'generally obnoxious' and 'one of the few men in public life who has been rude to me'.[18]

If Churchill was quintessentially English, Franklin Delano Roosevelt epitomised the United States. 'The Americans seemed to him the best of all possible people,' his Labor Secretary, Frances Perkins, wrote. 'Not necessarily the smartest or the most powerful . . . but the ones with more goodness per thousand of population than in other countries.' If the virtues of Americanism could be propagated around the globe, he believed, the outcome could only be beneficial for all.[19]

A patrician populist whose fifth cousin, Theodore, had preceded him to the presidency, Roosevelt found his destiny in leading the United States out of the Great Depression. Triumphing over his polio, he exuded the spirit of his age, with an infectious self-confidence and a mastery of public relations that perfectly fitted a land increasingly moulded by popular entertainment. Invariably positive in public, he believed that any problem could be solved. Encountering difficulty, his motto was: 'We can. We will. We must.'[20]

At the outbreak of war in 1939 he recognised the need to resist Fascism but was cautious about involving America. In this he echoed a nation which, while wanting to stop aggression, shrank from sending troops abroad. Once Pearl Harbor had solved that dilemma, the man described by the historian Warren Kimball as a 'subtle democratic imperialist' knew that – so long as he could keep it engaged in the world – the USA would be the indispensable global player and the 'receiver' of the fading European imperium.[21]

Roosevelt's dozen years in the White House marked him as a supreme political animal, starting with the blizzard of anti-Depression measures in his first hundred days. Manipulator and visionary, he played public opinion like a fly fisherman, leading his catch towards his ultimate net. He balanced coalitions of interest groups and took personal credit for everything that was to the administration's benefit, always weighing the electoral implications.

He was the only one of the Big Three to have gone to university, a man who escaped definition, a supreme egoist, who trusted only himself. He could be without scruple when it served his purpose, dropping long-time associates and switching tack with no compunction. 'Roosevelt's objectives were almost always benign, but his techniques, while bloodless, were not always much less ruthless, devious, and cynical than Hitler's or Stalin's,' according to Conrad Black, his generally admiring biographer. The President was 'almost an egomaniac in his belief in his own wisdom,' judged Eisenhower.[22]

Following his train of thought could be as confusing as the clutter on top of his desk, for both the British and his own Cabinet. He set subordinates to compete with one another, trusting that creative friction would spur them on. Churchill was moved to note the almost complete lack of businesslike methods on the American side, while Anthony Eden described a presidential statement on India as 'a terrifying commentary on the likely Roosevelt contribution to the peace, a meandering amateurishness lit by discursive flashes'.[23]

Impatient with detail, contemptuous of bureaucrats, the President was the ultimate big picture man. Secretary of War Henry Stimson likened dealing with the President to 'chasing a vagrant beam of sunshine round a vacant room'. Henry Morgenthau, the Treasury Secretary, called him 'a man of bewildering complexity of moods and motives'. The playwright Robert Sherwood, who served in the wartime administration, found his character 'was contradictory to a bewildering degree'. When he said 'yes, yes' to you, his wife noted, it did not mean that he agreed, but that he had heard what you had said. 'I understand each individual word that he says,' Albert Einstein remarked. 'But when he is finished I don't know. Does he mean yes or does he mean no?'

Unlike Churchill, who had travelled widely and knew the world, the President was overwhelmingly a domestic politician. After childhood visits to Germany, he only made two trips to Europe as an adult, both before entering the White House. 'A deeper knowledge of history and certainly a better understanding of the reactions of foreign peoples would have been useful to the President,' wrote the American diplomat Charles Bohlen, who interpreted at the Big Three summits and acted as liaison between the White House and State Department.[24]

Behind his relaxed exterior, Roosevelt was a control freak who kept his emotions on a very tight rein. Nobody was allowed to get close – he divided his correspondence among various secretaries, which meant none had a complete file. Deeply secretive behind his apparently open public face, he compared himself to a cat – 'I strike and then I relax.' Or he likened himself to a juggler who never let one hand know what the other was doing. He was not, Bohlen decided, a likeable man. After meeting him at a wartime summit, Joseph Stilwell, the chief US adviser to China, described him as 'a guy who greets me as "Joe" and reaches for a knife when I turn around.' When his secretary Marguerite 'Missy' Le Hand suffered a severe stroke in 1941, those around him were struck by how cool Roosevelt appeared – 'all President', devoid of human feelings, as one put it. Harry Truman would recall him as 'the coldest man I ever met. He didn't give a damn personally for me or you or anyone else in the world, as far as I could see.'[25]

Though Roosevelt was America's Commander-in-Chief, he left military matters to the Chiefs of Staff, making major strategic decisions but not interfering in the way Churchill did. From early on in the war, his mind was more on what would follow the conflict. Sure his country would emerge victorious, he accepted that global power meant global responsibility – indeed he relished it; the greater the first, the greater the second.

He held to a few specifics – the need for America's international involvement, the creation of the United Nations to safeguard the peace, the need to forge an understanding with the Soviet Union, anti-imperialism and free trade. When events clashed with these, he appeared at a loss as to how to proceed, trusting that he could use his skills to smooth his way through. While his political and social orientations were progressive, he was an island to himself. Not only did nobody know what he was aiming at; they could not tell if he himself had a clear idea. The danger was that, after so many years of success, Roosevelt would fall into wishful thinking based on faith in his persuasive powers, his intuition, and his reading of others, which bore less and less connection with reality.

Having risen from humble roots as the son of a drunken cobbler in Georgia, Josef Stalin, born Iosif Vissarionovich Dzhugashvili, studied at a Russian Orthodox seminary before becoming a revolutionary, robbing banks to fund the cause. Like Ivan the Terrible, when he achieved power he believed himself beyond human laws, and fostered a climate of denunciation in which tens of millions were killed or reduced to virtual slavery. His reserved, self-assured toughness – his assumed name meant 'Man of Steel' – contrasted sharply with the feline President and the mercurial Prime Minister, and deeply impressed Westerners. Anthony

Eden wrote that, if he had to pick a team to negotiate at a conference, the Georgian would have been his first choice.

'There was a composed, collected strength,' the American diplomat George Kennan wrote, while Harry Hopkins saw 'a perfectly coordinated machine, an intelligent machine' who looked like 'a football coach's dream of a tackle'. The American ambassador to Moscow, Averell Harriman, while calling him 'a murderous tyrant', found the dictator 'better informed than Roosevelt, more realistic than Churchill . . . the most effective of the war leaders.'[26]

At the first summit in Teheran he showed his cool confidence when Churchill spoke of a dream in which he became ruler of the world. By prearrangement, Roosevelt chipped in to say that he had dreamed of becoming master of the universe. 'And what did you dream of, Marshal Stalin?' the President asked. 'I dreamt that I did not confirm either of you,' replied Stalin casually.[27]

His understated style and his readiness to let the other leaders do most of the talking made an impression on the President and Prime Minister – he might be a dictator, but he was in striking contrast to Hitler and Mussolini. As late as 1944, Churchill could still call him 'that great and good man'. Roosevelt's son James recalled his father saying: 'Uncle Joe is smarter and stronger than I thought he was.' As for the principal foe, Adolf Hitler called Stalin 'one of the greatest living human beings'. The Soviet leader, he said, 'towered above the democratic figures of the Anglo-Saxon powers'.

The dictator was, as Churchill wrote to Roosevelt, never 'actuated by anything but cold-blooded self-interest and total disdain of our lives and fortunes'. It made no difference to him whether he allied with the Nazis or the democracies, so long as it suited his purpose. Given his own track record of betrayals and plots, he was bound to be highly suspicious of the intentions of others, but he was also the farthest-sighted of the Big Three in pursuing long-term aims, using the enormous bloodshed on the eastern front to consolidate his demands. He believed in the application of force on as large a scale as possible, and recognised from the start that the winners in the war would impose their systems on territories they conquered. Though he made much of frontier claims, what mattered most was that governments should be installed which would serve his aims after fighting ended.

Stocky, with a pockmarked face, honey-coloured eyes, discoloured teeth, dark hair flecked with grey, and a moustache that was twirled at the ends, Stalin was wary of public appearances, and tried to hide his double chin when caught by the camera. Soon after the Nazi invasion, a Russian interpreter was shocked by his limp handshake and tired face. In 1942, the British ambassador Archibald Clark Kerr saw 'a little slim, bent, grey man with a large head and immense white hands'. The Yugoslav Communist Milovan Djilas noted that his arms and legs seemed too long for his torso, and that he had a large paunch. Visitors noticed how the dictator avoided looking them straight in the face, gazing at their shoulders instead. His uniforms always seemed a bit too big for him.[28]

Stalin had even less experience of the world than Roosevelt. As a young agitator, he had made brief trips London, Finland and Poland. After that, he did not leave the Soviet Union until going to Teheran in 1943. Having grown accustomed to dominating the Kremlin, he set about doing the same with his allies, knowing how much they needed the Red Army to defeat Hitler – an American position paper in 1943 identified the USSR as the decisive factor in the war, and argued that 'every effort must be made to obtain her friendship'. Stalin wasted no words as he pursued his ends with laconic determination. An American general compared him to his six-year-old son who had insisted on ordering a rich dish in a restaurant despite repeated attempts by his parents to get him to change his mind – and who got his way in the end.[29]

Caught out by Hitler's attack in 1941, Stalin reinvented himself as the father of the nation leading a Great Patriotic War – the Russians, he observed, needed 'a Tsar they can worship'. For the West, he became 'Uncle Joe'. The 9 million casualties suffered by the Red Army gave him a moral advantage over the Western Allies, particularly before they launched the second front in France in the summer of 1944. Though Churchill resented being lectured by a man who had signed the 1939 pact with Hitler and stood by as Britain fought alone, Stalin could count on plenty of support from public opinion in the West.

When it came to evaluating his Western Allies, Stalin was haunted by the suspicion that they – Churchill in particular – were out to do a deal with Hitler to destroy the Soviet Union. He summed up the difference between the Prime Minister and President with a remark that 'Churchill would pick your pocket for a kopeck. Roosevelt is not like that. He dips in his hand only for bigger coins.' During his first summit with the other leaders, Stalin said he was sure of being able to guess what Roosevelt would do, but remarked of Churchill, 'you can expect absolutely anything from him'. He subsequently described the Prime Minister as 'a powerful and cunning politician [who] behaved as a gentleman and achieved a lot.' Churchill was, he added in 1950, 'the strongest personality in the capitalist world'.[30]

Molotov, his long-time lieutenant, categorised Roosevelt as a wily imperialist 'who would grab anyone by the throat' and Churchill as a man who had tried to use the Soviet Union for his own ends, only to be used by Moscow. But Stalin appears to have gained a certain feeling for Roosevelt; after calling on him at the Yalta summit in 1945, he remarked to Molotov: 'Why did nature have to punish him so? Is he any worse than other people?'[31]

As early as 1934, Stalin had spoken to the British writer H.G. Wells of the President's 'outstanding personal qualities . . . his initiative, courage and determination'. 'Undoubtedly,' he added, 'Roosevelt stands out as one of the strongest figures among all the captains of the contemporary capitalist world.' In later years, he privately called him 'a great statesman, a clever, educated, far-sighted and liberal leader who prolonged the life of capitalism'. A year after Roosevelt's death, as the shadows of the Cold War deepened, the Communist party newspaper *Pravda* hailed him as 'a friend of the Soviet Union . . . an enemy of isolationism as well as of those non-isolationists who considered and still consider today that United States policy mostly consists of power politics with the aim of establishing the domination of American interests throughout the world.'

As noted by George Kennan, whose scepticism about the Kremlin contrasted with the rosy view in Washington, Roosevelt had never met a man like Stalin before: 'I don't think FDR was capable of conceiving of a man of such profound iniquity, coupled with enormous strategic cleverness.' So deep was Roosevelt's wish to see what he wanted in the dictator that, after the Yalta summit, which clinched Stalin's achievement of his aims in eastern and central Europe, the President expressed the belief that, during the Georgian's days in the seminary, 'something entered into his nature of the way in which a Christian gentleman should behave'.[32]

The differences between the three men were evident in everything from their appearance to their working methods and habits. Roosevelt wore elegantly cut, double-breasted suits. Stalin contented himself with plain brown uniforms until he took to donning a marshal's outfit later in the war. Churchill's wide array of outfits ranged from military uniforms to sober black suits to one-piece, woollen 'siren suits' zipped from waist to neck like a baby's garment, and known to those around him as 'the Teddy Bear'.[33]

While Stalin was economical with words, Roosevelt frequently rambled and Churchill talked endlessly – at one summit, he lost his voice after perorating at dinner from eight in the evening to one-thirty the next morning. Methodical, hard working and with an insatiable appetite for detail, Stalin kept his large desk in his vaulted, wood-panelled office in the 'Little Corner' of the Kremlin free of clutter. Alongside, Lenin's death mask lay under a glass case. Outside sat his secretary and a senior secret police guard. As a master bureaucrat, he insisted on holding people to what he said they had agreed to, asking simple but piercing questions that cut through the Prime Minister's verbiage and the President's obfuscation.

Roosevelt preferred to talk rather than putting things in writing, permitting himself maximum deniability and a fog of laconic evasiveness. He could be extraordinarily informal – before sending Harry Hopkins on a mission to London, he tore a page from *National Geographic,* and drew a line to indicate where American warships would take over patrols from the Royal Navy in the western Atlantic. He signed important documents he had not read properly, and then expressed surprise at being confronted with them.

In the White House, he sat at a wooden desk presented to his predecessor, Herbert Hoover, by the Grand Rapids Furniture Association. Behind him were two furled American flags and dark blue and green curtains. To one side, stood a large globe. On the desk surface were a blotter, a jug of iced water, a double pen stand, an inkpot, a circular match stand, medicine bottles, a clock set in a bronze model of a ship's steering wheel, books and several model animals, including Democratic donkeys – one made of hazelnuts. The head of the Radio Corporation of America gave him a recording device with a microphone in a desk lamp, activated by a switch in a drawer, but he did not use it much. On the floor was a food dish, a red ball and a model of a foot for his dog, Fala.[34]

Churchill's work was organised by the British civil service. As if knowing of the danger of his flights of rhetoric, he ordered that none of his instructions were to be regarded as valid unless put in writing. He liked to have everything set down, dictating to secretaries even when lying in the bath. He could become disruptive as he insisted on going on speaking, and refused to listen to the reasoning of others. Clement Attlee described Cabinet meetings as 'not good for business, but . . . great fun.'[35]

When Downing Street was badly damaged by an air raid in October 1940, the Prime Minister moved into a nearby annexe. During air raids, he descended with ministers, commanders and aides to the War Rooms installed in an underground complex where he had his own small dining room and bedroom-cum-office, maps on the walls, a green quilt on the bed and an electric fire for warmth. Along the corridor were bedrooms for Attlee and Eden, a typing pool, rooms for the War Cabinet and Chiefs of Staff to meet and a set of map rooms from which the progress of the war was plotted.[36]

As a rule, Roosevelt stopped work before dinner, going to bed at a reasonable hour, often poring over his $80,000 stamp collection. He could become grumpy if kept up. In contrast, Stalin was nocturnal, sleeping till 11 a.m., and then working into the early hours, either at his dacha or in his Kremlin office. Churchill also went on well past midnight, fuelled by his determination to do everything possible in the time available to him, sometimes working eighteen-hour days before finally going to bed after drinking a bowl of consommé. When he had no morning appointments, he would read papers in bed in a multi-coloured dressing gown or a pink kimono over the silk vest in which he slept, one of his cats lying on the counterpane. After lunch, he would take a lengthy siesta, which gave him the energy to pore over battlefield reports and hold forth to guests into the early hours. After a Churchill visit, Roosevelt had to recuperate with ten hours' sleep for several nights. Much as he admired the British leader, Roosevelt's doctor, Vice Admiral Ross McIntire, came to regard him as 'Public Enemy Number One'.[37]

Except when in a rage, Churchill took a generally benevolent view of his fellow human beings, although he could maintain long-term dislikes – as well as likes – that skewed his judgement. On the other hand, Stalin derived pleasure from humiliating those around him, enjoying forcing subordinates to totter to their feet and exchange toasts when much drunk. Roosevelt's humour could contain 'viciousness', the Labor Secretary Frances Perkins noted. 'Sadistic magisterial puppeteering was one of the handicapped President's chief amusements (and possible psychological displacement),' according to Conrad Black. Averell Harriman judged that 'he always enjoyed other people's discomfort. I think it is fair to say that it never bothered him very much whether other people were unhappy.'[38]

The President was the only one of the three to take exercise. He boasted that this gave his upper body the physique of a boxer. On one visit by Churchill, he invited him to feel his biceps. His doctor said Roosevelt could out-swim any of his staff in the White House pool. He was a keen ocean fisherman, once landing a 235-pound shark after an hour-long battle – quite an achievement for a man who had no strength in his legs with which to brace himself. In contrast, Stalin disliked swimming and merely had a paddling pool at one of his country houses. He also played billiards. For recreation Churchill painted and built brick walls at his country home.[39]

Roosevelt liked to mix cocktails, often weak Martinis or whisky sours, but at times a gin and grapefruit mixture described by Hopkins as 'vile'. 'How they drink!' a Foreign Office official, Oliver Harvey, remarked in his diary during a visit to Washington in 1943 . . .'Incessant cocktails and highballs at all hours of the day between meals.' Churchill, who disliked cocktails, sometimes had to sip the concoctions out of politeness; on other occasions, when Roosevelt served a transparent gin drink, he would go to the toilet with his glass, replace the liquid with water and return to the room pretending to be drinking with enjoyment.[40]

The food and table service at the White House were notoriously poor. The *New York Times* sympathised with the President for having to lunch on salt fish four days in a row. Complaints got nowhere as his wife and the cook insisted that plain fare was fitting at a time of national difficulties. In contrast, while the people of Moscow queued for thin rations, Stalin presided over multi-course Kremlin banquets, at which endless courses of caviar, meat and fish were washed down with vodka, wine, cognac and champagne. Usually, the dictator did not drink much himself, filling his toasting glass with wine, but encouraging those around him to knock back the hard stuff. 'Apparently, he considered it a useful way to test people so that they would speak more frankly,' Molotov recalled. On the rare occasions that Stalin got drunk, he played records of Russian folk tunes and comic Georgian songs. When not presiding at lavish Kremlin banquets, he enjoyed raw white salmon from Siberia, with garlic and vodka.[41]

Though sensitive to the national mood, as rationing cut the availability of food in Britain, Churchill indulged himself in private or on state occasions – he was, after all, a man who had once said he had simple tastes, being 'quite easily satisfied with the best of everything'. On one occasion, his doctor found him breakfasting in bed on grouse and an omelette. A dinner on a wartime voyage consisted of oysters, consommé, turbot, turkey, melon and ice, cheese, fruits and petits fours.

Churchill consumed weak whisky and sodas from mid-morning, with vintage wines and Pol Roger champagne at meals, followed by brandy. Arriving at the British Embassy in Cairo at 7.30 a.m., he asked for white wine at breakfast, having already downed two Scotchs. At a summit, after sipping iced water he remarked that it tasted funny. 'Of course it does,' replied Hopkins, 'it's got no whisky in it.' Alexander Cadogan, the senior civil servant at the Foreign Office, noted in his diary how the Prime Minister 'armed up after his third glass of brandy' at a lunch at the Spanish Embassy. Returning from his first meeting with Roosevelt, Churchill capped lunch on the train with a Benedictine liqueur. Ten minutes later, he called for a cognac. The waiter reminded him he had just had Benedictine. 'I know,' Churchill said. 'I want some brandy to clean it up.'[42]

To defend him from charges of alcoholism, his colleagues insisted that his drinks were much watered, that he nursed them, and that he was never under their influence – a verdict contradicted by both Alan Brooke and the Soviet ambassador, among others. The writer and academic C.P. Snow quipped that Churchill was no alcoholic because no alcoholic could drink that much. His own remarks about drink being his servant, not his master, and how he had got more out of alcohol than it had taken out of him, have a defensive air about them. At the least, the amount he consumed on a daily basis, from late morning to the early hours, made him alcohol-dependent – or, as put by the British historian Richard Holmes, he went in for 'maintenance drinking'. That may not have affected his conduct of the war, but it could only add to the strain on a man already living beyond his physical means.

When it came to families, the Roosevelts had a daughter and five sons, one of whom died in infancy; the Churchills three daughters and a hard-drinking son; Stalin a daughter and two sons. Roosevelt's three sons served in the US forces; Churchill's son undertook intelligence work and fought with partisans in Yugoslavia; one of Stalin's sons killed himself in a German prison camp – his father refused an exchange for a Nazi officer – while the other was a drunken exhibitionist who served in the air force. The wife of Churchill's son had a wartime affair with Averell Harriman, and one of the

Prime Minister's daughters was divorced from her entertainer husband, of whom her father disapproved. The Roosevelt children chalked up a total of nineteen spouses. As a schoolgirl, Stalin's daughter, Svetlana, fell passionately for a Russian-Jewish writer, whom her father sent to a labour camp.

The Georgian was twice a widower. His first wife had died of illness in 1909; his second committed suicide in 1932 following a drunken dinner during which he flirted with an actress. Stalin said she had died as an enemy: Svetlana never forgave him for her mother's death. He then had a string of mistresses before retreating into what has been called 'austere sterility' as though it was too dangerous to let anybody get close to him.[43]

Roosevelt married Eleanor in 1905; she was a power in her own right, a liberal champion who used ground-breaking broadcasts, press conferences and a newspaper column to press the New Deal and internationalism. She constantly rolled out ideas on a plethora of subjects – during the war she suggested filling planes with bees, wasps and hornets which would be dropped on German and Japanese troops. Her earnestness could become rather too much for her husband, who erected a protective shield against her lobbying and instead liked to shoot the breeze with cronies like Hopkins.[44]

Roosevelt had an affair with his wife's social secretary Lucy Mercer during the First World War, and his son Elliott described his blue-eyed secretary 'Missy' Le Hand as his 'other wife', sitting in his arms on his lap in state rooms, though how far the relationship went sexually remains open to doubt.[45]

Eleanor discovered the Mercer affair when her husband returned ill from a trip to Europe at the end of the First World War and was taken to hospital. Unpacking his cases, Eleanor found letters from Mercer which made matters plain. She offered a divorce, which he declined. He promised to break off the relationship, but then took it up again, though Mercer had married a wealthy widower with six children called Winthrop Rutherfurd. He sent a limousine to drive her to a front row seat at his first inauguration, and resumed the relationship after Rutherfurd died in 1941, taking her with him to the health resort at Warm Springs in Georgia where he sought treatment for his polio. His cousin Margaret 'Daisy' Suckley called Lucy 'a lovely person, full of charm, and with beauty of character shining in her face; no wonder the Pres. has cherished her friendship all these years.'[46]

Eleanor had found life at the family estate at Hyde Park in Upper New York State cramped by the presence of her strong-willed, matriarchal mother-in-law, and lived her own existence for much of the time when in Washington. She had affairs with young men, including her bodyguard, and then with a woman reporter who moved into the White House. The Roosevelts 'treated each other with devotion, respect and tolerance', the biographer James MacGregor Burns wrote. Their son, James, called the relationship 'an armed truce' marked by her bitterness.[47]

On the other hand, Churchill's marriage was a source of strength to a man who seemed to the outside world to need nobody. Clementine, who had married the rising politician in 1908, subordinated her needs and those of their family to him, though she could become overwhelmed by his pace and often had to worry about the cost of his lavish lifestyle. In the mid-1930s, she appears to have developed a fondness for a handsome young art dealer she met on a five-month sea trip to Indonesia while her husband stayed at home. She described it in French as '*une vraie connaissance de ville d'eau*' ('a true spa town relationship'), implying a flirtation but no more. Churchill called Clementine his 'cat'; for her, he was her 'pug'. His biographer Roy Jenkins judged that he was 'probably the least dangerously sexed politician on either side of the Atlantic since Pitt the Younger' in the early 1800s.

None of the Big Three had much contact with everyday life. Roosevelt lived in the presidential bubble and Stalin was a distant figure, shuttling between his dachas and the Kremlin. Churchill's wife told his doctor that her husband 'knows nothing of the life of ordinary people' – he never took a bus, and on the one occasion he entered the London underground he could not find his way out and had to be rescued.[48]

Each enjoyed his country home. The President loved the family estate at Hyde Park in Dutchess County above the wide Hudson River, with its long lawns, bordered by pines, spruces, maple and magnolias outside the town of Poughkeepsie. He extended its grounds and expanded the residence where he had been born to thirty-five rooms; the third floor was given over to the children. Redecoration turned it from the Victorian country house bequeathed by his father into a colonial revival mansion, with white portico, green shutters, naval cannon by the door, and a dark, crowded interior full of heavy furniture, Chinese porcelain, stuffed birds, bookcases and sea paintings. To cope with the President's infirmity, ramps were fitted between the rooms; at the back of the entrance hall was a lift that ran on ropes. Roosevelt took pleasure in showing the grounds to eminent guests – George VI was served hot dogs on a picnic. Churchill slept in the Pink Room on the first floor, chatted to Roosevelt in the small snuggery, with an early television set in one corner,* and sat up late in the spacious, book-lined drawing room expounding on the war and the world.

After his re-election in 1940, Roosevelt had a special small stone house built for himself in Dutch colonial style in the grounds to 'escape the mob'. It was designed to be wheelchair-friendly, and he sat on the porch in a rocking chair looking out at what his cousin Margaret Suckley called the 'nicest hill in Dutchess County'. In 1944, he wrote to a friend: 'All that is within me cries out to go back to my home on the Hudson River.' He also sought rest and relaxation in a newly built government hideaway in the Catoctin Mountains, then called Shangri-La (later known as Camp David), or at Warm Springs in Georgia.[49]

Stalin grew ~~roses~~ in his native Georgia, and stayed in dachas outside Moscow – he wandered disconsolately around one after news of Hitler's attack was brought to him. His main retreat was set amid lawns beside a fir wood behind barbed wire and a closely guarded green stockade fifteen feet high. Clumps of raspberries dotted the grass. There were strawberry beds, fountains and a tank filled with goldfish. Lifts led to a ten-roomed air-raid shelter with marble walls and wood panels set in concrete eighty feet underground, with a kitchen, and, in case the electricity failed, heavy silver candelabras.[50]

As well as his official country residence at Chequers in Buckinghamshire, Churchill made use of Ditchley Park outside Oxford, a classic Georgian mansion dating from 1722 which had been restored in the 1930s. His own country home, at Chartwell in Kent, which he bought in 1922, was a fine brick building with a rose garden set in a shallow valley where he sought solace when bad news brought on depression. The view over the countryside comforted his essential belief in Britain. 'A day away from Chartwell is a day wasted,' he wrote.

All three men enjoyed a private showing of movies at night. Roosevelt

---

* Roosevelt did not think the new medium would take off.

viewed the latest Hollywood hits. Stalin was particularly keen on westerns. When news was brought to him after dinner of the landing in Scotland of the Nazi leader, Rudolf Hess, Churchill replied, 'Hess or no Hess, I'm going to watch the Marx Brothers.'

The Prime Minister and President retained a sentimental attachment to the sea from their time in charge of their countries' navies; Stalin, on the other hand, was very much a land animal. The first two – particularly Churchill – used aircraft increasingly as the war went on; the dictator, who disliked travelling, flew only once, on his way to the Teheran summit, and hated the experience.

All were confirmed smokers, and their means of absorbing nicotine became an integral part of their public personas. Roosevelt puffed Camels through a holder held at a rakish angle. He smoked several in bed before going to sleep, sometimes lighting one from another. Churchill's eight cigars a day were an essential prop, though he did not inhale and often let them go out. Stalin crumbled Balkan cigarette tobacco into the pipes that became central to his 'Uncle Joe' image – some with a white spot on their stems were imported from Dunhill's in London, which also provided Churchill's cigars. At crucial moments, he cradled the pipe in his hand like a comforter. If he ran the stem over his moustache, he was in a good mood; if he left it unlit, that was a bad sign. When the Red Army suffered major reverses in 1942, he tipped the tobacco from his pipe over the bald head of Nikita Khrushchev, whom he held responsible.

All had health problems which were exacerbated by the pressures of running a total war. Roosevelt's were most obvious, but Stalin, a hypochondriac, had caught smallpox as a boy while an infection of his left elbow seriously stiffened the whole arm, giving him rheumatic aches. He had pigeon toes, and bad corns, as well as suffering from tonsillitis and psoriasis. In 1944, he was found unconscious at his desk. Over the years, his acute suspiciousness hardened into paranoia and pathological cruelty that merged with the Georgian vendetta tradition.

From the end of 1941, Churchill suffered heart difficulties. He had several bad bouts of pneumonia, and was seriously overweight – in 1942, a new desk had to be made for him in the War Rooms below Whitehall because he had grown so fat. To sleep, he took barbiturates. In the background lurked what he called his 'Black Dog' of depression, and the effect of his constant drinking. In the autumn of 1944, Alan Brooke noted in his diary that it was 'doubtful how much longer he will last'.* Six months earlier, a specialist called in to examine Roosevelt had secretly concluded that his heart disease and high blood pressure made his lifespan questionable.[51]

Not only were the Big Three very different men, their countries were also quite separate. Air travel and telephone communications were in their infancy – when a scrambler line was set up between London and Washington during the war, the equipment required was so big that it occupied the whole of a large basement room below the London department store, Selfridge's.

The inter-war decades had seen America retreating into isolationism, the Soviet Union becoming the revolutionary outcast, and Britain holding aloof from Europe under Conservative governments that pursued rigorously hard-line economic policies that divided the nation. Churchill had denounced the 'botulism of Bolshevism', and called for intervention to overthrow the Soviet regime. Understandably, Moscow felt under siege. But trans-Atlantic relations were none too easy, either. Many Americans felt they had been suckered into the First World War by tricky Europeans and landed with unpaid debts, leading Churchill to lament the fraying of 'the majestic edifice of Anglo-American friendship' amid 'bitter waters of suspicion, a marsh of misunderstanding'. The British Prime Minister, Neville Chamberlain, was the most anti-American politician to have occupied 10 Downing Street.[52]

The three countries had other differences. Despite grave imperfections of racism and class, the United States and Britain were democracies; the Soviet Union was a dictatorship imbued with terror that infused everyday life. For all his executive authority, and re-elections in 1936, 1940 and 1944, Roosevelt had to work with a Congress that could be contrary and with a Supreme Court he had failed to pack. He could never put domestic politics from his mind. Churchill had not led his party to electoral victory, but inherited a Conservative majority won under the predecessor he had roundly criticised, and led a War Cabinet that included leading members

---

* The historian Richard Holmes suggests that he suffered from Asperger's syndrome, accounting for his lack of empathy or care for others, his monologues, his disorientation when disturbed, his obsessive determination to complete tasks and the skin sensitivity that caused him to don silk underwear. But medical experts say this is unlikely since other symptoms are a lack of humour, rigid adherence to structure and timetables, and an inability to engage in abstract thought – none of them evident in Churchill.

of the Labour Party. He faced several minor parliamentary revolts, and some by-elections that resulted in sharp defeats. On the other hand, at the head of a country described by Churchill as 'a riddle wrapped in a mystery inside an enigma', Stalin wielded virtually arbitrary power over life and death, personally marking lists of those to be eliminated. He could hardly be expected to fathom the way the Western nations worked; how the power to declare war lay with Congress, not the President, or how Churchill reported from summits to the War Cabinet. Equally, he found it impossible to understand the free press in the West, seeing newspaper criticism of Moscow as inspired by the White House or Downing Street. As he said at Yalta, one-party rule was much simpler.[53]

Not that British officials found the workings of Washington easy to understand. Anthony Eden called the US capital a madhouse, and contrasted its 'confusion and woolliness' with the businesslike ways of Moscow. 'No method, no organisation, working in bedrooms,' Oliver Harvey, his Private Secretary, noted. The ambassador Viscount Halifax summed up one British view of Americans as 'very crude and semi-educated', their leaders prone to 'soft words and fine thoughts that are not always reflected in action' and 'dangerously afraid of public opinion.' At the same time, he equated the intensity of New Dealers like the Vice President, Henry Wallace, to 'the new Islam divinely inspired to save the world'.[54]

'The American mind runs naturally to broad, sweeping, logical conclusions on the largest scale,' Churchill wrote in his memoirs. 'It is on these that they build their practical thought and action. They feel that once the foundation has been planned on true and comprehensive lines all other stages will follow naturally and almost inevitably. The British mind does not work quite in this way. We do not think that logic and clear-cut principles are necessarily the sole keys ... in swiftly changing and indefinable situations. In war particularly we assign a larger importance to opportunism and improvisation ... There is room for much argument about both views. The difference is one of emphasis, but it is deep seated.'[55]

Many Americans considered the British as coming from a stuffy, hidebound society, epitomised by plummy-voiced butlers and fops in Hollywood films. 'It is in the American tradition, this distrust, this dislike, even hatred of the British,' Roosevelt remarked during a dinner conversation soon after Pearl Harbor. On an earlier occasion, he remarked that 'European statesmen are a bunch of bastards' – presumably including the British among them. Isolationism was not just for suspicious minds from the sticks. The writer Edmund Wilson was an outspoken opponent of involvement with the old continent – asked why he was so anti-British, he replied, 'The American Revolution.' Powerful voices in Washington favoured fighting America's war in the Pacific rather than going to the aid of the British. Henry Stimson, the Secretary of War, wrote in his diary of Britain as decadent, run by a tired government which sought to block the 'young and vigorous nation' across the ocean. For some Americans the British epitomised the Machiavellian ways of the old continent – Roosevelt once remarked they were 'always foxy and you have to be the same with them'.[56]

As for the other ally, Roosevelt told Frances Perkins: 'I don't understand the Russians. I just don't know what makes them tick. I wish I could study them. Frances, see if you can find out what makes them tick.' Was he serious? she asked. 'Yes,' came the reply, 'find out all you can and tell me from time to time. I like them and want to understand them.' She did as she was told, delivering digests of information to the White House. 'You know,' Roosevelt told her several times, 'I want to go to Russia myself.'[57]

While he nurtured no illusions about what he called 'a dictatorship as absolute as any other dictatorship in the world', he believed that the inclusion of the Soviet Union was the key to lasting peace. Though warned by Harriman that 'the Slavic mind does not understand us any more perhaps than we understand them', the President thought the USSR would soften as it came into contact with the rest of Europe. He told the diplomat Sumner Welles that, if one regarded the American and Soviet systems as having been 100 points apart after the Bolshevik Revolution, a stage could be reached at which the US would have moved 60 points and the Soviets 40 towards a junction. He did not appreciate that Stalin was a believer in Marxism who thought that its tenets, if backed by force, would triumph in the struggle with capitalism.[58]

If Roosevelt was right to decide that the best path to post-war peace lay through an understanding with Moscow, he greatly overestimated the dictator's readiness to compromise. By the end, his trademark optimism resembled a refusal to accept reality. 'I do not think Roosevelt had any real comprehension of the great gulf that separated the thinking of a Bolshevik from a non-Bolshevik and particularly from an American,' the diplomat Charles Bohlen wrote.

Though he could get carried away by euphoria after a late-night conversation with Stalin, Churchill always had the need for a post-war balance of power in mind. So much so that he would reflect on how a defeated Germany might be needed as a counterweight in Europe. For Roosevelt, on the other hand, zones of influence were part of the old system that had caused wars and should be rejected – whatever the evidence from the battlefield. A supreme salesman with no time for 'isms', who believed he could talk anybody round, he was unable to accept the strength of ideological differences and the reality of 'Red Army Socialism'.

For all their differing views, none of the three could allow ideological differences to get in the way of victory. If Britain fell, America would lose its first line of defence, and the launching pad for the invasion of France. If the Soviet Union was defeated or was forced into a second pact with Hitler, the war in Europe would become unwinnable for the other two. If the United States turned its prime focus from Europe to the Far East, an invasion of France would be impossible and Hitler would be able to focus on the war with Russia while the Soviet and British war efforts would be sapped by reduced supplies from across the Atlantic.

This interdependence involved messy compromises, tough negotiations, hard words and betrayals of smaller allies. Necessity forced the three men and their nations together, and it was hard to see anybody stepping into their shoes. Though Truman would rise to the occasion and Attlee would oversee fundamental changes in Britain, neither could have filled the role at an earlier stage, while Stalin had made sure there was no successor in the Kremlin. Once forged, the alliance would triumph so long as it did not split. To achieve that, personal chemistry was vital. Though the Cold War which followed their victory is over, the way Roosevelt, Stalin and Churchill acted had repercussions which still mark the globe, and provide an object lesson in managing – and mis-managing – a global alliance.

2

The First Summit

PLACENTIA BAY, NEWFOUNDLAND
9–12 AUGUST 1941

'At last – we have gotten together.'

ROOSEVELT

I

Walking the Line

The weather in Washington was particularly oppressive in early August 1941. Roosevelt had been in low spirits for some time. As he worked in bed at the White House, he complained of 'feeling so mean', with none of his habitual pep. This was hardly surprising, he had been suffering from influenza, a cold, sinus trouble, intestinal disturbance, diastolic hypertension and iron deficiency caused by bleeding haemorrhoids. He was given two blood transfusions and iron injections. His mother had recently died – the *New York Times* reported subsequently that this led him to 'shut himself off from the world more completely than at any time since becoming President'. Though he did not look at her coffin as it was lowered into the vault, tears welled in his eyes when he went through her belongings.[1]

Visitors found his conversation rambling as he reminisced about the First World War, and worked on a design for a hurricane-proof house in Florida that he planned to share with Hopkins. The serious stroke suffered by his secretary 'Missy' Le Hand, who had become the virtual presidential hostess in the frequent absences of Eleanor, added to the gloom – before she was stricken, Le Hand said she thought her boss was being dragged down by 'sheer exasperation' at the argument about America entering the war. Harold Ickes, the Secretary for the Interior, warned that, unless the President exerted leadership, he would not retain his authority much longer.[2]

Roosevelt had no doubt about the need to counter the Nazis, whose armies had scored victories in the Middle East and were surging forward in Russia after the attack in June. Secret military talks were held with the British in Washington and Roosevelt agreed that the United States would equip and maintain 10 of their divisions. He ordered the production of arms for the United Kingdom to be stepped up. After initially turning down a request for warships from London, he had agreed, in September 1940, to provide 50 mothballed destroyers in return for ninety-nine-year leases on British possessions in the Caribbean and Newfoundland. The United States, he declared, should become the arsenal of democracy. The Neutrality Acts, which restricted exports to belligerent nations, were relaxed.[3]

After a lengthy appeal from Churchill at the end of 1940, when Britain was running out of money and German submarines had sunk 1,282 merchant ships in the Atlantic, Congress agreed to a $1.3-billion programme allowing the President to 'sell, transfer title to, exchange, lease, lend, or otherwise dispose of . . . any defence article' to any government whose defence he deemed vital to the defence of the United States. What became known as 'Lend-Lease' removed the requirement of the 1939 Neutrality Act that US supplies had to be paid for in cash, a vital consideration given Britain's dwindling reserves. Roosevelt likened the scheme to loaning a neighbour a garden hose if his house was on fire.* Britain needed all the help it could get – while Germany was geared up for a long war, British output lagged below full potential and gold and dollar holdings would have only covered half its projected monthly expenditures if it had to pay for supplies in cash.

In May 1941, Roosevelt declared 'a state of unlimited national emergency' – what this meant in practice was unclear. Still there could be no doubt about how he was moving America. He ordered the construction of 200 ships to carry aid. Training facilities were offered for RAF pilots.

* The image came from Harold Ickes.

Engineers and mechanics went to service planes, tanks and vehicles sent to British forces in North Africa. The United States undertook to pass on information about 'aggressive ships or planes', and extended its maritime protection zone in the Atlantic. The US navy determined that 'Axis naval and air forces within the Western Hemisphere will be deemed potential threats to shipping and will be attacked where ever found.' As army numbers jumped, an order for 1,500 four-engined Superfortress bombers was placed with Boeing. German and Italian assets in the United States were frozen. American troops were sent to garrison the Danish territories of Greenland and Iceland under an agreement signed with Copenhagen's Minister in Washington.

Still, Roosevelt would not ask Congress to go to war. Though a powerful group of Cabinet members, including the secretaries of the army and navy, urged him to take a tougher line, he knew how divided his country was. For all his statements about stopping the dictators and messages of sympathy to London, he was, as always, playing the game in his own way, manoeuvring from week to week, leaving the eventual outcome to be determined by events and public opinion, whose contradictions he reflected perfectly.

Though he told one of his secretaries in 1940 that even a day's delay in helping Britain might mean the end of civilisation, he assured the mothers of America in his re-election campaign that autumn: 'Your boys are not going to be sent into any foreign wars.'* Polls showed that 64 per cent of voters regarded the preservation of peace as vital for their country. Few Americans wanted to see Britain defeated. Fund-raising drives collected aid – one called 'Barkers for Britain' encouraged dog owners to contribute in return for receiving collars for their pets. But a majority opposed sending troops across the Atlantic.

While the choice of the internationally minded businessman, Wendell Willkie, as his Republican opponent in 1940, saved Roosevelt an all-out fight with an isolationist, anti-war sentiment was backed by a formidable coalition. The main group, America First, counted 800,000 members including Henry Ford, Charles Lindberg and the President's cousin, Theodore Jr. The Hearst press empire and the *Chicago Tribune* fanned

---

* Just as Woodrow Wilson ran on the slogan: 'He kept us out of war.'

feeling. The anti-Semitic radio priest Father Coughlin spewed vitriol to 15 million listeners. Roosevelt haters accused him of wanting to use war to assume monarchical powers. Left-wingers warned that Wall Street was pushing for hostilities to maximise profits. Internationalists blamed the Europeans for defeating their ideals after 1918.

Behind this lay a deep belief in America's exceptionalism as the standard bearer for liberty and a rejection of balance of power politics as practised in Europe. The Founding Fathers had warned against permanent, entangling alliance. Geography made Americans feel they were invulnerable, so long as they steered clear of the snares of global politics. 'I thank God for two insulating oceans,' the isolationist Senator Arthur Vandenberg declared. It was an approach Roosevelt had followed in his first term. Now, even if the Axis threat stirred him to see the need for greater involvement, he was constrained by the two-year election cycle, the power of Congress, and public opinion.[4]

London launched a substantial covert propaganda campaign in America under a programme known as British Security Coordination that fed stories to the US press aimed at increasing support for entry into the conflict. A map was forged showing a German plan to split Latin America into vassal Nazi provinces, one of which would contain the Panama Canal – Roosevelt cited this at one point though whether he believed in it may be doubted. The BSC also produced a fake American war plan against Germany which was leaked to an isolationist senator and, through him, found its way to the *Chicago Tribune*, which ran a big story headlined 'F.D.R.'s War Plans'. According to the account from the British side, the idea was to push Hitler into declaring war on the USA. But the Führer preferred not to let his strategy be dictated by an American newspaper story.

The aloof Lord Halifax hardly helped Britain's case with the American people, as he went fox-hunting and committed the faux-pas of leaving his hot dog behind at a baseball game as if American food was not good enough for him. The US desk at the Foreign Office was told that the envoy's standing had 'gone from zero to freezing'. There was some respite, however, when anti-war women pelted him with eggs. The British Embassy circulated the ambassador's alleged response – that Americans were fortunate to have eggs to spare when the British were rationed to one a month. The remark may have been invented by a press officer, but it made its point.

To handle his dilemma, Roosevelt stepped up his policy of bolstering

Britain without committing troops. This, he argued, was the best way of keeping hostilities 3,000 miles away. Polls showed half the electorate thought the President had got it about right, with the rest evenly divided between those who believed there was too great a commitment and those who thought not enough was being done. Dodging and weaving his way forward under a cloud of obfuscation, Roosevelt encouraged American opinion to evolve month by month towards readiness to go to war. Henry Kissinger would hail this as 'an object lesson on the scope of leadership in a democracy' while George VI wrote to the President in June 1941, to say how struck he had been 'by the way you have led public opinion by allowing it to get ahead of you'.[5]

America faced a second dilemma on the other side of the globe. In 1937, Japan had launched full-scale war against China, a nation with which the United States had strong links through religion, the media and trade. Tokyo was careful to describe the attack as an 'incident' so as to avoid the interruption of American exports which would have followed its true definition as a war – and Washington went along with the fiction.[6]

Madame Chiang Kai-shek, the charismatic, New England-educated wife of China's leader, used American radio broadcasts to ask why Washington had fallen into 'spell-bound silence' as 'all treaties and structures to outlaw war and to regularise the conduct of war appear to have crumbled, and we have a reversion to the days of savages.' Difficulty of access to the Nationalist wartime capital of Chungking, behind the Yangtze gorges, made supplying Chiang's forces difficult. But the Chinese leaders hammered away at how little assistance they were getting, comparing their treatment with that of the British and making veiled references to the strength of those in China who wanted to make peace with Tokyo.[7]

Roosevelt temporised, promising supplies but always putting Britain first. An oil embargo was slapped on Tokyo; Japanese assets in the United States were frozen. But the State Department pursued negotiations in the hope that the new government of General Tojo would become more reasonable.

Apart from public opinion, there was another major problem with going to war. Given its size and wealth, America was the most unmilitarised of nations. Though the navy was declared to be 'superior to any in the world', the running down of the army after the First World War meant that the US only just squeezed into the twenty largest forces on earth, with 174,000 men. Half its divisions were under strength. Training was poor. Joint operations were held only every four years. The draft had been introduced, but a tight vote was expected when it came up for renewal in Congress. While unexploited industrial capacity meant that military expansion offered an opportunity to mark the final chapter of recovery from the Great Depression, developing the military-industrial complex was still in an early stage.[8]

Given the trying circumstances and his health problems, what could be more natural for the President than to take a sea trip to revive himself? Journalists asked if he would be going ashore. 'I replied definitely in the negative,' Roosevelt recorded in an account he wrote for himself at the time.[9]

On Sunday 3 August, the presidential train left Washington for New London, Connecticut, where the yacht, the *Potomac*, waited. At sunset, the 165-foot 'Floating White House', a former coastguard cutter, headed into Long Island Sound, watched by a throng of people. Calling at South Dartmouth, Massachusetts, she took on the Crown Prince and Princess of Norway for a day's fishing – the President kissed the attractive Princess hello and goodbye. His son, James, hints at 'a romantic relationship', noting how he kissed her goodnight when she stayed at Hyde Park. In the evening, he personally drove a speedboat to take the party back to shore.[10]

The next morning, watchers saw the *Potomac* go through the Cape Cod Canal, its passengers sitting on the deck. One, wearing sunglasses, waved to them. The rakish angle of his long cigarette holder told them he was the President. In fact, the men on deck were sailor stand-ins. The previous night, Roosevelt's boat had sailed to a nearby bay where seven warships waited. The President had boarded the biggest one, the heavy cruiser *Augusta*.[11]

Waiting for him were America's top military commanders. With destroyer escorts, the 9,050-ton warship sailed east, and then north. Sharp blades hung from its bows to cut the cables of any mines in its path. Roosevelt cast his line, catching a large, ugly fish that nobody could identify. It was full of worms, and inedible; so he had it pickled and sent to the Smithsonian Institute in Washington.[12]

The President found his disappearing trick 'delightful'. 'Even at my ripe old age I feel a thrill in a get-away – especially from the American press,' he wrote to a cousin. Among those taken in was the head of his Secret Service detail who watched the *Potomac* move through the Cape Cod Canal. None of the Cabinet or White House staff knew where he was. His wife, Eleanor, thought he was, indeed, on a fishing trip.[13]

After a 250-mile voyage, the *Augusta* sailed into Placentia Bay on the pine-covered coast of Newfoundland, anchoring at Argentia Harbour, where the United States had acquired a base under the destroyers deal with Britain. The melancholy shore was dotted with small beaches and white wooden houses. While he waited, Roosevelt conferred with the Chiefs of Staff, bending over a map of the Atlantic to draw a line further extending the area for which the US navy would assume responsibility from Iceland to the Azores.

Under Secretary Sumner Welles joined the party. The previous year, Roosevelt had sent the tall, superior New Englander to see if Mussolini might act as a mediator between Hitler and the British. Welles found Il Duce looking fifteen years older than his age, his expression leaden, his movements ponderous, his eyes closing as they spoke. Italy's declaration of war on France after Germany's victory there in June 1940, dashed any hopes of a Roman negotiating channel. Washington, Welles advised, would have to work on its own if it wanted a 'practicable plan of security and of disarmament'.[14]

Averell Harriman flew across the Atlantic to be at the President's side. Franklin Roosevelt Jr, who was in the navy, sailed in aboard a destroyer – his father enrolled him as his Junior Naval Aide. Another son, Elliott, also turned up. Now all they had to do was to wait for their secret guest.

Winston Churchill was in ebullient form as he crossed the Atlantic on Britain's finest battleship, the *Prince of Wales*. He loved every moment of the voyage, behaving, one observer remarked, 'like a boy let out of school, and not a very good boy at that.' A British journalist thought that, in his blue naval uniforms and with his pink, happy face, the British leader 'belongs definitely to an older England, to the England of the Tudors . . . a warm and emotional England, too, an England as yet untouched by the hardness of the age of steel.'* Initially, Churchill installed himself in the admiral's spacious quarters in the stern of the ship; but, wakened by a storm one night, he made his way to a cabin on the upper deck, where he decided to stay, commandeering the warrant officers' mess as his sitting and dining room.[15]

This was the most important trip he had made since becoming Prime Minister. He was sailing to meet the leader of the nation that would determine Britain's future. Like a lover finally meeting the object of his

---

* The journalist H.V. Morton was famed for writing about the countryside. The choice of him for the trip was ironic since, privately, he agreed with Hitler on many things, including anti-Semitism.

attentions, he was nervous about the impression he would make. 'I wonder if he will like me,' he had remarked to Harriman.[16]

Though Churchill told the House of Commons that Anglo-American cooperation rolled on like Ole Man River, that Lend-Lease was the 'most unsordid act' in history, that the worth of the destroyers was 'measured in rubies', transatlantic relations had been touchy – and not only over the President's refusal to press Congress to declare war. Hard bargaining on aid by Washington aroused bad blood, particularly since the supplies still only amounted to a small proportion of British procurement. The insistence by the Treasury Department and the President on a fire sale of British assets in the United States at far less than their value to meet financial obligations went down badly. Eden saw the exchange of bases for old destroyers as 'a grievous blow at our authority and ultimately at our sovereignty'. Churchill's scientific adviser, Professor Lindemann, worried that 'the fruits of victory which Roosevelt offers seem to be safety for America and virtual starvation for us'. It has been calculated that, in return for an immediate credit of $1 billion and Lend-Lease, the United States appropriated British assets worth $13 billion. Beggars were not being allowed to have a choice.[17]

For all his pro-American feelings, Churchill could take umbrage. Four months after moving in to Downing Street, he had reflected acidly that the Americans were 'very good at applauding the valiant deeds done by others'. In 1941, he cabled Halifax that, if the US Treasury Secretary was going to have 'a bad time' in front of congressional committees asking about repayment of Lend-Lease, British cities being bombed by the Luftwaffe were 'having a bad time now'. On another occasion, he wrote to the ambassador of the United States wanting Britain 'not only to be skinned but flayed to the bone'. After Roosevelt insisted on British gold worth £30 million being shipped to the US from Africa as surety, Churchill prepared a message comparing the Americans with 'a sheriff collecting the last assets of a helpless debtor' – but then decided to strike out the passage.[18]

By May, matters had become so tangled that the leading British economist, John Maynard Keynes, was sent to Washington to discuss Lend-Lease and to try to obtain more dollars. Finding the going 'sticky', he returned home unsuccessful. A British minister negotiating with the Americans called them gangsters. On the other side, Roosevelt's domestic critics warned that Britain would use aid supplies to undercut US exports, and Senator Vanderbilt snorted: 'What "suckers" our emotions make of us.'[19]

The President's evasiveness could drive Churchill to his 'Black Dog' of depression. 'It seems to me as if . . . we are being very much left to our fate,' he wrote in a note to Eden. But the American card was the only way he could see of beating Hitler, so he had to 'keep buggering on'. As he left the Scapa Flow naval base in Scotland for the first summit, he sent Roosevelt a message noting that: 'It is twenty-seven years ago today that Huns began their last war. We must make good job of it this time. Twice ought to be enough.'[20]

II

The Fourth Man

The groundwork for the first summit between Roosevelt and Churchill had been laid earlier in the year by an unlikely emissary, the gangling, shambolic Harry Hopkins. The son of an Iowa saddle-maker, Hopkins had been the main administrator of welfare funds under the New Deal. His progressive ideas did not keep him away from smart resorts, night clubs, the race track, and luxurious homes of rich men. Travelling first class, he paid the difference from the government travel allowance out of his own pocket. When he took the film star Paulette Goddard to the White House there was gossip that he hoped to marry her; his first wife had divorced him after he had fallen in love with another woman, whom he married but who died five years later – a friend said that whatever 'Harry the Hop' had been born for, 'it couldn't be personal happiness'. A Democratic insider, Joseph Davies, described him as having 'the purity of St Francis of Assisi combined with the sharp shrewdness of a race-track tout'.[21]

In 1940, Hopkins fell ill at dinner at the White House, stayed the night, and remained for three years, occupying the Lincoln Room along the passage from the President. He annoyed Eleanor by burning cigarette holes in tablecloths, by asking the cook for more fancy food, including grapefruit with French dressing, and by his high living. He served his master with dogged devotion, even if he may have been motivated, in part, by the hope of running for president in 1940 if FDR did not stand again – though his health and status as a divorced man would have blocked him.

Hopkins lacked any formality – 'he doesn't even know the meaning of the word "protocol",' Roosevelt remarked. 'When he sees a piece of red tape, he just pulls out those old garden shears and snips it.' In wartime photographs, he usually hovers at the edge of the frame. Overwhelmingly, he existed to serve Roosevelt, identifying opportunities, setting up deals, producing the evidence his master intuitively wanted to hear. He said that he regarded the President as 'unlimited'. The war would make him the equivalent of today's National Security Adviser. His *raison d'être*, the journalist Marquis Childs wrote, lay in 'understanding, sensing, divining, often guessing – and usually guessing right – what is in Franklin Roosevelt's mind.' Churchill's doctor remarked that he 'knows the President's moods like a wife watching the domestic climate. He will sit patiently for hours, blinking like a cat, waiting for the right moment to put his point; and if it never comes, he is content to leave it to another time.'[22]

At some of the wartime summits, Hopkins acted as de facto Secretary of State, dismissing his country's diplomats as 'cookie pushers, pansies – and usually isolationists to boot'. 'When Hopkins was there, decisions went well, and towards good results,' the commentator Walter Lippmann wrote in an obituary. 'When he was absent, things went all to pieces.' The aide, he added, had the gift of 'cutting aside the details and coming to the crux of the matter, of finding swiftly the real issue . . . the sticking point at which pride, vested interest, timidity, confusion were causing trouble. He would bring it nakedly into the open, ruthlessly, almost cynically . . . often with tactlessness meant to shock men into seeing reality . . .' Churchill said that, if the American was ennobled, he should become 'Lord Root of the Matter'.[23]

Hopkins 'was also objective about himself, a characteristic all too uncommon to those close to the throne,' noted Charles Bohlen. The administration's enemies branded him a Rasputin who sought to make America a socialist state; for good measure, the *Chicago Tribune* wrote that he suffered from dandruff.[24]

His wartime performance was vital as the trusted presidential adviser who worked ceaselessly to open supply bottlenecks and bring order to Roosevelt's disparate administration – and as the carpenter of the alliance. This was all the more extraordinary because he was constantly ill after having two-thirds of his stomach removed in 1937 – the President referred to him as a 'half man'. As Hopkins himself said, he took pills 'by the bushel' and was frequently hospitalised. Even so, he smoked several packs of Lucky Strike a day – some said two, others four – and drank regularly, sometimes wandering through the White House corridors with glass in hand. Though politics and serving Roosevelt were his full-time occupation, he also had a love of English verse, particularly that of John Keats. 'I fairly walk on air,' he wrote to his daughter after finding himself passing the poet's home in Hampstead.

Following his preferred tack of dispatching personal emissaries, Roosevelt sent him to London after Churchill's lengthy plea for help at the end of 1940. Hopkins arrived in Britain so ill after the flight that he had to be carried from the seaplane. But he and Churchill got on famously over a long, well-lubricated Downing Street lunch. The American sat up late with the Prime Minister on visits to his country residences. One evening, he produced a box of records, and Churchill walked round the room in time to the music as if dancing on his own as he perorated. On another country weekend, Hopkins listened to the British leader delivering a speech which he crafted to accord with the visitor's political leanings. What would Roosevelt think of that? Churchill asked. 'I don't think the President will give a damn for all that,' Hopkins replied, causing a momentary frisson in the room. Then he added: 'You see, we're only interested in seeing that Goddamn sonofabitch, Hitler, gets licked.'*[25]

In a handwritten note to Roosevelt from his room at Claridge's Hotel he was unequivocal. 'The people here are amazing from Churchill down and if courage alone can win – the result will be inevitable . . . Churchill is the gov't, in every sense of the word – he controls the grand strategy and often the details – labor trusts him – the army, navy, air force are behind him to a man . . . I cannot emphasise too strongly that he is the one and only person over here with whom you need to have a full meeting of minds.'

Though he lived in a luxury hotel and stayed at Churchill's country homes, he saw the devastation bombing had wrought on British cities, and, in his way, shared some of the privation. During provincial trips, he was found curled up in his overcoat in front of a gas fire because of the coldness of British bedrooms. At Chequers, he read his papers in the bathroom because it was the only place with heated pipes; he said his victory present to the British leader would be central heating.[26]

Dining with Churchill at the Station Hotel in Glasgow at the end of

---

* The story was discounted by Hopkins's biographer Robert Sherwood, but figures in an account by a participant at the weekend.

February, 1941, Hopkins said the Prime Minister probably wanted to know what he was going to tell Roosevelt when he got home. He then quoted from the Book of Ruth – 'Whither thou goest, I will go; and where thou lodgest, I will lodge; thy people shall be my people, and thy God my God.' Dropping his already soft voice, Hopkins added, 'Even to the end.' Churchill dissolved into tears. It was, the Prime Minister's doctor noted in his diary, 'like a rope thrown to a drowning man'.[27]

Other American emissaries went to London in the first half of 1941, among them Wendell Willkie who bore from Roosevelt to Churchill the first lines of a Longfellow poem that came to be a symbol of the Anglo-American alliance:

> Sail on, O Ship of State!
> Sail on, O Union, strong and great!
> Humanity with all its fears,
> With all the hopes of future years,
> Is hanging breathless on thy fate.[28]

On Hopkins's second visit in July, Churchill made the unique gesture of inviting him to a Cabinet meeting, though he ushered the visitor out halfway through on the grounds that there was nothing more of interest on the agenda. In fact, ministers went on to discuss debate on US policy in the Far East which Churchill evidently did not think suitable for the envoy's ears.

On 19 July, he invited Hopkins to Chequers and, inadvertently, set off the next stage in the construction of the alliance. That same day, the Soviet ambassador, Ivan Maisky, received a message from Stalin for the Prime Minister calling for a landing in France to draw German troops away from the eastern front. Maisky drove to Chequers to deliver the communication. Receiving him in his study, Churchill expressed deep sympathy with the Soviet plight, but said it was impracticable to think of an invasion. Leading him out into the crowded drawing room, he introduced a man whom Maisky described as being 'tall, very thin . . . with a long face and lively eyes'. Though it was summer, Hopkins stood with his back to the fire, for warmth.[29]

As Churchill went to talk to other guests, Maisky recounted his conversation in the study. Hopkins put some questions. Then Mrs Churchill approached, and offered tea.

Two days later, Churchill told Stalin that the British Chiefs of Staff 'did not see any way of doing anything on a scale likely to be of the slightest use to you' though he did offer naval help in the Arctic and announced the sending of 200 fighters, up to 3 million pairs of ankle boots, rubber, tin, wool, cloth, jute, lead and shellac. In a subsequent cable, he made clear that he was ready to deplete Britain's resources 'in view of the urgency of your requirements'. If he expected to be thanked, he was disappointed. He had to wait till the beginning of September to hear further from Stalin. In his war memoirs, Churchill noted that 'the Soviet Government has the impression that they were conferring a great favour on us by fighting in their own country for their own lives. The more they fought, the heavier our debt became.'[30]

Realising the importance of the visitor he had met at Chequers, Maisky telephoned US ambassador John Winant to fix a lunch the following week. He used this to set out arguments for a second front, which Winant backed. Hopkins, according to Maisky, listened attentively and 'with obvious sympathy for the Soviet Union'.[31]

'We in the USA are a non-belligerent country now, and cannot do anything to help you in regard to a second front,' he said. 'But as regards supplies things are different. We are providing Britain with much in the way of armaments. Raw materials, ships and so on. We could give you too quite a lot. What do you require? Couldn't you tell me?'

'Mr Hopkins,' Maisky replied, 'could you, yourself, visit Moscow and there, on the spot receive from the Soviet Government all the information you require?'

That afternoon, Hopkins sent a 'For the President Only' message, saying that 'everything possible should be done to make certain the Russians maintain a permanent front even though they be defeated in this immediate battle'. This could be achieved, he suggested to Roosevelt, 'by a direct communication from you through a personal envoy'.[32]

Some historians have speculated that a Hopkins mission to Moscow had been cooked up in advance. But the lunch, and the tenor of the subsequent exchanges with Washington, suggest otherwise.

Would the President consider it 'important and useful' for him to go to Moscow? he asked. 'The stakes are so great that it should be done. Stalin would then know in an unmistakable way that we mean business on a long-term supply job.' As so often, Hopkins was telling Roosevelt what he wanted to hear. Bolstering Soviet resistance would facilitate the policy of leaving it to others to put men in the field to fight Hitler. Already, the President could see a world in which Moscow would keep the peace in conjunction with Washington.

On 26 July, Roosevelt approved the trip. He sent Hopkins a message to take with him that asked Stalin to treat the visitor 'with the identical confidence you would feel if you were talking directly to me'. It held out the prospect of 'a great deal of materiel'. In Washington, Henry Stimson described the Soviet ambassador as a crook and George Marshall warned that he would 'take everything we own'. But the President ordered the Cabinet to 'use a heavy hand, – act as a bur under the saddle and get things moving' on supplies to the USSR.[33]

Eight days after meeting Hopkins, Winant called on Maisky bearing three passports. He explained that Hopkins was going to take the sleeper train with two Americans to Scotland where they would board a flying boat for the arduous flight to the Soviet port of Archangel. 'A dangerous and difficult journey,' the US ambassador added, 'especially for such a sick man as Hopkins, but he doesn't reckon with anything.'

Maisky took out his pen and wrote in the passport, 'Harry Hopkins to be permitted to cross any frontier station of the USSR without examination of luggage, as a diplomatic person.' Signing the page, he stamped it with the embassy seal, and did the same with the other two. Winant raced to the station, arriving as the train was starting to move. He pushed the passports through the open window to Hopkins who had left so hurriedly that he had forgotten to settle his bill at Claridge's. In a message to the Kremlin Churchill described the American visitor as 'your friend and our friend' in whom burned 'a flame . . . for democracy and to beat Hitler'.[34]

In the Catalina seaplane, Hopkins sat at the back, looking very frail. He wore a grey homburg given to him by Churchill with WSC stamped into the band – he had mislaid his own. He slept a little on a canvas stretcher, helped with the cooking, and stared through the Plexiglas of the rear gunner's position, imagining shooting at Nazi planes. Arriving in Archangel, he looked forward to a restorative sleep. But his hosts took him to a four-hour banquet at which the vodka flowed. Hopkins worked out that the best thing was to eat a chunk of bread spread with caviar as 'a shock absorber' before knocking back each shot of alcohol. After two hours sleep, he left for Moscow at 4 a.m.

As he flew over Russia, nearly a million Red Army troops were trapped in the cities of Kiev and Smolensk. Minsk had fallen with the loss of 300,000 troops. The Germans were advancing on Leningrad. The Soviet secret police were conducting mass arrests, and executing anybody suspected of lacking the will to fight, along with thousands of political prisoners. Lenin's body, government offices and Stalin's library were evacuated eastwards as were foreign embassies, travelling five days and four nights on a train without a dining car or drinking water to the city of Kuybyshev in the Urals. Looking down at the vast expanses of forest on the flight from Archangel, Hopkins grasped an essential point. Not even the all-conquering Wehrmacht and Luftwaffe could master such a huge country, he thought.*

Despite the exhaustion of the trip, he was too excited to sleep when he got to the capital, sitting up for a long talk with ambassador Laurence Steinhardt, and then going on a sight-seeing drive. After which, he was driven to the Kremlin to meet Stalin.

Wearing a khaki uniform with unbuttoned collar, the dictator sat behind a large desk from which half a dozen differently coloured telephones connected with ministries. Molotov and the interpreter were the only other people in the room. After shaking hands, the dark-suited Hopkins said Roosevelt considered Hitler the enemy of mankind and was determined to provide the Soviets with all possible aid. In reply, the man who had entered into an alliance with Berlin to dismember Poland and had swallowed up the Baltic States, stressed the need for 'a minimum moral standard between all nations'. If governments did not fulfil treaty obligations, international society could not continue. Since they did not respect such a standard, the Nazis were 'an anti-social force in the present world'. Happily, he added, Soviet and American views on this matter coincided.[35]

During the two-hour meeting, Hopkins was struck by the size of his host's hands, 'as hard as his mind, his voice is harsh, but ever under control'. His 'quick, managed smile . . . can be cold but friendly, austere but warm . . . he curries no favours with you, he seems to have no doubts . . . he takes it for granted that you have no doubts, either.' Stalin spoke in simple sentences and occasionally broke into short, somewhat sardonic laughter. Hopkins found himself replying as tersely, and reflected

---

* Hitler observed in his will that Russia's size meant it could 'afford the luxury of time'.

how businesslike the conversation was, in contrast to the rambling discussions in Washington or London.[36]

In a picture taken of the two men by the American photographer Margaret Bourke-White, Stalin appears the more relaxed, gazing into the camera with a half-smile, his arms hanging by his side, his stomach pressing against the blouse of his uniform. Hopkins poses formally, looking off at an angle, standing almost to attention, his lips pursed. Faced with Stalin, he may have wanted to cut a tough figure.[37]

The Russians went out of their way to look after their guest. When German planes came overhead, he was taken to a shelter stocked with caviar, chocolate, cigarettes and vodka; Steinhardt observed that he never received such protection, drawing a laugh from Hopkins. His treatment, the ambassador added, 'clearly indicates the extreme importance attached to his visit'. Stalin had shown 'frankness unparalleled in recent Soviet history'.[38]

The second Stalin–Hopkins session lasted for four hours. The dictator greeted the visitor with a few quickly spoken words, shaking his hand firmly and smiling. They exchanged cigarettes. The Soviet leader predicted that the Soviet Union would have 350 divisions under arms by the spring of 1942, compared with a maximum of 300 for the enemy. He wanted as many soldiers as possible to be in action 'because then the troops learn that Germans can be killed and are not supermen'. Requesting arms and other supplies, he made notes on a small pad, and handed the sheets to the American.

Hopkins said that the US and Britain were willing to do all they could to help. But it would probably not be possible to produce and ship aid before winter. He stressed the need for Roosevelt and Stalin to deal with one another directly. This was particularly vital, he reported to Washington, because 'there is literally no one in the whole Government who is willing to give any important information other than Mr Stalin himself'.[39]

On the sensitive issue of whether the United States would enter the war, the Georgian said he had thought of sending a written note to the White House, but then decided it was better to use Hopkins as his channel. He thought it inevitable that America would come to grips with Germany. On their own, the USSR and Britain would find it very difficult to win, but Hitler's greatest weakness lay in the vast number of oppressed people who hated him and his regime. They could get the encouragement and moral strength to resist from only one source – the United States. The President had 'enormous' world influence. Germans would be so demoralised by a declaration of war that the fighting might end without the USA having to fire a shot.[40]

Stalin raised the possibility of troops under American command being posted to the Russian front. Hopkins replied that he doubted if the administration would want to send forces. Involvement would be decided largely by how far Hitler encroached on fundamental US interests, he added, side-stepping the matter of Japan – he knew of Stalin's anxiety not to be dragged into any hostilities with Tokyo: what he did not know was that the Soviet master-spy Richard Sorge, who had predicted Hitler's invasion, told Stalin that Tokyo would not be planning to attack the USSR.

As his visitor left, Stalin asked him to convey his respects to Roosevelt. Hopkins imagined that his host's smile as he departed was more friendly, a bit warmer than it had been before. He was particularly struck by his last view of – 'an austere, rugged, determined figure in boots that shone like mirrors, stout baggy trousers, and snug-fitting blouse.'[41]

His stay in Moscow, he wrote, drove home to him 'the difference between democracy and dictatorship'. But, on 1 August, a brief report to the White House, marked 'most secret', said he felt 'ever so confident' about the eastern front, having been impressed by the exceptional morale of the Russians and their 'unbounded determination to win.'[42]

Again it was what Roosevelt wanted to hear, over-riding pessimistic reports, and providing evidence to argue for the aid he intended to send to Moscow. Speaking to Elliott, the President summed up Churchill's view of Russia's ability to stay in the war by snapping his fingers. His son said he took it his father had more faith than that. 'Harry Hopkins has more,' Roosevelt replied. 'He's able to convince me.'[43]

His job done, the aide flew back to Archangel. Despite appalling weather, he insisted on taking off immediately for Scotland. He had a rendezvous to keep. Behind him, *Pravda* wrote that his visit demonstrated that Soviet–American cooperation had aroused 'an invincible and powerful force . . . which will annihilate Hitler for ever.'[44]

When Hopkins got to Scapa Flow after flying through Arctic storms, the waves were so high that the launch sent for him could not tie up alongside the seaplane. So he jumped from the observation dome into the tender where a sailor pulled him across the slippery deck with a boathook. His luggage, including papers on the war and on his conversations with Stalin, was tossed after him. Though he had a gift of caviar from the dictator in his suitcase, he had forgotten his medicine in Moscow.[45]

Exhausted, with dark circles under his eyes, Hopkins slept under sedation for eighteen hours on the *Prince of Wales*. The next day, Churchill arrived. Still pale and weak, Hopkins stood in the shadow of a gun turret as the Prime Minister came on board the battleship.

'Ah, my dear friend, how are you?' Churchill asked. 'And how did you find Stalin?'

'I must tell you about it,' the saddle-maker's son replied in a slow, weary voice. Linking arms, the two men went below.[46]

As he crossed the Atlantic, the Prime Minister conferred with the British Chiefs of Staff and worked on papers. He read C. S. Forester's novel *Captain Hornblower RN*, and dined off Scottish beef and grouse – ninety birds had been brought along. When Hopkins produced the caviar given to him by Stalin, Churchill remarked that it was good to have such a delicacy 'even though it meant fighting with the Russians to get it'.

Revived by the ocean air, Hopkins resumed his pattern of sitting up late with the Prime Minister, talking and playing games – he won seven guineas at backgammon. Each night, a film was shown in the warm, tightly curtained mess room. Churchill took out his handkerchief to dab his eyes as, for the fifth time, he watched Laurence Olivier's depiction of Nelson's death in *Lady Hamilton*. One night, in the interval while the film reels were changed, he called for a record of Noël Coward's 'Mad Dogs and Englishmen', and sang along with it. On the other side was the song 'To England!' with its vision of a country living in peace and dignity. When it ended, nobody spoke. Then the Prime Minister cried out, 'Here, here!'[47]

III

Charter Pie

At 7 a.m. on 9 August, Churchill stood on the bridge of the *Prince of Wales* as it entered Placentia Bay. He wore a romper siren suit. His sandy hair was unkempt – he had been in such a hurry to glimpse what lay ahead that he had not paused to comb it on getting up. Beside him was Hopkins, in his dressing gown. 'You'd have thought Winston was being carried up into the heavens to meet God,' he told friends.

In the morning mist a pilot came aboard to guide the battleship, but the *Prince of Wales* suddenly headed back out to sea. The captain had set his clocks to the wrong time and the ship had arrived early; Churchill was not pleased. Still, the delay meant he had time to don the blue, brass-buttoned uniform of an Elder Brother of Trinity House, the British lighthouse organisation. As the mist lifted, the *Prince of Wales* sailed back, dropping off Hopkins who took a destroyer to the *Augusta* to brief the President.

Observers were struck by the contrast between the spick-and-span American vessels and the camouflaged British vessel which bore the marks of damage inflicted in a sea battle. One ship came from a country that had been fighting for almost two years, the others from a nation that had little or no idea of the kind of war Hitler was waging. 'We were living in different time cycles,' the journalist H.V. Morton noted. As if to bring this home, Roosevelt had 1,500 cardboard boxes sent to the British containing an orange, two apples, 200 cigarettes, and half-a-pound of cheese, with a card reading: 'The President of the United States of America sends his compliments and best wishes'.[48]

Wearing a light-brown 'Palm Beach' suit, Roosevelt waited on the deck of the *Augusta* while the *Prince of Wales* sailed into the bay and dropped anchor. Looking across the water, he held his hat to his chest in salute. On the quarter-deck of the battleship, Churchill stood with his fingers raised to the peak of his naval cap. Bosuns' pipes shrilled. Sailors cheered. Bands played the national anthems.

Slipping his hand under Elliott's arm, and supported by the heavy steel leg braces that enabled him to stand, the President rose to his feet to greet the Prime Minister when he came aboard, a cigar clenched between his teeth. Roosevelt flashed his jaunty trademark smile, holding his head high in patrician fashion. The shorter Churchill appeared like a supplicant as he bowed slightly and held out a typewritten letter from George VI – in the Prime Minister's mind, the American leader was always a chief of state, as well as head of the executive. Such things counted with him.

The royal message conveyed best wishes. The King was sure the President would agree that his visitor was 'a very remarkable man' while the meeting would be 'of great benefit to our two countries in pursuit of our common goal'.[49]

The two men exchanged a handshake, Roosevelt taking a second longer than the British leader to extend his arm.

'At last – we have gotten together,' Roosevelt said.

'We have,' Churchill replied with a nod.

They went below for lunch, with Hopkins the only other person present.

At the opening conversation the two men got on well, though differences of intention and policy soon emerged. When Churchill pressed for a tough statement to deter further Japanese expansion, the President shied away from agreeing to any formal warning to Tokyo. On the issue of a declaration of war, Churchill could get no more than non-committal generalities. Having waited so long, the British leader wanted to sail home with something concrete; for his host, merely meeting, and getting an opportunity to size up the other man, was enough.[50]

Over the next three days, the talks moved between the two big ships. Hopkins attended all the sessions; Welles, Harriman, and the senior Foreign Office official, Alexander Cadogan, came in and out. Generals and admirals held parallel discussions. Churchill's crony Lord Beaverbrook arrived midway through the summit. He and the head of the British Purchasing Mission in Washington, Arthur Purvis, who had played a key role in ensuring supplies, had set off in separate planes from Scotland. The aircraft carrying Purvis crashed within minutes, killing all on board. Arriving safely in North America, Beaverbrook commandeered a train to get him close enough to be ferried out to the floating summit.

Also present was the Prime Minister's adviser Lindemann, who had just been ennobled as Baron Cherwell and was generally known as 'the Prof'. Drawing on his knowledge of British atomic research, he spoke of new forms of energy that could pack immense destructive power – Roosevelt expressed great interest and, soon afterwards, secretly approved an atomic project submitted to him by a US team. The British, who had set the ball rolling, were delayed by arguments between those, like Cherwell, who wanted to develop a strictly national weapon, and others who saw that cooperation with the US would be necessary.[51]

As was his after-lunch habit, Churchill took a two-hour siesta on the first afternoon back on the *Prince of Wales*. That evening, he returned to the

Augusta for a black-tie dinner, a row of medals pinned to his bow-fronted dinner jacket. Before going to table, the two delegations posed for photographs. The Prime Minister and President sat in the middle of the front row, with Roosevelt's Scottie dog, Fala, at his feet. At table, where he sat to his host's right, Churchill handed over copies of the first lines of the poem by Longfellow which Roosevelt had sent him at the beginning of the year. The words were in red, and with the first 'S' curled round an Elizabethan warship. Roosevelt signed the copies at the top, Churchill at the bottom and the assembled company added signatures between them.

To eat, there was roast chicken, spinach omelette, candied sweet potatoes, vegetable purée, tomato salad, chocolate ice cream and cheese. Churchill may have found the meal something of an ordeal given the no-alcohol policy of the US navy, though on this occasion the President allowed himself to mix Martinis of gin and Argentine vermouth. (In contrast, the bar on the *Prince of Wales* served liquor, and the British repaid the generosity of their hosts, who showered them with cigarettes, by inviting them over for a drink or three.)[52]

At the end of the meal, Roosevelt invited Churchill to review the war situation. The Prime Minister made the most of the opportunity. His eyes flashing, he sounded forth in rolling phrases, alternately leaning back in his chair, and then hunching his shoulders forward, gnawing on his cigar. Fiddling with his pince-nez, Roosevelt doodled on the tablecloth with a burned-out match. Churchill's message was plain – the US should enter the war. Roosevelt remained non-committal as proceedings broke up at a quarter to midnight.[53]

On Sunday morning a religious service was held in bright sunshine under the six big guns on the main deck of the *Prince of Wales*. Wearing a blue double-breasted suit, and grasping a cane, Roosevelt crossed from the *Augusta* in a tender, holding his hat against his chest when he came aboard, leaning on Elliott's arm as he climbed the gangplank. Once on the deck he insisted on walking unaided, his face showing his determination. Reaching his chair beside Churchill's, he hoisted a triumphant beam.[54]

Two hundred and fifty American sailors and marines joined him. The national colours were draped over the pulpit. Chaplains from each country officiated. The Prime Minister, who wore one of his quasi-naval uniforms and a cap that sat slightly askew, chose as hymns 'Onward Christian Soldiers' and 'O God Our Help in Ages Past' while the President picked 'Eternal Father, Strong to Save'. Among the readings were verses from the Book of Joshua advising 'be strong and of good courage'.[55]

Always prey to emotion, Churchill shed tears as the hymns rose from the deck. He told the War Cabinet that the service was 'a deeply moving expression of the unity of faith of our two peoples'. Nobody who saw it, he added, 'will forget the spectacle presented that sunlit morning'. Roosevelt's doctor considered that he had 'never listened to a more inspiring religious service'.[56]

Afterwards, the two leaders sat smiling and smoking as sailors clustered round to take photographs. Then they moved on to a second round of talks, followed by lunch of caviar and smoked salmon, turtle soup and grouse; Churchill presented a brace to his guest. A Royal Marines band played American marches, a Strauss waltz, and light operatic airs. At table, Hopkins turned over his menu card for Roosevelt and scrawled on the back a joke Churchill had told him – on hearing his speech appealing to the United States to 'give us the tools' to fight the war, the exiled Emperor of Abyssinia, Haile Selassie, had sent the Prime Minister a telegram saying he had the men but wondered 'what shall I do with the tools?'[57]

In the afternoon, Roosevelt was pressed again to take a tougher line towards Tokyo, with no success. As he left to return to the *Augusta*, the ship's cat ran across the deck to try to follow him. Churchill bent down to restrain the animal. Watching the American party sail away, he turned to the officers around him and said: 'You have seen a great man this day.' Then he remarked, 'On this lovely day . . . it is difficult for you and me to realise that we are fighting for our lives.' Later, he went ashore with Cadogan, 'the Prof', Harriman and his bodyguard. They clambered over rocks, and climbed a cliff from which Churchill rolled boulders. He talked incessantly; even a rain squall did not stop his flow. When he returned to the *Prince of Wales*, he carried a bunch of pink wild flowers.[58]

Though Churchill remained anxious about the impression he had made, he had no need to worry. Replying to the letter from George VI, Roosevelt wrote of the privilege it had been to come to know the visitor. 'I am very confident that our minds travel together,' he added.

'I like him – & lunching alone broke the ice both ways,' Roosevelt noted to his cousin Margaret Suckley. The ever-optimistic Churchill still hoped to achieve his ultimate aim. To H.V. Morton, he confided: 'I have an idea that something really big may be happening, something really big.'[59]

But the lack of commitment was evident throughout the US delegation. 'Not a single American officer has shown the slightest keenness to be in the war on our side,' noted Ian Jacob, a member of the War Cabinet staff. 'They are a charming lot of individuals but they appear to be living in a different world from ourselves.' The Americans, he added, were like 'reluctant bathers on the brink of a shark-infested sea' whose ideas had 'not got beyond how to avoid being bitten; they have not yet reached out to thoughts of how to get rid of the sharks'.[60]

The British military team was headed by the First Sea Lord, Dudley Pound, a sixty-four-year-old veteran of the Battle of Jutland in the First World War. Churchill was fond of the old sea dog with whom he had sat up drinking whisky in the early hours in the Admiralty. 'Pound', Churchill said, 'is necessary to me.' But the Admiral was showing his age. He suffered from deafness, and nodded off during meetings, the result of an undiagnosed brain tumour. Alan Brooke described him as looking 'like an old parrot asleep on his perch' only roused by key words like 'battleship'.[61]

The Americans fielded the pleasant, white-haired, pink-cheeked naval chief Harold Stark. Nicknamed 'Betty', he looked more like a bishop than a sailor. More fearsome was the Commander of the Atlantic fleet, Ernest King – 'tough as nails and carried himself like a poker,' a British general noted. One of King's daughters described him as 'the most even-tempered man in the Navy. He is always in a rage.' Protective of American naval resources and deeply suspicious of the British, he remarked that, when Churchill launched into his appeals for more help, he kept his hand on his watch.[62]

The solidly built General Henry Arnold, who had been taught to fly by the Wright Brothers, had converted the President to the importance of air power. Known for his cheerful nature, 'Hap' (for Happy) Arnold was the only top US commander to have been to England, watching a bombing raid from the roof of the sandbagged Dorchester Hotel. He got on well with the British Air Chief Marshal Charles Portal, a reserved pipe smoker with a small head and beaked nose. A historian of the conference, Theodore Wilson, describes the two airmen as being 'almost inseparable, neither taking much part in the general discussions'.[63]

George Marshall, the American Army Chief of Staff, immediately hit it off with Field Marshal John Dill, who was about to be replaced by Alan Brooke as Chief of the Imperial General Staff because of Churchill's impatience with him. Sent subsequently as head of the British Joint Staff Mission, Dill would become the senior liaison officer in Washington. He made the most of good contacts with Hopkins and Marshall to operate outside official channels, facilitating the flow of information and sometimes alerted by Hopkins to Roosevelt's thinking before the US Chiefs of Staff. The Americans so trusted him that, at one point, they said they would be ready to accept Dill as overall commander in Europe. Roosevelt called him 'the most important figure in Anglo-American co-operation'. 'A dear friend unique in my lifetime,' Marshall said after Dill's death in 1944. 'Never to be out of my mind.' Posthumously awarded the Distinguished Service Medal, he was buried in the military cemetery at Arlington, Virginia. But Churchill never changed his view of 'Dilly Dally', twice refusing him a peerage.[64]

The war would make Marshall a towering figure in American life, a future Secretary of State and architect of the plan for post-war European recovery. Just under six feet tall, with grey hair and piercing blue eyes, he forgot people's names and kept mislaying his spectacles – his orderly bought replacements at five-and-dime stores. A country boy from Pennsylvania, and a stickler for formality, he drove himself to the Pentagon in a small black saloon, stopping to give workers lifts. One secretary recalled that he had the shiniest shoes she had ever seen.[65]

He believed in clear lines of command – the antithesis of his commander-in-chief. Disliking the way Roosevelt called him by his first name, he showed his independence by refusing to laugh at presidential jokes. But he respected the President's authority, and never shared the opposition of the conservative military class for the New Deal – Hopkins became one of his closest friends. His main task in 1941 was to expand and modernise the army, promoting new men including Dwight Eisenhower, George Patton and others. A saying on Capitol Hill went 'Trust in God and George Marshall'. Churchill would call him 'the noblest Roman of them all'. In 1944, Roosevelt told him, 'I feel I could not sleep at night with you out of the country'.

The US military leaders, as a whole, were not well disposed towards the British, seeing them as old-fashioned masters of bureaucratic intrigue who would try to use American power to safeguard their Empire. Conscious of how unprepared his own forces were, a factor London had not properly appreciated, Marshall refused to pledge more aid. Though he hesitated to offer advice since, he said, the British were 'at this business every day – all day', he stressed the strain Lend-Lease put on US resources.[66]

The British produced a 'Review of General Strategy' that highlighted 'blockade, bombing, subversion' as the way to victory and called for the provision of 10,000 planes from America. Marshall and Stark dismissed the idea of beating Germany from the air. 'It should be recognised as an almost invariable rule that wars cannot finally be won without the use of land armies,' they said – the message was also aimed at the President who was flirting with bombing to avoid sending troops to Europe.

This pointed to a basic difference between London and the Pentagon. The bloodbath of First World War was always at the backs of the minds of British commanders and Churchill. They feared what the Wehrmacht could do to an invasion force – later calculations found that the Germans could inflict 50 per cent more casualties than they suffered from UK and US forces. This increased the British preference for attacking along the periphery in the Mediterranean and in Norway; with bombing pounding the Nazi heartland and destroying morale, the regime in Berlin would then topple. The nightmare for Churchill was that the Allies would invade France and be held or defeated, giving Hitler a second wind, and turning American opinion against the war in Europe.[67]

Marshall was not only doubtful about bombing, he was also sceptical about the Middle East and Mediterranean. To him the Russian front was much more important and worthy of receiving supplies. Longer term, he put his faith in a massive landing in northern France. Anything other than this thrust for the jugular was a sideshow, a diversion. He sought a Joe Louis knock-out punch – or, as Roosevelt would put it, 'hitting Hitler an uppercut right on the point of the jaw.'[68]

From the hour they met on the *Augusta* the President and Prime Minister looked ahead to the world they hoped would emerge from victory. Given the military position at the time, this was quite audacious. The German army was crashing through Russia. Hitler faced no challenge in western Europe. The Afrika Corps threatened Britain in the Middle East. U-boats were wreaking havoc with Atlantic shipping. Japan was threatening to expand into South East Asia, where it could capture the oil fields of the East Indies.

In this forbidding context, the two leaders set out to lay down principles to make it clear that the issues in the war went beyond the battlefield. However much hypocrisy this involved, their charter would be a key step in making the fight against the Axis powers a 'good war', pitting the forces of light against those of darkness. The job of working out a statement of those broad principles was given to the two senior diplomats present – Alexander Cadogan and Sumner Welles. The Foreign Office man was the epitome of an aristocratic mandarin; Churchill's bodyguard called him 'the coldest [man] I ever met – a real oyster'. Welles was a heavy drinking, hard-working, high-class operator, whose expression suggested that old fish was lodged in his moustache. He had known Roosevelt since their schooldays and used his privileged channel to the White House to engage in what a colleague called a 'guerilla front' with his boss, Secretary of State Cordell Hull, who, with his lisp, called him an 'all-American thun of a bitch'. The animosity was so sharp that they did not attend the same cocktail parties. The poor health of the septuagenarian Hull meant he had to take leaves of absence, during which Welles ran the department. But Roosevelt's favourite was on a personal tightrope.[69]

The previous September, travelling on the presidential train in Alabama, he had made drunken approaches to male, black sleeping-car porters, offering them money for sex. A similar indiscretion followed a few weeks later. William Bullitt, a former ambassador to France, loathed Welles and went to the White House with affidavits from the porters. The President listened for a while, pressed the button for a secretary and said, 'I don't feel well. Please cancel my appointments for the rest of the day.' Welles survived, claiming the porters had been bribed by Bullitt, but Roosevelt ordered him to be put under surveillance.[70]

By Sunday night, Welles and Cadogan had completed a draft of general principles for discussion by the leaders the following morning.[71] The Americans had no wish for anything resembling a treaty, which would cause trouble with Congress. All they required was a statement of intent, phrased so that isolationists could not object. There would be no hint of any commitment to enter the war.

On the Monday morning, Roosevelt and Churchill were joined in the admiral's quarters on the *Augusta* by Welles, Cadogan, Beaverbrook and Hopkins, who was suffering from near-total exhaustion but insisted on being present. Bright sunshine streamed through the portholes.

Roosevelt wore an open-necked shirt and grey suit; Churchill was in naval uniform. The Americans worried that Britain might be making secret agreements on post-war territorial arrangements. The State Department had reminded Roosevelt of how Woodrow Wilson had been confronted at Versailles by unexpected secret pacts. Roosevent had specifically asked Churchill for assurances before Placentia Bay – to which he got no reply.[72]

Returning to the issue, he called for a declaration that no future commitments were being made. Apart from the question of principle, he needed to be able to refute allegations by political opponents that he was conniving with the British. Churchill said that ruling out commitments risked discouraging resistance movements in occupied countries. The British people would also be put off if they thought their future was uncertain.

Roosevelt compromised. He thought it would be enough if he could say that nothing had come up which had not already been indicated in his public statements. Welles passed round a fresh draft, which satisfied both sides for the time being. But the issue would resurface before long in tense exchanges between London and Washington.[73]

Egged on by the imperial-minded Beaverbrook, the Prime Minister homed in on an American-inspired commitment in the draft statement for the two nations to 'endeavor to further the enjoyment by all peoples of access, without discrimination and on equal terms, to the markets and to the raw materials of the world which are needed for their economic prosperity'. Did that apply to the preferential system of the British Empire? he asked.[74]

It was a key issue. Britain saw the preferential trading system between the dominions and colonies as a sovereign matter for it and them. Washington was intent on making free trade a plank of the post-war world. Cordell Hull regarded commerce on American lines as a stepping stone to global peace, and 'a knife to open that oyster shell, the Empire'. As the historian Warren Kimball puts it, 'eliminating imperial preference had become a neoreligious quest'. Roosevelt agreed with this thrust. In addition, he told Churchill, such a clause would assure the German and Italian peoples that they would get a 'fair and equal opportunity of an economic character' after their defeat.[75]

The Prime Minister responded that he, himself, was in favour of free trade. But he knew the political storm such a commitment would arouse at home. So he played for time by saying he could not decide on his own since Canada, Australia, New Zealand and South Africa were also involved. It would take at least a week to get their opinions.

Welles objected that modification of the clause 'would destroy completely any value in that portion of the proposed declaration'. A vital principle was at stake. If the United States and Britain could not agree, 'they might as well throw in the sponge and realize that one of the greatest factors in creating the present tragic global situation was . . . to continue unchecked in the post-war world'.

Churchill returned to his difficulty with the Dominions – there was a certain irony in this since, despite their important contributions to the war effort, he never sought to bring them into arrangements for mutual benefit. At one point, the Labour Prime Minister of Australia, John Curtin, said his country looked to the United States rather than 'to our traditional links with the United Kingdom'. Australian First World War losses at Gallipoli rankled, as did the thought that Churchill was deploying its troops far away when the homeland needed to be defended.

The imperial issue came up again at dinner when Roosevelt remarked that a pre-condition of peace should be the greatest possible freedom of trade.[76]

His head lowered, Churchill, who had been knocking back brandy, watched the President steadily from his armchair.

'No artificial barriers,' Roosevelt said, according to Elliott, who was present. 'As few favoured economic agreements as possible. Opportunities for expansion. Markets opened for healthy competition.'

'The British Empire trade agreements are . . .' Churchill interposed.

'Yes,' the President interrupted, 'those Empire trade agreements are a case in point. It's because of them that the people of India and Africa, of all the colonial Near East and Far East, are still as backward as they are.'

Reddening, Churchill crouched forward. The trade that had made England great should continue, he declared – by Elliott's account – 'under conditions prescribed by England's ministers'.

'You see,' Roosevelt said slowly, 'there is likely to be some disagreement between you, Winston, and me. I am firmly of the belief that if we are to arrive at a stable peace, it must involve the development of backward countries . . . It cannot be done, obviously, by eighteenth-century methods. Now . . .'

'Who's talking eighteenth-century methods?' Churchill interrupted. Hopkins grinned.

'Twentieth-century methods involve bringing industries to these colonies,' Roosevelt said. 'Twentieth-century methods include increasing the wealth of the people by increasing their standard of living, by educating them, by bringing them sanitation – by making sure that they get a return for the raw wealth of their community.'

With Churchill looking increasingly apoplectic, Roosevelt insisted that the war on Fascism had to go hand in hand with freeing people all over the world from colonialism.

'What about the Philippines?' Churchill asked, trying to score a point on US colonialism there. Roosevelt pointed out that education and sanitation had been promoted.

When Churchill invoked the sanctity of imperial agreements, Roosevelt again waved them aside as artificial.

'They're the foundation of our greatness,' the British leader grunted.

'The peace cannot include any continued despotism,' Roosevelt ploughed on. 'The structure of the peace demands and will get equality of peoples. Equality of peoples involves the utmost freedom of competitive trade.'

Smoking a last cigarette in bed after the dinner ended at 2 a.m., Roosevelt grunted to Elliott: 'A real old Tory, isn't he? A real old Tory, of the old school.' He thought he would be able to work with Churchill – 'We'll get along famously.' But he forecast more talk about India – 'And Burma. And Java. And Indo-China. And Indonesia. And all the African colonies. And Egypt and Palestine. We'll talk about 'em all. Don't forget one thing. Winnie has one supreme mission in life, but only one. He's a perfect war-time prime minister. His one big job is to see that Britain survives this war . . . He changes the subject away from anything post war . . . His mind is perfect for that of a war leader. But Winston Churchill lead Britain after the war? It'd never work.'*

The conversation rankled with Churchill. The following night, at the end of dinner, he got up and walked round the room, talking and

* Churchill once remarked: 'Those who can win a war well can rarely make a good peace and those who could make a good peace would never have won the war.' (Churchill Museum, London)

gesticulating. Stopping in front of Roosevelt, he waved a stubby finger at him.

'Mr President,' he cried, according to Elliott's memoir, 'I believe you are trying to do away with the British Empire. Every idea you entertain about the structure of the post-war world demonstrates it. But in spite of that – in spite of that – we know that you constitute our only hope.

'And you know that we know it,' he went on, his voice dropping to dramatic effect. 'You know that we know that without America, the Empire won't stand.'

Having recognised Britain's dependence, Churchill came up with a diplomatic solution, suggesting a phrase to state that the agreement on trade paid 'due regard for our present obligations'. This would cover him while not fatally weakening the declaration of principle. Roosevelt accepted the wording. Hull was less accommodating; from Washington, he warned that the US would act unilaterally if necessary to get a stronger statement. The threat in the background was that this might be made a condition of Lend-Lease supplies. Churchill played for time, and the ambassador in London pointed to the danger of negative reaction in Britain where 'a lot of people . . . are beginning to feel that we are slow about coming in [to the war].'[77]

Another ambiguity was in a clause expressing 'the right of all peoples to choose the form of government under which they will live'. For Churchill, this applied to those under Fascist rule, not to the Empire. The Americans could interpret it as referring to colonialism in general.

The President expressed pleasure at a British suggestion to include a point on welfare, improved working conditions and economic growth. The idea had not been Churchill's. It had come in a message from Clement Attlee, who had called a Cabinet meeting at 3 a.m. London time to approve the draft of the charter, sent from Placentia Bay.

Churchill wanted a commitment to an 'effective international organisation' for the post-war world. Though he would later make the creation of the United Nations a key to his post-war world, Roosevelt said he could not agree because this would look like reviving the League of Nations, and arouse opposition in the United States. It was Churchill's turn to give ground, so the clause just spoke of the need to disarm nations that might threaten aggression 'pending the establishment of a wider and permanent system of general security'.[78]

On that note, the most intense negotiation of the conference broke up. Welles and Cadogan left to polish up the wording of what became known as the Atlantic Charter – Churchill went through the final draft presented to him, making half a dozen stylistic alterations in red ink.[79]

The last summit session took place on the *Augusta* on Tuesday, 12 August, over a lunch attended by Churchill, Roosevelt, Hopkins and Beaverbrook, who was becoming a key figure in supply matters. It was agreed that an Anglo-American mission should go to Moscow in September. Beaverbrook would be one of its two leaders. Hopkins's health was too bad for him to make the trip, so Harriman would replace him.

Lunch over, the two leaders went on the quarter deck to bid farewell. Supported by his two sons, Roosevelt walked down a line of British and American officers shaking their hands. Churchill did the same. They exchanged signed photographs, and clasped hands. Then, as the band on the *Augusta* struck up 'God Save the King', the British party climbed down to a motor launch and crossed to the *Prince of Wales*.

Accompanied by a US destroyer escort, the battleship left at 5 p.m. under grey skies and through a drizzle, the band playing 'Auld Lang Syne'. Roosevelt watched from the deck of the *Augusta*. At sea, Churchill sent a message: 'God bless the President and the people of the United States.' To which the reply was, 'Good luck to each and every one of you'.

On the way home, the Prince of Wales passed through a convoy of 72 ships. 'The forest of funnels looked almost like a town', Cadogan noted in his diary. The cargo ships carried military supplies and food. Some had aircraft lashed to their decks. As the great battleship sped past, the crews cheered and waved their caps. Churchill gestured back, his fingers split in his first flashing of the V-sign. When the Prince of Wales moved ahead of the convoy, he ordered it to circle back and pass through the convoy again. Flags on the tramp steamers and tankers echoed his V message. 'A delectable sight,' Churchill breathed.[80]

The summit had been invaluable in enabling Churchill and Roosevelt to get to know one another. Despite their differences, they had hit it off. The President wrote to his cousin Margaret Suckley that the meeting had 'contributed to things we hold dear. We hope the country will approve.' Democrats hailed the document. The *New York Times* said it was expected to be followed by 'further declarations and actions'. The Supreme Court Justice Felix Frankfurter called it truly historic, 'grandly conceived and finely executed', creating what the presidential speechwriter, Robert Sherwood, dubbed 'the Common Law Alliance'.

Towards the end of his life, Roosevelt would refer to the Charter as a beautiful idea. When it was drawn up, he said, 'the situation was that England was about to lose the war. They needed hope, and it gave it to them.' But despite pressure for greater involvement from leading Cabinet members the President went into a cautious crouch. He instructed his Press Secretary not to make any comment when issuing the text of the Atlantic Charter. Though the Chiefs of Staff were pushing ahead with plans for an army of 6 million, a navy to dominate the Pacific and Atlantic and an air force of 50,000 planes, there had been a sombre warning of congressional opinion when the House of Representatives renewed the draft by one vote.[81]

The conference had been an 'interchange of views, that's all. Nothing else,' the President told reporters when he got back to Washington. Was the US any closer to going to war? they asked. No, was the reply. Blithely ignoring what had happened in Europe in the two previous years, he added that declarations of war were out of fashion. Having finally agreed at the end of the summit to issue a warning to Tokyo, he put nothing in writing. Only a watered-down version was passed on to the Japanese ambassador – verbally.[82]

As usual, the President was in step with public opinion. Though polls reported strong approval of the Charter, a Gallup survey reported that 68 per cent thought America should avoid war in all circumstances. A leading Republican, Robert Taft, said that even the collapse of Britain would be preferable to 'the participation for the rest of our lives in European wars'.[83]

Churchill, naturally, made all he could of the summit. He hailed it as representing '. . . the deep underlying unities which stir and at decisive moments rule the English-speaking peoples throughout the world . . . the marshalling of the good forces of the world against the evil forces . . . which have cast their cruel spell over the whole of Europe and a large part of Asia?'[84]

On the 'evil' side, Hitler was not impressed. Meeting Mussolini a week after Placentia Bay, he dismissed the summit as unimportant. Nor were Churchill's private feelings up to his public celebration. He had gained some new undertakings, such as American naval escorts for British convoys, with orders to attack U-boats even if they were 300 miles away. He could speak of Washington waging war without declaring it. But he had been taught a lesson. 'The President, for all his warm heart and good intentions is thought by many of his admirers to move with public opinion rather than to lead and form it,' he told his son, Randolph.

In a cable to Hopkins from London on 29 August, he wrote of a 'wave of depression through Cabinet and other informed circles here about the President's many assurances about no commitments and no closer to war etc. . . . If 1942 opens with Russia knocked out and Britain is left alone again, all kinds of dangers may arise . . . Should be grateful if you could give me any sort of hope.'[85]

Hopkins showed the President the message, warning that, if the British concluded the US was not going to enter the conflict, 'that would be a very critical moment in the war and the British appeasers might have some influence on Churchill'. But, visiting Washington after Placentia Bay, Beaverbrook concluded: 'There isn't the slightest chance of the U.S. entering the war until compelled to do so by a direct attack on its own territory.' This, the press lord feared, might not happen until Britain and the Soviet Union had been defeated. The first summit had come and gone. The two leaders had agreed on a grand set of principles. But the full alliance was elusive.[86]

3

Uncle Joe

'There is still a long and hard path to be traversed'

ROOSEVELT AND CHURCHILL

THREE DAYS AFTER THE Placentia Bay summit ended, the American and British ambassadors in Moscow delivered a message from their leaders to Stalin, assuring him that they recognised how vital 'the brave and steadfast resistance of the Soviet Union' was to defeat Germany. The 'very maximum of supplies' would be sent – a seven-ship convoy was about to leave Iceland for Archangel. To show how much importance he attached to this, Roosevelt put Hopkins in charge of expediting aid to the USSR. But there was also a note of caution. It was important to decide where resources could best be used, the message said. Every gun for the eastern front was one less for US and British forces.

To ensure efficient allocation of supplies, Roosevelt and Churchill proposed sending to Moscow the joint mission they had discussed. After which, the three leaders should jointly consider policy, 'since there is still a long and hard path to be traversed before . . . victory without which our efforts and sacrifices would be wasted.'[1]

Expressing gratitude for the supplies, Stalin told the ambassadors he was ready to facilitate a three-power meeting. He certainly required all the help he could get. The Red Army was about to cede the Ukrainian capital of Kiev, at the cost of 650,000 men. Leningrad was under siege. Another great defeat at Smolensk brought the loss of 300,000 men and 3,000 tanks. An attack on

Moscow was in preparation. Many Western observers forecast a Soviet implosion within weeks, the latest in a long line of defeats that stretched back through the collapse in 1917, the defeat by Japan in 1905 to the loss of the Crimean War. And in the Winter War of 1939–40 against Finland, the Red Army had performed badly against the far less numerous Finns.

Though Churchill gave Russia no more than an even chance of lasting the winter, Soviet survival was vital to both Washington and London. This meant doing all they could whatever the political and ideological differences. The US Chiefs of Staff concluded that 'only Russia possesses adequate manpower, situated in favourable proximity to the center of German power' to attack Hitler's heartland on the ground. Roosevelt told the Secretary of War, that sending arms to the USSR was important 'for the safety and security of America'. In terms of proxies, the Soviet Union could be even more useful than Britain – so long as it held out. Beyond that, Roosevelt counted on it becoming a partner in the post-war world as it emerged from its revolutionary purdah.[2]

Roosevelt's adoption of the USSR as a new proxy led to the prospect that, if Stalin held out, Churchill's goal of getting America into the war might be even further delayed. Still, Soviet survival was vital for Britain in diverting German forces from the western front. London and Moscow signed a treaty pledging to help one another and undertook not to negotiate or conclude an armistice or peace with Berlin except by mutual agreement. This did not signify any change in Churchill's view of Communists; on the day after the signing of the accord, he described them as barbarians unconnected with humanity. But he could draw a distinction between the creed, which he abhorred, and the ally he needed. As he put it, if Hitler had invaded Hell, he would have found it in himself to 'make a favourable reference to the Devil in the House of Commons'.[3]

Not that there was much practical cooperation. A Soviet military delegation to London adopted a peremptory and truculent manner – Dill described them as 'like a lot of pig stickers'. A British military mission to Moscow was cold shouldered.[4]

Churchill found it hard to forget Moscow's pact with Hitler in 1939, or how the Red Army invaded Poland from the east, attacked Finland and stood by while the Nazis conquered Western Europe – on a visit to Berlin in 1940, Molotov had talked of carving up the Empire with Germany. Stalin ignored a message sent by Churchill soon after he took office proposing collaboration; the dictator promptly reported the démarche to Hitler. As the Wehrmacht surged forward through Russia, Churchill conjured up fears of a second German–Soviet pact. Though this was conjecture, Stalin did twice tell the secret police chief Lavrenty Beria to try an indirect approach to Berlin to ask about armistice terms; but Hitler had no interest in peace.

The memory of 1939–41 made it even more galling for the Prime Minister to receive messages from the Kremlin blaming Hitler's ability to move troops to the east on the absence of a front in the west. Churchill could argue that Britain's presence in North Africa and the Middle East tied down significant Nazi forces. But this cut no ice in the Kremlin. Stalin wanted an attack in the Balkans or France, plus 30,000 tons of aluminum within weeks and minimum monthly supply of 400 planes and 500 tanks. 'Without these two forms of help,' he warned, 'the Soviet Union will either suffer defeat or be weakened to such an extent that it will lose for a long period any capacity to render assistance to its Allies by its actual operations'.[5]

When Maisky delivered this message, Churchill reacted sharply. 'Remember that, only four months ago, we in this Island did not know whether you were not coming in against us on the German side,' he retorted. 'Whatever happens . . . you, of all people, have no right to make reproaches to us.' Writing to the British ambassador in Moscow, Stafford Cripps, he said Stalin would have 'remained utterly indifferent' if Britain had been invaded. 'If they harbour suspicions of us it is only because of the guilt and self-reproach in their own hearts,' he added.[6]

Though some Cabinet colleagues favoured opening a front in the west, the Prime Minister would have none of it. He told Stalin there was no chance of a British offensive in France or the Balkans. 'Action, however well-meant, leading only to costly fiasco would be of no help to anyone but Hitler,' he added in an argument he was to deploy repeatedly – with the Americans as well as with the Kremlin. The Georgian replied that, if no attack could be mounted in the west, Britain should send 25 to 30 divisions to Archangel or the southern Soviet Union – an idea seen in London as 'a physical absurdity'.*

The issue of a second front would become a recurrent theme over the

---

* Churchill's wife took the helm of an Aid to Russia appeal which raised £8 million.

following three years, with Stalin returning repeatedly to the failure of America and Britain to land troops in France. But there must be doubt as to whether he really expected action in 1942 or 1943. The Western Allies lacked men and landing craft, and Hitler still had superior forces across the Channel. 'From the first, I did not believe they would do it,' Molotov told an interviewer towards the end of his life. 'This was a completely impossible operation for them . . . I don't doubt that Stalin too believed they would not carry it out.' At the Teheran summit, Stalin acknowledged at one point that the mere threat of landing in northern France had pinned down 25 German divisions. But, Molotov added, 'our demand was politically necessary and we had to press them for everything.' It was too useful a political tool not to be used to ensure that the Western Allies would compensate by pumping supplies to the eastern front.[7]

For Britain, the danger was that this would divert desperately needed American supplies, and strain its own domestic production. The service ministers and chiefs of staff made their feelings plain at an evening meeting in Downing Street on 19 September. Churchill said the importance of the eastern front meant making a fair offer of help – he had already told Stalin Britain would send 240 Hurricane fighters on top of 200 American Tomahawk planes.

Annoyed when the military men tried to limit the supplies, Churchill hunched over in his seat, scowling deeply, his head sinking low over the table. After a break for dinner, however, he was in a better mood. Showing off a large cigar cabinet he had received as a gift from the President of Cuba, he remarked that he had had some difficulty getting it through Customs. He handed a cigar to each man at the meeting, warning that it might contain deadly poison. Lighting up, the group went back into the Cabinet room. In half an hour everything had been settled.[8]

Still, three days later, Churchill wrote to Roosevelt of 'feeling very blue about all we have to give up to Russia'. More than a year after the USSR entered the war, he would note in his memoirs, 'she presented herself to our minds as a burden and not as a help'. The services, he recalled, felt the diversion of supplies 'like flaying off pieces of their skin'.[9]

As envoys to Stalin, two men were chosen as far removed from Communism as could be imagined. The gnarled, gnome-like Beaverbrook, born Max Aitken, made a fortune in his native Canada before moving to Britain, where he became owner of the *Daily* and *Sunday Express*, and aspired to play an important political role. Known for his political scheming and high living, the sixty-two-year-old Minister for Air Production was a fervent believer in the Empire, who said he used his newspapers 'for propaganda not profit'.

Beaverbrook was unpopular with colleagues, and one of her husband's cronies that Clementine thoroughly disapproved of – in a note to him in 1942, she described Beaverbrook as a 'microbe which some people fear is in your blood – Exorcise this bottle Imp & see if the air is not cleaner & purer'. But Churchill saw his work on boosting fighter output in 1940 as a key element in winning the Battle of Britain. Nothing, the Prime Minister's doctor noted, could 'shake the P.M.'s faith in his genius'. In a letter to Stalin which he gave Beaverbrook to deliver, Churchill described the Canadian as 'one of my oldest and most intimate friends.'[10]

His companion on the trip was an even richer man, though he was tight with his money. Six weeks from his fiftieth birthday, Averell Harriman had inherited $100 million from his father's Union Pacific Railroad fortune, and was a Wall Street figure before becoming a Hopkins protégé. In the spring of 1941, he was sent to London to handle Lend-Lease affairs, by-passing the embassy. In his letter to Stalin, Churchill called him 'a remarkable American, wholeheartedly devoted to the victory of our common cause.'[11]

The American also had a personal link with Churchill, though one which was kept discreet. Harriman was having an affair with the wife of Churchill's hard-drinking, indebted son, Randolph. The alluring, auburn-haired Pamela had married Randolph in October 1939, and given birth to a son a year later. Six months on, she and Harriman slept together for the first time during an air raid after a dinner at the Dorchester Hotel in honour of Fred Astaire's sister, Adele. At the time, she was twenty-one – two years younger than Harriman's daughter, who arrived in London soon afterwards. Pamela remembered the lantern-jawed American as 'absolutely marvelous with his raven black hair . . . very athletic, very tan, very healthy'. Others recalled him as a middle-aged man with a slight stoop and mournful brown eyes who wore rumpled suits and had the gaunt air of an undertaker, when not flashing his broad smile. The Soviet diplomat Maxim Litvinov asked how a man with a hundred million dollars could look so sad.*[12]

The aid mission, which included Churchill's military aide, General

Hastings 'Pug' Ismay, sailed to the Arctic city of Archangel on a two-funnelled cruiser, HMS *London*. There was no escort since it was feared that this might draw German attention. The passengers took 1,000 pounds of luggage – the Foreign Office advised packing soap. Churchill's farewell message said they bore with them 'the hope of the world'. He warned Beaverbrook not to divulge 'our special source of information' – the Ultra monitoring of German military communications.[13]

After a five-hour flight from Archangel the party gathered in Beaverbrook's room at the Hotel National, in Moscow. To beat the microphones they assumed were planted in their quarters, they turned on the wireless at full volume, tapped wine glasses with forks as they spoke and dropped their voices so low that they almost had to lip read.[14]

On the night of 28 September, Harriman and Beaverbrook drove through the blacked-out city to the first high-level meeting of the three powers. With them were the two ambassadors, Stafford Cripps and the American Laurence Steinhardt. Outside the Kremlin, a huge piece of canvas had been erected as camouflage. Guards shone torches into the car before opening the heavy gates. The visitors were taken to Stalin's office, dominated by portraits of Lenin, Marx and Engels, with a table big enough to seat twenty people.[15]

Wearing a mottled brown tunic, their host gave a correct but reserved greeting, Molotov standing beside him. The interpreter Litvinov came in – the visitors were taken aback by his shoddy appearance, but the dangerously cosmopolitan former Foreign Minister, who was married to an Englishwoman, was lucky to have survived the purges.

The ambassadors were sent away. Hopkins had warned Harriman that Stalin disliked Steinhardt, who was the first envoy to try to bring some realism to Washington's rosy view of the USSR but who was out of step with the White House in his belief that the Soviet Union would fall to the Germans. Beaverbrook did not want Cripps present so that he could start with a clean slate. He felt uncomfortable with the austere, self-righteous, left-winger – Stalin also took a cautious view of those who drank little or not at all.

---

* They married thirty years later. After Harriman died in 1986, she became US ambassador to France. Her lovers included the Ali Khan, Gianni Agnelli of Fiat, the broadcaster Ed Murrow and his boss at CBS, Bill Paley.

Stalin said he needed 1,400 tanks a month, but would settle for 500. He also wanted Spitfires, anti-tank guns, armour plating and barbed wire. As he spoke, he looked at Litvinov rather than at the visitors. In the gaps for interpretation, he sketched wolves on a napkin.[16]

The Soviet leader then suggested London might send troops to fight in Ukraine. Beaverbrook said British forces in Iran might be diverted to the Caucasus. 'There is no war in the Caucasus,' Stalin replied. 'But there is in the Ukraine.' It was past midnight when the visitors left. They felt 'more than pleased' at this first contact; Beaverbrook sent an exuberant message home for factories that would make tanks for Russia – 'Boys, Oh Boys, you have raised the roof and lifted the lid and beaten the band.'[17]

When the visitors returned to the Kremlin for their second meeting, Stalin was sallow, tired, almost emaciated. Rude and surly, he appeared under intense strain as news came in of a fresh German advance. Walking round the room, he smoked continuously, breaking off three times to pick up a telephone and dial a number, probably to get the latest tidings from the front. When Beaverbrook handed him a letter from Churchill, he ripped open the envelope, and tossed aside the paper inside without reading it. After Molotov reminded him about it, he stuffed the sheet back in the envelope, and handed it to a clerk.

'The paucity of your offers clearly shows you want to see the Soviet Union defeated,' he said. Harriman felt deeply discouraged. Beaverbrook feared the political consequences for himself of failure. Radio Berlin reported that the talks had fallen apart.[18]

Though under great strain, the Soviet leader may have been acting up to get the most out of the visitors. He certainly had an effect. After being told of the conversation, Roosevelt sent Harriman a 'Most Secret' cable agreeing to step up the supply of tanks.[19]

At the third session, Stalin reverted to his friendly routine. It was, the American recalled, 'all business' as they went through a list of seventy items the Russians wanted. When Beaverbrook asked if he was pleased with what was now on offer, Stalin puffed on his pipe, smiled and nodded. Bounding from his chair, Litvinov cried, 'Now we shall win the war!'[20]

The Soviet Union was promised 200 planes, 250 tanks and 1,000 trucks a month, plus $340 million worth of steel, armour plate, aluminum, barbed wire, rolled brass, copper tubes, ferro-silicon, hard alloys, cutting tools, tin plate, abrasives, telephone equipment, electric cable, jeeps, woollen clothing, wheat and sugar, and $15 million of medical supplies. 'On most of these items, every day counts,' Harriman told Washington.[21]

Capitalising on the good mood, he urged Stalin to develop a personal relationship with Roosevelt by writing directly to him. The Georgian said he would be glad to do so.

Beaverbrook suggested he invite Churchill to Moscow.

'Will he come?' Stalin asked.

'He might well if you ask him,' the Canadian replied.[22]

The meeting broke up in the friendliest fashion possible, Harriman reported. Beaverbrook wrote of 'scenes of complete happiness . . . sunshine after rain'. There was even time for a jocular exchange about ambassadors. Harriman said the Soviet envoy in Washington, Constantin Oumansky, 'talked too much and ran around the capital creating more irritation than good will'. As for Cripps, Beaverbrook said there was nothing wrong with him except that he was a bore. 'In that respect, is he comparable to Maisky?' Stalin asked. 'No, to Madame Maisky,' came the reply – the ambassador's wife being known as a compulsive talker. Stalin enjoyed the joke.[23]

Harriman got the impression that the Soviet leader was a nationalist, not a revolutionary and that aid and personal relations might eradicate suspicions between the governments. Beaverbrook described Stalin as 'a kindly man' and 'a faithful friend'.[24]

However, parallel military talks proved sticky. The Russians divulged little or no information. When the Westerners asked how many anti-tank guns a Soviet division had, the answer was: 'It depends on what sort of division.' When they suggested an infantry division, the reply was: 'That depends on where it has to fight.' Ismay felt that the West should tell Stalin that, if he was going to demand everything and give nothing, he would be left to handle Hitler as best he could. But Washington and London chose to avoid confrontation.[25]

Between the sessions, the visitors attended a party with gypsy music at the US Embassy, and *Swan Lake* at the Bolshoi Theatre. Like Hopkins two months earlier, a German air raid forced them to go to a shelter in Moscow's ornately decorated underground railway, where they were served food from their hotel, and played cards, Beaverbrook cleaning up at gin rummy.[26]

On their last night, they were invited to the eighteenth-century Catherine Hall in the Kremlin, with its green silk wallpaper and chairs bearing the empress's monogram. Stalin appeared wearing soft leather boots, baggy trousers and a tunic that seemed to hang off his body. Ismay likened him to 'a wild animal in search of prey . . . his eyes shrewd and full of cunning'.[27]

Sitting between Beaverbrook and Harriman at the banquet as anti-aircraft batteries opened up outside, he chatted amiably and defended the pact with Germany as a last resort forced by Britain's unwillingness to join an anti-Nazi alliance. The occupation of Poland had, he said, been necessary to keep the Wehrmacht as far away as possible. Leningrad would hold, as would Moscow. The danger point was Ukraine, where he admitted that there was great hostility to the Soviet regime. Raising the matter of the second front, Stalin baited Beaverbrook with a taunt he would repeat over the years. 'What is the point of having an army if it doesn't fight?' he asked. Harriman thought this 'supremely tactless', but felt it inadvisable to have an argument.[28]

The banquet consisted of hors d'oeuvres, caviar, soup, fish, suckling pig, chicken, game, ice cream, cakes and fruit flown in from the south, washed down with red and white wines. Champagne was served with the deserts, followed by Armenian brandy. Stalin ate well, nibbling caviar from his knife. Thirty-two pepper vodka toasts were drunk, but the host preferred wine. When a champagne bottle was put in front of him, he placed a glass on top of it to keep in the bubbles. After the meal, two films were shown while more champagne flowed. The dictator saw off his guests at 1 a.m. As they flew out the next day, the Germans were surrounding the Red Army at the city of Orel, 200 miles south-west of Moscow. 'For all military purposes Soviet Russia is done with,' the Nazi press chief Otto Dietrich proclaimed: 'The British dream of a two-front war is dead.'[29]

But, when Beaverbrook and Harriman went to Chequers to report on their talks, Churchill seemed greatly reassured by Stalin's determination to fight. He sent a cable to the Kremlin promising regular convoys to Archangel, the first with 160 heavy tanks, 290 fighters plus 250 guns and ammunition. He began his message with the Latin tag 'Bis dat qui cito dat' ('Help in time is double help'). Still, there was a considerable gap between what Stalin wanted and what the West could offer. A shipment in mid-October consisted of 100 bombers and 100 fighters, plus 94 light tanks and 7 medium tanks – far short of the volume agreed by the Harriman–Beaverbrook mission. Though Roosevelt decided to declare the defence of the Soviet Union vital to the defence of the USA, which qualified the USSR for Lend-Lease, he grew irritated with shipment delays. On the bottom of one memo, he scrawled 'Hurry, Hurry, Hurry!' To Stalin, he wrote: 'We are going to bend every possible effort to move these supplies to your battle lines.'*[30]

To strengthen Russia's dollar position, he authorised the purchase of Soviet gold worth $30 million, followed by an interest-free $1-billion loan on which repayment would not start until five years after the end of the war. A supply expert was named to replace the sceptical Steinhardt as ambassador – an old Rooseveltian friend, Rear Admiral William Standley.

The President still had to deal with significant American reservations about Moscow. Writing to Churchill, Hopkins noted there were 'an amazing number of people here who do not want to help Russia and who don't seem able to pound into their thick heads the strategic importance of that front.' Senator Harry Truman wrote to his wife that the Soviets were 'as untrustworthy as Hitler and Al Capone' – he thought America should help Russia if Germany was winning, and Germany if Russia was winning, so as to 'let them kill as many as possible'. To counter the hostility of Catholics to godless Communism, Roosevelt sent an envoy to urge the Pope to be more accommodating towards the USSR; the Vatican bent slightly with a doctrinal statement allowing a distinction between Russia, as a nation, and Communism.[31]

For his part, Stalin dispatched Litvinov as ambassador to the US to replace the unpopular Oumansky. But, if he was anxious for smooth relations with Washington, he was ready to play a rougher game with Churchill, whose country carried less weight. Complaints began over Britain's reservations about declaring war on Finland, Romania and Hungary, which had joined in the attack on Russia. Stalin called leaks to the British press on the issue 'intolerable', and asked if London's aim was

---

* More than 100 vessels took supplies on the Arctic route by the end of 1941, threatened by U-boats and planes from German bases in Norway as they sailed in constant light in summer and intense cold in winter.

'to demonstrate the lack of unity between the USSR and Britain'. When Churchill replied that he would not divulge Britain's military plans to the Kremlin 'any more than you can tell me about yours', he received what he would call a 'chilling' response. Maisky translated the message personally before taking it to Downing Street. He asked that Anthony Eden be present. As he handed the message over, the Ambassador urged the Prime Minister to treat it 'with all possible calm'.[32]

Stalin's message blamed the lack of clarity in relations on two failings:

(a)   There is no definite understanding between our two countries on war aims and on plans for the post-war organisation of the peace.

(b)   There is no agreement between the USSR and Great Britain on mutual military assistance against Hitler in Europe.

As long as there is no accord on both these questions, there can be no clarity in Anglo-Soviet relations. More than that to be frank, as long as the present situation exists there will be difficulty in securing mutual confidence.[33]

As for a proposal by Churchill to send the Russian-speaking commander in India, Iraq and Iran, General Wavell, and his deputy, General Paget, for talks in Moscow, Stalin said he could not find time to see them unless they came to discuss the two fundamental questions he had outlined.

On reaching this passage, Churchill jumped from his chair, and marched round the room in what Maisky described as 'a state of extreme excitement'.

'What!' he shouted. 'I send Stalin my best men, and he doesn't want to receive them. I try to meet him in every possible way, and he replies by letters like that. I can't understand what Stalin wants. Bad relations? A rupture? Whom will that benefit? Now, when the Germans are at the gate of Moscow and Leningrad is ringed with blockade!' Sitting down, he said heavily: 'We shall think this one.'

Beaverbrook went to the Soviet Embassy, seeking to promote a reconciliation. The vital thing was to prevent Churchill from replying in anger, he said.

Maisky must have sent word to Moscow, because Stalin relaxed. The ambassador told Eden that Stalin wanted it to be known that his earlier message was prompted only by a desire to be businesslike. He had not intended to cause offence.

Cooling, Churchill replied with a cable that began by referring to his personal correspondence with Roosevelt, and added that his only wish was 'to work on equal terms of comradeship and confidence with you'. He said that he was trying to get Finland to stop fighting. Receiving no positive reply from Helsinki, Britain declared war two weeks later, as well as on Romania and Hungary.[34]

As for the post-war settlement, Churchill, well aware of American feelings on the subject, merely said that, once Germany was defeated, there should be a conference of the three allies. Its first object would be to prevent Germany launching another war. Beyond that he was silent, except for adding that political differences did not constitute 'any obstacle to our making a good plan for our mutual safety and rightful interests'.

The Foreign Office thought Stalin suspected that the old anti-Bolshevist wanted to see the USSR so weakened by the war that it would be largely excluded from a peace dictated by Washington and London. What could seem more logical to a leader who had been ready to see Germany and Britain fight to a standstill to the benefit of his regime? To clear the air, Churchill proposed that Eden should go to Moscow to 'discuss every question relating to the war'. Stalin agreed.

As he was navigating the Soviet rapids, Churchill had to face the fact that Placentia Bay had produced meagre results. He rejoiced at a further amendment of the Neutrality Acts allowing the arming of US merchant ships. But, on the core issue of asking Congress to declare war, Roosevelt was as elusive as ever. Churchill's doctor, Charles Wilson, became frightened as he watched him walking round 'head thrust forward, scowling at the ground, the sombre countenance clouded, the features set and resolute, the jowl clamped as if he had something between his teeth and did not mean to let it go'. He wondered in his diary how long his patient could go on like that.[35]

Despite German submarine attacks on American naval ships, one of which was sunk with the loss of all 115 hands, Roosevelt would do no more than ratchet up his rhetoric, calling Hitler a 'rattlesnake', which should be crushed before it could strike. The President, concluded Robert Sherwood, the White House speechwriter, 'had run out of tricks. The hat from which he had pulled so many rabbits was empty.' Mussolini remarked to his Foreign Minister, Count Ciano, 'It is quite clear that Roosevelt is barking because he cannot bite.'[36]

Though Churchill urged 'a plain declaration' to warn Japan against further expansion, Roosevelt and Hull declined to go beyond economic sanctions, including an oil embargo, and continued tortuous negotiations with Tokyo. The fear in London was that Britain might find itself at war with Japan in Asia while America stayed on the sidelines. In Washington, Hopkins warned of giving the impression that 'we only sent notes and talked'.[37]

Around 20 November, Roosevelt wrote notes for Hull in pencil proposing a resumption of economic relations with Japan, including a partial lifting of the oil embargo, if Tokyo would undertake not to send more troops abroad and agree not to attack America. As for China, Roosevelt proposed: 'U.S. to introduce Japs to Chinese to talk things over but U.S. to take no part in their conversation.' This would have meant an abandonment of the Nationalist regime on the scale of the desertion of Czechoslovakia by Britain and France at Munich. Nonetheless, the scheme was initially endorsed by US military planners, who wanted time to build up their forces.[38]

Roosevelt's initiative was, however, criticised by some senior Cabinet members. Chiang Kai-shek warned that his country was at the most critical phase of its four-year-old war. Japan had moved troops into Indochina, and was now poised to cross the frontier into the Chinese province of Yunnan. Prompted by Eden, Churchill sent Roosevelt a message noting the 'very thin diet' being offered to the Nationalists, and the danger presented by the collapse of China. The President dropped his proposal, ordering US forces in the Philippines to be strengthened. But he was no nearer to asking Congress to declare war. Once again, the moves that would change history came from the Axis.[39]

4

World War

WASHINGTON, CHEQUERS, MOSCOW,
CHUNGKING, ROME, BERLIN
6–12 DECEMBER 1941

'We are all in the same boat now'

ROOSEVELT

ON THE NIGHT OF 6 December 1941, Roosevelt was working on his stamp collection and chatting to Harry Hopkins in the Oval Office. A naval officer brought in the translated intercept of the first thirteen parts of a lengthy cable sent from Tokyo to the embassy in Washington. The fourteenth and final part had not yet been deciphered.

'This means war,' Roosevelt said after reading the sheets, handing them to Hopkins. Five Japanese divisions were sailing south of the island of Formosa, which Japan had colonised half a century earlier. Convoys were in striking distance of Thailand and Malaya. 'We might be at war with Japan though nobody knew [it],' the President added.[1]

Hopkins regretted that the US was not in a position to strike the first blow.

'No, we can't do that,' the President said. 'We are a democracy and a peaceful people.'

Then, raising his voice a little, he added: 'But we have a good record.'[2]

At 10.30 a.m. on Sunday 7 December, he was handed the final section of the message from Tokyo. It said there was no point in further negotiations since 'obviously it is the intention of the American Government to conspire with Great Britain and other countries to obstruct Japan's efforts towards the establishment of peace through the creation of a New Order in Asia.'

Hopkins strolled in, wearing slacks and a sweater. As the two men sat down to a sandwich lunch, the Navy Secretary, Frank Knox, telephoned. A message from Hawaii reported an attack on Pearl Harbor. Eyewitnesses variously described the President as calm, serene, tense, excited, and shaken – he was probably all of those as his war moment came at last.* At 8.40 p.m., the Cabinet met for what he said was the most important session since the Civil War. Some proposed declaring hostilities on Germany and Italy, as well as Japan, but Roosevelt rejected the idea. Congressional leaders arrived to be briefed. Outside crowds sang 'God Bless America', 'My Country 'Tis of Thee' and 'America the Beautiful'.[3]

Then Roosevelt kept a previously arranged meeting with Edward Murrow, whose radio reports from London had alerted American opinion to Britain's fight. Hopkins joined them. At the end of the session, Murrow accompanied the aide to his bedroom. As he got into his pyjamas, Hopkins said the Japanese attack was a godsend because no other event could have united America in going to war. Sitting on the side of his bed, he pondered what lay ahead. 'Oh God – if I only had the strength,' he whispered.[4]

After a sound night's sleep, Roosevelt castigated the attack as having marked a 'date that will live in infamy'. Congress approved a declaration of war against Japan with the single dissenting voice of a Republican pacifist. 'We are going to win the war, and we are going to win the peace that follows,' Roosevelt declared on the radio.

Three thousand miles away, Churchill was dining at Chequers on the Sunday night with Averell Harriman. Ambassador Winant was the other guest. Known as 'Gil', he was developing a passion for Churchill's daughter Sarah, who was separated from her entertainer husband, Vic Oliver. The British leader seemed tired and depressed, immersed in thought. From time to time, he plunged his head into his hands. Just before 9 p.m., his butler, Sawyers, brought in a small flip-top radio, a gift from Hopkins, so that the diners could listen to the BBC news. The main items were about the Russian front and fighting in Libya. Then, the newsreader, Alvar

---

* The conspiracy theory that Roosevelt and Churchill had known of the attack and waited for it to provoke war is succinctly demolished by Warren Kimball in *Forged in War*, p.121.

Liddell, was handed a flash – the White House had just announced the attack on Pearl Harbor.[5]

At first, Churchill did not take it in. Sawyers reappeared to say that the staff had heard the news on the wireless in the kitchen. Winant suggested getting confirmation.

When their call reached the White House, Roosevelt told the ambassador what had happened.

Winant said he had a friend with him who wanted to speak to the President. He handed over the receiver.

'What's this about Japan?' Churchill asked.

'It's quite true,' Roosevelt replied. 'They have attacked Pearl Harbor. We are all in the same boat now.'

Winant took the receiver to speak to the President, then Churchill reclaimed it.

'This certainly simplifies things,' he said. 'God be with you' – or, as he added in his account, words to that effect. Later, he called Pearl Harbor 'a blessing . . . greater good fortune has rarely happened to the British Empire.' That night, as he wrote, he 'slept the sleep of the saved and thankful'. 'One hopes that eternal sleep will be like that,' he added in a sentence which he deleted from the published edition of his history of the war. The next day, he rushed to get Parliament to declare war on Japan – even before Roosevelt had gone to Congress.[6]

In Moscow, the news arrived through Western news agencies. The attack presented Stalin with a problem. Though the Red Army was holding the Wehrmacht outside Moscow, the military situation was fraught, and the Georgian saw the neutrality pact the USSR had concluded with Tokyo in April as vital in heading off a two-front war.

When Roosevelt proposed working together, Stalin suspected a trick to drag him into war in the Pacific. He did not respond to a suggestion of an Allied military conference in Moscow, and saw Roosevelt's warning that Japan was preparing to attack the Soviet Union as an attempt to push him into pre-emptive action. When Washington proposed establishing a US base in Siberia, the Kremlin replied firmly that it would do nothing to increase the risk of finding itself at war in the Far East.[7]

In London, Charles de Gaulle had no doubt of the importance of Pearl Harbor. 'Of course, there will be military operations, battles, conflicts, but the war is finished since the outcome is known from now on,' he judged. 'In this industrial war, nothing will be able to resist American power.'[8]

In China, Chiang Kai-shek greeted the news by playing a gramophone recording of 'Ave Maria'. On 9 December, China declared war on Germany, Italy and Japan – Tokyo's four-year-old invasion of its territory finally ceased to be an 'incident'. The Generalissimo suggested that he should take charge of the Allied war effort in Asia and that Japan should be blockaded while its forces were destroyed – how, he did not state.

Adolf Hitler was eating his evening meal at his bleak 'Wolf's Lair' in the East Prussian forest when news of Pearl Harbor reached him. Just as he had not told Tokyo of the invasion of Russia, so Japan had not informed him of its attack in advance. The Führer had been in low spirits as the advance on Moscow was checked. He looked aged and grey. Operation Barbarossa had cost Germany nearly 750,000 casualties, including 160,000 dead. Domestic morale had plummeted, and he had put off his end-of-year report to the Reichstag in Berlin.

The entry of the United States faced the Axis with a huge new opponent, even if it was only at war in the Pacific. With its European allies, Germany had more people than the USSR, sat on more coal and turned out more steel. But the Nazi economy was more fragile than it appeared, with shortages of reserves of oil, coal, steel, ammunition and weapons, a lack of foreign currency and a backward farm sector, as the economic historian Adam Toose has demonstrated. American industrial resources and manpower aggravated the equation – the US produced more than twice as much steel as Germany and Austria. With the build-up of American forces, the Allies would be able to put more than 30 million men in the field, compared with 17.5 million for the Axis. By the later stages of the war, the Allies would have three times as many planes and twice as many tanks.[9]

But Hitler was elated. Pearl Harbor was a dramatic coup after his own heart. In the past, he had spoken scathingly of the Japanese, calling Emperor Hirohito 'a lacquered half-monkey'. Now, he decided that 'the East Asia conflict falls to us like a present in our lap'. He had, earlier, conjured up the vision of Operation Orient in which German troops would slice through the Middle East and Iran to reach the border of India while the Japanese advanced from the east. Now this might become reality. Germany had an ally which had not been conquered in 3,000 years, he declared – even though he admitted to feeling it strange that it would be Japan which would help to 'destroy the position of the white race in East Asia and that England fights against Europe with the Bolshevik swine.'[10]

Hitler was 'beaming again with optimism and confidence in victory', the Nazi propaganda chief Josef Goebbels noted in his diary. 'A complete shift in the general world picture has taken place.' The abstemious Führer was even seen with a glass of champagne in his hand to celebrate. Though he envied the size and wealth of America, he condemned it as a 'half Judaized, half negrified' country 'which had a concept of life inspired by the most vulgar commercialism and had no feeling for any of the most sublime expression of the human spirit'. Its leader was, he thought, a criminal manipulated by Jews, suffering from syphilitic paralysis which was driving him insane. Returning to Berlin, Hitler ordered U-boat attacks on US shipping to be stepped up, and had the communications of the embassy in Berlin cut.[11]

War in the Pacific would, he reasoned, bog down America, and force it to reduce aid to Britain and the Soviet Union. Its troops would be driven from the Philippines. As for Stalin and Churchill, there was nothing to fear. Though the first was 'one of the most extraordinary figures of world history', the system he headed would crumble under a renewed onslaught in the spring, reducing the 'Slavic rabbit' people to slavery. The second was a drunken wreck from the past, 'an utterly amoral repulsive creature'. German military pressure would drive him from office as Britain reeled from defeats by Japan. A pliant government would be installed in London, which would be allowed to hold on to India for the time being, but would keep out of Fortress Europe run by the Nazis. That, Hitler noted, was only natural since 'England had always felt itself to be an insular power. It is alien to Europe, or even hostile to Europe. It has no future in Europe.'[12]

Still, he took a couple of days to consider his next move. A secret pact committing each of the three Fascist powers to go to war with the US if any one of them did so had been drawn up on 4 December – three days after the order to attack Pearl Harbor was issued in Tokyo. But it had not been signed when the raid took place. Instead, there was agreement that none of the three would conclude an armistice with Washington without mutual consent. As frequently happened, cooperation between the Axis powers was confused – what counted for them was action.[13]

After lunch on 12 December, Hitler drove to the Kroll Opera House in Berlin which was used for parliamentary sessions. As he waited while his deputy Hermann Göring went through the formalities, the leader of the third Axis power jumped the gun in Rome.

Walking on to a balcony overlooking the Piazza Venezia, Benito Mussolini addressed a crowd of 150,000, his words relayed by radio to assemblies in the squares of other Italian cities. Some of the throngs carried placards reading 'A Basso Roosevelt' and 'A Basso Churchill'. The Duce denounced the President as 'a democratic despot' who had prepared for war with 'diabolic tenacity' and 'infinite provocations'. 'Italians, men and women, stand erect,' he thundered. 'Be proud of this great hour. We shall win!' But his Foreign Minister noted that the crowds were not very enthusiastic, which he attributed to it being a cold day and to their not having eaten lunch.[14]

In Berlin, just after 2 p.m., Göring appealed to his leader, 'Führer, speak to us.' Wearing his habitual brown uniform, Hitler walked to the dais on the semi-circular platform, illuminated by spotlights. Film cameras were trained on him, and microphones picked up his words for live broadcast.

As he started his speech with a review of the war on the eastern front, his former ally in Moscow lifted the special green telephone connected to Molotov's office. An interpreter was providing an instant translation of the radio broadcast from Berlin. Stalin wanted to know if Hitler had said anything about the United States. Not yet, Molotov replied.[15]

He soon would, contrasting himself – 'the child of a small, poor family' – with Roosevelt, who enjoyed the pleasures of 'those who do business while others bleed'. The New Deal had been the biggest failure ever experienced by one man, he said, and would have led to the President being put on trial anywhere else. But the Jews had protected him to enable them to use the United States as a way of gaining revenge on European nations 'which were becoming increasingly anti-Semitic'. Having embraced 'the full diabolical meanness of Jewry', Roosevelt had created conflict by ordering US ships to provoke German submarines, launching personal attacks on the Führer, and inciting Japan to war.[16]

His voice rising to frenzy against the backdrop of wild clapping, Hitler declared that the President planned to attack Germany and Italy in 1943 on behalf of 'the Jewish-Capitalist World and Bolshevism'. So the Axis powers had decided to wage a joint war to create a new world order. Cheering engulfed the semi-circular auditorium as the eighty-eight-minute address ended. Taking the microphone, Göring said a world war had broken out 'in the truest sense of the word – a war between the powers of construction and the powers of decay.'[17]

In the US Embassy, the staff, having burned the secret codes, closed the metal shutters on the ground-floor windows as a crowd gathered in the street outside. The diplomats feared an attack on the building, but all they got was a telephone call from the Foreign Ministry summoning the chargé d'affaires, who was told by Ribbentrop, 'Your President wanted war, now he has it.' The Gestapo took the diplomats to a detention centre near Frankfurt where they were held for five and a half months before being exchanged for their German counterparts in the US.[18]

In the Kremlin, the translator reported that Hitler had announced war with the United States. Molotov lifted the telephone to tell Stalin. Would Japan now attack the Soviet Union, the Georgian asked. Unlikely, was the reply, in view of the 'lesson the Germans were being taught outside Moscow'. Still, old fears remained. *Pravda* warned that Hitler might try to drive a wedge between the Soviet Union and its allies. This, the party newspaper added, would be 'squeezed out'.[19]

In London, where the news from Berlin did not dent a Stock Exchange rally, Churchill wrote to King George VI that 'taking it all together, I am enormously relieved at the extraordinary changes of the last few days.' The danger of America going to war in the Pacific but not in Europe had been removed. A War Department memorandum identified the North Atlantic as the principal theatre of operations. It urged that American forces in Britain should be built up. Full US involvement, Churchill told Eden, 'makes amends for all, and with time and patience will give certain victory.' When somebody advocated handling Washington carefully, he said with a leer, 'Oh! That is the way we talked to her when we were wooing her; now that she is in the harem we talk to her quite differently.'[20]

In Washington, two German diplomats went into the grey French Renaissance-style State Department to hand over the declaration of war. Declining to see them, Hull sent them to the Europe Department. As they got in the lift to leave, three photographers crashed in. 'This is not very dignified,' the chargé d'affaires remarked.

The Senate agreed unanimously to 'recognize the existence of a state of war' between the United States and Germany and Italy. In the House of

Representatives, the only member who had opposed war with Japan absented herself, so the vote was unanimous there, too. The White House housekeeper bought material for blackout curtains and the *New York Times* advised readers on what to do if there was an air raid. 'We are now engaged in the greatest war ever fought by the American people,' observed the isolationist *Chicago Tribune*. 'They must win it and win a peace which will protect them and their future.'[21]

Roosevelt was at the helm of a global fight. His country was behind him as never before. The prospect of action enlivened him. As he put it in his message to Congress: 'The long known and the long expected has thus taken place. The forces endeavouring to enslave the entire world now are moving toward this hemisphere. Never before has there been a greater challenge to life, liberty, and civilization. Delay invites greater danger. Rapid and united effort by all the peoples of the world who are determined to remain free will insure a world victory of the forces of justice and of righteousness over the forces of savagery and of barbarism.' Vitally, he did not seek to define American war aims in national terms. He saw his country's best interest and the best hope of winning the war as lying in the alliance. Preserving that association would, therefore, become his fundamental purpose, with fundamental repercussions on the world to come.[22]

5

Four Men Talking

MOSCOW, WASHINGTON, LONDON
9 DECEMBER 1941–14 JANUARY 1942

'A declaration I regard as algebra. I prefer practical arithmetic.'

STALIN

I

Sailing West

After Pearl Harbor, Churchill's first thought was to go to Washington. Some thought that he should not be away at the same time as Eden was in Moscow. But he told the King that a top-level British presence in both capitals would 'make the settlement of large-scale problems between the three great Allies easier'.[1]

What he did not take into consideration was how welcome he would be. Roosevelt was fully occupied with the aftermath of Pearl Harbor and the subsequent attack on the Philippines. He had public opinion to lead, plans to consider. Replying to Churchill's proposal to cross the ocean, he expressed concern about the risks of such a trip. The Prime Minister dismissed this with a neat turn of phrase about the greater danger lying in not having a full discussion. To wait for another month would be disastrous, he added. Roosevelt continued to worry about the other man's safety – 'for the Empire needs you at the helm and we need you there'. In the end, they agreed to meet before Christmas.

On 14 December, wearing a double-breasted blue reefer coat and yachting cap, Churchill boarded the new battleship, the *Duke of York*, at Greenock in Scotland to cross the Atlantic, leaving Attlee to head the government. Twenty-seven cypher staff kept him in constant touch with London. The new Chief of the Imperial General Staff, Alan Brooke, did not make the trip but his demoted predecessor, John Dill, joined the group, along with Harriman and Beaverbrook.

The Germans branded the trip a 'penance to Canossa' forced by the military position. A cable from Clementine to her husband lamented: 'It's a horrible World at present, Europe over-run by Nazi hogs & the Far East by yellow Japanese lice.' But Churchill was in fine form. His doctor, Wilson, who was also on board, noted in his diary; 'To be Prime Minister of England in a great war, to be able to direct the Cabinet, the Army, the Navy, the Air Force, the House of Commons, England herself, is beyond even [Churchill's] dreams. He loves every minute of it . . . The tired, dull look has gone from the eye; his face lightens up as you enter the cabin.' Resolutely upbeat, Churchill cabled Roosevelt: 'Now, suddenly, the war is as good as won and England is safe.'[2]

In fact, the situation was dire. Europe was under Fascist domination; U-boats continued to take a high toll of Atlantic shipping. Though Britain scored successes against the Italians in Libya, Rommel's Afrika Corps would soon advance. Tokyo's forces were racing over the Philippines, the Dutch East Indies and Britain's imperial positions in Malaysia, Singapore, Burma and Hong Kong. Three days after Pearl Harbor, an air attack off Malaya sank the *Prince of Wales*, the great warship on which Churchill had travelled to Placentia Bay. 'In all the war, I never received a more direct shock,' he recalled. 'Japan was now master of the Pacific and the Indian Ocean, and we everywhere were weak and naked.'[3]

So impatient was he to get to Washington that he told the battleship to sail ahead of its slower escort vessels. Crossing the main German submarine lane during a pitch-black night, with hatches battened down and high waves beating on the decks, the *Duke of York* headed out on its own.

During the day, Churchill worked with the service chiefs on position papers setting out how to win the war. They would remain the core of British grand strategy and the cause of fundamental differences with the Americans. A landing in North Africa was the immediate priority, followed by an offensive in Europe in 1943 after Germany had been pummelled from the air. In the Pacific, supremacy would be achieved in 1942. Overall victory could come in 1943 or 1944 by pursuing 'Closing the ring; Liberating the populations; Final assault on the German citadel'.[4]

In his war memoirs, Churchill took issue with the 'tales . . . of my rooted aversion from large-scale operations on the Continent'. Disingenuously, this avoided the main point separating the British from the American wish to concentrate on an invasion of northern France as the prelude to an assault on Germany. He hoped peripheral attacks and bombing would do the job, with the focus on the Mediterranean, which, as Roosevelt would note, the Prime Minister saw as 'an area under British domination'.[5]

Another paper looked to 'the liberation of the captive countries of Western and Southern Europe by the landing at suitable points . . . of British and American armies strong enough to enable the conquered populations to revolt'. Still, one uncertainty gnawed at the British. Could they persuade the Americans that 'the defeat of Japan would not spell the defeat of Hitler, but that the defeat of Hitler made the finishing off of Japan merely a matter of time and trouble'? As the battleship heaved its way through gales and heavy seas, Churchill told Harriman that it was in the hands of the United States to make it a long or short war. 'If you defend each town on the Pacific with fighter aircraft it will be a long war – five years,' he said. 'If you will be courageous – let the raiders come; what does it matter? – it can be finished in two years.'[6]

II

Redrawing the Map

While Churchill sailed westwards, Eden headed through bitterly cold weather to Murmansk on the cruiser *Kent*. He was suffering from gastric influenza – his only illness of the war years. He was none too happy that Churchill's insistence on going to Washington threatened to overshadow his mission to Moscow. He was also aware that he did not have much to offer. In his diary, Brooke described him as 'like a peevish child grumbling because he was being sent off to see Uncle Stalin without suitable gifts.'[7]

Peevishness was a quality others would detect in the handsome, charming forty-four-year-old. Born into the minor aristocracy, he had fought in the trenches in the First World War, and then rose swiftly as a politician, becoming the Golden Boy of the Conservative Party. Following seven years in government, he walked out of the Foreign Office in 1938 after clashing repeatedly with Neville Chamberlain, particularly over policy towards Eden's *bête noire*, Mussolini. Though not the firmest opponent of the Axis dictators, his resignation set him apart from the appeasers. In 1940, Churchill named him Secretary of State for War, a post he held till he became Foreign Secretary when Halifax went to the embassy in Washington early in 1941.

Churchill described Eden as 'the most resolute and courageous figure in the administration'. But he was vain, and could grow nervous, flying into petulant tempers, particularly when he thought he had been slighted. While calling him the best negotiator he worked with, Alexander Cadogan noted within a week of his return to the Foreign Office: 'A in rather a flap . . . I fear that here he is getting as jumpy as ever.' While Roosevelt would describe him as 'the nicest type of Englishman, very clever', Molotov called him 'spineless, too delicate, quite helpless'.[8]

Though Churchill insisted in his memoirs on their closeness, Eden bridled at the 'monopolistic' behaviour of the Prime Minister, particularly in the vital transatlantic relationship. Needing a garden of his own to cultivate, he turned his sights to Russia. He had met Stalin on a visit to Moscow in 1935, and his Private Secretary, Oliver Harvey, thought him the one man in England who was ready to put the Soviet case given Churchill's feelings about Communism and the 'violently anti-Soviet' attitude of Labour members of the Cabinet.[9]

By late 1941, Eden had come to feel that, since London and Moscow 'should have a common enemy and a common interest', Britain should begin the second front in France for political, rather than military, purposes. To dispel Soviet fears that London and Washington sought to exclude Moscow from their longer-range plans, he wanted a British declaration promising post-war collaboration. He hoped that Stalin would reciprocate by sticking to the Atlantic Charter, respecting non-intervention in the affairs of other states, and agreeing to confederations of weaker European states to buttress them after the war. This approach raised a very real danger for him – not with the Soviet leader but with Churchill who was banking all on his relationship with Roosevelt.[10]

Landing in Murmansk in minus 20 degrees of frost, Eden shielded himself from the cold with a large sheepskin coat and fur hat. He and his party boarded a train for the sixty-hour trip to Moscow, accommodated in plush compartments with silk curtains. Between each carriage was a flat car with an anti-aircraft gun. As soon as the train started, caviar, smoked salmon, ham, sausage, and bread, butter and cheese were served, with tea and wine. Maisky, who was with them, presented Eden with a small black bag full of roubles. When the visitor declined to accept it, Maisky looked downcast, locked the bag and took it away.[11]

In Moscow, Eden settled into the old-fashioned, French-style National Hotel looking out at the Kremlin wall, Red Square, St Basil's Cathedral and the Lenin Mausoleum. There was a grand piano in his suite; the bathroom taps squirted water in all directions. Gunfire boomed from the battle outside the capital. When an air-raid alarm sounded one lunchtime, the visitors were taken to a shelter in one of the lavish underground stations, with cubicles fitted with beds and telephones.[12]

Eden found Stalin in a confident mood following the Red Army's success in turning back the attack on Moscow – at one point, he remarked that Russian forces had reached Berlin twice in the past, and would now do so a third time.* 'Stalin is a quiet dictator in his manner,' the visitor noted. 'No shouting or gesticulation.'[13]

The Soviet leader handed over two draft treaties, one for a military alliance and the other on post-war Europe, with a secret protocol on frontiers. It was the first time a Westerner had heard directly what Stalin was after, and he was blunt. Just as Roosevelt and Churchill had looked beyond the war in drawing up the Atlantic Charter, so Stalin ignored the battlefield position to seek post-war territorial arrangements.

In Germany, Prussia and the Rhineland would be separated, and a Bavarian state might be created. Poland would get East Prussia while mainly German Sudetenland would be restored to Czechoslovakia. The Anschluss with Austria would be dissolved. Yugoslavia might gain territories from Italy. There would be some shifting of the border between Greece and Turkey. Bulgaria would be punished for joining the Axis by losing land to its neighbours. Hungary would hand border regions to Czechoslovakia and Romania.[14]

---

* The previous occasions were during the Napoleonic and Seven Years Wars.

The Soviet Union would resume control of the Baltic States, Bessarabia and Bukovina. It would also recover territory lost to Finland in the Winter War of 1940. Romania would grant Moscow base facilities. The Soviet frontier with Poland would follow the Curzon Line drawn up by the British politician of that name after the First World War, but not implemented – this would give it 70,000 square kilometres of land and, on the last census, 10 million inhabitants. Poland was a particularly sensitive issue for Moscow because it lay on the route to and from Germany and because of the Polish fight against the Bolsheviks after the 1917 revolution.

A scheme on a grand scale reminiscent of Tsarist plans to gain territory and construct a deep security zone beyond Russia's frontiers, all this ran completely counter to the Atlantic Charter, to which the Soviets had subscribed. While Roosevelt and Churchill had talked of broad principles, Stalin was strictly concrete. In a spirit of realpolitik, he said he would support the establishment of British bases in France, Belgium, the Netherlands, Denmark and Norway. After four hours, he let the visitors leave to consider what he had put to them.

Meeting again the next day, Stalin took from his pocket a small sheet of paper as, in Eden's words, he showed his claws – as if he had not done so with the territorial proposals.[15]

'You will not object if we add a small protocol to our agreements on post-war reconstruction,' he said as if the British had signed up to his vision of post-war Europe. The paper guaranteed the frontiers Stalin had achieved under the pact with Hitler. He said he would be happy if Washington would also agree.

'I doubt whether they would do that,' Eden responded, noting that Britain had not recognised the 1941 borders. All he was authorised to do was seek a general declaration, he explained.

'A declaration I regard as algebra,' Stalin replied. 'I prefer practical arithmetic.'

Eden said Britain could not commit itself on any territorial issues.

'A pity,' came the response. Poland remained open, Stalin told the Foreign Secretary. 'I do not insist on settling that now,' he went on. 'What I am most interested in is the position in Finland and the Baltic States and in Romania. It is very important for us to know whether we shall have to fight at the peace conference in order to get our western frontiers.'

Eden suggested leaving territorial matters until the three powers met to discuss the post-war world. However, referring to the Baltic States, he said that, if they were so important to his host, he would try to get a favourable answer. Churchill had ruled that Britain would not accept any territorial changes made during the war, he noted. But 'it may be that this particular change is an exceptional one and if you wish it I will consult the British Government on that basis and let you have an answer' – though he also recalled the Atlantic Charter, which would have excluded such a blatant contradiction of self-determination.

Stalin seemed surprised at how much his visitor was making of the issue. 'We are fighting our hardest and losing hundreds of thousands of men in the common cause with Great Britain as our ally,' he said. 'I should have thought that such a question as the position of the Baltic States ought to be axiomatic and ought not to require any decision . . . All we ask for is to restore our country to its former frontiers. We must have these for our security and safety.'

Indeed, he was so 'surprised and amazed' at the British position that he had to compare it to the behaviour of the pre-war government. As for London having to consult Washington, he added woundingly that he 'believed your Government to have more freedom of action in these matters. That is perhaps why it is difficult to reach an agreement.'

'You would not respect me if I were to go back upon the arrangement with President Roosevelt,' Eden replied.

Picking up on the mention of the Atlantic Charter, Stalin said he had thought it was 'directed against those people who were trying to establish world dominion. Now it looks as if the Charter was directed against the USSR.'

'No; that is certainly not so,' Eden responded. 'It is merely a question of your putting forward certain views as to your frontiers and of my being unable to give you an immediate reply and asking you to allow me time to get the answer.'

'Why does the restoration of our frontiers come into conflict with the Atlantic Charter?' the Soviet leader persisted.

'I never said that it did,' was all Eden could answer.

Returning to their hotel rooms, the British shouted indignantly about what Stalin had said for the benefit of the microphones. 'Russian ideas were already starkly definite,' Eden noted later. 'They changed little during the next three years, for their purpose was to secure the most tangible physical guarantees for Russia's future security.'[16]

The next morning, Maisky came to the hotel to tell them Stalin insisted on a mention of the 1941 frontiers in any communiqué. The British thought it was 'a try-on'. But Oliver Harvey reflected that, while the Baltic States could not be 'signed away without any further thought', if the Red Army occupied them at the end of the war, no one was going to fight to turn it out. Within a month of the war becoming global, the West was confronted with a dilemma that would dog it to beyond the end of the defeat of Germany.[17]

Churchill was at sea when he received a report on Eden's talks. He cabled Attlee to note how Stalin was directly contravening the first three articles of the Atlantic Charter. Yet his doctor recorded him as saying that, while the Baltic demands would 'dishonour our cause', he did not feel this moral position could be physically maintained because 'in a deadly struggle it is not right to assume more burdens than those who are fighting for a great cause can bear.'[18]

In 1940, the British had considered acknowledging Moscow's de facto authority over the Baltic States and part of Poland as the price for weaning Stalin away from Hitler. But now the situation had changed. Britain was no longer alone, and Churchill had to remember the opposition Roosevelt had expressed at Placentia Bay to territorial understandings before the end of the conflict. Just before Eden left London, Cordell Hull had stressed that it would be unfortunate if any of the Big Three nations 'were to express any willingness to enter into commitments regarding . . . the postwar settlement'. Since the British were keeping the US Embassy in Moscow informed of the discussions with Stalin, word of the Soviet proposals would get back to Washington where the Prime Minister foresaw a 'sharp and negative' reaction.[19]

Churchill told Attlee that there could be no question of reaching an understanding in Moscow without prior agreement with Washington. To Eden, he cabled, 'Naturally you will not be rough with Stalin. We are bound to the United States not to enter into secret and special pacts. To approach President Roosevelt with these proposals would be to court a blank refusal, and might cause lasting trouble on both sides . . . Even to raise them informally with President Roosevelt at this time would, in my opinion, be inexpedient.' Better to end the Moscow talks inconclusively than create a secret understanding to get a joint declaration, he added.

After a day at the front, Eden had a final meeting where a draft statement was produced that did not contain any contentious passages about Russia's frontiers. Stalin was ready to bide his time so long as Western aid flowed in. He also knew that, if the Red Army defeated the Wehrmacht, his territorial gains would be much greater than those he had obtained from Hitler. 'It would not be in the power of the United States or Great Britain by any physical pressure to stop them,' Sumner Welles told Halifax.[20]

Anxious to preserve relations with Moscow, Eden undertook to discuss the possibility of some concessions to Soviet aims with Churchill and the War Cabinet. In his memoirs, he explained that he could see a situation in Europe in which, with Germany defeated and France weakened, Russia's position would be unassailable, and most countries would find themselves with Communist governments. This made it wise to try to tie Moscow down with prior agreements as soon as possible.[21]

After the last round of talks, it was time for a Kremlin banquet. As usual, it was a highly fuelled occasion, with thirty-six toasts to drink and caviar, sturgeon, borsch, meat and suckling pig among the dishes on offer. Gazing at a bottle of a yellowish liquid that looked like Scotch, Eden asked what it was.[22]

'This is our Russian whisky,' Stalin replied, with a sly glance.

'I should like to try it,' the visitor said.

Stalin poured a big glass. Eden took a large mouthful. His face turned red, his eyes bulged and he started to choke.

'Only a strong people can take such a drink,' Stalin said of the pepper brandy. 'Hitler is beginning to feel this.'

As midnight chimed, Eden got to his feet to toast the dictator's sixty-second birthday that day. Stalin drank to Churchill's health, and spoke warmly of the Prime Minister. When Marshal Voroshilov, the commander of the north-west front, slumped over in an alcoholic haze, Stalin asked the Foreign Secretary if British generals got drunk.[23]

'They don't often get the chance,' Eden replied.

'The better my generals are,' Stalin said, 'the more drunk they get.'*

The British left the Kremlin at 5 a.m. after two films had been shown. Eden sent a message to Churchill saying he felt he had allayed some of Stalin's suspicions. He believed the Russians sincerely wanted military agreements, but would sign nothing till they got their way on frontiers. To recover from the banquet, he slept till 3 p.m. That evening, he paid a brief farewell call on Stalin, and then left with his delegation for Murmansk by train. On Christmas Day, they sailed for home, Eden expressing concern at how Churchill's visit to America would get more publicity than his trip. 'All prima donnas,' Cadogan noted in his diary.[24]

III

Washington Christmas

As Stalin was bidding Eden farewell, the *Duke of York* neared the United States. There had been no announcement of the summit. Roosevelt merely told his wife to expect 'some guests'. He did not name them, but gave instructions to make sure there was 'good champagne and brandy in the house and plenty of whiskey'.[25]

Churchill took a plane for the forty-five-minute flight to Washington through a cloudy night. Roosevelt waited at the airport. The two men shook hands, and were driven to the White House in a black limousine confiscated from Al Capone.

Anxious to be in good form for the talks, Churchill went to bed early – for him. But, at midnight, he called his doctor into his room. The bedclothes were thrown back and the floor strewn with newspapers. Churchill asked for sleeping pills. Wilson allowed him two 'reds' – barbiturates.

Roosevelt did all he could to make their second summit harmonious, so much so that the two men laid the seeds for future discord by avoiding difficult decisions. The meeting, optimistically codenamed 'Arcadia', stretched over three weeks, with occasional breaks. Churchill spent two of those weeks in the White House, sleeping in a room down the corridor from the President – Hopkins was on the same floor. The Prime Minister examined several bedrooms before settling on one that suited him, giving instructions to the staff that he was to be served two glasses of sherry at

---

* An alternative version of the exchange, given by Brooke, has Eden responding that British generals might 'have a better capacity for drink, but they have not the same ability for winning battles'.

breakfast, two glasses of whisky at lunch, good French champagne at dinner and old brandy afterwards. He also made clear that he would not tolerate any whistling in his presence.[26]

Churchill installed his travelling map room, on which he kept track of the progress of the war, next to Hopkins's quarters. Roosevelt ordered a similar room to be put together for him, with three big charts of the world, a double desk for military clerks and a coding machine hotline to London.[27]

The two men frequently popped into one another's rooms. After dinner, taking the role of a caring friend, Churchill pushed the President's wheelchair into the lift to go up one floor to his bedroom. In one incident related by Hopkins, Roosevelt wheeled himself in as the visitor was emerging from the bathroom 'stark naked and gleaming pink'. When he started to apologise, and made to leave, Churchill remarked: 'The Prime Minister of Great Britain has nothing to conceal from the President of the United States.' Asked about the story later, Churchill denied it; then added that he never received Roosevelt without a bath towel around him. A modified version had the towel falling to the ground as Roosevelt came in. Whatever the truth, the anecdote is symptomatic of the personal relationship between the two.[28]

Churchill was buoyed by good news from North Africa, which he trusted would convince the Americans that Britain had an army that could beat the Wehrmacht. But, though much the more experienced war leader, he was still the suitor. 'For the first time I have seen Winston content to listen,' his doctor noted. 'You could almost feel the importance he attaches to bringing the President along with him . . . he has become a very model of restraint and self-discipline . . . and when he does say anything it is always something likely to fall pleasantly on the President's ear.' In a note to Clementine Churchill at the end of the visit, Hopkins wrote: 'You would have been quite proud of your husband on this trip. First because he was ever so good natured. I didn't see him take anybody's head off and he eats and drinks with his customary vigor, and still dislikes the same people. If he had half as good a time here as the President did having him about the White House he surely will carry pleasant memories of the past three weeks.'[29]

The morning after Churchill's arrival, Roosevelt introduced him to the White House press corps, the Prime Minister standing on a chair so that all

200 reporters could see him. His buoyant mood went down well, kindling a love affair with the American media. 'If we manage [the war] well, it will only take half as long as if we manage it badly,' he said. Asked if US entry was one of the 'great climacterics', he put on a Southern drawl to say 'I sho' do.'

At the formal opening of the summit, the Americans confirmed the 'Europe First' strategy. 'Germany is still the key to victory,' their Chiefs of Staff stated. 'Once Germany is defeated, the collapse of Italy and the defeat of Japan must follow.' The President said everything possible would be done to save the Philippines, and Singapore must be held. Archibald Wavell was appointed Supreme Commander in the Far East – the Japanese advance severely reduced the geographical scope of the job, and, aware that the United States would lead the fight-back in the Pacific in due course, the British saw it as a token gesture. Roosevelt proposed a Supreme War Council of the United States, Britain, the Soviet Union and China, but this never took off, in part because of the unwillingness of Stalin and Chiang Kai-shek to cede authority. That could only boost Churchill's vision of a privileged transatlantic relationship, which would carry over into the NATO alliance. But it also left Roosevelt free to pursue relations with Stalin and Chiang as he wished.[30]

The British went along with a proposal that a joint Anglo-American military planning body should be located in Washington; a combined intelligence committee was also established. This decision further fuelled the rise of George Marshall. According to Charles Wilson 'neither the P.M. nor the President can contemplate going forward without Marshall.' Still, US planning remained quite rudimentary, and the Pentagon lacked the British skills at running meetings as became apparent when Churchill presented the papers he had drawn up while crossing the ocean.

Roosevelt said he liked the notion of an attack in North Africa though his Chiefs of Staff thought it a thoroughly bad idea that would distract from the use of maximum force in France. They worried that the President was falling under Churchill's spell. In fact, North Africa had already been in his mind – receiving Attlee before Pearl Harbor, he pointed at Algiers on a map, and said: 'That is where I want to have American troops.'[31]

On Christmas Eve, the worries of Marshall and his colleagues about their Commander-in-Chief were dramatically deepened. Roosevelt invited himself to a meeting at which the British were discussing the Far East. Japan's advance meant US reinforcements for the Philippines might not be able to arrive there in time. In that case, the British, apparently led by Churchill, wondered if they could go to Singapore. The President agreed this would be discussed.[32]

When the visitors proposed the idea to Marshall and the US Chiefs of Staff, the Americans were aghast. It ran counter to their planning, and would involve using US forces to defend the British Empire.

Alerted by Marshall, Stimson telephoned Hopkins. If this was the way Roosevelt intended to conduct the war, the Secretary of War said, he would resign. Getting the greatly respected Republican to cross party lines to join the Cabinet in 1940 had been a considerable coup for Roosevelt; to lose him at the outset of war would be a grave blow. Hopkins went to see the President and Prime Minister to try to sort things out.

Roosevelt denied having discussed diverting troops. Stimson sent him a note on the original conversation drawn up by the British. The President replied that he had no intention of holding forces back from the Philippines. Hopkins assured Stimson that Roosevelt sympathised with him. The President let a few hours pass; then called in Hopkins and others to dismiss the British note. 'This incident shows the dangers of talking too freely in international matters . . . without the President having his military and naval advisers present,' Stimson noted in his diary.[33]

Trouble then broke out with news that the Free French had taken the islands of St Pierre et Miquelon off Canada from collaborationist forces. Earlier in the month Washington had insisted that no attack should be mounted – it still recognised the Vichy regime. Enraged, Cordell Hull denounced the 'so-called Free French'. He suggested asking the Canadians to re-take the islands and hand them back to Vichy. But Roosevelt let matters rest, so annoying the Secretary that he was spotted clearing papers from his desk into a waste-paper basket as if preparing to walk out.[34]

Washington's hostility towards the London-based French was again evident a few days later at one of the grand moments of the Arcadia summit – the signing of what was known as the United Nation Pact by twenty-six nations, including China and the Soviet Union as well as the US and UK.* They all pledged to uphold the principles of the Atlantic Charter and use their full resources against Axis powers with which they were at war – a wording designed to cater for Moscow's non-aggression pact with Japan. The signatories would cooperate, and not make a separate armistice or peace. The Free French were excluded on the grounds that they did not constitute a government.

When Churchill proposed changing the wording from 'governments' to 'authorities' to include them, Litvinov vetoed the idea on the grounds that he lacked authorisation from Moscow. Losing his temper, the Prime Minister said he was 'not much of an ambassador if he didn't have power to add a word like this'. Hull insisted the Free French were ineligible and Churchill stepped back, leaving de Gaulle to reflect how strange it was 'that, as soon as America entered the war the Free French were eliminated from the Allied conferences in spite of the military effort which they were making'.[35]

On the evening of Christmas Eve, Roosevelt went outdoors with Churchill for the ceremonial lighting of the tree in the garden of the White House. A crowd of 30,000 gathered in the unseasonably warm weather. Churchill said in his speech that, though far from his country and family, he did not feel far from home. 'I cannot feel myself a stranger here in the centre and at the very summit of the United States,' he went on. 'I feel a sense of unity and fraternal association which, added to the kindness of your welcome, convinces me that I have a right to sit at your fireside and share your Christmas joy.'[36]

'Almost the whole world is locked in deadly struggle,' he reflected. 'But amid all the tumult, we have tonight the peace of the spirit in each cottage home and in every generous heart . . . for one night, each home throughout the English-speaking world should be a brightly lighted island of happiness and peace. Let the children have their night of fun and laughter. Let the gifts of Father Christmas delight their play. Let us grown-ups share to the full in their unstinted pleasures before we turn again to the stern task and the formidable years that lie before us, resolved that, by our sacrifice and daring, these same children shall not be robbed of their

---

* The others were: Australia, Belgium, Canada, Costa Rica, Cuba, Czechoslovakia, Dominican Republic, El Salvador, Greece, Guatemala, Haiti, Honduras, India, Luxembourg, Netherlands, New Zealand, Nicaragua, Norway, Panama, Poland, South Africa, Yugoslavia.

inheritance or denied the right to live in a free and decent world. And so, in God's mercy, a happy Christmas to you all.'

Coming in from the terrace for a dinner of Virginia ham, Churchill told his doctor he had suffered palpitations. Wilson took his pulse – it was 105. Lisping with excitement, the Prime Minister said, 'It has all been very moving. This is a new war with Russia victorious, Japan in, and America in up to the neck.' The next morning, the President took his visitor to sing hymns at a Methodist church. Churchill said it put his mind at rest. He needed comfort; the Japanese had just taken Hong Kong. As the British Chiefs of Staff sipped cocktails mixed for them by Roosevelt that evening, he read out a quotation from the 112th psalm – 'He shall not be afraid of evil tidings; his heart is fixed, trusting in the Lord.'[37]

At dinner, Roosevelt was, Wilson noted in his diary, 'like a schoolboy, jolly and carefree. It was difficult to believe that this was the man who was taking his nation into a vast conflict.' Churchill was unusually quiet, appearing preoccupied by an address he was to make to Congress the next day. Following a war film after the meal, he excused himself to go to work on his speech. In his absence, carols were sung, starting with 'O Come All Ye Faithful'.

In the morning, Churchill was still making finishing touches to his address as he was driven from the back entrance of the White House, the car's siren wailing and two security men on each running board. A few people cheered and waved. Wilson accompanied him.

At the Capitol, they went up in a lift to wait in a small room. Churchill sat, deep in thought. Then he got up and paced the room.

'Do you realise we are making history?' he said, his eyes popping.[38]

Called to the chamber, he donned shell-rimmed spectacles to read his thirty-five-minute speech. Roosevelt listened to the live radio transmission.

Churchill began by saying that, if his father had been American and his mother British instead of the other way round, he might have got to Congress on his own. That earned laughter. Applause followed when the visitor turned to the war, though he warned of a long, hard conflict. Of Japan, he said to cheers: 'What sort of people do they think we are?' At the end, he gave his V-sign, to which the Chief Justice Harlan F. Stone raised his arms in an echo, while congressmen cheered and waved papers. Sweating heavily afterwards, Churchill told Wilson a great weight had been lifted from his chest. The press reaction was ecstatic. *Time* wondered if

Congress had ever heard such a moving speech; the *New York Times* described the visitor as a 'new hero'; *Life* wrote that he had 'sold Washington on Britain, and America on himself'. But, the hero was in for some personal pain.[39]

On the night of 27 December, Wilson was called to the White House. His most famous patient looked worried. Churchill said he had got up to open the window. It was very stiff and he had had to use 'considerable force', becoming short of breath. Then he added: 'I had a dull pain over my heart. It went down my left arm. It didn't last very long, but it has never happened before. What is it? Is my heart all right?'[40]

A quick examination showed Wilson symptoms of coronary insufficiency, though another doctor, after reviewing Churchill's medical history much later, concluded that it was more likely to have been muscle strain. Treatment would mean six weeks in bed, Wilson thought. That was unthinkable. Also, if Churchill was told he had heart trouble, his confidence would be diminished. To gain time, Wilson listened twice through his stethoscope.[41]

'Well,' asked the Prime Minister, 'is my heart all right?'

'There is nothing serious,' the doctor said economically. 'You have been overdoing things.'

'Now, Charles, you're not going to tell me to rest,' Churchill replied. 'I can't. I won't. Nobody else can do this job. I must. What actually happened when I opened the window? My idea is that I strained one of my chest muscles. I used great force. I don't believe it was my heart at all.'

'Your circulation was a bit sluggish,' Wilson said, having decided not to tell the full truth. 'It is nothing serious. You needn't rest in the sense of lying up, but you mustn't do more than you can help in the way of exertion for a little while.' At which point, Hopkins knocked at the door, and Wilson slipped away.[42]

Though he continued to quiz his doctor about his heart, Churchill went ahead with a visit to Ottawa. He delighted Canadians by donning a local beaver fur hat and made a celebrated reference to a prediction by Maxime Weygand, the French Marshal, in June 1940, that Britain was a chicken about to have its neck wrung by Hitler. 'Some chicken, some neck,' Churchill chortled. He told journalists on the train back to Washington: 'Here's to 1942! Here's to a year of toil – a year of struggle and peril, and a long step forward towards victory! May we all come through safe and with honour!'[43]

In London, Eden raised the post-war Soviet frontiers with the War Cabinet, advocating making an accommodation with Moscow. Facing resistance, he cabled Churchill suggesting the Prime Minister should present Roosevelt with the case for recognising the 1941 frontiers as a matter of 'stark realism'. This would be 'an acid test of our sincerity' towards Moscow.

'Your telegram surprised me,' Churchill replied. 'All territorial matters must be left for a peace conference to follow Germany's defeat.' He rejected Eden's idea that Moscow would dominate Europe after victory; on the contrary, he thought it probable that the USA and the British Empire would be the most powerful grouping in the world while 'the Soviet Union will need our aid for reconstruction far more than we shall need theirs'.[44]

For a rest, Churchill flew in Marshall's plane to Florida while Roosevelt went to Hyde Park. The Prime Minister stayed in a house owned by Edward Stettinius, the Lend-Lease administrator. He travelled as 'Mr Lobb,* an invalid requiring quiet', but nobody who saw him could doubt his real identity.[45]

The Palm Beach air was balmy, the ocean warm. Without a swimming costume, Churchill told his private detective, Walter Thompson, the beach was private enough for him to swim naked. 'You could be seen through glasses, sir,' Thompson replied.

'If they are that much interested,' said Churchill, 'it is their own fault what they see.'[46]

Going to the shore wrapped in a large towel, he took it off and launched himself into the water where he basked half-submerged – 'like a hippopotamus in a swamp,' his doctor noted. At one point, a shark was reported, and the visitor kept to shallow water thereafter, telling Thompson to keep watch.

Despite the sea and sun, Churchill was, according to Wilson, under strain, 'hitting out blindly, like a child in a temper'. The reason was a flood of bad war news. Britain's position in the Mediterranean had deteriorated. He was worried about Singapore after the loss of airfields in Malaya. There was concern about arms production; Beaverbrook, who was accompanying

---

* The firm of John Lobb was Churchill's shoemaker in London.

Churchill, sent Roosevelt dire warnings, which helped to jog him into some streamlining of supplies.

However, at a final meeting in the White House on 12 January, Churchill took comfort from Roosevelt's backing for a landing in North Africa. Each country would commit 90,000 men with 'considerable' air support. Churchill forecast that French troops would desert Vichy and back the Allies.[47]

Roosevelt proposed to send 30,000 men to Northern Ireland to free British troops for deployment elsewhere, 50,000 to defend Australia and 25,000 to New Caledonia. But Marshall's focus on France showed through in an agreement that 'only the minimum of forces necessary for . . . other theatres should be diverted from operations against Germany'. This ambiguity was Rooseveltian – and necessary. As the President told Marshall, 'I am responsible for keeping the Grand Alliance together. You cannot, in the interests of a more vigorous prosecution of the war, break up the alliance.' But avoidance of a clear decision led to a dispute which would cause the greatest strain between the United States and Britain.[48]

Bidding his host farewell on 14 January 1942, Churchill handed him a dedicated volume of his book *The River War*, about South Africa written forty-three years earlier. The dedication read: 'In rough times, January 1942'.

'Trust me to the bitter end,' Roosevelt responded.[49]

6

Undecided

'Stalin hates the guts of all your top people.'
ROOSEVELT TO CHURCHILL

THE DIFFERENCES WHICH HAD hovered over the meetings in Moscow and Washington at the turn of the year flared into the open in the following eight months, producing strains that could have broken the anti-Axis front. Despite Churchill's pursuit of transatlantic entente, the Americans and the British locked horns on the second front and Soviet territorial demands. Stalin's presence hovered in the background of both, and the dictator did not relax his pressure on the other two leaders, steadily buttressing his position as the most resolute of the Big Three.

There were major reverses on the battlefields. The Japanese inflicted what Churchill called 'the greatest disaster in our history' by taking Singapore. In North Africa, Rommel swept forward. In Russia, the Wehrmacht launched huge new offensives. Atlantic shipping losses rose alarmingly. But the Arcadia summit had left the two Western leaders in contented frames of mind. As he flew home in a well-appointed seaplane, Churchill told his doctor he felt he had 'done a good job of work with the President'. On the last day of January, Roosevelt, whose birthday it was, sent him a message declaring simply: 'It's fun to be in the same decade as you.'

On his return, the Prime Minister found that, despite his high popularity ratings, critics were accusing him of running too much of a one-man band, and of being a poor organiser. There were suggestions he should relinquish the Ministry of Defence. For many traditional Tories, he remained suspect while some younger men saw him as a figure from the past who might be disposed of now the great danger of invasion had passed.

'He seems quite incapable of listening or taking in even the simplest point but goes off at a tangent on a word and then rambles on inconsecutively,' Leo Amery, the Conservative Secretary of State for India, an old foe, wrote in his diary. Eden told a confidant that he was 'much troubled about the present method of conducting the war' and at the centralisation of authority in Churchill's hands. But he was not ready to strike, and nobody else had the backing needed to launch a coup. A no-confidence motion in the Commons received one vote.[1]

In mid-February, Churchill shuffled the seven-man War Cabinet to widen the representation of the left. Cripps was brought back from Moscow to become Lord Privy Seal and Leader of the Commons. With a 70 per cent approval rating in the polls, the austere socialist was the second most popular candidate after Eden to move into Downing Street if Churchill went. At fifty-two, he was fourteen years younger than the British leader. Critical of the Prime Minister's power, he was also a strong supporter of closer relations with the USSR.

Attlee, aptly described in a newspaper profile as 'the first-class captain of a first-class cricket side who is not himself a headliner', was given the formal title of Deputy Prime Minister while a third member of the left, former trade union leader Ernest Bevin, held the Labour Ministry. After a running dispute over his authority, Beaverbrook resigned – his bad asthma was given as the official reason. Though the Canadian could be as difficult to deal with as Churchill himself, the Prime Minister was soon floating the idea of appointing the press lord as ambassador in Washington, a proposal the Foreign Office torpedoed.[2]

The military situation hit morale. 'Nothing but failure and inefficiency everywhere,' Cadogan wrote in his private journal. 'I am running out of whisky and can get no more drink of any kind. But if things go on as they are going, that won't matter.' Even Churchill was downhearted. 'Papa is at a very low ebb and he is worn down by the continuous crushing pressure of events,' his daughter Mary recorded after lunching with her parents. The Prime Minister could see the irony. 'When I reflect how I have longed and prayed for the entry of the United States into the war,' he wrote to Roosevelt, 'I find it difficult to realise how gravely our British affairs have deteriorated by what has happened since December seven. Other misfortunes will come thick and fast upon us. Your great power will only become effective gradually because of the vast distances and the shortage of ships.'[3]

Despite the bad news from the Pacific as MacArthur was forced from the Philippines, the President felt able to reply in buoyant form: 'We must constantly look forward to next moves that need to be made to hit the enemy. I hope you will be of good heart in these trying weeks . . . I think of you often.' However, as he wrote, twin Anglo-American discords were breaking out.

Churchill's sternly worded message from Washington about Soviet territorial demands did not make Eden abandon his belief that the issue should be used to foster relations with Stalin. Cadogan noted that the man seen as an apostle of anti-appeasement was adopting an 'amoral real politik line' and was 'quite prepared to throw to the winds all principles which he has not drafted'. Eden had two very different allies. Cripps believed in recognising Moscow's claims to the three Baltic States, Bessarabia and Moldavia, plus bases in Finland. In Washington, Halifax had urged Churchill to tell Stalin Britain would back him on the Baltics. Playing what he must have imagined to be a trump card, the ambassador told Sumner Welles that Roosevelt had come up with a similar notion on his own initiative in a conversation.[4]

After this news was relayed to London, the Foreign Office – despite Cadogan's reservations – warned the State Department that a refusal to satisfy Russian demands 'may be the end of any prospect of fruitful co-operation with the Soviet Government.' It might 'encourage Soviet policy to revert to the pursuit of purely selfish aims with incalculable consequences for the post war period.' The British suggested a tripartite agreement granting frontier recognition. A group consisting of Eden and the Russian and American ambassadors should deal with such issues – a useful counterweight to the Combined Chiefs of Staff in Washington.[5]

This was not at all to the liking of Welles, who was running the State Department while Hull was on sick leave. He wanted the Atlantic Charter to be respected. Like others round Roosevelt, he was suspicious of old habits he could see surfacing across the Atlantic. On top of which, a principled defence of the American position could do him no harm during his tenure in charge of the State Department.

Whatever Halifax may have gathered from Roosevelt, he should have known how dangerous it was to take what he heard at face value. Nor did he grasp the way the men running American diplomacy saw a new world dawning after the war which would have a very different complexion from Churchill's vision of a transatlantic partnership. Though the United States had been pushed into war by Japan and Germany, the global struggle became a matter of spreading American values for the President and some of those around him. The United States would, they assumed, become the beacon for the world.

Hopkins, for instance, thought the defeat of Hitler could only be achieved by a new order of democracy that would extend the New Deal to the whole planet. Hull saw free trade and an end to imperial systems as the key to peace. In a speech in the spring, Welles declared that 'the age of imperialism is ended', and that the war was being fought for the liberation and sovereign equality of the peoples of the world – the President said Welles's words were authoritative. The Assistant Secretary of State, Adolf Berle, pictured the struggle as a 'people's war' which would be won by the Chinese, Russians and Americans – and the Indians 'if they can be galvanised into doing so'. 'In this spectrum,' he added in his diary, 'Britain falls into her place; and it is by no means the dominant place. Gone is the ideal of the "English-speaking world"; and, on dead reckoning, the era of Anglo-American operations will be pretty short.'[6]

Such thinking led naturally to a readiness to embrace the Soviet Union as the preferred partner in building a new world. It was an approach Roosevelt would increasingly adopt. If that meant questioning some of the convictions of the ally in London, so be it. He was merely picking up the revolutionary impulse which, as the writer Ian Burama has noted, lies under the surface of American idealism.[7]

Some New Dealers were ready to take exceptional steps to win Moscow's confidence. According to a former member of the Moscow spy centre, Vasili Mitrokhin, Hopkins 'established a remarkable reputation in Moscow for taking the Russians into his confidence', probably using a Soviet agent at the embassy in Washington as a back channel. He may have provided

Stalin with information on an Anglo-American summit to encourage the dictator to feel that he could count on the Americans. He warned the Soviet Embassy that the FBI had bugged a meeting between a Soviet spymaster and an American Communist, and endeavoured to displace American officials regarded as anti-Soviet. However, Mitrokhin rejects claims by Soviet intelligence that Hopkins was one of its agents – characteristically, the aide was motivated by a mixture of idealism and guile, not treason.[8]

Others were much closer to being spies. Harry Dexter White, Assistant Treasury Secretary for international financial policy, was, to all intents and purposes, a Soviet agent, passing information to a contact at the embassy in Washington and gathering no fewer than three codenames from Moscow – Lawyer, Jurist and Richard. Other well-placed helpers included a White House aide, Lauchlin Curie, and Alger Hiss at the State Department. When Adolph Berle drew up a list of suspected Soviet agents, including these three, Roosevelt showed no interest, and the note was pigeonholed.

Meeting Halifax on 18 February, Welles was blunt. 'It appears that our two governments are at a crossroads,' he said, according to the official record. The British suggestion of an agreement on frontiers was 'a complete repudiation of the principles for which we stand. I cannot conceive of this war being fought in order to undertake once more the shoddy, inherently vicious, kind of patchwork world order which the European powers had attempted to construct during the years between 1919 and 1939. Could it be conceivable that any healthy and lasting world order could be created on a foundation which implied the utter ignoring of all of the principles of independence, liberty, and self-determination? . . . I do not believe that the people of the United States would wish to be parties thereto.'

Halifax had a realpolitik reply – 'We need to have Russia as a balance for Germany after the war.' This, Welles noted later, epitomised 'the worst phase of the spirit of Munich'.

'The only hope for the future lay in a new world order based on proper principles', he told the ambassador. 'What peace can be envisaged if . . . the British Government and ourselves agree upon selling out millions of people who look to us as their one hope in the future, and if that new world order is based upon the domination of unwilling, resentful and potent minorities by a state to which they would never give willing allegiance?'

After Halifax had left, Welles spent ninety minutes discussing the British ideas with the President. Roosevelt told him to tell Halifax that the proposal to agree to Stalin's wishes brought only one word to his mind – 'provincial'. When informed of this, Halifax was shocked. What was notable was that Roosevelt's hostility was directed entirely at London, not Moscow, the source of the demands Washington rejected. Having decided that the future must be based on US–Soviet understanding, he did not want a fight with Stalin. Rather, matters should be put on ice until the war ended and, if Britain threatened to upset that or cause him domestic political trouble, the President would use his authority to whip Churchill into line.

Anyway, he told Morgenthau, the Treasury Secretary, Stalin had good reason not to trust the Prime Minister because 'every promise the English have made to the Russians, they have fallen down on'. On the other hand, 'the only reason we stand so well with the Russians is that up to date we have kept our promises.' Maintaining that state of affairs was becoming Roosevelt's prime concern, whatever strain it caused with London.[9]

To make matters even worse for the British, Welles told Halifax that Roosevelt intended to address Stalin directly on the frontier question. Clearly relishing the conversation, Welles warned that, if the American people knew the British were proposing a secret territorial agreement with Moscow, 'the most serious crisis in the relations between the United States and Great Britain . . . would undoubtedly take place. Such an agreement would be seen as a shameful violation of one of the chief objectives for which the American people believed they were fighting.' He did not add that Roosevelt had no desire to alienate millions of voters of Polish, Baltic or East European stock who would be going to the polls in mid-term elections in November.[10]

In London, Cadogan sensed great danger, noting in his diary: 'We shall make a mistake if we press the Americans to depart from principles, and a howler if we do it without them . . . We're annoying and disgusting Roosevelt. And to what purpose?' But Eden argued that, if the West delayed, it might well find a hostile Stalin in control of Europe, including Germany, with no treaties to restrain him. Aware of the split, Moscow urged Britain to disregard 'American interference'.[11]

Crucially, Eden's persistence induced Churchill to change tack. At dinner with the Foreign Secretary on 6 March, he agreed to suggest to Roosevelt that they should not interpret the Atlantic Charter as denying the borders Russia had acquired under the Molotov-Ribbentrop Pact. The gravity of the war situation justified this, he added. Even more surprising, the Prime Minister let Stalin know what he was doing. 'I have sent a message to President Roosevelt urging him to approve our signing the agreement with you about the frontiers of Russia at the end of the war,' he told the Kremlin.[12]

With Churchill on board, the deeper issue arose of how far London was ready to let its policy be made in Washington. While Roosevelt could legitimately claim that Britain should not make decisions without consulting him, could he put the ally into a straitjacket? 'He cannot properly claim that he can over-rule our foreign policy or deny us a foreign policy at all,' Oliver Harvey wrote in his diary. It was a question not only for the war, but for the decades to follow.[13]

There was also a domestic political issue at play. The Soviet cause was popular in Britain, and Churchill could not exclude the possibility of a move by Eden, Cripps and others. The Conservatives lost three by-elections in a row, one with a negative swing of 35 per cent. Beaverbrook was organising big rallies and using his best-selling newspapers to call for 'Second front Now!' If Churchill could get an accord with Stalin, he might quieten the pro-Soviet lobby, short-circuit Eden and Cripps, and show Moscow he was not Roosevelt's poodle.

Emboldened by Downing Street's support, Eden informed Washington that Britain could not neglect any opportunity to establish close relations with Moscow. His message parroted the line that 'the adherence of Stalin to the Atlantic Charter was undertaken upon the understanding that the Soviet Union was to be regarded as being entitled to its 1940 frontiers and that consequently the Baltic States were part of Russian territory.' It would be catastrophic if the Kremlin took a hostile attitude to London because of a refusal to recognise the pre-Barbarossa frontiers, Eden added. Halifax told Welles this was an allusion to what would happen if the war continued to go badly and Russia negotiated a separate peace with Hitler; Churchill would probably be replaced by Cripps whose administration would follow a 'frankly Communist, pro-Moscow policy'.[14]

Roosevelt was unmoved. Agreeing to Stalin's demands 'would mean that

I tear up the Atlantic Charter before the ink is dry on it. I will not do that,' he told Welles. He assured the Polish government-in-exile that the US would not go along with what Moscow wanted. When Halifax asked to see the President, Roosevelt said he saw no useful purpose in discussing the frontier issue further since he had expressed his views. The rebuff was complete.[15]

Though Cadogan continued to disapprove, the War Cabinet authorised negotiations for a new treaty with Moscow. Halifax was told to inform the President that Britain intended to go ahead because the frontier question was standing in the way of frank dealings with Stalin. If he did not feel able to approve, London hoped he would not make his views public.

Strongly backed by Hull and Welles, Roosevelt would not budge. The Secretary of State believed an Anglo-Soviet agreement would constitute a 'terrible blow' to the alliance. He told Litvinov that, though America would support 'legitimate measures of security' for the Soviet Union, public opinion would disapprove of anything affecting the Baltic States. There could be no defining of frontiers until the fighting ended. The President resented the way Stalin and the British were communicating between themselves without involving him. When Hopkins and others raised the matter with him, Roosevelt grew cross, and refused to listen.[16]

Churchill had let himself be led up a dangerous path. He risked destroying the trust he had sought to instil in Roosevelt, and he had let Stalin know that the Western leaders were split. He had also frightened the Polish leaders-in-exile with a course of action that might well suggest to resistance movements in other occupied countries that Britain would be ready to sell them out. Above all, he had shown weakness at a time when the alliance needed maximum strength – and he had done so when Washington and London were engaged in several other disputes.

One involved finance and trade. In the week after Pearl Harbor, at the US Treasury, Harry Dexter White had been set to work on a proposal for an inter-Allied stabilisation fund as the basis for post-war monetary arrangements. Though the British had a similar idea, the American plans aroused concern, particularly after John Maynard Keynes had failed to get understanding on international finance during his trip to Washington the previous summer. Then there was a fresh flare-up on trade and imperial preference – Churchill told Winant that while he himself was open to discussion, three-quarters of the Cabinet 'felt they should not barter away Empire sovereignty on a payment basis to meet a debt obligation'. Welles waded in to warn that it was 'fast becoming a very serious issue'. Some in Washington feared the British Empire might survive to become a major global rival after the war. The President said that, in due course, there would need to be 'bold, forthright and comprehensive discussions' so that Washington could pursue its vision of commerce helping to open the door to peace.[17]

At the same time, and despite his opposition to the frontier demands, Roosevelt saw himself moving into the driving seat in contacts with Stalin, thus undermining Churchill's hopes of playing the pivotal role with Moscow. The President told the Prime Minister that he could easily come to an agreement with the dictator since they were both realists. 'I know you will not mind me being brutally frank when I tell you I think I can personally handle Stalin better than your Foreign Office or my State Department,' he added. 'Stalin hates the guts of all your top people. He thinks he likes me better, and I hope he will continue to do so.'[18]

The problem in this was its fundamental incompatibility with the position Roosevelt was taking on the frontier question. Supremely self-confident, he thought he could juggle the two, and fixed on the second front as an avenue forward – an approach that had the added attraction of embracing George Marshall's strategic vision. The American Chiefs were told to press ahead with plans for an offensive in France, and the President made clear to Litvinov that he was fighting to persuade the British. The ambassador's report to Moscow quoted him as saying it was hard to deal with London, but much easier to come to an agreement with Stalin 'since we both speak one and the same language'.

This meant abandoning the compromise reached at Arcadia. 'We've got to go to Europe and fight – and we've got to quit wasting resources all over the world – and still worse – wasting time,' Dwight Eisenhower, the chief military planner, had written in a position paper. 'If we're to keep Russia in, save the Middle East, India and Burma, we've got to begin slugging with air at Western Europe; to be followed up by a land attack as soon as possible.' Marshall and Stimson insisted that Western Europe was the only place where the Allies could launch a powerful offensive and where American and British troops could act together with air superiority. Though the landing would not be for another year, planning should start immediately, and a smaller attack could be mounted in the autumn if Russia looked like collapsing.[19]

After a meeting on 1 April, Roosevelt told Marshall and Hopkins to take the American news to London. Before flying out of Baltimore, the aide sent Churchill a cable, asking, 'Please start the fire.' Whether he was remembering his days shivering on previous visits, or was looking for the kindling of military action was not clear. But Roosevelt left the Prime Minister in no doubt about the weight of the mission. 'What Harry and Geo. Marshall will tell you all about has my heart and mind in it,' he cabled. 'Your people and mine demand the establishment of a front to draw off pressure on the Russians, and these people are wise enough to see that the Russians are to-day killing more Germans and destroying more equipment than you and I put together. Even if full success is not attained the big objective will be.'[20]

If Roosevelt remained firm on refusing territorial agreements, Churchill was equally wedded to the peripheral strategy he had put forward on his visit to Washington. Despite the campaign in Britain in favour of a second front, a significant section of opinion thought Stalin was expecting too much, particularly given his past pact with Hitler. The writer A.P. Herbert penned a poem appealing for 'less nonsense from the friends of Joe'. If Hitler had not attacked it, would Russia be in the war today, it wondered. Churchill told a joke about a British visitor to Moscow. 'This is Winston Churchill Square, late Adolf Hitler Square,' a guide said; then 'This is the Eden Hotel, late Marshal Goering Hotel'; then 'This is Beaverbrook Street, late Himmler Street.' When the guide offered him a cigarette, the visitor replied: 'Thank you comrade, formerly bastard.'[21]

American plans for a Normandy landing also faced a formidable opponent in the person of the new Chief of the Imperial General Staff, the hawk-faced, stoop-shouldered Alan Brooke. The general, who escaped from the pressures of war by birdwatching, came from a Northern Irish family, but had been brought up in south-west France by his mother. Rigorous to the point of dogmatism, his nickname was 'Shrapnel'. Presented with a proposal that did not appeal, he would simply say 'I flatly disagree' and snap the pencil in his hand. His diary, strewn with exclamation marks, is bitingly critical of some of those he worked with, and, in particular, of US strategy. It represented a safety valve for the tightly coiled general, often reflecting exhaustion resulting from a relentless workload.[22]

The novelist Anthony Powell had one of his characters observe Brooke's 'hurricane-like' impact in Whitehall as he burst from his staff car and 'tore up the steps of the building at the charge, exploding through the inner door into the hall. An extraordinary current of physical energy, almost of electricity, pervaded the place.' Behind his steely exterior, there lurked more human feelings which he rarely allowed to escape – his diary contains yearning references to weekends with his wife at their Hampshire home.[23]

The fifty-eight-year-old general, who spoke so fast in an idiosyncratic accent that Americans sometimes found him hard to follow, had become CIGS at the end of 1941 when Churchill decided to replace Dill. The Prime Minister had known Brooke in his previous job in charge of home forces, and offered him the top post after the two men left the table at a dinner party at Chequers. Brooke thought of his predecessor, whom he greatly admired, and of the nature of the task at that point of the war. Churchill tried to reassure him, and then rejoined the other guests. Brooke went down on his knees to pray for guidance. At 2 a.m., Churchill came to his bedroom, took his hand and, looking into his eyes, said: 'I wish you the very best of luck.' On taking over, Brooke was appalled by the way 'we worked from day to day, a hand to mouth existence . . . every wind that blew swung us like a weathercock.'[24]

He and Churchill were continually at odds as military logic clashed with the politician's flights of imagination and impatience. When the Prime Minister thumped the table, Brooke thumped back, matching glare for glare. Constantly exasperated by Churchill's methods, he told him as little as possible because 'the more you tell that man about the war, the more you hinder the winning of it'. 'It is impossible for soldiers and politicians ever to work satisfactorily together,' he judged. 'They are, and always will be, poles apart.'

In 1942 Churchill told Ismay: 'I cannot work with him. He hates me.' Pug replied that, Brooke thought it his duty to disagree when justified, but really loved the Prime Minister. 'Dear Brooke,' Churchill murmured, tears in his eyes.[25]

On 8 April 1942, the American team arrived in London, bringing with it two crates of fresh farm produce. Unfortunately, the military staff who had supplied the food had picked one of the few fresh vegetables easily available in Britain at the time – Brussels sprouts. Hopkins was in poor health again, and Roosevelt told Marshall: 'Please put Hopkins to bed and keep him there under 24-hour guard by Army or Marine Corps. Ask the King for additional assistance if required on this job.' Still, he slipped out of Claridge's at night in search of gin rummy or other diversions. He also found time to savour the springtime – only when you saw the countryside in that season did you 'understand why the English have written the best goddamn poetry in the world,' he wrote to his daughter.[26]

Hopkins was invited to address the House of Commons, which was sitting in Church House in Westminster because of bomb damage to its home across the way. He stressed American industrial power, but struck rather too informal a note for some of those present. He also renewed his habit of sitting up late with Churchill – usefully when his early morning presence headed off an explosion after Roosevelt sent the Prime Minister a message urging talks with Indian nationalists. Enraged, the British leader spoke of resigning. Hopkins calmed him down, and the next day Churchill sent a 'purely private' message to the White House saying he would not even put the idea to the War Cabinet. 'Anything like a serious difference between you and me would break my heart and would surely deeply injure both our countries at the height of this terrible struggle,' he added.[27]

The code name of Modicum given to the US party suggested modesty, but the plan it unfolded to Churchill and Brooke provided for an attack in France by 48 divisions, 7,000 landing craft and 5,800 combat planes. In advance, 'ruses and raids' would destabilise the enemy. The first wave would land by sea and air between Boulogne and Le Havre, followed by 100,000 men the following week.[28]

The year's wait until such an undertaking could be launched irked the Americans. Roosevelt was anxious to get troops into the field against the Germans as soon as possible. The public expected dramatic action – with potentially difficult mid-term congressional elections in early November, the administration wanted troops fighting Germans by the end of October. So a smaller offensive was envisaged, either against the port of Brest or on the Cotentin peninsula. Known as Sledgehammer, the original idea was that this would be launched if there were signs of collapse – either by Germany or Russia. But it took on a life of its own as the weeks went by, offering a way of meeting the President's call for autumn action in Europe ahead of the bigger landing, codenamed Roundup*, which would follow in the spring. One thing was clear to

Marshall, full-scale invasion in 1943 meant no diversion of troops to North Africa or elsewhere.[29]

Brooke foresaw disaster. The shortage of landing craft meant that only 4,000 men could be taken over the Channel at any one time for Sledgehammer. They would have to cross at least 70 miles of sea under threat from the Luftwaffe. The Germans had three dozen fighting divisions in the West, and could pour in many more men. On top of which, Sledgehammer would be a primarily British operation; given London's strategic views, this presented an obvious problem of motivation.

The atmosphere between Brooke and Marshall was chilly. The American thought the Ulsterman lacked Dill's brains while the CIGS was not impressed by the visitor's intelligence, and found him 'rather over-filled with his own importance'. Four days into the talks, the British general softened to the extent of noting in his diary: 'The more I see of him, the more I like him.' But liking did not mean agreement. 'The more I saw of him, the more clearly I appreciated that his strategic ability was of the poorest,' Brooke wrote later. 'In fact in many respects he is a very dangerous man whilst being a very charming one!'[30]

There was also the danger that a premature landing ending in defeat would deter the American public, and Roosevelt would switch the primary focus to the Pacific, where Japan had conquered Burma amid feuding between the British, Chiang Kai-shek and the US adviser Joseph Stilwell, who abandoned his disorderly Chinese troops and walked through the jungle to India. Like Roosevelt, Churchill had to consider the wider issue of alliance solidarity – and take pains not to alienate the ally across the ocean. Whatever its weaknesses, the American plan represented a commitment to Europe – indeed, Marshall was pushing that commitment further than the British wanted. So, as he put it later, Churchill needed 'to work by influence and diplomacy in order to secure agreed and harmonious action'. He could leave it to Brooke to lead the opposition while he, himself, waited for what he dubbed 'strategic natural selection' to swing things his way.[31]

---

* It appears in various style in wartime exchanges – Round Up, Round-Up, Roundup. The style here is that adopted by Roosevelt in his first message to Churchill. In the messages cited in the text, the names of operations are usually spelled out in CAPITAL letters. For easier reading, I have used upper and lower cases.

So, when the Roundup–Sledgehammer plan came before the Joint Defence Committee on 14 April, Churchill said he had 'no hesitation in cordially accepting' it – though he did not mention the autumn landing by name. Brooke expressed his doubt that a salient around Cherbourg could be held through the winter, and put scornful inverted commas round the word 'plan' in his diary. After a tête-à-tête with Marshall, he noted that the Americans had not thought of what would happen after the Roundup landing. 'Whether we are to play baccarat or *chemin de fer* at Le Touquet, or possibly bathe at Paris Plage is not stipulated!' he added.[32]*

* A reference to the smart beach at the resort, not the more recent stretch set up in summer along the Seine in Paris.

7

The Commissar Calls

MOSCOW, LONDON, WASHINGTON
MAY–JUNE 1942

'We simply cannot organize the world between the British and ourselves without bringing the Russians in as equal partners.'

HOPKINS

HOPKINS, HARRIMAN, BEAVERBROOK and Eden had all been to Moscow. Now, it was time for Stalin to send an emissary to the West. On 20 May, 1942, Molotov arrived in Scotland in the rain, his four-engined Soviet bomber having flown across Scandinavia. The trip followed a suggestion by Roosevelt that the Commissar for Foreign Affairs, who travelled under the codename of 'Mr Brown', should visit Washington. Hoping for a new treaty with Britain which would include agreement on his frontier demands, Stalin proposed that he go via London. Though the Red Army was suffering another huge reverse at the Battle of Kharkov, the visitor was, according to Eden, in 'cracking form, all smiles in a smart brown suit'. A decade later, the secret police would allege that, during the train trip from Scotland to London, he had been recruited as a British spy – he was saved from the consequences by Stalin's death.[1]

Molotov, fifty-one at the time, had fought in the Bolshevik Revolution, and then become the epitome of a Soviet bureaucrat. Tireless and unrelenting in negotiations, he was dubbed 'stone bottom' or 'iron arse' by Lenin. A member of the Politburo since 1924, he had changed his name from Skriabin to Molotov, meaning hammer. In an ironic reference to him, the Finns, resisting the Soviet invasion of 1939–40, named the improvised incendiary bombs they threw at Red Army tanks 'Molotov cocktails'. As

Prime Minister until 1941, he was Stalin's right-hand man in repression of the kulak peasantry, and was unswervingly loyal – he abstained when the Central Committee voted against his wife, Paulina, who was in charge of the perfume industry, and later divorced her at Stalin's bidding before she was arrested and exiled. To the end of his life, he raised a toast 'To Stalin, Paulina and Communism'. The only leading figure on the Allied side to have met Hitler, his appointment to the Foreign Ministry in 1939 to replace Litvinov had marked a toughening of policy. A believer in 'Red Army socialism' – the expansion of the Communist sphere by military force – he said that his task was 'to expand the borders of our Fatherland', giving Moscow the right to police the internal affairs of states it liberated from the Nazis. Though nationals would make up their governments, the tradition of imperial rule from Moscow would be perpetuated.[2]

Better educated than many of his colleagues, Molotov spoke with a slight stammer, his face immobile, his eyes cold. One of his few known personal characteristics was a taste for shelled walnuts. Meeting him in the Kremlin in 1941, Harriman found 'a man of great energy, totally lacking in humour or flexibility, literal-minded and less open to compromise than Stalin himself'. With subordinates, he was coldly polite, almost never raised his voice or used bad language. But, a Soviet interpreter recalled, his dressings down could cause his targets to pass out; Molotov revived them by sprinkling cold water from a carafe on their faces before having guards take them away.[3]

The atmosphere between Moscow and London had warmed somewhat in the months before Molotov flew in. Apart from changing course on the frontier issue, Churchill had assured Stalin he had given orders that supplies to Russia must not be delayed or interrupted; the dictator said he was pleased with the speed and efficiency with which Britain was acting. After Maisky, the ambassador, mentioned over lunch that the Germans might use gas in their spring offensive, Churchill said Britain would react by dropping gas bombs on Germany.[4]

The new ambassador in Moscow, Archibald Clark Kerr, got on better with Stalin than Cripps had done. For one thing, he was not a teetotaller. During a two-and-a-half-hour talk in a Kremlin air-raid shelter, he and Stalin discussed their mutual taste for pipe smoking and exchanged sex stories. Stalin said he 'favoured the use of the stick' to keep spouses in line, a somewhat sensitive subject with the ambassador whose wife had left him. As the talk continued, the Soviet leader paced up and down, seeking to disguise the loud rumbling of his belly. Afterwards he sent the envoy a large supply of his personal tobacco. Clark Kerr reported the dictator as being 'convinced that our joint work will proceed in an atmosphere of perfect mutual confidence'.[5]

But the wind in London was shifting again. Churchill had taken note of the strength of American opposition to promising Stalin what he wanted on frontiers. Even Eden was having second thoughts, realising that Britain should not sell out Poland. At a meeting of the War Cabinet on 7 May, Churchill took the moral high ground. Russia's demands were bad, he said. 'We oughtn't to do it, and we shan't be sorry if we don't,' he added. The Foreign Office drafted an alternative treaty, omitting any mention of frontiers.[6]

Churchill took considerable pains with the Molotov delegation, handing over Chequers for the stay, where they were served breakfasts of York ham and kedgeree. But the Commissar was not much impressed by the house or gardens, and remarked on the lack of a shower in the bathroom. His party demanded the keys to the bedrooms, and kept them locked. Two women members of the party took over the cleaning duties for their quarters. When Chequers staff did get into the rooms, they found revolvers under some pillows. A pistol was laid out at night alongside Molotov's dressing gown and briefcase.[7]

Churchill took the visitor to his map room to explain the limitations under which Britain was operating. He accompanied him to an RAF station while an operation was going on, and raised a luncheon toast of 'Workers of the world unite! Hitler is forging you new chains.' At one lunch, he underlined this country's privation by serving oatmeal and substitute coffee made of barley – when Molotov told him about this, Stalin said the meal was 'nothing but a cheap show of democracy . . . he was just pulling your leg.'[8]

The Foreign Minister soon reverted to form, showing, Cadogan noted, 'all the grace and conciliation of a totem pole'. He pressed relentlessly for the immediate opening of a second front, which he said was more important than an Anglo-Soviet treaty. Truthfully, if disingenuously, Churchill replied that preparations were being made for a landing later in the year, but warned that it was unlikely to have as much of an effect as Moscow hoped. On post-war matters, the visitor wanted recognition of pre-Barbarossa frontiers, and a secret protocol letting the USSR station troops in Finland and Romania.[9]

'There is no way we can accept this,' Churchill told him. In a cable to

Stalin, which must have been received with some surprise given his earlier position, he explained: 'We cannot go back on our previous undertakings to Poland, and have to take account of our own and American opinion.' Eden noted that the Russians were 'opening their mouths very wide'. Oliver Harvey wrote in his diary that the proposals for Finland and Romania had 'a bad smell'.

Molotov insisted that the Polish issue would be settled between Moscow and the post-war government in Warsaw. If Poland was to take 15,000 square miles from Germany in East Prussia, Britain should accept Moscow swallowing the Baltic States. He rejected Eden's suggestion that the Balts should be allowed to emigrate.

Washington watched with concern. Winant told the Foreign Office he could not exaggerate the bad effect a frontiers agreement would have in the United States. Hull warned that it would deal 'a terrible blow to the whole cause of the United Nations'. The State Department prepared a dissenting statement to be issued if the British did cave in. Roosevelt approved this, though it would have split the alliance asunder less than six months after it had come into being.[10]

The combination of the tougher British line and an awareness of US feelings got through to Molotov. At 6 p.m. on Sunday 24 May, he telephoned Winant suggesting a talk the next day. The ambassador said it should be sooner. An appointment was fixed for 10 p.m. Maisky came, too.[11]

When Winant stuck to the hard line against a frontiers agreement, Molotov acknowledged that Roosevelt's position was 'a matter for serious consideration'. As Winant was leaving, Maisky telephoned Eden to ask him to see Molotov the next day. Eden agreed, and called Churchill who was, he recorded in his diary, 'greatly cheered'. During the night, Molotov consulted Stalin. Facing a major German offensive and needing all the help he could get, the dictator gave instructions to reach an accord, even if this meant dropping any mention of frontiers and the secret protocol. He knew that, if a steady flow of Western supplies helped the Red Army to advance beyond Russia, he could impose his wishes, whether or not there had been any prior agreement.[12]

Molotov looked cheerful again as he told Eden he accepted the British treaty draft, which was signed two days later. Article Five constituted a milestone in the hypocrisy of the alliance as it stated that the two parties would 'act in accordance with the two principles of not seeking territorial aggrandisement for themselves and non-interference in the internal affairs of other states.' At a lunch at the Soviet Embassy, many toasts were drunk. 'Somehow,' Brooke noted in his diary, 'the whole affair gave me the creeps and made me feel that humanity has still many centuries to live before universal peace can be found.'[13]

Elated by what he called his 'biggest day yet', Eden took Harvey to the Ritz for a celebration dinner. The atmosphere around the talks was good enough for the Polish leader General Sikorski to attend a function at the Soviet Embassy. The Poles saw US intervention as decisive; their ambassador in Washington called on Welles to congratulate him – Hull later told him about the British, 'we certainly had to give them hell.' 'We have done a great deal of beating down of barriers between our two countries,' Churchill cabled Stalin. The dictator 'was almost purring,' he recalled – like a tiger relaxing before preparing its next hunting foray.[14]

At the end of May, Roosevelt had a teasing conversation with his cousin Margaret Suckley. He was, he said, about to receive 'a visiting fireman' who knew no English, 'comes from Shangri-La and speaks nothing but Mongolian'. He heard that the visitor was 'not very pleasant and never smiles'.[15]

Molotov's seven-year-old bomber blew a tyre as it landed in Washington. Greeted at the airport by Hull, the Foreign Minister stood on the tarmac with his overcoat folded neatly over his arm while the national anthems were played. Meeting Roosevelt, Molotov explained that he would deal with military matters as well as political questions since the military expert in his party had been obliged to stay in London after breaking his kneecap in a car accident.[16]

The President was ill at ease at the first session not knowing how to handle the visitor. The interruptions for translation cut into his usual conversational style. Though the atmosphere was cordial, Hopkins noted it was 'pretty difficult to break the ice'. As the conversation did not seem to be getting anywhere, the aide suggested the visitor might like a rest. This led to a debate between Molotov and Litvinov. The Soviet ambassador wanted his boss to stay at Blair House, the residence for diplomatic visitors. But his successor had his heart set on a night in the White House, where he was given a room across the passage from Hopkins. A young woman from the Soviet party joined him. As at Chequers, his luggage included a pistol, as well as sausage and black bread.

Mixing cocktails before dinner that night, the President told Molotov of his vision of a world policed by the US, the UK, the USSR and China. He said American planners were working on the idea of Washington, London and Moscow creating a global economic framework to underpin the United Nations and eradicate the economic causes of war. Germany, Japan, France, Spain, Belgium, the Netherlands, Scandinavia, Turkey and Eastern Europe would be disarmed, though France might be allowed to regain great-power status after ten to twenty years. When Roosevelt said he was glad the frontier issue had been dropped from the treaty, Molotov replied that he had given way in deference to Britain and because of what he understood to be the President's position.[17]

After the meal, Roosevelt took the visitor to his study where they talked on the sofa. Molotov asked about the image of the Soviet Union in the United States.

The public was probably more friendly than Congress, Roosevelt replied.

Hopkins chipped in that the American Communist Party was made up of 'largely disgruntled, frustrated, ineffectual and vociferous people – including a comparatively high proportion of distinctly unsympathetic Jews'. This, he added, misled the average American as to the character of Communists in the Soviet Union.

'On this,' the US interpreter's record went on, 'the President commented that he was far from anti-Semitic, as everyone knew, but there was a good deal in this point of view.'

At which Molotov volunteered that 'there were Communists and Communists'.[18]

That night, Hopkins wandered into the visitor's bedroom with some advice. He should paint a black picture of the military situation to underline the importance of a landing in France. But, Hopkins added, Roosevelt could not act without British agreement.

When the talks resumed on the Friday morning with Marshall and Admiral King, who had become the commander of the US Navy after Pearl Harbor, Molotov excluded Litvinov. 'We didn't trust him,' he explained later. 'He was intelligent, first rate, but we didn't trust him . . . Litvinov remained among the living only by chance.' The ambassador was cut out of the information loop, and barred from making speeches.[19]

Laying out reasons for a second front, the visitor said that, without action in France, the danger was that Hitler would be able to inflict a crushing blow in the east – though they did not know it, the Führer had just told gauleiters the war there had been won.[20]

'If you postpone your decision,' Molotov went on, 'you will have eventually to bear the brunt of the war, and if Hitler becomes the undisputed master of the continent, next year will unquestionably be tougher than this one.' If, on the other hand, 40 Wehrmacht divisions could be drawn from the east, Germany would be doomed, and might even be beaten in 1942.

In response, the President went in for some play-acting.

Turning to Marshall, he asked if they could tell Stalin a second front was being prepared. As far as he knew, the matter had been settled positively at the talks in London the previous month.

'Yes,' the general replied on cue.

As if unveiling a new policy rather than stating what he believed had already been agreed, Roosevelt said Stalin might be informed he could expect the 'formation' of a front later in 1942. Over lunch, he laid out the plans for the two-stage invasion of France. Molotov was pleasurably astonished.

The President then remarked that the Russian had spoken to Hitler more recently than anybody else on the Allied side, and asked for his impression of the Führer. After thinking for a moment, Molotov said it was possible to arrive at a common understanding with almost anyone. But he had never met two more disagreeable people to work with than Hitler and Ribbentrop. When Roosevelt mentioned that the German Foreign Minister had previously sold champagne, Molotov responded that Ribbentrop was no doubt better at that than diplomacy.[21]

At the weekend, the visitor made a trip to New York where he queued to see the show at Radio City Music Hall. While denouncing Americans as obsessed with money, he was impressed by the country's speed and efficiency. Unlike Chequers, he noted that there was a shower in his quarters in Washington.[22]

Though Cordell Hull found the visitor 'quiet-mannered [and] very agreeable', Molotov was gruff and assertive as Lend-Lease supplies for Russia were discussed on Monday, with Roosevelt proposing that these should be cut back to enable ships to be diverted for the second front in France. The session ended when the President had to host a lunch for the Duke and Duchess of Windsor. Before he left, Molotov sought confirmation of what he had been told about the second front three days earlier.

Roosevelt replied that the Western Allies were consulting on landing craft, food for troops and other issues. He insisted that the date of 1942 should be included in a joint statement which spoke of 'full understanding' on the matter. In a cable to Churchill reporting that the visit had generated 'candor and . . . friendship as well as can be managed through an interpreter', the President added: 'I am especially anxious that Molotov shall carry back some real results of his mission and give a favourable report to Stalin.'

In his notes on the Molotov talks, Hopkins wrote that 'he and the President got along famously . . . There is still a long way to go but it must be done if there is ever to be any real peace in the world. We simply cannot organize the world between the British and ourselves without bringing the Russians in as equal partners . . . I would surely include the Chinese too. The days of the policy of the "white man's burden" are over. Vast masses of people simply are not going to tolerate it and for the life of me I can't see why they should. We have left little in our trail except misery and poverty for the people whom we have exploited.'[23]

From Washington, Molotov flew back to London. In a long after-dinner conversation, Churchill set out the problems of a landing in France. But Roosevelt's endorsement of the second front meant he had to follow suit. An Anglo-Soviet statement on 11 June repeated the US-Soviet phrase about 'full understanding' on the matter, including a mention of 1942.

'The piece of paper had vast political significance,' Molotov recalled. 'It raised our spirits, and in those days this meant a lot.' He thought the West would probably not fulfil its undertaking. But this could be turned into 'a great victory' against them. 'We took them in: "You can't? But you promised" . . . That was the way. This undermined faith in the imperialists. All this was very important to us.'[24]

Churchill considered that the statement could be useful if it led Hitler to retain troops in France, bolstered Russian morale – and kept London in step with Washington. But, pursuing the double game he had been playing since April, he made sure he kept his options open, in private, at least. Meeting Molotov alone in the Cabinet Room, he handed him an aide-memoire which made plain the difference between the 'full understanding' mentioned in the communiqué and actual action.[25]

It talked of preparations for action in the autumn and the landing of 1.5 million troops in Europe in 1943. But it also warned of the problem of assembling sufficient landing craft, and reiterated the argument that action for action's sake would not help if it ended in disaster. 'It is impossible to say in advance whether the situation will be such as to make this operation feasible when the time comes,' the note added. 'We can, therefore, give no promise in the matter.'[26]

As Molotov left Downing Street after a final champagne toast, Churchill walked him to the garden gate. There, by his own account, he gripped the Russian's arm and they looked one another in the face. 'Suddenly he appeared deeply moved,' Churchill recalled. 'Inside the image there appeared the man. He responded with an equal pressure. Silently we wrung each other's hands. But then we were all together, and it was life or death for the lot.'

As Molotov's bomber took off on the dangerous trip home – it would be attacked by German fighters – the newsreel commentator cried: 'Come again, and bring Comrade Stalin with you!'[27]

8

Torch Song

HYDE PARK, CHUNGKING, WASHINGTON, LONDON
JUNE–JULY 1942

'A rather staggering crisis in our war strategy'
MARSHALL

ON 18 JUNE 1942, Roosevelt wheeled himself into the library at his country home at Hyde Park, and told Margaret Suckley that 'Mr Weinstein' was on his way across the Atlantic. That day, the man in question was walking along the quayside at the Scottish naval base of Stranraer humming a song to himself – 'We're here because we're here.' He boarded a launch that took him out to a Royal Mail flying boat, fitted with full-length bunks and armchairs. The craft flew through magical skies, the red glow of the sun shining over the horizon. Its main passenger was, once again, happy as a schoolboy to be on his way to meet the President. On 18 June, the plane landed on the Potomac river like a great swan.[1]

The Washington weather was sweaty, and 'Mr Weinstein' relished the air-conditioning at the embassy during an overnight stay, before flying to Hyde Park. Roosevelt was waiting at the nearby airfield in his specially equipped, dark-blue Ford Phaeton convertible which he could operate by hand gears without needing to use the foot pedals – there was even a device on the steering column to dispense lighted cigarettes. The plane made a bumpy landing, and then Churchill had a second cause for concern when the President veered across the grass verges above the steep drop to the Hudson as he drove him to his house.[2]

The car trip enabled the two men to talk in the way they both relished. Churchill was glad to have the President to himself. 'Though I was careful not to take his attention off the driving,' he recalled, 'we made more progress than we might have done in formal conference.'[3]

The three-storey house seemed big and empty after the death of the President's mother, who had dominated life there. The visitor occupied a small suite known as the Pink Room, with large English prints and wallpaper decorated with roses. He had a bed made from rosewood, a couch, a desk, and a rocking chair. Harry Hopkins slept in a spartan room along the corridor.

The two leaders talked in a study decorated with paintings of ships, or went to Top Cottage, Roosevelt's retreat. Suckley saw real friendship and understanding. At one point, the visitor decided to use the swimming pool. A pair of sufficiently large trunks was found. He stuck cotton in his ears, and jumped into the water, bouncing about like a rubber ball. Getting out, he donned a wide-brimmed sun hat, and lay in the shade as a bottle of brandy was brought. Later, he thought of hunting butterflies, but no net could be located.[4]

According to Churchill, he and Roosevelt agreed to pursue joint development of the atom bomb, a project codenamed 'Tube Alloys'. There is no record of the discussion, and the historian David Reynolds, in his authoritative analysis of the war memoirs, argues that the author was thinking of another meeting at Hyde Park in 1944. Though talks on the matter began later in 1942, they became deadlocked by mutual suspicions – the Americans thinking London was after a cheap ride and the British fearing Washington sought a monopoly on atomic weapons.[5]

On the matter of the second front, Churchill felt no need to beat around the bush. Meeting British commanders at the end of May, he had accepted Brooke's argument that Sledgehammer could not work given the lack of landing craft. Two principles had been laid down: '(a) No substantial landing in France unless we are going to stay; and (b) No substantial landing in France unless the Germans are demoralised by another failure against Russia.' Churchill had sent to Washington Admiral Lord Louis Mountbatten, the dashing head of British Special Operations, who outlined the case against Sledgehammer to the President, and reported that Roosevelt agreed. US military chiefs were not invited to the meeting, nor were they told what had transpired.

At Hyde Park, Churchill told the President that 'no responsible British military authority has so far been able to make a plan for September 1942 which had any chance of success unless the Germans become utterly demoralized, of which there is no likelihood.' Did the Americans have a plan, he asked. 'If so, what is it? What forces would be employed? At what points would they strike? What landing-craft and shipping are available? What British forces and assistance are required?' The President did not reply.[6]

Returning to Washington by train, the two leaders joined their military chiefs for their third summit, codenamed Argonaut. Marshall and his colleagues were still holding to the decision they thought had been reached in London. Hopkins talked of a 'second, third and fourth front to pen Germany in the ring of our offensive steel'. The formidable seventy-four-year-old Henry Stimson was pressing to get US troops into battle against Germany as soon as possible, if only to make up for their ally's weakness. 'I have come to the conclusion that, if this war is to be won,' the Secretary of War wrote in his diary, 'it's got to be won by the full strength of the virile, initiative-loving, inventive Americans, and that the British really are showing decadence – a magnificent people but they have lost their initiative.'[7]

Seeking to impress the visitors, Marshall invited Churchill and Brooke to a military exercise in South Carolina. As the British group arrived at the airport to fly out, a plainclothed policeman was seen fingering his pistol and saying he would 'do in' Churchill. He was arrested.

Squinting into the glare, the British watched a simulated armoured battle and a parachute drop by 600 men. Brooke noted that they were 'fine looking' but wondered if the Americans realised how much training was needed. Ismay said it would be murder to put them up against the Germans. The Prime Minister thought they would learn very quickly, but added that it took two years or more to produce a proper professional army.[8]

Churchill wore a light-coloured suit, the jacket of which was buttoned so tightly that it broke into a ripple of creases. With the brim of his panama hat turned up all the way round, he looked, according to Brooke, 'just like a small boy in a suit of rompers going down to the beach to dig in the sand.' As he prepared to disembark from the return flight, his butler

Sawyers, who had made much of the alcoholic hospitality, positioned himself in front of his employer, barring his progress.[9]

'What's wrong, Sawyers?' Churchill asked. 'Why are you getting in my way?'

In a very thick voice, waving his arms as he spoke, the butler replied: 'The brim of your hat is turned up; does not look well; turn it down.'

Red-faced and angry, the Prime Minister complied. 'That's better, much better, much better,' the butler muttered, standing aside. At the White House, Churchill sat up working till 3.45 a.m.[10]

When the two leaders discussed military plans with the generals and Hopkins, there was agreement on the necessity of staging an offensive in 1942. While plans for France should be pursued with all possible speed, energy and ingenuity, if detailed examination showed that success was improbable, an alternative must be prepared. A sentence in the final summit agreement, drawn up by Ismay, stated that, if political conditions were favourable, this should be against North Africa, and so 'plans should be completed in all details as soon as possible'. The wording left no room for Marshall to mount a counter-argument. Sledgehammer–Roundup still had priority – if he could convince Roosevelt it would succeed. But the President had picked up Churchill's insistence that Allied troops should not 'stand idle' against the Germans in 1942, and North Africa could be mounted before Roundup. Though the American planners argued that it would not draw a single German soldier, tank or plane from the Russian front, Churchill had the wind in his sails.[11]

Marshall and company knew they were put at a disadvantage by the way Churchill and his military men communicated as they pressed their strategy, in sharp contrast to how Roosevelt told them so little. Their suspicion of their ally's tactics was such that army planner Albert Wedemeyer was authorised to install a recording machine in his office which he could activate with pressure from his knee to tape what the British said; he played Marshall one conversation in which they made unreasonable demands while invoking the names of Roosevelt and Hopkins to seek to overawe him. As Dill put it, the US Chiefs suspected they were being led 'down the Mediterranean garden path to a cul-de-sac'. Given that, North Africa represented a major gamble for Churchill – if it went wrong, he would face unpopularity at home, and the prospect of losing Roosevelt's trust amid recriminations from Marshall.[12]

The Prime Minister was sitting with Roosevelt, Hopkins and Ismay in the Oval Office after breakfast when a naval aide came in to hand the President a sheet of pink paper.

After reading it, he said quietly: 'Show this to Winston.'

The aide took it, and crossed to the couch where Churchill was sitting.

Scanning the message, the Prime Minister winced. The colour drained from his cheeks. The note reported that the British had surrendered to Rommel at Tobruk in Libya; 25,000 men had been taken prisoner.*

Churchill was appalled. 'Defeat is one thing; disgrace is another,' he would write. After the loss of Singapore, his country's reputation was at stake. The Western Desert was one region where Britain still had a significant army facing the enemy. Now a nightmare opened up of being caught between Rommel advancing on Egypt and the Wehrmacht driving through the Caucasus.

No wonder that Churchill described himself as being the most unhappy Briton on American soil since General Burgoyne, the defeated commander in the War of Independence. But Roosevelt's reaction showed how their relationship could produce instant positive decisions.

'What can we do to help?' he asked.[13]

'Give us as many Sherman tanks as you can spare and ship them to the Middle East as quickly as possible,' Churchill replied.

Roosevelt called in Marshall, and told him what was being requested.

The Shermans were only just coming into production, Marshall said. 'It is a terrible thing to take the weapons out of a soldier's hands,' he added. 'Nevertheless, if the British need is so great, they must have them; and we could let them have a hundred 105 mm self-propelled guns in addition.'

Three hundred Shermans, in which the engines had not yet been installed, were loaded on fast ships, along with the guns – when a vessel carrying the engines was sunk by a U-boat off Bermuda, Roosevelt ordered a fresh set to be sent. At a subsequent meeting, the President went so far in imagining further help that Marshall strode from the room.[14]

*

* The total number would turn out to be 33,000.

The Tobruk disaster led Churchill to cut short his visit. At home he faced bad political news as the Conservatives lost a by-election in Maldon, Essex, in which their candidate won only 6,226 of the 20,000 votes. The seat was taken on a 22 per cent swing by Beaverbrook journalist Tom Driberg, who called for a reorganisation of the government and more help for Russia. A censure motion in the Commons got the backing of 25 MPs, still a tiny number, but a large increase on the single dissenter in January – the critics shot themselves in the foot by suggesting that the Duke of Gloucester, widely regarded as the thickest member of the royal family, should become Commander in Chief. 'Good for you,' Roosevelt cabled when he heard of the vote. But approval of the conduct of the war in British polls fell below 50 per cent. A report by Cripps spoke of 'profound disquiet and lack of confidence of the electors'.[15]

There was further cause for depression when German submarines and aircraft attacked a convoy of 34 ships taking supplies to Russia, sinking 23. The bad news was compounded when it became known that the Admiralty had ordered the withdrawal of the cruiser escort and the dispersion of the PQ-17 convoy because of a false report that the German battleship *Tirpitz* had left Norway to attack it. To Stalin's fury, Churchill suspended Arctic convoys until the autumn. After the string of reverses on land and sea since he had taken office, he needed a convincing victory. With so few alternatives, he had to trust that Roosevelt would throw himself behind the invasion of North Africa, and that this would mark a turning of the tide. If it did not, he told Eden, 'I'm done for.'[16]

The interest Roosevelt had shown in an invasion of North Africa was distinctly unpalatable to Marshall, Hopkins and Eisenhower. Stimson believed it had become the President's 'great secret baby'. Marshall wrote of being reduced to 'a defensive, encircling line of action for the continental European theatre'.[17]

On 8 July, Churchill told Roosevelt the Cabinet had voted against Sledgehammer. Marshall got the news from Dill, not the President. It was, he told Stimson, 'a rather staggering crisis in our war strategy'. He was 'very stirred up' and tired of 'these constant decisions which do not stay made'. It was time to invoke the Far Eastern threat.[18]

American confidence in the Pacific had been boosted by the navy's victory in the Battle of Midway in June. 'It is fun to win a victory once in a while,' Hopkins noted. 'Nothing that I know of quite takes its place.'

While agreeing on the importance of holding the 'citadel and arsenal' of Britain, Admiral King was pushing for more resources to press the advantage in the Pacific. The attack on Guadacanal in the Solomon Islands to start the island-hopping advance towards Japan was approved. Against this backdrop, Marshall proposed to Roosevelt that the focus should switch to operations against the Japanese if there was be no landing in Europe. As Roosevelt studied the plan at Hyde Park, Dill warned London that, if Britain persisted with North Africa to the exclusion of everything else, Washington would switch to the other war front – the recipients did not know that Marshall had co-written the message.

It is virtually certain that the Chief of Staff was bluffing. He remained wedded to the Europe First policy. But he could see that Sledgehammer and Roundup were in danger. By seeming to press for resources to go to the Pacific, he hoped to keep the President in line, and force Churchill to agree with him.

Roosevelt rejected the 'Pacific Ocean alternative' in a terse note that showed his global vision. 'My first impression is that this is exactly what Germany hoped the United States would do after Pearl Harbor,' he wrote, accurately reading Hitler's thinking in December 1941. 'Secondly it does not in fact provide use of American troops in fighting except in a lot of islands whose occupation will not affect the world situation this year or next. Third: it does not help Russia or the Near East. Therefore it is disapproved as of the present.' Signing the note 'Roosevelt, C-in-C', he told Marshall to go to London with Hopkins and King to resolve this alliance-threatening dispute.

Harry Hopkins usually enjoyed his trips abroad. This time, he was less keen. He was due to be married for the third time. The ceremony had been set for 30 July; when he left for London, his bride-to-be told him, 'You better keep that date.'[19]

The night before he flew out, the aide dined alone with the President, who was 'somewhat disturbed' by the British attitude which he characterised as a 'readiness to give up 1942'. If Sledgehammer could not be staged, another theatre of war should be identified 'where our ground and sea forces can operate against the German ground forces in 1942'. Marshall had come round to the extent of producing a paper noting that action in North Africa would have both the 'great advantage' of US forces engaging with the Germans and offering 'the beginning of what should be the ultimate control of the Mediterranean.'

In his orders to the delegation, Roosevelt set out three cardinal principles – 'speed of decision on plans, unity of plans, attack combined with defense but not defense alone.' In addition, promises of supplies to Russia must be carried out in good faith. The team was to investigate moves which 'would definitely sustain Russia this year [and] might be the turning point which would save Russia.'[20]

Getting American forces into action against the Germans in 1942 was 'of such grave importance that every reason calls for accomplishment of it,' he told Hopkins, Marshall and King. 'You should strongly urge immediate all-out preparations for it, that it be pushed with utmost vigor, and that it be executed whether or not Russian collapse becomes imminent.' If such a collapse looked probable, it would be imperative to divert the Luftwaffe from the eastern front. 'Only if you are completely convinced that Sledgehammer is impossible of execution with reasonable chances of serving its intended purpose, inform me,' Roosevelt went on. 'If Sledgehammer is finally and definitely out of the picture, I want you to consider the world situation as it exists at that time, and determine upon another place for U.S. troops to fight in 1942.' The Commander-in-Chief inserted the final part of this sentence into the typed version of the order in his own handwriting.[21]

There was a contretemps after the US party's plane landed in Scotland. The weather was too bad to fly on, so Churchill provided a special train for the visitors, which was to stop at the station near Chequers. But Marshall, Hopkins and King chose to go straight to the capital to confer with Eisenhower, who headed the American military effort in Britain, working from sixteen rooms on the fourth floor of Claridge's and a brick building in St James's Square.[22]

Churchill took umbrage, insisting that the visitors had gravely breached protocol. Speaking to Hopkins on the telephone, he read the war regulations to make his point, tearing out each page after he had finished with it. He 'threw the British Constitution at me with some vehemence,' Hopkins reported to Roosevelt. 'As you know, it is an unwritten document so no serious damage was done.' Churchill was 'his old self and full of battle.'[23]

At meetings on 20 and 21 July, each side stuck to its guns. Marshall feared that Roosevelt was 'all ready to do any sideshow' at Churchill's bidding. Brooke was unyielding. Sledgehammer would simply lead to the loss of 6 divisions, with no result. The bridgehead could not hold through the winter. That led King, his face like a sphinx, to talk of switching the focus to the Pacific. The CIGS stared into the distance through his heavy spectacles. Hopkins reached for a sheet of Downing Street notepaper and scrawled on it 'I feel damn depressed', passing it to his colleagues. 'Br. say no, we say yes,' he noted at another point. Churchill said he would have to consult the Cabinet. When it met two hours later, with Brooke laying out his argument, ministers unanimously rejected the US proposal. Eisenhower called it 'the blackest day in history'.[24]

Marshall, King and Hopkins had to report back to Roosevelt. As they waited for his response, they were guests at a dinner given by the British at Claridge's. 'On the whole, went well,' Brooke noted in his diary. In Washington, Stimson bombarded the White House with notes and telephone calls. In his diary, he again depicted British policies as those of 'a fatigued and defeatist government which has lost its initiative, blocking the help of a young and vigorous nation whose strength has not yet been tapped.' Sending troops to North Africa would isolate them there at just the time they would be needed in France, he insisted.[25]

It was too late. Roosevelt had made up his mind, at last. He told the delegation that some other offensive must be worked out to get American troops into action against the Germans and offer 'the best chance of success combined with political and military usefullness'. His anxiety for action was reflected in his list of possible operations – against Algiers, Morocco, Egypt, Iran, Norway and the Caucasus. 'Tell our friends we must have speed in a decision,' he concluded.[26]

When the two sides reassembled, Churchill announced that Roosevelt had sent him a message saying he accepted that an attack on France in 1942 was off. Turning immediately to North-west Africa, he pressed for urgent action, citing intelligence reports that Vichy forces were strengthening coastal and air defences.[27]

That day was Brooke's fifty-ninth birthday, and he dined alone with Marshall in what he called a 'very pleasant and friendly mood'. The next day, Hopkins cabled the President: 'We are naturally disappointed but good will prevails nevertheless. Now that the decision has been made we are hard at work on the next steps.' Even so, Marshall did not entirely give up, proposing that preparations for cross-Channel action in 1943 and for the North African landings should continue simultaneously, with a final decision to be taken in the middle of September when the situation on the eastern front should be clearer. In this, he came up against an unexpected opponent, Hopkins.

As on his previous trips to London and Moscow, the aide was filling the position of his master *in absentia*, and showing why the President so valued him. Putting off a decision till September could make any operation in October or November impossible. Now that the President had come down for it, the landing in North Africa had to be pursued with all possible speed. Hopkins suggested 30 October as the latest date, meaning preparations would have to start immediately. 'Full speed ahead,' Roosevelt replied. Folding his hands as if in prayer, he was heard to say, 'Please make it before election day.'[28]

'Besides reaching complete agreement on action,' Churchill told him, 'relations of cordial intimacy and comradeship have been cemented between our high officers. I doubt if success would have been achieved without Harry's invaluable aid.' In fine form, Churchill took the visitors to a dinner at the Royal Naval College at Greenwich which ended with the singing of sea songs and the two national anthems. The next night, he hosted a farewell dinner at Chequers, after which he showed them Cromwell's death mask and Queen Elizabeth's ring. When the Americans left, he settled down with Ismay and Brooke to watch a film, *The Younger Pitt*, followed by two hours of conversation before it was time for bed at 2.45 a.m.[29]

The business in Britain concluded, Roosevelt urged Hopkins to get back fast for his marriage. 'Tell Winston that not even he can stop that wedding,' he cabled.[30]

The bride, Louise Macy, was a former fashion editor who worked as a nurse's aide after Pearl Harbor. She met Hopkins while seeking other war work. Seventeen years younger than her husband at thirty-five, she was described as having good looks, a bright, ready smile, and a tactful nature. The ceremony took place in Roosevelt's White House office, the only one held there. In a white linen suit, Roosevelt sat watching from the side. The bride wore blue. The room was decked with palm fronds and white flowers.

Hopkins, according to a guest, 'trembled like an aspen leaf', his fingers shaking as he fished the wedding ring from a trouser pocket. Marshall asked the bride to 'curb [her husband's] indiscretions and see that he takes the necessary rest'.

They honeymooned in Connecticut – hostile newspapers reported falsely that the coastguard had requisitioned a yacht for them to take a sea cruise. Then they returned to Washington and took up residence in the Lincoln Room. The new Mrs Hopkins found life at the White House less congenial than her husband who, whatever his devotion to his new partner, could not give up on his old one. Eleanor was less than charmed by the new ménage, who invited friends for early cocktails and sometimes got 'really quite high'.[31]

Thus, Sledgehammer was abandoned, and Roundup shelved, though this was not spelled out. The North African landing, codenamed Torch, had Roosevelt's full backing. Marshall had learned a lesson in the conjunction of politics and strategy, and of how his chief worked. 'I did not realize how in a democracy the public has to be kept entertained,' he remarked.[32]

Winning the tussle was a considerable feat for Churchill. He had achieved the right military outcome; the raid on Dieppe by Canadians in August would show the hazards of a cross-Channel operation – half the 5,000 men were killed or captured. Though some Americans still held that the decision delayed victory in Europe by a year, the hazards were demonstrated by the difficulties the Allies would face after they did land in France in 1944 with far larger forces – 'blunt evidence that the invasion would certainly have ended in defeat if it had begun a year earlier,' as military historian Richard Holmes puts it.[33]

Having achieved his goal of overturning the American's plan without damaging the alliance, Churchill was ready to deploy a deftly obsequious touch in writing to Roosevelt of North Africa as 'your great strategic conception'. 'I cannot help feeling that the past week represented a turning point in the whole war and that now we are on our way shoulder to shoulder,' the President replied. But there was one outstanding issue to be addressed – Moscow had to be told.

Not knowing what had been decided, Stalin insisted 'most emphatically' that he could not tolerate a delay in the second front until 1943. Taking the message to Downing Street, Maisky found Churchill in a bad temper, having received news of fresh advances by Rommel. 'Through grief, Churchill had evidently overdone it a little with the whisky,' Maisky recalled. 'This could be seen from his face, his eyes, his gestures. At times his head jerked in a strange sort of way, and one felt that in reality he is already an old man . . . and that only a frightful concentration of will and consciousness maintain [his] capacity to act and fight.'[34]

Thinking Stalin was making an implied threat of withdrawing from the war, Churchill growled: 'Well, we've been alone before. We went on fighting. It is a wonder that this little island of ours stood up.' Calming down, he insisted Britain was doing all it could. The Soviet Union was under intense military pressure as the Wehrmacht advanced on two fronts against Stalingrad and the Caucasian oilfields. British intelligence had warned of the offensive, and a plane carrying plans for the campaign had crashed behind Soviet lines; as in 1941, Stalin dismissed both as disinformation. Hitler moved his headquarters from East Prussia to a mosquito-infested base known as 'Werewolf' in Ukraine to be closer to the front. His decision to order a two-pronged offensive would eventually prove a major error in splitting German strength. But, initially, it looked like another great success.[35]

Roosevelt cabled London to underline the need to look after 'Uncle Joe'. 'We have got always to bear in mind the personality of our ally and the very difficult and dangerous situation that confronts him,' he added.[36]

On the night of 30 July, Churchill called Maisky to Downing Street. He received him in his study, wearing a black and grey dressing gown over his siren suit. Eden was there, in a green velvet jacket and slippers. Churchill said he was about to fly to Cairo, and could go on to Russia for a meeting with Stalin to 'survey the war together and take decisions hand-in-hand'.

When the Georgian replied that he could not leave Moscow, Churchill decided to go to the Soviet capital. Cabling Roosevelt, he depicted his mission as 'a somewhat raw job'. Stalin would not like the news about the second front, he told his doctor. 'I'm not looking forward to it.'[37]

9

Midnight in Moscow

MOSCOW
AUGUST 1942

'The man has insulted me. From now on he will have to fight his
battles alone.'

CHURCHILL

THE TWELFTH OF AUGUST 1942 was a sultry, windless day in Moscow. As
Molotov and the frail, aged Soviet Chief of Staff, Marshal Shaposhnikov,
lined up on the turf apron of the Central Airport, bees buzzed round
them, birds chirped, and the air bore the scent of hot wormwood. They
watched a speck in the air turn into a Liberator bomber gliding in over the
rooftops. After it touched down and taxied to the grass verge, a ladder was
lowered and a pair of legs in heavy boots and crumpled trousers emerged,
followed by a bulky body. Finally, the welcoming party saw Churchill's head.

Given the codename of 'Mr Green' for the trip, the Prime Minister had
travelled via Cairo and Teheran in the converted American B-24 bomber.
The engine noise was deafening. The plane was unheated. Draughts
whistled through the fuselage. Sleeping facilities were two shelves in the
rear. Above 12,000 feet, those on board had to don oxygen masks –
Churchill had his adapted to accommodate a cigar, so other passengers
claimed.

In Cairo, he had replaced the Supreme Allied Commander in the
Middle East, Claude Auchinleck, whose caution he blamed for Rommel's
advances. In his place he appointed the debonair Harold Alexander, while
Bernard Montgomery was named as leader of the Eighth Army. 'There will
be no more belly aching and no more retreats,' 'Monty' declared, ordering

the destruction of plans for withdrawal. It was just what Churchill wanted, and morale improved as he visited troops in the desert.

After a stopover in Teheran where he called on the Shah, he headed for Moscow. With him were Averell Harriman, who had met Stalin the previous autumn and would act as Roosevelt's representative, his bodyguard, Commander Thompson, and his doctor, Charles Wilson. When Churchill called for food, Thompson produced a ham sandwich from a basket provided by the British Embassy in Teheran. Churchill asked for mustard. Thompson said there was none. 'Ten demerits,' his boss said, 'you should know that no gentleman eats ham sandwiches without mustard.'*[1]

Emerging from the plane, he looked round cautiously; 'Like the bull's, the PM's eyes were bloodshot and defiant, and like the bull he stood and swayed as if uncertain where to make the first charge,' wrote Archibald Clark Kerr, the ambassador. 'But the charge came from the crowd, headed by Molotov, and the bull was lost in a wild scrum.'[2]

After a military band played the Soviet, American and British national anthems, Churchill made a short speech pledging to fight with the Russians until the Nazis were 'beaten into the ground'. Then he inspected an honour guard of steel-helmeted soldiers, peering intently at their faces as if trying to read the extent of their determination. Following formal photographs, Molotov ushered the visitor into a Lend-Lease Packard limousine to be driven at great speed through virtually empty streets. Churchill was silent, abstracted and short-tempered. Winding down the window for air, he noted that the glass was more than two inches thick – Molotov thought such protection prudent, explained the interpreter, Vladimir Pavlov. In all, 120 bodyguards were assigned to protect the Prime Minister.[3]

The destination was State Villa No 7, at Kuntsevo, six miles outside the city. It had been built for Stalin, though the visitors did not know this. An elderly concierge took Churchill to a large bedroom and equally spacious bathroom on the first floor. Wilson was lodged in the nursery below, lined with cupboards full of toys. Elderly servants in white jackets stood by smiling, waiting to be summoned.[4]

---

* After Molotov mentioned the sandwiches to Stalin, the dictator said: 'What a hypocrite Churchill is! He wanted to convince me that all he is eating now is sandwiches – with a figure like his!'

As Churchill decided to draw himself a bath, Wilson heard shouts. Going upstairs, he found the Prime Minister sitting in the tub, shivering and cursing. The lettering on the mixer tap was in Cyrillic. Not understanding the labels, he had run cold water. Nor were things helped by the lack of a plug. A hot bath was eventually arranged, after which Churchill went downstairs where caviar, suckling pig and side dishes awaited him on fine porcelain, accompanied by wine and hard liquor. But he was in no mood for a feast. His message to Stalin that there was not going to be a second front in 1942 was, he reflected, 'like carrying a large lump of ice to the North Pole.'

At 7 p.m. on the warm summer night, Churchill and Harriman were driven to the Kremlin. With them was Clark Kerr, an Australian-born Scot who had come to Russia after a successful posting in China.* His rich, vivacious Chilean wife had left him during their time in China, and he found life dull in the Ural city of Kuybyshev, to where embassies had been evacuated – though he was anxious to meet a Turkish diplomat who had left a visiting card with his name 'Mustapha Kunt'. During the summer, he worked in the garden wearing only a pair of black shorts; as a result his face was bright red and his torso deeply tanned – that, with his broken nose and fitness, led the Russians to nickname him 'the Partisan'.[5]

As Churchill's car pulled up, Pavlov, the short, balding interpreter, stepped forward to escort the visitors to the second floor office overlooking the river. Stalin waited with Molotov and Marshal Voroshilov, an old army crony, together with a second interpreter, Valentin Berezhkov, who heard the dictator murmur 'there's nothing to get thrilled about' as the British approached.[6]

The door opened. After a lifetime of enmity and fourteen months of enforced alliance, Churchill was face to face with the leader of the 'botulism of Bolshevism'.

Wearing a brown tunic and ill-pressed trousers tucked into his boots, Stalin looked grim and absorbed. He stood by his desk, examining the visitors. Harriman found him older and greyer than the previous autumn.[7]

Hesitating in the doorway, Churchill's eyes ranged over portraits of Tsarist commanders, which had been put up to evoke patriotism alongside

---

* Ennobled as Lord Iverchapel, Clark Kerr was ambassador in Washington from 1946 to 1948.

Lenin on the wall of the long, rectangular room. Then he looked at his host.

Stalin walked slowly across the thick red carpet. He held out a limp hand. Churchill shook it energetically.

'Welcome to Moscow, Mr Prime Minister,' Stalin said in a hoarse voice, his face impassive.

Replying how glad he was to visit Russia and meet its leader, Churchill hoisted a broad smile.

Stalin sat down at the top of a long table covered with a green cloth. His chair had arms, the others did not. Boxes of cigarettes, bottles of mineral water and glasses lay in front of them. Stalin gestured to Churchill to sit to his right, Harriman to his left. The chairs were hard and uncomfortable, with white covers on the backs. The curtains on the windows were heavy.

The dictator began in a sombre mood, saying news from the front was 'not encouraging'. He had been surprised by the quantity of troops and tanks the Germans had thrown at the Soviet Union. He thought the Führer had 'pumped all he can out of Europe' to turn against the USSR. The message was plain – what was the West going to do to help by diverting the Nazis?

'I believe you would like me to address the question of the second front,' Churchill said, picking up his 'lump of ice'.

'As the Prime Minister wishes,' Stalin replied.

Saying he hoped they could talk frankly and as friends, the visitor recalled Molotov's visit to London, and the memorandum he had handed over making clear there could be no promises of action across the Channel in 1942. But London and Washington were planning to build up twenty-seven divisions for an operation the next year, he added.

Stalin looked very glum. Hitler did not have a single worthwhile division in France, he said. When Churchill disputed this, Stalin shook his head and looked even grimmer. The British would wonder if, in his desire to return home with the best possible news, Molotov had failed to reveal the reservations Churchill expressed in the memorandum.

The conversation grew 'bleak and sombre', in Churchill's words as Stalin fell back on a familiar tactic of insulting his interlocutor.

'No risk, no gain,' he said, according to Berezhkov's account. The British should not fear the Germans; they were not supermen. 'Why are you so afraid of them?' he asked rudely. Ignoring Churchill's offended look, he added that opening a new front in 1942 would enable the British and Americans to test their troops in battle. 'This is what I would do in your place,' he went on. 'Just don't be afraid of the Germans.'

Chewing on his cigar, Churchill replied heatedly that his country had not flinched when it stood alone in 1940.

Stalin said London had not helped Poland, or gone on the offensive against Germany. The dictator, Harriman reported to Roosevelt, expressed himself 'with bluntness almost to the point of insult'. But Churchill was 'at his best and could not have handled the discussion with greater brilliance'.[8]

As proof of the difficulty of mounting a cross-Channel operation, he pointed to the way Hitler had not tried to invade Britain in 1940.

No analogy with the present situation, Stalin responded. The Nazis would have met British national resistance, whereas the French would be welcoming.

All the more reason, Churchill rejoined, not to expose them to Nazi vengeance by a premature operation, and to harbour their support for 1943.

Each of the leaders was restless. Stalin kept getting up and walking across to a writing table, opening a drawer for cigarettes. He tore them apart and stuffed the tobacco into his curving pipe. From time to time, he gathered up the pencils on the table in front of him and rolled them across his palms. Churchill rose from his seat several times, pulling at the fabric of his trousers, which had stuck to his buttocks in the warmth of the summer night.[9]

To show what Britain was doing, the Prime Minister spoke of the bombing of Germany. Civilian morale was a military target, he added. He 'hoped to shatter almost every dwelling in almost every German city'. Stalin noted that morale was fading among German civilians, whom he wanted to 'blast out of their homes'.[10]

Unrolling a map of Southern Europe, the Mediterranean and North Africa, Churchill said a second front did not have to be in northern France. Under strictest secrecy, he was going to disclose what he and Roosevelt planned. For the first time, Stalin grinned. When the Prime Minister stressed the importance of secrecy, the Soviet leader's face wrinkled with amusement as he said he hoped the British press would not break the story.

As Churchill began to outline the plan for Operation Torch, Stalin held up his hand to stop the flow of words and asked about the timing.

The end of October at the latest, the British leader replied. If possible, by the seventh of that month. Molotov said September would be better. But he, Stalin and Voroshilov looked relieved. Even more so when, to make his point, Churchill drew a picture of a crocodile to illustrate how France was its hard snout but the Mediterranean a soft underbelly which could be pierced*.[11]

Harriman chimed in to say that, despite the war in the Pacific, Roosevelt would support the Allied effort in Europe to the limit. The two visitors painted an optimistic picture of French collaborationist forces not firing at American troops because Washington had maintained relations with Vichy. When the question of de Gaulle came up, Churchill said he would not be involved in Torch, and would 'probably do what he told him to do'.

'May God help this enterprise to succeed,' the former seminarist now head of the atheistic Communist state, exclaimed, by Churchill's account. His interest was 'at a high pitch' as he saw Torch hitting Rommel's army in the back, overawing Spain, provoking fighting between Germans and French, and exposing Italy. Walking over to a globe, Churchill added a fifth aim, the opening up of the Mediterranean. Stalin's reaction was, he recalled, just what he wanted – 'He saw it all in a flash.'

Berezhkov tempered this upbeat account in recording that the conversation left 'a sour taste'. After hearing about Torch, he noted, Stalin brought the talk back to Western Europe, and did not budge from insisting that there was a commitment to a landing in France later that year.[12]

Still, as they drove off, the visitors were 'delighted with the talk', according to Harriman. Reaching the dacha at midnight, Churchill sat down to a huge meal, nursing his head in his hands between courses. When he had finished, he lit a cigar, but soon put it across a wine glass. Yawning, he got up, and stretched. It was nearly twenty hours since he had left Teheran. He was ready for bed. As he undressed, he congratulated himself to Wilson on his tactics. The Soviet leader had appreciated his

---

* Churchill would also use the analogy of a crocodile in talking of relations with Communists. It was, he said 'like wooing a crocodile. You do not know whether to tickle it under the chin or to beat it over the head.' (Churchill Museum, London)

frankness, and 'ended in a glow' over Torch. That, alone, made the trip worthwhile.[13]

Having woken, according to some accounts, with a hangover, Churchill told his doctor as they walked in the fir woods in the morning that the talks should be 'plain sailing'. He felt he had established the human relationship he sought. Back in the villa, he was warned that the rooms were probably bugged, but showed his confidence by declaring: 'The Russians, I am told, are not human beings at all. They are lower in the scale of nature than the orang-utang. Now then, let them take that down and translate it into Russian' – he added that he hoped the listeners would pass this on to Stalin.*

At dinner, he still appeared unaware – or unworried – about being listened to as he described Stalin as a peasant whom he could handle. A member of his party scribbled '*Méfiez-vous*'† on a menu, which he passed up the table. Reading it, Churchill glared back.[14]

The rest of the British party, including Cadogan and Brooke, arrived in a Douglas aircraft furnished with armchairs, a radio gramophone and Persian carpets, and flown by a daredevil Russian colonel who delighted in swooping on the airport before landing, scattering the welcoming party on the ground. Over the Caucasus, the pilot's low flying gave Brooke, a dedicated twitcher, a chance to see unfamiliar marsh birds, but also to note the rudimentary nature of the defences.[15]

Churchill now fell out with the ambassador. After the first meeting in the Kremlin, Clark Kerr struck a cautionary note. This clashed with Churchill's optimism, fuelled by Harriman's sunny view – 'the sustained bumsucking of Harriman made me feel and probably look like an angry ram,' the envoy noted. As they exchanged hostile looks, Churchill pawed theatrically at the American, saying, 'I'm so glad, Averell, that you came with me. You are a tower of strength.' He decided not to include Clark Kerr in the second Kremlin meeting. 'What a bloody day!' the ambassador wrote in his diary.[16]

---

* Churchill included a reference to this, though not the words he used, in the original draft of his memoirs. He cut it from the published version for diplomatic reasons – Stalin was still alive and he was hoping to return to power and negotiate with the Soviet leader. (Reynolds, *History*, pp. 326–7)

† 'Be careful'.

At 11 p.m., Churchill drove up for his second meeting with Stalin. He was accompanied by Brooke, Cadogan, Air Marshall Arthur Tedder, Wavell, Colonel Jacob of the Cabinet staff, an interpreter, and Harriman. On the other side, Stalin and Molotov were alone, apart from their interpreter.

The Soviet leader began by producing an aide-memoire, signed by himself. Pavlov read out a translation. It began by recording that there would be no second front in France in 1942, though, 'as is well known', this had been agreed during Molotov's visit. Soviet military plans were based on the belief that there would be such an attack. So the decision 'inflicts a mortal blow to the whole of the Soviet public opinion' and 'complicates the situation of the Red Army at the front and prejudices the plan of the Soviet Command'. There was no mention of the memorandum Churchill handed over in London. Ignoring arguments about the difficulties of an offensive, Stalin insisted that conditions were 'most favourable' because Hitler had moved the bulk of his forces, including his best troops, to the east.*[17]

Saying that he would deliver a written reply in due course, the Prime Minister tried to discuss more positive matters. But, leaning back and pulling on his pipe, his eyes half-closed, Stalin unveiled a litany of complaints. Churchill found him 'most unpleasant' as he charged that the British and Americans considered the eastern front of secondary importance. They had sent him little in supplies and had not recognised the price being paid by the Red Army, with 10,000 men sacrificed each day. Going back to the start of the previous night's talk, he said the Western Allies should be able to land 6 to 8 divisions on the peninsula around Cherbourg. Then he reverted to insults, saying that, if the British army had been fighting the Germans as much as the Russians had, it would not be so frightened of them.

Holding himself back, Churchill replied that he pardoned this slur because of the bravery of Soviet forces. But, he added tartly, the proposal to land around Cherbourg overlooked the existence of the Channel.

Stalin cut off the discussion by inviting the visitors to return for dinner the next night. Churchill accepted, but said he would be leaving at dawn

---

* That very day Hitler stressed to Albert Speer, the Armaments Minister, the importance of building an 'Atlantic Wall' of 15,000 concrete bunkers to guard against a landing in France. This would use 13 million square metres of concrete and 1.2 million tons of steel, largely to defend ports which the Allies would bypass when they landed in Normandy.

the morning after that. Stalin appeared surprised, asking if he could not stay longer. Non-committally, the Prime Minister said he could remain another day if it would be useful.

Cracking his hand on the table, he then launched into what, with studied understatement, he later described as a 'somewhat animated' outburst. 'I have come round Europe in the midst of my troubles – yes, Mr Stalin, I have my troubles as well as you – hoping to meet the hand of comradeship; and I am bitterly disappointed,' he said. 'I have not met that hand.' He talked of Britain's lone fight in 1940 and insisted on the aid being provided in a dramatic outburst. The British interpreter was unable to keep up. Cadogan, who had scribbled down some of Churchill's words, began to read them out for translation.[18]

Stalin held up his hand. 'I do not understand the words, but by God I like your spirit,' he said.

The atmosphere improved as Stalin vaunted the merits of Russian trench mortars and asked for an exchange of information about each country's inventions. He outlined the position in the Caucasus on a relief model. But when Harriman asked if he was satisfied with plans to deliver aircraft, Stalin replied curtly that wars were not won by making plans, and that no planes had arrived.

Watching Stalin and Churchill spar, Brooke noted that they were 'poles apart as human beings'. 'I cannot see a friendship between them such as exists between Roosevelt and Winston,' he wrote in his diary. 'Stalin is a realist if ever there was one, facts only count with him, plans, hypotheses, future possibilities mean little to him, but he is ready to face facts even when they are unpleasant. Winston, on the other hand, never seems anxious to face an unpleasantness until forced to do so. He appealed to sentiments in Stalin which do not I think exist there.'[19]

Churchill wondered at the change in his host's attitude, sitting up with Harriman till 3.30 a.m. to discuss it. Their conclusion was that the 'Council of Commissars' might have adopted a harsher line when their leader reported on the first session of talks – an explanation that showed ignorance of the authority Stalin exercised. Allowances had to be made for the stress on the Russians, the Prime Minister would tell the Cabinet. He was certain Stalin's 'surefooted and quick military judgment' made him a strong supporter of Torch.[20]

Still, he was 'downhearted and dispirited' by the harshness of the second session. His talk of North Africa had not shifted the Soviet insistence on a landing in France. Recounting the meeting to his doctor, he pressed his lips together and muttered 'I can harden too.' But when Cadogan asked if he should tell the Kremlin Churchill was thinking of turning down the dinner invitation in protest, he replied: 'No, that is going too far, I think.' Still, at 4 a.m., he told Wilson that, if his host wrecked the talks and the alliance, his government would fall. 'I am going to leave that man to fight his own battles,' he muttered.

The next day, Cadogan delivered the British reply to Stalin's note, reiterating the argument against a landing in France and rejecting the idea that Red Army planners could have been misled by the conversations with Molotov in London. As he did so, the diplomat took the opportunity to say that Churchill had been 'puzzled and disheartened' by the Soviet leader's attitude. Harriman took a more sanguine view. 'I cannot believe there is cause for concern and I am confidently expecting a clear-cut understanding before the Prime Minister leaves,' his cable to Roosevelt added. Later, he linked Stalin's mood to the military situation in the Caucasus – 'they were really desperate. Stalin's roughness was an expression of their need for help.'[21]

Churchill stayed in a lowering mood. At lunch at the dacha, he sat slumped and silent, his head in his hands or low over his plate. Once again, he directed his ire at Clark Kerr. 'It was difficult to sit through the meal with any semblance of patience and good manners,' the ambassador wrote. 'I felt like giving him a good root up the arse. My respect for him and faith in him have suffered sadly.'[22]

That night, at a nineteen-course banquet in the Kremlin, Stalin sat with Churchill on one side, Harriman on the other, and Molotov opposite. Though cheerful, Stalin appeared tired. Sipping wine from a small vodka glass, he ate only one potato and a little cheese, telling Harriman he had already dined. John Reed, the Head of Chancery at the British Embassy, thought he might be drunk. Jocularly, he raised toasts to 'British Intelligence Officers present', warning of the terrible fate their work might bring. Churchill's bodyguard was so overcome by the food and drink that he slumped back in his chair, sending a dish of ice cream being carried by a waiter crashing to the floor.[23]

Addressing Churchill, the Soviet leader referred to himself as 'a rough man, not an experienced one like you'. He recalled that, when a British visitor praised Chamberlain, he predicted the British would call back 'the old war horse' in their hour of need. Then he remembered how he had been told that Churchill had misled the British government of the day to intervene against the Bolsheviks in the Russian civil war.

There was much in that, the Prime Minister responded. 'I was very active in the intervention, and do not wish you to think otherwise.'

Stalin smiled.

'Have you forgiven me?' his visitor asked.

'All that is in the past, and the past belongs to God,' came the reply.

Stalin walked down the table to where Brooke was sitting beside Marshal Voroshilov, who was drunk on fiery yellow vodka in a jug with a large red chilli – the CIGS kept sober by surreptitiously filling his vodka glass with water. Sweat pouring from his forehead, Voroshilov stared straight ahead. Stalin stood by his chair, toasting him. This meant Voroshilov had to struggle to his feet, holding the table for support. Lunging forward, he clinked glasses with his master. Then he sank back into his chair with a deep sigh.

Cadogan noticed how Churchill became increasingly bored as the toasts and speeches dragged on, with Molotov paying tribute to each general at the table. When Stalin proposed his health, Churchill's response was short. During the meal, he recalled to his host his immediate support for the Soviet Union in 1941: 'When the Germans declared war on you, I consulted nobody, but made my broadcast speech.' In his thoughts, he returned to wondering what would have happened if Britain had lost the war when Stalin 'was giving Hitler so much valuable material, time and aid.'

Sensing that it would be wise to bring proceedings to a close, Cadogan made a final toast of 'death and damnation to the Germans'. Nobody could top that. As they got up from table, Stalin insisted on being photographed with Churchill. In the picture, he smiled broadly as did Harriman; Churchill's lips were pursed.

The Prime Minister suggested an immediate private meeting between the two of them, but Stalin declined to leave the party. So the British leader stumped to a side table where he studied a document. According to an account by a Russian air force general, he had drunk so much that he 'was literally carried from the table to get some rest'.

Out of Churchill's earshot, Stalin complained to Harriman that the

British army and navy had lost their initiative, comparing the suspension of convoys and the loss of Singapore with the way Americans were fighting in the Pacific. When the Georgian proposed watching a film called *The German Rout Before Moscow,* Churchill declined, and went on reading even after his host joined him. At 1.30 a.m., the Prime Minister stood up, and said, 'Goodbye.' His wording was deliberate.

Shaking hands, Stalin remarked that they only differed as to the method of best fighting Germans. Churchill replied that Britain would do its best to remove those differences by deeds. Then he left the crowded room, his face overcast. Walking down the passage outside, he reached out to strike a match on the wall, and lit his cigar.[24]

Stalin hurried after him. He had almost to trot to keep up as they went through the vast, ornate chambers to the door where the big ZIS limousine was waiting. Stalin managed to bid a second farewell, but, as he rode to State Villa No 7, Cadogan beside him, Churchill exploded in resentment.

'I don't know what would have happened at the Kremlin if the party had gone on much longer,' the diplomat said. 'He was like a bull in the ring maddened by the pricks of the picadors,' he added, adopting the same imagery as Clark Kerr. 'He declared that he really did not know what he was supposed to be doing here. He would return to London without seeing Stalin again.'

At the dacha, Churchill's bad temper was aggravated by an argument with Cadogan about the wording of the communiqué to be issued at the end of the trip. Churchill objected that the Russian draft contained no reference to offensive action by Britain. He thought this made clear disagreement between the Allies, which it would be disastrous to reveal. But, in the end, he told the diplomat to do as he wished, while insisting that his views should be recorded. After a silence, he went up to his room. Stripped to his silk vest, he sat in an armchair, staring at the floor. Then he noticed that Wilson had come in, as he usually did last thing at night.[25]

'Stalin didn't want to talk to me,' Churchill said. 'I closed the proceedings down. I had had enough. The food was filthy. I ought not to have come.'

Getting up, he paced up and down. Stopping in front of his doctor, he clutched at a straw, saying: 'I still feel I could work with that man if I could break down the language barrier. That is a terrible difficulty.'

Should he make another attempt, he wondered. He might be snubbed.

That was a necessary risk, Wilson replied.

No, Churchill said, he would not go near Stalin again. He had deliberately said 'Goodbye' rather than 'Goodnight' on leaving the banquet. If there was any fresh move, it must come from the other side.

Climbing into bed, he put on a black eyeshade, and settled his head on the pillow. Wilson turned out the light, and left the room. It was 3.45 a.m.

Back in the Kremlin, Stalin told the aviation chief he would have the Prime Minister 'wriggling like a carp in a frying pan'.[26]

When he woke, Churchill debated whether to leave Moscow. To one British officer, he speculated that perhaps Stalin had not meant to be so insulting and that there had been a translation problem. In another conversation, he said he was 'damned' if he was going to submit to more Soviet complaints.

In this fraught context, Clark Kerr became the key player. Known for his ability to charm others into agreement without giving up anything substantial, the ambassador once said that what was needed at the embassy in Moscow was diplomatic 'cock-teasing'. Convinced of the disastrous consequences if Churchill flew out, he went to work on him, comparing the Prime Minister to a spoiled child.[27]

Clark Kerr's account of his 'furious battle' on 'a hell of a day' provides a good illustration of the way Churchill's mind and emotions worked, his pride and susceptibility, his self-indulgence and desire to parade his toughness – and the way he could be talked round by those brave enough to stand up to him.

When Clark Kerr arrived at the dacha, Wilson told him of the previous night's events. One of Churchill's weaknesses, the doctor observed, was that he was surrounded by too many yes-men, and 'only listens to what he wants to listen to'.

Deciding to be a no-man, the sixty-year-old ambassador reflected that the worst that could happen to him was to be sacked. 'It was clear that some plain speaking was needed and I was probably the person to do it,' he wrote in his journal. 'Golly! I should be taking a great risk.'

First, he had 'a little feast of raspberries' from the garden. Then Cadogan called him in to see Churchill. 'The minotaur was ready for his next victim,' as the envoy wrote.

Wearing a grey siren suit, Churchill was lowering and sullen.

'I hear you want to see me,' he said.

Clark Kerr suggested a walk to discuss matters. Putting on a ten-gallon hat, the Prime Minister picked up a walking stick.

'May I be frank?' Clark Kerr asked as they went outside.

'Frank?' Churchill responded, staring at him. 'Why not?'

'I may say something that is unpleasing to you.'

'I've been used to that all my life. I'm not afraid.'

As Churchill stumped ahead of him through the fir trees, Clark Kerr addressed his hunched shoulders, saying he thought he was going about the whole business with Stalin in the wrong way. The British leader stopped walking several times to look him in the face, and then moved off again. Clark Kerr said it would be Churchill's fault if his mission ended in failure. He had thrown away his 'matchless gifts' in talking to Stalin. The Soviets were rough men who thought aloud, and said harsh and offensive things. He had let this anger him, and affect his judgement.

'The man has insulted me,' was the reply. 'From now on he will have to fight his battles alone.'

Clark Kerr said the talks could not be allowed to fail. The Prime Minister must meet the dictator halfway.

'But the man has insulted me,' Churchill repeated as he walked on. 'I represent a great country, and I am not submissive by nature.'

What would happen if Stalin was left to fight alone, and Russia was beaten? the ambassador asked – 'How many young British and American lives would have to be sacrificed to make this good?'

'The man thinks he can upset my government and throw me out,' Churchill replied. 'He is very much mistaken.'

Clark Kerr warned that, if he abandoned Russia, Churchill would find his political strength ebbing away. He would be the man who had thrown the Soviet Union to the Nazis. 'What a pity to have come so far, and to have made a mess of things,' he added.

'A mess of things?' Churchill echoed as they emerged from the wood to walk abreast towards the dacha. 'You mean you think it's all my fault?'

'Yes. I am sorry but I do.'

'A mess of things?' Churchill stabbed the ground with his stick, looking down. 'Well, and what do you want me to do?'

Clark Kerr said he should immediately propose another meeting with Stalin.

'But I am not a submissive man.'

'I don't ask you to be submissive. I merely ask you to be yourself.'

'Myself,' Churchill repeated, striding into the house.

Soon afterwards Churchill said he wanted to discuss plans with Cadogan. Putting on 'a baby's bottom face', Churchill said that Clark Kerr believed the problem with Stalin was all his fault. He chuckled. Cadogan laughed.

Pavlov was told that Churchill wanted to see Stalin again – alone. The Kremlin replied to British telephone calls by saying that the Soviet leader was out for a walk. Finally, at 6 p.m., the message came that Churchill would be received an hour later. This meant delaying a dinner appointment with the Polish General Anders – the Poles would always play second fiddle to Stalin for the West.

Following up his concern about the language barrier, Churchill decided to change interpreter. Clark Kerr recommended Major Birse from the embassy staff. On the way to the Kremlin in a large ZIS, Churchill told Birse that some of his previous conversations with Stalin had been rather tense. Though it might be difficult, he wanted to put his host in a better temper before leaving Moscow.

Stalin kept his eyes lowered as he shook hands though he glanced briefly into Birse's face. He waved the visitors to the long table. The two leaders were alone except for the interpreters.[28]

The Georgian returned to the second front, but Churchill moved the conversation to other subjects – the Caucasus, Torch, Arctic convoys. Stalin doodled on a pad, rarely glancing up. When something Birse translated sparked his interest, he looked at the interpreter, at first with no expression but then 'something like a look of approval seemed to emerge, like the sun breaking through the dark clouds.' Birse found the Georgian accent and low voice made Stalin's simple Russian sound like another language.[29]

After an hour, Stalin's mood lightened. Gesturing over a map, he vowed that the Red Army would halt the Wehrmacht in the Caucasus, and spoke of the importance of Operation Torch.

'May God help you,' he added.

'God, of course, is on our side,' Churchill said.

'And the devil is, naturally, on mine, and through our combined efforts we shall defeat the enemy,' Stalin chuckled.*

Churchill asked Birse if he was getting the message over. The interpreter said he believed so. 'I think you are doing well,' Churchill assured him.

When the Prime Minister said it was time for him to go, Stalin asked:

'Why don't we stop in my Kremlin apartment for a drink?'

'I never refuse offers like that,' the British leader replied.

Accompanied by NKVD guards, the Georgian led the way along the corridors, across a small yard and a street until they reached his quarters, where an old woman in white overalls and a headscarf was laying for four. Bottles stood in the middle of the table. The bookcases were empty – their contents had been taken away for safe keeping during the attack on Moscow.

Stalin had given instructions for the meal to be prepared that afternoon, planning to get Churchill into a more relaxed environment. He had told his pretty, sixteen-year-old daughter Svetlana to stand by. When conversation turned to offspring and the two men found they each had a red-haired daughter, she was summoned. After kissing her father, who handed her a gift, she hovered for a while. Stalin glanced at Churchill to see how he reacted. 'I confess that I acquired a quite definite physical impression,' the Prime Minister wrote later. He told Stalin and his daughter that he, too, had had red hair as a boy. When the talk turned to war, she was sent away.

The dinner began with radishes, followed by caviar, salmon, sturgeon and mushrooms. Later came beef, chicken and pork. Though the room was rather stiff and cold, Birse recalled the atmosphere as 'very homely and pleasant'.

Stalin filled glasses with vodka, Caucasian champagne and wine. As he talked, he kept touching an even number of glasses superstitiously with his fork. Then he poured a special light brown vodka into a small glass, saying it was much better than the usual drink. But, after a quiet warning from Birse of 'vicious stuff', Churchill declined to try it.

They agreed that a meeting with Roosevelt should be arranged. 'We have no antagonistic interests,' the Prime Minister said. Stalin agreed.

If they met in Iceland, Churchill added, the Soviet leader should visit Britain. Stalin recalled he had been in England with Lenin for a Socialist conference in 1907.

'Had Trotsky also been there?' Churchill asked.

'Yes,' Stalin replied, but he had left as 'he did not represent anybody.'[30]

Stalin called in Molotov who was still in his office. The Foreign Minister, he noted, was an expert drinker. The fourth place had, evidently, been laid in advance for him.

* According to Eden, this exchange was repeated at the Big Three meeting in Teheran eighteen months later. It evidently appealed to the two men. (Eden, *Reckoning*, p. 427)

Churchill asked if Stalin knew that his colleague had visited New York during his trip to America. 'He did not go to New York,' the dictator replied. 'He went to Chicago to meet the other gangsters.'[31]

When the ill-fated PQ-17 Arctic convoy came up, Stalin wondered if the Royal Navy had had no sense of glory. 'You must take it from me that what was done was right,' his visitor replied. 'I really do know a lot about the Navy and sea-war.'

'Meaning,' Stalin responded, 'that I know nothing.'

'Russia is a land animal, the British are sea animals,' Churchill said.

When Churchill asked to go to the toilet, Stalin accompanied him through his simply furnished bedroom. Returning to the dining room, he and Molotov questioned Birse on his knowledge of Russia and Russian. After Churchill came back, the conversation turned to history. The British leader mentioned his ancestor, Marlborough. Stalin put on a mischievous look and said that he thought Wellington an even greater general – the Iron Duke's campaigns against Napoleon in Spain could, he added, be regarded as a second front.

As midnight passed, the talk took on a more sinister tone when Churchill asked if the war was as bad a stress as the collectivisation of Soviet agriculture in the 1930s.

'The collective farm policy was a terrible struggle,' his host responded.

'I thought you would have found it bad. You were not dealing with a few score thousands of aristocrats or big landlords, but with millions of small landholders.'

'Ten million! It was fearful! For four years it went on. But it was absolutely necessary for Russia if we were to avoid periodic famines and to supply enough tractors for the countryside.'

'These were what you call kulaks?'

'Yes. It was all very bad and difficult – but necessary.'

'What happened to them?'

'Well, many of them agreed to join us. Some got plots of land . . . but they didn't put down new roots there. They didn't get along with the local people. Eventually, their own farmhands finished them off.'

Churchill did not challenge this ludicrous version of events – though, in his memoirs, he wrote that he shuddered inwardly.

Returning to the war, the two men agreed that an operation in Scandinavia, one of Churchill's pet schemes, would be useful. By then, the atmosphere was sufficiently relaxed for Churchill to ask why Moscow had ended talks with the West in 1939 and signed the pact with Germany. Stalin said that, given Britain's lack of forces and the poor state of France's army, he had not believed those two countries would go to war. He knew Hitler would attack him in due course, and, by taking East Poland, he thought he had gained time. He told a story about Molotov visiting Berlin during an RAF raid. In the shelter, Ribbentrop talked of the end of the British Empire. 'Then why are we down here now?' Molotov asked.

Back at the dacha, Clark Kerr was asleep on a sofa while the Polish General Anders sipped whisky. A telephone call from the Kremlin summoned Cadogan to come with a draft of a communiqué. Arriving at 1 a.m., he found a scene of great good humour. A suckling pig was brought in. Stalin offered the head to Churchill which was refused. So the host fell on it, cleaning out the inside with a knife, cutting slices from the cheeks and eating them with his fingers.[32]

He then disappeared for twenty minutes to read reports from the fronts, before returning to review the communiqué. An English typewriter was fetched, on which Birse tapped out a clean copy. 'A number of decisions were reached covering the field of the war against Hitlerite Germany and her associates in Europe,' it began, pledging the two governments to use all their power to destroy Hitlerism and any similar tyranny. The talks had been marked by 'cordiality and complete sincerity' and reaffirmed 'the existence of close friendship and understanding between the Soviet Union, Great Britain and the United States of America, in entire accordance with the Allied relationship existing between them.'[33]

It was 2.30 a.m. when the party broke up. Stalin and Churchill had been together for almost seven hours. At the door, the Prime Minister said Molotov should not come to the airport to see him off three hours later. They could say farewell there and then.

'Oh, no,' said Stalin, 'he is a younger man. He will see you off.'

Reaching the dacha, Churchill was glowing. He dismissed Anders after saying he would see him in Cairo. Flinging himself on a large sofa, he chuckled and waved his legs in the air as he told Clark Kerr he had cemented a friendship with 'that great man' in the Kremlin. 'I was taken into the family,' he exulted. 'We ended friends.'[34]

Hearing the water running for a prime ministerial bath, the ambassador made to go. Churchill told him to stay, stripping to his silk vest, below which the envoy saw 'a penis and a pair of wrinkled cream buttocks'. In the margin of his journal, he sketched what must be the only portrait by a British ambassador of a Prime Minister naked from the waist down.[35]

Two hours later, Molotov arrived, bleary eyed, to accompany the British party to the airport. Churchill, suffering from a splitting headache, lined up for the farewell ceremonies on the tarmac, wearing a chalk-striped three-piece suit. His plane took off at 5.30 a.m., the Prime Minister sleeping as it headed for Teheran. On wakening, Churchill called for food. His bodyguard produced a lunch basket packed by the Kremlin staff. When he found that it contained caviar and champagne, Churchill erased the demerits he had imposed on Thompson for the lack of mustard on his ham sandwich on the flight to Moscow.[36]

From Teheran, he thanked Stalin for his comradeship and hospitality. 'I am very glad I came to Moscow,' he added, 'firstly because it was my duty to tell the tale [about the non-second front in 1942] and secondly because I feel sure our contacts will play a helpful part in furthering our cause. Give my regards to Molotov.' He assured Roosevelt of his success in 'getting Joe in the bag'.

'On the whole, I am definitely encouraged by my visit to Moscow,' he cabled the War Cabinet. 'I am sure that the disappointing news I brought could not have been imparted except by me personally . . . Now they know the worst, and having made their protests are entirely friendly; this in spite of the fact that this is their most anxious and agonising time. Moreover, Stalin is entirely convinced of the great advantage of "Torch".' Churchill could congratulate himself on having led Roosevelt to back the landing in North Africa, and then opened a personal channel to the Kremlin. But his views on the eastern ally had not altered. 'It would be a measureless disaster,' he wrote to Eden, 'if Russian barbarism overlaid the culture and independence of the ancient States of Europe'.

Nor had the convivial night in the Kremlin dispelled Soviet suspicions. When Moscow's spy ring of Cambridge graduates failed to come up with evidence of Churchill's anti-Soviet plotting, Moscow concluded that Philby, Burgess, Maclean and others were British double agents. 'All of us in

Moscow have gained the impression that Churchill is aiming at the defeat of the USSR, in order then to come to terms with the Germany of Hitler or Brüning [the pre-Nazi Chancellor] at the expense of our country,' Stalin wrote to Maisky.[37]

10

★ ★ ★

As Time Goes By

NORTH AFRICA, MOSCOW, CASABLANCA
OCTOBER 1942–JANUARY 1943

'Unconditional surrender. Uncle Joe might have made it up himself.'

ROOSEVELT

CHURCHILL CALLED the autumn and winter of 1942 to 1943 'the end of the beginning'. Though the Wehrmacht reached the first oilfields in the Caucasus, the Russians blew up the wells before retreating. On 25 September, the Germans got to Stalingrad, but were halted there, with hugely extended supply lines. This meant that Hitler could not depend on drawing further resources from conquered territory to fuel his war machine and compensate for the weaknesses of the German economy. Arctic convoys resumed though 10 of the first 40 merchant vessels were sunk. In the Pacific, 16,000 US Marines landed at Guadalcanal. Britain and the US began to share decrypts of German and Japanese messages. In Washington, the atom bomb programme was formalised under the name of the Manhattan Project; the first experiment would be conducted in December.

Most heartening for Churchill, British and Dominion troops under Montgomery scored a victory in the Western Desert at El Alamein. The peppery general was turned into a popular icon. On 18 November, church bells rang throughout Britain in celebration; a year earlier they would have been warning of invasion.

However, after returning to London from Moscow, Churchill received what he called a 'bombshell' from Washington about Operation Torch. The US Chiefs of Staff argued that lack of men and landing craft meant there could be only two landings – at Casablanca on Morocco's Atlantic coast and Oran in western Algeria. This did not fit at all with the British aim of taking Tunis and Bizerta to the east. After Churchill made his case, Roosevelt agreed, ordering a three-pronged landing – at Algiers as well as Oran and Casablanca.[1]

'Hurrah!' he cabled Churchill.

'OK. Full blast,' the former naval person replied.

But Roosevelt added that there was no intention of abandoning plans to invade France later – Sledgehammer might be dead; Roundup was still at the core of American strategy.

Though Churchill had got his way again, there was tension between Washington and London over France ahead of Torch. The President had established a personal link with a leading Vichy figure, the ambitious, unscrupulous Admiral François Darlan, who had been the number two figure in the collaborationist regime until German pressure led to him being replaced by the veteran politician Pierre Laval. This made him ready to blow with the American wind. Darlan's son suffered from polio, and the President invited him to the treatment centre he used. Through a go-between, the admiral told Washington he could rally the French in North Africa to the Allied cause.

The one point in Darlan's favour was that he had not handed the French fleet over to the Germans in 1940. Otherwise, before losing power, he had agreed to a series of concessions to Hitler, sometimes without consulting Marshal Pétain. He set up military cooperation in the Middle East and North Africa, and allowed U-boats to use the French base at Dakar to attack Atlantic shipping. Under his authority, a Commission on Jewish Affairs was set up, which strengthened anti-Semitic legislation and persecution.[2]

Washington justified cooperation with him on the grounds that, once he had smoothed the way for Allied troops, he would be replaced in liberated North Africa by a less tarnished figure, General Henri Giraud, who had escaped from German captivity earlier in the year.* Whether the admiral

---

* Giraud told Brooke his wife had sent him wire hidden in butter tins which he used to descend the walls of his prison in Germany, having previously obtained civilian clothes. A contact met him with false papers. Regaining France, he made his way by submarine to Gibraltar.

would step aside was, however, extremely doubtful, while Giraud lacked political skills, as a military man interested only in military matters.

Stalin approved of the US decision, quoting a Russian proverb about needing to be ready to use 'even the Devil himself and his grandma'. For the sake of Allied solidarity, Churchill also defended it, though the admiral was strongly anti-British because of the Royal Navy's attack on the French fleet at Mers-el-Kebir in 1940. But he was sensitive to friends asking him: 'Is this what we are fighting for?' Eden was strongly opposed. Cadogan dismissed the policy as 'the Vichy French telling the Americans what they want, and the Americans giving it to them with both hands'. The Prime Minister worried about the lack of British influence in North Africa, where Roosevelt sent a pro-Darlan diplomat, Robert Murphy, as his political representative. On 22 December, he appointed Harold Macmillan, Junior Minister at the Colonial Office, to join Eisenhower's command, with ministerial rank, reporting directly to Downing Street.

In his London headquarters in Carlton House Terrace overlooking St James's Park, de Gaulle strode up and down in a rage. Free French forces were not being invited to take part in the liberation of French territory. Power had been handed to a leading Vichy figure. Giraud was a potent rival. It was his darkest hour since he left France in 1940.

A professional soldier all his life, and a veteran of the First World War, de Gaulle had been Deputy Minister of Defence at the time of the defeat. He was the only Allied leader to have seen service at the front, having led a tank attack on the advancing Germans. Sent to seek reinforcements from London, the tall, gawky Frenchman had taken a last-gasp proposal to Churchill for a Franco-British union which the Cabinet had agreed, but which was shot down by armistice-seeking ministers in France. As Pétain sued for peace, de Gaulle unfurled his flag of resistance with his broadcast call to the French people on 18 June 1940.

His intransigence could make him his own worst enemy, as Churchill told him. In reply, the fifty-two-year-old general pointed out that the Free French leaders were 'necessarily somewhat difficult people. Or else they would not be where they were.' Churchill believed in the need for a strong France after the war, and saw de Gaulle as the man who could achieve that.

---

* Often attributed to Churchill, the phrase came from Edward Spears, the British general who brought de Gaulle from France in 1940, but then fell out with him.

Though he would be referred to, after his movement's symbol, as the Prime Minister's 'Cross of Lorraine'*, the British leader could empathise with a man who had refused to give up.

On the other hand, there was little common ground between the intensely patriotic Frenchman and Roosevelt, who maintained an embassy at Vichy and toyed with the idea of splitting off North-east France (where de Gaulle had been born) to combine it with Belgium in a new country. For de Gaulle cooperation with Vichy was anathema; but Roosevelt seemed ready to work with anybody, even Laval, if this would weaken the Germans. Though the Free French were eventually allowed to join the United Nations, the President thought their chief was a dictator in the making, a 'well-nigh intolerable figure' with a messianic complex who threatened the Allied cause. When de Gaulle offered America the use of West African bases held by his movement, he got no reply.[3]

Taking a line he would pursue two decades later in the Elysée Palace, the Frenchman believed that the United States was already too powerful and wanted to be more so. He blamed America's isolationism and aid to Germany for facilitating the rise of Hitler, and was highly critical of its failure to enter the war in 1940. Nor did he have any illusions about where Churchill's ultimate loyalty lay. The British would do nothing without the agreement of Roosevelt, he forecast.

On 7 November, nearly 700 ships landed 107,000 men in North Africa in the biggest amphibious invasion ever staged. Expecting the attack to be directed at a Mediterranean island, the Germans had not sent in reinforcements. So the landings were relatively easy. Within three days, the Allies controlled 1,500 miles of coast. Darlan ordered Vichy troops to stop firing. He himself was confirmed as the principal French political figure in North Africa. Two days later, the Governor of French West Africa rallied, bringing with him the Dakar naval base.

Torch was Dwight Eisenhower's first field command. The fifty-two-year-old West Point graduate had moved slowly up the staff hierarchy before being spotted by Marshall and put in charge of Pentagon planning. His diplomatic nature and insistence on Allied unity marked him out as the man to lead the first Anglo-American land offensive.

Roosevelt was with guests at his retreat Shangri-La, a former Marine base with simple pine cabins, when news of Torch was telephoned through to him. Still wearing his mourning band for his mother on his sleeve, he trembled as his secretary, Grace Tully, passed him the receiver.[4]

'Thank God,' he said. 'Congratulations!' Then, turning in his chair, he told the guests: 'We are striking back.'

He had finally got US troops into action against the Germans, even if it had been later than he had hoped, after the US Chiefs of Staff had advised that Torch could not be staged before the mid-term elections, which had not been good for him. Though his party retained control of Congress, its share of the vote dipped, while the defeat of liberals strengthened the conservative wing of the Democrats. Republicans gained nine governorships, and held states which would make a majority of the electoral college in the next presidential poll.

Still, Roosevelt was in high spirits. He had got a troublesome political fight out of the way, and could concentrate on the war. He did, however, take note of rising criticism of the cooperation with Darlan; Willkie came out against it, and Adolf Berle of the State Department warned of a looming storm of protest at the installation of a 'semi-Fascist' government. As a result the President told Eisenhower: 'It is impossible to keep a collaborator of Hitler . . . in civil power any longer than is strictly necessary.'

In Britain, Torch and Montgomery's victory at El Alamein greatly boosted morale. Churchill's popularity soared to over 90 per cent; polls showed approval of the conduct of the war leaping from 41 per cent in September to 75 per cent. 'There is a long road still to tread,' the Prime Minister told a visitor, 'but the end is sure.' He saw off several political challenges, notably from Stafford Cripps, who resigned from the War Cabinet, being replaced by a more orthodox Labour figure, Herbert Morrison.

Hitler heard of the first major Allied counter-attack when Ribbentrop boarded his train in the Thuringian forest, as he travelled to Munich for a celebration of the anniversary of his attempted beer hall putsch in 1923. Ribbentrop suggested exploring the prospects of a peace agreement with Stalin. Hitler rejected the idea. 'From now on, there will be no offers of peace,' he declared. In his speech in Munich, he said that, while the Kaiser had given up at a quarter to midnight in the First World War, he always ended at 'a quarter past twelve'.[5]

In September, Roosevelt sought to massage US–Soviet relations by sending Willkie on a goodwill mission to Moscow. Stalin produced his usual list of demands, and the President undertook to dispatch vehicles, explosives, grain, and monthly consignments of 15,000 tons of frozen meat, 10,000 tons of canned meat, 5,000 tons of soap, 10,000 tons of vegetable oil, and 12,000 tons of lard. He told Churchill he wanted to be able to say that 'we have carried out our obligations one hundred per cent.'[6]

Willkie, an ebullient backer of a second front, toured factories, went to a safe distance from the front, and after a performance of *Swan Lake* jumped on to the stage with a bouquet for the prima ballerina . He claimed to have drunk fifty-three vodkas at a dinner Stalin hosted for him – and to have walked to his car unaided. Before he did so, Marshal Voroshilov produced a tommy gun and, playing on the British ambassador's nickname, asked Clark Kerr if he knew how to use it like a 'partisan'. The envoy made a show of raking Stalin and Willkie. Then Stalin took the gun and said he would demonstrate how a politician would fire, sweeping it round the room as if to kill everybody.[7]

Patrick Hurley, a former Republican Secretary of War, who was now the US representative in New Zealand, followed Willkie in November. A lawyer with a penchant for shouting Native American war cries, his brief was to talk to the Soviets about the war in the Pacific – but he was told the USSR was not in a position to confront Japan, and Stalin did not want to switch resources from the war in Europe.[8]

Keeping up the pressure for aid and for a second front, the Soviet leader rounded on Britain as the Soviet press accused London of acting 'with customary duplicity' against the emergence of a strong USSR. He wrote to Maisky that the Prime Minister 'belongs, apparently, to those people who are quick to give promises, only to forget them as quickly, or to break them . . . Well, we will know for the future what sort of allies we have.'[9]

Litvinov reported that Stalin feared that the Western Allies and Hitler would reach an agreement to sacrifice the Soviet Union. Clark Kerr, on the other hand, worried that it might be the dictator who reached an agreement with Berlin. Visiting London, he was not clear how the government wanted him to proceed with the Kremlin. 'You want a directive?' Churchill growled. 'All right. I don't mind kissing Stalin's bum, but I'm damned if I'll lick his arse.'[10]

Undaunted, Roosevelt cabled the Kremlin in early December saying the Big Three should meet. There should be 'some tentative understanding' about what to do if Germany collapsed. But the most compelling reason was, 'I am very anxious to have a talk with you.'

The President proposed mid-January, at 'some secure place in Africa', with only a few senior staff present. 'If the right decision is reached, we may, and I believe will, knock Germany out of the war much sooner than we anticipated,' he added. Stalin replied that he could not leave Moscow because of 'affairs at the front'. Roosevelt offered to send air force units to help the Red Army in the Caucasus, but the Soviets said this was not needed.[11]

By Christmas, Roosevelt had to accept that a Big Three summit would have to wait, though he told the Chiefs of Staff Stalin probably 'felt out of the picture . . . and that he has a feeling of loneliness.' In fact, the Georgian was focusing all his attention on winning the Battle of Stalingrad. For that, he had no immediate need for an Allied conference. Better to wait till the Red Army gave him the military edge. So, when the planned summit assembled in January 1943, it was, again, confined to Roosevelt and Churchill.[12]

At ten p.m. on 12 January 1943, Averell Harriman drove to an RAF base near Oxford where the Liberator in which he and Churchill had flown to Moscow was lined up. Over a late dinner in the base canteen, he said that he and the two aides were going to Algiers to deal with Lend-Lease matters. The Americans climbed into the plane, but it did not take off. At midnight, a convoy of cars arrived with blaring sirens; the lead limousine had the brightest lights Harriman had ever seen – and this during a blackout. The idea had been for the Americans to provide a cover story for the Liberator's real mission. But, as the base commander exclaimed: 'Good God, the only mistake they made was they didn't put it in the newspapers. No one could make that much noise except the Prime Minister.'[13]

Clambering into the plane, Churchill took off his blue commodore's uniform and stripped down to a silk vest before lying on a mattress on the floor. To reduce the cold at high altitudes, a petrol heater had been installed with heating points round the fuselage. At 2 a.m., Churchill was woken by one of these points, which had become red hot and was burning his toes. Worried about the fire risk, he crawled down the plane to wake Air Chief Marshal Portal. They found two more red-hot points.[14]

Churchill climbed into the bomb bay, oblivious of his nakedness from the waist down. He discovered two men servicing the petrol heater.

Deciding it was better to freeze than burn, he told them to turn it off. Then, shivering at 8,000 feet, he tried to fix a blanket on the fuselage to stop the draughts. From his place on the floor, his doctor, who had just been ennobled as Lord Moran, watched the British leader on his hands and knees cutting 'a quaint figure with his big, bare, white bottom'.

Arriving in Morocco after the nine-hour flight, Churchill noticed a second plane coming in to land, carrying members of his staff. Despite the security risk, he insisted on waiting for it on the tarmac, drawing on his cigar. As he stepped down from the second plane, Ismay remarked: 'Any fool can see that it is an air commodore disguised as the Prime Minister.'[15]

Roosevelt flew in two days later. The forty-eight-hour journey chalked up a series of firsts – the first time the US leader had been in the air since flying to Chicago to accept the 1932 nomination, the first flight by an incumbent president on official business, his first intercontinental trip, and his first wartime journey outside the United States. He had flown down to Brazil, across the Atlantic to the British colony of the Gambia, and then to his ultimate destination, Casablanca – the new film of that name had been shown at the White House at New Year. Hopkins compared the President to a sixteen-year-old on a first-class holiday. 'He loves the drama of a journey like this,' the aide wrote. 'They are always telling him that the President must not fly; it is too dangerous. This is his answer.' Roosevelt brought with him detective stories, copies of the *New Yorker*, and the script of the play *The Man Who Came to Dinner*, which Missy Le Hand observed could have applied to his right-hand man who had stayed over in the White House since 1940.[16]

Security in Casablanca was heavy. Harold Macmillan was struck by the 'terrifying' machine guns, tommy guns and sawn-off shotguns carried by rings of sentries. A strong barbed-wire fence surrounded the site. When Roosevelt was driven in from the airfield, mud was smeared on the car windows to conceal him. The main participants were referred to by codenames – Churchill was Air Commodore Frankland, while Roosevelt and Hopkins were Admiral Q and Mr P (Q for Quixote, P for Panza).[17]

Given the codename of Symbol at Churchill's suggestion, the fourth American–British summit was held in an idyllic oasis outside the city called Anfa. It continued the small-circle pattern set at Placentia Bay and in Washington. Apart from the military chiefs and the political officers Murphy and Macmillan, Churchill brought with him from London only one member of the government, Lord Leathers, the Minister of War Transport. Roosevelt was accompanied by Harriman and Hopkins, whom Churchill found looking twice as fit as 'before the combined restoratives of blood transfusions and matrimony were administered to him'. The President took pains to exclude Hull, describing him as a 'ringer' who would be a nuisance. This meant Eden could not attend either. Harriman was sent to persuade Churchill of this, which he did only after being, as he put it, 'beaten up' by the Prime Minister.[18]

Macmillan described Anfa, a mile in circumference, as 'a kind of Roman camp' and the conference as 'a curious mixture of holiday and business in these extraordinarily oriental and fascinating surroundings'. He was struck by the quantity of food, drink, cigarettes, chewing gum and toilet requisites. Churchill noted the free availability of eggs and oranges, which were strictly rationed in Britain. The British leader, Macmillan noted, ate and drank enormously, played cards by the hour, 'and generally enjoyed himself', though he wrote to his wife of suffering indigestion and 'housemaid's elbow'.[19]

At the President's villa, Macmillan recorded, there was 'a lot of bezique, an enormous quantity of highballs, talk by the hour and a general atmosphere of extraordinary good will.' Harriman pretended that he did not know how to play bezique, one of the Prime Minister's favourite card games, but still won several rounds against the father-in-law of his mistress. Both the President's sons arrived, as did Randolph Churchill, who came in from the Western Desert where he was part of a commando force operating behind German lines.[20]

The two leaders occupied villas fifty yards apart. Churchill's, called Mirador, was fitted with a ramp so that the President could be wheeled in. Roosevelt's, called Saada, had a high living room surrounded by a gallery, large French windows, steel shutters, a garden with oleanders and bougainvillea, and a swimming pool that had been turned into a makeshift air-raid shelter. The ground-floor suite had frilly decorations, a huge bed and a bathroom with a sunken black marble tub – 'all we need is the madam of the house,' said the President, whistling as he was shown in. The owner was a prisoner of war in France; his wife and children had been moved to a hotel.[21]

The summit began with a preliminary dinner during which Hopkins arranged for five black soldiers to sing. Admiral King got drunk, and delivered a lecture on how to deal with the French in North Africa. Not realising the American's condition, Churchill took him seriously, and began to argue. 'Most amusing to watch,' Brooke noted in his diary.[22]

At 1.30 a.m., there was an air-raid alarm – Casablanca was in the Luftwaffe's range. The lights were extinguished, leaving the company sitting in the light of six candles. Churchill and Roosevelt debated if Stalin might put in a last-minute appearance. The President thought not, but forecast that, if he did arrive, he would have only one subject in mind – the second front.

The first formal session was held in beautiful weather on 15 January. Harold Alexander, whom Churchill had promoted to command British and Dominion forces in North Africa the previous summer, came from his desert headquarters unshaven, weary, tanned and in battledress. He brought with him good news of Montgomery's progress across the desert.

The Chiefs of Staff held strategy sessions each day in the large dining room of the Anfa hotel. Familiar themes emerged as the British pressed for the invasion of Sicily, leading to an attack on Italy, not France. When Marshall pressed the case for Roundup, Brooke responded that no more than 27 divisions could be assembled. Laying it on extremely thick, he said a cross-Channel operation would mean giving up the attack on Sicily, stopping convoys to the USSR, delaying action in Burma, shelving operations in the eastern Mediterranean and reducing bombing of Germany. Better to apply pressure in South Europe, increase air raids, and try to get Turkey into the war.[23]

Marshall replied that he was 'most anxious not to become committed to interminable operations in the Mediterranean', while King grumbled that the British 'have definite ideas as to what the next operation should be, but do not seem to have an overall plan for the conduct of the war'. If Britain was counting on the Soviet Union to beat Hitler, perhaps more aid should be sent to Russia, he added – and, by implication, less to the United Kingdom. Churchill said he was not reneging on a landing in France, but continued to put the Mediterranean first. Again, Roosevelt sided with him in backing the invasion of Sicily, even alluding to Churchill's crocodile image by suggesting that the operation should be codenamed 'Belly' – the Prime Minister substituted the more staid 'Bellona' though this was later changed to 'Husky'. Falling into line, King said he could find the landing craft. But the American Chiefs, Harriman recalled, agreed only 'with marked reluctance'.[24]

There was also prolonged sparring over China and Burma with Marshall warning that reverses in the Far East might necessitate the transfer of resources from Europe. Chiang Kai-shek had complained to Roosevelt of the 'demoralizing doubts on the part of my officers who concluded that . . . China is treated not as an equal like Britain and Russia but as a ward.' The Nationalists hinted they might be forced to seek a truce with Tokyo if more help was not forthcoming – fast. The forceful, articulate and alluring Madame Chiang Kai-shek, nominal head of her country's air force, had pressed for more planes in talks with the US adviser, 'Vinegar Joe' Stilwell. She and her husband were annoyed that aircraft destined for China had been diverted to North Africa. Why did Britain 'always have to have somebody else to pull her chestnuts out of the fire', she asked. In retaliation, the Nationalist leader issued what were known as the Three Demands – the US should reopen the land supply route to south-west Yunnan province; send 500 planes; and pledge 5,000 tons of Lend-Lease supplies a month. Until that was agreed, China would not join in any operations in Burma.[25]

A personal element had been added to the equation by a night Chiang Kai-shek's wife spent with Wendell Willkie when he went to the wartime capital of Chungking after his visit to Moscow – the publisher, Gardener Cowles, who accompanied him, recorded that he returned 'cocky as a young college student after a successful night with a girl'. Still Stilwell's reports from China were gloomy, as the Nationalist army, with some notable exceptions, refrained from fighting the Japanese and hoarded its strength for the post-war struggle with the Communists. Vinegar Joe castigated the regime's incompetence and corruption, but Roosevelt was intent on building up China as a great power to fill the Asian vacuum that would be left by Tokyo's defeat. The Americans planned to launch air raids on Japan from a huge airbase being built in Sichuan province, and saw a landing in Burma as the way to get supplies into south-west China.

Brooke viewed the Burma plan as a threat since it would take away landing craft from the invasion of Sicily. Given the way Roosevelt had swung behind the Mediterranean policy, it was difficult for the British to lay down a veto, but the CIGS insisted that it must not 'prejudice the earliest possible defeat of Germany', a neat echo of American reservations about British strategy in southern Europe.[26]

In addition to Sicily, the Chiefs recommended continuing to build up forces and landing craft in England for a cross-Channel thrust 'in the event that the German strength in France decreases, either through withdrawal of her troops or because of an internal collapse'. Every effort was to be made to get Turkey to commit itself. Operations would continue in New Guinea and the Marshall Islands. The timing for Burma was set at the end of 1943.

Brooke noted 'definite progress'. Well he might, for superior British committee work once more won the day. 'We came, we saw, we were conquered,' commented the American planner, Albert Wedemeyer.[27]

That left the thorny issue of France. The situation there and in North Africa had evolved since Torch. The United States no longer had an embassy in Vichy. Hitler had ordered German troops to occupy the collaborationist zone. On Christmas Day, a French royalist, coached by the British, had assassinated Admiral Darlan – Roosevelt called it 'murder in the first degree' but Churchill noted how the Allies were relieved of an embarrassment, while retaining the advantage of his collaboration.[28]

However, Roosevelt showed no hesitation in meeting ex-Vichy officials. At a session with the resident governor in Rabat, General Noguès, he discussed the future of Jews in North Africa in a conversation that was all the more extraordinary for coming at a time when there could be no doubt of the Nazi genocide.[29]

Ceilings should be fixed for the number of Jews in professions in line with their percentage of the overall population, the President said. They should not overcrowd those professions, he added. Noguès replied that it would be 'a sad thing for the French to win the war merely to open the way for the Jews to control the professions and business world of North Africa'.

Enlarging on his quota idea, Roosevelt said it would eliminate 'the specific and understandable complaints which the Germans bore towards the Jews in Germany, namely, that while they represented a small part of the population, over fifty per cent of the lawyers, doctors, school teachers, college professors etc, in Germany were Jews.' The 'understandable' was, at best, another sign of his irresponsibility and loose use of language to soft-soap whoever he was meeting. More likely, it represented a terrible blindness to the fate of European Jewry.

After Darlan's death, the American protégé Henri Giraud was put in charge of military and civilian affairs, but soon showed his limitations. The tall general, with his fine curled moustache and ramrod back, let himself be led by former collaborationists, who had local resistance figures arrested on trumped-up grounds. He also proposed to continue with Darlan's scheme to appoint as Governor General in Algiers a former Vichy interior minister who had applied anti-Jewish legislation, and had signed the death sentence for de Gaulle.

Roosevelt wanted a Committee for the Liberation of France with de Gaulle and a civilian – Hopkins favoured the banker and civil servant Jean Monnet, the future 'Father of Europe'. According to the US account, Giraud reacted enthusiastically, saying he was certain he and de Gaulle could work out a military arrangement between them.[30]

When the President pressed him to 'get your problem child down here', Churchill replied that de Gaulle was on his high horse. 'Refuses to come down here. Refuses point blank. . . . He's furious over the methods used to get control in Morocco and Algeria and French West Africa. Jeanne d'Arc complex.'

In his bedroom that night, the President poured out his feelings to his son. He accused the Free French leader of wanting to impose a dictatorship. 'I can't imagine a man I would distrust more,' Elliott recorded him as saying. Returning to the theme as the summit went on, he said he had produced the groom in Giraud; Churchill must bring the bride for a shotgun wedding.

But de Gaulle was not a man to be easily bidden. Called to the Foreign Office by Eden to be handed a message from Churchill urging him to fly to Casablanca, he read it in silence until he came to a mention of a former Vichy general who was organising the imprisonment of resistance figures.[31]

'Ah, they're going to bring in even that one!' he exclaimed.

He said the only choice was between Vichy and his movement – Giraud represented nothing. Returning to his headquarters, he sent a refusal in writing. 'This, I should think, is the end of the Free French movement,' Cadogan judged.

But Roosevelt had been unimpressed by Giraud. 'I am afraid we are leaning on a very slender reed,' he told Elliott. 'He's a dud as an administrator. He'll be a dud as a leader.' For its part, Giraud's group was shocked by the President's appearance, describing him as 'a very ill man . . . with a grey, ravaged face'.

Pressing Churchill to get rougher with the Free French leader, Roosevelt hit on a new argument. 'I asked W.S.C. who paid de Gaulle's salary,' he wrote to Margaret Suckley. 'W.S.C. beamed – good idea – no come – no pay!'[32]

In a cable to de Gaulle, Churchill said the invitation had come from the President, as well as from him. Continued refusal would have negative consequences, alienate public opinion and sabotage British efforts to reconcile Roosevelt with the Free French. If the general did not change his mind, Britain would have to 'review' its attitude and 'endeavor to get on as well as we can without you'. Churchill advised Eden: 'For his own sake you ought to knock him about pretty hard.'[33]

The Foreign Secretary told the Cabinet of the message, and, before it was given to de Gaulle, it was toned down. The Free French National Committee voted in favour of the trip. De Gaulle told an aide that he would not have gone for Churchill alone, but would do so to meet Roosevelt. He used his message of acceptance to lay out complaints – the French had not been involved in Torch; Vichy officials had been retained; he had no idea of how the talks would be organised.[34]

Churchill walked to Roosevelt's villa to deliver the news with a smile. 'Congratulations,' the President replied. 'I was sure you'd succeed.'[35]

For dinner that night, Roosevelt invited five members of the US Women's Army Auxiliary Corps. 'Awfully nice girls,' he wrote, 'but very military & efficient!' Churchill, Harriman and Alexander joined in at 11 p.m., and sat up talking with Hopkins till 2 a.m.[36]

He also gave a dinner for the Sultan and Grand Vizier of Morocco which put Churchill in a bad mood. A photograph before the meal shows the Prime Minister looking querulous as he sat on a sofa in his three-piece dinner suit. In deference to the religious customs of the Moroccans, no alcohol was served. In a note to Hopkins on his programme, Churchill wrote that he would follow the dinner, 'dry alas!' by 'recovery from effects of above'.[37]

As if that was not bad enough for a man who once said that his own religion prohibited him from not drinking before, after and during meals, the President used the occasion to attack the way the French and British profited from their colonies, and proposed that American universities could train Moroccan engineers. Moving smoothly from politics to business, he suggested that the Sultan might engage US firms to carry out development programmes 'on a fee or percentage basis'. The ruler said he would ask for development aid after the war. Glowering, Churchill bit into his cigar.

In a conversation later that night, Elliott Roosevelt recorded his father as saying: 'When we win the war, I will work with all my might and main to see to it that the United States is not wheedled into the position of accepting any plan that will further France's imperialistic ambitions or that will aid or abet the British Empire in its imperial ambitions.' He had been shocked by what he had seen on the stopover in the Gambia; people there were 'treated worse than the livestock,' he told his son. 'Their cattle live longer!' As for Britain sucking out India's wealth and leaving the population to starve, 'Churchill may have thought I was not serious, last time. He'll find out this time.'

Meanwhile, trouble had flown in. From the start, de Gaulle was sharply negative. He saw the way the windows of his car were covered with mud as evidence that his hosts wanted to hide his presence from local people. He viewed the heavy American security presence as an insult to his nation – French soldiers should be guarding their territory. At lunch with Giraud, he exploded. It was, he said, 'odious that they should finally get together behind barbed wire manned by foreigners'. After refusing to sit at table until French soldiers had replaced the American sentries, he insisted that all former Vichy officials must be sacked, and criticised the Americans and British. Then he went for an icy tête-à-tête with Churchill at which he was warned he would be abandoned if he was not more cooperative.[38]

De Gaulle hardly seemed interested. He said the American plan for Giraud to take overall charge and for ex-Vichy officials to remain in place 'might seem adequate at the level of American sergeant-majors', but could not be taken seriously. Neither the US nor Britain should presume to decide on the attribution of power in the French Empire. At the end of the meeting, he stalked out through the garden, his head high in the air. Churchill could not conceal his admiration. 'His country has given up fighting, he himself is a refugee, and if we turn him down he's finished,' he told his doctor. 'But look at him! Look at him! He might be Stalin, with 200 divisions behind his words . . . France without an army is not France. De Gaulle is the spirit of that army. Perhaps the last survivor of a warrior race.'

Late that night, after the dinner for the Sultan, Roosevelt had his first session with de Gaulle. Armed American secret service men stood hidden behind drapery round the gallery above the living room in case the general attacked the President.

De Gaulle was 'cold and austere', Hopkins wrote. Roosevelt did most of the talking. Despite his antagonism to the Free French leader, he could not lay aside his innate tendency to massage whoever he was talking to.

'I am sure that we will be able to assist your great country in re-establishing its destiny,' he began.

Sitting stiffly in his chair, the Frenchman grunted.

'And I assure you, it will be an honour for my country to participate in the undertaking,' Roosevelt went on.

'It is nice of you to say so,' de Gaulle replied in a low voice.

The President stressed the importance of French unity against the Germans. He said that none of the various factions could presume to possess sole legitimacy to rule France, to which de Gaulle replied that Joan of Arc had drawn her legitimacy by taking action and refusing to lose hope.

Ploughing on, Roosevelt explained why he felt North Africa should be held in trusteeship by America and Britain till the war ended. To illustrate this, he used a metaphor that could hardly have been more calculated to enrage his visitor. According to the US record, 'the President stated that France is in the position of a little child unable to look out and fend for itself and that in such a case a court would appoint a trustee to do the necessary.'

Yet, de Gaulle contained himself, and the meeting ended after half an hour in a more relaxed mood. The American record says the general left 'with some show of cordiality'. The Frenchman told an aide afterwards that he had just met 'a great statesman. I think we understood one another well.' Macmillan reported that Roosevelt had been impressed. Churchill's doctor, Moran, wrote in his diary, without citing a source, that Roosevelt had been attracted by 'a spiritual look' he detected in the other man's eyes. This did not stop him inventing and retailing a story that de Gaulle had compared himself to Joan of Arc, Georges Clemenceau and other great figures of French history. When word of this reached its target, he was considerably annoyed.

After de Gaulle left, Roosevelt, Churchill and Hopkins spent an hour comparing notes. Sensitive, as always, to domestic opinion, which had a good view of the Free French, the President sensed the need to temper his hostility. Using so many ex-Vichy in the administration in North Africa was attracting widespread criticism in the bundles of American press clippings delivered to his villa each day. Eisenhower, dogged by a bad cold and depressed by the politics around him, feared that French resistance might be provoked. So Roosevelt decided to try to resolve the quarrel between the two men by offering them equal footing, and leaving it to a future French assembly to choose between them. 'De Gaulle will oppose it, obviously,' he predicted.

He did, indeed, reject the idea. Apart from anything else, it was yet another unacceptable piece of interference in French matters. All he would do was to agree to meet the President and Prime Minister again.

Before that, however, he underwent a harangue from Churchill. Having fortified himself with a bottle of white wine at breakfast, the British leader was at breaking point. Receiving de Gaulle at the Mirador villa, he thundered that he was ready to denounce him in the Commons and on the radio as the man who had prevented agreement. He would turn the British public against him, and tell the French what had happened. It was, de Gaulle recalled, their roughest session of the war. Churchill did not mention it in his memoirs.

The general gave as good as he got. Churchill was 'free to dishonour himself', he said. To please America at any price, Britain was embracing a cause unacceptable for France. This was worrying for Europe, and regrettable for Britain.

While words were flying at the Mirador, Roosevelt was greeting Giraud for their third session fifty yards away. Elliott and Hopkins were present. The former American go-between with Vichy, Robert Murphy, hovered.

Giraud handed Roosevelt two memoranda. One provided for him to be recognised as the man responsible for managing 'French interests in the military, economic, financial and ethical spheres'; the other said the President would assure French forces of military supplies as a matter of priority, and help him achieve their unity. Roosevelt had no time to discuss all this – a press conference was due in an hour's time and he had to have something to announce. So he signed the papers without reading them properly, and got down to business.

'We must have your assurance, General,' he told Giraud, according to his son's account, 'that you will sit down with de Gaulle and –'

'That man! He is a self-seeker,' Giraud interrupted.

'If I told you that I share with you some of your misgivings, that this is precisely why I urge that you –'

'And a bad general. I need only support for the armies I can raise –'

'– must sit down with him and work out a joint plan for the interim.'

Crossing from Churchill's villa, de Gaulle waited in the hall.

Inside, Giraud gave way. 'It is understood, Monsieur le Président,' he said. 'It is understood.' Walking out, he brushed past his rival. But he did not leave the villa, waiting to see what would happen.

'The ground had been paved, but the prima donna wanted urging,' Elliott recalled. 'Like the girl in the story, he was playing hard to get. Father moved by degrees from charm to suasion to urgency to direct demand.' In the end, like Bogart in the movie, he fell back on the simple appeal – 'Trust Me.'

Calm and confident, de Gaulle argued that Giraud should serve under him. Hopkins found himself liking the Frenchman who never gave up.

Roosevelt said how sorry he was at the lack of understanding between the two generals.

'Leave me be,' the visitor replied. 'There will be a communiqué, even if it is not yours.'

At that moment, a secret service man came in to say that Churchill was outside talking to Giraud. The Prime Minister then came in. Hopkins ducked out, thinking that, if he could get the four men together, they might reach agreement. Roosevelt nodded to his son who followed Hopkins, and beckoned to Giraud to come back.

De Gaulle looked 'somewhat bewildered' at the other Frenchman's reappearance, Hopkins recalled. Waving his finger, Churchill bellowed in improvised French: '*Mon Général, il ne faut pas obstacler la guerre!*'

Roosevelt was all charm, turning to de Gaulle to ask if he would agree to be photographed with him, the Prime Minister – and Giraud.

'Naturally, because I have the greatest esteem for this fine soldier,' de Gaulle replied, by his own account.

'Will you go as far as to shake hands with General Giraud in our presence and in front of the cameras?' Roosevelt repeated.

'I shall do that for you,' came the response – in English.

The two Frenchmen looked stiffly at each other, and circled like suspicious dogs. At the President's urging, they exchanged a brief handshake.

Roosevelt beamed.

'We have agreed,' de Gaulle said, 'we have agreed that we will do our best to work out a satisfactory plan of action . . .' He paused, then uttered the tough word – 'together.'

Giraud nodded. They would, de Gaulle added, draw up a joint statement.

'Come on,' Roosevelt cried, 'pictures!'

The four went to the terrace behind the villa for the noon press conference. Roosevelt was carried to his seat. He suggested the generals shake hands for the cameras. As shutters clicked and movie cameras turned, the two tall Frenchmen stepped forward, arms outstretched at the greatest possible distance, each showing clearly he was as reluctant as the other.

Their statement said: 'We have met. We have talked. We have registered our entire agreement on the end to be achieved which is the liberation of France . . . This end will be attained by a union in war of all Frenchmen.' De Gaulle called the whole show ridiculous – 'a handshake in front of the photographers – no, that does not interest me any more.' In his memoirs, Churchill remarked that the photograph of the two generals 'cannot be viewed . . . without a laugh'. But Roosevelt looked greatly relieved as he sat back in his chair with a broad smile. The alliance's great impresario had got the public show of agreement he sought, however little it meant.

At the press conference following this pantomime, Roosevelt and Churchill said they had agreed to send all possible aid to the USSR, help China and unite the French to fight the Axis. Then Roosevelt added that getting the French generals together had been as difficult as arranging the meeting of the Union and Confederate commanders, Grant and Lee, in the Civil War. Spinning an imaginative web, he said he had suddenly recalled that Grant had been known as 'Old Unconditional Surrender', and he used the three words to define Allied policy towards the enemy.[39]

Churchill heard this with surprise, and told Harriman later that he was offended Roosevelt should make an important announcement in such a way. But, at the press conference, he loyally followed suit, anxious that no crack should appear. In fact, according to Elliott Roosevelt, his father had mentioned the phrase at a lunch with Churchill and Hopkins.

The presidential aide had said he liked the words.

Churchill munched his food, frowned thoughtfully, and then said 'Perfect! And I can just see how Goebbels and the rest of 'em'll squeal.'

'Of course, it's just the thing for the Russians,' the President added. '. . . Unconditional surrender. Uncle Joe might have made it up himself.'

Churchill would write that he had no recollection of this conversation – anything from Elliott was calculated to raise his hackles. But, at a meeting with the Combined Chiefs of Staff and Roosevelt on 18 January, he had proposed a public statement that the war effort would not be relaxed 'until the unconditional surrender of Germany and Japan has been achieved'. A message to the War Cabinet said he and Roosevelt proposed to include such a phrase in a statement to the press 'at the proper time'. It would declare their intention 'to continue the war relentlessly until . . . the "unconditional surrender" of Germany and Japan.'

For Roosevelt, the words were anything but improvisation. Before leaving Washington, he had told the Chiefs of Staff he was going to discuss whether to tell Stalin that 'the United Nations were to continue on until they reach Berlin and that their only terms would be unconditional surrender'. At the press conference, he had in his lap carefully prepared notes, which contained a reference to unconditional surrender as 'a reasonable assurance of world peace for generations'. 'One thing about Roosevelt's famous statement is certain – he had his eyes wide open when he made it,' the speechwriter Robert Sherwood judged. Apart from anything else, the Supreme Court judge and former Attorney General Robert Jackson would note a subsidiary factor – 'There was a very large Jewish influence in public sentiment that favored a very strong or severe peace, to which unconditional surrender was preliminary.'

Roosevelt's nature made him prefer to pass this major policy statement off as improvisation. The juggler needed to conjure up the illusion that he could reach into his box of tricks at a moment's notice, masking substance by style.

Once uttered, the phrase decided the strategy of the Western Allies. It contributed to ensuring that this would be a 'good war' with no compromises to achieve victory. Set on an absolute triumph, Roosevelt wanted to head off any possible negotiations with dissident Germans, making it impossible to argue, as after 1918, that the Reich had been betrayed by defeatists. At the same time, he hoped to give a reassurance that the Darlan deal was not a precedent. So policy had to be blunt and absolute; when the State Department proposed talks to provide greater definition, Roosevelt gave a flat rejection.

Did the policy prolong the war in Europe, discouraging those in Germany who might have tried to overthrow Hitler and seek a negotiated peace? And to what extent did it pave the way to Soviet domination of eastern and central Europe by making the outcome of the war solely dependent on the progress of armies?

Stalin came to fear that it would stiffen German resolve. According to his son, the Soviet police chief Beria thought it a 'huge blunder as the Germans' resistance would be galvanised'. After the D-Day landings in 1944, Eisenhower expressed reservations. The British military historian Basil Liddell Hart judged that the policy 'was bound to leave England, and Western Europe, in utter dependence on America and confronted with Communist domination of the larger part of Europe and Asia'.

Speaking to Churchill on the evening of the Casablanca press conference, Harriman gained the impression that he feared the announcement might make the Germans fight all the harder. The American diplomat Charles Bohlen, who framed the 1944 State Department suggestion to Roosevelt, judged that it was one of the great errors of the war, prolonging the conflict and leading to the loss of many lives. It certainly fitted perfectly with Hitler's Valhalla mentality of complete victory or complete defeat. In another of the many what-ifs of the war, other historians dismiss the idea that a German surrender would have been facilitated without it, and that Soviet control of eastern Europe would have been avoided.

The lack of notice before Roosevelt uttered the words continued to rankle with Churchill, according to Harriman. But the President was increasingly less ready to defer to the older man's feelings. On the last night of the summit, smoking the final cigarette of the day in his bedroom with Elliott, he reflected that the British had always been good at choosing allies, so 'they've always been able to come out on top, with the same reactionary grip on the peoples of the world and the markets of the world . . . they must never get the idea that we're in it just to help them hang on to the archaic, medieval Empire ideas . . . I hope they realise they're not the senior partner; that we're not going to sit by, after we've won, and watch their system stultify the growth of every country of Asia and half the countries in Europe to boot . . . Great Britain signed the Atlantic Charter. I hope they realise the United States government means to make them live up to it.'

After the conference, the two leaders drove 150 miles through the desert to Marrakech, a favourite spot which Churchill wanted to show the President. They stayed in a luxurious house occupied by the American Vice Consul, Kenneth Pendar, set in an olive grove, which Churchill described to Clementine as 'a fairyland villa'. Beside it was a tower with a fine view over the city and out to the Atlas mountains. Two aides carried Roosevelt to the top, their arms crossed to support him. Moran recorded how his legs were 'dangling like the limbs of a ventriloquist's dummy, limp and flaccid'. Churchill followed up the stairs, singing, 'Oh, there ain't no war, there ain't no war.' The two men looked out over the rooftops to the mountains.[40]

'It's the most lovely spot in the world,' Churchill murmured. As the evening temperature dropped, he called for Roosevelt's coat, and draped it over his shoulders. Among the orange trees in the garden, he remarked, 'I love these Americans. They have behaved so generously.'

That night, the two leaders and their colleagues feasted on lobsters. Churchill was in fine form. Looking tired, Roosevelt discoursed on how Morocco would enjoy independence, with education, birth control and immunisation. When the subject of de Gaulle came up, Churchill said: 'We call him Jeanne d'Arc, and we are looking for some bishops to burn him.' There were affectionate toasts. Then the Prime Minister burst into song, and the President joined in the choruses. They sat up till 3.30 a.m., drafting an eight-point message to Stalin on their summit which concluded with the assurance: 'Our ruling purpose is to bring to bear upon Germany and Italy the maximum forces by land, sea and air which can be physically applied.'

Four hours later, Roosevelt was wheeled into Churchill's bedroom before setting off for home. The Prime Minister insisted on accompanying him to the airfield, donning a romper suit, slippers and a red, green and gold dressing gown with black velvet collar and cuffs and embroidered dragons. Returning to the villa, he rested in his ornate Moorish chamber, with a green, blue and gold fresco and religious candles on either side of the bed. Then he climbed to the top of the tower, and began work on the only canvas he completed during the war.

As Churchill painted, the President flew to West Africa and Brazil on his way back to the United States. Arriving home, he telephoned his cousin Margaret Suckley to ask after his dog, Fala, which he had entrusted to her. That day, the Germans surrendered at Stalingrad. *Time* magazine made Stalin its Man of the Year.

11

Stormy Weather

'The Red Army alone is bearing the whole weight of the war.'

STALIN

BOTH WESTERN LEADERS fell ill when they got home from Marrakech. Roosevelt was confined to bed for five days – 'I think I picked up sleeping sickness or Gambia fever or some kindred bug in the hell-hole of yours called Bathurst,' he wrote to Churchill. However, five days of rest at Hyde Park left him 'feeling like a fighting cock'. The Prime Minister was more seriously affected, though not immediately. He went first to Cairo, surprising the British ambassador's wife on arrival at 7.30 a.m. by asking for white wine with breakfast, and telling her that he had already downed two whisky and sodas on the flight. He made a fruitless trip to try to get Turkey to join the Allies before visiting Montgomery's army in the desert.[1]

Reflecting on the shape of the post-war world, he set down what he called his '*pensées matinales*' – morning thoughts. He envisaged a global organisation, embodying the spirit of the League of Nations but free of its weaknesses. Though they might quarrel, the victors would do all they could to extend their association after the war. 'Great Britain will certainly do her utmost to organise a coalition resistance to any act of aggression committed by any Power, and it is believed that the United States will co-operate with her, and even possibly take the lead of the world,' he added in a note to himself. As well as the global body, there should be regional organisations. In Europe, Britain would play the major role, but America should also be involved to give his country added weight in the face of the USSR.[2]

Getting back to London on 8 February, Churchill had a bad attack of pneumonia. A patch was discovered on his left lung – he was amused when a consultant told him his illness was known as the old man's friend 'because it takes them off so quickly'. Agreeing to cut back his workload, he read *Moll Flanders* as he lay feverishly in bed. After a week, he was well enough to get up to watch a film Stalin had sent him of the Battle of Stalingrad.[3]

Despite the handshake on the lawn at Casablanca, the French imbroglio was far from settled. Continuing US opposition to de Gaulle became clear when Robert Murphy produced a document signed by Roosevelt recording an agreement with Churchill that Giraud should be given all facilities to bring about the union of Frenchmen. The Prime Minister said he had not seen or approved any such documents – it may have been a variation of the two papers Roosevelt had signed at a meeting with Giraud without having read them properly. 'Sharp work by Murphy!' noted Oliver Harvey, of the pro-de Gaulle Foreign Office. A new version was drawn up laying down equal roles for the two generals. But Washington took its time confirming this, and relations were further harmed when de Gaulle issued a statement implying that Eisenhower had prevented him from going to North Africa.[4]

There was also an Anglo-American brush over atomic research as Churchill wrote to Hopkins that data was being withheld. If the United States did not fully respect their cooperation agreement, Britain would have to go it alone, he warned. This, he added, would be a 'sombre decision'. The reply was qualified – information would be given to those who needed it and who could use it in furtherance of the war effort. In May, Roosevelt agreed to resume the exchange, but the project was clearly evolving into one led by Washington, which moved responsibility from the scientists to the War Department.

The American military made fresh noises about shifting resources to the other main theatre of war. 'Their hearts are really in the Pacific,' Brooke noted in his diary. As they rolled off the Boeing assembly line in Kansas, the most advanced US warplanes, the Superfortress bombers, were allocated to bomb Japan, not Germany. Apart from the pressure from Admiral King and the Asia-Firsters, running two wars put an enormous strain on shipping – the US had more tonnage available in the Pacific than the Atlantic. Any attempt to drive the Japanese from Burma and to bolster

Chiang Kai-shek would mean diverting even more landing craft, planes and supplies.

Meanwhile, Stalin was back on the warpath, as fears surfaced in the West that he might capitalise on the victory at Stalingrad to clinch a fresh deal with Germany. In a message to the armed forces in February, he made no mention of the Western Allies and included Latvia, Lithuania and Estonia when talking of the liberation of Soviet soil. 'In the absence of a second front the Red Army alone is bearing the whole weight of the war,' he added. The slowing down of the advance in Tunisia, where the Allies were held back by bad weather, a single track road and German resistance, had, he claimed in a message to the Western leaders, enabled Hitler to move 36 divisions to Russia. Uncertainty about the cross-Channel operation, the Soviet leader said, 'arouses great anxiety in me, about which I feel I cannot be silent.'[5]

'If we do not . . . avail ourselves of the present moment to further our common interests, it may so happen that the Germans, having obtained a breathing spell and gathered their forces, will be able to recover,' he concluded. 'It is clear to both of us that such an undesirable miscalculation should not be allowed.'[6]

All Roosevelt could reply was that he understood the importance of a major effort 'at the earliest practicable date'. That was hardly going to satisfy Stalin. Relations were further damaged when Admiral Standley, the ambassador, who was fed up with being bypassed by Roosevelt and wanted to go home, made incautious public remarks accusing the Soviet authorities of concealing the true extent of US aid from the public. Clark Kerr reported that the atmosphere had grown so frosty that, when he made jokes at meetings with Molotov, the Foreign Minister reacted by removing his spectacles, wiping the lenses and putting them back on again.[7]

In this difficult context, the US Minister in Stockholm forwarded a report that Germany had used Japanese channels to offer Stalin a return to the 1939 frontiers, Soviet possession of Bessarabia and a Russian sphere of influence in the Near East. Moscow and Japan were to split India after Britain's defeat. Stalin was said to favour this, though Molotov did not. The Soviet leader, the report added, had asked for four months to consider the proposal. The Soviet Embassy in Washington reassured the State Department, but talked of an attempt by Tokyo to broker a deal between Moscow and Berlin which would enable Germany to move forces to the west.[8]

Things were made worse when planning for the invasion of Sicily diverted shipping from convoys to Russia. Stalin, who had assumed the rank of Marshal, called this catastrophic. Then a fresh test for the alliance emerged after the German discovery of mass graves of Polish officers at Katyn in western Russia.

Though Stalin had agreed to let 115,000 Polish troops, who had been taken to the USSR in 1939–40, leave for Iran on their way to join the Western Allies, relations between Moscow and the London Poles had not improved. A million Poles remained trapped in Russia, where they were declared Soviet citizens. Visiting Washington, the Polish leader, Sikorski, told Roosevelt he hoped Western troops would move through the Balkans to liberate his country. In early April, he informed Churchill he had proof that the bodies found at Katyn were Russia's doing. On 17 April, the Poles in London asked for a Red Cross inquiry. The Germans offered to allow an international investigation. But the Red Cross said it could only send a team if the Russians invited it. Moscow refused to do so, blaming the massacre on the Germans, and turned violently on the London Poles, accusing them of being pro-Nazi and were playing Berlin's game.[9]

While Churchill was spending a night at Chartwell at the end of April, Maisky arrived in a perturbed state with a message from the Kremlin saying that, as a result of their attitude, Moscow was renouncing its agreement with the Poles in London. From now on, it would back a rival exile group based in the USSR.

'The . . . revelations are probably true,' Churchill said at a Downing Street luncheon. 'The Bolsheviks can be very cruel.' But he told Stalin Britain would certainly oppose any Red Cross investigation in territory under German authority. Urging the Kremlin not to break relations with the London Poles, he argued that, far from being in any way sympathetic to Hitler, Sikorski was under pressure from compatriots who thought he was not tough enough with Russia. 'If he should go,' he added, 'we should only get someone worse' – a prediction borne out after Sikorski died in a plane crash three months later; Churchill wept when he heard the news.

Roosevelt told the Soviet leader he could 'well understand your problem' but hoped he would merely suspend talks with the London Poles. The President added that he did not think Sikorski had acted in any way with 'the Hitler gang'. He noted that the several million Americans of

Polish extraction were bitterly anti-Nazi and 'knowledge of a complete break between you and Sikorski would not help the situation.'

Stalin dug in his heels, and Churchill decided the alliance came first. 'We have got to beat Hitler,' he told Maisky. 'This is no time for quarrels and charges.' As with the transatlantic link, the key element for him was to preserve a relationship which gave Britain the hope of being on the victorious side. If smaller allies suffered, that was the price of waging a global struggle.

Still, Churchill warned Stalin that Britain could not recognise a government-in-exile on Soviet territory and pointedly remarked on the 'double occupation' of Poland in 1939. In reaction, Stalin accused the London Poles of trying to play off the Allies against each other. They thought they were clever, he added, 'but God has given them no brains'.

Another strand in the Anglo-American patchwork was spun in March when Eden went to his first meeting with Roosevelt, who got to like him. Conversations over two weeks ranged across a wide field of wartime issues, including, unusually at the time, the Jewish question. At a meeting attended by Roosevelt, Hull, Eden, Welles, Hopkins and Halifax, the possibility of helping 60 to 70,000 Jews leave Bulgaria came up. Eden warned that this could lead to pressure from Jewish organisations seeking to get people out of Poland and Germany. Hitler might accept such approaches, but there would not be enough ships to move them, and German agents might be infiltrated into the refugees. Britain was ready to take 60,000 Jews in Palestine, but Eden stressed the transport problems.[10]

At dinner on 15 March, Roosevelt shifted ground on the Soviet frontiers. While speaking of the desirability of holding plebiscites, which Eden said Stalin would refuse, the President said he realised that the West might have to agree to Soviet absorption of the Baltic States and domination of Finland, though he added that 'if we did, then we should use it as a bargaining instrument in getting other concessions from Russia.' Germany, they agreed, should be dismembered – Roosevelt thought into three or four zones, policed by the Allies. Eden felt Stalin wanted the US and Britain to be involved in post-war Germany because he did not wish to handle it on his own.

Showing a disregard for sovereignty that contravened the Atlantic Charter, Roosevelt said the big powers would decide the shape of Poland; he 'did not intend to go to the Peace Conference and bargain with Poland

and other small states.' The two men agreed that Warsaw should get East Prussia from Germany. Eden reported that the Polish government-in-exile in London expected Russia to be so weakened by the war, and Germany so crushed, that it would become the most powerful force in that part of the world.

The President brought out his idea of joining Belgium and Luxembourg with north-east France in a new country to be called Wallonia while Serbia, Croatia and Slovenia would be separate nations. Eden took a dim view of this, pointing out that post-war Europe would do better to have fewer states rather than more – Churchill was worrying about 'the Communisation of the Balkans'. The Foreign Secretary thought that, while Stalin would prefer post-war cooperation with Britain and America in Europe, the Kremlin was preparing plans to deal with a US withdrawal. He also reiterated London's reservations about China – a recent speech by Churchill which had omitted it from the great powers had ruffled feathers in Washington. Having thus dealt with the post-war world, Eden and Hopkins left the President, and went for late-night oysters at the Carlton Hotel – the visitor said how surprised he was at finding Roosevelt in such a degree of agreement with him.

At another meeting, Roosevelt outlined his vision of a world organisation with an annual general assembly, an advisory council of the Big Four and regional representatives. A committee at its heart would be run by the USA, the USSR, Britain and China. Only they would be allowed to have armaments. It should be a simple organisation which he would chair with Hopkins and Winant as his assistants, he told his cousin Margaret Suckley. Between sessions, the secretariat would operate on a 'small island with a good airfield'.

In his press conference at the end of Eden's visit, Roosevelt looked back to 1918. He said the tempo then 'seemed to be that of a lady who is told at noon that she is to accompany her husband on a month's trip on the three o'clock train that afternoon'. Now, preparations were being made for the peace well in advance, and the Allies were 'about 95 per cent together'.

That was a considerable overstatement, even for the salesman in the White House. The issue of post-war frontier arrangements remained to be settled with Stalin. The other three Allied leaders were at odds with Churchill on the future of the British Empire. Free traders and defenders of imperial preference were at loggerheads. London and Washington were tussling over the post-war international financial structure. There was no way of denying the fundamental incompatibilities of the Western system and Stalinism. But Roosevelt was on a high, buoyed by polls showing that 65 per cent of those questioned thought he should be re-elected for a fourth term the following year, and that only 16 per cent of Americans believed their country should not play a larger part in world affairs.

Apart from his sensitivity about Eden horning in on his domain, Churchill had rather different views about global arrangements after the conflict ended. His doubts about China's fitness to play the 'policeman' role in Asia were as strong as ever. While seeing the need for a global organisation to keep the peace, he feared that Britain would be out-voted on matters such as the Empire. He also believed in strong regional bodies, enabling Britain to play the key role in Europe – and to use its presence in Asia to make its voice heard there. Above all, his vision of the post-war world rested on the transatlantic link whereas Roosevelt increasingly put his faith in a three- or four-power structure in which Britain would be an important ally, but not the privileged partner.[11]

To keep his finger on the pulse of the transatlantic relationship, Churchill decided it was time to cross the ocean once again for his fifth summit. He embarked on the *Queen Mary* on 5 May with a 100-strong party, including the British Chiefs of Staff, Harriman, Beaverbrook, Leathers, the Shipping Minister, and Moran. There were also 3,000 American troops returning home, and a contingent of German prisoners. Departure was delayed when the liner was found to be full of vermin and had to be cleaned up. Churchill told Harriman that he had ordered a machine gun to be mounted on the lifeboat he would use if the ship was torpedoed, so that he could go down fighting the enemy.

Brooke, who was recovering from an attack of influenza, was in a particularly depressed and acerbic mood. 'I am very *very* tired,' he wrote in his diary, shuddering at the 'useless struggle' that lay ahead in Washington.[12]

On 12 May, Churchill opened the summit, codenamed Trident, by noting the striking change since a year earlier when he had sat in the same room at the White House and learned of the surrender at Tobruk. Victory had been clinched in Tunisia, with nearly 250,000 enemy prisoners taken.

While Atlantic shipping losses remained high, the number of new vessels soared beyond those lost. More U-boats were being sunk. American victories in the Pacific lifted the threat of Japanese invasion of Australia and New Zealand.[13]

The Prime Minister said the difficulties involved in a cross-Channel operation must not be underestimated, and insisted that, after Sicily had been taken, Allied forces in the Mediterranean should not remain idle. His mind on Italy, not Normandy, he reached back to the First World War. The withdrawal of Bulgaria from that conflict had brought about Germany's collapse, he said – the same might be true of Italy now.

According to Hopkins, this made little impression on the President. 'The fighting in Italy does not make sense to him,' the aide told Moran. 'He wants the twenty divisions, which will be set free when Sicily has been won, to be used in building up the force that is to invade France in 1944.'

Roosevelt's attitude took Churchill aback, and the strategic difference came up sharply when the Chiefs of Staff met. The Americans, Brooke wrote, were 'taking up the attitude that we led them down the garden path taking them to North Africa! That at Casablanca we again misled them by inducing them to attack Sicily!! And now they are not going to be led astray again. Added to that the swing towards the Pacific is stronger than ever and before long they will be urging that we should defeat Japan first.'

The CIGS thoroughly alarmed the Americans by saying that no major operation in France would be possible until 1945 or 1946. This implied that the Mediterranean would continue to be the only theatre of war against the Germans. Such a prospect was too much for Marshall.[14]

'I find it very hard even now not to look on your North African strategy with a jaundiced eye,' he told the British general as they walked together to a meeting.

'What strategy would you have preferred?' Brooke asked.

'Cross-Channel operations for the liberation of France and advance on Germany. We should finish the war quicker.'

'Yes, probably, but not the way we hope to finish it.'

Brooke listed reasons for his depression in a diary entry which, even if coloured by the extreme irritation 'Shrapnel' felt towards anybody who did not agree with him, reflects the disarray among the Western Allies.

a) King thinks the war can only be won by action in the Pacific at the expense of all other fronts.

b) Marshall considers that our solution lies in a cross Channel operation with some 20 to 30 divisions, irrespective of the situation on the Russian front, with which he proposes to clear Europe and win the war.

c) Portal considers that success lies in accumulating the largest air force possible in England and that then, and then only, success lies assured through the bombing of Europe.

d) Dudley Pound on the other hand is obsessed with the anti-U-boat warfare and considers that success can only be secured by the defeat of this menace.

e) AFB [Brooke] considers that success can only be secured by pressing operations in the Mediterranean to force a dispersal of German forces, help Russia, and thus eventually produce a situation where cross Channel operations are possible.

f) And Winston??? Thinks one thing at one moment and another at another moment. At times the war may be won by bombing and all must be sacrificed to it. At others it becomes essential for us to bleed ourselves dry on the Continent because Russia is doing the same. At others our main effort must be in the Mediterranean, directed against Italy or Balkans alternatively, with sporadic desires to invade Norway and 'roll up the map in the opposite direction to Hitler'! But more often he wants to carry out ALL operations simultaneously irrespective of shortages of shipping!

Interestingly, he did not mention Roosevelt.

In the end, the invasion of Sicily was confirmed for July. After that, the next step would be whatever was 'best calculated to eliminate Italy from the war and to contain the maximum number of German forces'. Hopkins said that, if Churchill wanted to get a firmer statement on Italy from Roosevelt, he would have to spend another week in Washington, 'and even then there is no certainty'.[15]

'The President is not willing to put pressure on Marshall,' Churchill told his doctor. 'He is not in favour of landing in Italy. It is most discouraging.' Still, he did not lose confidence in his persuasive powers, suggesting Marshall should accompany him on a visit to North Africa after the summit. This was agreed. Churchill hoped sustained exposure to his rhetoric and the sight of the Allied forces on the spot would sway the general.

A new target was set for the cross-Channel invasion – 1 May 1944, nearly two years after the date envisaged by the American plan for Sledgehammer. The name was changed to Roundhammer – it was to be bigger than Sledgehammer but smaller than Roundup, and was to draw some troops from the Mediterranean after the invasion of Sicily. The continual delays in the plans for France led to a joke that circulated in Washington. Stalin telephones Downing Street without giving his name: 'Churchill speaking,' the Prime Minister says. 'This is Joe at this end,' the other voice announces. 'Joe who?' 'Joe Stalin.' 'Hello, Joe, where are you?' 'Oh, I am at Calais.'

Irritated as he was with the US attitude, Brooke knew he had to be careful in handling Marshall. The Army Chief of Staff had enormous bipartisan support on Capitol Hill. Getting on the wrong side of him risked arousing legislators' suspicion of Britain. In addition, Marshall might side with the pro-Pacific party – he said that, if time was going to be wasted in the Mediterranean, US forces might be better used against Japan. There was another reason why the Far East loomed large at Trident.

Chiang Kai-shek's wife, Meiling, spent the first half of 1943 in the United States, first undergoing medical treatment and then barnstorming the country on behalf of her husband's regime. She addressed a joint session of Congress, the first woman and the first Chinese person to do so. Roosevelt invited her to stay at the White House – the youngest daughter of one of Shanghai's richest families, she brought her own silk sheets and annoyed the staff by snapping her fingers for attention.[16]

Roosevelt did not let her sit beside him on the sofa in his office, but set up a chair for her opposite with a card table between them to make sure she didn't 'vamp me'. She flattered him by categorising Willkie as 'an adolescent' in contrast to the President's sophistication though the Chinese princess committed a faux pas by telling him not to bother to get up as she was leaving the room.

Roosevelt found her 'hard as steel' – when he asked what happened to strikers in China, she drew her fingers across her throat. The President arranged a meeting with Churchill over lunch at the White House, but 'Snow White', as the FBI codenamed her, was in New York and declined to make the trip.

Madame Chiang, who celebrated her forty-fifth birthday during the visit, exerted her charm on all she met, telling Stimson that he had the most beautiful hands she had ever seen as she tried to induce him to send more planes to China. Hollywood stars paid tribute when she went to California. She discussed the nature of her sex appeal with Joseph Kennedy. Wendell Willkie, her partner for the night in Chungking the previous autumn, introduced her as 'an avenging angel' at a rally in Madison Square Gardens. She hatched a scheme to use American aid money to buy the White House for him, after which they would rule the world between them – her wild notion evaporated when the Republican died of a heart attack.

Though Roosevelt soon tired of this combination of Dragon Lady and New England college graduate, her impact on the public could not be gainsaid, and speculation grew that it might swing opinion behind an Asia-First policy. At the very least, this meant that the President had to be seen to be supporting Chiang and the Nationalists, even if they were not fighting much against the Japanese. The matter of China was further reinforced at the summit by the two main US military advisers – the acerbic general 'Vinegar Joe' Stilwell, and the good ole boy airman Claire Chennault, who was close to Madame Chiang.

The two Americans detested one another, and were constantly feuding for Lend-Lease supplies. When Roosevelt asked him what he thought of Chiang, Stilwell replied that he was 'a vacillating, tricky, undependable old scoundrel who never keeps his word'. Chennault called him 'one of the two or three greatest military political leaders in the world today'. Roosevelt tried to square the circle by promising each of the advisers supplies. 'Continual concessions have confirmed Chiang in the opinion that all he needs to do is to yell and we'll cave in,' Stilwell noted in a private account of the conference. 'Churchill had Roosevelt in his pocket. They are looking for an easy way, a short-cut for England and no attention must be diverted from the Continent at any cost. The Limeys are not interested in the war in the Pacific, and with the President hypnotized they are sitting pretty.'

The reference to Roosevelt being under Britain's spell said much about Stilwell's ignorance. Nor did he know of a meeting at which his Commander-in-Chief expressed 'very strong dissatisfaction with the way our whole show is running in China'. Stilwell 'obviously hated the Chinese',

Roosevelt added, and should be replaced. Marshall, who admired Vinegar Joe, opposed promoting Chennault because he was too close to Chiang. So things were left as they were. Month by month, American policy in China was unravelling.

At a British Embassy lunch attended by Vice President Wallace, Stimson, Welles and other senior figures, Churchill re-iterated his idea of a 'three-legged stool' of regional councils for Europe, the Americas and the Pacific under an over-arching association of the United States, the Soviet Union and Britain – if Washington insisted, China could be included though 'she was not comparable to the others'. No doubt it would be necessary for America to be associated with the policing of Europe, he said. But the obvious implication was that its overall authority would be limited by the regional groupings. Though this would serve to defend Britain's interests, it was hardly in tune with Roosevelt's vision and left the issue of the Empire unresolved.[17]

Churchill made another successful speech to Congress, comparing the situation with the Civil War after Gettysburg – some legislators complained that the only time they found out what was going on in the war was when he addressed them. Then he escaped with Roosevelt from the heat and humidity of the capital for a weekend at Shangri La. The President's daughter, Anna, recalled the Prime Minister picking his teeth throughout dinner, and making liberal use of snuff, which set off sneezing that 'practically rocked the foundations of the house', then blowing his nose with a noise like a foghorn. Wearing a fawn sweater and dark checked shirt, Roosevelt took his guest to fish in the cool woods – Churchill sticking to his overcoat – but they caught nothing.[18]

On the road trip to the hills, his visitor spotted a sign advertising a brand of sweets named after a Civil War heroine, Barbara Fritchie, and asked who she was. Roosevelt recited two lines of poetry about her, which Churchill picked up as he recalled the whole long poem – whether his query had been entirely innocent or designed to allow him to show off his memory is not clear. His anxiety to keep in favour was such that he sat silently for half an hour in the evening watching Roosevelt stick stamps into an album – though he recorded his 'great interest' in his memoirs, it must have been like watching paint dry.

*

Each of the three Allies made gestures at the time which, however hollow, served a propaganda purpose. Britain and the US renounced extra-territorial rights wrested from the Qing Empire in China in the previous century – it had no immediate effect since Japan occupied the foreign concessions. Moscow announced the dissolution of the international Communist organisation, the Comintern. Stalin ruled that 'it was impossible to direct the working-class movement in all countries from a single international centre'. This enabled national parties to claim that they were not acting at the behest of a foreign power, but the Kremlin kept a close watch on their activities to ensure that, whatever their roles during the fighting, foreign affairs would fall in with Soviet interests when the war ended. The Foreign Office took the decision as evidence of a real desire on Stalin's part to cooperate in the reconstruction of Europe. But Maisky told the US Embassy that the Comintern had been moribund for half a dozen years. More to the point, Moscow showed how it intended to move in territorial matters with the formation of the Lublin Committee, made up of trusted Poles to try to keep Warsaw under Stalin's thumb.[19]

There was fresh trouble during the Trident summit over de Gaulle. As he gained the upper hand over Giraud, Washington accused him of having used British funds to bribe French sailors to desert. Hammered daily by Roosevelt, Churchill agreed that the general's behaviour at Casablanca had been preposterous. Fearing that sticking up for de Gaulle would cause a rift with the President, he sent three messages to London containing the US allegations, and proposing Britain should withdraw its support.

Attlee immediately called a Sunday night session of the War Cabinet, which turned down the idea. Churchill bowed to this, and agreed to wait to see how the de Gaulle–Giraud talks ended. He may have calculated on the reaction in London, but he showed himself ready to go through the motions of ditching an ally to keep in with Roosevelt. Reflecting Foreign Office opinion, Oliver Harvey noted in his diary: 'It is high time the old man came home. The American atmosphere, the dictatorial powers of the President and the adulation which surrounds him there, have gone to his head.' At the final lunch of the summit, according to Stilwell, Churchill launched into a panegyric of his host – 'Mr President, I cannot but believe that an all-wise Providence has draped these great events, at this critical period of the world's history, about your personality and your high office.'

'Frank', added the general, using a rare diminutive for the President, 'lapped it up.'[20]

Still, Churchill asked Moran if he had noticed that Roosevelt was 'a very tired man' – 'his mind seemed closed; he seems to have lost his wonderful elasticity.' His condition was certainly worse – his secretary, Grace Tully, noted signs of 'cumulative weakness', including dark circles under his eyes, slumped shoulders and tremors of his hands, which forced him to use a mug twice the size of the one he had before so he would not spill his coffee.[21]

What Churchill did not know was that, while he was meeting Roosevelt, a different form of Allied contact was being discussed that was specifically designed to exclude him. During Trident, the strongly pro-Soviet former ambassador in Moscow Joseph Davies called at the Kremlin. Davies was in Moscow to promote a film about his time in the Soviet Union which even some Kremlin officials found sycophantic – Davies's enthusiasm for the Communist regime may have been fanned by the way he was allowed to buy works of art from museums for symbolic sums.[22]

In the greatest secrecy, he handed Stalin a letter from Roosevelt. It proposed an 'informal and completely simple' meeting in the Bering Straits at which 'you and I would talk very informally and get what we call a meeting of minds.'

Roosevelt picked the Arctic to keep the meeting a strictly US–Soviet affair. A summit in the Atlantic, he noted, 'would make it difficult not to invite Churchill'. 'Three's a crowd and we can arrange for the Big Three to get together thereafter,' he told Davies. 'Churchill will understand. I will take care of that.'

The initiative was a sign of the way his mind was set on the post-war situation which would be shaped by him and Stalin, not Churchill. He had no need to worry about the Prime Minister's ultimate loyalty; whatever differences might come between them, the British leader was not going to shatter the alliance. What mattered was to win over Moscow as a post-war collaborator. At a picnic at Hyde Park before Trident, he murmured to Margaret Suckley that he thought Stalin would have a better understanding than Churchill of his plan for a global police force run by the Big Four, as well as the need for self-determination for colonies.

Initially, Stalin seemed interested in a bilateral meeting. Davies reported that he half-agreed to an encounter in mid-July – a German offensive expected in the summer meant he could not leave Moscow earlier. Then he was told of the Trident decision to delay again the landing in France. This put a brake on a bilateral summit. 'Your decision creates exceptional difficulties for the Soviet Union,' Stalin told Roosevelt and Churchill. Ignoring Torch and the planned invasion of Sicily, he said the Red Army was being left to fight alone. Moscow could not 'align itself with this decision which . . . may gravely affect the subsequent course of the war.'

'I quite understand your disappointment,' Churchill replied, repeating his argument about it being pointless to throw away a hundred thousand lives in a disastrous expedition. 'The best way for us to help you is by winning battles and not by losing them,' he added. That produced a lengthy message from the Kremlin which Harriman characterised as being of 'surpassing bitterness'.

It began by listing cables from Churchill about action in 1943, and then drew attention to the way the fresh delay had been decided without consulting Moscow. 'It goes without saying that the Soviet Government cannot put up with such disregard of the most vital Soviet interests in the war against the common enemy,' Stalin went on. Then he concluded: 'You say that you "quite understand" my disappointment. I must tell you that the point here is not just the disappointment of the Soviet Government . . . One should not forget that it is a question of saving millions of lives in the occupied areas of western Europe and Russia and of reducing the enormous sacrifices of the Soviet armies, compared with which the sacrifices of the Anglo-American armies are insignificant.'

Receiving Maisky, Churchill said he was 'getting rather tired of being scolded'. Though the diplomat urged him not to attach importance to the Kremlin's tone, the Prime Minister feared the worst. In a 'personal and secret' message to the embassy in Moscow, he wrote that Stalin's reference to not putting up with such treatment 'raises various questions in experienced minds' – presumably, a reference to a new deal between Moscow and Berlin. 'Personally, I feel that this is probably the end of the Churchill–Stalin correspondence from which I fondly hoped some kind of personal contact might be created between our two countries,' he added.

To pre-empt the danger that Stalin might make his summit proposal known, Roosevelt sent Harriman to break the news to the Prime Minister after he got back to London; not that the strictly bilateral nature of the proposal can have been made clear, for Churchill immediately asked to be included. On 12 June, he wrote plaintively to Roosevelt saying he was 'anxious to know anything you care to tell me about your letter sent to [Stalin] by Mr Davies and the answer which has been received'. He was, he added, ready to go anywhere the President wished for a meeting.

Sixteen days later, Roosevelt replied with a straight lie. 'I did not suggest to U.J. [Uncle Joe – i.e. Stalin] that we meet alone but he assumed (a) that we would meet alone and (b) that we agreed that we should not bring staff to what would be a preliminary meeting.'

There were, he wrote, 'certain advantages in such a preliminary meeting which I know you will appreciate. First, that without staffs there will be no military collisions in regard to demands for an immediate Roundup. Second, that he will not think that we are demanding a Russian offensive this summer if the Germans do not attack. Third, that in my opinion he will be more frank in giving his views on the offensive against Japan now and later. Fourth, that he would also be more frank in regard to China. Fifth, that he would be more frank in regard to the Balkan States, Finland, and Poland.

'I want to explore his thinking as fully as possible concerning Russia's postwar hopes and ambitions. I would want to cover much the same field with him as did Eden for you a year ago.'

As Roosevelt knew very well, there was a world of difference between the Foreign Secretary's trip to Moscow and a full-blown bilateral summit that excluded Britain. Not surprisingly, as Eden recorded, Churchill was 'considerably upset that the meeting would be *à deux*.'

As a palliative, Roosevelt suggested that after seeing Stalin he would meet Churchill in Quebec, and that all three would gather in the autumn. 'Of course, you and I are completely frank in matters of this kind,' his message concluded blithely.

The following day, Churchill replied that, if a bilateral encounter with Stalin could be arranged, 'I should no longer deprecate it. On the contrary in view of his attitude I think it important that this contact should be established.' Still, it was a bitter pill which pointed to the way in which alliance politics were shifting.

*

On 25 July 1943, as Churchill was watching the film *Sous les Toits de Paris* after dinner, he received news that Mussolini had been overthrown. He immediately called a post-midnight meeting of the War Cabinet that lasted until 4 a.m. Though Il Duce would be rescued from captivity by German paratroopers to head a rump government and Hitler poured in troops to hold Rome, a new Italian government sought an armistice.

Two weeks later, Churchill embarked once more for North America. He spent a weekend with Roosevelt at Hyde Park, where the weather was so hot that he could not sleep. For a picnic, he donned a Stetson hat, and brought along a small pail of ice to cool his drinks. 'He is a strange looking little man,' Margaret Suckley recorded. 'Fat & round, his clothes bunched up on him. Practically no hair on his head.'[23]

Despite the wrangles with Stalin and Roosevelt's attempt to bypass Churchill, the Allies had a good deal to celebrate. With Mussolini's overthrow, the Mediterranean strategy was producing dividends. On 10 July 160,000 Allied troops successfully invaded Sicily – though more British than American troops were involved, Eisenhower retained overall command, with Harold Alexander as the main battlefield chief. The Russians had won the world's greatest tank battle at Kursk. US forces advanced across the Solomons, and Japan suffered heavy losses of ships and planes. 'Isn't there some way, some place, where we can win a real victory over the Americans?' asked a plaintive Emperor Hirohito. 'The massed, angered forces of common humanity are on the march,' Roosevelt declared in a Fireside Chat radio broadcast. 'They are going forward – on the Russian front, in the vast Pacific area, and into Europe – converging on their ultimate objectives, Berlin and Tokyo.'[24]

Roosevelt and Churchill travelled by train from Hyde Park to Quebec for another summit, codenamed Quadrant. Eden joined the meeting at the Citadel, the Governor General's summer residence overlooking the St Lawrence River. For once, Roosevelt let Cordell Hull come along.[25]

The summit produced agreement to bring the atomic project 'to fruition at the earliest moment'. Restrictively, Roosevelt got an undertaking that any industrial or commercial exploitation would be a matter for the President to determine. A Combined Policy Committee was set up in Washington, including a representative of Canada, to supervise research. The two countries pledged not only not to use the project against one another, and 'not use it against third parties without each other's consent'. This appeared to be in direct contravention of Congress's authority to decide if America went to war.

Roosevelt also agreed to recognise the French Committee of National Liberation. Forecasts that de Gaulle would dominate it were soon borne out – Giraud held on till November, but then resigned as Co-President, remaining Commander-in-Chief, but clearly second fiddle.

Differences surfaced once again over strategy in what Churchill's memoirs call a 'somewhat sharp' manner. After meeting British leaders in London, Henry Stimson reported that, though they rendered lip service to the landing in France, their hearts were not in it. Hopkins made sure Roosevelt saw Stimson's report. In retaliation, the US Chiefs raised a familiar threat – if London delayed the invasion of France, they would cut the build up in Britain and focus on Japan.

Brooke, as he later acknowledged, was nearing a nervous breakdown. 'How I hate those meetings, and how weary I am of them!' he wrote in his diary. 'I now of course know the limitations of Marshall's brain and the impossibility of ever making him realise any strategical situation or its requirements.'

Churchill gave the CIGS another reason to remember Quebec as an unhappy experience. During the summer, he had promised Brooke command of the invasion of France – a prospect that thrilled the general.[26]

But Churchill had not obtained Roosevelt's approval. At Hyde Park before the summit, the President made clear an American should be in charge. The reason was not only nationalistic – he wanted his own man to check any British backsliding.

Before lunch on 15 August, Churchill asked Brooke to go out with him on to a terrace of the Citadel, where he broke the news that he would not get the job. As they walked up and down above the river, the CIGS said he 'could not feel anything but disappointed'. That the job would probably go to Marshall must have compounded his emotions – not to mention the trade-off by which the command in south-east Asia went to Mountbatten, for whom he had little time, either. In his memoirs, Churchill recalled that Brooke 'bore the great disappointment with soldierly dignity'. In fact, the CIGS recalled it as 'a crashing blow' which left him 'swamped by a dark cloud of despair'. He took months to recover.

The military arguments at the summit grew so heated that junior officers were told to leave the room while their superiors wrangled. This produced a rare moment of comedy. With Churchill's enthusiastic backing, the British had been working on a scheme to build 2,000-foot long floating aircraft bases from an indestructible mixture of ice and wood pulp. Weighing 2 million tons, these islands could house 150 planes. Mountbatten brought a sample of the ice-pulp mix to the summit, and staged a display for the senior officers in the drawing room of the Frontenac Hotel. A revolver was fired at ordinary ice, which shattered. A shot was then directed at the sample – it bounced off and ricocheted like an angry bee round the room between the legs of the Chiefs of Staff. 'Good Heavens,' one of the junior officers outside cried, 'they've started shooting now.'

In the end, 1 May 1944 was confirmed for the landing in northern France, codenamed Overlord. The Americans proposed another offensive in the south of the country to draw off German troops. Though he did not like this much since it would divert troops from Italy, Churchill went along with it for the time being for the sake of Allied amity. It was agreed that Eisenhower should strike from Sicily to the Italian mainland while negotiating with the Badoglio government – though, officially, any surrender had to be unconditional. Bombing of Germany was to be stepped up by the US air force. The Americans were to press the advance across the Pacific.

Churchill was in a peevish mood; Brooke suspected that he was reacting badly to growing American power – he referred to himself to Roosevelt as 'your lieutenant' for the campaigns in North Africa and Sicily. He came up with the idea of an Anglo-American offensive in the Balkans to block Soviet influence, and developed an obsession with a scheme to stage a landing in Northern Sumatra after working out with a pair of dividers that Singapore could be bombed from there. He summoned the daredevil leader of the guerrilla force sent into Burma, Orde Wingate, whose Long Range Penetration Strategy had impressed him. Roosevelt ordered the formation of a similar force under Frank Merrill, which would also be deployed in Burma, where its leader subsequently suffered a heart attack while Wingate died in a plane crash.

Though Churchill had insisted that Stalin should not be invited to Quebec, the Soviet Union hovered in the background of the discussions. Hopkins produced a paper which identified it as the decisive factor in the war, and argued, that every effort must be made to obtain Moscow's friendship. Since the USSR would dominate Europe after the defeat of

Hitler, the note added, 'it is even more essential to develop and maintain the most friendly relations with Russia . . . Should the war in the Pacific have to be carried on with an unfriendly or negative attitude on the part of Russia, the difficulties will be immeasurably increased and operations might become abortive.'

Roosevelt and Churchill sent a message to Moscow suggesting a tripartite summit at Fairbanks in Alaska. But Stalin, who had just made only his second visit to the front, was still in a tough mood, as he showed by replacing both Maisky and Litvinov with harder liners. Litvinov was succeeded by the chargé d'affaires, Andrei Gromyko, while the London post was given to Fedor Tarasovich Goussev, whose English seemed limited to shouting 'How are you', and who became known in Whitehall as 'Frogface'.

Despite a request from Roosevelt, Stalin withheld permission for American bombers to make emergency landings in southern Russia after attacking Romanian oil-fields until a week after a disastrous raid that caused the loss of most of the planes involved. As well as backing its own Polish government-in-exile, the Kremlin formed a National Committee for a Free Germany of German Communists and high-ranking prisoners of war, which held a convention in Moscow.

Stalin also took umbrage at what he considered a lack of information about the campaign in Italy. 'I have to tell you that it is impossible to tolerate such a situation any longer,' he warned, calling for a tripartite military committee in Sicily to consider how to deal with Axis allies that broke with Germany. The danger in this for the West was that, if Stalin could accuse it of keeping him in the dark, he would have an excuse to withhold information about eastern Europe.

Roosevelt shared Churchill's annoyance. 'We are both mad,' he told Harriman before one dinner at the Quebec summit. After the President had gone to bed, Churchill remarked to those still at table that there would be 'bloody consequences' from Russia's attitude.[27]

When Eden suggested that things were not so bad, Churchill ticked him off, saying, 'There's no need for you to attempt to smooth it over in the Foreign Office manner.'

'Stalin is an unnatural man,' he added. 'There will be grave troubles.'

After Quebec, Churchill spent six days in Washington, where news was received from General Alexander that 'the last German soldier was flung out of Sicily and the whole island is now in our hands'. Enemy losses were put at 167,000 men, 37,000 of them Germans compared with 31,158 Allied dead, wounded or missing.

As Churchill and Roosevelt sat talking after dinner one evening, Admiral Dudley Pound, a man Churchill was close to, came in to discuss a naval matter. When Roosevelt asked him questions, he gave vague answers. The next morning, Pound went to Churchill's bedroom to say that he had had a stroke which had largely paralysed his right side, and was tendering his resignation – he was also suffering from an undiagnosed brain tumour. He was succeeded by Admiral Andrew Cunningham, who had excelled in the Mediterranean.

Despite his obvious sadness at Pound's medical news, and though suffering from a cold, Churchill did not moderate his behaviour. According to Cadogan, he was in high-strung, muddled form, spending 'a large part of the day hurling himself violently in and out of bed, bathing at unsuitable moments and rushing up and down corridors in his dressing gown'. This behaviour did not please his host who had returned from Quebec tired and with rings under his eyes. 'I'm nearly dead. I have to have my sleep,' he told the Labor Secretary Frances Perkins. 'I have to talk to the P.M. all night and he gets bright ideas in the middle of the night and comes pattering down the hall to my bedroom in his bare feet.' To get away and recuperate, he headed for Hyde Park, on his own.

Churchill, meanwhile, went to Harvard with Clementine to receive an honorary degree, suggesting in his speech that common citizenship might be established for the Americans and British, an idea he had already mentioned to Roosevelt. On the way back to Washington, he flashed V-signs at passing trains, and rushed out on to the rear platform in his dressing gown to chat to people at stations, making his wife do the same.

In Roosevelt's absence, he convened a meeting of the Combined Chiefs of Staff in the White House, at which he pressed for faster action in Italy. In a summary of the global outlook, he forecast the USSR would be the most powerful nation on earth after the defeat of Germany and Japan, but hoped that the 'fraternal association' of the British Commonwealth and the United States would prove 'a friendly balance' – at least during post-war reconstruction. Churchill also showed a premonition of the dangers in the triangular relationship. He told British Embassy staff that it was important 'not to allow the Russians to try to play the US and the UK off against each other'.

Before heading home, he went to Hyde Park for a weekend, leaning into Roosevelt's car as he left to say: 'God Bless You'. Roosevelt replied, 'I'll be over with you, next spring.'

It was an empty promise. Though his wife had measured the doorways of a Mayfair flat during a visit to London to make sure they would be wide enough for her husband's wheelchair, he never reciprocated Churchill's transatlantic visits.

12

Russian Overture

MOSCOW
OCTOBER 1943

'We shall do as we like'
STALIN

THE SHIFTING BALANCE of power across the Atlantic was shown very clearly in the autumn of 1943. After American newspapers reported that Marshall was to be put in overall military charge in Europe, including the Mediterranean, Churchill wrote to Hopkins saying the American should not have authority beyond the Overlord landing in Normandy. On 1 October, he told Roosevelt of his understanding that Alexander would hold the Mediterranean command. Otherwise, he predicted an explosion in Britain. On 1 November, Roosevelt decided to defer the decision, aware of the hole Marshall would leave in Washington.

Another irritant came when a group of senators issued a statement accusing London of unfair behaviour, including passing off US Lend-Lease aid to Russia as coming from Britain. Churchill expressed his regret at such unfounded accusations to Hopkins, and said publicly that the matter would be investigated. But he saw no point in getting involved in this 'wordy warfare'.

More gallingly, Roosevelt delivered a sharp rebuff to Churchill's latest hobby horse – an invasion of Rhodes as part of his east Mediterranean strategy. 'It is my opinion that no diversion of forces or equipment should prejudice "Overlord" as planned,' the President wrote. This produced what Churchill called 'one of the sharpest pangs I suffered during the war'. But he had to submit. In his memoirs, he gave an alliance reason – 'I could not risk any jar in my personal relations with the President.'

There was also what he called Stalin's 'increasing bearishness' to deal with. When the British declined to accompany the resumption of convoys with a binding commitment to continue shipments, the dictator fired off a stiff reproach. Receiving this as he worked in bed, Churchill said he would stop the convoys. Calming down, he called in the new Soviet ambassador later in the week, and put the 'offensive' message in his hand as he left, uttering the diplomatic formulation '*nul et non avenu*' to signal its non-reception. There was also a row with Moscow over British sailors who had been arrested after knocking the hats off locals in an Arctic port. 'It is disheartening to make so little progress with these people,' Churchill reflected. By the beginning of October, he was telling the War Cabinet: 'We mustn't weaken Germany too much – we may need her against Russia.'[1]

Yet, progress was on the horizon. Unexpectedly, it came from 'Bruin' as Churchill called Stalin. Since the three chiefs had not been able to fix a meeting, Stalin suggested their Foreign Ministers gather. This could pave the way for a summit.

Roosevelt and Churchill were both keen, though they insisted it should only be 'exploratory' – they reserved final decision-making power for themselves. In a transparent move, Roosevelt said he would not want the septuagenarian Cordell Hull to make a long journey to Europe because of his poor health and age. He proposed to send Sumner Welles instead, together with Harriman. This was a sign of how, for all his acute political antennae, Roosevelt could live in a world of his own – an Under Secretary of State would have been seen by Stalin as insulting and he would have nominated a more junior diplomat than Molotov to represent the USSR.

The President was saved from himself by Hull being spurred into action against his deputy. Secretary of State for a decade, he had grown even more irritated by the superior Yankee – not just because of Welles's close contacts with Roosevelt, but also by the way he dealt directly with diplomats of foreign governments without reference, and made speeches setting out US policy off his own bat. In August, the *New York Times* reported that the feud was causing a 'lack of cohesive policy' – and blaming Hull.

Though the Secretary was always highly deferential to the office of the President, the prospect of being replaced by his rival at the highest-level meeting of all three major Allied powers to date, must have been too much. Welles's enemies resumed the campaign against him over his sexual advances to the Pullman porters. There was a threat to leak the story to a newspaper, and Roosevelt felt obliged to let the axe fall before the story came out. The President also felt he needed Hull's clout in the Senate in case his plan for a global organisation ran into trouble as the League of Nations had. At a meeting in his office, Hull suggested that Welles might go to Moscow to prepare for the meeting of foreign ministers. The Under Secretary was not in the business of preparing meetings for him. Getting up, he crossed the room, shook hands, and headed for a retreat in Maine. At seventy-two, the Secretary of State would finally get his chance to play a major role in the alliance.

Born in a log cabin in Tennessee, Hull had sat in the House of Representatives for twenty-four years before being appointed to head the State Department in 1933. Tall and lean, he had a reserved, almost shy, manner. A former judge, he believed in broad principles which he assumed would be respected by those who signed up to them. Eden referred to him in his diary as 'the old man' while Cadogan described him as 'the old lunatic'.

Churchill offered London as a venue for the conference, but Stalin insisted on Moscow; Molotov's other duties meant he could not leave the Soviet capital, he explained. The British and Americans bowed to his wishes, and, when Eden proposed a preliminary Anglo-American session in London, Hull turned down the idea. Eden sent a message to Washington saying that, from his experience 'Moscow is not a very good place for confidential discussions'. What the British did not grasp was that the Americans were positively anxious not to see them in advance for fear of giving Stalin reason to suspect a Western stitch-up.

On 18 October, the Foreign Ministers met in the Kremlin. The weather was bright and crisp. On the war front, American progress continued in the Pacific while the Red Army was poised to cross the Dnieper into Ukraine, confirming the significant improvement in its military capacity and skill. Berlin Radio admitted the military situation in Russia was 'extremely grave'. Shipping losses dropped, and more U-boats were being destroyed as Portugal gave permission for the Allies to use the Azores as a base in the Battle of the Atlantic. Corsica was taken, but Italy was proving tougher than had been expected. Though the Badoglio government had surrendered, and declared war on Germany, the Wehrmacht held Rome. Much to Churchill's chagrin, the Nazis had taken Rhodes and other islands in the east Mediterranean.[2]

The former Public Prosecutor in the purge trials, Andrei Vyshinsky, joined the conference as Molotov's deputy. White haired and red-faced, with hard eyes behind his spectacles, he lost his temper at times, and stalked from the chamber. He assured the Americans that Moscow had 'no interest in any territory beyond the Soviet frontiers and there is no real obstacle to the closest kind of cooperation'. Litvinov also attended, but in a subordinate role.

Eden was assisted by Ismay, and a senior Foreign Office figure, William Strang, as well as Clark Kerr and Oliver Harvey. Hull was accompanied by Harriman, flying in to take up the ambassadorial post, and General John Deane, who was to become head of the American military mission in Moscow. As interpreter, Hull took with him the new head of the Russian section of the State Department, Charles 'Chip' Bohlen; at other times, he used Arthur Birse, which the Englishman found a trial given his unfamiliarity with US policy and Hull's low voice, southern accent and labyrinthine thinking.

The three delegations met for two or three hours each afternoon in the marbled, gilded Spiridonovka Palace – experts then laboured on late into the night on the details. The proceedings were well organised, following a set agenda in a businesslike manner. The ministers sat at a large round table with national flags in the centre. Brightly decorated boxes of Russian cigarettes and water carafes were in reach. As well as portraits of Lenin and Stalin, there was a painting depicting the signature of the Anglo-Soviet Treaty in London the previous year which Molotov pointed to with pride. Birse recalled that, from time to time, the Foreign Minister's pince-nez slipped from his nose.

On the first day, proceedings were interrupted by a ninety-minute lunch. There were breaks for tea and wine in an adjoining room or in the garden where Hull recorded having 'private and fruitful conversation with Molotov'. If delegates wanted to move round Moscow, they were provided with heavily armour-plated limousines – Eden recalled that the interior of his was 'scented'. Hull was accustomed to working in overheated rooms and on the first day called for his overcoat. The Soviet organisers turned the heat up so high the next day that Eden thought he was going to faint. 'Happily the three Powers were able to agree on a compromise temperature,' he recalled.

On the evening of 21 October, at his suggestion, Eden was received by Stalin who said glumly that Churchill was 'offended' with him and had refused to take his letter about convoys from the ambassador. If the Prime Minister did not want to correspond further, 'let it be so.'

Eden explained that the British leader had resented the tone and content of the message, but had told him to discuss the issue further. After that, things brightened up, and agreement was reached to renew the supply route. Still, Eden worried that Britain's contribution to the war effort was not recognised by the Russians. He found Stalin personally friendly, even jovial. 'A meeting with him would be in all respects a creepy, even a sinister experience if it weren't for his readiness to laugh, when his whole face creases and his little eyes open,' he noted in his diary. 'He looks more and more like a bruin.'

At Eden's suggestion, the conference agreed to establish an Advisory Commission for Europe – the British could take pleasure in its location in London. A joint body was set up for Italy to meet Soviet complaints about not being informed on events there. Moscow's demands on the Baltics were, in effect, accepted by both Washington and London. The Foreign Secretary carried a note by Churchill recognising that Moscow's accession to the Atlantic Charter had been 'based on the frontiers of June 11, 1941', and taking note of 'the historic frontiers of Russia before the two wars of aggression waged by Germany in 1914 and 1939.'

Eden was keen to provide as many safeguards as possible for small states likely to be liberated by the Red Army. It would be the test of his policy of giving Stalin some satisfaction, and then seeking to tie him down to post-war commitments. He even tried to derail a treaty which the Czechoslovak government-in-exile in London proposed to sign with the USSR. His big idea was that the three powers should encourage the formation of federations of smaller European states to help them avoid being overwhelmed singly.

Molotov said it was too soon to discuss post-war arrangements, as if Stalin's proposal put to the Foreign Secretary at the end of 1941 had never existed. With the radical change in the military situation on the eastern front, the Kremlin had no need of agreements; the dictator could count on

Red Army Socialism imposing itself. If he chose, he could put up his own candidates to run countries. There was no way Moscow would agree to Eden's idea which could lead to a cordon sanitaire round the USSR.

Accordingly, Molotov made plain that his country reserved the right to take unilateral action in the region if its interests were threatened, and to conclude agreements on matters affecting its border security. On Poland, he refused to give any commitments, or to try to improve relations with the government-in-exile in London. The frontier issue was a matter for Moscow and whichever government ruled in Warsaw after the war, he repeated.

Hull pleased the Russians by advocating that 'Hitler and his gang' should get a summary trial and then be shot. But he gave Eden very little support – in part, this reflected the fact that he had no authority to agree to anything beyond broad principles. What he wanted from the conference was a grand declaration on the post-war international organisation. The future of smaller European nations was of no concern to him – 'I don't want to deal with these piddling little things,' he told Harriman, adding that Poland was a 'Pandora's box of infinite trouble' best left unopened. At one point, his lack of interest in the future of eastern Europe was such that Eden slipped him a note reading: 'I am sorry to take your time, but behind all this is a big issue: two camps in Europe or one.' As Harriman noted, the Secretary's silence may have led the Kremlin to believe that Washington would not raise serious objections in the future over frontiers.

Nor did Hull inspire confidence when he suggested that China and Brazil should join the Allied commission for Italy; this idea died a natural death. A further irritant for the British came when, without telling Eden, Hull gave the Russians a proposal that the Allies should commit themselves to independence for colonies. The memorandum had been rejected by Britain, and Eden said he would not discuss it. Tactfully, Molotov moved on to the next item.

As the conference neared its end, Eden made a last try on Europe, proposing a declaration in favour of democracy and national independence and against spheres of influence. Litvinov said the Atlantic Charter bound the three governments to the first two principles, and that none of them had any intention of establishing spheres of influence. Hull did not demur. Eden withdrew.

Having done nothing to discomfort Molotov, Hull got his declaration committing the Allied powers to a post-war global body in which they would collaborate in peace as they had in war, act together on the surrender and disarmament of the enemy, agree to regulate arms, and work 'on the principle of the sovereign equality of all peace-loving states, and open to membership by all such states, large and small, for the maintenance of international peace and security'. Hull then campaigned to get Soviet agreement for China to sign the statement warning that leaving it out would have 'the most terrific repercussions' in the Pacific and on US public opinion. He even threatened that supplies might be diverted from Russia to Chiang Kai-shek if Moscow proved obdurate. The Kremlin gave way, and China's ambassador was invited to sign on behalf of the Nationalists. Stalin then offered the Americans another reason for Pacific satisfaction.

At a banquet, he leaned behind Hull's back, and beckoned to the interpreter, Berezhkov.[3]

'Listen to me very carefully,' he said in a barely audible whisper. 'Translate this to Hull word for word. The Soviet government has studied the situation in the Far East and has decided that immediately after the end of the war in Europe . . . it will come out against Japan. Let Hull transmit this to President Roosevelt as our official position. But, for the time being, we want to keep this a secret. So you, too, speak in a low voice so that no one overhears you. Understand?'

'Yes, Comrade Stalin,' Berezhkov whispered back.

Hull sent the information to Roosevelt in two different codes for the sake of secrecy – and did not tell the British, whom he regarded as too leaky to be trusted.

As the Foreign Ministers met, Churchill launched another bid to put the brakes on the landing in France. In a lengthy message to Roosevelt, he warned of 'grave defects' in the strategy for 1944. If the operation went wrong, Hitler might be able to stage 'a startling comeback'. 'My dear friend,' he added, 'this is much the greatest thing we have ever attempted, and I am not satisfied that we have yet taken the measures necessary to give it the best chance of success.' He felt he was 'in the dark at present, and unable to think or act in the forward manner which is needed.' A summit with Stalin would clarify matters.[4]

Hull warned that any delay of Overlord could undo the benefits of the Moscow conference while Harriman pointed to the danger of 'a large section of Russians firmly believing we waited till the last possible moment and let Russia bleed'. Molotov stressed that Moscow expected the Western Allies to carry out their promise this time.

However, military difficulties in Italy convinced Churchill that troops and landing craft should be kept in the Mediterranean. Meeting Stalin, Eden read out the report from Italy and a message from the Prime Minister expressing concern about plans for 1944. He admitted that this might mean putting off the attack on France. Stalin reacted with surprising calm; he was in a benign mood, and had been reassured by the American determination to go ahead.

But trouble was in store after the US military attaché in Moscow alerted Eden's team to the way Churchill had not included in his message a dissenting – and more upbeat – note from Eisenhower. Then the British team learned that the Prime Minister had written to Roosevelt to suggest a bilateral Anglo-American summit in Cairo, turning down a suggestion from the President that the Russians should be invited to send a representative to join the American and British Chiefs of Staff in military talks.

'The P.M. is untameable,' Harvey wrote in his diary. 'He cannot leave well alone and he loathes the Russians. He would torpedo A.E.'s conference light-heartedly . . . The wicked old P.M. will bring our labours to naught yet.' In Washington, Stimson concluded that it showed 'how determined Churchill is with all his lip service to stick a knife in the back of Overlord'. Hopkins was put out, too, and Roosevelt called Churchill's behaviour 'improper'. The net result was that the British leader was storing up difficulties for himself by deepening American suspicions.

On 7 November, Molotov ended the conference and celebrated the anniversary of the Bolshevik Revolution with his largest party of the war. The host, who got very drunk, wore a gold-trimmed black dress uniform, with a small dagger hanging from the belt. The jewels, furs and gold braid on display recalled pre-revolutionary days. The American and British ambassadors were honoured guests – the Japanese envoy was hustled into a side room. Clark Kerr and Harriman were taken into a chamber where the Soviet trade negotiator, Anastas Mikoyan, and a Russian general were deputed to drink them under the table; the only food on offer was a bowl of apples.[5]

At midnight, the American left, shepherded out by his daughter,

Kathleen, who reckoned that their ability to leave on their feet won them respect; her father spent the next day in bed. Clark Kerr, in formal wear with a large blue and red sash, was less fortunate. Rising to offer a final toast, he fell on to the table, landing amid the glasses and empty bottles and cutting his forehead. Rising, the British envoy managed to make his exit, only to wake the next morning on the floor of his embassy study with his head in the fireplace.

Roosevelt hailed the Moscow meeting as 'a genuine beginning of British–Russian–US collaboration which should lead to the defeat of Hitler'. Hull told Congress there would be no need for spheres of influence, alliances, balances of power 'or any other of the separate alliances through which in the unhappy past, the nations strove to safeguard their security or to promote their interests'. Eden, whose memoirs pull a veil over the extent of his rebuffs, pointed to the European Commission as a channel through which Britain could play an influential role in shaping the continent, though Washington sought to limit the organisation's remit from the start.

The real winner was Molotov – and, behind him, Stalin. The Soviets had headed off any agreements that would restrict them in eastern Europe. The way was open to impose the deep security zone they had always sought and, whatever Hull said, to extend Communist influence over more than half-a-dozen states. 'Now the fate of Europe is settled,' Stalin remarked, according to Beria's son. 'We shall do as we like, with the Allies' consent.'[6]

To capitalise on the Moscow encounter, Roosevelt and Churchill proposed meeting Stalin in Cairo. Referring to the conference of Foreign Ministers, the President wrote of the 'psychology of the present excellent feeling' which made a meeting essential even if it lasted only two days. He had just received a fillip with the 85–5 vote in the Senate for the establishment of an international organisation and America's post-war international role. Now, he proposed to make the conference in Cairo all the more global by including Chiang Kai-shek.[7]

Stalin refused to attend for three reasons – distance, fear of provoking Japan by meeting the Chinese leader, and reluctance to meet in the quasi-colonial domain of Egypt. So Roosevelt suggested Basra in Iraq, but the dictator would not go so far. Writing as if bound by those around him, he told Roosevelt that, 'My colleagues in the government consider that my travelling beyond the borders of the USSR at the present time is impossible due to [the] great complexity of the situation at the front.' Instead, he proposed that Molotov could take his place, and then gave way to the extent of saying he could go to Teheran, which was under Anglo-Soviet control.

There were worries in Washington about air travel over the mountains to the Iranian capital. In addition, as Roosevelt explained in messages to Stalin, constitutional responsibilities meant he had to be able to receive documents from Congress to sign and return within ten days, which might be difficult to arrange so far away. Such niceties cut little ice with Stalin, who talked of delaying the meeting. As over the Foreign Ministers' meeting, he got his way. Roosevelt and Churchill agreed to see Chiang on their own in Cairo, and then go on to Iran. If the President had to deal with a congressional bill, he would fly to Tunis. Nearly thirty months after Hitler had dragged Stalin into the war on the Allied side, and two years after Japan had done the same for Roosevelt, the Big Three would finally come together.

13

Pyramid

Cairo
21–26 November 1943

'Some of us are beginning to wonder whether the invasion will ever come off.'

HOPKINS

AT 9.30 P.M. ON THURSDAY, 11 November 1943, Roosevelt was driven from the White House to repeat the vanishing trick he had employed to get to Placentia Bay twenty-seven months earlier. An hour after leaving Washington, he arrived at the Marine base at Quantico, Virginia. There he boarded the presidential yacht, *Potomac*, which sailed for five hours to reach Cherry Point in North Carolina. As dawn came up, the bulk of a 58,000-ton battleship, the *Iowa*, could be glimpsed five miles out to sea. At 9 a.m., Roosevelt was wheeled up a special gangway on to the warship, where the three Chiefs of Staff were waiting.[1]

Though the *Iowa* was ready to sail at 10.20 that night, the President observed an old maritime superstition against setting off on a Friday. So the voyage began at six minutes after midnight. Three destroyers acted as escorts; two carriers provided air cover.

Roosevelt had turned down a request from his wife to join him. Hull was also left behind. No journalists had observed the transfer to the battleship. As far as America knew, its President was still on the yacht, taking a relaxing sea cruise.

Enjoying the fine, if cold, weather, Roosevelt changed into an old pair of trousers and a fishing shirt. At a meeting with the military men, he drew three lines on a *National Geographic* map of Germany to mark where each of the Allies would have its occupation zone. He predicted that Churchill would try to get America to take the southern area, landlocked and dependent for communications on routes through France. But he said he would insist on a zone in the north-west, including the ports of Hamburg and Bremen. Otherwise, the British would 'undercut every move the US made'. Quite what he meant was not plain, but it denoted a suspiciousness Marshall felt he had to rebut.

Roosevelt also remarked that 'the United States should have Berlin'. Its forces must win what he forecast would be a race with the Red Army for the German capital. At which, Hopkins chipped in to suggest putting two airborne divisions on stand-by to drop into the city 'two hours after the collapse of Germany'. American occupation forces in Europe would number around a million men, the President went on. How long would they stay, Marshall asked. 'For at least one year,' was the reply. 'Maybe two.'

On the second day of the voyage, a cry of 'Torpedo defence!' rang out as Roosevelt sat on deck in clear weather watching an anti-aircraft gunnery practice, cotton wool stuffed into his ears. One of the accompanying destroyers, the *William D. Porter*, had been using the battleship as an aiming point, and had released a torpedo by mistake. 'It's the real thing!' an officer shouted. Secret agents prepared to lift the President into a lifeboat. Did he want to go inside? Hopkins shouted. Roosevelt told his valet: 'Take me over to the starboard rail. I want to watch the torpedo.' A shockwave from an underwater explosion hit the hull. It did no damage, but Admiral King ordered the sacking of the destroyer captain. Though Roosevelt countermanded this, Hopkins noted, 'I doubt that the Navy will ever hear the last of it.'[2]

As the *Iowa* headed into the Atlantic, Churchill took the train to Plymouth to board the 26,500-ton battlecruiser, HMS *Renown*, for a five-day voyage to Malta. With him were Ismay, Winant, Moran and Cunningham, the First Sea Lord. As aide-de-camp, he took his daughter, Sarah, who was in the women's air force; a dancer, she had appeared in West End revues and would make the film *Royal Wedding* with Fred Astaire. At twenty-two, she had married an Austrian-born actor and entertainer, Vic Oliver, eighteen years her senior, whom Churchill found 'common as dirt' and from whom she had split by this time.[3]

The British leader had a heavy cold and sore throat, and was suffering from the after-effects of cholera and typhoid inoculations. He was, his doctor noted, 'in the doldrums'. His wife wrote urging him not to get angry at the summits, adding: 'I often think of your saying, that the only worse things than Allies is not having Allies.'[4]

As was his habit, Churchill used the long sea voyage to draw up a lengthy note to present to Roosevelt and the American Chiefs to reinforce his strategic arguments. In his memoirs, the text begins by extolling the alliance as exhibiting 'harmony and mutual comprehension' unique in history, though 'certain divergence of views, of emphasis rather than principle, have opened between the British and American Staffs'. He argued for a fresh push in Italy, and an offensive to the east Mediterranean to take islands in the Aegean Sea. Problems in Italy he attributed to the movement of forces to England for Overlord. 'In the Mediterranean alone are we in contact with the enemy and able to bring superior numbers to bear upon him now,' he added. 'It is certainly an odd way of helping the Russians, to slow down the fight in the only theatre where anything can be done for some months.'[5]

In fact, as the historian David Reynolds shows in his analysis of Churchill's memoirs, the version of this note published in 1952 was edited to rebut American accounts which depicted the Prime Minister as ready to renege on the commitment to Overlord. The full version made plain his priorities:

(a) Stop all further movement of British troops and British and United States landing craft from the Mediterranean.

(b) Use all possible energy to take Rome.

(c) Bring Turkey into the war . . . Meanwhile prepare an expedition to take Rhodes before the end of January.

(d) Seize a port or ports and establish a bridgehead on the Dalmatian coast, and carry a regular flow of airborne supplies to the Partisans. Use the British 1st Airborne Division and all the Commandos available in the Mediterranean . . . to aid and animate the resistance in Yugoslavia and Albania and also capture islands like Corfu and Kefalonia.

Only then did he add '(e) Continue and build up Overlord without prejudice to the above.'

Stopping over in Malta, where he was kept awake by street noise and the mooing of cows, Churchill, according to Brooke, launched 'a long tirade on the evils of the Americans'. If they would not provide more support for Mediterranean operations, he would threaten to withdraw British forces from Overlord. If Washington threatened to shift forces to the Pacific, he would tell them to go ahead. His vehemence was such that the CIGS found himself in the unusual position of siding, in his mind, with the Americans against the Prime Minister.[6]

Stalin was still in the Kremlin. On 9 November, he had received a message from Roosevelt dated the previous day saying he had cleared away difficulties in going to Teheran. Churchill only learned this after Harriman informed Clark Kerr. He sought to attribute this snub to 'a most unfortunate misunderstanding'. 'I rather wish you had been able to let me know direct,' he added in a message to Washington.[7]

Stalin, too, showed a preference for bilateral communication that left out Churchill, who learned from Roosevelt that the Georgian had agreed to go to Teheran. A cable from the Kremlin arrived two days later. Typically, Roosevelt used a light form of words in passing on the dictator's decision – 'Thus endeth a very difficult situation, and I think we can be happy'. That was hardly a sentiment the Prime Minister could share given the way he had been treated by the other Allies. He could no longer harbour any illusions about his place in the relationship between the Big Two.

'I have held all along – as I know you have – that it would be a terrible mistake if UJ* thought we had ganged up on him on military action,' Roosevelt cabled him in answer to a suggestion of preliminary bilateral meetings. Relations with Moscow were, the President added, of 'paramount importance' – Soviet suspicions were shown when Molotov asked Harriman if his closeness to the British was based on a secret treaty. Roosevelt had been told of remarks in July by the Soviet ambassador to Mexico that Stalin regarded Churchill as irrationally anti-Soviet, and feared that a Big Three summit would be an Anglo-American stitch-up. The pro-Soviet current in Washington was so strong that the head of the State Department's Russian section, Loy Henderson, resigned in frustration at the way his realistic assessments were ignored as a division opened up in the

* Uncle Joe.

foreign service between those who recognised the nature of Stalin's regime and those who went along with Roosevelt and Hopkins in preferring to keep quiet about the purges and gulags.

Roosevelt gave Churchill a general assurance about holding 'many meetings' before Teheran. What he actually did was to invite Molotov and a Red Army representative to join them in Cairo. This, he wrote to the Prime Minister, meant that 'they will not feel that they are being given the "runaround". They will have no staff and no planners. Let us take them in on the high spots.'

Churchill objected, and wrote that a Soviet general would have no authority, and 'simply bay for an earlier second front and block all other discussions'. 'Considering they tell us nothing of their own movements,' he went on, 'I do not think we should open the door to them as it would probably mean they would want to have observers at all future meetings and all discussions between us would be paralysed.' Instead, he stressed the 'fundamental and vital' rights of the British and Americans to hold bilateral meetings given the nature of the 'very great operation' planned for 1944 which would involve no Russian troops. Invoking 'the intimacy and friendship which has been established between us and our High Staffs' and voicing the fears in his mind, he added: 'If that was broken, I should despair of the immediate future.'

Desperate to get time alone with Roosevelt, Churchill suggested a variety of places and dates where they might meet bilaterally. He got nowhere. Instead, Roosevelt gave Chiang Kai-shek the dates of 20 to 25 November to be in Cairo – the full length of the conference. Nor did he hurry to get to Egypt, stopping to visit troops in North Africa on his way.

But his plans to bring the Russians into the tent were aborted when Churchill revealed to Stalin that Chiang would be at Cairo; Roosevelt had not mentioned this to the Kremlin. Whether the Prime Minister calculated on the result of this revelation is not clear, but he must have had a good idea of the reaction. Stalin replied that he was ill, so Molotov had to stay in Moscow to deal with everyday matters. In a subsequent message to Roosevelt, he dropped the mention of his health, simply saying that the Foreign Minister could not go to Cairo 'due to some circumstances, which are of a serious character'. The 'circumstances' were that he was still anxious not to provoke Japan by meeting Chiang, and did not regard China as fit to attend a great power meeting. In a message to London, he underlined the second point by saying that the Teheran summit would consist only of the Big Three, and 'the participation of any other countries must be absolutely excluded.' 'I understand your position,' Churchill replied, 'and I'm in full accord with your wishes.'

There were other sources of Anglo-American tension as the summit approached. Roosevelt expressed concern at 'chaotic conditions developing in the Balkans' where, he noted, anti-German guerrillas appeared to be fighting each other, not the enemy. The one man who could bring them together, the President said, was the US secret operations chief, William Donovan. This could only irritate Churchill given his personal interest in the area, and the British responsibility there.

France also came up again. The Free French had annoyed the British by unilateral arrests of members of the government in Lebanon, which Churchill reversed. He again suggested withdrawing support from de Gaulle, but was turned down by the War Cabinet. Meanwhile, Roosevelt gave Vyshinsky, the Soviet Deputy Foreign Minister, who called on him on his way to join the Mediterranean council in Algiers, a lengthy explanation of why he had no confidence in de Gaulle.[8]

On 21 November, Churchill flew to Cairo where he moved into a luxurious villa in the Mena Hotel enclave outside the city, which was somewhat spoiled by the large number of insects and the smell of burning camel dung used for fuel. Anti-aircraft batteries and searchlights had been set up, and large amounts of food and drink were brought in, including 22,000 pounds of meat, 78,000 eggs and 360 bottles of whisky, as well as half-a-million cigarettes and 1,500 cigars. The weather was pleasantly warm during the day, and cool at night.[9]

The following morning, Churchill went back to the airstrip to welcome Roosevelt, who had travelled via Tunis where he had had talks with Eisenhower. The President flew in an adapted C-54 aircraft known as the 'Sacred Cow' fitted with a stateroom measuring twelve feet by seven and a half. In the centre was a conference table bearing an inlaid presidential seal. An elevator had been installed for the President's wheelchair, and impediments to his movement round the aircraft had been removed. With Admiral Leahy and Hopkins, Roosevelt settled into the ambassador's villa, some three miles from Churchill. He had immediate legislative business to deal with, signing twenty-seven congressional bills, and vetoing two others.

To save him from having to move around, it was agreed that the main meetings of the summit would be held in his villa. Chiang Kai-shek, who had been the first to arrive, accompanied by his wife and three generals, was lodged conveniently close by.

As he might have feared, Churchill had few opportunities to talk to the President alone. 'Lengthy, complicated and minor' Chinese matters 'occupied first instead of last place,' he complained in his memoirs. Chiang had six meetings with Roosevelt at which the Chinese leader refused to commit himself, and constantly changed his mind. The President also busied himself seeing the Kings of Greece and Yugoslavia, high Egyptian officials, the US ambassador to Turkey and commanders in the Middle East. On two nights, he dined with close aides and played cards afterwards.[10]

The British got the Americans to agree to a unified command in the Mediterranean, and headed off the appointment of a single commander for both Overlord and the Mediterranean. Otherwise, Churchill and his delegation suffered a series of rebuffs that led him to categorise Roosevelt to Eden as 'a charming country gentleman' who lacked businesslike methods. As a result, he added, he had to play the role of a courtier and seize opportunities as they arose, though he had to go through another anti-imperial discourse from the President who told him: 'Winston, you have four hundred years of acquisitive instinct in your blood and you just don't understand how a country might not want to acquire land somewhere if they can get it. A new period has opened in the world's history and you will have to adjust yourself to it.'

Eden was disconcerted, too, when the Americans advised him not to make too much of the London-based European Commission, which he had brought into being. The Cairo summit, he would recall, was among the most difficult he had attended – 'there was nothing for it but to wait and hold up our end as best we could'. Nor were matters improved when Cadogan discovered that Hopkins had handed the Chinese a draft of the communiqué, without having consulted the British on the wording. This obliged the Foreign Office official to spend time arguing for changes.

It was as if the Americans were out to put their ally in its place, with the Army Chief of Staff playing a key role. Roosevelt remarked to his son, Elliott, that Marshall was being 'very patient, very polite, and very firm' in pressing 'the strategy of hitting Hitler an uppercut right on the point of the jaw . . . General George is still the best man at the conference table.'[11]

The General stood firm when Churchill pressed his pet plan to attack Rhodes and other Aegean islands. 'All the British were against me,' the American recalled. 'It got hotter and hotter.'

Clutching the lapels of his jacket, Churchill positioned himself in front of the Chief of Staff.

'His Majesty's Government can't have its troops staying idle,' he thundered. 'Muskets must flame.'

'God forbid if I should try to dictate,' Marshall shot back. 'But not one American soldier is going to die on that goddamned beach!'

Churchill calmed down, but the impression he was creating was counter-productive. Moran found Hopkins 'full of sneers and jibes' about the way the British leader went on about 'his bloody Italian war'. 'Some of us are beginning to wonder whether the invasion will ever come off,' the aide snarled. 'You're not going to tell me that Winston has cold feet.' In his diary that night, the doctor wrote: 'What I find so shocking is that to the Americans, the P.M. is the villain of the piece; they are far more sceptical of him than they are of Stalin.'[12]

The Anglo-American row was not simply a matter of Overlord versus Italy. Churchill's plans for the Aegean introduced a new element in the equation. The US chiefs wanted a two-pronged offensive in Burma – on land by American-trained Chinese troops crossing the border from Yunnan and by water over the Andaman Sea. Chiang insisted that 'Burma is the key to the whole campaign in Asia'. But, it would be impossible to stage all four operations, the troop build-up for Overlord was already falling well short of targets. So, the Combined Chiefs had what Brooke described as a 'father and mother of a row'. As at Quebec, junior officers were told to leave the room.[13]

'Brooke got nasty and King got good and sour,' Stilwell noted in his diary. 'King almost climbed over the table at Brooke. God he was mad. I wish he had socked him.'

Marshall objected that a million tons of supplies stockpiled in Britain would go to waste if the Overlord timing was not respected. Then, once again, he raised the threat of switching efforts to the Pacific. Brooke pointed out that dropping the Burma project would enable 'the full weight of our resources to bear on Germany' – just the argument employed so often by the Americans against the British Mediterranean strategy. What neither general knew was that Roosevelt had given the Chinese a promise to land in Burma.

Chiang and his wife called on Roosevelt on the afternoon of his arrival, returning for a second conversation that night. Churchill learned of the first meeting when he sent his private detective round with an invitation to the President to dine with him. Walter Thompson returned to say he had not been able to deliver the missive because the President was meeting the Chiangs. 'He cannot do this to me,' Churchill complained. 'He cannot do this to me.'

Still, he was impressed by the Generalissimo's 'calm, reserved and efficient personality' – a highly misleading verdict on a leader who flew into rages and presided over a regime marked by corrupt incompetence. Brooke found the fifty-six-year-old Chinese leader 'a cross between a pine marten and a ferret. Evidently with no grasp of war in its larger aspect and determined to get the best of the bargain . . . a shrewd but small man . . . very successful at leading the Americans down the garden path.'[14]

Madame Chiang, also known by her maiden name of Soong Meiling, contributed an unusual note to the proceedings. The forty-six-year-old American-educated daughter of one of Shanghai's richest families used her perfect English to break into the discussions, repeatedly correcting the interpreters, and speaking on the side to the Generalissimo, chain-smoking all the while. Brooke felt that she was 'a study in herself, a queer character in which sex and politics seemed to predominate, both being used indiscriminately, individually or unitedly to achieve her ends'. When the three leaders posed for group photographs, she joined them.

Receiving her at his villa on his first day in Cairo, Churchill said he supposed she regarded him as a scoundrel and imperialist out to grab more colonies.

'Why are you so sure what I think of you?' she replied evenly. Wearing a white jacket with a spray of rubies, and jade and pearl earrings, she handed him a gift of a long Ming-era scroll. Churchill found her 'most remarkable and charming', and wrote to his wife that he took back anything bad he had said.

At the first full session of the summit, Madame (never Mrs) Chiang appeared in a black slit satin dress, with a yellow chrysanthemum pattern, and a neat black jacket, big black tulle bows at the back of her head, hat and black veil, light stockings and black shoes with large brass nails. At one point, she shifted position, showing what Brooke called 'one of the most shapely of legs' through the slit in her dress. 'This caused a rustle among those attending the conference and I even thought I heard a suppressed neigh coming from a group of some of the younger members,' the CIGS added.

On the night of 23 November, Roosevelt invited the Chiangs to dinner. The Chinese account recorded the following highlights of the exchanges, as interpreted by Madame Chiang. Roosevelt opened by saying that China should be an equal member of the Big Four. This was very much what Chiang wanted to hear, but he turned down a suggestion that his country should play a leading role in the occupation of Japan, though he wanted its industrial plant, merchant ships, trains and rolling stock to be transferred to China, with which the President was in accord.

During the three-hour conversation, it was agreed that Manchuria, Formosa and the Pescadores Islands would be returned to China. The Ryukyu Islands would be split with the Soviet Union. Chiang requested Lend-Lease aid for 90 divisions, a $1 billion loan and payment of $100 million in gold for labour to build the airbase in Sichuan province from which the US air force would bomb Japan. In his diary, Stilwell noted that the Nationalist leader also asked for 600 planes, and Roosevelt promised him 12,000 tons of supplies each month over the 'Hump' route across the Himalayas. In a subsequent conversation with Hopkins, Chiang made clear that China would hold on to Tibet and did not want Moscow to take over Outer Mongolia – the aide scrawled himself a note that they were 'afraid of [the] British'.

Roosevelt pledged an amphibious operation against Burma. But he held back from asking Chiang why 200,000 Nationalist troops were encircling the Communists in northern China rather than fighting the Japanese, or why, despite the huge size of his army, Chiang was launching so few offensives. Nor did he enquire why the Nationalists were asking for $1 billion when they still had nearly $500 million in American aid funds in bank accounts in America.

Chiang had every reason to feel content when he and his wife left Roosevelt's villa at 11 p.m. He had been accorded recognition as one of the Big Four and had obtained promises of substantial territorial gains. Roosevelt said he favoured the return of Hong Kong to China – Chiang responded that he would make it a free port. He also got the Americans to agree to send an undercover mission to work with his secret police, nominally to fight the Japanese but, as anybody without rose-coloured spectacles could have foreseen, to persecute domestic critics. The headquarters of this joint operation outside Chungking became notorious for torture and barbarous conditions.

When the matter of democracy arose at a subsequent meeting with Roosevelt, Madame Chiang deflected the conversation by expounding on what was being done for education in China, a highly dubious proposition. A report from the US Embassy shortly afterwards noted that the Nationalists seemed to have no intention of introducing representative government, and that the trend appeared to point in the opposite direction. Still, Roosevelt felt able to cable Hull that he 'had a very satisfactory conference with Chiang Kai-shek and liked him'.

The Chiefs of Staff got a more realistic impression of the Chinese. The three generals Chiang brought with him were anything but forthcoming, although they felt a need to assure the Americans that aid would be used for military purposes rather than being hoarded or sold. When presented with the plan for Burma, they remained silent. Then their spokesman stood up to say: 'We wish to listen to your deliberations.' After another silence, Brooke explained that the Western Allies had completed their planning. It was for the Chinese to express their views. After more whispering, the spokesman rose to repeat: 'We wish to listen to your deliberations.'[15]

The CIGS felt that everyone in the room was looking at him with suppressed amusement as they waited to see how he would handle this. Rising, he suggested that the Chinese take twenty-four hours to study the proposals. 'Before we had time to realise it they had all slipped out through the door and disappeared,' he recollected.

Turning to Marshall, he said: 'That was a ghastly waste of time!'

'You're telling me!' his counterpart replied.

When the Chinese returned the next day, one of their queries involved the number of British troops to be involved in Burma. Stilwell noted with satisfaction that this question 'got under their [British] skin'. But, when the Chinese spoke of their right to aid, Marshall called them sharply to account. 'Now let me get this straight,' he said. 'You are talking about your "rights" in this matter. I thought these were *American* planes, and *American* personnel, and *American* material. I don't understand what you mean by saying that we can or can't do thus and so.'

For all his frustrations, Churchill savoured two occasions on which the old intimacy with the President came back to life. On the first full day of the conference, 23 November, he asked his daughter to arrange for a car to take the two leaders to the Pyramids. When he went to tell Roosevelt, the President leaned forward on the arms of his chair as if about to rise to his feet. Then he sank back. It was, Sarah Churchill wrote to her mother, as if Churchill was able to make him feel for a moment that he was able to walk.[16]

'We'll wait for you in the car,' Churchill said, going out with Sarah. 'I love that man,' he told his daughter in the sunshine, tears in his eyes. Whatever their differences on strategy, the Empire or de Gaulle, he would not put the relationship at risk. Nor would he imperil the Anglo-American alliance. His problem was that Roosevelt knew this, and could take the British leader for granted while he cast his line in Stalin's direction.

Reaching the Pyramids at sunset, Churchill, in a three-piece cream suit, dark bow-tie and straw hat with a broad black band, climbed from the car and stood looking at the scene with one foot on the running board, as Roosevelt peered from inside. A guide recounted the history of the monuments as dusk fell.

Two days later, Roosevelt threw a Thanksgiving Day dinner to which he invited Churchill and Sarah, but not the Chiangs. His son, Elliott, and his son-in-law, John Boettinger, attended, as did Hopkins and his serviceman son, Robert. After cocktails, twenty people sat down at table. Wearing a dinner jacket in contrast to Churchill's blue siren suit, Roosevelt carved two large birds. Propped up in his chair, he placed the meat on plates, which were passed round – some of the guests had finished eating before the President finished carving, but he reserved just enough to make sure he had some for himself. There was champagne, and Hopkins got an American military band to play. Churchill requested 'Ol' Man River' and 'Carry Me Back to Old Virginny'. Roosevelt responded with a request for 'The White Cliffs of Dover'. When the orchestra went into the 'Marine Hymn', Roosevelt sang along and Churchill jumped to his feet flashing a V-sign.

Towards the end of the meal, the American leader lifted his glass for a toast which concluded 'I, personally am delighted to be sharing this Thanksgiving dinner with Great Britain's Prime Minister.' As Churchill rose to respond, Roosevelt silenced him by adding: 'Large families are usually more united than small ones . . . And so, this year, with the peoples of the United Kingdom in our family, we are a large family and more united than ever before. I propose a toast for this unity, and may it long continue!' Churchill recalled that he had 'never seen the President more gay'.

After the meal, everybody went into the drawing room, where records were played. As the only woman present – and an accomplished dancer – Sarah Churchill was in great demand. Churchill waltzed with the presidential appointments secretary, 'Pa' Watson, watched with delight from the sofa by Roosevelt who, according to one observer, laughed enough 'to wake the Pharaohs'.

It was an evening during which, as Churchill put it, 'we cast care aside'. But he knew that, trying as the seventh Anglo-American summit had been, an even greater test lay immediately ahead. The next evening, the last at Cairo, Roosevelt chose to dine with his doctor, Watson, and two other aides before going to bed at 10 p.m., maintaining his arm's-length attitude to alliance business rather than having a last discussion with the Prime Minister before they flew to meet Stalin. 'Sure we are preparing for a battle in Teheran,' Hopkins told Churchill's doctor. 'You will find us lining up with the Russians.'[17]

14

★ ★ ★

Over the Rainbow

TEHERAN
28 NOVEMBER–1 DECEMBER 1943

'The centre of the world.'

CHURCHILL

I

28 November

'At last! I am glad to see you,' said the leader of the world's most powerful nation, stretching out his arms to the only man who might challenge his supremacy. 'I have tried for a long time to bring this about.'[1]

It was 3 p.m. on a bright Sunday afternoon. A few minutes earlier, Stalin had left the Soviet Legation in Teheran, wearing a mustard-coloured tunic with the Order of Lenin pinned on his chest, red-striped trousers and gleaming soft Caucasian leather boots with built-up soles. He appeared to have put on a little weight. Accompanied by Georgian bodyguards and an interpreter, he walked clumsily, like a small bear, across the courtyard to the villa where the President was staying. Guards from the NKVD secret police stood among the trees outside the white-columned, yellow stone building. Red and gold leaves on the lawns had been left unraked so that they would crackle under the feet of any intruder. A young American army officer went out to meet the dictator, saluting and ushering him past Hopkins and Harriman. Roosevelt, in a blue suit in his wheelchair, reached up to shake hands.[2]

The room was decorated in Tsarist gilt and Communist red stars. On one wall was a photograph of the Soviet leader puffing his pipe.

Stalin observed that he had wanted for a long time to meet the President. 'It was not my fault,' Roosevelt countered. 'I did my best to meet sooner.' Stalin accepted blame for the delay; he had, he said, been immersed in military concerns. Their conversation jumped over half a dozen subjects as they sized up one another. Pointing at the photograph on the wall, Roosevelt sought to put his visitor at ease by remarking that he wanted a photograph of the Three (he did not call them the 'Big' Three) as smokers – Stalin with pipe, Churchill with cigar, himself with cigarette in its holder.[3]

Was he comfortable? Stalin enquired. Could he be of service? Roosevelt noticed that the Georgian was looking curiously at his legs and ankles. To Elliott, he described him as having 'a kind of massive rumble, talks deliberately, seems very confident, very sure of himself, moves slowly. Altogether quite impressive, I'd say.'

Roosevelt offered the visitor a cigarette, and they spoke about the advice doctors gave against smoking and for the benefits of fresh air. Then the President turned the conversation to the war. How was the situation at the front? he enquired. Not too good in the Ukraine, came the reply. The Germans had been able to bring up new divisions – an implicit reference to the lack of a second front in the west.

Did the Russians hold the initiative? Roosevelt asked.

Yes, apart from the Ukrainian sector.

The President said he wished it was in his power to draw thirty or forty Nazi divisions from the eastern front. Such a transfer would be of great value, Stalin concurred, stating the obvious.

In his usual mercurial manner, Roosevelt veered off to raise the prospect of part of the American and British merchant fleets being put at the disposal of the Soviet Union after the war. Stalin said that, if the United States sent equipment to the USSR, it could expect to receive a plentiful supply of raw materials in return.

Roosevelt moved on to China and his talks with Chiang Kai-shek. The Chinese had fought very badly, Stalin observed. In his opinion, the fault lay with their leaders. He then asked about the Lebanon, which gave Roosevelt a chance to denounce the Free French for causing trouble there. The Soviet leader said he did not know de Gaulle personally, but thought he was 'very unreal in his political activities'. Though he represented the 'symbolic soul of France', he had no contact with the 'physical France' which, under Pétain, was putting its resources at the disposal of Hitler. France should be punished for this. Meanwhile, de Gaulle was acting as though he was the head of a great state.

No Frenchman aged more than forty should be allowed to take a position of authority after the war, Roosevelt suggested. No member of the country's ruling class should enjoy the benefits of peace, Stalin added. The President volunteered that he did not share Churchill's belief that France would be reconstructed very quickly. It would take 'many years of honest labour'. The first necessity was for the French to become 'honest citizens'.

This led the conversation to one of France's colonial possessions, Indochina, which both agreed should not be returned to Paris after the war. The people there were worse off than they had been before the Europeans arrived, Roosevelt remarked. Trusteeships, which he saw as a means of enabling colonies to develop independent political systems under tutelage from the international community, would be the best avenue to explore. Mentioning the scheme which had caused an Anglo-American chill at the meeting of foreign ministers in Moscow, he said Washington was working on the idea of a committee to visit colonial possessions each year and use 'instrumentalities of public opinion' to correct any abuses they found. Warming to the anti-colonial theme, Roosevelt added that he would like to have a bilateral discussion on India at a future date, but warned that this was not an issue to raise with Churchill. The best solution for India, he felt, would be to 'reform from the bottom, somewhat on the Soviet line'.[4]

That was a bit much even for Stalin. India was a complicated matter, with different levels of culture and castes, he said. Reform from the bottom would mean revolution.

When the Soviet leader left, Roosevelt had a brief session with Molotov. Then it was time for the first plenary.

'I'm sure we'll hit it off, Stalin and I,' the President told Elliott. 'A great deal of the misunderstandings and the mistrust of the past are going to get cleared up during the next few days – I hope once and for all. As for Uncle Joe and Winston . . . I'll have my work cut out for me, between those two. They're so different. Ideas, temperaments.'

The defender of the Empire sat on his own in the British Legation, a Victorian-era building with a large garden a couple of hundred yards away

1

Prayer service: The President and Prime Minister attend a Sunday morning service on the *Prince of Wales* in Placentia Bay, August 1941. (Behind them, in hat, is the senior Foreign Office civil servant, Alexander Cadogan.)

Military men: From the start there were wide and often sharp strategic differences between the American and British Chiefs of Staff led by George Marshall (second left) and Alan Brooke (far right).

Empire first: Churchill was joined at Placentia Bay by his crony, the press baron Lord Beaverbrook (left), who urged him to defend the British Empire.

Superior person: Sumner Welles (seen here with Eleanor Roosevelt) handled the detailed negotiations for Roosevelt at the first summit. An American aristocrat, he harboured a sexual secret that would eventually bring him down.

5

The dictators: German Chief of Staff Alfred Jodl flanked by Hitler and Mussolini with General Keitel planning dispositions in January 1942.

6

The Emperor: Hirohito reviews his troops as Japan sweeps across the Far East.

Alliance builder: Harry Hopkins laid the groundwork for the Anglo-American entente with a visit to London in January 1941. (Behind him and Churchill stands the Prime Minister's crony, Brendan Bracken).

Side by side: Hopkins flew to Moscow in August 1941, meeting Stalin for six hours of talks and then advising Roosevelt to back the USSR.

The master watches: The Soviet ambassador to Britain, Ivan Maisky, helped to set up the Hopkins trip to Moscow and had to handle rough exchanges between the dictator and Churchill.

The Blitz: Churchill inspects bomb damage at the House of Commons.

Siren song: As soon as America entered the war, Churchill flew to Washington, in late December 1941, for a second summit with Roosevelt during which he took time out to demonstrate his trademark romper 'siren suit' for Hopkins' daughter, Diana, who seems more interested in Roosevelt's dog, Fala.

Kremlin summit: After the Western allies decided to put off their landing in France, Churchill took the news to Stalin in August 1942. Roosevelt's trouble-shooter, Averell Harriman, sits between the two leaders. Foreign Minister Molotov shows a rare public smile on the right.

Stripped down: Churchill prepares to take a bath at the end of his trip to Moscow in 1942 – sketched by the watching British Ambassador.

Invasion now! Roosevelt sent Hopkins and Marshall to London in April 1942 to press for a landing in France that autumn, a probable disaster which Churchill deflected with great diplomacy.

15

French handshake: At their summit in Casablanca in January 1943, Roosevelt and Churchill got the rival French leaders, Charles de Gaulle and Henri Giraud, together and induced them to shake hands.

16

Free Frenchman: Roosevelt was hostile to de Gaulle but, despite intense irritation at times, the British continued to back him.

17

Unconditional surrender: Roosevelt announces the policy during a press conference at Casablanca, pretending that the idea had just popped into his mind.

Four-power pact: The Soviet, American and British Foreign Ministers met for the highest-level tripartite conference to date in Moscow in October 1943. After strong argument by Cordell Hull (third left) China's ambassador (far left) was allowed to join the signing ceremony (centre: Molotov, right: Eden).

18

19

Chinese walls: Chiang Kai-shek and his wife, Meiling, attend the Cairo summit of December 1943, with Roosevelt and Churchill.

20

Vinegary relations: Despite the smiles for the camera, the Chiangs were at odds with their peppery US adviser, 'Vinegar Joe' Stilwell, who was eventually recalled.

21

At last: Stalin, Roosevelt and Churchill finally met at Teheran in December 1943. Here, the Soviet leader rises to greet the Prime Minister's daughter, Sarah. Harriman stands behind. At right are Eden and the British ambassador to Moscow, Archibald Clark Kerr.

22

Birthday cheer: Churchill gives a lavish dinner for his birthday during the Teheran summit. Roosevelt looks far away.

23

Stalingrad sword: The dictator kisses a crusader sword presented by the British at Teheran to honour the courage of the people of Stalingrad.

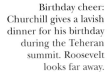

24

Troubles ahead: By the time they meet in Quebec at the beginning of 1944, differences are evident between Roosevelt and Churchill, undermining the Prime Minister's vision of Anglo-American unity.

25

D-Day: On 6 June, American and British forces launched the biggest landing in history on the beaches of Normandy.

26

Ike and the GIs: Roosevelt decided to entrust command of the Overlord landing to Dwight Eisenhower instead of George Marshall.

Picnic time: Churchill, Brooke and Montgomery in the field.

The manager: Hugely respected, Marshall was the key figure in organising America's war on two fronts, and became *Time* magazine's Man of the Year for 1944.

Stiff occasion: De Gaulle visits Washington in July 1944, but Roosevelt remains suspicious of the Free French leader. Seen here with the visitor are (left to right) Secretary of the Navy James Forrestal, Secretary of State Cordell Hull, Navy chief Ernest King and Treasury Secretary Henry Morgenthau.

30

The plan: Treasury secretary Morgenthau seeks to impose a Draconian programme on Germany after its defeat. A fierce departmental battle ensues pitting him against Secretary of War Henry Stimson (right) while Secretary of State Hull wavered.

31

Financial agent: Morgenthau's assistant, Harry Dexter White, used his bureaucratic skills to set up the IMF and pushed for harsh treatment of Germany – it was not known that he was a Soviet agent.

Naughty notions: Churchill went to Moscow for the second time in October 1944. He proposed splitting Eastern Europe with Stalin, an idea the Americans would have rejected out of hand. Here, Stalin and Molotov see off the British visitors (far left, Eden).

Pacific thrust: American confidence was heightened by the advance across the Pacific, with bloody fighting for islands such as Iwo Jima.

34

Together again: The Big Three meet for their second summit at Yalta in February 1945. Whatever their differences, the three leaders always posed for group photographs, with or without their civilian and military staffs. The American photographer at Yalta was Hopkins' son, Robert.

35

Cigar to the fore: Though his influence was declining by the second tripartite summit, the Prime Minister usually managed to put on a brave face.

36

Toasting time: The summits were marked by long dinners, filled with toasts and speeches extolling the alliance. At this Yalta night, Roosevelt's look suggests his failing health. (Left, Secretary of State Stettinius).

Paying tribute: Roosevelt's death on 12 April 1945 shook America, his bad health having been kept secret. Churchill did not attend the funeral, but later went to the grave at the President's estate in Upper New York State.

Bad tidings: Former US ambassador to Moscow Joseph Davies (right) was used by Roosevelt to try to open up a secret bilateral channel with Stalin. In June 1945, the new President, Harry Truman, sent him to London to say he wanted to do the same thing. Highly critical of Britain, the visitor made a bad impression on Churchill and Eden (left).

39

Victory in Europe: Soviet troops face the badly damaged Reichstag building in Berlin.

40

On the steps: Churchill, Truman and Stalin (left to right) hold the last summit at Potsdam outside Berlin in July and August 1945, by which time the Cold War is taking shape.

41

New faces: Churchill flew home during the Potsdam conference to learn that the Conservatives had lost the general election. The Labour leader, Clement Attlee (seated, left), replaced him at the summit. He was accompanied by the tough Foreign Secretary Ernest Bevin (standing, second left) while Truman brought the new Secretary of State, James Byrnes (standing, second right). Molotov stands on the right and the White House Chief of Staff Admiral Leahy on the left.

from the Soviet quarters. Churchill had laryngitis, and had dined in bed the previous night, forcing the cancellation of a dinner of the Big Three – Roosevelt proposed eating alone with Stalin, but the Georgian said he was too tired. Though the Prime Minister would subsequently write to Roosevelt of 'our sunlit days in Teheran', storm signals were flying. Moran noted that he had been full of misgivings as he flew in. His daughter Sarah thought him nervous and apprehensive.[5]

The loss of the island of Leros in the eastern Mediterranean might have given him pause for thought about his Aegean strategy, and could only increase Turkey's doubts about joining the Allies. Still, writing to his wife, Churchill complained that lack of support for Mediterranean operations meant he had to fight with 'my hands tied behind my back'.

He had wanted to meet Stalin as soon as he arrived in Teheran, and to have a preliminary session with Roosevelt on military matters. But his cold and loss of voice ruled out the first, even if the dictator had been willing, and the President declined to see him alone. When Moran asked Harry Hopkins if Roosevelt's preference for a bilateral session with Stalin would encourage the dictator to think that the Western Allies were divided, the aide blew up. What possible objection could there be? he asked hotly. His boss had travelled to Teheran to come to terms with Stalin, and was not going to allow anything to interfere with that. 'The mathematics of this is two to one,' the doctor noted in his diary.

Refusing to acknowledge that, and the evidence of the past weeks, Churchill attributed the way Roosevelt was avoiding him to the work of officials round the President. Nor was everybody on Roosevelt's team that convinced of Stalin's malleability. Marshall was surprised that none of his colleagues had read about the Soviet leader's violent early career. Categorising the Georgian as 'a rough SOB who made his way with murder and everything else', the Chief of Staff thought he should be dealt with as such. Bohlen felt that Stalin would have taken for granted that the British and Americans were closer in their thinking than they could ever be to him, and was probably amused by the President's attitude.

Warned by Ismay of Churchill's ill temper, Harriman went on a pacification mission while Roosevelt was cloistered with Stalin. He found Churchill 'grumbling but whimsical'. He claimed the right to chair the summit since he was the oldest of the Big Three, because the first letter of his name came ahead of the others in the alphabet, and on account of the 'historic nature of the British Empire'. But he was ready to waive his right so long as he could hold a dinner for his sixty-ninth birthday in two days' time, and get thoroughly drunk.

Stalin had been the first of the Big Three to arrive in Teheran. He set out from Moscow in special train number 501 to Stalingrad and then on to the Caspian. With him were Molotov and Marshal Voroshilov, who was to handle talks with the American and British Chiefs of Staff despite having been relieved of his command for incompetence in 1941. The sixty-two-year-old soldier, whom Stalin had humiliated at the Kremlin banquet during Churchill's visit to Moscow, had been a member of the Communist Party since 1921 and had played a prominent role in the military purges of the 1930s – Khrushchev would describe him as 'the biggest bag of shit in the army'. The Americans saw him as a Stalin stooge, chosen because he would faithfully follow orders. At one point, when military matters came up, the Soviet leader remarked: 'I've only got Marshal Voroshilov. I hope he'll do.' Also in the party were the police chief, Beria, who brought his personal assassin, plus the head of Stalin's security, the Georgian's doctor and a dozen bodyguards.[6]

At the Caspian oil city of Baku, Stalin boarded an aircraft for the first time in his life. At the last moment, he decided not to take the plane assigned for him, which would be piloted by a general. He preferred an aircraft commanded by a colonel, saying: 'It seems to me that colonels have more experience than generals where flying is concerned.' Twenty-seven fighter planes provided the escort. Stalin was terrified when the aircraft hit an air pocket. Landing in Teheran, he was constantly surrounded by guards. Gun holsters could be seen poking from the bottom of the uniform jackets of the Soviet servants.

Churchill's passage from the airfield to the city had been flanked by cavalry, but the Prime Minister noted that 'there was no kind of defence at all against two or three determined men with pistols or a bomb.' Crowds stood four or five deep only a few feet from the car. As the spectators pressed in on the vehicle, Sarah put a hand on her father's knee; he covered it with his palm. Stuck in a traffic jam, Churchill grinned at the locals staring at him – 'and on the whole they grinned at me', he recalled.[7]

Fog had delayed Roosevelt's departure from Cairo, but there was time for a swing over Jerusalem to allow an aerial inspection of the Holy City.

From Teheran airport, the President travelled in a car fitted with bullet-proof glass. In keeping with the security deceptions that shrouded his trips abroad, a double travelled in a larger vehicle. At the American Legation, a large ramp had been built to enable the President to be wheeled to the door.

In view of Roosevelt's disability, the initial plan was for all meetings to be held in the US Legation. But the building was some way from where Stalin and Churchill were staying. This raised the danger of a possible attack by German agents as the two leaders drove through the narrow, crowded streets. 'All three of us would be taking unnecessary risks . . . if we were staying so far from each other,' the President wrote to Stalin. 'Where do you think I should live?'[8]

Both the Russians and the British invited him to move into their compounds. All Churchill could offer was a bedroom and sitting room. The Russians, on the other hand, had a suite of six rooms. If Roosevelt moved, the proceedings could all take place in the Soviet quarters. After midnight, Molotov called in Harriman and Clark Kerr to impart grave news – German agents in Teheran were planning to stage a 'demonstration' – or even an assassination attempt. Neither ambassador believed the story. All enemy agents were reckoned to have been rounded up by police. But Harriman decided to play along, and inspected the rooms set aside for Roosevelt who agreed to move. In the morning, a decoy car swept out of the US Legation to drive around with the presidential lookalike in the back, complete with fedora and cigarette holder. Roosevelt and Hopkins left by the back door. However, bodyguards riding on the running board of their car, holding tommy guns in gangster fashion, gave the game away.

Thus, the Soviet compound contained two of the leaders. With Churchill across a street closed off with barbed wire and screens. The two buildings, he noted, 'might be said to be for the time being the centre of the world'. On his return to Washington, Roosevelt told Frances Perkins that he did not believe there had been a plot. But being in the Soviet buildings meant it would be easier for him to meet Stalin informally – that is, without Churchill.

The compound had once been the home of an Iranian magnate. Built of light stone and surrounded by a wall, it was set in a large, shady park, with big cedars, willows reflecting in ponds and plane trees. A portico with white Doric columns led to the entrance of the main building. Stalin and his delegation moved into smaller houses in the compound, one of them a former harem now filled with camp beds and files and dossiers.

Teheran would see Hopkins acting as a 'paramount' influence on Roosevelt, as Charles Bohlen put it. Cadogan noted that Hopkins seemed to be 'the only practical and more or less effective member of the [American] entourage, even if his methods are a trifle unorthodox . . . his language is refreshingly emphatic.' But he was in uncharted territory, trying to bring his experience of years in Washington to bear in dealing with a dictator who saw no reason to compromise and for whom the moralism and legalism which infused the American approach to foreign policy meant nothing.

The President's rooms were conveniently placed beside the main meeting room. Its toilet was particularly valuable since there was only one lavatory for the conference chamber. One day, just after Churchill went into this convenience, Stalin strode up. He rattled the knob so fiercely that a Russian-speaking US officer feared it would come off in his hand. He rushed over to tell Stalin that Churchill was inside. '*Tchort vozmi!*' Stalin muttered – 'The devil take it.'

Roosevelt's quarters were fitted with listening devices by the Soviet secret service. Sergio Beria, son of the police chief, was in charge of summarising the recordings. The dictator called the job 'delicate and morally reprehensible'. But, he added, 'I must know everything in detail, be aware of all the shades of meaning. I am asking you for all that because it is now that the question of the second front will be settled. I know that Churchill is against it. It is important that the Americans support us in this matter.'[9]

At 8 a.m. each day, the handsome Sergio, with whom Stalin's daughter would fall in love, briefed the Georgian. 'He prepared himself carefully . . . having at hand files on every question . . .' Sergio wrote in his memoirs. 'He even went so far as to ask for details of the tone of the conversations: "Did he say that with conviction or without enthusiasm? How did Roosevelt react? Did he say that resolutely?" Sometimes he was surprised: "They know that we can hear them and yet they speak openly!" One day he even asked me: "What do you think, do they know that we are listening to them?"'

'I can only say this,' Sergio Beria replied. 'That it is impossible to spot the microphones that we use. We ourselves couldn't do it.'

'It's bizarre,' Stalin said. 'They say everything, in fullest detail.'

According to Sergio, who was rewarded for his work with a Swiss watch, Roosevelt always expressed a high opinion of Stalin when talking to his delegation. When Admiral Leahy, the White House Chief of Staff, urged him to adopt a firmer line, he responded: 'Do you think you can see further than I can? I am pursuing this policy because I think it is more advantageous. We are not going to pull the chestnuts out of the fire for the British.'

Though this pleased Stalin, it is entirely possible that the President was playing a double game, aware of being bugged and saying what he knew would reassure the Soviet leader. In which case, a triple play is also possible in which Stalin, thinking that Roosevelt would guess the presence of microphones, would regard what Beria brought him as phrased to mislead. None or all of this may have been the case. It made little difference. Stalin was pathologically suspicious of everybody while Roosevelt's main aim at Teheran was to bring the Soviet Union into the global community of nations, and avoid 'a Russia excluded, aggrieved and driven in on itself to prepare for the inevitable war of continents'. That could be done, he was sure, by establishing a personal relationship.

Beaming, Roosevelt welcomed the 'new member of the family circle' as he, Stalin and Churchill met together for the first time at 4 p.m. on 28 November. Arthur Birse, the British interpreter, thought the President looked 'very much like a kind, rich uncle paying a visit to his poorer relations'. Having walked from the British Legation in pleasant sunshine, flanked by Sikh troops, Churchill shook Stalin's hand and went over to do the same with Roosevelt. Though the venue had been moved to the Soviet Legation, Stalin and Churchill agreed that the American should chair the plenaries.[10]

The session was held in a spacious room decorated in heavy, imperial style, with tapestries on the walls. The leaders and their three main aides sat in upright armchairs upholstered in striped silk at a large round table specially made for the occasion – the carpenters were fed a cover story about it being for a wedding. Soviet secret police stood guard. In the centre of the table was a wooden stand with the flags of the three countries. Notebooks and sharpened pencils lay in front of each participant.

Harriman sat at Roosevelt's right, Bohlen, the interpreter, at his left, Hopkins beside him. Stalin greeted the aide warmly; they had not met since his ice-breaking trip to Moscow twenty-seven months earlier. His subsequent leaks of information had cemented his reputation in the Kremlin as a friend of the Soviet Union. Harriman recalled that, 'Stalin showed Hopkins a degree of personal consideration which I had never seen him show anyone else except Roosevelt and Churchill.' Admirals King and Leahy, General Deane from the mission in Moscow, and a navy secretary completed the US delegation. Marshall and Arnold were absent because they had misunderstood the time of the meeting and were out sightseeing.

Stalin sat across from the President, flanked by Molotov, Voroshilov, Pavlov, and a secretary. Churchill brought Eden, Ismay, Brooke, Dill and the Navy and RAF Chiefs, Cunningham and Portal. His interpreter was Birse.

Roosevelt began by quipping that, as the youngest of them, he had the privilege of welcoming Stalin and Churchill. 'We are sitting around this table for the first time as a family, with the one object of winning the war,' he went on. He hoped they could achieve 'constructive accord' to maintain close touch during the fighting and after the war. Perhaps the Prime Minister would like to say something about 'matters pertaining to the years to come'.

The three leaders, Churchill observed, had the future of mankind in their hands. 'I pray that we may be worthy of this God-given opportunity,' he added.

Roosevelt invited Stalin to speak. The Georgian was in unusually affable form at the summit. He smiled, and softened his language, even indulging in jokes, some of which would prove hard to take. Though he sometimes read from a document, he usually spoke without notes, and without raising his voice; sometimes he talked so quietly that he was barely audible. Self-contained, he rarely consulted Molotov or Voroshilov. As he listened to Roosevelt and Churchill, he smoked and doodled wolves on his pad in red pencil.

'I think that history will show that this opportunity has been of tremendous import,' he said. 'I think the . . . power which our people have invested in us can be used to take full advantage within the frame of our potential collaboration. Now let us get down to business.'

The President launched into a general survey of the war by talking about the Pacific, anxious to underline the extent to which America was committed on two fronts, with most of its naval power and a million men fighting Japan. Gesturing from time to time with his pince-nez, he noted how China had to be kept actively involved in the war, and the great importance of getting 'at Japan with all possible speed.' In Europe, he added, transport difficulties had prevented a definite date for an offensive across the Channel, which was an unpleasant body of water – Churchill interrupted to note that the British had been very glad of this at one time. Lack of landing craft meant it was impossible to conduct large-scale operations in both the Mediterranean and in northern France. But Overlord should not be delayed beyond May or June; in the meantime, consideration could be given to stepping up the Italian campaign or launching operations in the Adriatic or Aegean seas.

Churchill intervened to say that there were no differences between Britain and America except on 'ways and means' – the fact that he felt a need to state this was significant. He asked what could be done to help the Soviets most. Before answering, Stalin gave Roosevelt what he so much wanted to hear. Though Soviet forces in the Far East were sufficient for defensive purposes, he said, they would have to be tripled for offensive action. This could not be done until Germany had capitulated. But '*then* we shall be able by our combined front to beat Japan'.

Turning to the war with Germany, he said the Red Army had achieved more progress than expected in its current offensive, but the Germans still had 210 divisions of 9,000 men each on the eastern front alongside nearly 50 divisions from their Finnish, Romanian and Bulgarian allies. Against this, the Soviet Army had 330 divisions. While the attack on Italy had freed the Mediterranean for shipping, he said he did not think operations there were of great value in furthering the war against Germany. The best thing would be for an attack in France – either the north-west or the south, though 'the Germans will fight like devils'.

As his remarks were translated, the Soviet leader took a pipe with a curved stem from his tunic pocket, opened a box of Flor Balkan cigarettes, removed several, slowly broke them up and sprinkled the tobacco into the pipe. He lit up, and looked round the table. According to the interpreter Berezhkov, when Stalin's eyes met those of Roosevelt, the President smiled and winked.

When the time came for his main opening statement, Churchill followed the usual pattern of speaking at much greater length than either of the other two. Though he pursued a logical path, his verbosity may have created a negative impression, and bored Roosevelt, who remarked on his return to Washington that the Prime Minister had 'developed a tendency to make long speeches which are repetitions of long speeches he has made before'.

Churchill said the Western Allies were resolved to launch an operation in France in the late spring or early summer of 1944. They were putting together a force of a million men. Since Britain's strength was fully stretched, the rest of the build-up would have to come from the United States. Pausing from time to time to re-light his cigar, he observed that the summer of 1944 was six months away. A renewed offensive in Italy could cut off up to a dozen German divisions. But this would not be enough. More aid to the partisans in Yugoslavia could hurt the enemy. It was also important to bring Turkey into the war, which could force the Germans to evacuate Greece.

To the irritation of Hopkins, Roosevelt talked of a possible operation in the north-east Adriatic, leading to an offensive towards the Danube and a meeting with the Red Army. 'Who's promoting that Adriatic business that the President continually returns to?' the aide scribbled in a note to King. 'As far as I know, it is his own idea,' the Admiral replied. Churchill pointed out that such an advance could follow operations in Italy. But Stalin was hostile.

He had come to Teheran with one major military aim in mind, he said – to agree an early date for the landing in Normandy. He noted that the Anglo-American plan laid down that the Wehrmacht would not have more than 12 mobile divisions in northern France at the time of the landing, and should not be able to build up more than 15 divisions in the succeeding two months. Would the operation be halted if the enemy had 13 or 14 mobile divisions in France and more than 15 available from elsewhere? he asked ironically.

'Certainly not,' Churchill replied. But Stalin had made his point. The Western Allies were too cautious. Like the century's other great mass-murdering autocrats Hitler and Mao, he put great stress on what could be achieved by an exercise of will – so long as it was his will. He dismissed Churchill's Mediterranean plans as worthless scattering of forces. The

Allies should remain on the defensive in Italy; Rome could be taken later. Overlord should be the basis of operations in 1944; other actions should be considered as diversionary. A landing in southern France might enable a link with troops from Normandy – he did not mention that this would rule out an Anglo-American incursion into the Balkans, which he wanted to avoid. As for Turkey, he was convinced it would not enter the war.

When Stalin first pressed for a second front in 1941, the Soviet position had been dire. That he made it the core of his demands two years later at Teheran provides a strong argument that he set limits on what he wanted to obtain at the end of the war – a deep security zone achieved by the Red Army in eastern and central Europe. So long as he could also be sure that Germany would not re-emerge as a threat, that would be enough. Churchill might raise the spectre of Soviet domination of all Europe, and Communist troops on the Channel coast, but Stalin was ready to see the west of the continent remain outside his grasp as the Soviet Union was reconstructed. If he had had ambitions to see the Red Army sweep beyond the middle of Germany, he would not have wanted Anglo-American forces in its path. Longer term, he probably envisaged an inevitable war between the capitalist powers, and knew that friendly parties in countries like Italy and France could turn their resistance credentials into solid domestic political positions.

The President said a landing in the South of France was of considerable interest to him, and added that he was 'particularly desirous' to avoid any delay in the attack on Normandy. Churchill did not give up. He said he wanted to go on record that it would be 'difficult and impossible to sacrifice all activity in the Mediterranean in order to keep an exact date for Overlord'. Shortage of shipping meant that 20 divisions could not be moved out of the Mediterranean. They should be used to stretch the Germans to the utmost. When Roosevelt repeated that an operation against southern France should be studied, Churchill said they should also work on Turkey, which was an important supplier of chrome to Germany's war machine.

Stalin waved this aside. All neutral states, he said, regarded the belligerents as fools. Ankara would be mad not to join the winning side, Churchill observed. Some people were mad, Stalin responded. At that, the first plenary session ended after three hours and twenty minutes.

Seeing Churchill afterwards, Moran found him deeply dispirited. Eden was 'rather in despair about this hazy conference' when he met British officials. He feared that much of the progress made by the Foreign Ministers in Moscow was being undone as Roosevelt promised everything Stalin wanted – and that Churchill was being isolated as the target of Soviet suspicions. Cadogan worried about presidential indiscretions and amateurism, while Brooke thought the American leader was 'in Stalin's pocket'. 'We were reaching a very dangerous point where Stalin's shrewdness, assisted by American short-sightedness, might lead us anywhere,' he reflected in the gloss to his diary.

That night, after signing four congressional bills, Roosevelt invited the two other leaders to a steak and baked potato dinner in his quarters. Eden, Clark Kerr, Hopkins, Harriman and Molotov also attended, along with the interpreters. As usual, Roosevelt mixed cocktails of gin and vermouth before the meal. Stalin, who drank only moderately, sipped his drink, winced and remarked: 'It's all right, but cold on the stomach.'[11]

Sitting beside the President, Stalin made reference to his infirmity by saying he now understood what it had meant for him to make such a long journey. 'Tell him that next time I will go to him,' he instructed the interpreter.

Stalin and Roosevelt went into a denunciation of France, leading Churchill to object that it had suffered the horrors of occupation. He could not conceive of a civilised world without a flourishing, lively France. To which Stalin responded that, though charming and pleasant, it could not play any important part on the post-war scene.

When it came to Germany, the Soviet leader seemed to regard as inadequate whatever was proposed. When Roosevelt said the use of the word 'Reich' should be banned, he intervened to say that this was not enough – 'the very Reich, itself, must be rendered impotent ever again to plunge the world into war'. He had no faith in the possibility of the Germans reforming themselves, telling a story of 200 German workers who failed to leave a station in Leipzig to attend a mass meeting in 1907 because there had been no station controllers to punch their tickets. With unconscious irony for a dictator, he said he thought the German mentality of discipline and obedience could not be changed.

Germany should be dismembered, Stalin insisted. But he also wondered if the unconditional surrender principle, 'merely served to unite the

German people'. With specific terms, however harsh, German capitulation would probably come sooner. He also disagreed with Roosevelt's evaluation of Hitler as mentally unbalanced; the German leader was, he said, a very able man but not basically intelligent, lacking in culture and with a primitive approach to political issues.

Suddenly, Roosevelt turned green. Great drops of sweat rolled down his face. He put one hand to his forehead. Hopkins feared he was going to faint, and had him wheeled to his room. His doctor diagnosed an attack of indigestion, and he did not return to the dinner.

In his room, he told his son-in-law John Boettinger that he felt a great deal had been accomplished on the first day. 'He was thoroughly satisfied in every way,' the young man wrote to his wife. He saw no reason to vary his tactics towards Stalin and Churchill. When the Prime Minister suggested a bilateral session the next morning, Roosevelt sent Harriman to explain that he did not want Stalin to see them meeting without him. 'It is not like him,' Churchill told Moran, recording that he thought, 'we all three should treat each other with equal confidence'.

But he was not going to miss the opportunity for a talk with Stalin after Roosevelt had left the dinner. He drew the Soviet leader to sit beside him on a sofa for coffee. The two men went into a routine. 'God is on our side,' Churchill said. 'At least I have done my best to make Him a faithful ally.' 'And the devil is on my side,' Stalin chipped in. 'Because, of course, everybody knows that the devil is a Communist and God, no doubt, is a good Conservative.'[12]

Stalin then reiterated his fear of Germany. The country had recovered very quickly after Versailles, and there was every possibility of this happening again. 'We must therefore establish a strong body to prevent Germany starting a new war,' he added.

How soon did he think Germany might provoke a fresh war? Churchill asked.

'Within fifteen to twenty years.'

'We would have betrayed our soldiers if the world was made safe for only such a short period,' Churchill observed.

The Germans were able, industrious and cultured, Stalin said. Their manufacturing capacity should be restrained. At which, Churchill proposed forbidding Germany to have any planes, and outlawing its military General Staff system.

'Would you also forbid the existence of watchmakers and furniture factories for making parts of shells?' Stalin asked. 'The Germans produced toy rifles which were used for teaching hundreds of thousands of men how to shoot.'

'Nothing is final,' Churchill replied. 'The world rolls on. We have learned something. Our duty is to make the world safe for at least fifty years.' That could be achieved by disarmament, preventing re-armament, supervision of German factories, forbidding all aviation and through far-reaching changes.

'There was control after the last war, but it failed,' Stalin remarked.

'We were inexperienced then,' Churchill responded. 'The last war was not to the same extent a national war, and Russia was not a party at the peace conference. It will be different this time.' Prussia should be dealt with more severely. Bavaria, Austria and Hungary might form 'a broad, peaceful cow-like confederation'.

'All very good, but insufficient,' Stalin said.

Churchill noted that Russia would have its army, Britain and America their air forces and navies – none of the three powers should disarm. 'We are the trustees for the peace of the world. If we fail, there will be perhaps a hundred years of chaos,' he added.

The conversation moved to Poland, for which Britain had declared war in 1939. Nothing was more important than the security of Russia's frontier with its western neighbour, Churchill said. He wanted a heart-to-heart discussion on this. Stalin said he did not feel the need to ask himself how to act.

If Poland was given territory which 'trod on some German toes' to compensate for losing land to the USSR, that could not be helped, Churchill went on. 'Are we to try to draw frontier lines?' he asked.

'Yes.'

The Prime Minister pointed out that he had no power from Parliament to define borders – nor, he believed, did Roosevelt. He made no reference to the Atlantic Charter or to past Anglo-American agreements not to discuss territorial arrangements. Rather, according to the British record, he suggested that the three of them might see if they 'could form some sort of policy which might be pressed on the Poles, and advise them to accept.' (In his memoirs, Churchill uses the word 'recommend' rather than 'pressed'.)

Stalin asked if the British thought he was going to swallow Poland. Eden, who had joined the conversation, replied that he did not know how much the Russians were going to eat. How much would they leave undigested? The Soviets 'did not want anything belonging to other people, although they might have a bite at Germany,' Stalin replied.

Churchill took out three matches to represent Russia, Poland and Germany, and used them to demonstrate how the Polish frontier with Germany could move westwards. This, the British account recorded, 'pleased Stalin'.

II

29 *November*

When the Chiefs of Staff met the following morning, Brooke advanced the British argument for a landing in Italy and a drive on Rome. Voroshilov said he would like to hear Marshall's views. The American replied that his country had plenty of supplies and men – 1.6 million men for Europe and 1.8 million for the Pacific. More than 50 divisions were waiting to be deployed overseas. The problem was moving them.[13]

Did the British join Marshall in considering Overlord of first importance? the Russian asked. Did the Western Allies think the cross-Channel landing must be carried out, or did they consider that it might be replaced by some other operation?

When Marshall replied that all preparations were under way for Overlord for 1 May 1944, Voroshilov wondered if Brooke was as wedded to the operation as Marshall was. It was of vital importance, the British general responded. But he knew the defences of northern France and did not wish to see the operation fail, which it was bound to do, unless auxiliary operations were conducted in the Mediterranean.

Marshall remarked on the difference between a river crossing – such as those the Red Army had been conducting – and a sea landing. Failure of a river crossing was a reverse; failure of a landing from the sea was a catastrophe because it meant the almost utter destruction of landing craft and personnel. Before the present war, Marshall added, he had never heard of any landing craft except a rubber boat. Now he thought about little else.

'If you think about it, you will do it,' the Soviet commander told him.

'That is a very good reply,' Marshall said. 'I understand thoroughly.'

The American might have ended on a diplomatic note, but Brooke felt 'more like entering a lunatic asylum or a nursing home than continuing with my present job. I am *absolutely* disgusted with the politicians' method of waging a war!! Why will they imagine they are experts at a job they know nothing about! It is lamentable to listen to them! May God help us in the future prosecution of this war, we have every hope of making an unholy mess of it and of being defeated yet!'

At 2.45 p.m. on 29 November, Stalin arrived in Roosevelt's quarters for a second tête-à-tête, described in the US log as 'an informal talk'. He gave the President a Russian cigarette with a two-inch cardboard holder. Roosevelt, who had invited Elliott to sit in at the forty-five-minute meeting, began by handing over what he called a 'most interesting report' on the situation in Yugoslavia followed by a memorandum on the granting of airbase facilities for up to 1,000 four-engined bombers in the maritime territories of Soviet Asia to attack Japan. After that, he moved to the post-war global organisation. Countries which had signed up to the Atlantic Charter would be the founding members, he said. Thirty-five would meet periodically and make recommendations to a smaller group of the United States, the Soviet Union, Britain, China, plus two other European states, one from South America, one from the Far East, one from the Near East and one from the British Dominions.[14]

Would this committee's decisions be binding on others? Stalin asked.

Yes and no, Roosevelt replied. It could make recommendations to resolve disputes; but this could only be in the hope that those concerned would accept such guidance. He could not see Congress accepting the decisions of the committee as binding. On the other hand, the US, USSR, Britain and China would have 'the power to deal immediately with any threat to the peace and any sudden emergency which requires this action'. If the threat came from a small country, it might be quarantined by closing its frontiers and embargoes. If the threat was more serious, the Big Four might issue an ultimatum and, if this was ignored, stage 'bombardment and possible invasion'.

Stalin expressed doubts that smaller European states would like the idea. They would resent China's presence. Better to set up a separate organisation of the United States, the Soviet Union and Britain for Europe, possibly plus one other European nation.

This, Roosevelt noted, was somewhat similar to the proposal Churchill championed of separate committees for Europe, the Far East and the Americas. He doubted, however, that Congress would want the United States to participate in a European group which might be able to require the despatch of troops across the Atlantic. The furthest he would go in a future crisis in Europe would be to send planes and ships – it would be up to the Soviets and British to supply land forces.

Roosevelt's invocations of the legislature cut no ice with Stalin, who could have little comprehension of the American political process. On one occasion, an interpreter heard him tell Molotov, 'He thinks I will believe he is truly afraid of Congress, and that this is why he is unable to make concessions to us. He just does not want to do it, and he is using Congress as an excuse. It is all nonsense! He is their military leader and commander in chief. Who would dare to object to him? It is just convenient for him to hide behind Congress. But he won't take me in.'

Stalin reiterated the concern about Germany he had expressed to Churchill the previous night, telling Roosevelt of the sofa conversation. According to the American record, he thought the country would recover completely in fifteen to twenty years – 'therefore we must have something more serious than the type of organization proposed by the President.' What was needed was the control of 'certain strong physical points either within Germany along German borders, or even farther away; to prevent aggression.' The same method should be used on Japan, with the islands round it remaining under Allied control.

Arthur Schlesinger, the American historian, has suggested that Roosevelt had a fall-back position in mind if his main scheme for the global body went wrong. With great armed forces, a network of overseas bases, peacetime universal military service and the atom bomb, the United States would be able to confront the Soviet Union if necessary. Such thoughts may or may not have been in Roosevelt's mind, but they certainly did not lead him to allude to any kind of deterrent potential at Teheran. Gently tapping the fingers of his right hand on the arm of his wheelchair at the end of the second tête-à-tête, Roosevelt said he agreed one hundred per cent with the Soviet leader.

*

Churchill and his staff had, meanwhile, gathered in the main conference room. British and Soviet honour guards stood to attention on either side of the chamber, the first with fixed bayonets and the NKVD troops carrying tommy guns. Churchill, in the uniform of an air commodore, smiled happily. Molotov looked into the room and went to fetch Stalin.

The Soviet leader was in his mustard-coloured marshal's dress with gold epaulettes, a single star on his breast, his face impassive as he walked forward slowly, followed by the Foreign Minister and Pavlov. At the other end of the chamber, Roosevelt was wheeled in by his valet.[15]

An orchestra played the national anthems. A British officer handed a huge, two-edged crusader sword in a scabbard to the Prime Minister. Dedicated, as the inscription along the blade said, to 'the steel-hearted citizens of Stalingrad', it had been shown round Britain before being flown to Teheran. Churchill presented it to the Soviet leader as a gift from George VI and his people.

Stalin took it, and held it for a long moment. Roosevelt, who called the occasion 'very magnificent, moving and sincere', saw tears in the dictator's eyes as he kissed the weapon, saying in a husky voice: 'On behalf of the citizens of Stalingrad, I wish to express my appreciation.' He walked over to Roosevelt to show him the weapon. Then he passed it to Voroshilov, at an oblique angle. The sword slipped from the scabbard. Witnesses differ on whether it actually clattered to the floor or whether Voroshilov managed to catch it in mid-descent. Stalin frowned, before hoisting a forced grin. The sword was borne from the room by a Russian honour guard.

Voroshilov stammered his apologies, then suddenly wished the Prime Minister a happy birthday the next day, followed by 'a hundred more years of life with the same spirit and vigour'.

'Isn't he a bit premature?' Churchill whispered to an interpreter. 'Must be angling for an invitation.'

The three leaders went outside to sit for group photographs. In the centre, the blue-suited Roosevelt had a partly upholstered chair of modern design. To his right, Stalin was on an official swivel chair with thick arms. On the other side, Churchill sat back in a stuffed period seat. Stalin, his hands folded on his stomach, looked into the camera for the trio shot, confident and even a trifle superior; he had pulled down the flaps of his tunic and arranged his feet and the line of his trousers for the occasion.

Roosevelt gazed off to his right. Churchill, his RAF hat perched on one knee, had his eyelids lowered and bore a vaguely worried expression, anything but a bulldog. Then he turned to look at Stalin while Roosevelt smiled up to the sky.

When other members of their parties joined them on the portico, Churchill put on his hat. Flashing a broad smile, the President turned to shake the hand of Sarah Churchill in her Women's Auxiliary Air Force uniform. Churchill took her across to introduce her to Stalin, who got up and bent over her hand with an air kiss. Roosevelt recalled that, compared to the American greetings of 'Howdy' and 'Hello, Sarah', the Georgian's courtly manner gave him 'the best of the moment'.

In the row behind the leaders, Molotov stole a sideways look at Ms Churchill. Harriman grinned. Hopkins stood on the margin, almost out of the frame.

Who would command Overlord? Stalin asked as the second plenary began.[16]

This had not been decided, Roosevelt and Churchill replied. 'Then nothing will come out of these operations,' the Soviet leader forecast.

The British had agreed that the Supreme Commander should be American, Churchill said. The dictator added that he did not presume to take part in the appointment, but simply felt this should be done as soon as possible. Leaning over to Admiral Leahy, Roosevelt murmured: 'I just can't tell him yet because I have not made up my mind.'

Stalin returned to Overlord. Roosevelt said 1 May would be a good date. If that could not be achieved, the operation should take place no later than 15 or 20 May. Churchill dissented from giving such a firm date, but Stalin insisted that the landing should be staged in the suitable weather of May. Failing to get a definite answer, he rose to his feet.

'Let's not waste our time here,' he told Molotov. 'We've got plenty to do at the front.'

Reddening, Churchill muttered something about having been misunderstood. Roosevelt induced the Soviet leader to sit down.

Stalin then gave a lesson on his approach to decision making. If a committee was set up on Overlord, it should be told that the landing must be carried out by a set date, with a landing in the South of France a month or two earlier. An invasion of Rhodes or other operations would be off the agenda. The appointment of the Supreme Commander should be made forthwith. In fact, a committee was unnecessary, he added, since the Big Three could solve everything between themselves. Anyway, he wanted to leave by 2 December, preferably the day before.

It was a breathtaking performance, in effect telling the Western Allies how to proceed in a huge military operation in which no Soviet forces would be involved. It is inconceivable that Stalin would have put up with anything like this from Roosevelt or Churchill. But he was not finished. To put the British on the spot, he looked at Churchill and asked, 'Do the Prime Minister and the British Staff really believe in Overlord?'

Churchill was visibly irked. 'Provided the conditions previously stated for Overlord are established when the time comes, it will be our stern duty to hurl across the Channel against the Germans every sinew of our strength,' he replied. The conditional start to the response underlined for Stalin the divergence between the two Western Allies. Soviet intelligence, and the bugging reports from Sergio Beria, told him that the President's mind was set. The force of the dictator's words carved through Churchill's conditional rhetoric like a knife through whipped cream while the President sat by and agreed with him as the session came to an end.

The plenary left Churchill in a grim mood. Pacing his room, he murmured that 'nothing more can be done here'. On the other hand, Hopkins told Moran that Roosevelt now knew that Stalin was 'get-at-able', and was sure they were going to get along fine. The aide kept repeating the word 'get-at-able'.[17]

'Gets things done, that man,' Roosevelt said of Stalin when chatting with Elliott before dinner. 'He really keeps his eye on the ball he's aiming at. It's a pleasure working with him. There's nothing devious. He outlines the subject he wants discussed, and he sticks to it.'

Tired by the discussions, he felt like a nap before the meal, but told his son he was 'too tired and on edge' to do so. Closing his eyes, he rubbed them with both hands. Then, sighing, he reached out for a cigarette. After a while, he asked for an Old Fashioned cocktail of whiskey, vermouth and bitters. As he sipped it, he ruminated.

'Our Chiefs of Staff are convinced of one thing, the way to kill the most Germans, with the least loss of American soldiers, is to mount one great big invasion and then slam 'em with everything we've got. It makes sense to me. It makes sense to Uncle Joe. It makes sense to all our generals. It's the quickest way to win the war. That's all.

'Trouble is, the P.M. is thinking too much of the post-war, and where England will be. He's scared of letting the Russians get too strong. Maybe the Russians will get strong in Europe. Whether that's bad depends on a whole lot of factors.

'The one thing I'm sure of is this: if the way to save American lives, the way to win as short a war as possible, is from the west and from the west alone . . . and our chiefs are convinced it is, then that's that! I see no reason for putting the lives of American soldiers in jeopardy in order to protect real or fancied British interests on the European continent. We're at war, and our job is to win it as fast as possible . . . I think – I hope – that he's learned we mean that, once, finally, and for all.'

As host at the banquet that evening, Stalin dominated proceedings as he sniped at Churchill for being 'pro-German' and provoked the British leader's walk-out. After fetching him back, he said he was glad the Prime Minister was not a liberal, pronouncing the word in a contemptuous voice. Once more evoking a familiar religious theme, he announced that 'the Devil is Communist, and my friend God a Conservative'.[18]

As the talk turned to the post-war world, Churchill insisted Britain would hold on to Hong Kong and Singapore, and would dictate the political future of its possessions. Stalin said Britain might expand the area it held round Gibraltar. Indeed, he suggested that Washington and London might like to replace Franco in Madrid, as if they could switch Spanish rulers at will. This led Churchill to enquire about Moscow's territorial demands. 'There is no need to speak at the present time about any Soviet desires,' the host replied. 'When the time comes, we will speak.'

When Churchill remarked on his own age, Stalin interjected, 'You need not boast about that. I'm only four years younger.' But Churchill acknowledged he was 'pretty nearly all-in'.

Back in the British Legation after midnight, he received a visit from Hopkins who told him that he was fighting a losing battle in seeking to delay Overlord. The Americans and Soviets were equally firm on the timing, so he should yield with grace. It was not clear whether Hopkins was acting on instructions from Roosevelt, or had decided to try to prevent a break-up of the alliance less than six months before the planned landing.[19]

After Hopkins left, Churchill, his eyes closed, talked in a tired, slow voice to Eden, Clark Kerr and Moran. As they sipped whisky, he spoke of the danger of 'a more bloody war'. 'I shall not be there,' he went on, according to Moran. 'I shall be asleep. I want to sleep for billions of years. But you will be there.' He stopped for a moment, before adding: 'When I consider the vast issues, I realise how inadequate we are.'[20]

'You mean a war with Russia?' one of the others asked. Getting up to pace the room, Churchill did not answer immediately on that point. Moran thought the 'black dog' of depression had settled on him. Relighting his cigar, he turned abruptly to his future, recounting that the President had told him: 'You may go at the election, but I shan't.' Then he veered off on another track, saying: 'I told Stalin we wanted nothing. We desired no new territory. Stalin didn't agree with me. . . . You see, it would make it easier for Russia if we took something.'

What would be vital after the war, he went on, would be supremacy in the air. 'If we are strong in the air, other countries, remembering this war, will hesitate to attack us. Moscow will be as near as Berlin is now.'

When Moran asked about Roosevelt's behaviour, Churchill hesitated, then replied: 'Harry Hopkins said the President was inept. He was asked a lot of questions and gave the wrong answers.'

After Eden and Clark Kerr left, Moran took his patient's pulse, which was high. The doctor told him his health problems were due to his drinking, and that he ought not to go on at this rate. When they got to his bedroom, Churchill turned apocalyptic. 'I believe man might destroy man and wipe out civilisation,' he said, his eyes popping. 'Europe would be desolate and I may be held responsible.' Turning away with an impatient gesture he asked: 'Why do I plague my mind with these things? I never used to worry about anything . . . we are only specks of dust, that have settled in the night on the map of the world. Do you think my strength will last out the war? I fancy sometimes that I am nearly spent.'

The Prime Minister got into bed. After a few minutes, Moran asked if he wanted the light to be put out. There was no answer. Churchill was already asleep.

III

30 November

In the morning, the British leader met Stalin for half an hour in a small room in the Soviet Legation. He opened by telling the Georgian that what he was going to say was not to be understood as disparaging the Americans. Noting the preponderance of British troops in the Mediterranean, he wished to use them all the time. But Roosevelt wanted a landing in Burma in March. If that was cancelled, there would be enough landing craft for both the Mediterranean and Normandy. The choice was not between the two European operations, but between an early Overlord and Burma. The United States was 'very touchy about the Pacific', he noted. 'Unfortunately' Chiang Kai-shek's presence at Cairo had meant Chinese questions had dominated that conference.[21]

Turning to Overlord, he underlined the preparations Britain was making. But he also talked of a big landing he hoped would relaunch the Italian campaign. Stalin responded with a warning of the consequences of reneging on northern France. Disappointment could only create bad feeling. Russia was war-weary.

Churchill reassured him, but then entered a caveat. If the Germans built up their forces in France to 30 or 40 divisions, the Western Allies would not be able to hold out. The actual landing did not worry him so much as what would happen on the thirtieth, fortieth or fiftieth day. On the other hand, if the Red Army went on engaging the enemy, and the Germans were held in Italy – and, possibly, if Turkey came into the war – the alliance could win.

Stalin discounted the prospect of more German forces moving into France. The transfer of troops to the east was still continuing, he said. The Germans were afraid of the Soviets. The Red Army would advance if it saw that help was coming from the west. 'When would Overlord begin?' he asked again. Churchill replied that he could not answer without Roosevelt's accord.

At noon, the American and British Chiefs of Staff told Roosevelt and Churchill what they had agreed. Their paper said the Western Allies should:

advance in Italy to a line between Pisa and Rimini, retaining 69 tank-carrying landing craft which had been due to have been sent to Overlord until mid-January

launch an operation in the South of France on as big a scale as the availability of landing craft allowed, to be planned at the same date as Overlord

tell Stalin that Overlord would be launched during May in conjunction with the operation in Southern France[22]

It is not clear exactly how Stalin was informed. Moran's diary says that, in what could be seen as a case of twisting the knife, Roosevelt asked Churchill to read the recommendation to Stalin before lunch, while he visited the Shah of Iran. Churchill carried out his mission without flinching, and found Stalin 'reasonably affable', his doctor recorded. 'He can be quite friendly when he gets what he wants,' the British leader told Moran later in the day.

In his memoirs, however, Churchill says the news was broken by Roosevelt at lunch. Whichever version is correct, Stalin was obviously pleased. He promised simultaneous offensives by the Red Army, before returning to the question of the command. This would be decided in three or four days, Roosevelt replied – that is to say after the Teheran meeting had ended. However, one report says that, in an aside, Roosevelt told Stalin the job would go to Marshall.[23]

When the question of concealing such a big operation from the Germans was brought up, Stalin outlined how the Red Army had used deceptive measures to mislead the enemy, with up to 5,000 dummy tanks and 2,000 fake planes. 'Truth deserves a body guard of lies,' Churchill observed. 'This is what we call military cunning,' Stalin added.

As the talk flowed across the table, the President doodled a design on a sheet of paper in front of him. He drew three circles, the one on the left contained the words '40 U.N.', for the number of member states, the one in the centre 'Executive', and the one on the right '4 Police'. Such was his structure for the post-war world.

That night, Churchill gave a banquet for his birthday in the British Legation at which a cake with sixty-nine candles was set before him. It was the social highlight of the summit, going on till 2 a.m., and was marked by genuine good humour on all sides. Though relegated to third place in the alliance, the host could still lay on a grand celebration, which he recalled as 'a memorable occasion in my life'. Still, Soviet suspicions were evident. The NKVD searched the legation from top to bottom, 'looking behind every door and under every cushion', as Churchill put it. Fifty Soviet guards posted themselves at the doors and windows. When Stalin arrived and a servant tried to take his coat, one of his bodyguards reached for his pistol. Behind the dictator's seat, a six foot, four inch NKVD general kept watch, dressed in the white jacket of a waiter.[24]

The forty-five-foot long dining room was in oriental style lit by candles – it might have been the interior of a Persian temple. The walls were covered by mosaics of small pieces of glass set at angles, with pictures of the British Royal Family hanging at intervals. The heavy curtains were deep red. The table was covered with fine silver and crystal. Iranian waiters wore blue-and-red uniforms and white cotton gloves, most of which were too big for their hands, leaving them with flapping fingertips. The cook was said to be the best in Teheran.

There were cocktails before the banquet; Stalin asked Birse what was in them and asked for a simpler drink. Birse suggested whisky, which the Georgian drank neat, saying it was good, but ordinary vodka was better.

Churchill sat Roosevelt on his right and Stalin on his left. Eden, Molotov and Hopkins were opposite. A family note was added by the presence, at the end of the table, of Elliott Roosevelt, Hopkins's son Robert, and Sarah and Randolph Churchill – though the Prime Minister wrote in his memoirs that his son was not present, the seating plan shows him between Elliott and Marshall. John Boettinger, an army major, was at the other end, next to Ismay. Sarah wrote to her mother that she had wanted to get up and propose her father's health, but she was held back by inhibition. She added that Randolph, who had fought with a unit which operated behind enemy lines and was twice wounded, also felt a restraint. (His father had failed to back him up over his wife's affair with Harriman – the couple would divorce in 1945.)

Stalin was still in uniform with a single star pinned below his left shoulder. Roosevelt wore black tie, and Churchill a three-piece dinner suit. Stalin gave Churchill a porcelain sculpture representing a Russian fairy-tale theme. Roosevelt presented the host with a blue-and-white Persian porcelain vase, which Harriman had bought at cost price from an American curator in Teheran. Unfortunately, the vase was broken into fragments on the journey home, though subsequently put together again – some kind of metaphor, perhaps. Harriman gave Churchill an eighteenth-century print on cloth of mounted warriors with lions in the background.

At the start of the meal, Stalin seemed ill-at-ease. 'This is a fine collection of cutlery!' he said to Birse. 'It is a problem which to use. You will have to tell me, and also when I can begin to eat. I am unused to your customs.' The interpreter told him to eat as he liked, and he relaxed, sitting back in his chair.

Churchill proposed that the dinner should be 'in the Russian manner; with anybody making a toast when he felt like it'. Glasses were never permitted to stand empty, Boettinger wrote to his wife: 'the champagne consumed would float a battleship.' The first toast was proposed by Roosevelt to Sarah Churchill. Stalin went round the table to clink glasses with her. She walked over to thank the President. 'I'd come to you my dear,' he said. 'But I can't.'

As the Big Three raised their glasses to one another, the British leader hailed 'Stalin the Great' and 'Roosevelt the President – my friend!' while Stalin toasted 'My fighting friend Roosevelt'. When Stalin asked if he might call his host 'My great friend', the reply came: 'Call me Winston.' Roosevelt celebrated 'our unity – in war and peace!' When the Prime Minister toasted Hopkins, Roosevelt said: 'Dear Harry, what would we do without you?' Bohlen recalled it as the only occasion he heard Roosevelt express appreciation for his closest aide.

At one point, as Stalin lit a cigarette, the pipe-smoking Clark Kerr leaned across the table to say: 'It's cissy to smoke cigarettes.' Stalin stubbed it out, and lit his Dunhill pipe with its trademark white dot.

Churchill said that the whole political world was now a matter of tints and that his country could be said to have now quite a pink look. 'A sign of good health,' Stalin observed.

Picking up the theme, Roosevelt said the effect of the war would be to blend all the world's many tints, shades and colours into one rainbow where their individuality would be lost in an emblem of hope. That led somebody to remark that, while neither Roosevelt nor Churchill was a Red, they had both grown pink during the dinner. To which Stalin responded that rosy cheeks were a sign of good health.

Roosevelt then brought the spotlight to Brooke with a toast referring to how their fathers had known one another. Stalin followed by saying the summit might have convinced the Chief of Staff to be less suspicious of Russians.

This took Brooke aback; he suspected that Harriman had been bad-mouthing him to the Soviets in the hope of scoring points – the American acknowledged having become 'scared to death' at the antipathy the CIGS was showing towards the invasion of Normandy.

In reply, Brooke evoked Churchill's remark in the afternoon plenary about the need to give truth a bodyguard of lies in wartime. Then he told Stalin: 'You have failed to observe those feelings of true friendship which I have for the Red Army, nor have you seen the feelings of genuine comradeship which I bear towards all its members.'

'That is possible, even probable,' Stalin responded, turning to Churchill to say: 'I like that man. He rings true.'

Still, instead of toasting Voroshilov as had been expected, Brooke chose to raise his glass to Admiral Leahy.

The *pièce de résistance* for the meal was an elaborate dessert consisting of two vast ice creams on large plates edged with friezes of icing sugar. Two of these were mounted on ten-inch-high pillars of ice, reinforced with metal and with the centre hollowed out to accommodate a religious nightlight. 'When lit up and carried in by white gloved hands with long white fingertips the total effect was beyond description,' Brooke recalled. The two concoctions were paraded round the table as Stalin raised a toast. When one was carried towards him, the CIGS noticed that the heat of the light was eating away at the ice, making the whole thing lean like the Tower of Pisa. He grabbed his American neighbour, and shouted at him to duck. They buried their faces in their empty plates as 'with the noise of an avalanche the whole wonderful construction slid over our heads and exploded'. In front of him, the ice cream splattered the Russian interpreter, Pavlov, from head to toe but he did not dare to stop translating Stalin's words. Brooke called for towels, and, with the help of the waiters, mopped him down. Pavlov was later made a Commander of the British Empire (CBE) for his work at the summit.

Towards the end of the meal, Stalin poured the waiter who had served him a glass of champagne and wished him good luck. The waiter did not know what to do. Birse told him to drink it.

Offering his last toast, Stalin remarked that 'the most important things in this war are machines. The United States has proven that it can turn out from 8,000 to 10,000 airplanes per month. Russia can only turn out at most 3,000 airplanes a month. England turns out 3,000 to 3,500, which are principally heavy bombers. The United States, therefore, is a country of machines. Without the use of those machines, through Lend-Lease, we would lose this war.'

To round things off, Roosevelt referred back to the remarks about the political complexions. 'We have proved here at Teheran that the varying ideals of our nations can come together in a harmonious whole, moving unitedly for the common good of ourselves and of the world.

'So, as we leave this historic gathering, we can see in the sky, for the first time, that traditional symbol of hope, the rainbow.'

The meal over, the diners moved into an antechamber furnished with armchairs and sofas where they milled about in groups. Brooke went up to Stalin to repeat his disappointment at the accusations levelled against him. 'The best friendships are those founded on misunderstandings,' the Soviet leader replied, shaking him warmly by the hand. The two men ended up, Brooke recalled, 'almost with our arms round each other's necks!' It seemed to Churchill a good portent.

Roosevelt left just before midnight but the Soviet and British teams stayed on for another two hours, Churchill wreathed in cigar smoke, Stalin, flanked by Voroshilov, almost boisterous.

'I want to call you my friend,' he told the Prime Minister. 'I'd like to be allowed to call you my good friend.'

'I drink to the proletarian masses,' Churchill responded.

'I drink to the Conservative Party.'*

When the British leader finally went back to his room, he called in Birse to ask how he thought Stalin had enjoyed himself. The interpreter said he was sure he had been agreeably surprised by the good fellowship round the table, and had gone away happy. But a storm was brewing. Pacing quickly up and down, Churchill handed Moran a cable from Atlee

---

* Subsequently, sending Churchill the new Soviet national anthem, Stalin would suggest that he should whistle it to members of the Tory Party (Sergei Kudryashov, *History Today*, May 1995). Evidently, he did not know that the Prime Minister detested whistling, one of the few things he had in common with Hitler.

about the freeing of the British fascist leader Oswald Mosley from prison, which had been ordered on health grounds. Ernest Bevin, the powerful Minister of Labour, was 'kicking', Churchill said. 'The Government may go out.'[25]

Moran grew worried about his patient. 'He has been profligate of his resources on this trip,' he wrote. 'I don't know where this will end.'

For his part, Churchill recalled: 'I went to bed tired but content, feeling sure that nothing but good had been done. It certainly was a happy birthday for me.' But, in a message to his wife, he described the meetings with Roosevelt and Stalin as 'grim and baffling'. He would have been even more concerned had he known what Roosevelt was calculating.

IV

1 December

The President felt that he had not made the connection he sought with Stalin. 'Nothing human to get hold of,' he later told Frances Perkins, the Labor Secretary. 'I felt pretty discouraged. If it was all going to be official paper work, there was no sense in my having made this long journey . . . What we were doing could have been done by the foreign ministers.'[26]

So he decided 'to do something desperate'.

On his way to the conference room on the morning of 1 December, he told Churchill: 'Winston, I hope you won't be sore at me for what I am going to do.' Shifting his cigar in his mouth, Churchill grunted.

When he got into the chamber, Roosevelt had a private word with Stalin. Lifting his hand in front of his mouth and dropping his voice to a whisper, he said: 'Winston is cranky this morning, he got up on the wrong side of the bed.'

As a vague smile appeared in Stalin's eyes, Roosevelt decided he was on the right track. At the start of the plenary session, he teased Churchill about his Britishness, John Bull, his cigars, his habits. 'It began to register with Stalin,' he recalled.

Scowling, Churchill grew red. The more he coloured, the more Stalin smiled, letting out a deep, hearty guffaw. 'For the first time in three days I saw light,' Roosevelt told Perkins.

He continued to goad Churchill, Stalin laughing along with him. Roosevelt then called the dictator 'Uncle Joe' to his face. 'From that time on our relations were personal and Stalin himself indulged in an occasional witticism,' he told Perkins. 'The ice was broken and we talked like men and brothers.'

There is no way of telling how accurate Roosevelt's account was. His intention, and his readiness to use personal cruelty on his old ally, can, however, be in no doubt. Naturally enough the Prime Minister made no reference to the episode in his memoirs. Roosevelt said Churchill 'behaved very decently afterwards'. But even somebody as resilient as the British leader could hardly fail to have been wounded. His daughter Mary recalled that he had been very hurt at being so obviously cast as the odd man out.*

Launching a discussion on Germany, Roosevelt said this could be dealt with in 'three or fifteen ways'. With a grin, Stalin suggested that Churchill was not listening 'because he was not inclined to see Germany split up'. In response, the Prime Minister said he considered that 'the root of the evil lay in Prussia, in the Prussian Army and General Staff'.[27]

The President outlined his idea of dividing Germany into five self-governing areas, with two regions under United Nations control – one made up of the northern ports of Hamburg, Kiel and its canal, the other of the heavily industrialised Ruhr and Saarland. This, Churchill observed, was 'a mouthful'. The vital thing was to isolate Prussia and detach the southern regions of Bavaria, Württemberg, Saxony, Baden and the Palatinate, which he would like to see in a Danubian confederation. The people of these parts of Germany were 'not the most ferocious'. If they were allowed tolerable lives, they would feel differently in a generation. South Germans were not going to start a war, and 'we would have to make it worth their while to forget Prussia'.

Stalin preferred the American plan as it was more likely to weaken Germany. Taking issue with Churchill, he said Germans were all the same. Prussian officers provided the cement, but, fundamentally, there was no

---

* In his biography, Conrad Black says Roosevelt 'undoubtedly embellished' the story which he calls a 'fraudulent account', noting that it is not mentioned by others present, including Churchill – hardly surprising. It may have been 'puerile', as Black says, but was in keeping with Roosevelt's behaviour at the time. (Black, p. 882)

difference between northerners and southerners – 'they all fight like beasts'. Austria and Hungary must be kept apart; a new federation would be unwise. 'Far better to break up and scatter the German tribes,' he advised. The danger of reunification should be neutralised by economic measures and, if necessary, by force. This was the only way to keep the peace.

So, Churchill asked, did Stalin envisage a Europe of small, disjointed states? Not for the whole of the continent, came the reply, but Germany must be split up. Roosevelt chipped in that Germany had 'been safer when she was divided into 107 small principalities'. Evidently fearing the other two would produce a *fait accompli*, Churchill noted that the discussion was 'only a preliminary survey of a vast historical problem'. Certainly very preliminary, Stalin agreed. But he knew that, whatever progress the Western Allies made after Overlord, the Red Army's advance would put him in a strong position to determine the shape of Germany once Hitler was beaten.

That was even more the case with the next topic – Poland, which was to become a major source of discord, and disenchantment, between the Allies. Churchill produced a formula fixing the 'home of the Polish state and nation' between the Curzon Line in the east which gave Moscow large amounts of territory, and the Oder River in the west, which would give Poland German territory in compensation.

Harriman had warned the President that, unless he raised the matter, Poland would 'probably go by default'. But Roosevelt wanted a private word with Stalin before he discussed it. So, ignoring Churchill, he went on with Germany, proposing a three-power commission to study the future of the defeated enemy.

Churchill objected that Poland was a much more urgent question. The Poles, he said, would 'make a clatter'. Why not agree a formula by which he could say to the government-in-exile in London, 'I do not know if the Russians would approve, but I think that I might get it for you. You see you are being well looked after.' However, he reflected that the Poles would never say they were satisfied.

Moscow, Stalin said, would like to take the warm-water Baltic port of Königsberg* to put Russia 'on the neck of Germany'. Sketching a line on a map, he said that, if he got this, he would be ready enough to agree to Churchill's formula.

At lunch, Stalin launched into another heavy-handed jibe at Churchill. 'I can't understand you at all,' the dictator said in reference to his backing for intervention against the Bolsheviks. 'In 1919, you were so keen to fight and now you don't seem to be so at all. What happened? Is it advancing age?'

Afterwards, the American and Soviet leaders had their third meeting without Churchill. Eden recorded that the British did not learn what was said till 'long afterwards'.[28]

As Harriman noted, Roosevelt 'consistently shows very little interest in Eastern European matters except as they affect sentiment in America'. According to Clark Kerr, he said at one point during the summit: 'I don't care two hoots about Poland. Wake me up when we talk about Germany.' Now, he remarked to Stalin that a presidential election would take place in 1944. He said he did not want to run, but might have to if the war was still on. There were six to seven million American voters of Polish origin, whose votes he did not want to lose – Hopkins had told Eden that Poland would be electoral dynamite. Stalin said he understood.[29]

There were also voters whose roots lay in Latvia, Lithuania and Estonia, which the Red Army was fast approaching, Roosevelt added. Americans would want to see some expression of the will of the people – perhaps not immediately after the reoccupation by Soviet forces, but some day. He was, he said, confident that those states would vote to join the Soviet Union.

Stalin did not like the sound of this. He reached back into history to point out that the Balts had enjoyed no autonomy under the last Tsar. He did not understand why the matter of public opinion was being raised now.

The truth of the matter, Roosevelt replied, was that the public neither knew nor understood. Well, they should be informed, Stalin said. Propaganda work should be done. He could not agree to any form of international control.

Roosevelt assured Stalin that he would not go to war over the Baltic States. The stern, moralistic line on the frontiers of 1942 was long forgotten; there was no mention of the Atlantic Charter. Still, the President stressed that a declaration about future elections would be 'helpful' for him.

* Now Kaliningrad.

Unwilling to commit himself, Stalin said merely that there would be plenty of opportunities for such an expression of the will of the people.

Roosevelt changed the subject to his proposal for a global organisation to keep the peace noting that it was premature to raise them with the British leader. In response to this fresh indication of the bilateral nature of presidential thinking, Stalin added another strike against the Prime Minister by saying he had come to the conclusion that the organisation should be worldwide and not regional, as the British wished.

When the plenary resumed to discuss Poland, Roosevelt was silent. Stalin accused the government-in-exile in London of being in contact with the Germans and of killing partisans. He was 'by no means sure that [it] was ever likely to become the kind of government it ought to be'.[30]

Churchill responded that he wanted to be able to tell the London Poles the Soviet plan was a good one, and the best they were likely to get. His aim was a strong and independent Poland, which was friendly to Russia.

When Stalin said he adhered to the 1939 frontier, which appeared to be ethnologically right, Eden asked if this meant the line agreed in the Ribbentrop–Molotov Pact. 'Call it whatever you like,' the dictator replied. Bohlen went to get maps the Americans had brought with them. One showed the ethnic divisions of eastern Poland. Examining it, Stalin commented that it appeared to be based on Polish statistics. Grunting, he drew lines with his red pencil to show what Russia would get and what would be returned to Poland. Bohlen thought him 'somewhat contemptuous'.

Churchill undertook to inform the London Poles that they would be fools not to accept the offer. Turning to Stalin, he added that he did not think they were very far off in principle.

As the last session entered its final phase, Churchill got agreement that Austria would be treated independently from Germany, opening the door to its post-war neutrality. There had been a possibility of another day of talks, but weather reports indicated that, if Roosevelt did not leave in the morning, cloud conditions might block his departure. So it was decided to wind up the summit.

During the plenary, Hopkins had written a note to Roosevelt asking what he thought of 'letting the Russians give dinner tonight – your last chance at Russian food'. Roosevelt scribbled his agreement, but added that he would have to leave early. So Stalin was host at the meal, after the leaders had initialled a document setting out the military agreements, including that 'Overlord would be launched during May 1944, in conjunction with an operation against Southern France'.

Round the table, the three leaders discussed the final communiqué and a declaration guaranteeing the independence of Iran. Stalin was exhausted, and not in the best of humours. When he was examining the text of the communiqué with Molotov and Pavlov, Roosevelt sent Bohlen across with a message. Hearing Bohlen approach, but not looking round to see who was coming, Stalin said over his shoulder: 'For God's sake, allow us to finish this work!' Turning, he sighted the American diplomat and, for the first and only time during the conference, showed embarrassment.[30]

As the dinner ended, Roosevelt told Stalin, 'We came here with hope and determination. We leave here as friends in fact, in spirit, in purpose.' At 10.30 p.m., he said he had to go. Gusts of wind blew leaves round the park of the Soviet compound as he was wheeled to the portico, smiling with his cigarette holder at its usual angle, a crumpled hat on his head; a waterproof was thrown over his shoulders, above his habitual black cape fixed with a gold chain between lion-head buckles. The Russian interpreter, Berezhkov, noted the fatigue on his face. The President was lifted into a waiting jeep, a tartan rug laid across his knees. Stalin and Churchill went to bid him farewell. 'I think we have done some great work here,' he said. To which the dictator replied: 'No one can doubt now that we shall win.' The driver started the engine. Four secret service men jumped on to the running boards, two brandishing sub-machine guns. As the jeep drove off through the trees, Roosevelt smiled and raised his right arm, with a victory sign. After spending the night at a US camp outside Teheran, he was driven in a staff car over dusty dirt roads to the airport to fly back to Cairo.[31]

Four days later the joint declaration was published. Again, it ignored the realities of the USSR and its government, looking to the 'day when all peoples of the world may live free lives, untouched by tyranny, and according to their varying desires and their own consciences.'

The biggest thing had been to make clear to Stalin that the United States and Great Britain were not allied in a bloc against the Soviet Union, Elliott Roosevelt recalled his father saying. 'I think we got rid of that idea once and for all,' he went on. 'I hope so. The one thing that could upset the apple-cart, after the war, is if the world is divided again, Russia against England and us. That's our big job now . . . making sure that we continue to act as referee, as intermediary between Russia and England . . . Our principal job was to come to agreement as to what constitutes the area of general security, in the post-war world, for each of our countries. That job is still before us but we've made a start of it.'

For security reasons, Churchill left the British Legation lying out of sight on the back seat of a beaten-up army truck with battered trunks around him. Then he was flown to Cairo for meetings with Roosevelt and the Chiefs of Staff on bilateral issues.[32]

Stalin flew back to Baku, suffering ear trouble from the air pressure. On arrival, he donned an ordinary soldier's greatcoat and cap before being driven to take a special train. It made one stop on the way to Moscow, for the dictator to pay his only visit to the city named after him. As his car drove through the ruined streets of Stalingrad at high speed, it collided with a vehicle driven by a woman who was terrified when she saw him. 'It's not your fault,' he said as he got out of the car. 'Blame it on the war. Our car's armoured and didn't suffer. You can repair yours.'

Though he had misgivings about the political conversations at the summit, Harriman reported a 'revolutionary' change in the tone of the Soviet press towards the alliance. Newspapers hailed the 'historic decisions' taken at Teheran. Sergio Beria recalled his father as saying that Stalin considered he had won the game. He had got a date for Overlord and a commitment to a landing in the South of France. He had obtained accord in principle to the Soviet Union taking a big chunk of Polish territory, and had been able to gauge the weaknesses and divisions of the other two leaders. His forceful tactics had, in effect, made him the motor of decisions they had been unable to nail down for so long.[33]

Back in Washington, Roosevelt told the Cabinet, 'You know, I really think the Russians will go along with me about having no spheres of influence and about agreements for free ports all over the world.' But Bohlen submitted a starkly realistic memorandum to Harriman when they got back to Moscow. 'Germany is to be broken up and kept broken up,' he wrote. 'The states of eastern, south-eastern and central Europe will not be permitted to group themselves into any federations or association. France is to be stripped of her colonies and strategic bases beyond her borders and will not be permitted to maintain any appreciable military establishment. Poland and Italy will remain approximately their present territorial size, but it is doubtful if either will be permitted to maintain any appreciable armed force. The result would be that the Soviet Union would be the only important military and political force on the continent of Europe. The rest of Europe would be reduced to military and political impotence.'

By the end of 1943, the NKVD had arrested 931,000 people in territories taken by the Red Army, and launched mass ethnic cleansing of minorities deemed to be unreliable to the Soviet state. As he waited with Hopkins to fly out of Iran, Admiral Leahy, remarked: 'Well, Harry, all I can say is, nice friends we have now.'

★ ★ ★

Ill Wind

'We've got to do something with these bloody Russians.'

CHURCHILL

THE PRESIDENT HAD TWO KEY decisions to make in Cairo before returning to Washington. The first was whether to go ahead with the landing in Burma he had promised Chiang Kai-shek. The second was whether to appoint Marshall to command Overlord.

Though concerned about the effect of cancellation on Chiang and Chinese morale, Roosevelt gave ground little by little to those who thought the Burma operation was a waste of resources needed elsewhere. At 5 p.m. on 5 December he told the American Chiefs of Staff that he had decided to end the 'argumentation', and call off the landing. Like his backing for Torch rather than Sledgehammer, it was a sensible outcome. But, just as the decision in 1942 had been awkward to break to Stalin, so Roosevelt needed to exercise care in informing Chiang, who had not been told of the Teheran decisions for security reasons. A message drafted by Roosevelt and Hopkins spoke only in general terms of 'a combined grand operation on the European continent giving a fair prospect of terminating the war with Germany by the end of the summer of 1944'. As a result, the requirement for heavy landing craft in Europe made the Burma action impracticable.[1]

The next morning, Joseph Stilwell, who had stayed in Cairo during the Teheran summit, took a political adviser from China, John Paton Davies, to talk to Hopkins about China. Looking frail, the aide was in bed under a green counterpane. He said China should be made into a great power, though the British preferred to re-build Japan. Just before lunch, Roosevelt called in the two men for a half-hour conversation that showed the difficulty of pinning him down, and the hazy nature of his thinking on the nation he wanted to be the Fourth Policeman.[2]

Stilwell asked about policy towards China.

'Well, now, we've been friends with China for a gr-e-e-at many years,' the President replied, according to the general's diary.

What would the United States do if Chiang's regime disintegrated? Davies enquired.

'How long do you think Chiang can last?' the President countered.

'A fresh Japanese offensive might overturn him.'

'Well, then we should look for some other man or group of men, to carry on.'

There was no obvious successor, they said. Any alternative rulers 'would probably be looking for us,' Stilwell observed. Though neither knew it, this was just what was happening. A group of young officers who wanted to keep Chiang as a figurehead but get rid of the more corrupt and inefficient of his associates had planned to kidnap him on his return from Cairo, and force him to act as they wished. They hoped for US backing. But the secret police discovered the plot, and sixteen of the plotters were executed.

The Chinese really liked the Americans, but not the British, Roosevelt went on. 'Now, we haven't the same aims as the British out there. For instance, Hong Kong. Now, I have a plan to make Hong Kong a free port: free to the commerce of all nations – of the whole world! But let's raise the Chinese flag there first, and then Chiang can the next day make a grand gesture and make it a free port. That's the way to handle that! I'm sure that Chiang would be willing to make that a free port, and goods could come through Siberia – in bond – without customs examinations.'

Hauling the conversation back to Burma, Stilwell observed that Chiang would have trouble explaining to his people the failure of the Allies to do as Roosevelt had promised. 'We need guidance on political policy on China,' he insisted.

'Yes, as I was saying, the Chinese will want a lot of help from us – a lot of it,' Roosevelt responded, only to veer off into a lengthy tale about an occasion on which the Prime Minister, H.H. Kung, had asked him for a $50-million loan to develop China's transport system. He talked about a scheme to buy up Chinese currency on the black market to raise its value. When Hopkins came in and switched the talk to Japan, Roosevelt told anecdotes about an ancestor of his who had been to Japan when the Mikado had been without power. At other points, he rambled on about his forebears who had traded in China. As he drove off with Davies, Vinegar Joe held his head in his hands. 'A brief experience with international politics confirms me in my preference for driving a garbage truck,' he reflected.

Chiang took more than two weeks to tell Roosevelt that the decision to renege on the pledge made in Cairo had 'given rise to serious misgivings on all sides'. As a result, he would not go ahead with a planned offensive into northern Burma from south-west China. Never known for his consistency, the Generalissimo did, in fact, allow the attack to take place, under Stilwell's command and with the participation of the American commando force set up following the Quebec summit known as 'Merrill's Marauders'. After two months, it took a Japanese base, and opened the Ledo Road for supplies to reach China by land.[3]

Stilwell was made a four-star general, one of only five in the US Army. But his relations with the Nationalist leader reached rock-bottom as he sought to reform the Chinese army. Chiang fought a determined battle for his autonomy while the adviser lambasted the regime for 'greed, corruption, favouritism, more taxes, a ruined currency, terrible waste of life, callous disregard of all the rights of men'. The cure for China, he decided, was the elimination of the Generalissimo. He recorded that, in Cairo, Roosevelt had been 'fed up with Chiang and his tantrums and said so. In fact he told me in that Olympian manner of his: "If you can't get along with Chiang and can't replace him, get rid of him once and for all. You know what I mean. Put in someone you can manage."' But no such person was to be found, and the Nationalist leader hung on, waiting for America to defeat Japan so that he could turn back to the elimination of the Communist rivals he had been pursuing since 1927.

To many, the appointment of George Marshall to command Overlord seemed a foregone conclusion. But the President dithered.[4]

In two years of war, he had come to treasure the Chief of Staff for his skills, integrity and loyalty. Politically, he was a huge asset. Even the President's most vociferous critics respected him. *Time* magazine was about to name him Man of the Year. 'He armed the Republic' read the cover line while the story inside declared that 'the secret of American democracy is the stuff Marshall is made of'. However, the general's respect for the political process made him awkward to deal with in a system where people usually pushed their own case. If he had made clear his preference for going to Europe or staying in Washington, Roosevelt could have followed his lead. But Marshall insisted that this was a matter for his Commander-in-Chief. Still, his wife had started packing.

Sent by the President to see the general on Sunday 5 December, Hopkins told his good friend that Roosevelt was 'in some concern of mind' about his appointment to command Overlord. Marshall replied that he would go along with whatever the President wanted. The conversation must have been especially opaque. Hopkins did not know what Roosevelt wanted. Marshall refused to reveal what he wanted. The two men parted in a fog of uncertainty.

The next day, at Churchill's behest, the President and Prime Minister went on a trip to the Pyramids and the Sphinx. Almost casually, Roosevelt said he had decided he could not do without Marshall in Washington. So Eisenhower would command Overlord. Was this acceptable to the British? he asked. The Prime Minister replied positively. He may have thought that the diplomatic Ike would be easier to get on with than the steely Marshall.

That afternoon, the President called in the Chief of Staff. After beating round the bush, he asked the general what he wanted to do. Marshall said Roosevelt should act as he wished in the best interests of the United States, and not consider his feelings. At which, Roosevelt blurted out, 'I feel I could not sleep at night with you out of Washington.'

Churchill thought Roosevelt believed that Overlord, on its own, was not a big enough job for Marshall, who deserved overall command in Europe. So he preferred to keep him in Washington. Eisenhower had put great stress on cooperation with the British and was, as the President told Elliott, 'the best politician among the military men. He is a natural leader who can convince other men to follow him.' He also had experience of commanding major amphibious operations – and he had Marshall's backing. The Army Chief of Staff accepted the end of his hopes of leading Overlord without a word.

*

The presidential log recorded the second Cairo meeting as having been in 'delightful weather' though 'the mosquitoes and flies were bothersome'. Three rounds of talks were held with the Turkish President, Ismet Inonu, to try to bring Ankara into the war on the Allied side. Inonu kissed Churchill on the cheek as he left, but there was no commitment, as Stalin had forecast at Teheran. After Eden remarked that a kiss on the cheek was not much of a result for fifteen hours of discussions, the Prime Minister told his daughter: 'The truth is I'm irresistible. But don't tell Anthony, he's jealous.'[5]

Getting Roosevelt alone, Churchill raised the matter of Britain's gold and sterling balances, which had been rising. The American plan for the post-war financial system would have capped them at \$1 billion; the Treasury in London felt this would hobble recovery. The President was non-committal.

At 8.30 on the morning of 7 December, Roosevelt flew westwards to Tunis to meet Eisenhower. The general had received a garbled message from Marshall referring to a change of assignment. He thought this meant returning to Washington to take over his patron's job. But, as soon as he met Eisenhower, the President told him: 'Well, Ike, you are going to command Overlord.'

'Mr President, I realise such an appointment involved difficult decision,' came the reply. 'I hope you will not be disappointed.'

Despite Churchill's positive reaction, the War Cabinet in London predicted that public opinion would be 'surprised and rather uneasy' to hear that Eisenhower had got the job, rather than Marshall. The ministers also insisted on the senior British role for Montgomery instead of Harold Alexander, a step Churchill accepted on the grounds that the victor of El Alamein was a public hero.

Harriman was nervous that Stalin might react badly to the command decision, given his high opinion of Marshall. Handing a message with the news to Molotov, he asked how soon he could get the Soviet leader's views. The Foreign Minister picked up the internal Kremlin telephone, and, after stuttering that he hoped he was not disturbing the Georgian, relayed the information. 'Marshal Stalin is satisfied with this decision,' Molotov told the ambassador. 'He considers Eisenhower a general of experience, particularly in directing large forces and amphibious operations.' To reassure Moscow of Western strategy after Teheran, Roosevelt sent messages about the cancellation of the landing in Burma and to say that he and Churchill had decided to give the highest priority to the bombing offensive against Germany – a five-day aerial attack on Hamburg killed 42,000 people and set the city alight.

On the 1,300-mile flight from Teheran to Cairo, the Prime Minister had sat with his head in his hands, his cigar out, seemingly lost in thought, too weary to read. Though clearly exhausted, he kept insisting that he must go to Italy to see General Alexander. Moran told him this would be madness. 'You don't understand,' Churchill stormed. 'You know nothing about these things. . . . We've got to do something with these bloody Russians.'[6]

In Cairo, he had a bad attack of diarrhoea as well as a head cold. After taking his frequent baths, he made no effort to dry himself, but lay on his bed wrapped in a towel. When Harold Macmillan went to see him in the evening, he was in bed – quite usual for the morning but not for 6 or 7 p.m. Lunching with Brooke at a small card table among the flower beds of the garden of the palatial British Embassy, he said he felt very flat, tired and had pains across his loins. Wearing a grey siren suit and a vast sombrero, he swatted flies, and spoke inconclusively about the Mediterranean command, telling the CIGS he should be made a Field Marshal – the promotion was announced on 1 January. Despite this, 'Shrapnel' recalled the meal as a nightmare.

Churchill was still weary as he flew to Tunis in his converted York bomber on 11 December to meet Eisenhower. When they landed, there was no welcoming party. Getting out of the plane, he sat on his ministerial boxes, took off his hat and looked gloomily around. Cold wind blew in his hair; his face shone with sweat. His plane had landed at the wrong aerodrome. Getting into Eisenhower's car after finding the right airfield, he told the general: 'I am afraid I shall have to stay with you longer than I had planned. I am completely at the end of my tether.' Arriving at the American's headquarters, he collapsed into the first chair he reached.

Churchill moved into a villa outside Tunis called the White House, with large rooms and terraces. Unable to sleep on the first night, he went to his doctor's room, swathed in a dressing gown. 'I've got a pain in my throat, here,' he said, putting his hand below his collarbone. 'It's pretty bad.' In the morning, the pain had gone but he had a temperature of 101. Moran cabled to Cairo for nurses and a pathologist. When they arrived, the patient's temperature had dropped to 99. 'What have you been up to?' he said to the doctor. 'I'm not ill, and anyway what's wrong with me?'

An X-ray showed a considerable opaque area at the base of the left lung. 'Do you mean I've got pneumonia again?' Churchill asked impatiently. Indeed, he had. His temperature and pulse rose, and the doctor prescribed an antibiotic sulphonamide. The patient then complained that his heart 'feels to be bumping all over the place'. Moran's account mentions only prescribing pills known as M&B from their manufacturer's name, in which he had great faith. But the head of a British Quaker Ambulance Unit later recounted that his team had treated the Prime Minister with penicillin flown out from an experimental laboratory in Oxford. When the question of where the needle should be inserted came up, according to this colonel, Churchill replied that he had 'an almost infinite expanse of arse'. If this is correct, it would have made the British leader a guinea pig in the use of penicillin on humans.

Through it all, the patient insisted on working, even when his temperature rose again to 101, writing a long message to the War Cabinet on command issues. Sitting by his bed, Sarah read *Pride and Prejudice* to him. At one point, he told her, 'Don't worry; it doesn't matter if I die now, the plans for victory have been laid, and it is only a matter of time.' Randolph and Clementine flew in. 'He's very glad I've come, but in five minutes he will forget I'm here,' she told Moran.

'Am stranded amid the ruins of Carthage,' Churchill cabled Roosevelt. 'With fever which has ripened into pneumonia . . . I do not pretend I am enjoying myself.' That day, Macmillan recorded in his diary that Churchill had a heart attack. Moran told the minister he had thought the British leader was going to die. Three days later, Churchill's temperature returned to normal, making him more difficult to handle; at one point, Moran told his patient not to shout at him, and walked out of the room. As he recovered, the British leader fired off messages to London and bombarded Macmillan at his office in Algiers with telephone calls, sometimes getting so excited that the minister thought he was going to have an apoplectic fit.

On Christmas Day, he presided from his bed over a conference of Mediterranean commanders, including Eisenhower, who flew out afterwards. Wearing his quilted blue-and-gold dragon dressing gown, he then left his room for the first time since falling ill, and lunched with

Clementine, Sarah, Randolph, Macmillan and six generals. Soup, turkey, plum pudding and champagne were served. That evening, he ate in his room, but came down afterwards to join a buffet supper for Coldstream Guards at the villa. He was, Macmillan noted, 'in capital form'.

As he recuperated, Churchill's mind focused on the blocked Italian front. He fixed on an amphibious operation as the way forward. On Boxing Day, he sent a message to the British Chiefs of Staff mooting the idea of putting off the landing in northern France until 6 June – the first time this date was mentioned. He then cabled Roosevelt: 'Having kept these fifty six L.S.T.s [landing craft] in the Mediterranean so long, it would seem irrational to remove them for the very week when they can render decisive service. What, also, could be more dangerous than to let the Italian battle stagnate and fester on for another three months? We cannot afford to go forward leaving a vast half-finished job behind us. If this opportunity is not grasped we must expect the ruin of the Mediterranean campaign of 1944.'[7]

Waiting for the response from the White House, Churchill flew with Clementine and Moran to Marrakech where he received the welcome news that the Royal Navy had sunk the German battlecruiser *Scharnhorst*, off Norway. He sent Stalin a message about the victory and saying his health was better. 'I shake your hand firmly,' the Soviet leader replied.

The British Chiefs of Staff thought Washington would veto the new Italian landing, and Churchill recalled 'the dull, dead-weight resistance, taking no account of timing and proportion that I had encountered about all Mediterranean projects.' However, on 28 December, the President agreed, while insisting that the schedule set for the landing in northern France must be adhered to. As so often, Roosevelt was seeking to have his cake and eat it. But Churchill eagerly grasped this as a sign of renewed Anglo-American partnership. 'I thank God for this fine decision, which engages us once again in whole hearted unity upon a great enterprise,' he replied. The Italian operation was given the name of Anzio.

Still extremely weak, he lay in bed for eighteen hours a day, and could not summon up the strength to use a painting kit flown out for him. With his old friends Beaverbrook and the Duff Coopers, plus Moran's son, who had all joined the party, he was driven on picnics in the Atlas Mountains – at one, local children picked up the scraps of food the visitors left behind. On another occasion, when Churchill could not manage to climb up a steep, rocky path, Diana Cooper folded the picnic tablecloth into a rope, and put it round his stomach. A detective and Moran's son pulled him up from the front while the doctor and Duff Cooper pushed him from behind. Another member of the party carried his cigar.[8]

He invited de Gaulle to spend the night at the villa; the reply was that the general would only sleep in an official French residence. Still, the Frenchman came to lunch. Duff Cooper noted in his diary that he was stiff and unhelpful, but thawed after two hours of conversation. De Gaulle spoke English while Churchill used French. 'Now that the General speaks English so well he understands my French perfectly,' remarked the Prime Minister.[9]

Churchill was also visited by the Czechoslovak leader, Eduard Beneš, who was on his way back to London from Moscow. Talks with Stalin had convinced him that the Soviets would work with the London Poles if 'irreconcilable reactionaries' were purged from the administration in exile. The Kremlin no longer wanted to extend Bolshevism, and would conclude treaties that respected governments in the region, he believed. According to Beneš, Churchill was enthusiastic, saying that, when he got to London, he should contact Eden and, jointly, they should urge the London Poles to accept the offer from Moscow.

There was a somewhat testy exchange with Roosevelt about giving Italian ships to the Soviet Union, ending with agreement that Moscow should get a battleship, a cruiser, eight destroyers, four submarines and 40,000 tons of merchant shipping. More seriously, the timing of Overlord raised its head once again. Eisenhower came to Marrakech for talks and a dinner, at which he was in a very bad temper because his chauffeur and mistress, Kay Summersby, was not invited. (Roosevelt's son, Franklin Jr, had developed a fancy for the driver, but the President's intuition told him where her affections lay after seeing her with the general.) Churchill sent a cable to the White House, invoking military opinion to say that the full moon at the beginning of June looked like marking the earliest practical date. 'If now the June date is accepted as final I do not feel that we shall in any way have broken faith with [Stalin],' he added. 'The operation will anyhow begin in May with feints and softening bombardments, and I do not think U.J. is the kind of man to be unreasonable over forty-eight hours.' Even so, he advised that Stalin should not be told for several weeks.[10]

Roosevelt replied that his understanding was that the Soviet leader had been given a promise of Overlord in May, supported by a landing in the South of France. No decision should be made at this point to defer operations. 'I think the psychology of bringing this thing up would be very bad, in view of the fact that it is only a little over a month since the three of us agreed on the statement in Teheran,' the President added. Churchill blithely replied: 'I am very glad to see that we are in complete agreement.' Manifestly, they were not but, once again, the Prime Minister sought refuge in the pretense of accord.

On 14 January 1944, the Prime Minister began the journey home, stopping in Gibraltar and then sailing in a warship to Plymouth. He had been away for more than two months. The War Cabinet and the Chiefs of Staff 'really seemed quite glad to see me back,' he recalled in his memoirs. On his return, he told his old friend Lady Violet Bonham-Carter of his realisation at Teheran of 'what a small nation we are'. Then he made his remark about being 'the poor little English donkey' between the Russian bear and the American buffalo, but 'the only one of the three, who knew the right way home.'[11]

In Washington, domestic troubles awaited Roosevelt when he got back, including threats of major steel and railway strikes. At an off-the-record meeting with journalists, George Marshall made an unusual – and unusually heated – political intervention, swearing at the strikers and banging his fist on the desk as he warned that the stoppages might endanger hundreds of thousands of military lives. As it turned out, the effects were less drastic, particularly after Roosevelt granted the War Department power over train tracks. But Marshall found himself in the middle of a storm when his remarks were leaked in the press. Further angered by protests at the way US troops were using flame-throwers in the Pacific, he made a broadcast in which he stressed that 'our soldiers must be keenly conscious that the full strength of the nation is behind them'.[12]

Roosevelt passed on his satisfaction at the Teheran summit in his Christmas Eve broadcast in which he referred to Churchill's illness, and added 'the heart felt prayers of all of us have been with this great citizen of the world'. He called Stalin 'a man who combines a tremendous, relentless determination with a stalwart good humour . . . I believe he is truly representative of the heart and soul of Russia, and I believe that we are going to get along very well with him and the Russian people – very well indeed.' In his last press conference of the year, he said that America had switched from being 'Dr New Deal to Dr Win the War'.

But domestic politics continued to intrude. A storm blew up after he vetoed a pro-business congressional tax bill, saying it would 'rob the needy to enrich the greedy'. The Senate Majority leader resigned in protest, and was then re-elected by his peers. The veto was overridden by a vote of 72 to 14. Stalin might regard the President's talk of Congress as a smokescreen, but Roosevelt knew otherwise – and had to ensure bipartisan support for his war policy.

Showing his concern not to give hostages to electoral fortune and despite his desire to foster relations with the Kremlin, he turned down a suggestion for a swap of intelligence teams with Moscow. Harriman considered this a considerable breakthrough, but Roosevelt instructed him to tell Stalin that 'for purely domestic political reasons which he will understand it is not appropriate – just now – to exchange these missions'. Harriman concluded that he feared the presence of an NKVD mission in Washington in an election year, could have been embarrassing.

Though Roosevelt was visibly tired when he got back from Teheran, his doctor, Ross McIntire, said in his end-of-year report that he had enjoyed 'one of the best years since he entered the White House'. This was a lie, particularly at the moment it was issued. His patient knew that if the truth of his condition was made known, he was likely to find himself ruled out of a fourth term. So the news was kept under wraps, with Roosevelt referring to his complaints simply as 'the grippe'. In fact he was suffering from a persistent cough and cold symptoms, and abdominal pains. His face turned sickly grey and he sweated heavily. His wife feared that he was succumbing to invalidism. White House staff found him looking tense and tired. His secretary, Grace Tully, noticed him nodding off over his mail during dictation with his mouth open and his sentences left unfinished.[13]

For Hopkins, the return from Teheran marked a momentous point in his personal life. After three years in the White House, he took up a residence with his new wife, Louise, at a small and cosy house in Georgetown – his enemies charged, falsely, that he had used his influence to be given a refrigerator for the kitchen. During a party there on 1 January 1944, the aide drooped, and went up to bed. He was suffering from influenza, but a hospital examination suggested something more serious – his weight was down to 126 pounds. After a month in a naval hospital, he was told to rest in Florida, while doctors argued about whether he should have a stomach operation.[14]

The day before he took the train south, Hopkins composed a letter to his younger son, Stephen, a marine who was taking part in a Pacific island landing. Characteristically, the aide minimised his own problems. 'It has been nothing serious but I seemed to have had more difficulty in bouncing back this time . . . Do write if you get a moment, but I presume you will be pretty busy . . . so I will not expect to hear from you. At any rate you know that I wish you the best of luck.'

The letter was never delivered. As he travelled to Florida, Hopkins received a telegram from Roosevelt telling him that Stephen had been killed in action and had been buried at sea. 'I am confident that when we get details we will all be even prouder of him than ever. I am thinking of you much. F.D.R.,' the message concluded.

Stephen Hopkins had been hit by a sniper's bullet the day before his father had written to him. Aged eighteen, he was carrying ammunition to an isolated machine-gun unit. 'Harry, this war has hit you very hard,' John Dill wrote. 'I know of no one who has done more by wise and courageous advice to advance our common cause. And who knows it? Some day it must be known. George Marshall and I have been talking today of the great part which you have played and are playing. So may this sorrow not weigh you down too much and may you soon be fit and well to rejoice your friends and continue your great work.'

Marshall suggested that Hopkins's other son, Robert, who was serving in Italy, should be temporarily removed from the thick of the fighting. 'I hope you will not send for him,' Hopkins replied. 'The last time I saw him in Tunis he said he wanted to stay until we get to Berlin.'

Churchill sent a scroll engraved with Stephen's name and a quotation from the last scene of Macbeth:

> Your son, my lord, has paid a soldier's debt:
> He only liv'd but till he was a man,
> The which no sooner had his prowess confirm'd
> In the unshrinking station where he fought,
> But like a man he died.

To Roosevelt, Churchill wrote of the man he first met in London three years earlier: 'He is an indomitable spirit. I cannot help feeling anxious about his frail body and another operation. I shall always be glad for news about him for I rate him high among the Paladins.'

Returning to Washington, Hopkins insisted on a stomach operation to determine if he had cancer. 'OK boys, open 'em up,' he said as he was wheeled into the operating theatre. 'Maybe you'll find the answer to the Fourth Term.' No cancer was found, and the surgeons repaired Hopkins's intestines as best they could. Marshall arranged for him to convalesce at an army centre in West Virginia. Critics seized on this as an example of cronyism. The complaint died the death it deserved, and Marshall wrote to Hopkins, urging him to 'be more careful, to conserve your energy and not to overdo and I am also prepared to damn you for your cigarettes, your drinks, and your late hours. Confine your excesses to gin rummy.'

Hopkins had turned down a proposal from the President to increase his annual salary from $10,000 to $15,000 because of the criticism this could bring against his master. But he now accepted a raise to $12,000. A letter from Roosevelt advised that the first thing for him to focus on was 'connect up the plumbing and put your sewage system into operating condition. The second is . . . that you have got to lead not the life of an invalid but the life of common or garden sense.' He did not want him to show his face in Washington until the middle of June at the earliest, he wrote, adding: 'Tell Louise to use the old fashioned hat-pin if you don't behave.'

On 21 January 1944 the US Fifth Army carried out the Anzio landing in Italy Churchill had conceived. Though the Germans were taken by surprise, the dilatoriness of an American army corps in advancing from the beach enabled the Wehrmacht to regroup and pour in reinforcements, pinning down the allied troops. Meanwhile, the Germans were showing their skills by holding the British in bitter fighting in rocky inland terrain around strong fortifications at Monte Cassino. Both were the kind of highly professional performances which had contributed to British caution about landing in Northern France. However, the Pacific yielded better news as planes from US carriers pummelled the Mariana Islands in preparation for a Marine attack on Saipan.

Set on pressing ahead with the relationship he believed he had with Stalin at Teheran, Roosevelt told Harriman to inform the Soviet leader that he was hopeful of finding a solution to the problem of Poland, which would be kept out of 'politics'. He thought the Kremlin should give the London government-in-exile 'a break'.[15]

Moscow agreed to a plan for shuttle-bombing of Germany by US planes from its territory. An American embassy official who was taken to see a grisly display of the corpses dug up at Katyn, designed to show that the Germans were responsible, found that 'on balance, and, despite the loopholes, the Russian case is convincing'. The Kremlin provided some intelligence information about Japan, and Stalin told the ambassador of a peace feeler from Tokyo, to which the reply had been: 'Go to the devil.'

On 14 February, Roosevelt sent a memorandum to the Secretary of State laying down that: 'Russia continues to be a major factor in achieving the defeat of Germany. We must therefore continue to support the USSR by providing the maximum amount of supplies which can be delivered to her ports. This is a matter of paramount importance.' Lend-Lease to Moscow was set to rise by 200 per cent, with planned delivery of 7,800 planes, 4,700 tanks, 170,000 vehicles and other supplies, including six million pairs of shoes. Beyond that, Molotov asked Harriman if Washington would be ready to help post-war Soviet reconstruction. With the backing of Hull and Hopkins, Roosevelt told the ambassador to open preliminary discussions about a $500-million loan at 2–3 per cent annual interest repayable over twenty-five to thirty years.

This was not simply altruistic. Harriman thought it could give Washington leverage with Moscow, and pointed out that the United States could obtain 'a competitive advantage' in the Soviet Union to provide orders for US companies at a time when domestic demand fuelled by the war effort would be tailing off – two decades earlier, he had been one of the first American businessmen to look for opportunities in the Bolshevik heartland. Just as the huge American build-up to fight the war had capped the New Deal recovery, so the Soviet Union could ensure continued peacetime prosperity for the USA. 'It will certainly be of enormous value in cushioning the shock from war to peace if we are prepared to put into production Russian orders immediately on the cessation of hostilities,' Harriman wrote. A note from Hull in the spring named Dupont, General Electric, Westinghouse, the Radio Corporation of America and the Standard Alcohol Company as among firms which were in talks with the Russians, or were about to do so.

Moscow submitted a list of requirements totalling $1 billion. Washington drew up a draft list of supplies ranging from metals and chemicals to live animals, tractors, office machinery, plumbing equipment and light fittings. But the proposal ran into problems over the extension of Lend-Lease after the end of the war, while the Treasury objected to making a loan at a lower rate of interest than the federal government paid to raise money. The new Soviet ambassador in Washington, Gromyko, complained that getting what Moscow wanted out of the Americans was like pulling teeth.

While some of his subordinates had reservations about the relationship Roosevelt was seeking with Moscow, a more generally held view was that the most likely coming conflict was between Britain and the Soviet Union. 'It would seem in the highest degree unlikely that Britain or Russia, or Russia alone, would be aligned against the United States,' Admiral Leahy wrote to Hull. So, 'it is apparent that any future world conflict in the foreseeable future will find Britain and Russia in opposite camps.' The USSR would be the stronger of the two, Leahy went on. America might be able to defend Britain, but could not, under existing conditions, defeat Russia. 'In other words, we would find ourselves engaged in a war which we could not win even though the United States would be in no danger of defeat and occupation.' So the utmost efforts should be made to get Moscow and London to cooperate. That meant, Leahy concluded, Washington should avoid making any agreements with Britain without consulting the USSR since this 'might well result in starting a train of events that would lead eventually [to] the situation we most wish to avoid.'

Churchill had drawn comfort from Roosevelt's agreement to the Anzio landing, even if it turned out to be far from the quick success he had envisaged, but a series of Anglo-American differences surfaced on other issues.

The Prime Minister invoked difficulties in Italy to modify his support for the landing in the South of France on the grounds that it would draw off troops. He told Marshall the new Italian campaign had sucked in eight more German divisions, so 'there has been cause for rejoicing as well as disappointment'. If more troops were allocated to France, they should go to the west of the country where they would be closer to the Normandy landings, he wrote to Hopkins. To which the reply was simple: 'It would be a great mistake to change strategy now.'[16]

Then there was the question of whether the Free French should be involved in the Normandy landings. 'It is very difficult to cut the French out of the liberation of France,' Churchill wrote to the President ten days before the operation. Roosevelt replied that he hoped de Gaulle would help, but 'without being imposed by us on the French people as their Government'. Nor did Roosevelt agree with London's argument that bombing of railway targets in France should be modified because collateral damage to civilians would sow 'a legacy of hate' and turn the population against Overlord.

There was also a tussle over the Italian government. Churchill defended King Victor Emmanuel and Marshal Badoglio while Roosevelt wanted new men, whom he eventually got with the abdication of the monarch and the entry of new ministers, including the Communist Palmiero Togliatti. Further east, Churchill warned the President against sending a military mission to the pan-Serb Chetnik resistance in Yugoslavia since the British had decided to back Tito. (Randolph Churchill had parachuted in to meet the Communist leader and was appointed to head the British military mission to Croatia – the plane flying him there crashed, killing ten of the nineteen people on board and injuring him.)

There was, in addition, an Anglo-American difference over the future occupation of Germany, where each country wanted a zone in the north. Detailed discussions on the issue were held in the European Advisory Commission (EAC) set up after the Foreign Ministers met in Moscow. The Russians backed a British plan which left Berlin in the Soviet area. Though the city was to come under an Allied Control Commission, no provisions were made to guarantee access for the West.

Eden viewed the London-based commission as a key element in his country's post-war influence and a forerunner to a regional council for the continent. But Washington wanted to limit its authority, seeing it as detracting from Roosevelt's global body. Hull found British ideas about the EAC 'frankly disturbing', insisting that it should restrict itself to drafting surrender terms for Germany and working on the control mechanism for defeated enemy countries.

The divergence was so great that Ambassador Winant told the State Department it should be concealed from the Russians. The Americans dragged their feet, taking more than six months even to comment on a British draft of the surrender terms, and ensuring that the EAC never lived up to Eden's hopes. Halifax attributed the American attitude to a desire to retain the centre of war planning in Washington.

Reflecting his intention of bringing US troops back from Europe as soon as possible after the end of hostilities, Roosevelt told Churchill he was 'absolutely unwilling to police France and possibly Italy and the Balkans as well. After all, France is your baby and will take a lot of nursing in order to bring it to the point of walking alone.'

It was a line Roosevelt would repeat, speaking of West European countries as Britain's post-war 'children'. He greatly overrated London's ability to fulfil such a role, but he was adamant. 'I do not want the United States to have the postwar burden of reconstituting France, Italy and the Balkans,' he wrote. 'This is not our natural task at a distance of 3,500 miles or more. It is definitely a British task in which the British are far more vitally interested than we are.' That did not denote a return to isolationism, but it was a major threat to Churchill's wish to keep an American presence in Europe to balance Soviet power – in May, he spoke to Eden of his worry about the 'Communisation of the Balkans and perhaps of Italy'.

Just as he had attributed Stalin's toughening during the talks in Moscow to forces operating behind the scenes in the Kremlin, so Churchill now developed the notion that negative signals from the White House were the doing of Roosevelt's advisers. 'I cannot believe that any of these telegrams come from the President,' he told Eden at one point. 'They are merely put before him when he is fatigued and pushed upon us by those who are pulling him about.' As for the attitude Britain should adopt, he added that 'all this frantic dancing to the American tune is silly. They are only about their own affairs and the more immobile we remain the better.'

He had fresh cause for disappointment when Roosevelt turned down his proposal that the two of them spend Easter together in Bermuda. Instead, the President suggested a meeting of the Chiefs of Staff. That was not what Churchill had in mind. A meeting of the Chiefs would not be worth holding 'without your being there', he wrote. Apart from the desire not to risk arousing Stalin's suspicions of an Anglo-American cabal, the President had a very good reason for not wanting to travel – his health.

On 27 March, at the urging of the Roosevelt family, the naval physician Ross McIntire had approached Dr Howard G. Bruenn, a heart specialist, and asked him to examine the President. Bruenn was to make his conclusions known only to McIntire. As Roosevelt prepared to leave the White House for the hospital, his doctor asked him how he was. 'I feel like hell,' was the reply.[17]

He was suffering from an accumulation of physical ailments, and what is known as 'post-polio syndrome' which affects some survivors after two or three decades of living with their condition, bringing together muscular atrophy and traumatic stress disorder as the whole physical system starts to fall apart. Bruenn found hypertension, hypertensive heart disease, congestive heart failure and chronic bronchitis. Roosevelt's blood pressure was 186/108. He had anaemia and signs of long-standing pulmonary disease, breathing trouble and could not lie flat without discomfort. His heart disease and high blood pressure 'made his lifespan questionable' the doctor added.*

Bruenn recommended that he should take to his bed for one or two weeks, reduce appointments, and follow a special diet. McIntire rejected this because of the demands on the President, and agreed only to some rest and cough syrup with codeine. Roosevelt's bright, attractive daughter, Anna, gave up her job with a newspaper in Seattle to move into the White House to tend to her father.

McIntire kept the state of the President's health secret, and did not tell the patient how ill he was. Nor did Roosevelt appear to want to know – he never questioned Bruenn about the frequency of his visits or asked why he was being given digitalis treatment or furnished with a special bed with a raised head to ease breathing.

The simultaneous illnesses of Roosevelt and Hopkins meant that two of the three men who guided the American war effort were out of commission, while the Prime Minister across the Atlantic was recovering from the most serious illness of his life. Though he began to drink more heavily at dinners in the Kremlin, only Stalin was in reasonable physical shape as the Red Army pushed to the border with Estonia, destroyed Nazi forces on the Dnieper River, advanced into Romania and lifted the siege of Leningrad after 900 days and the death of a million inhabitants. In the spring, Soviet forces moved into the Crimea, retaking Odessa and Sevastopol. That signalled the end of Hitler's dream of obtaining huge supplies of food and raw material, as well as an endless stream of slave labour, by extending German frontiers in the east as America had done in

---

* Post-polio syndrome was not generally recognised in Roosevelt's day. His exercise regime was likely to have made matters worse by exacerbating atrophy. The phenomenon is examined in Marc Shell, *Polio and its Aftermath* (Cambridge: Harvard University Press, 2005, pp. 206–8.)

its west. The Soviet advance also made the question of the post-war settlement in eastern Europe even more pressing, while the emergence of anti-government groups in Italy and a looming three-sided conflict in Greece involving Communists, Royalists and another resistance group showed just how tough the post-war situation threatened to be.

Poland loomed as the trickiest of these situations. At the end of January, Churchill met the London Poles to tell them, 'The British Government takes the view that Poland must be strong, independent and free', before quickly adding, in-line with the discussion in Teheran, 'from the Curzon Line to the Oder.' He warned Stalin against interfering in the future Warsaw government. 'I feel like telling the Russians that personally I fight tyranny whatever uniform it wears or slogans it utters,' Churchill remarked in March. This attitude worried Roosevelt, who thought the Kremlin might suspect a bid by Britain to install a government which 'rightly or wrongly they regard as containing elements irrevocably hostile to the Soviet Union'.[18]

Stalin was obdurate. When Clark Kerr saw him in early February bearing tobacco and a pipe as presents, he had to listen to two hours of denunciation of the government-in-exile and a demand for the removal of three of its leading members. In a further discussion, Stalin sniggered at the London Poles in what the envoy described as 'a dreary and exasperating conversation'. The Soviet Embassy in London briefed newspapers with anti-Polish information. When Churchill told the Commons that territorial settlements must await the end of the war, Stalin accused him of reneging on the Teheran agreement, and of 'renouncing the liberative character of war of the Soviet Union against German aggression'. On April Fool's Day, he sent a lengthy cable to Downing Street saying that earlier messages from London and a statement by the ambassador 'bristle with threats against the Soviet Union'. Accusing Churchill of backsliding on the Curzon Line, he concluded: 'I fear that the method of intimidation and defamation, if continued, will not benefit our co-operation.' Clark Kerr raised the possibility of being recalled to show London's displeasure, but Churchill backed off from further confrontation.

With Poland put on the shelf for the time being, Britain and the Soviet Union moved towards a de facto accord that Britain would control events in Greece, where Churchill was intent on blocking the Communist resistance movement, while the Soviet Union would have a free hand in Romania, which Stalin saw as part of his country's *cordon sanitaire*. The dictator would have liked a formal agreement on this, but the British, knowing the inevitable American reaction to territorial agreements, steered clear of any such thing.

Starting to feel better, Roosevelt decided to rest on the South Carolina estate of his friend, the financier Bernard Baruch. He told reporters he had thought of going to Guantánamo Bay, but decided against it because 'Cuba is absolutely lousy with anarchists, murderers, et cetera, and a lot of prevaricators.' The stay at Baruch's estate was meant to last for two weeks but stretched to twice that length. Roosevelt went fishing and cruising. He cut his smoking from twenty or thirty cigarettes a day to five or six, limited his cocktails to one-and-a-half a night, and adopted a low-fat, 1,800 calorie diet. He was cheered by the presence of his mistress, Lucy Rutherfurd. But he suffered gall-bladder trouble, and, on a visit, Eleanor found that he had no pep. He did no work on his stamps, nor did he read the detective novels he took with him.[19]

Still, when he got back to Washington his face had a better colour and he looked less weary. In a letter to Hopkins, he said he planned to take life more easily, spending three days a week in the capital, moving for the rest of the time between Hyde Park, Shangri La and sailing on the *Potomac*. 'I had a really grand time at Bernie's – slept twelve hours out of twenty four, sat in the sun, never lost my temper and decided to let the world go hang,' he added. 'The interesting thing is the world didn't hang.' Still, Baruch advised White House staff to conduct important business in the morning and it was noticed that, in Cabinet, the President was flippant and ill-informed.

In mid-May, Allied troops advancing overland in Italy finally linked up with the force at Anzio, and thus could start the drive on Rome. The Italian fighting meant there were insufficient forces to mount the landing in the South of France as planned. On 14 May, at Roosevelt's suggestion, the Western leaders sent Stalin a message telling him this. The reply was emollient: 'You can best decide how and in what way to allocate your forces. The important thing, of course, is to ensure complete success for "Overlord".'

When Harriman visited him in the White House on 17 May, the President was bubbling over with messages for Stalin. But with less than a month to go to Overlord, Churchill was still worried. Speaking to Harriman as he travelled through London, he noted that 'if Overlord failed, the United States would have lost a battle, but for the British it would mean the end of their military capability.'[20] Taking John McCloy from the US War Department to the bombed-out House of Commons, he recalled how many of his contemporaries had died in the 'hecatombs of World War One'. Writing to Stalin after visiting Eisenhower's headquarters, the Prime Minister noted 'the difficulties of getting proper weather conditions'. Speaking to Brooke, he observed that while he 'could still sleep well, eat well and especially drink well,' he did not jump out of bed as he used to do. As for Roosevelt, Churchill added that the President was 'no longer the man he had been'.

16

★ ★ ★

Triumph and Tragedy

LONDON, WASHINGTON, NORMANDY, PARIS, WARSAW
JUNE–SEPTEMBER 1944

'A source of joy to us all'

STALIN

AT 4 A.M. ON 6 JUNE, Eisenhower said, 'OK. Let's go' to launch the great
military operation across the Channel, involving 5,000 ships and 600,000
men. Having delayed the landing by twenty-four hours because of the
weather, the Supreme Commander scribbled a note to himself about
what to say were D-Day to fail. 'If any blame or fault attaches to the
attempt it is mine alone,' concluded the general, who was smoking
heavily and suffered from headaches, high blood pressure, insomnia and
eye trouble.[1]

The night before Overlord was finally launched, Churchill dined alone
with his wife. They went to his Map Room. 'Do you realise,' he said to her,
'that by the time you wake up in the morning, twenty thousand men may
have been killed?' As for Brooke, he feared it might be 'the most ghastly
disaster of the war'.

Marshall, who was in England, rang the White House at 3 a.m.
Washington time. Eleanor woke the President. He put on an old grey
sweater, sat up in bed and stayed on the telephone for the next six hours.

'How I wish I could be with you to see our war machine in operation,'
he cabled Churchill, to whom he sent a present of two electric typewriters
to mark the occasion. That night, he broadcast to the nation in the form
of a prayer beseeching God for victory and 'a peace that will let all men live

in freedom, reaping the just rewards of their honest toil'. It was just two years since he had promised Molotov a second front.

Stalin hailed 'a source of joy to us all and of hope for further success'. He inscribed photographs of himself in uniform for the Western leaders, telling them the offensive he had pledged at Teheran would start in mid-June on the Byelorussian Front into Poland. To which Churchill responded with a series of messages noting that the 'Teheran design' was being implemented with coordinated attacks from west and east, and adding that Washington and London would despatch a convoy of thirty ships with supplies to Russia in mid-August. 'I hope you will observe that we have never asked you a single question because of our full confidence in you, your nation and your armies,' he wrote in a tart reference to Stalin's questioning of his commitment to Overlord.

By the end of 6 June, 155,000 Allied troops had landed. Among them was the President's one-time isolationist cousin Theodore Roosevelt Jr, who had joined the army and fought with distinction in Italy. He was the oldest man on the beaches, supporting himself with a cane.[2]

Four days later, Montgomery reported that it was safe for Churchill to cross to France for an inspection visit, accompanied by Marshall, Brooke and King. The peppery British general greeted the party as it scrambled from a landing craft in brilliant weather. During lunch in a tent outside Montgomery's headquarters, three miles behind the front, Churchill asked if the Allied line was continuous. No, Montgomery replied. So what was to stop a German armoured column breaking up their meal? Churchill enquired. Later in the day, when the visitors went further forward, two German soldiers in hiding chose to give themselves up rather than shooting at them.[3]

The advance through the hedgerows of Normandy was more difficult than expected, but Stalin hailed the 'brilliant success' of taking Caen and Cherbourg, where Theodore Roosevelt Junior became Military Governor before dying in his sleep from a heart attack at the age of fifty-seven. For their part, the Western Allies welcomed the 'glorious victory' of the Soviet army at Minsk and in the Baltics. But Hitler hit back by launching the first flying bombs on London, leading to a British discussion of whether to unleash poison gas attacks on German cities – the Chiefs of Staff turned down the idea. Churchill now considered it time to broach a matter he knew was likely to raise hackles in Washington.

He wanted an agreement with Stalin to safeguard British interests in the eastern Mediterranean, and to stop the Communists taking over in Greece. Eden went to see the ambassador in London with a proposal that 'the Soviet Union should take the lead in Roumania [sic] and the British should do the same in Greece'.[4]

The proposal was very much in line with Stalin's thinking. He wanted a free hand in Romania, on Russia's south-western frontier, and had little interest in Greece. He recognised the British-backed Greek government-in-exile in Cairo, and appears to have actively discouraged the Greek Communists from vying for power.

Stalin asked Churchill to solicit Roosevelt's views. Writing to the President at the end of May, the British leader presented his initiative as the way to deal with 'disquieting signs of a possible divergence between ourselves and the Russians in regard to the Balkan countries and in particular towards Greece'. Disingenuously, he added that there was no intention of carving the region into zones of influence. The Big Three powers would retain their rights and responsibilities towards the countries involved.

At the State Department, Hull said the Allies should stick to declarations of broad principles. Roosevelt told Churchill that, far from calming differences, the proposal would mean 'the division of the Balkan region into spheres of influence'. Instead, there should be 'consultative machinery to dispel misunderstandings and restrain the tendency toward the development of exclusive spheres'.

The Prime Minister replied immediately that he was 'much concerned' by this. Consultations would paralyse action and be out-run by events. The Red Army was about to invade Romania where the Americans and British had no troops. So Stalin would be able to do as he wished. On the other hand, Britain had put itself in a position from which it could supervise the evolution of Greece, whose king and government were under its protection. 'Why is all this effective direction to be broken up into a committee of mediocre officials?' Churchill asked. 'Why can you and I not keep this in our own hands?'

He proposed a three-month trial of the Romania-Greece arrangement, after which it would be reviewed by the Allies. Roosevelt agreed, though he insisted that 'we must be careful to make it clear that we are not establishing any postwar spheres of influence'.

Churchill cabled Stalin proposing the trial which would be 'only a working arrangement to avoid as much as possible the awful business of triangular telegrams which paralyses action.' In reply, the dictator noted that Washington 'has certain doubts about the matter', but the deal was done. The division of Europe was taking shape, nearly a year before the Yalta Conference. Four years later, George Orwell wrote to his publisher that he got the idea of the global blocs in *1984* from the Teheran summit and what followed.[5]

Having been excluded from Torch eighteen months earlier, de Gaulle was told about the landing in his country only two days before D-Day. He reacted calmly enough to begin with. Then Eisenhower said that, on Washington's instruction, a proclamation would be dropped on France as troops landed, naming him as the new authority and making no mention of the Free French, the Resistance or de Gaulle.[6]

That sent the Frenchman into a rage. He vetoed the use of 200 Free French agents to guide Allied troops. When he was not given first place among leaders of governments-in-exile, he refused to broadcast to the French people. It was the turn of Churchill and Marshall to explode.

Trying to smooth over the row in the hours before the landing, the Free French ambassador Pierre Viénot asked to see Eden. The Foreign Secretary was at Churchill's bedside; some accounts say the Prime Minister had drunk more than usual and had retired early – for him. At 1 a.m., Viénot went to Downing Street to plead that there had been a misunderstanding. From under the covers, Churchill harangued him about de Gaulle's 'treachery in battle'. Viénot responded that he would not be talked to in that way, and walked out. At 3 a.m., an hour before Eisenhower's order to launch Overlord, Churchill telephoned an aide and ordered that the Free French chief should be flown to Algiers 'in chains if necessary'. The aide ignored the instruction. When Viénot reported to him, de Gaulle evidently considered he had gone far enough, agreeing both to broadcast and to allow the liaison agents to work with Allied troops. A week later, three days short of the fourth anniversary of his flight to London from his collapsing country, he returned home to be received in triumph in the old Norman town of Bayeux.

Even so, when he visited Washington from the 6th to the 8th of July, the Frenchman was received as a military leader, not a head of government.

Roosevelt greeted him by saying in French, '*Si content de vous voir*'; but the visit was 'devoid of trust on both sides', as the Free French representative in New York, Raoul Aglion, put it. The two men spoke at, rather than to, each other. Roosevelt refused to accord France the great power status the general saw as hers by right. Nor could de Gaulle accept the Four Policeman order propagated by the President which excluded France. He told Aglion America was 'already trying to rule the world' and that 'Britain will always accede to its wishes'.

The presence at the White House talks of Leahy, who had been the US ambassador to the Pétain regime, was a reminder to de Gaulle of how Roosevelt had worked with his enemies. Things were not improved when, as tea was being served, his host turned to Leahy to say: 'For you, Admiral, Vichy [water] would be more appropriate.' After the visit, Eleanor forbade their grandson from playing with a large model submarine de Gaulle had presented as a gift on the grounds that it came from a head of state. Roosevelt chipped in to say it was only from 'the President of some French committee or other'.

However, the American leader relaxed his hostility to the extent of agreeing that the French Committee in London could be granted 'temporary de facto authority for the civil administration of France', on two conditions – that Eisenhower should have complete power to do what he felt necessary for military operations and that the French should be allowed a free choice as to their future government. Eisenhower took a less circumspect line. He saw de Gaulle's value in rallying popular support, and preventing disturbances that might hamper military efforts. When Allied troops entered Paris on 24–25 August, Eisenhower let French forces be the first into the capital – on the 26th de Gaulle led a triumphant procession down the Champs-Elysées. After Stalin said he was ready to acknowledge de Gaulle as ruler of his country, and under pressure from Marshall and Eisenhower, Roosevelt caved in, though he took his time approving a draft recognising the new regime in Paris. Cadogan blamed the foot-dragging on the 'spiteful old great-aunt' Leahy. Churchill took up an invitation to visit Paris, and had an emotional stay, speaking at length in his idiosyncratic French, and taking delight in the gold bath in his suite, installed for Hermann Göring.[17]

In talks with the British, de Gaulle made plain that he envisaged his country becoming an equal partner in the post-war world. Together, he said, the two nations would be able to stop anything happening they did not accept. The US and the USSR would be too taken up by their rivalry to counter them. Other smaller countries would be supportive. 'Eventually, England and France will create peace together,' he concluded. Churchill demurred – he saw the Anglo-American alliance as the major force in the post-war world. As soon as the Prime Minister had left, de Gaulle arranged a trip to Moscow.

As the Allied armies advanced, Churchill visited Italy, meeting the generals and the Pope, bathing at Capri and getting sunburned. He met the Italian Communist leader Palmiero Togliatti who had been told by Stalin to support the government. He also spent a day with Tito, who looked uncomfortable in a splendid blue-and-gold uniform.[8]

Much as he relished the trip, this was a frustrating time for the Prime Minister which brought out the fraying of his relationship with Roosevelt. From Italy, he wrote to his wife, reflecting his frustration at the role his country was playing in the alliance. Two-thirds of British forces are being mis-employed for American convenience, he charged. He told Roosevelt he deplored the way in which the Italian campaign was being 'bled white' by the transfer of US troops for the Anvil landing in South of France. 'Let us resolve not to wreck one great campaign for the sake of winning the other,' he added. He sought to enlist Hopkins, with no success – the aide, who had returned to Washington to work two or three hours a day, noted to Dill that 'the Prime Minister sounds a little jittery'. Roosevelt replied that Eisenhower wanted Anvil by the end of August, so it should be launched as soon as possible.[9]

'We are deeply grieved by your message,' Churchill wrote back in one of the more strongly worded messages he had begun to send to Washington. Not enough resources were available to make Anvil a success, he warned. He recalled a remark by Eisenhower after Teheran about the importance of 'continuing the maximum possible operations in an established theatre', and added a message from Stalin calling the Italian offensive 'worthy of the greatest attention and praise'. 'If you still press upon us the directive of your Chiefs of Staff to withdraw so many of your forces from the Italian campaign and leave all our hopes there dashed to the ground, His Majesty's Government, on the advice of their [sic] Chiefs of Staff, must enter a solemn protest,' he concluded. 'It is with the greatest sorrow that I write to you in this sense.'[10]

Roosevelt responded in friendly language, but gave no ground. He insisted on Anvil going ahead as soon as possible, and hoped that the reduced forces in Italy would be able to achieve 'great things'. He rejected any idea of a thrust into the Balkans through the mountain gap by the city of Ljubljana in Slovenia which Churchill reasoned could lead the Allies to Vienna. 'I honestly believe that God will be with us as he has in Overlord and in Italy and in North Africa,' Roosevelt concluded. 'I always think of my early geometry: "A straight line is the shortest distance between two points."'

There was nothing Churchill could do. For the sake of Allied solidarity, he had to pledge to 'make a success of anything that is undertaken'. When the landing in the South of France, renamed Dragoon, was launched on 15 August and proved successful, he cabled the White House that he wished it 'success from my heart'. But, to Moran, he called it 'sheer folly'. 'Good God, can't you see that the Russians are spreading across Europe like a tide? . . . They have invaded Poland, and there is nothing to stop them marching into Turkey and Greece.'

To try to restore harmony, he sought a fresh meeting with Roosevelt. 'I am sure that if we could have met, as I so frequently proposed, we should have reached a happy agreement,' he wrote. 'That we must meet soon is certain.' It would be better if Stalin joined in. If not, the two of them must confer. Hopkins warned Roosevelt that a bilateral summit might be construed as having 'left Russia out in the cold'. Roosevelt wrote to Stalin proposing a tripartite meeting in the north of Scotland. But the dictator said he could not leave his command – 'my colleagues consider it absolutely impossible'.

In a message to Churchill at the beginning of June, Roosevelt had noted that 'over here new political situations crop up every day but, so far, by constant attention, I am keeping my head above water.' That month, Congress passed a key plank in completing the reforming agenda of the New Deal, the G.I. Bill of Rights, which made subsidised university education available to veterans – by the late 1940s, half the male college students in the United States were on the programme. It had been Roosevelt's idea, proof that, amid his machinations, his spirit was firmly on the side of progress which could serve the country's needs and interests. But he failed to get through a measure to allow all servicemen to vote; Southern Democrats saw that it would open the floodgates to the end of

Jim Crow restrictions on black enfranchisement, and Republicans knew that most of those at war would vote for Roosevelt.[11]

On 20 July, plotters tried to kill Hitler with a bomb and General Kuniaki Koiso, a harsh military man known as the 'Tiger of Korea', was appointed Prime Minister of Japan. That same day, Roosevelt was nominated by the Democratic Convention to run for a fourth term. Senator Harry Truman of Missouri became the vice-presidential candidate. Given the state of Roosevelt's health, it was one of the most important nominations ever made for the number two post but it was the result of party feuding and alliances rather than a consideration of who might succeed to the White House.

During the convention, Roosevelt set off by train on a lengthy journey to meet military chiefs running the war in the Far East, notably Douglas MacArthur. Unusually, he left Marshall behind, which was not to the liking of the Chief of Staff who sent his own emissary to see the Pacific commander. On the journey, the President collapsed on the floor of his railway carriage with angina.

MacArthur had intimated that he could be available to be drafted as the Republican candidate. When a Nebraska congressman wrote to him denouncing the 'monarchy' of left-wingers and New Dealers in Washington, the general replied that this was 'sobering and calculated to arouse the thoughtful consideration of every true patriot'. Roosevelt knew he had nothing to fear from MacArthur as a politician, and the general's ambitions soon fizzled out. On top of which, MacArthur wanted presidential backing to fulfill his pledge to return to the Philippines rather than following the strategy advocated by Admirals King and Chester Nimitz, the navy Commander in the Pacific, who wished to aim straight for Japan after US forces had sunk three Japanese aircraft carriers and destroyed 400 of their planes in the Battle of the Philippine Sea. Roosevelt sided with MacArthur.

Getting back to the East Coast, the President made a radio address from the deck of a destroyer floating in a flooded dry dock. With ten thousand workers assembled to hear him, he put on his heavy leg braces, which he had worn less and less frequently. Because he had lost weight, they did not fit. The deck was curved. A crisp wind blew. Roosevelt had to grasp the lectern. For the nation he had led for eleven years, it was the first intimation of the decline in his health. His voice was mushy and muffled; his delivery uncertain and rambling. His speechwriter Sam Rosenman listened with 'a sinking sensation'. Roosevelt was suffering what Dr Bruenn would call a 'substernal oppression with radiation to both shoulders'. It could have been muscle spasms or angina. An examination reported 'no unusual abnormalities' – a phrase which, given his record, meant little.

Roosevelt's election opponent was the sharp, energetic, forty-two-year-old crime-busting prosecutor and New York Governor, Thomas Dewey. A short, dapper man with a pencil moustache, he was described woundingly by a Roosevelt relative as looking like the groom on a wedding cake. It was going to be a rough campaign, in which the incumbent would have to keep the state of his health hidden from voters – and from himself – as he put himself forward as the champion of the American fighting man and the leader who could fashion a new world. Roosevelt, who had not personally disliked his previous opponents, developed a deep distaste for Dewey, privately calling him a 'son of a bitch' and saying publicly that he would not pronounce his name 'because I think I am a Christian'. The Republicans accused him of molly-coddling domestic Communists, and of having diverted a destroyer to pick up his dog, Fala, which had supposedly been left behind on an island during the West Coast trip. Roosevelt roused the country to laughter with a speech in which he said that, while he was used to malicious falsehoods about himself, he had 'a right to resent, to object to libellous statements about my dog'.

As the electoral battle moved into gear, representatives of the Big Four powers met in a Washington mansion, Dumbarton Oaks, to plan the post-war global organisation that was to keep the peace. For fear of irritating Tokyo, the Soviets refused to sit down with the Chinese, who had to wait their turn till the US and British completed their work with the Russians.[12]

Exhibiting all his diplomatic skills, Cadogan headed the British team. Gromyko led the Soviet side, displaying the toughness that was to mark his long career. Though Cordell Hull was involved from time to time, Welles's successor as Under Secretary of State, the former Lend-Lease administrator Edward Stettinius, ran American operations, drawing heavily on planning carried out since 1939 by a Russian-born official, Leo Pasvolsky, a man with an unusually large, egg-shaped head known as 'the brain that walks like a man'.

Roosevelt consented to modifications of the power of the Four Policemen by giving authority to a council in which seven other countries would sit on a non-permanent basis. He also agreed that France could take a permanent seat on the council in due course. Moscow and Washington both wanted the big powers to have a veto in matters involving their own interests. Cadogan pointed out that this would make the organisation seem like a dictatorship. When Roosevelt cabled Stalin on the matter, the reply was that unanimity of the three main allies had been implied at Teheran. Gromyko insisted Moscow's position was 'final and unalterable'. Then the Kremlin threw in a demand for all sixteen constituent USSR republics to sit in the General Assembly.

Hull asked Harriman if he thought Stalin had decided to reverse the policy of cooperation Washington believed it had obtained. The ambassador did not think so, but counselled that it could be difficult to grasp the Soviet concept of what had been agreed. Molotov had indicated to him that, if the West did not raise objections to a Soviet plan, he and Stalin saw this as compliance. 'Then, too, words have a different connotation to the Soviets than they have to us,' the envoy added. To enable the Western Allies to go to a swift session with the Chinese, it was decided that the crucial issue of the veto would be left until the Big Three met again.

The Red Army had launched its summer offensive on 22 June, the third anniversary of the start of Operation Barbarossa. In keeping with the patriotic feeling Stalin was seeking to evoke, it was named after a heroic Tsarist general, Bagration, who had fought Napoleon across Europe and perished after repulsing French charges at the Battle of Borodino in 1812. A total of 1.7 million troops were involved, with 6,000 planes, 2,715 tanks, 24,000 artillery pieces and 70,000 lorries. In the first week, more than 150,000 Germans were killed or captured. By the beginning of August, Soviet forces held a line stretching from Riga on the Baltic through Lithuania and East Prussia to the outskirts of Warsaw and then south to the Hungarian border.

Just before Bagration began, Roosevelt had several meetings with the Prime Minister of the London Poles, Stanisław Mikołajczyk, who had taken the post after the death of Sikorski in a plane accident in Gibraltar. The President said Poland must be free and independent. He opposed dividing the country along the Curzon Line in the east. He would mediate an agreement to give Silesia, East Prussia and other important areas to Warsaw. The Poles should understand that the United States and Britain had no intention of fighting Russia, but he was certain Stalin was not an imperialist. The Soviet leader did not want to annihilate Poland, and knew how important it was to the Western Allies. 'I will see to it that Poland will not be hurt in this war, and will emerge strongly independent,' he promised. 'Here is the perfect idealist,' Mikołajczyk thought. 'But his faith in Stalin is tragically misplaced.'[13]

In a message to the Kremlin, the President stressed that there was no attempt on his part 'to inject myself into the merits of the differences which exist between the Polish Government and the Soviet Government'. Mikołajczyk, he added, struck him as 'a very sincere and reasonable man whose sole desire is to do what is best for his country' and who wanted to foster cooperation between the Polish underground and the advancing Red Army. Roosevelt ended by suggesting a visit to Moscow by the Polish leader while taking care to state that he was not trying to press his views in any way.

In reply, Stalin wrote that a 'reconstruction' of the government-in-exile was vital for all Polish groups to work together. So was recognition of the Curzon Line by which Warsaw would cede large swathes of territory to Russia. To Churchill, the Soviet leader wrote that, as the Red Army moved into Poland, the Kremlin had 'seen fit to get in touch with the Polish Committee of National Liberation'. This was play-acting. The Committee had been organised under Soviet auspices at the end of 1943, and was at Stalin's beck and call. It was already setting up shop in the city of Lublin which had been taken by the Red Army. 'We have not found in Poland other forces capable of establishing a Polish administration,' Stalin told Churchill. 'The so-called underground organisations, led by the Polish Government in London, have turned out to be ephemeral and lacking in influence.' He was, however, ready to meet Mikołajczyk, even if he thought it better for him to see the National Committee first. 'This seems to me the best ever received from U.J.,' Churchill commented to Roosevelt while insisting on the 'utmost importance' of not deserting the London Poles. Eden told the Commons that London continued to recognise Mikołajczyk and his colleagues, though he wished to say no more 'since we are here concerned with relations between two of our Allies'. The Foreign Secretary believed Washington would do nothing for the Poles. Roosevelt might make 'vague and generous promises', but it would be a delusion to put faith in them, Eden forecast privately. The government-in-exile in London agreed. It accused Moscow of intending 'to impose on the Polish people an illegal administration which has nothing in common with the will of the nation'. It called on Britain to make a démarche to Stalin. Knowing that the West was not going to intervene militarily in the east, the Home Army of the London Poles was preparing to rise against the Nazis as the Red Army moved in on Warsaw.

At the end of July 1944, Mikołajczyk made a circuitous flight to Moscow. The fourty-four-year-old leader of the main peasant party was among the more moderate figures of the London government, standing apart from the die-hard anti-Communists. Known for his stubbornness, the balding, thick-set politician could expect to head the largest parliamentary group in a democratic regime. He was under several disadvantages, however. The Lublin group had already started operating on Polish territory, with Soviet backing. The NKVD was purging supporters of the London Poles in areas taken by the Red Army. Despite verbal assurances from the Americans and British, he had no way of knowing how far they were ready to go in standing up to Stalin – or how prepared the dictator would be to compromise. As the historian Norman Davies has noted, his position as leader of a peasant party would have meant that Stalin would have classed him with the kulak rural bourgeoisie he had liquidated in the Soviet Union.[14]

'Why are you here?' Molotov asked when the Polish leader called on him. The Soviets advised him to see the Lublin Committee, but Mikołajczyk insisted on meeting Stalin first. That entailed a three-day wait, during which a German threat to deport men from Warsaw sparked the Warsaw Rising on 1 August, starting a two-month battle which would ravage the city while, in the words of Norman Davies, 'the largest army in the world pretended not to be there,' despite having broadcast calls for the Poles to rise in revolt. The death toll of 30,000 resistance fighters and Germans was far outweighed by more than 200,000 civilians who perished.

The leaders of the Home Army counted on help from the Russians, but, with its supply lines highly extended and its troops exhausted, the Red Army was planning to rest and regroup before entering the city. The Poles felt they could not wait, however. They were anxious to make their mark in the capital before Soviet troops arrived, if only to establish their political claims against the Lublin group. Stalin paced his office, uncertain what to do. Could the army advance? he asked. His generals said a pause was essential. Stalin conferred with Beria and other aides. The decision was to accept the military advice. This may have been play-acting to establish an alibi against accusations that he did not want to help the Poles; but the commander at the front, the part-Polish Rokossovsky, said the rising would have only made sense if his forces had been about to take the city, and that this point had not been reached. Faced with a German counter-offensive east of the Vistula, the Soviet leader ordered the Red Army to halt on 2 August – the order was later concealed.[15]

The following day, Mikołajczyk got to see the dictator. When he asked for help for the insurgents, Stalin initially agreed, but then said he would not allow any operations beyond Red Army lines, dismissing the underground for not having fought the Germans in the past but 'skulking in the woods'. However, according to Mikołajczyk's later account, he said the Soviets expected to enter Warsaw on 6 August; Molotov had told him they were ten miles from the city.

Mikołajczyk had two meetings with the Lublin group. First, they told him there was no fighting in Warsaw; then they attacked the Home Army for acting without consulting Moscow. Mikołajczyk should resign, they said, so that they could form a government. If he returned to his homeland, he would be arrested. Still, there was a slender hope – Stalin's initial offer of help. Mikołajczyk must have communicated this to the British, because, on 5 August, the head of the military mission in Moscow asked the Soviet General Staff for information about 'the decision' to fly arms and ammunition into Warsaw. The letter was forwarded to Stalin.

On 9 August, Mikołajczyk saw Stalin again. The dictator was cordial, speaking warmly of Soviet–Polish relations. According to the account Mikołajczyk gave to Clark Kerr, the Soviet leader said he had no intention of 'communising' Poland, which should have ties with the West as well as an alliance with the USSR. As for the prime enemy, he added that Communism was 'no more fit for Germany than a saddle for a cow'. He agreed to provide the rising with 'the most rapid assistance possible', though he wondered how realistic this was given the German counter-attack. Thinking he had obtained a commitment, the Polish leader left as soon as he could for London.

Stalin wrote to Roosevelt that the meetings could be considered as the first stage in the relations between the Polish Committee and Mikołajczyk and his colleagues. He added that the London Poles had been offered four ministerial portfolios in a post-war government, including the post of Prime Minister. How accurate that was in the light of the harsh attitude taken by the Lublin Committee is open to question. But Churchill noted to Roosevelt that the mood of the message was 'more agreeable than we have sometimes met'.

The previous day, the Red Army commander, Rokossovsky, had drawn up a plan to cross the Vistula River to take Warsaw and drive on towards Berlin. This was approved by his superior, Marshal Zhukov. The Lublin Committee issued a declaration proclaiming that 'the moment has arrived for the liberation of our capital'. But Stalin hesitated. Reports from the field showed strong support for the London Poles. Their partisans were shooting members of the Lublin group. The leaders of the rising were unlikely to prove friends of Moscow while the German counter-attack showed that the Wehrmacht was not on the run.

So, instead of following the Rokossovsky–Zhukov plan, Stalin switched priority to an attack on Romania, an easier target. From Churchill's message in May, he knew that he would have no trouble with the West. An advance to the Balkans would block any lingering British plans to intervene there. On 13 August, Tass news agency issued a statement denying any contact between the Home Army and the Soviet command. 'Full responsibility for the events in Warsaw will fall exclusively on Polish émigré circles in London,' it ended.

Five days later, Stalin told Churchill that, after his second meeting with Mikołajczyk, he had ordered intensive arms drops on Warsaw. But he had concluded that 'the Warsaw Action represents a reckless and terrible adventure which is costing the population large sacrifices. This would not have been if the Soviet command had been informed before the beginning of the Warsaw action and if the Poles had maintained contact with it. In the situation which has arisen the Soviet command has come to the conclusion that it must disassociate itself from the Warsaw adventure as it cannot take either direct or indirect responsibility for the Warsaw action.'

Britain tried drops on Warsaw with planes flying from Italy, but a third of the aircraft were lost, and the RAF declined to fly more sorties. Any help would have to come from US bombers from England, flying on from Warsaw to land in Ukraine. Churchill sought to rouse Roosevelt to action with a message referring to 'an episode of profound and far-reaching gravity. If, as is almost certain, the German triumph in Warsaw is followed by a wholesale massacre no measure can be put upon the full consequences that will arise.' He proposed a joint approach to Moscow. The victory in

Normandy far exceeded any single Russian battle, he went on, so 'I'm inclined to think that they will have some respect for what we say so long as it is plain and simple. It is quite possible that Stalin would resent it but even if he did we are nations serving high causes and must give true counsels towards world peace.'

Stirred to action, the Americans pressed for landing rights for relief planes at airfields it was using in Ukraine for shuttle bombing of Germany. But Vyshinsky, the Deputy Foreign Minister, said this could not be agreed to because the rising was 'a purely adventuristic affair to which the Soviet Government could not lend its hand'. When Harriman and Clark Kerr asked to meet Molotov, they were told he was unavailable. Seeing Vyshinsky again on 15 August, they pointed out that, even if the rising had been premature, the Poles were killing Germans and that Moscow's obstructionism was bound to have a bad effect on Western opinion. But Stalin had made up the Kremlin's mind.

Harriman sent a message to Roosevelt saying: 'I am, for the first time since coming to Moscow, gravely concerned by the attitude of the Soviet Government. If [its] position . . . is correctly reflected by Vyshinsky, its refusal is based on ruthless political considerations – not on denial that resistance exists nor on operational difficulties.' He urged Roosevelt to contact Stalin to seek reconsideration, pointing out the risk to 'the belief of the American public in the chances of success of postwar cooperation and of world security organization'.

On 17 August, Harriman and Clark Kerr got to see Molotov. He was unyielding, pointing to Western newspaper criticism of the Soviet Union as the work of the London Poles. Nothing could be done to save the fighters in the streets of Warsaw from their own folly, Molotov said, American use of the airfields in Ukraine would have to stop as winter approached. Reporting to Roosevelt, Harriman depicted Molotov and his deputy as men 'bloated with power [who] expect they can force acceptance of their decisions without question on us and all countries'.

Washington instructed Harriman to ease off for fear of jeopardising military cooperation with Moscow. A major general from the US air force in Europe warned Hopkins that London was trying to manipulate the Americans, and said only 5 per cent of supplies dropped on Warsaw would reach the underground. The State Department told Harriman, 'there is a tendency on the part of the British to go considerably farther than the

President is prepared to go.' The ambassador, who was working till 6.30 a.m., did not give up. 'In our long-term relations with the Russians,' he cabled Roosevelt and Hull, 'we should impress our views on them as firmly as possible and show our displeasure whenever they take action of which we strongly disapprove.'

Roosevelt bent to the extent of agreeing to a joint message with Churchill to Stalin which said: 'We are thinking of world opinion if the anti-Nazis in Warsaw are in effect abandoned. We believe that all three of us should do the outmost to save as many of the patriots there as possible. We hope that you will drop immediate supplies and munitions to the patriot Poles in Warsaw, or will agree that our planes should do it very quickly. We hope you will approve. The time element is of extreme importance.'

Whatever the President's personal feelings, domestic politics were in play. At Teheran, he had invoked the Polish vote as a reason for not committing himself. Now, in his re-election campaign, he could see the electoral danger if he was portrayed as having done nothing to help the Warsaw rising. On 23 August he sent Churchill a message that 'we must continue to hope for agreement by the Soviet to our desire to assist the Poles in Warsaw'. What they got was a broadside from Stalin. 'Sooner or later the truth about the handful of power-seeking criminals who launched the Warsaw adventure will out,' he wrote. 'Those elements, playing on the credulity of the inhabitants of Warsaw, exposed practically unarmed people to German guns, armour and aircraft. The result is a situation in which every day is used, not by the Poles for freeing Warsaw, but by the Hitlerites, who are cruelly exterminating the civil population.'

Churchill suggested replying with a proposal that the US planes would land in Ukraine without Moscow being officially told where they had been. 'The massacre in Warsaw will undoubtedly be a very great annoyance to us when we all meet at the end of the war,' his draft to Stalin added. 'Unless you directly forbid it, therefore, we propose to send the planes.' If there was no reply, he felt they ought to proceed and see what happened.

There were limits to how far Roosevelt was ready to go. 'I do not consider it advantageous to the long-range general war prospect for me to join with you in the proposed message to U.J.,' he replied. He was not going to let the Warsaw rising imperil his relations with Stalin. Hopkins put his faith in the Red Army. 'The problem of Warsaw will be handled by the sure victories on Germany's eastern front,' he advised.

On 4 September, Churchill returned to the charge. He told Roosevelt that the War Cabinet was 'deeply disturbed at the position in Warsaw and at the far-reaching effect on future relations with Russia of Stalin's refusal of airfield facilities'. The defeat of the rising would destroy any hope of progress towards a political settlement, and fatally undermine Mikołajczyk.

The Prime Minister told his secretary he wanted to threaten 'drastic action' on supplies to the Soviet Union if Stalin did not help the rising. 'Seeing how much is in jeopardy we beg that you will again consider the big stakes involved,' he told Roosevelt in another message. In a cable to Clark Kerr, which was copied to the White House, the War Cabinet said it wanted the Kremlin to know how moved British opinion was by events in Warsaw.

'Our people cannot understand why no material help has been sent from outside to the Poles in Warsaw,' the cable went on. 'The fact that such help could not be sent on account of your Government's refusal to allow United States aircraft to land on aerodromes in Russian hands is now becoming publicly known. If on top of all this the Poles in Warsaw should now be overwhelmed by the Germans, as we are told they must be within two or three days, the shock to public opinion here will be incalculable . . . Your Government's action in preventing this help being sent seems to us at variance with the spirit of Allied cooperation to which you and we attach so much importance both for the present and for the future.'

Roosevelt was not to be moved. His response to London said US intelligence reported the 'fighting Poles' leaving Warsaw, with the Germans in full control. In fact, the rising did not end for a month; but Roosevelt's message concluded that 'the problem of relief for the Poles in Warsaw has therefore unfortunately been solved by delay and by German action and there now appears to be nothing we can do to assist them. I have long been deeply distressed by our inability to give adequate assistance to the heroic defenders of Warsaw and I hope that we may together still be able to help Poland and be among the victors in this war with the Nazis.'

In mid-September, the Allies finally went into action. Soviet planes dropped food and bombed German positions. US bombers parachuted down supplies which did fall mainly in areas controlled by the Wehrmacht. Hull told Harriman: 'From the political point of view, we feel that it is of the highest importance that there should be no hesitation on our part . . . in order to avoid the possibility of our being blamed in the event that the aid does not arrive in time.'

Though Stalin now claimed he had been misinformed about the reasons for the rising, the Red Army still did not advance as anti-Communist Polish forces in the city were reduced to a handful. The deadly inaction had done the Lublin Committee's work for it. Reporting to Washington, Harriman concluded that Stalin did not want the Poles to take credit for the liberation of Warsaw, and wished the underground leaders to be killed by Nazis or stigmatised as enemies who could be arrested when the Russians entered. 'Under these circumstances,' he added, 'it is difficult for me to see how a peaceful or acceptable solution can be found to the Polish problem.'

'I have evidence that they have misinterpreted our generous attitude as a sign of weakness, and acceptance of their policies,' the envoy reported to Roosevelt. 'Time has come when we must make clear what we expect of them as the price of our goodwill. Unless we take issue with the present policy there is every indication the Soviet Union will become a world bully wherever their interests are involved.' He advocated that Washington should be ready to stand up to the Kremlin on vital issues. In the last analysis, he thought, Stalin would back off. Churchill reflected that the world was 'full of wolves and bears'.

17

The Plan

WASHINGTON, QUEBEC
12–16 SEPTEMBER 1944

'I have not the faintest recollection of this at all!'

ROOSEVELT

HENRY MORGENTHAU, the American Treasury Secretary since 1934, was a professorial-looking, fifty-three-year-old with a domed, bald head and pince-nez who owed his position to his long acquaintance with the President. Shy, sometimes inarticulate, generally uncharismatic, and a sufferer from migraine attacks, he was referred to in private by Roosevelt as 'the Morgue'. His father had been a successful real-estate developer, but Henry Jr had preferred a quieter life running his farm close to the Hyde Park estate before being appointed to the Treasury. A prominent New York Jewish political donor commented that the President had found 'the only Jew in the world who doesn't know a thing about money'.[1]

But Morgenthau proved to be an efficient manager, and Roosevelt valued his loyalty. 'You and I will run this war together,' he told his neighbour in 1942. Given the advanced ages of Hull and Stimson, the Treasury Secretary could nurture the ambition of rising to an even higher post. He was adept at dealing with the vagaries of the Roosevelt court, and knew how to protect himself – he used a recording machine in his office to capture conversations. He also had powerful assistance in the shape of his driving number two for international affairs, the stout, abrasive, ping-pong-playing Harry Dexter White, son of Lithuanian Jewish refugees, who had changed his name from Weit and added Dexter.

White was the Morgenthau's intellectual motor, and an expert at soothing his boss's self doubts with flattery. Morgenthau said he wanted international financial policy to be 'all in one brain, and I want that brain to be Harry White's'.

Morgenthau and White achieved great success in July 1944, at the conference held in Bretton Woods, New Hampshire, which established the International Monetary Fund and the International Bank for Reconstruction and Development (later the World Bank) to encourage post-war global recovery and mould the future international financial system. Though forty nations attended, it was mainly an Anglo-American meeting. Under White's leadership the American team showed itself a better bureaucratic operator than the British under the sickly, less focused John Maynard Keynes. The United States put up a third of the $9.1 billion subscribed to the fund, and its corresponding share of the votes made it dominant, enabling it to press its agenda of convertible currencies, fixed exchange rates based on gold, and free trade. Much to White's satisfaction, a Soviet delegation took part in the talks, but Stalin decided not to join the new system or its institutions.

What Morgenthau did not know was that White was a Soviet agent, passing classified information to Moscow. He acted out of genuine admiration for the USSR and from a belief that it should be helped in the search for a better world. But, however much White was driven by idealism, or resentment at the anti-Semitism he encountered in America, there is no doubt he committed treason, even letting the Russians have the printing plates for US occupation currency in Germany.[2]

The only Jew close to Roosevelt, Morgenthau had been brought up in a secular environment, and prided himself on being 'one hundred per cent American'. But the growing evidence of the Holocaust strengthened his Jewish identity. He held the German people as a whole responsible, and, in the words of his son, became 'the avenging angel for the remnant of world Jewry'. The rise of Hitler, he decided, had been made possible by the weak behaviour of the Allies in the 1920s. Germany must not be allowed to escape maximum punishment this time.[3]

Morgenthau faced a sceptical Washington establishment. Nazi killing of Jews was still seen as part of general 'German criminality'. When first informed of the Final Solution in September 1942, Roosevelt did not believe it, telling the Supreme Court judge Felix Frankfurter that Jews were being sent to the east to build fortifications. At the War Department, Stimson and his assistant, John McCloy, felt strongly that military resources should not be diverted to saving them – the way to help the Jews, they said, was to defeat Hitler. The State Department actively obstructed moves to draw attention to what was happening, blocking attempts to help Jews escape Europe. Breckinridge Long, the Assistant Secretary of State responsible for refugees, was an anti-Semite who urged steps to stop entry into the USA of those fleeing Nazi persecution. He argued that 'the absorption of new arrivals will have to be kept to a small scale or resistance will develop and spread rapidly, thus inviting attacks on the position of Jews already established'. Hull's wife was half-Jewish, something he tried to conceal; he had been attacked in the past for being a 'slave' of the Jews and using his office to 'satisfy the greed of the moneychangers'. As a result, he preferred to avoid the issue.

While Roosevelt declared himself no anti-Semite and attracted most Jewish votes, his attitude could be ambivalent as shown by his remarks to the Vichy official at Casablanca about Jewish professional quotas, and the 'understandable complaints which the Germans bore towards the Jews'. At a lunch with Churchill and Hopkins in 1943, he remarked on his success in adding four or five Jewish families to Hyde Park and the area round the hot springs he used in Georgia. The locals 'would have no problems if there were no more than that', he added. Just after Pearl Harbor, he told Morgenthau and a Catholic official that the United States was a Protestant country and 'the Catholics and Jews are here under sufferance'. Until 1944, he refrained from referring to persecution of the Jews when denouncing Nazi oppression. The matter had not come up at Allied summits; Churchill suppressed news of the Holocaust 'lest this incite an increase in anti-Semitic feeling'.

But Morgenthau got a concerned official from his department appointed to head a newly created Refugee Board and, in March 1944, confronted Roosevelt with a demand to take action against the 'plain anti-Semitism' at State. This drew a presidential statement denouncing 'one of the blackest crimes in all history . . . the wholesale systematic murder of the Jews of Europe [which] goes on unabated every hour'. The United Nations, he vowed, would pursue the guilty and deliver them up to justice.

Four months later, he finally agreed to authorise European Jews to enter the United States – just 1,000 to a camp in New York State. But he turned down pleas to bomb Auschwitz. As John McCloy recalled, in an exchange with Morgenthau's son, the President was 'irate' at the suggestion. 'Why the idea!' he exclaimed when McCloy took it to him. 'They'll say we bombed these people, and they'll only move it down the road a little way and [we'll] bomb them all the more. If it's successful, it'll be more provocative, and I won't have anything to do [with it]'.

The month after Bretton Woods, Morgenthau and White went to London and France. Unknowingly, they were about to set off a multi-layered alliance drama. At the time, the War Department was pressing for Lend-Lease to be cut back heavily after Germany's defeat; in particular, it wanted to halt civilian assistance and anything else that could help Britain to compete economically in the period before Japan was also beaten. Aware of the concern this aroused in London, Hopkins suggested to Churchill that he raise the issue with Morgenthau.[4]

The Prime Minister told the visitor his country was completely bankrupt and could only produce half the food it needed. Despite his plea to Roosevelt during their second conference at Cairo, Bretton Woods had limited Britain's dollar holdings to one billion, increasing its dependence on the United States. Hull and Hopkins saw the makings of a deal. In return for giving London help, they would insist on the victory of free trade over imperial preference. Hopkins advised the President it was important for him to 'tell the Prime Minister how strongly you feel about knocking down some of the trade barriers . . . I rather think that he thinks that . . . this program in America lies with Secretary Hull, while the truth of the matter is that it is a program that, from the beginning, has been pushed by you.' When Morgenthau told him of Britain's problems, Roosevelt replied: 'This is very interesting. I had no idea that England was broke. I will go over there and make a couple of talks and take over the British Empire.'

On the flight to London, White had handed the Treasury Secretary a memorandum from the State Department arguing that Germany would be needed for the revival of Europe; so its industry must be preserved and supported. White, probably motivated in part by a desire to help the Soviet Union, wanted a weak Germany. He judged, rightly, that the memo would stir up his boss. By the time their converted bomber landed, Morgenthau was, indeed, convinced something had to be done to head off the State Department.

His concern was heightened when he read the draft of a handbook for US occupation forces emphasising the establishment of efficient and orderly administration under German supervision. What he did not know was that the planners in Washington were working in the dark since Roosevelt had not informed anybody about the Teheran discussions on Germany. On the trip to Britain, he became the first Cabinet official to find out about this. At a Sunday afternoon tea party on the lawn of Eden's country home, also attended by White, the Foreign Secretary referred to the agreement for dismemberment of the enemy. Morgenthau asked if he could see the Teheran papers. Knowing the importance of gaining support on Lend-Lease, Eden felt he could not refuse.

At the Foreign Office two days later, he read the record of the summit to the two Americans. He was clearly embarrassed at what he had blundered into. He asked Morgenthau to tell Roosevelt he had not meant to discuss Germany with the visitors. Morgenthau replied that he had not come to Britain to talk about Germany, but would raise the matter when he got home. State Department plans for a unified, reviving Germany were clearly in breach of Teheran. He could use this to press Roosevelt into the much tougher policy he wanted towards the enemy.

The first priority, Morgenthau decided, was to demolish the industrial heartland of the Ruhr. 'Just strip it,' he told White. 'I don't care what happens to the population . . . I would take every mine, every mill and factory and wreck it . . . Steel, coal, everything, just close it down . . . I am for destroying first and we will worry about the population second.'

The argument that Germany might be needed as a buffer to Russia's expansion carried no weight with him. He had, his son added, 'a rather romantic view of the Soviets as liberators of the Russian people from czarist tyranny'. Paying no heed to the Keynesian analysis of the harm done by reparations on Germany after the First World War, Morgenthau and White waved aside arguments from Whitehall about the importance of Germany for a healthy European economy as an attempt to safeguard British exports.

Henry Stimson felt very differently. The Secretary for War believed that the harsh treatment of Germany after 1918 had helped the advent of the Nazis. What he termed 'mass vengeance' after Hitler's defeat would lead to a similar result. While recognising that Morgenthau was 'understandably very bitter', he felt his colleague was letting personal resentment lead him down a dangerous path. A weak Germany, he thought, would leave a vacuum for Moscow to fill.

At seventy-six, Stimson was a much respected Republican, an old-fashioned figure who refused to have divorced people in his house. His presence in the Cabinet was particularly important in establishing the bi-partisan nature of the war effort. Alongside Marshall, 'the Colonel', as he was known from his service in the First World War, was one of the few people with whom Roosevelt did not dare to trifle. This made his opposition a major threat to Morgenthau's plans.

However, the Treasury Secretary scored an opening point on Stimson's own turf by bringing the army handbook to the attention of the President who said it was 'pretty bad', and sent the War Department a 'spanking letter'. (The book was subsequently rewritten to sound tougher, but the War Department included loopholes which would enable it to appoint local figures to administer the first cities to be occupied, such as Aachen.)

On the broader question of the treatment of Germany, Roosevelt asked Hopkins to chair a committee of Morgenthau, Stimson and Hull to produce a recommendation on US policy. Its deliberations produced a vivid example of how top-level policy-making was conducted in the administration, as senior figures battled for the approval of a President who chose to dodge and weave for weeks.

Though Stimson was implacably opposed to his ideas, Morgenthau believed he had Hull's backing. On his return to Washington, he had told the Secretary of State what he had learned from Eden. 'Henry, this is the first time I have heard this!' Hull gasped. Morgenthau said he did not want to intervene in a field that was not his, but noted that nobody was working along the lines agreed in Teheran.

'I am not told what is going on,' Hull explained. 'When they talk about Germany, I am not consulted.'

Where did Hull stand? Morgenthau asked. In reply, the Secretary of State recalled his proposal at the Foreign Ministers' meeting in Moscow for a secret trial of 'Hitler and his gang' before shooting them.

The fourth member of the committee, Hopkins, disliked Morgenthau, whose closeness to the President had increased while the aide was recuperating from his operation. But Hopkins seemed to be on the side of toughness, and would, in the end, do whatever his boss wanted. It was difficult to read the Roosevelt runes. After Teheran, the President had said that the United Nations had no intention of enslaving the German people, who would be given a chance to develop in peace as 'useful and respectable members of the European family'. But, in August, he told the Cabinet Germans should have only 'a subsistence level of food' after defeat. There was, he added, no reason the country could not go back to 1810 'where they would be perfectly comfortable but wouldn't have any luxury'. On a visit to the Morgenthau farm, Roosevelt told his host that Germany should not be permitted to keep a single plane, 'not even a glider', that 'nobody should be allowed to wear a uniform', and that no marching would be permitted. How serious he was is a matter for debate; the Treasury Secretary lapped it up.[5]

Roosevelt's administration was always marked by departmental rivalries, but this reached a particularly high pitch as the State, Treasury and War departments battled over the plans for post-war Germany. Stimson found the committee meetings the most difficult and unpleasant he had attended in the three years since he returned to government. At times, the discussions grew so frosty that participants dropped their habit of calling one another by first names and reverted to titles. The War Secretary did not help matters by telling Morgenthau that the reconstruction of Germany would require 'kindness and Christianity'. When the proposal to destroy the Ruhr came up, he insisted: 'I cannot treat as realistic the suggestion that such an area in the present economic condition of the world can be turned into a non-productive ghost territory.' He could not conceive of reducing 'such a gift of nature into a dust heap'. Europe, he stressed, would need speedy reconstruction if it was to avoid further convulsions.

The President kept all balls in the air. When he met the foursome, he began by looking at Stimson and saying that Germans could be fed from soup kitchens, before rambling on about how his ancestors had lived without luxuries. When the War Secretary impatiently turned the discussion to the Ruhr, Roosevelt said there was no particular hurry to reach a decision, and added that the region might be used to provide raw materials for Britain. Though he told his close staff he was heartbroken at not getting his way, Morgenthau vowed: 'I'm not licked.' At a subsequent tête-à-tête, Roosevelt told him: 'Don't be discouraged.' The Treasury Secretary had White draw up a fourteen-point memorandum, which became known as the Morgenthau Plan. When White's treasonable contacts with Moscow were later revealed, one obvious conclusion was that he was acting to boost the Soviet post-war position. He certainly backed harsh treatment of the defeated enemy, but he hardly needed to egg on his boss. When White suggested introducing some vagueness into the paper, the Treasury Secretary replied: 'I am not going to budge an inch. I don't know any other way than going to the heart of the thing which is the Ruhr.'

The plan provided for immediate dismantling of all factories and equipment which would be transported to Allied nations as restitution. Germans were to be liable to forced labour abroad. Schools and universities were to be shut – elementary schools would be reopened when suitable teachers and books had been located, but higher education bodies were to stay closed 'for a considerable period of time'. The media were to be shut down until the right people could be put in to run them. The victors would control Germany's trade and capital flows for at least twenty years. East Prussia would be split between Russia and Poland; the Saar would go to France; the Ruhr would be put under international control; the rest of Germany would be split into two zones. Even Roosevelt's remark about banning gliders, parades and uniforms was included.[6]

Copies were distributed to the President and members of the committee in black, loose-leaf books for a meeting on the morning of Saturday 9 September. There was no time to digest it in advance. Looking grey and exhausted, Roosevelt read out one heading: 'It is a Fallacy that Europe Needs a Strong Industrial Germany'. He agreed with this.[7]

'It would breed war, not peace,' Stimson said of the plan: 'It would arouse sympathy for Germany throughout the world.'

Hull began to shift ground. He was concerned that the Treasury was making the running on a major issue he regarded as State territory. Hull had made it known that he would not attend a conference with Churchill which had been fixed for Quebec later in the month because of his health and because it was meant to be confined to military matters – not that Roosevelt had invited him along. But the President noted that, if financial matters emerged at the summit, 'I will want Henry to come.' This increased Hull's worry as it would enable Morgenthau to push himself and his ideas on Germany. The Treasury Secretary's position would be all the stronger since, in deference to a complaint from State about how he took Hopkins and Harriman to international meetings rather than professional diplomats, Roosevelt had decided not to invite them to the summit.

Hull's irritation deepened when he learned that Churchill insisted on Cadogan coming to Quebec from the Dumbarton Oaks discussions. He called this a 'tragic mistake', fearing that Stalin would think Roosevelt and Churchill were plotting to turn the global organisation to their own ends. On top of this, it then transpired that Eden was also going to Quebec, supposedly only in his role as Deputy to Churchill as the Minister of Defence.

'The Conference has opened in a blaze of friendship,' the Prime Minister cabled the War Cabinet from Quebec on 13 September. The tide of the war in Europe was clearly with the Allies though there was a set-back when Montgomery launched a parachute drop to try to seize the bridge over the Rhine at Arnhem in Holland. This led to a defeat in which more than 7,000 men were killed or taken prisoner. But, in the Pacific, the American advance captured islands from which Japan could be bombed.[8]

Roosevelt was the first to arrive in Quebec for the conference, codenamed Octagon. He was waiting at the station in an open Phaeton to greet Churchill, who swung his cane as he walked from the train in a blue uniform and naval cap. Neither man was in the best of health. Before leaving for Canada, the President told Margaret Suckley he felt 'like a boiled owl'. He was suffering from stomach trouble, fell into dozes and had an alarmingly low haemoglobin count. Churchill found him very frail. Noting his loss of weight, Moran noted in his diary: 'You could have put your fist between his neck and his collar.'

Churchill had again contracted pneumonia before leaving Britain on the *Queen Mary*, and was in a bad mood on the voyage across the Atlantic, accusing the Chiefs of Staff of misleading him, alleging that they were scheming with their US counterparts and talking obsessively of a landing in the Adriatic, spouting what Brooke described in his diary as 'absurdities'.

Sitting with his head in his hands on the ship, Churchill looked old, unwell and depressed – Brooke blamed the after-effects of the M&B drugs Churchill had taken for pneumonia. After one session, the general noted: 'It was hard to keep one's temper with him, but I could not help feeling

---

* In the published version of his diary, Brooke noted that part of his criticism of Churchill was 'unnecessarily harsh' and had been written in exasperation and desperation. (Alanbrooke, pp. 590–1)

frightfully sorry for him. He gave me the feeling of a man who is finished, can no longer keep a grip of things, and is beginning to realize it'.*

For the only time, both leaders were accompanied by their wives. Mrs Churchill took the occasion to buy some nylon stockings, which, if available at all, were strictly rationed in Britain.

On the second day of the meeting, Churchill sent Roosevelt a note saying they should discuss the issue of continuing American aid to Britain after the defeat of Hitler, known as Lend-Lease Two. 'In which case I hope you could have Morgenthau present,' he suggested. The President cabled the Treasury Secretary to fly in, which he promptly did, accompanied by White.[9]

Learning this, Hull exploded. 'In Christ's name,' he exclaimed, 'what has happened to that man?' Stimson found it 'outrageous' that Roosevelt had taken with him 'a man who really represents the minority and is so biased by his Semitic grievances that he is really a very dangerous adviser to the President at this time'.

Churchill wanted a commitment to fund the reconstruction of his country. The British thought that their early resistance to Hitler merited consideration beyond strict accounting or congressional reservations. Outlining the scale of spending since 1939 to Morgenthau, Keynes had written that it 'no doubt makes up collectively a story of financial imprudence which has no parallel in history. Nevertheless, that financial imprudence may have been a facet of the single-minded devotion without which the war would have been lost. So we beg leave to think that it was worthwhile – for us, and also for you.'

When Churchill pressed the matter, Roosevelt rambled off into a string of anecdotes which so irritated the Prime Minister that he burst out: 'What do you want me to do? Get up on my hind legs and beg like Fala?' In the end, the President agreed verbally that Britain should continue to receive aid to cover 'reasonable needs'. But the $5.5 billion package sent to Congress was linked to the war, not to reconstruction. White summed up American concerns when he wrote that 'a vague commitment to England's future prosperity would threaten both the financial and political position of the United States in the post-war world.'

Roosevelt sent Hull a memorandum saying London should be told that aid would depend on 'the soundness of the course adopted by the British Government with a view to restoring its own economy, particularly with regard to measures taken to restore the flow of international trade.' But, when State and Treasury issued a joint statement on the extension of Lend-Lease into 1945, they stated specifically that they had not covered 'problems of post-war foreign trade'.

At a three-hour summit dinner on 13 September, Churchill slumped in his chair in an irascible mood. Roosevelt suggested that Morgenthau outline his ideas on Germany. When he complied, the Prime Minister burst out: 'Unnatural, un-Christian and unnecessary.'[10]

'You cannot indict a whole nation,' he added in a vitriolic tone. 'Kill the criminals but don't carry on the business for years.'

As the talk veered off to another subject, Roosevelt steered it back to Germany. Churchill did not want any of this. Truculently, he said the plan would mean 'chaining himself to a dead German'.

'Is this what you asked me to come all the way over here to discuss?' he grunted. Talking to Stimson on his return to Washington, Morgenthau said the Prime Minister had been even angrier than the Secretary of War about his plan.

The Treasury Secretary spent a sleepless night. In the morning, he found an ally in Churchill's violently anti-German adviser, Cherwell, who saw how the proposal could be presented to appeal to his master. The destruction of German industry could save Britain from the spectre of post-war bankruptcy as former German markets opened up for British goods. Leaving Morgenthau, the Oxford scientist turned prime-ministerial adviser went to see Churchill and explained the advantages of eliminating German competition – later, Stalin would remark to the Bulgarian Communist Georgi Dimitrov that the British were bombing Germany so heavily in order to 'destroy their competitor'.

'Somebody must suffer for the war,' the 'Prof' added. 'It is surely right that Germany and not Britain should fit the bill.'

When the summit reassembled at noon, Churchill said Britain could step into Germany's economic shoes after the war. But he still insisted on confirmation of a second phase of Lend-Lease. Cherwell told a Treasury official that Britain was 'very much more likely to get the loan if he got Winston to sign the [Germany] document'. From the US side, White saw a definite link.

Given Churchill's awareness of the need to maintain a balance in Europe, it is unlikely that his change of heart was genuine. Rather he calculated that he would get the aid while Morgenthau's proposals would prove too radical to be put into practice. This was in line with the way he had handled the US plan to land in France in 1942, opening the door for the President to adopt a strategy different from the one he had originally agreed with those around him.

When he came to write his war memoirs, Churchill again felt a need to be extremely guarded. As the apostle of the unity of the English-speaking peoples, anxious to hold up his partnership with Roosevelt as a shining example, all he could include was a pregnant subordinate clause on the plan: 'At first, I was violently opposed to this idea. But the President, with Mr Morgenthau – from whom we had so much to ask – was so insistent that in the end we agreed to consider it.'

Having made his switch, Churchill took command, dictating a paper that went further in some ways than Morgenthau and White. The document began by saying that the two leaders had agreed that the future of the Ruhr and the Saar were an essential element in preventing German rearmament. (Morgenthau was pleased to hear Roosevelt say in an aside that he didn't just have those two regions in mind, but the whole of Germany.)

'The ease with which the metallurgical, chemicals and electric industries in Germany can be converted from peace to war has already been impressed upon us by bitter experience,' Churchill went on. 'It must also be remembered that the Germans have devastated a large portion of the industries of Russia and other neighbouring allies, and it is only in accordance with justice that these injured countries should be entitled to receive the machinery they require in order to repair the losses they have suffered.'

Their industries closed down, the Ruhr and the Saar would come under a United Nations body, he said, before adding a flourish of his own. Morgenthau and White had provided for the break-up of big landed estates and their redistribution. Churchill provided the words which were to be associated with the Morgenthau Plan for ever – 'The program for eliminating the war-making industries in the Ruhr and the Saar is looking forward to converting Germany into a country primarily agricultural and pastoral in its character.'

As he was dictating, Eden came into the room. Morgenthau, wrongly, saw the Foreign Secretary as an ally in view of his help in London. But he had been advised by Whitehall that the plan would hurt world trade and British exports.

'You can't do this,' he objected.

Britain would take over Germany's export trade, Churchill replied.

'How do you know what or where it is?' Eden asked, suggesting that Hull should be asked to comment, an idea that irritated Churchill, who rarely took issue with the Foreign Secretary in front of third parties.

'Well,' the Prime Minister said testily. 'We will get it wherever it is. Now I hope, Anthony, you're not going to do anything about this with the War Cabinet. After all the future of my people is at stake, and when I have to choose between my people and the German people, I am going to choose my people.'

When the typed-up, 226-word 'Program to Prevent Germany from Starting World War III' was brought back, Roosevelt leaned forward, and scrawled 'OK'. Churchill added his initials with the date.

Some writers have argued that the President could not have believed in such an extreme scheme, and signed only to try to convince Stalin of his toughness towards Germany. That may have been in his mind but, at Teheran, and in other conversations, Roosevelt had made plain his strong views about the treatment of the enemy. The Morgenthau Plan was the logical extension of his line of thinking, though, as so often, it is hard to gauge if he knew quite how he intended to proceed. Another explanation may have lain in his health; how far he knew what he was doing at times must be open to question.

On other matters, as well, the two leaders were in accord. Roosevelt agreed to the British occupying northern Germany while the US took a zone in the south. Churchill sweetened the pill by offering the US access to the sea through Bremen and Bremerhaven.[11]

As Hull had feared, the two leaders did talk about the United Nations. However, their discussion 'rambled', Cadogan wrote in his diary. Churchill was now tending to side with Stalin on the primacy of the Big Three veto while Roosevelt would warm to a compromise dreamed up by Cadogan which would have limited their ability to block the first stages of investigation of disputes. Anyway, nothing could be done until they met Stalin. 'It's quite impossible to do business this way,' the diplomat noted.

China was a matter of concern once again. Roosevelt's decision at the second Cairo conference to cut back on the Burma offensive had, in effect, scuppered Stilwell's grand plan for an offensive in southern China. When the Japanese launched a major sweep from the north, codenamed Ichigo, the Chinese crumbled, and the Americans were forced to abandon their airbases. A pitched battle raged over supplies between Stilwell and Chennault of the air force, who accused Vinegar Joe of precipitating the defeat of the one Nationalist army which put up a good fight by withholding fuel from the air force to fly in its support.

Marshall drew up a message to Chiang Kai-shek, which Roosevelt signed, telling the Generalissimo to let Stilwell command the Chinese army. Though the American exulted when he delivered it, this proved a step too far. Chiang was worried that Stilwell would undermine his military power base, and that the Americans would send aid to the Communists in northern China. After biding his time for a few weeks, the Generalissimo played the sovereignty card. How could Roosevelt proclaim his anti-imperialist sentiments if he was trying to dictate to China's legitimate government? Since he could not get rid of Chiang, removing Stilwell was the only way for the President to seek a new start. At a dinner in Washington, Chiang's brother-in-law gathered from Hopkins that Roosevelt might be ready to drop the adviser. Stimson noted bitterly that the President's envoys to China had 'filled his head with poison on the subject of Stilwell'. In October, the axe fell; Vinegar Joe was recalled, and replaced by the more emollient Albert Wedemeyer.

After the summit, Roosevelt and Churchill spent the weekend at Hyde Park, where they talked over sharing the results of research into atomic weapons – three months earlier they had signed an agreement to establish the innocuously named Combined Development Trust, which contracted to buy 3.4 million pounds of uranium oxide from Belgium's Union Minière du Haut Katanga. An aide-mémoire by Roosevelt recorded agreement to continue Anglo-American cooperation after the war. It also raised the prospect of the bomb being used against Japan 'after mature consideration'. The work was to stay under heavy wraps – Stimson, who was one of the few informed, called it 'the best kept secret I ever knew'. Roosevelt would not inform Truman, and Churchill kept Attlee in the dark.[12]

The third paragraph said that enquiries should be made into the activities of the prominent nuclear scientist Niels Bohr, who had been smuggled out of his native Denmark. Seeing how the atom bomb would change warfare, Bohr believed it should be subject to a global agreement. During the summer, he had met Democratic elder statesman Felix Frankfurter, subsequently sending him a memorandum which included the information that he had been invited by a fellow scientist to go to Moscow. Frankfurter had already discussed the question with Roosevelt who, he recalled, had been receptive to sharing atomic secrets with the USSR. Bohr saw Churchill in London. The two men did not get on. Churchill believed America and Britain should keep their monopoly on atomic weapons, and cabled Cherwell, who was in Washington, that the Dane 'ought to be confined or at any rate made to see that he is very near the edge of mortal crimes'.

Bohr then called on Roosevelt who treated him with greater respect. According to historian Robin Edmonds the President 'seems to have agreed that Stalin must be approached in this matter'. Frankfurter sent him a handwritten letter arguing that Moscow should be told of the research. Since its atomic work was far behind what was being done in the West, 'appropriate candor would risk very little,' he wrote. 'Withholding, on the other hand, might have grave consequences.' But, at Hyde Park, Roosevelt swung behind Churchill. The last sentence of his aide-mémoire said steps should be taken to ensure that Bohr 'is responsible for no leakage of information, particularly to the Russians'.

There were two other visitors to the Roosevelt estate. The Duke of Windsor, the monarch to whose cause Churchill had nailed his colours in the abdication crisis of 1936, came to lunch, and Harry Hopkins also turned up. The aide confided to Churchill that he was not what he had been; Morgenthau had taken his place as the man to whom the President spoke most. Roosevelt turned down his proposal that he should become High Commissioner in Germany on health grounds – sensible enough, but a blow to somebody who had done so much despite his continual stomach problems. When Hopkins arrived for lunch a little late, Churchill noted that the President did not greet him. But then the atmosphere grew more cordial, and the Prime Minister felt it was 'like old times'.

'It was remarkable how definitely my contacts with the President immediately improved and our affairs moved quicker as Hopkins appeared to regain his influence,' he wrote in a passage that implies that he was finding it more difficult to deal with Roosevelt. For his part, the President may have begun to view his aide as a man of the past, even sicker than himself and not quite up to the historic, global role he saw himself fulfilling.

After Churchill left Hyde Park, to sail home on the *Queen Mary* from New York, Roosevelt slept round the clock. Getting up, he practised walking with his braces and then took the train back to Washington to plunge into campaigning for a fourth term.

At 9.30 a.m. on 20 September, Morgenthau, accompanied by White, met Hull and Stimson in the State Department to brief them on the Quebec summit. He had returned to Washington feeling 'terrifically happy'. 'We got just what we started out to get,' he told his staff. The summit had been 'unbelievably good . . . the high spot of my entire career in government.'[13]

When Stimson asked about a connection between the acceptance of the plan for Germany and the extension of Lend-Lease, Morgenthau denied any link. He stressed that, while Roosevelt had been ready to agree there and then, he had insisted on a committee being set up to consider the aid issue. According to White's note, Hull was 'very disturbed that the President made the decision on lend-lease with Britain without prior consultation with the men who had been working on the problem for a long time.' The State Department memorandum on the meeting recorded that Hull 'expressed his shocked feelings at the way such vital matters were settled without any consultation with our Government experts or regard for what has gone before'. Not only had the summit produced yet another incursion into his territory by a fellow Cabinet member, but the accord meant the continuance of aid could not be used as 'bait' to get the British in line on free trade.

When the conversation came back to Germany, Hull pointed out the danger that Stalin would think Roosevelt and Churchill were hatching policy without him. Sounding bitter, the Secretary of State said he was rapidly losing interest in the whole matter since he was being kept out of discussions and decisions. His health was getting worse, and he had held his job for a record twelve years, he remarked. Given his own ambitions, Morgenthau could only take note.

Stimson was celebrating his seventy-seventh birthday – Roosevelt sent him a bouquet of roses. Deeply troubled by what had happened and what it said about the decision-making process, the old-school Republican felt it was terrible to 'think of the total power of the United States and the

United Kingdom . . . in the hands of two men, both of whom are similar in impulsiveness and their lack of systematic study.' He dismissed Churchill's 'Prof' as 'an old fool . . . a pseudo scientist.' Morgenthau, he thought, was driven by 'Semitism gone wild for vengeance and, if it is ultimately carried out (I cannot believe that it will be), it as sure as fate will lay the seed for another war in the next generation.'

With a 'heavy cloud' over his head, the War Secretary sat down to write a letter to the President calling the Morgenthau Plan 'a crime against civilization' comparable to what the Nazis wanted to do to their victims. Under the Atlantic Charter, the vanquished, as well as the victors, were entitled to freedom from want, he added. 'The sum total of the drastic political and economic steps proposed by the Treasury is an open confession of the bankruptcy of hope for a reasonable economic and political settlement of the causes of war,' the letter charged.

Then the Treasury Department shot itself in the foot. Exultant, and seeking to tie the President publicly to its plan, it leaked the contents of the Quebec document. A column in the *Washington Post* portrayed Morgenthau as the winner against Stimson and Hull. That was too much for the Secretary of State. His department called in the senior *New York Times* writer, Arthur Krock, for a briefing. The resulting column depicted the Treasury Secretary as 'the central civilian government official' concerned with post-war Germany. This made Morgenthau vulnerable to charges of overreaching himself, and pinned down his department's responsibilities. Krock dug in the knife by reporting that, at Quebec, the British had been interested in the advantages they could gain from the de-industrialisation of Germany, and making points about what Lend-Lease had cost. The suggestion was that Morgenthau had been ensnared by the wily ally.[14]

The press war escalated. The *Wall Street Journal* reported that the Treasury plan entailed 30 million Germans leaving their country. An Associated Press despatch detailed the split in the administration. Seeing the political danger, particularly in an election year, Roosevelt dissolved the four-man Cabinet committee. But the *New York Times* threw further fuel on the fire with a report that the President and Morgenthau had 'bribed' Churchill to accept the plan with the promise of new Lend-Lease aid.

In London, the War Cabinet reacted negatively, and Churchill did not formally table the scheme for discussion. The British Treasury Representative in Washington called it 'lunatic'. As the Prime Minister recalled in a post-war speech, it 'just dropped on one side' as far as Britain was concerned. In a conversation in 1947, John McCloy recorded, Churchill 'damned Morgenthau and the Prof. Said they were Shylocks.' In Moscow, according to the police chief's son, Beria detected an unreasonable 'act of vengeance by the Jews against the German people'. In Berlin, Goebbels brandished the scheme to show what lay in store if the Nazis fell. 'Roosevelt and Churchill Agree to Jewish Murder Plan', one German headline read. Picking this up, Dewey said it was as valuable to Hitler as 10 fresh divisions, and cost American lives by stiffening German resistance. Privately, Marshall agreed.[15]

Deeply troubled, Morgenthau tried to telephone Roosevelt at Hyde Park. The President declined to take his calls for three days. Eventually, the Treasury Secretary got Hopkins to ring for him, but Roosevelt rebuffed his suggestion of a statement saying he was mulling over advice.

Returning to Washington, the President spoke to Stimson, and backed off from the plan. Morgenthau prepared another line of attack by telling White to look in the records for dirt on Stimson's attitude to German reparations and Mussolini when he had been Secretary of State.

On the morning of 29 September, Morgenthau walked to the White House and took a seat outside Roosevelt's quarters. The President was in bed, with a high temperature. His daughter-chatelaine Anna, who disliked the visitor, came out into the hall. Morgenthau produced press clippings favourable to his scheme, but recognised the storm was 'bad politically and bad from the Jewish angle'.

'I think [the President] ought to get Hull, Stimson and me together,' he said, 'and stop us talking.' He would wait while Anna went to see her father with the idea.

'All I know is that the President definitely doesn't want to see you,' she said when she returned. Putting her hand on Morgenthau's arm, she moved him out.

Later that day, Roosevelt sent Hull a memorandum saying that 'the real nub of the situation is to keep Britain from going into complete bankruptcy at the end of the war . . . I just cannot go along with the idea of seeing the British Empire collapse financially, and Germany at the same time building up a potential re-armament machine to make another war possible in twenty years. Mere inspection of plants will not prevent that.'

He blamed the mess on press leaks, telling Hull that he wished he could catch whoever was responsible 'and chastise him'. Despite what had been said at Quebec, he added that 'no one wants to make Germany a wholly agricultural nation again' and that 'no one wants the complete eradication of the German industrial productive capacity in the Ruhr and the Saar'.

'Henry Morgenthau pulled a boner!' the President exclaimed at a particularly friendly lunch with Stimson at the beginning of October, as if the whole thing was nothing to do with him. All he had wanted was to help Britain financially, he added. When Stimson read the Quebec document to him, Roosevelt replied: 'Henry, I have not the faintest recollection of this at all!'

Despite everything, Roosevelt followed his usual pattern of taking Morgenthau on a drive along the banks of the Hudson River on the eve of the election, and invited him to Hyde Park as the results came in the following night. He got 53.4 per cent of the popular vote and a 439 to 99 margin in the electoral college.*

The row over the plan chipped away at Morgenthau's status, and opened the door for Hopkins to return to favour. The Iowan's position was strengthened when Hull resigned in November, and was replaced by Edward Stettinius. Still only forty-four years of age, but with a distinguished thatch of white hair, he had gained high-level business experience as a senior figure at both General Motors and US Steel before becoming the Lend-Lease administrator, where he worked well with Hopkins. In foreign affairs, however, he lacked authority or depth of knowledge. Roosevelt had shown the kind of successor to Hull he wanted when he rejected the powerful Democratic politician James Byrnes as 'too independent'. Charles Bohlen, the interpreter at Teheran, was appointed as liaison between the State Department and the White House, reporting to Hopkins. The aide now had a twin power base from which to pursue his role as the President's prime alliance agent and was the one senior figure in Washington who could rise above departmental divisions.

Morgenthau did not relent. He castigated a British draft of policy towards post-war Germany for failing to deal with 'the elimination or destruction of heavy industry in Germany'. The State Department commented that the note would be 'most disturbing if there was any prospect of its being taken seriously by the British'.

---

* Compared to 54.7 per cent and 449 to 82 in 1940 and 60.8 per cent and 523 to 8 in 1936.

Roosevelt remained ambivalent. 'We should let Germany come back industrially to meet her own needs, but not to export for some time until we know better how things are going to turn out,' he told the State Department. But he also spoke to Keynes of going 'pretty far in de-industrializing the Ruhr and eliminating many . . . basic industries'. A State memorandum in November provided for 'a rock-bottom standard of living for Germans', but said the economy 'should be operated as nearly as possible as a unit during the occupation period'. The first part of the document played to the gallery; the second put forward a very different approach that would affect the shape of Western Europe for decades to come.

The real test came when Anglo-American troops surrounded the Ruhr in the spring of 1945. Eisenhower told Stimson he did not have enough men both to deal with the region and to press on with winning the war. Marshall advised him to make his decision without taking into account the argument for turning Germany into a pastoral state. Eisenhower got on with the war.

But Morgenthau was unyielding. In his last conversation with Roosevelt in 1945, he said he was going to continue to fight for his ideas because 'a weak economy for Germany means that she will be weak politically, and she won't be able to make another war . . . I have been strong for winning the war, and I want to help win the peace.'

'Henry, I am with you one hundred per cent,' the President replied.

18

Percentage Points

'The United States claims too many rights for itself'

STALIN

SITTING IN THE KREMLIN late at night on 9 October 1944, Churchill did something naughty.[1]

He had flown in with Eden earlier in the day for the summit with Stalin, codenamed Tolstoy. Dressed in military uniform with rows of medals, the Prime Minister aimed not only at reaching agreements with the dictator but also at re-establishing his own position in the alliance. 'Let us settle about our affairs in the Balkans,' he told the Soviet leader, according to his memoirs. 'Your armies are in Roumania [sic] and Bulgaria. We have interests, missions, and agents there. Don't let us get at cross-purposes in small ways. So far as Britain and Russia are concerned, how would it do for you to have ninety per cent predominance in Roumania, for us to have ninety per cent of the say in Greece, and go fifty-fifty about Yugoslavia?'

The deal he had suggested to the Soviet leader in May to swap influence in Greece for a Soviet sway over Romania had worked out satisfactorily as far as he was concerned. While the Red Army had taken the Romanian oilfields and prepared to advance on Bucharest, British forces had landed in the Peloponnese and moved into Athens as the Germans evacuated the city. According to the Soviet interpreter, Berezhkov, he stated that Britain must be 'a leader in the Mediterranean', which Stalin recognised.

Still, the Prime Minister pointed to the need to avoid phrases like 'division of spheres of influence' since, as he noted, this would antagonise the Americans who would be shocked by how crudely he was speaking. In an echo of Roosevelt's conduct at Teheran, he said that, while he welcomed the presence of Harriman at some of his meetings in Moscow, this should not prevent private Anglo-Soviet talks, such as this opening session without the US ambassador. According to the British record, which Churchill did reproduce in his memoirs, he went on to remark that Stalin was a realist while he, himself, was not sentimental and 'Mr Eden was a bad man'. Making clear that this was his personal initiative, the Prime Minister stated that he had not put his ideas to the Cabinet, let alone the Commons.

Just as he had got in digs at Churchill in Teheran, the Soviet leader now said he thought 'the United States claims too many rights for itself leaving limited opportunities for the Soviet Union and Great Britain. Yet our two countries have a treaty of mutual assistance, do we not?' It was all the Prime Minister could have hoped for.

There are two versions of what came next. Churchill wrote that, as the conversation was being translated, he took half a sheet of paper and set down his proposal, adding that there would be a fifty-fifty share in Hungary and that Bulgaria would be 75 per cent under Russian influence. Berezhkov had Churchill reaching into his breast pocket to bring out a paper folded four times which he smoothed on the table, saying: 'I have this naughty document here with some ideas of certain people in London.' Both versions agree that he pushed the sheet over to Stalin.

The Soviet leader paused to examine the numbers. He picked up a blue pencil to tick the top left corner of the paper before pushing it back. Churchill did not pick it up. There was a long silence broken by the Prime Minister.

'Might it not be thought rather cynical if it seemed we had disposed of these issues so fateful to millions of people, in such an off-hand manner?' he asked. 'Let us burn the paper.'

'No, you keep it,' Stalin replied. Churchill did.

Given the military situation in the east, the deal was, in many respects, being overtaken by events. At best, it was an attempt to get a toehold in countries which would fall under Soviet influence. There was no way the British could keep Stalin to any of the divisions outlined on the paper. Still, in talks that resembled a bridge bidding game, the matter was 'flogged out' by Eden and Molotov, as Churchill put it. Berezhkov reported that the

Soviet minister began by saying that Moscow's share of influence in Yugoslavia and Hungary should increase to 75 per cent.[2]

'That is much worse than what was agreed on,' Eden objected.

'Then let the percentage for Bulgaria be ninety and ten, for Yugoslavia fifty-fifty and as for Hungary, we'll work out agreement at a later date.'

'We are prepared to accept your proposal for Hungary, but we would like to have more influence in Bulgaria.'

'If the ratio for Hungary is seventy-five by twenty-five, let the same ratio apply to Bulgaria, too. But then it must be sixty by forty for Yugoslavia. This is our limit and we won't go down any further.'

Eden countered with eighty–twenty for Bulgaria, but insisted on equality in Yugoslavia which partly fell into what Britain considered its zone of interest. He complained about Bulgarian action against the British in frontier regions of Greece. Molotov hit back by stating that, if Moscow agreed to equality in Yugoslavia, it would want ninety–ten in Bulgaria.

Tiring of the argument, Eden said he did not much care for numbers, and took issue with a secret visit to Moscow by Tito, which the British had only just been told about. When the session finished at 9 p.m., he learned with horror that he was expected for dinner at the Prime Minister's dacha, a forty-five-minute drive away. Over the meal, Churchill listened unhappily to his report on the discussion with Molotov. He thought it had dispelled the good atmosphere fostered the previous day. 'I explained that this was the real battle and I could not and would not give way,' Eden wrote in his diary.

The next meeting with Molotov was, he recorded, 'as smooth as it had been rough yesterday'. Moscow would 'summon Bulgaria out of Greece and Yugoslavia tonight,' the Soviet minister said.

But Churchill was getting worried about what he had proposed, the repercussions if it leaked, and how to break the news to Roosevelt. To prepare the ground, he wrote to the President about the importance of reaching a common position on the Balkans to head off civil wars in which they would find themselves backing the opposite side to Stalin. Lifting a corner of the veil over his guilty secret, he added: 'Nothing will be settled except preliminary agreements between Britain and Russia, subject to further discussion and melting-down with you. On this basis I am sure you will not mind our trying to have a full meeting of minds with the Russians.'[2]

He then worked on a letter to Stalin intended to limit what the Russians might read into his proposal, and to ensure secrecy. The percentages proposal was, he wrote, 'no more than a method by which in our thoughts we can see how near we are together, and then decide upon the necessary steps to bring us into full agreement. As I said they would be considered crude, and even callous, if they were exposed to the scrutiny of the Foreign Office and of diplomats all over the world. Therefore they could not be the basis of any public document, certainly not at the present time. They might however be a good guide for the conduct of our affairs. If we manage these affairs well we shall perhaps prevent several civil wars and much bloodshed and strife in the small countries concerned.'[3]

The aim should be to let each country have the form of government its people preferred. All he wanted was to 'adumbrate the degrees of interest which each of us takes in these countries with the full assent of the other, and subject to the approval of the United States, which may go far away for a long time and then come back unexpectedly with gigantic strength.'

Harriman got wind of Churchill's idea during a Kremlin dinner and called on the British leader on the morning of 12 October to learn more. The Prime Minister was in bed working on his letter to Stalin. When he read it out, Harriman said he was sure Roosevelt would repudiate the initiative.

Eden came in, and Churchill told him the American thought the letter to Stalin should not be sent. It was not. The percentages were never mentioned again. Though Harriman had been let in on the secret, there is no record of a message about it to Washington. He may have deemed the matter too sensitive to commit to paper; due to fly home to report to Roosevelt, he could save it for a verbal report.

Churchill later characterised his decision not to send the letter to Stalin as 'deeming it wiser to let well alone'. But he must have realised that he had risked opening up a major fissure in the Western alliance. With the presidential election less than a month away, Roosevelt would have had to have disowned his ally if the scheme had become known. The alliance had again narrowly avoided a potentially fatal crisis.

'Stalin will get what he wants,' Churchill said privately. 'The Americans have seen to that.' His own attitude to Moscow was complex. He retained his innate hostility to Communism, recognised the reality of the Red Army's advance, and saw the need for a strong Western Europe to avoid Soviet domination after the war. At the same time, he still believed that, if he could establish a good personal rapport with Stalin, the alliance could prosper to their mutual benefit. He told Harriman his main aim was to 'create good feelings'. 'We can settle everything, we three, if we come together,' he said at a meeting with Eden and Clark Kerr. 'If we don't there'll be years of diplomatic wrangling and suspicion.'[4]

The concern lay, rather, in Washington. Worried that Stalin might think Churchill was speaking for both Western Allies, Hopkins had drafted a message which Roosevelt sent to Harriman to take to the Kremlin before Churchill arrived in Moscow. 'I am sure you understand that in this global war there is literally no question, military or political, in which the United States is not interested,' it told Stalin. 'I am firmly convinced that the three of us, and only the three of us, can find the solution of the questions unresolved. In this sense, while appreciating Mr Churchill's desire for the meeting, I prefer to regard your forthcoming talks with the Prime Minister as preliminary to a meeting of the three of us.'[5]

This puzzled Stalin. 'I had imagined that Mr Churchill was coming to Moscow in keeping with an agreement reached with you at Quebec,' he replied. 'It appears, however, that my supposition is at variance with reality.'[6]

The Warsaw Rising had ended a week earlier with capitulation to the Germans, and Churchill wanted to use his visit to find a solution to the Polish question. He summoned the Polish Prime Minister from London to Moscow, making it plain that if he did not come, Britain would withdraw support from his group. After a preliminary meeting with the British, Mikołajczyk and his colleagues went to the Soviet Government Hospitality House to see Stalin, Molotov, Churchill, Eden and Harriman.[7]

Acting as chairman, the Soviet Foreign Minister gave a short introduction, and invited Mikołajczyk to speak. The Polish leader had little room to negotiate. His Cabinet in London had laid down that its country must have as much territory after the war as before, including sources of raw materials and cultural centres in eastern regions. The government in Warsaw should contain five main parties, four of which were in London. Laying down a marker as regards the Lublin group, Mikołajczyk began by saying that his

---

* The fullest version of the dialogue is in Mikołajczyk's memoirs. When Moran put these to Churchill after their publication in 1948, Churchill did not demur. His own memoirs and those of Eden and Harriman are more truncated as if it was not a matter they wished to dwell upon during the Cold War.

aim was to produce 'an agreement between Poland and Russia, not between Russia and a handful of Poles, arbitrarily chosen by a foreign power'.*

Stalin expressed doubt that the underground had considered any plan given recent events.

'Marshal, perhaps you forget that as a younger man, you, too, were in the underground,' the Pole replied by his own account. 'Yet you remained active and made plans and programmes which affected the future of your country.'

The Soviet leader grinned.

Had the Lublin group been consulted? Churchill asked.

Mikołajczyk said his consultation had been with the Polish people.

'The Lublin government should have a bigger share in the post-war Polish government,' Churchill interjected.

Stalin said the Lublin group had 'done good work', but was being ignored. Nor was the Curzon Line being recognised. 'These two flaws must be corrected,' he insisted.

'You accuse me of ignoring the Lublin Committee,' Mikołajczyk objected. 'You're ignoring the Polish government which has fought the Germans, our common foe, for five years. You're ignoring the Polish government which created strong armies, a navy and an air force, and which now fights on all fronts!'

'I recognise this,' Stalin replied. 'I have given the proper credit.'

'But you haven't.'

'I want no argument.'

'Nor do I. But you mention the "good work" of the Lublin Committee. Yet it has permitted your agents to arrest and deport some of the very Home Army men who helped the Red Army liberate parts of Poland.'

'Things are bad everywhere.'

'Anyway,' Mikołajczyk said, 'I cannot accept the Curzon Line. If I agreed to cede forty per cent of Poland's pre-war territory and five million people, everyone would have the right to say, "It was for this that the Polish soldiers fought? A politician's sell-out."'

'You're an imperialist,' Stalin answered, noting the scale of Soviet losses. To which, the Pole replied that, proportionately, his country had suffered even worse.

'Who is threatening the independence of Poland?' the Soviet leader asked. 'Soviet Russia?'

Thinking back, Mikołajczyk believed he might have replied 'Yes.'

'But all this was settled at Teheran,' Molotov barked, staring at Harriman and Churchill, who said nothing.

'If your memories fail you, let me recall the facts to you,' the Foreign Minister went on. 'We all agreed at Teheran that the Curzon Line must divide Poland. You will recall that President Roosevelt agreed to this solution and strongly endorsed the line. And then we agreed that it would be best not to issue any public declaration about our agreement.'

Remembering how Roosevelt had told him that he did not support the line, Mikołajczyk was shocked. He looked at Churchill and Harriman, willing them to deny what Molotov had said. Given Roosevelt's avoidance of the Polish issue at Teheran, this could have been a case of what the ambassador had warned about, a Soviet tendency to take silence for acquiescence. Harriman kept silent, looking at the floor and deciding that his role of observer meant it would not be right for him to speak.

'I confirm this,' Churchill said in a quiet voice.

Growing angry at having been put on the spot, he insisted that the Poles must agree to Stalin's demands. British aid made it their duty to accede to what he was now supporting.

'I didn't expect to be brought here to participate in a new partition of my country,' Mikołajczyk shouted.

No public announcement was necessary, Churchill said. Seeking compromise, he said the Curzon Line might be regarded as a temporary frontier against which Warsaw could appeal at a peace conference. Far from calming the atmosphere, that brought Stalin to his feet.

'I want this made very clear,' he said gruffly. 'Mr Churchill's thought of any future change in the frontier is not acceptable to the Soviet government. We will not change our frontiers from time to time. That's all!'

Wheezing, the Prime Minister held out his hands, looking at the ceiling in despair. The session was over. In subsequent conversations with the London Poles, Churchill blamed them for not coming to an agreement with Stalin that would have cut the ground from under the Lublin Committee. When Mikołajczyk referred to the Atlantic Charter, the British leader replied that he would tell Parliament he and Stalin were in agreement. 'Our relations with Russia are much better than they have ever been,' he said. 'I mean to keep them that way.' Mikołajczyk added a demand for the Baltic port of Stettin (Szczecin), with which

Churchill was ready to go along with, though Eden demurred. Then the Poles went too far by demanding the city of Lvov, across the proposed border in Ukraine.[8]

Churchill exploded, berating the Polish Prime Minister for sacrificing his country for a single city and sowing the seeds of a future war. Striding up and down, he cursed, 'I will have nothing more to do with you . . . I don't care where you go . . . I will indict you.'

Recalling a remark by the Polish General Anders about fighting the USSR once Germany had been beaten, he stormed: 'If you think you can conquer Russia, well, you are crazy, you ought to be in a lunatic asylum. We shall tell the world how unreasonable you are. We shall not part friends.'

Mikołajczyk refused to give way.

'Then I wash my hands of this,' Churchill riposted, by the Pole's account. We are not going to wreck the peace of Europe . . . you wish to start a war in which twenty-five million lives will be lost!'

'You settled our fate at Teheran,' the Polish leader objected.

'Poland was *saved* at Teheran,' Churchill replied.

'I am not a person whose patriotism is diluted to the point where I would give away half of my country.'

'Unless you accept the frontier, you're out of business for ever!' Churchill exclaimed. 'The Russians will sweep through your country, and your people will be liquidated. You're on the verge of annihilation. We'll become sick and tired of you if you keep arguing.'

Eden calmed things down for a moment, but Churchill was soon back on the attack. 'You are *bound* to accept the decision of the Great Powers,' he insisted.

When the Pole referred to Churchill's speeches decrying the taking of territory by force, the Prime Minister denounced his government as callous people who wanted to wreck Europe. 'I shall leave you to your own troubles,' he thundered. 'You have no sense of responsibility when you want to abandon your own people at home. You are indifferent to their sufferings. You have only your miserable, petty selfish interests in mind.'

Mikołajczyk had had enough. In his memoirs, he recalled that he was 'furious at the man, and could not conceal it'. He asked Churchill to let him parachute into Poland to join the anti-German resistance.

'Why?' the Prime Minister asked, taken aback.

'Because I prefer to die fighting for the independence of my country, rather than be hanged later by the Russians in full view of your British ambassador!'

Churchill walked from the room. Mikołajczyk thought he had hurt him more than he wanted to. But, after a few minutes, he was back, putting an arm round his shoulder. Both men were on the verge of crying. Telling Moran that night of the Pole's request to be dropped into his homeland, Churchill had tears in his eyes.

When the British leader met representatives of the Lublin Committee with Stalin, Molotov and Eden present, the Soviet-backed group demanded between two-thirds and three-quarters of seats in government in return for agreeing that Mikołajczyk should be Prime Minister. As its members made lengthy, wandering, cliché-ridden statements, Stalin looked at his guest and smiled mischievously. Eden seemed incredibly bored, whispering 'the rat and the weasel' to Churchill at one point about two of the group. Molotov was impassive. Having had as much as he could endure, his face darkening, Churchill got up and walked to a side table where glasses and plates had been arranged for refreshments. He rearranged them with such a clatter that the noise drowned out the Pole who was speaking. Laughing, Stalin told the group they talked enough. Churchill later compared them to the Quisling collaborators in Norway.

Writing to his wife, Churchill noted the 'great cordiality' he was shown. 'Life is however the same and I did not get to bed till 4 a.m. this morning,' he added. 'I have had very nice talks with the Old Bear. I like him the more I see him. Now they respect us here and I am sure they wish to work with us – I have to keep the President constantly in touch and this is the delicate side.'

Reporting to Roosevelt, he stressed the 'extraordinary atmosphere of goodwill' he found in Moscow. Moran noticed that every time his patient returned from a talk with Stalin, he seemed in a good mood. He allowed himself to josh with the dictator – when Churchill observed that Mikołajczyk was a peasant and very obstinate, Stalin noted that he, too, was a peasant, at which Churchill said, 'You can be as obstinate as any of them.' Still, he recognised to the doctor that it was 'all very one-sided. They get what they want by guile, flattery or force.'

The British scored a notable social success when Stalin dined at their embassy on 11 October, the first time he had gone to a foreign legation in Moscow. The NKVD searched the gardens, the cellars, the attics and the out-houses.

Servants were questioned. A searchlight was mounted on the roof of the British building, which was ringed with guards.[9]

Stalin stepped from his car wearing a long grey military overcoat with red facings and a peaked cap with a red band. Underneath, he had on his usual marshal's tunic with a single star – the interpreter Birse noticed that the sleeves reached down to his knuckles. The visitors variously found him looking thinner, older, sprucer and more ashen than when they had last seen him.

Molotov, in diplomatic uniform, gazed suspiciously at a man scribbling notes; Birse explained that he was the single journalist allowed to witness the proceedings. Vyshinsky pointed to the Soviet guards and said: 'I see the Red Army has had another victory. It has occupied the British Embassy.' When Churchill asked Lazar Kaganovich, the Prime Minister, how the USSR kept its transport system running, the Russian slashed his fingers across his throat, smiled and said: 'If a locomotive engineer does not fulfil his responsibilities, he gets this.'

The meal was English style, preceded by sherry and cocktails. Stalin said he could not understand why Westerners weakened whisky by adding water. During the dinner, he stared at portraits of George V and Queen Mary on the wall, and asked if the man was Tsar Nicholas II. When Churchill recounted the cheers he had received during his visit to Italy on the way to Moscow, the dictator observed that the people had been applauding Mussolini only a short time before.

As the leaders went into a private room after the meal, guns outside fired to celebrate a Red Army victory. Fireworks exploded from the Kremlin walls opposite the embassy, bathing it in light. According to Berezhkov's account, Churchill spoke of 'our three great democracies' which were 'committed to the lofty ideals of freedom, human dignity and happiness'. That, he added, was why he attached such importance to a good atmosphere between the USSR and Poland. Noting that Poland was a Catholic country, he said the situation there could not be allowed to complicate relations with the Vatican.

'How many divisions does the Pope have?' the Soviet leader asked.

Raising the question of the Warsaw Rising, Stalin insisted that only military problems held the Red Army back from intervening – though he said he had not been able to admit this at the time. Churchill declared that he had never believed anything else. Harriman chipped in to claim that the same was true for the people of America. So, as over Katyn, alliance solidarity triumphed over truth. Stalin could but take note.

The conversation moved to Yugoslavia, a country which clearly presented a major problem of national cohesion after a war in which collaborationist Croats had slaughtered Serbs, Serb partisans had slaughtered royalists and some Muslims had sided with the Germans. Both leaders were firm in backing Tito, but Stalin warned that the partisan leader thought the Croats and Slovenes might not agree to work with the Serbian monarch and his government-in-exile in London.

When the talk drifted to the British general election, which would be held when the war ended, Stalin said he had no doubt the Conservatives would win (though recent by-elections had shown voters turning against them). He put the Labour Party in the same bag as the Mensheviks who had been overcome by the Bolsheviks in 1917. If Churchill had been in power at the time of Munich, he added, things would have turned out differently. At one point, he offered Eden 200 cases of Russian wine. When the Foreign Secretary said there was no room on the plane to transport them, Stalin offered to get them to London by his own methods.

On what was to be a more sinister matter given their fate, the Soviet leader said he would be grateful if London could arrange to send home Russians who had fought for the Germans and were being held as prisoners in Britain. Eden replied that the government would do all it could, despite pressure on shipping. In return, he asked for Moscow's good offices in ensuring the repatriation of British prisoners of war held in Poland and Germany. Stalin said that 'every care and attention would be given to our men', Eden recalled. He could have had little doubt about what would happen to the Russians sent home.

Stalin stayed for six and a half hours, finally leaving at 4 a.m. The social entente continued on the night of 14 October, when Churchill was guest of honour at a command ballet and opera performance at the Bolshoi. Suddenly and unexpectedly, Stalin appeared through a side door to slip into the box. It was the first time the Soviet leader had been to the theatre since the German attack. The audience – 'undoubtedly handpicked', Berezhkov noted – cheered loudly. Stalin stepped back into the shadows, leaving Churchill alone in the limelight. The British leader sent Vyshinky to pull his host forward. When Stalin walked to the rail, the audience unleashed a salvo of cheers described by Kathleen Harriman as 'like a cloudburst on a tin roof'.

In the interval, there was supper of cold cuts, caviar, crabmeat, Georgian chicken and nuts, suckling pig, sweets, fruit, wine, vodka, tea and coffee. Molotov toasted Stalin with familiar phrases, leading Stalin to observe: 'I thought he was going to say something new about me.' When somebody compared the Big Three to the Holy Trinity, Stalin said Churchill must be the Holy Ghost because 'he is flying all over the place'.

Before regaining their places, the Prime Minister and Foreign Secretary went to the toilet. There, Churchill started to talk excitedly about Poland. Outside, the third bell rang for the start of the second half. Stalin sent Berezhkov to fetch them. Eden explained to him that Churchill had become so carried away with his ideas that he had not heard the ringing. The performance was held up until they got back.

Afterwards, Stalin left as unobtrusively as he had arrived. A late-night meeting at the Kremlin, attended by military leaders, reviewed Anglo-American plans to drive up into north-west Europe, progress across the Pacific and the situation on the eastern front. Stalin said the Red Army would push vigorously into Germany, and added that Moscow would enter the war against Japan 'several months' after the Nazis had been defeated.

The next day, Churchill suffered from diarrhoea and his temperature rose to 101. Taking his place, Eden went to the Kremlin to pass on the Polish demand for Lvov. Stalin and Molotov replied that the city was part of Ukraine, which would be 'an independent state'; so nothing could be done. In his diary, Eden described the talks as 'the stiffest negotiations I have ever known'. Clark Kerr wrote in his journal: 'Mik (Mikołajczyk); Christ god damn fuck and bugger.' Not surprisingly, when the Poles made what – for them – was a concession of talking about agreeing to the Curzon Line provided they got Lvov and oil and potash deposits, Stalin would have none of it.[8]

Still, Churchill remained optimistic. He told Roosevelt the Polish leader was going to recommend acceptance of the Curzon Line and drop the claim to Lvov. 'I am hopeful that even in the next fortnight we may get a settlement,' he added. Roosevelt asked to be consulted if an agreement was reached so that publication could be delayed until after the presidential election.

Meeting Mikołajczyk before he left for London, Stalin said he could not agree to Lvov being ceded, but went on to say Poland was fortunate he was not asking for more.

Did he want to make Poland a Communist state? Mikołajczyk asked. 'Absolutely not,' Stalin replied. 'Communism does not fit the Poles. They are too individualistic, too nationalistic . . . Poland will be a capitalist state.'

Seeing the surprise of his visitor, he went on: 'There is no middle system. Capitalism can assume many forms, have many different controls. But what is not Communism is capitalism.' After the war, Poland would not be 'disturbed by fratricidal fights between Communists and non-Communists though there are certain people – both Left and Right – that we cannot allow.'

'But Marshal,' Mikołajczyk objected, 'one cannot dictate who will be in public life.' Stalin looked at him as if he was mad.

In his reports to Roosevelt, Churchill wrote that Stalin wanted Poland, Czechoslovakia and Hungary to form 'a realm of independent, anti-Nazi, pro-Russian States' with the first two possibly uniting. The Soviet leader no longer objected to the British notion of a Danubian federation of Austria, Bavaria, Württemberg and Baden with Vienna as its capital – though he did not want Hungary to join. In Germany, the Ruhr and Saar should probably be put under international control, as should the Kiel Canal. The Rhineland was to be a separate state. 'I am not opposed to this line of thought,' Churchill wrote, 'however, you may be sure that we came to no fixed conclusion pending the triple meeting.'

Going out of his way to be a good host, Stalin even changed his tune on the punishment of Germans by saying there should be no executions without trial. He gave his guest a brooch of British and Soviet flags with 'Liberty' written beneath them in Russian – a present from Svetlana for Sarah Churchill. He reassured Churchill that, 'We Russians are not as clever as you think; we're simple, rather stupid. No one in Europe can be persuaded that England is either simple or stupid.'

He described himself as a 'rough man and not much good at compliments.' 'I do not speak much but drinking eases the tongue,' he reflected. Churchill told his doctor it would be 'a catastrophe' if anything happened to the Soviet leader.

For their final meeting, Churchill, accompanied by Eden, arrived at the Kremlin at 10 p.m. for dinner in Stalin's private quarters. As they entered the entrance hall, the dictator nodded to a door and, recalling the interval delay at the Bolshoi, said: 'That is where you can wash your hands if you want to, the place where, as I understand it, you English like to conduct your political discussions.'[10]

They talked of the diplomatic methods of different nations, and Churchill mentioned the Morgenthau Plan – he knew it had been abandoned, but must have wanted to impress the Soviet leader with the readiness of the West to be tough with Germany. Stalin reminisced about his time as a political prisoner in Siberia. He recalled how he caught a big sturgeon by floating a log decked with hooks down a river. When he put it in a pool with several smaller fish, it ate them. Churchill told Moran later that Stalin's sense of humour was his strongest characteristic.

Referring to his backing for intervention against the Bolsheviks, which seemed to haunt him, the Prime Minister said, 'I am glad now that I did not kill you.'

Stalin replied with a proverb – 'A man's eye should be torn out if he can only see the past.' Churchill made to leave at 3 a.m. The dictator kept him an hour more, growing ever more animated and expansive. As for Churchill, Eden told Oliver Harvey he was 'very garrulous and repetitive'.

The weather was cold with heavy rain as the British flew out. Stalin waited in the rain, in a light green overcoat and marshal's cap.

Standing in front of the cameras, clad in a double-breasted greatcoat and military cap and carrying a stick, Churchill stressed the importance of his 'many long and intimate talks with my friend and war comrade Marshal Stalin'. He was sure that 'the warrior statesman and head of Russia will lead the Russian people, all the peoples of Russia, through these years of storm and tempest into the sunlight of a broader and happier age for all.'

The two leaders walked together to the plane. Churchill invited the dictator to inspect the interior. After which, Stalin said he now knew why his visitor enjoyed flying round the world so much. Then the plane taxied down the runway, the Prime Minister doffing his military cap behind the window. As it took off, the Soviet leader waved his handkerchief.

19

Red Blues

LONDON, WASHINGTON. MOSCOW, ATHENS,
PARIS, CHUNGKING
NOVEMBER 1944–JANUARY 1945

'All would therefore rapidly disintegrate as it did last time'

CHURCHILL

HIS RE-ELECTION VICTORY meant that Roosevelt had won 'the referendum of 1944 for American participation in a stronger United Nations', as his biographer John MacGregor Burns put it. The spectre of a renewal of isolationism after victory receded. But, while the Democrats picked up twenty-two new seats in the House of Representatives, they lost one place in the Senate, meaning that the President would have to continue to contend with a conservative majority there.[1]

The war in the Pacific was going well. MacArthur's troops had landed in the Philippines and the Japanese navy had been defeated once more in the Leyte Gulf. But the deterioration of Roosevelt's health meant that a race was on between his survival and his ability to shape the post-war world. Though he had campaigned vigorously, he had lost 23 pounds; his hands shook; his shoulders stooped. He would suddenly grow pale, his jaw slack, his eyes glassy. Frances Perkins likened him to 'an invalid who has been allowed to see guests for the first time and the guests had stayed too long.' Though Admiral McIntire continued in denial, the patient was becoming more aware of his condition. 'Well, what did you expect?' he asked his son when Elliott showed his shock at his father's appearance.

After the election, he went to Warm Springs in Georgia for treatment. At Thanksgiving, he began carving the turkeys at a dinner attended by 110 other patients. They found him looking old and ill, coughing and shaking as he told his usual string of stories. Though he could be bright and engaged, at times he looked awful, falling asleep in his chair, and complaining of headaches. His blood pressure was still very high, he continued to lose weight, his teeth troubled him, and his appetite was poor – Dr Bruenn prescribed egg-nogs. Though keen for another summit, he said this should be after he was inaugurated for a fourth term in January.

Poland does not seem to have swayed many votes in America – Roosevelt did well in cities with high Polish immigrant populations. But Churchill was keen to close the running dispute with Moscow. On 2 November, he called in the government-in-exile to urge it to reach agreement with Moscow. 'Like a big sheep-dog, watchdog, rather, he barked imperiously at his Polish flock, who were spared neither warning bites nor shafts of sarcasm,' the ambassador Count Raczynski wrote. London would withdraw its guarantees to Poland if he did not get their accord on the Curzon Line, Churchill warned. The Poles stuck to their rejection of Stalin's conditions.[2]

Nor did Mikołajczyk get any help from Washington. When he wrote to Roosevelt raising Molotov's assertion about his attitude at Teheran, the reply said US policy was to decline to guarantee any specific frontiers, which would be the concern of the future world organisation. Talking to Harriman, when he visited Washington, the President said once more he considered European problems so impossible that he wanted to stay out of them as much as he could, except for Germany.

Still, he added that he could act as an arbitrator between the USSR and Poland and Finland. But only one aspect of the Polish issue seemed to interest him – the future of Lvov – as he evolved a fantastic notion of an international authority for the city of Poles on Ukrainian territory. Finally, he said he would not object to the Curzon Line if the Poles, Russians and British all agreed to it. At the embassy in Moscow, the tough-minded George Kennan, who felt that the West should have had 'a full-fledged and realistic political showdown' with Moscow over its failure to help the Warsaw Rising, grieved that there was 'something frivolous about our whole action on this Polish question. I reflected on the lightheartedness with which great powers offer advice to smaller ones in matters affecting the vital interests of the latter.' When a former US ambassador to Warsaw urged

Roosevelt to take a strong line, the President sighed: 'Do you want me to go to war with Russia?'[2]

Caught between the extremist hawks among the London Poles, Stalin's obduracy and lack of support from the West, Mikołajczyk resigned on 24 November. Meeting him a few days later, Churchill assured him, 'Don't worry, I'll never forget Poland.' But the British leader wrote to Stalin that London would take a 'cold' attitude towards the new government-in-exile, headed by an old socialist who had fought the Russians in the First World War and had been smuggled out of his homeland. When Churchill expressed a hope that Mikołajczyk might return, Stalin dismissed him as 'incapable of helping a Polish settlement. Indeed, his negative role has been revealed.'

As Kennan had put it that autumn, the USSR was set on becoming the dominant power in central and eastern Europe while being committed to a vague policy known in the West as collaboration. 'The first of these programmes implies taking. The second implies giving,' Kennan wrote with unfashionable realism. 'No one can stop Russia taking, if she is determined to go through with it. No one can force Russia to do the giving, if she is determined not to go through with it.'

In one instance, however, Stalin did give – on a tough-minded calculation of Soviet interests. When the 50,000-strong Greek Communist army tried to seize power in December from the London-backed government installed in Athens, Moscow told it to expect no help. Showing fealty to the percentages agreement, he also demonstrated that he was ready to subordinate indigenous Communists to broader Soviet interests – in Yugoslavia, he delayed recognising Tito's movement as the legitimate government until he established that this would not alienate the Western Allies. Greece was marginal for him. If he could get British acceptance of Soviet control of much more important Romania, he would sacrifice the Greek Communists.[3]

Still, the revolt in Greece went well at first. The small British contingent was besieged as fighting flared through the streets of Athens. Leftist forces spread out across the country. Alexander flew in, and decided to send reinforcements from Italy. It was the only time when Western troops fought to prevent Communist rule in a European country, a demonstration of *realpolitik* by Churchill with Stalin's acquiescence.

This aroused criticism in Britain – though a vote of confidence in the Commons was won by 279 votes to 30. On Christmas Eve, Churchill decided to fly to Athens – driving Clementine to tears at the abandonment of the family celebration. He, Eden and Moran drove to Northolt aerodrome outside London to travel via Naples from where the Prime Minister sent a cable home with his Christmas love – 'I am sorry indeed not to see the tree,' he wrote. Arriving the following evening, the British party travelled by armoured car to a cruiser, the *Ajax*, which was to be its headquarters.

At discussions attended by Macmillan, Alexander reported that British troops were advancing slowly in house-to-house fighting. Churchill said the only way out was a round table with the Greeks, including the leaders of the revolt.

In the morning, shells landed near the cruiser before he was driven to the British Embassy. As he arrived at the legation, a woman was shot dead in the street. Clambering out, Churchill stood gazing up at a house, his fingers raised in a V-sign to people looking out of the windows.

The British group went on to the Foreign Ministry where they were met by an old man who showed them to a room with a huge table on which hurricane lamps flickered. The Archbishop of Athens sat in the centre. The Greek Prime Minister, George Papandreou, and his government were opposite. The extremely tall, black robed, long bearded cleric rose with a welcoming speech – Churchill reckoned that, with his hat, he stood seven feet high. The Prime Minister replied that Britain would not shrink from preserving Athens from anarchy.

At that point there was a knock on the door. Three men from the Elas Communist movement came in, their leader wearing a grey waterproof coat and brown muffler over a British uniform. Papandreou did not look at them. Moran noted that the Communists seemed much more lively than the haggard, scrawny ministers. Churchill told the meeting Britain wanted no territory in Greece, but could not leave until the crisis had been settled. The Communist leader, Partsalides, said the rising had been undertaken because those involved 'believed in the destruction of Fascism, in the right to live free upon a basis laid down in the Atlantic Charter'. He referred to Britain as 'our great ally' even as his men were fighting its soldiers in the streets outside.

Having brought the warring Greek parties together, Churchill said it was time for him to withdraw to let them try to find a solution. He walked round the table, shaking hands with the members of the government.

Forgetting his previous vows not to do the same with the Elas representatives, he grasped their hands too. On the way back to the ship he said they were different from the Lublin Poles. Had they not wrung his hand? If the three of them could be got to dine with him, all difficulties might vanish. Of one thing he was sure, he wrote to his wife, the hatred among the Greek factions was so intense that 'a frightful massacre would take place if we withdrew'.

The next day, the archbishop told Churchill all the parties had agreed he should become regent in place of the king, a deeply divisive figure. Churchill accepted this, despite fears that the cleric might become a second de Gaulle. Back in London, the Prime Minister and Eden talked to the monarch-in-exile till 4.30 a.m., finally getting him to submit to the regency and to undertake publicly not to return home unless a plebiscite showed he was wanted. The British gained the upper hand over the rebels in Athens, and advanced into other cities, while anti-Communist Greek forces were victorious in the north. In mid-January, the Communists gave up. Rightists in the army and police took their revenge with a 'white terror' that sought to destroy the remnants of their organisation – unsuccessfully since left-wing guerrilla attacks began in 1946 and the country then descended into civil war, which would produce the enunciation of the Truman Doctrine on limiting the spread of Communist by force, if necessary.

That was being far from the American attitude at the end of 1944, and the British intervention came in for heavy criticism across the Atlantic, arousing all the old fears about British imperialism, Churchill's bellicosity, and spheres of influence. Linking Poland and Greece, the new Secretary of State, Stettinius, told Eden that events in the two countries were 'causing great resentment' in the United States. 'Military people were going so far as to say that we ought to withdraw from Europe and "go to the Pacific now and win the war there".' Press reports presented the Communists as resistance fighters being attacked by Britain on behalf of Greek reactionaries and in pursuit of its own east Mediterranean ambitions. Warsaw, it could be argued, was on the road to Berlin; Athens led nowhere, and was important only in the scheme of British designs for the region.

'It grieves me very much to see signs of our drifting apart at a time when unity becomes ever more important, as danger recedes and faction arises,'

Churchill cabled Hopkins. On 9 December, Admiral King had commanded American landing craft to stop helping British forces in Greece. Learning of this, Churchill drafted a message to Roosevelt warning of 'a disaster of the first magnitude' threatening to 'endanger all the relations between Great Britain and the United States'. He was, he added, sure the President had not seen the naval orders and would 'have them stamped upon at the earliest moment'. Deciding not to send the message, Churchill telephoned Hopkins, using his cover name of John Martin. The line was so bad that the aide could not understand what he was talking about. The following morning, Hopkins became aware of the Admiral's decision, and suggested to Leahy that it should be reversed. The White House Chief of Staff agreed. Hopkins told Churchill Roosevelt had not been aware of what King had done.

There was also concern in Washington when Churchill referred to the agreement to leave territorial arrangements for a post-war peace conference, except for 'changes mutually agreed'. This raised the question of whether such mutual agreements had been made by London in secret. Another storm broke out when Churchill's secretary, John Colville, sent a message from the Prime Minister to the British commander in Athens, calling the Greek capital 'a conquered city'. Colville should have marked the message with the notation 'Guard' used for messages relating to purely British matters which should not go to the Americans. But, sending the cable to the Foreign Office for despatch at 5 a.m., Colville forgot. Leaked to the *Washington Post*, this aroused fresh criticism of Britain which Churchill tried to calm by a note to Hopkins assuring him that 'I certainly do not want to fight another war.'

'British troops fighting against the guerrillas who fought the Nazis for the last four years. How the British can dare such a thing!' Elliott recalled his father saying in private. 'The lengths to which they will go to hang on to the past! Killing Greek guerrillas! Using British soldiers for such a job!' To London, he was much more moderate, explaining that the adverse reaction in American public opinion meant he could not 'stand with you in the present course of events in Greece'.

Churchill's response showed his disappointment: 'We desire nothing from Greece but to do our duty by the common cause. In the midst of our task of bringing food and relief and maintaining the rudiments of order . . . we have become involved in a furious, though not very bloody, struggle. I have felt it much that you were unable to give a word of explanation for our action but I understand your difficulties.' Six weeks later, he wrote to his wife that 'the bitter misunderstandings which have arisen in the United States, and in degenerate circles at home [over Greece], are only a foretaste of the furies which will be loosened about every stage of the peace settlement.'

While the Greek crisis blew up, the Western Allies had to face their first major reverse on the European battlefield. On 6 December, Churchill wrote to Roosevelt of 'the serious and disappointing war situation' as their troops fell behind schedule in the move to the Rhine. Ten days later, things got worse when 250,000 German troops attacked in the Ardennes, advancing 60 miles. By Christmas, the offensive had been halted and the progress towards Germany resumed. In the east, despite tough resistance, the Red Army was steadily moving to the German frontier.

Against this background, a briefing paper by the State Department argued that tension was rising in Europe because of Moscow's suspicions that Britain was promoting right-wing, anti-Russian regimes while London viewed 'with apprehension the possibility that the Soviet Government will endeavour in its turn to install and support left-wing totalitarian governments'. In the circumstances, it added, Washington should be ready to take part in inter-Allied commissions to ensure free elections, civil liberties, and economic and social reforms. A Provisional Security Council for Europe should be established made up of the US, the USSR, Britain and France, to guarantee that provisional governments in liberated countries represented the broad sweep of opinion, and that free elections were held.[4]

Roosevelt was getting increasingly rigorous advice as to what lay over the rainbow he had evoked in Teheran. George Kennan thought that the line should be drawn with the USSR though he did not say where. There would be fireworks but 'should the Western world stand firm . . . Moscow would have played its last real card.' Noting that Stalin was making no practical distinction between countries which had sided with Germany and those whose governments-in-exile had backed resistance, Harriman reported that the USSR was using 'occupation troops, secret police, local communist parties, labor unions, sympathetic leftist organizations, sponsored cultural societies and economic pressure to assure the establishment of regimes which . . . actually depend for their existence on groups responsive to all suggestions emanating from the Kremlin.'

The US Embassy in Moscow found that military success was making the Soviets overbearing. Stalin dragged his feet when asked for more information on his intentions and did not divulge plans drawn up by the Soviet High Command for a forty-five-day advance on Berlin. The secrecy about Red Army plans in the Far East was such that a war game room was set up in the American embassy ballroom where officers took on the roles of Japanese and Soviet commanders to try to see what each side would do.

In a letter to Marshall in December, John Deane, head of the US military mission, expressed the frustration built up over the three years in Moscow. 'I have sat at innumerable Russian banquets and become gradually nauseated by Russian food, vodka and protestations of friendship,' he wrote. 'Each person high in public life proposes a toast a little sweeter than the preceding one on Soviet–British–American friendship. It is amazing how these toasts go down past the tongues in the cheeks. After the banquets, we send the Russians another thousand airplanes, and they approve a visa that has been hanging for months. We then scratch our heads to see what other gifts we can send, and they scratch theirs to see what else they can ask for.'

In this context, the State Department noted that 'American interests require that every effort be made by this Government to assist France . . . to regain her strength and her influence . . . with a view toward enabling the French to assume larger responsibilities in connection with the maintenance of peace.'[5]

The shape of de Gaulle's policy was already evident. Though France was anchored in the Western camp, the general sought leverage by positioning himself between Washington and Moscow, pursuing policies he would follow until the late 1960s. He gained ground in obtaining an occupation zone in Germany and in getting favourable frontier arrangements. France was admitted to the European Advisory Commission. Washington agreed to equip eight French divisions to join the final fight in the west. Hopkins went to Paris to see de Gaulle, who was chilly because he was going to be excluded from the next Roosevelt–Stalin–Churchill summit. The American envoy suggested a subsequent rendezvous with the President which the French leader accepted.

At the end of 1944, de Gaulle visited Moscow for talks with Stalin to establish his country's international position and sign a Franco-Soviet friendship treaty. He did not inform Churchill or Roosevelt in advance – they learned of the proposed treaty from the Kremlin.

The Russians did not make the journey easy, refusing to let de Gaulle fly in to the capital and forcing him to take a four-day train journey in the bitter cold. But Harriman noted that Stalin treated the Frenchman with respect. Learning that the Soviet leader was pressing the visitor to recognise the Lublin Committee as the price for agreeing to the treaty, Harriman went to see the general to warn him of the adverse reaction this would provoke in Washington. At a reception later in the day, de Gaulle took the ambassador aside to say he had told Stalin he would take no action on Poland without consulting Washington and London. All he would agree to was to post a military officer to the Soviet backed group.*

He added that, after the war, smaller European nations would have to rally round France to avoid Soviet domination. Britain was an island; America was far away; so France would assume a leadership role.

In a toast at the final banquet, the Soviet leader urged the visitors to 'drink more wine and then everything will straighten out'. His guest was one of those moderate drinkers he distrusted. He raised his glass to Roosevelt as 'the great leader for peace as for war' and Churchill as 'a man of indestructible fighting spirit' but ignored the Frenchman. Drunk, the Georgian went round his entourage saying they would be shot if they did not perform satisfactorily. Seeing Molotov and the French Foreign Minister, Georges Bidault, discussing details of a new draft of the Franco–Soviet treaty, he cried out: 'Bring the machine guns. Let's liquidate the diplomats.'

After the meal, de Gaulle sat through the usual film, but left when a second was shown. In the early hours, he was called back to the Kremlin, and presented with the original version of the friendship pact to sign. 'France has been insulted,' the furious general replied, starting to stalk from the room. Stalin told Molotov to get a new draft, which was signed at 6.30 a.m. As the Frenchman left, Stalin called after his interpreter: 'You

---

* De Gaulle had gone to Poland in 1919 as part of a Western military mission to help Warsaw fight the Bolsheviks. Unlike Churchill's recurrent references to his support for intervention in Russia, there is no record of this having been mentioned during the Moscow talks.

know too much. I'd better send you to Siberia.' On his way out, de Gaulle looked back; Stalin was sitting alone at a table, eating again.

In January 1945, as the British gained the upper hand in Greece, the Lublin Committee proclaimed itself Poland's provisional government, winning peasant support by breaking up estates and distributing land. Stalin promptly recognised the new administration. There was no point in dealing with émigré groups, he advised the West. Though there should have been nothing surprising about this, Roosevelt told the Kremlin he was 'disturbed and deeply disappointed' that the Soviets had not waited until the Big Three had had a chance to discuss the situation. The State Department defined US policy as aiming at 'the eventual establishment by the Polish people of a truly democratic government of their own choice'. Churchill told Stalin he was 'distressed'.[6]

The ensuing border changes gave the Soviet Union 70,000 square miles of territory, with 10 million inhabitants, according to the last census which did not take account of wartime deaths. Poland gained 27,000 square miles of land in East Prussia, Danzig, Pomerania and Silesia, containing some 15 million people, the overwhelming majority of them German, many of whom fled westward in one of the biggest population movements Europe had seen. Absorbing the new territory would make Warsaw even more dependent on Soviet help, while the huge refugee influx would place an added burden on Germany. As the logic of their Polish policies played out, Roosevelt and Churchill could only hope that Stalin would prove more flexible when the Big Three met.

Apart from Poland, Moscow had taken over the Baltic States, and held Finland in thrall. A 'Fatherland Front' was installed in Bulgaria after the Red Army invaded that country. Stalin got his quid pro quo for Greece when Romanian Communists took power in Bucharest, supervised by Vyshinsky – Churchill sent Eden a memo saying Britain must not 'press our hand too far' there, and adding: 'Remember the percentages we wrote out on paper . . . It is an awful thing we cannot have it both ways.' Though the installation of controlled regimes in Hungary and Czechoslovakia would take longer, the future of the first appeared to have been determined, and the second teetered on a knife edge. Tito was on his way to controlling Yugoslavia, and the National Liberation Army had taken over from the departing Germans in Albania.

Stalin had enough. Austria's neutrality, presaged at Teheran, was respected; it was treated as the first of Hitler's victims, rather than a country where the union with Germany in 1938 had been widely welcomed. West European Communist parties were told to disband resistance forces, and join the democratic process. This was the message Togliatti had taken back to Italy from Moscow in the summer. Seeing the French party leader Maurice Thorez, Stalin instructed him to 'pursue a left bloc' line in a form appropriate for France, not to defy de Gaulle, to cultivate socialists and moderate parties, and to back the rebirth of a militarily and industrially powerful France, with a united army in which he should try to get good positions for Communist resistance veterans.

Despite his annoyance over Moscow's recognition of the new government in Warsaw, Roosevelt was still focusing on improving relations with Stalin. So, when Molotov resurrected the matter of a loan, first mooted at the beginning of 1944 but dropped for technical reasons, Washington reacted positively. The Foreign Minister handed Harriman a note mentioning a $6-billion credit. Dropping earlier Treasury objections, Morgenthau raised this to $10 billion – his pro-Soviet feelings were still strong. Then the State Department brought the proposed amount back down to the Soviet figure. Talks began through the embassy in Washington, and Harriman expected it to figure at the next Big Three summit. But, for some reason, it did not, and his hopes that it might offer both leverage and business for US companies came to nothing.[7]

At the end of 1944, the President repeated to Churchill his intention of bringing troops home as rapidly as possible once the fighting ended. That, the Prime Minister replied, 'causes me alarm'. If US forces went home and France had not yet formed a proper army, 'how will it be possible to hold down western Germany beyond the present Russian occupied line?' he asked. 'All would therefore rapidly disintegrate as it did last time.' Roosevelt responded that there should be no problem in providing a French army with equipment taken from the Germans, while Harriman recalled that Marshall and Eisenhower trusted the Russians because they had kept their word militarily. Such was Roosevelt's desire not to ruffle the Kremlin that, when the OSS secret service got hold of a book of Soviet intelligence codes, he ordered it to be returned, without notes having been made of its contents – the OSS boss, William Donovan, copied it all the same.

*

China remained a major problem. Despite US efforts, Chiang Kai-shek and Mao Zedong were intent on renewing their civil war. The Generalissimo remarked pointedly to Patrick Hurley, who had become the US ambassador, that he did not want a repetition in his country of what had happened in Poland and Yugoslavia. His perennial concern about the reliability of American support was deepened by the discovery of an OSS plan to train and equip the Communists.[8]

He would have been even more concerned had he learned that Stalin had raised with the Americans his desire to regain Tsarist-era railway rights in Manchuria, as well as island territories north of Japan. Harriman noted that Red Army troops would probably be sent in to guard the lines, extending Soviet influence to the region. This would also open a channel for aid for the Chinese Communists, whose strength lay mainly in the north. With China's economy in ruins, society ripped apart by eight years of war, endemic corruption, no convincing leadership from Chiang, and regional barons resisting his control, Roosevelt's Fourth Policeman looked ever less able to fit the role he had laid out for it.

When it came to international organisations, the allied picture was mixed. The Bretton Woods conference had laid down the post-war international monetary system on American-led lines. Other talks covered cooperation in areas such as food supplies, health and labour. An American bid to force through a civil aviation agreement that would have opened up world routes to its companies ran into stiff British opposition; the argument became so heated that Roosevelt and Churchill had to step in to formulate a compromise that led to the US making bilateral arrangements. Such incidents deepened suspicions in Congress and the administration that London would be an unwilling partner in the new world.[9]

After the inconclusive end of the Dumbarton Oaks talks during the summer, Leo Pasvolsky, the Russian-speaking State Department official, held protracted discussions with the Soviet ambassador, but Gromyko gave no ground. At the end of December, Stalin rejected an American suggestion for the Big Three to show moral leadership by agreeing to abstain from voting on a dispute in which they were involved. 'The unanimity of permanent members is necessary in all decisions of the Council in regard to a determination of a threat to peace,' he insisted.

The State Department warned that agreement on complete unanimity would be seen as surrender to the Kremlin, and 'gravely alienate many sincere supporters of the Dumbarton Oaks'. Stettinius stressed the 'urgent need' for an accord as delay would bring 'slackening of interest and possible growth of opposition'. The spectre of Wilson and the League of Nations hovered.

With such tensions and uncertainties in the air, a Big Three summit was clearly needed. The Western leaders suggested the Mediterranean, or Jerusalem. Stalin insisted on the Crimea. The President said he wanted to sleep on a warship, but that navigating the Dardanelles would be troublesome, requiring escort vessels needed elsewhere. Hopkins, who was in London, sent Roosevelt a message relaying Churchill's remark on the Crimea: 'If we had spent ten years on research, we could not have found a worse place in the world.' But, the aide added, the Prime Minister felt 'he can survive it by bringing an adequate supply of whisky. He claims it is good for typhus and deadly on lice which thrive in those parts.'

Stalin told Harriman his doctors advised him against making a long trip, and mentioned that he had suffered from ear trouble incurred on the flight from Teheran. Once more, he got his way with an agreement to meet in Yalta in February.

It would be only the second meeting of the Big Three, but also the last. The conference would go down as the moment at which the world was divided among the victors. The reality was that the contours of the Cold War were largely set even before the three leaders met. The task for Roosevelt and Churchill was to make the best of the situation on the ground, even before the hot war had been won.

20

Yalta

'It was the best I could do'
ROOSEVELT

I

Getting There

The sun glistened on the waves and a light breeze blew as the President's
heavy cruiser, the *Quincy*, entered the harbour of Valetta on the island of
Malta at 9.30 a.m. on 2 February. Spitfires flew overhead. Bands on British
ships played 'The Star-Spangled Banner'. Roosevelt sat on the deck, his
black cape draped on his shoulders, a cotton cap on his head, acknowledging
the salutes from warships and the cheering from crowds on the quayside; all
the island was out to greet him. Passing the British cruiser *Orion*, the American
leader spotted Churchill. The two leaders waved to one another. Roosevelt
held much of the world's fate in his hands, Eden wrote in his diary.[1]

He had gone through his fourth inauguration on 20 January. He
insisted on standing for the ceremony and, despite the bitter cold, did not
wear a coat, hat or waistcoat. Before the lunch that day, he suffered an
angina attack – to revive himself, he drained half a glass of whisky as if it was
a soft drink. Passing his chair at the occasion, Frances Perkins said she
would pray for him. 'For God's sake, do,' he replied. 'I need it.'

Two days later, he boarded the *Quincy* at the naval base at Newport

News. The big ship took him 4,883 miles across the Atlantic and through the Mediterranean to stop at the British island on the way to the summit in the Crimea. He celebrated his sixty-third birthday at sea on 30 January – among the gifts was a package from Lucy Rutherfurd and Margaret Suckley containing useful gifts for the trip, such as thermometers, pocket combs and a cigarette lighter for use in the ocean wind.

Hopkins said later that most of those around Roosevelt opposed the journey and 'could not understand why the President of the United States should cart himself all over the world to meet Stalin'. Suckley recorded that her cousin 'doesn't relish this trip at all – thinks it will be very wearing & feels that he will have to be so much on the alert in his conversations with Uncle Joe and WSC. The conversations will last interminably & will involve very complicated questions.'

Perkins recalled that his appearance veered sharply, with very brief fainting fits. 'From looking badly and looking as if he were a ghost, in a couple of hours later, you'd see he'd be all right . . . he'd look fine again – his eyes bright,' she wrote. 'The change in appearance had to do with the incoming of a kind of glassy eye, and an extremely drawn look around the jaw and cheeks, and even a sort of dropping of the muscles of control of the jaw and mouth, as though they weren't working exactly . . . close to, you would see that his hands were weak.'

When he boarded the *Quincy* in Malta, Averell Harriman was 'terribly shocked' to see the President's physical deterioration since their last meeting in Washington in the autumn. Roosevelt admitted that his 'ticker trouble' was far more serious than generally thought to his daughter, Anna Boettinger, who was accompanying him to Yalta – she was lodged in the admiral's quarters. Charles Bohlen, who had been with Hopkins on his tour of western Europe, found the one-time Happy Warrior 'not only frail and desperately tired, but ill'.

The hand of death was on the President, but his desire to do all he could to make the summit a success was such that he accepted the argument from the Kremlin that it was Stalin's state of health which meant they had to meet at Yalta. That this was an initial power play – and also pandered to the dictator's dislike of flying – was evident. Yet, the President must have sensed that he might not have much time left in which to achieve his global aims, so he made the long journey.

*

Travelling under the codename of Colonel Kent, Churchill had flown from snowy London to Malta on 30 January, with his daughter Sarah. Sitting huddled in his greatcoat on his converted bomber, he looked like 'a poor hot pink baby about to cry,' she reported to her mother. Developing a high temperature once again, he rested on a British warship after arriving, sitting, his daughter noted, like 'a dejected lump' on his bed before stretching out and 'sleeping like a lamb'.[2]

Churchill read a book on India, which made him depressed. He wrote to Clementine that he was determined to make sure the imperial flag was 'not let down while I am at the wheel'. 'The world is in a frightful state,' he told her in a cable. 'The whole world appals me and I fear increasingly that new struggles may arise out of those we are successfully ending.' Moran recorded in his diary that, at one point, his patient turned his face to the wall and called out for his wife. He ended his message to her:

> Tender Love my darling
> I miss you very much
> I am lonely amid this throng
> Your ever loving husband.

By 2 February, Churchill was well enough to cross to the American cruiser to see Roosevelt. The two men lunched with their daughters and Eden and Stettinius. Roosevelt had a small candle set by his visitor's place to light his cigars.[3]

Strong pressure from Downing Street over the previous month – 'pertinacity' Churchill called it – had induced the American leader to agree to the bilateral encounter before they met Stalin. Churchill, who counted on a follow-up meeting after the Big Three summit, greeted this by drafting a couplet reading:

> No more let us alter or falter or palter.
> From Malta to Yalta, and Yalta to Malta.

He thought better of employing the rarely used verb at the end of the first line, meaning, according to various definitions, 'to mumble, babble, shuffle in statement or dealing', 'to act or talk insincerely or deceitfully', and 'to haggle in bargaining'. 'Perhaps it was as well that I did not send it,' he wrote in his memoirs. Instead, his message declared: 'No more let us falter! From Malta to Yalta! Let nobody falter!'

Before the two leaders arrived in Malta, the Combined Chiefs of Staff held half a dozen meetings to review war plans, during which Eisenhower's staff outlined the push on the Rhine. Sitting on either side of a long, rectangular table with a globe positioned at one end, they agreed that the most likely date for victory was 20 June 1945, though it was possible that the Soviet offensive might advance this to the middle of April. There was a sharp clash over strategy, with the British wanting to go faster and the Americans insisting on a broad front approach.

Eden and Stettinius met for a day of talks. The main matter was Poland, on which Eden was pleased to find the Secretary of State and Hopkins 'fully alive' to the seriousness of the issue. Stettinius warned that an 'equitable solution' was needed to satisfy US public opinion, particularly Catholics. Simple recognition of the Lublin Committee was out of the question; what was needed was a council of all groups.

As for Roosevelt, while acquiescing to the meeting in Malta, he was in no hurry to talk substance, setting off after lunch on a thirty-mile motor tour of the island. When he and Churchill did hold a session with the Chiefs of Staff, it lasted just fifty minutes. Brooke wrote in his diary that the Prime Minister had not read the briefing paper and 'made the most foolish remarks'. Though disinclined to be involved in details, Roosevelt did get Churchill's reluctant accord to withdraw 2 British divisions from Greece, and to send 3 divisions from Italy to north-west Europe. Dinner on the *Quincy* that night was a social occasion. After it, Roosevelt was driven to the airfield and was hoisted on an elevator into his converted bomber where he went to bed, awaiting the 3.30 a.m. take-off for the Crimea – there was, he said, 'an awful day ahead,' but he had succeeded in avoiding the kind of planning session Churchill so desired.

Eden pointed out to Hopkins 'that we were going into a decisive conference and had so far neither agreed what we would discuss nor how to handle matters with a Bear who would certainly know his mind'. The British could only note, in the Foreign Secretary's words, how Roosevelt 'moved out of step with us, influenced by his conviction that he could get better results with Stalin direct than could the three countries negotiating together.'

It was not a matter of the President trusting the Marshal, rather of seeking to manoeuvre him into positions that suited American ends. This was not a game Roosevelt could refrain from. 'What he thought he could do was to outwit Stalin as he had done with so many interlocutors,' as Walter Lippmann wrote. At Yalta, he wanted agreement on the United Nations and a firm commitment of Soviet entry into the war in the Pacific. Apart from Germany, he was not greatly concerned about Europe, and did not wish to see issues such as Poland clouding his main targets or, even worse, endangering his post-war plans.

For his part, Stalin came to Yalta with clear aims – to maintain the deep security zone conquered by the Red Army in eastern Europe, to assert his country's position as a great power, and to ensure that Germany would not be able to attack Russia again. 'We are interested in decisions and not in discussions,' as he said at one point. He would show himself a self-assured master of negotiation, he and Molotov forming a perfect team.

Churchill's position was much weaker, as the other two leaders well knew. He could still speak strongly and eloquently, making very valid points. But his country was the least powerful of the Allies, and had long lost its aura of 1940. The Americans and Soviets both felt they had the wind of the future in their sails; the Prime Minister, all too easily, appeared to be a man of the past, desperate to hold on to what he had and knowing that his country's power and status would depend on him being able to manoeuvre between the other two. Though there was the usual bonhomie when the Big Three met for the second and last time, he and the other two were, as Bohlen wrote, 'waging a fierce struggle on the shape of the postwar world'.

II

2–3 February

On the night of 2 February, a flight of 25 aircraft flew the 700 Americans and British over the Mediterranean, Aegean and Black Seas to Saki airfield in the Crimea.[4]

Roosevelt's 'Sacred Cow' arrived first, with a fighter escort. The

President stayed in the plane until Churchill landed twenty minutes later after what he described as 'a long and cold flight'. Wearing his dark cape and a trilby hat, the American leader was lowered to the slushy ground, and put into an open jeep from which he leaned forward, smiling broadly to chat with Hopkins. Molotov stood beside them, his right hand stuck into his black overcoat. A Soviet driver drove the President past an honour guard, the Prime Minister walking alongside.

Roosevelt appeared frail and ill, Churchill recalled. Moran noted that he looked straight ahead with his mouth open, 'as if he was not taking things in'. Churchill tried to raise summit issues, but the Soviet microphones bugging them picked up Roosevelt telling him everything had been discussed and decided.

After being served vodka, champagne, caviar, smoked sturgeon and black bread, the visitors boarded a fleet of Lend-Lease Packards with Russian drivers for the eighty-mile road from Saki to Yalta through deep valleys, with torrents rushing down from the mountains. The going was slow on the bumpy, snowy road. The countryside was bleak; only a few peasants were to be seen. Soviet troops, some of them women, stood guard, raising their rifles at a 30-degree angle in salute. As the cars climbed to a 2,500-foot mountain pass, the lowering clouds gave way to bright sunshine. When not snoozing, Roosevelt stared at gutted buildings, burned out trains and wrecked tanks – it was his first sight of the devastation of the war. In the separate British motorcade, Churchill asked Sarah how long they had been going.

'About an hour,' she replied.

'Christ,' he exclaimed. 'Five more hours of this.' He began to swear as his daughter worried about the lack of toilet facilities.

Two hours later, the British stopped to eat stale ham sandwiches brought from Malta, with soup and a swig of brandy. 'The call of nature was pretty desperate by now!' Sarah wrote to her mother. 'I scanned the horizon: cars in front – press photographers behind!! Obviously no future in that!'

Driving on, they reached a rest house where they were led to a small room with tables covered with food and wine – and a toilet. The Americans had not stopped, but the British ate what they could. Continuing their journey, they found the countryside more attractive crossing the mountains and descending through cypress trees towards the Black Sea. Churchill recited Byron's *Don Juan* before falling asleep.

Famous for health cures and its association with Chekhov, Yalta was badly damaged in fighting before the Germans withdrew, taking everything with them down to the doorknobs. Given the destruction, Churchill described the resort as 'the Riviera of Hades'. Four NKVD regiments guarded the town. Anti-aircraft batteries were set up, and 160 fighter planes deployed. More than 70,000 local inhabitants were checked, and 835 arrested as security risks. A thousand workers were drafted in to repair the accommodation. Hotel staff came from Moscow, bringing plates and cutlery. Bakeries were set up. A US naval delousing team arrived, but Anna Roosevelt found insects in the beds.[5]

Roosevelt and senior members of his party occupied the twenty-one-room Livadia Palace, overlooking the sea, its white walls camouflaged. The former summer home of the last Tsars, who had been visited there by Mark Twain, it had been a rest home before the war and was then taken over by the German commander. The American leader's ground-floor suite consisted of a living room, dining room and a bedroom in the Tsar's study. As at Teheran, he had the single private bath – Kathleen Harriman and the President's daughter shared a small room opposite it. Anna wrote to her husband, John Boettinger, that the mattress was so thin she could feel the springs. A Soviet military officer, she added, 'tried to pet me'. Roosevelt described him as 'a most sinister-appearing pest' who resembled some big businessmen he had known. Hopkins told Anna that Kathleen had had a torrid affair with Franklin Roosevelt Jr. She informed her father.[6]

George Marshall was in the Tsar's bedroom while Admiral King was ribbed for occupying the Tsarina's boudoir. The rest of the American party stayed in recently renovated, whitewashed rooms on the upper floor or in houses on the surrounding estate. Sixteen colonels shared one room.

Down the coast, the British had a light-brown, late Tsarist-era mansion built for a prince in a mixture of Gothic and Moroccan styles. Outside stood six large stone statues of lions. In the conservatory, there was a fish tank, which was empty, but was filled with goldfish by the Russians after Charles Portal remarked on it being unfilled – Sarah Churchill saw the RAF chief feeding them with bluebottles he caught in the library.

The villa looked 'a bit like a Scottish baronial hall inside and a Swiss Chalet plus Mosque outside', she wrote to her mother. 'Though the ablutions question is grim, it is warm and light, and Russian hospitality leaves little to be desired . . . Papa is very sweet and insists on me sharing his bathroom which I do – but if you were a spectator along the bedroom corridors here at about 7.30 in the morning, you would see 3 Field Marshals queuing for a bucket!' Cadogan called the mansion 'of indescribably ugliness . . . with all the furnishings of an almost terrifying hideosity'. At least he got to share Eden's bathroom. Again, there were bugs in the beds; Churchill was bitten in the foot. But Brooke was pleased by the birds on the shore in front of the house, spotting a great northern diver among the gulls.

Stalin settled into a villa on an estate once owned by the assassin of Rasputin, set in formal gardens with large pools and statues. The building had twenty rooms, and a 77-square-foot hall. A bomb shelter was constructed and a telephone exchange installed so that he could keep in touch with the Kremlin and the war fronts.

Snow-capped mountains rose behind all three mansions, offering protection from the wind. The Black Sea stretched in front, a promenade running along the shore. The town was surrounded by woods, vineyards, fruit farms and shingle beaches. Most of its houses were roofless shells.

There was caviar at breakfast, lunch and dinner, and decanters of vodka in the bedrooms – Sergio Beria recalled that the American and British guards regularly drank themselves under the table, and had to be carried to bed. Communication with the Russian staff was difficult as they did not speak English. After much pantomime, Hopkins's son, who was there as an army photographer, got over the message that he liked to start the day with eggs. He was brought a dozen, fried – along with a saucer of caviar. Soviet secret police kept a close watch. When Anna, Kathy and Robert Hopkins went for a walk and gave a child a chocolate bar, a soldier following them forced the infant to return it. 'Russian children aren't in need of food,' he said. After one meeting, Stalin went to the toilet when the guards were not looking. Two of them rushed up to Bohlen yelling 'Where's Stalin? Where has he gone?' They calmed down when the American told them.

III

4 February

Arriving by train on the morning of Sunday 4 February, Stalin called on Churchill and Roosevelt separately in the afternoon. He told the Prime Minister that he was optimistic about the progress of the war, reporting that the Soviet forces had established bridgeheads across the Oder River on Poland's western frontier. This put them only fifty miles from Berlin.[7]

Meeting Stalin in a small anteroom off the main entrance hall of the Livadia Palace, Roosevelt grinned and shook his host's hand warmly. The dictator gave a slight smile. They sat down on a plush couch with an inlaid table in front of them. Roosevelt, wearing a light suit and brightly coloured tie, mixed Martinis, and handed over a glass, apologising for the lack of lemon peel. The following morning, the Americans found a huge tree with 200 lemons standing by the door, flown in from Georgia.[8]

With Molotov and the two interpreters the only other people in the room, Roosevelt remarked that he had made bets aboard the *Quincy* that the Red Army would get to Berlin before the Americans reached Manila. Stalin gave a rather different report from what he had just told Churchill – hard fighting was holding up Soviet forces. Roosevelt said Eisenhower would not cross the Rhine till March because floating ice would cause difficulties earlier. Referring to the destruction he had seen on the drive to Yalta, he added: 'I'm more bloodthirsty than a year ago.'

When the talk turned to de Gaulle's visit to Moscow the President added he was going to say something indiscreet he would not mention in front of Churchill. The British were 'a peculiar people' who thought of artificially building up a French army against Germany. In this, they wished 'to have their cake and eat it'. They seemed to think the US should restore order in France, and then hand them political control.

What about France getting its occupation zone in Germany? Stalin asked.

Only out of kindness, the President replied.

That would be the *only* reason to give France a zone, Stalin concurred.

There was an element of play-acting in this. During his visit to Paris, Hopkins had undertaken that France would get a zone, which he would not have done without Roosevelt's authorisation. Stalin may well have learned of this from Communists in the administration in Paris. But bad-mouthing the French always has its appeal.

The Big Three then walked into their first full session with the military men. A lengthy paper from the Soviet General Staff described the eastern front campaign. Stalin said the Red Army had, out of 'our duty as allies', moved sooner than planned to help relieve pressure on the Anglo-American forces when they came under attack in the Ardennes. Churchill responded that Stalin could be depended on to do the right thing.

When the Russians asked for more air attacks on German communications lines to stop Hitler moving troops to the east, the British and Americans agreed to step up raids on Berlin, Leipzig and Dresden.[9]

The Americans were the first dinner hosts at the summit. By Russian standards, the menu was modest – caviar, consommé, sturgeon, beef, sweet cakes, fruit, vodka, five varieties of wine. For once, Roosevelt did not mix cocktails.[10]

The pressures of war were being felt by all three – Churchill was seventy, Stalin sixty-five, Roosevelt the youngest at sixty-three but in the worst health. Still, the US record reported that they 'appeared to be in very good humour throughout'. But Eden found the President 'vague and loose and ineffective', while Churchill talked too much. There were serious moments at the meal. Stalin said small countries should not have rights to enable them to contradict the big states; the Big Powers could not be put on the same rung as Albania. Roosevelt said the Big Three should write the peace. At which Churchill recited a verse: 'The eagle should permit the small birds to sing and care not wherefore they sang.'

When the Prime Minister raised his glass to the proletarian masses, the talk turned to the rights of people to govern themselves and get rid of leaders. Vyshinsky told Bohlen Americans should learn to obey their leaders and not raise questions. The diplomat replied that he would like to see the Russian go to the United States and say that. Vyshinsky responded that he would be glad to do so.

Roosevelt then said the American people would not let him keep troops in Europe after the war. Stalin could not have missed the import of this, but merely remarked that the West's weakness was that its people did not delegate permanent rights such as the Kremlin enjoyed.

Then there was an awkward moment when Roosevelt mentioned that he and Churchill referred to the Soviet leader in telegrams as 'Uncle Joe'.

According to Roosevelt's account of the time when he needled Churchill at Teheran to win over Stalin, he had mentioned the nickname then without provoking a reaction. But now the dictator asked angrily: 'When can I leave this table?'

'Half an hour,' Churchill replied.

James Byrnes, the Director of the Office of War Mobilization, saved the day. 'After all,' he said, 'you do not mind talking about Uncle Sam, so why should Uncle Joe be so bad?'

Stalin subsided. Molotov said later his boss understood the joke.

IV

5 February

At 3.55 p.m. on the Monday, as a Soviet newsreel cameraman at the entrance to the Livadia put it: 'first the huge cigar entered, which was followed by Winston Churchill, accompanied by his adjutant and his daughter Sarah.' A doorman, half concealed by the cloud of smoke, took his coat and fur hat. Seeing the cameraman, the British leader, who was in uniform with two rows of medals, pushed Sarah forward.[11]

Stalin was hardly visible among the throng of taller generals surrounding him. He wore his marshal's tunic with gold shoulder boards and walked slowly through the hall, waving from time to time to photographers. Finally, the half doors of the President's quarters opened and Roosevelt, who had been conferring with Hopkins, was wheeled out by a valet. He smiled, and shook hands with the other leaders. Then they went into the one-time Tsarist ballroom.

Twenty-six men sat at the table or on lines of chairs behind, the sun shining on them through French windows. At one end of the table, Stalin was flanked by Molotov, Vyshinsky, Maisky, Gousev and Gromyko. Eden sat beside Churchill at the other end of the table. The rest of the British party consisted of Cadogan, Clark Kerr and Sir Edward Bridges, the Cabinet secretary. On the other side of the table, Roosevelt was surrounded by Hopkins, Stettinius, Harriman, Byrnes, Leahy and H. Freeman Matthews, head of the State Department's European section. Bohlen, Pavlov and Birse interpreted.

Given Stettinius's lack of experience, Hopkins, who took the room next to Roosevelt's suite, continued to play a key role, even though he spent most of the summit in bed, and lost eighteen pounds. He had fallen ill again with dysentery during his trip to Europe, and had been drinking too much. He joked that his health had been fine until he had met the Pope. Moran described him as 'only half in this world . . . his skin was a yellow-white membrane stretched tight over his bones.' Getting up for plenary sessions, he sat behind Roosevelt. Back in bed, he held meetings with the delegation.

The leaders met each afternoon, for three or four hours from 4 p.m. The military chiefs held sessions in the morning. The Foreign Ministers gathered at lunchtime, their discussions delayed by toasts – seventeen on one occasion.

There was no orderly agenda. Issues were brought up, and dropped or shunted off. This could be confusing; but, in the best Rooseveltian manner, it meant arguments usually broke off below boiling point. Though the State Department had drawn up detailed 'black books' on topics which would arise, it became obvious that the President had not studied them closely.

Stalin was well informed about the thinking of the other participants by the Soviet spy ring in Britain and moles in Washington. He had also been supplied with psychological profiles of the two leaders. As at Teheran, microphones bugged the visitors. The listeners anticipated that Roosevelt would be wheeled out from time to time into the gardens of the Palace, so they traced a route, and placed microphones along it. The Americans were warned that, if they deviated from the paths, they might be blown up by unexploded mines.

The first subject for political discussion was Germany. Roosevelt handed out a map of the occupation zones. He rambled on about his youthful visits to Germany, talking of the evils of centralisation in what Bohlen called an 'inconclusive statement that didn't even hang together'. It was, the diplomat thought, 'the one place where I felt that his ill health might have affected his thinking'. His remarks were met with polite indifference from Stalin and boredom from the British. Churchill fiddled with his cigar, tapping his fingers on the table, Eden looked into the distance.[12]

In contrast, Stalin was all business. He wanted to know how Germany was to be dismembered – into five zones as he and Roosevelt had envisaged at Teheran or into Prussian and Austrian–Bavarian federations with the Ruhr and Westphalia under international control, as Churchill had suggested on his visit to Moscow. The Prime Minister objected that such decisions would take more than the five or six days of the summit, and he said he would find it difficult to do more than give assent to the principle of dismemberment. A month earlier, he had noted to Eden the danger of 'having a poisoned community in the heart of Europe'. He felt it best to leave the long-term future of Germany till later, he told the Foreign Secretary, rather than trying 'to write out on little pieces of paper what the vast emotions of an outraged and quivering world will be either immediately after the struggle is over or when the inevitable cold fit follows the hot.'

At the suggestion of Hopkins, Roosevelt shuffled off the issue by proposing that the Foreign Ministers should be asked to produce a plan in twenty-four hours – nothing came of this, leaving the military situation on the ground largely to decide the outcome. Bohlen thought none of the Big Three had his heart in dismemberment. The President had lost interest and 'was just giving lip service to a dying idea'. Churchill could see the need for Germany, as well as France, to balance Soviet power.

Confirming what Hopkins had told de Gaulle, Roosevelt agreed with Churchill that France should be given an occupation zone, carved out of US and British areas. Stalin said he had no objection so long as the French did not participate in the Control Commission that would supervise Germany.

Paris should share in helping to 'keep Germany down', Churchill remarked, since it was not known how long the United States would remain in its zone.

'I should like to know the President's opinion,' Stalin said.

'I can get the people and Congress to cooperate fully for peace but not to keep an army in Europe a long time,' was the reply. 'Two years would be the limit.'

In his memoirs, Churchill described this as 'a momentous statement'. In the meeting, he said he hoped it would be according to circumstances, adding: 'At all events we shall need the French to help us.'

'France is our ally,' Stalin interjected. 'We signed a pact with her. We want her to have a large army.' But he opposed Paris taking part in the control machinery.

'If the French are to have a zone, how can they be excluded from the control machinery?' Eden broke in. Molotov ended the discussion by saying it was agreed that France should have an occupation zone but that the Foreign Ministers should consider its relation to the control machinery.

Though the Morgenthau Plan was dead, Stalin told Maisky to set out Moscow's draconian scheme for reparations. Factories, machinery and rolling stock, amounting to 80 per cent of heavy industry, were to be removed in the two years after the war ended. Payments in kind would go on for ten years. All plants used to make weapons, including aviation factories, would be taken out of the country. Churchill recalled how little reparations had yielded after the First World War. He was haunted by the spectre of a starving Germany. If you wished a horse to pull a wagon, you had at least to give it fodder, he remarked. Right, Stalin replied, but take care the horse does not turn round and kick you.

That night, before going to sleep, Churchill told his daughter: 'I do not suppose that at any moment in history has the agony of the world been so great or widespread. Tonight the sun goes down on more suffering than ever before in the world.'[13]

V

6 February

At the next plenary the following afternoon, the first subject was the global body, on which Roosevelt pinned his hopes for peace. Some of the American team were disconcerted to find that Stalin had not read the proposal about voting Security Council procedures sent by Washington two months earlier. 'That guy can't be very interested in this peace organisation,' Hopkins remarked.[14]

Churchill reassured Stalin that, while the behaviour of the great powers could be criticised verbally, the veto system would make it virtually powerless for the organisation to act against the US, the USSR, Britain or China. Stalin asked if it would be unable to move against Britain over Hong Kong or British interests in Egypt. Churchill told him this was so.

Still suspicious, Stalin recalled how the League of Nations had expelled the USSR after its attack on Finland in 1939.

That would now be impossible, Eden said.

'Can we create even more obstacles?' Stalin asked.

There would be differences between the great powers, Roosevelt noted. Open discussions would demonstrate confidence between their governments, and strengthen unity. True, said Stalin. But, while Roosevelt foresaw 'a peace which will command good will from the overwhelming masses of the peoples of the world', the dictator wanted to ensure that the new organisation would be another brick in the USSR's defensive wall and could not become a Western tool against Moscow.

He knew the value of not agreeing immediately. So he said he wanted to study the scheme further, and discussion turned to the most sensitive issue on the table – Poland. With Churchill's support, Roosevelt floated the idea of a council of all Polish parties to prepare elections.

Stalin asked for a ten-minute break, and then launched into a bravura performance. He stressed that the security aspects of a Polish settlement were a life and death matter for the Soviet Union. Then he pointed out that the new eastern frontier he advocated between Poland and his country had been suggested by the British and French at the end of the First World War; how could he return to Moscow and be accused of getting less than Curzon and Clemenceau had proposed?

As for the new Polish administration, how could the Big Three act without the participation of the Poles? 'I am called a dictator and not a democrat, but I have enough democratic feeling to refuse to create a Polish government without the Poles being consulted – the question can only be settled with the consent of the Poles,' Stalin said. The Lublin Committee had at least as strong a democratic base as de Gaulle. The Red Army needed a secure rear area as it advanced on Germany, but agents of the London Poles were attacking its units. 'When I compare what the agents of the Lublin government have done and what the agents of the London government have done I see the first as good and second as bad,' he concluded.

It was a brilliant, supremely cynical, show, turning his puppets into a democratic, patriotic group, and picturing the London Poles as a danger to the war effort. Churchill said his information was different; in any case, Britain could not recognise the Lublin Committee as the government. Roosevelt tap-danced away, saying merely: 'Poland has been a source of trouble for over five hundred years.' To which Churchill responded: 'All the more must we do what we can to put an end to these troubles.' But the President was keen to end the discussion, so they adjourned for twenty-four hours.

That night, Roosevelt wrote a letter on Poland to Stalin after consulting Churchill, who stiffened its language. He warned that the differences of views could create the impression of a breach among them. Failure to reach agreement would be lamentable. So why not invite to Yalta two Lublin representatives and two or three from other Polish groups to seek an accord on a joint provisional government to prepare free elections?[15]

Ever alert to the domestic political daisy-chain, Roosevelt could see the danger that open discord on Poland might jeopardise his other plans by turning US opinion against cooperation with Moscow and putting the United Nations at risk. He warned Stalin that Americans would ask: 'If we cannot get a meeting of minds now when our armies are converging on the common enemy, how can we get an understanding on even more vital things in the future?' Thus, he put his finger on the fault line of the alliance.

VI

7 February

Anxious to get the Polish roadblock removed, Roosevelt began the following day by saying he was more concerned by the nature of the government in Warsaw than by frontier issues. Stalin responded that he had been unable to contact members of the Lublin Committee to get their reaction to Roosevelt's suggestion to invite them to Yalta. Molotov had drawn up some proposals to Poland, he added, but they had not been typed up. So why did they not talk first about the global body?[16]

Molotov had good news – he announced Soviet agreement to the American scheme for voting in the Security Council. He also scaled down Moscow's call for additional seats in the assembly from sixteen to three, Ukraine, Lithuania and White Russia (Byelorussia). Before leaving Washington, Roosevelt had told the Cabinet that, if Moscow demanded additional seats, he would ask for forty-eight for the United States. An American note listed three objections* –the Soviet Republics had not signed the United Nations Declaration of 1942; the Soviet constitution did not let them control foreign policy; and Roosevelt had said that the matter should not come up until the organisation was actually formed. But the British were on tricky ground here as Churchill wanted the Dominions plus India to sit in the assembly. Requiring Moscow to limit itself to a single seat, he told Attlee in a cable, 'is asking a great deal'. The Soviet request was passed to the Foreign Ministers, and, eventually, agreement was reached on two additional seats – White Russia and Ukraine. Bohlen thought that Roosevelt, 'ill and exhausted after days of arguing', simply made a mistake, but Stalin assured him in a note that he would approve an increase in the number of seats controlled by Washington.

Roosevelt told Stettinius to cable Chiang Kai-shek to get his accord to the voting system. The President suggested that the meeting to set up the organisation should be held the following month. Churchill thought that was too fast; they should wait till the fighting ended. But Roosevelt and Hopkins did not want to risk losing momentum. In a note to his boss, the aide called the British objection 'rot', which the President crossed out and replaced by 'local politics' – that is, the general election to be held in Britain at the end of the war in Europe.

After a diversion on Iran, Molotov produced his proposals on Poland. As well as the usual frontier demands, this added that 'it was deemed desirable to add to the Provisional Polish Government some democratic leaders from Polish émigré circles.' Molotov said that, since it had still not been possible to reach members of the Lublin group, the Poles could not be invited to Yalta. Rather, Clark Kerr, Harriman and Molotov should discuss enlargement of the Warsaw administration when they got back to Moscow. Roosevelt and Churchill accepted the fiction that the Soviet leadership had been unable to contact its puppets. 'In better health, FDR might have decided to stay in Yalta until the thing was done,' Harriman wrote. 'Some more acceptable compromise might have been worked out if [the Polish leaders] had been brought down to Yalta.'

---

* The note was drawn up by Alger Hiss, a member of the State Department team, who, Stettinius wrote, 'performed brilliantly' at the summit (Stettinius, p. 37).

Roosevelt and Churchill welcomed the Soviet ideas, though they took issue with the word 'émigré' – Churchill did not like its French Revolution connotations.

But there was still uncertainty about how far west Poland should reach. References to the Neisse River as the frontier with Germany had not taken into account that there were two waterways of that name: Moscow naturally wanted to adopt the westerly one while the other two Allies plumped for the easterly one. Churchill warned that moving the frontier too far might shock British public opinion. It would, he added, be 'a pity to stuff the Polish goose so full of German food that it got indigestion'. Stalin observed that most Germans across the line had run away. That simplified matters, Churchill responded, calculating that the refugee population Germany would absorb would be about equal to its war casualties.

VII

8 February

The next afternoon, Stalin called on Roosevelt, who had eaten lunch off a tray in his room with his daughter. The President began with the main subject on his mind now that he had agreement on the United Nations – the war in the Far East. It is easy to underestimate how large this loomed at the time. Military planners expected fighting to continue for a year and a half after Germany's defeat. Roosevelt hoped Tokyo could be beaten by bombing, but reports of Japanese determination to fight to the last made him particularly anxious to see the Red Army used in Asia. Stalin laid out his conditions.[17]

He wanted the thirty-two Kurile Islands stretching out from Japan towards the Soviet Kamchatka peninsula, and the southern half of Sakhalin Island. The latter had been seized by Japan from Russia in 1904, and the Kurile had been ceded by peaceful treaty in 1875. Stalin's next demand was more sensitive since it involved the territory of the China. He wanted to resume Tsarist-era rights to railways in Manchuria, together with use of the port of Dairen (now Lü-ta) at the end of the line. Without the railway concessions, it would be hard 'to explain to the Soviet people why Russia was entering the war against Japan', he said. He required agreement in writing before leaving Yalta.

Though Stalin had put his demands to Harriman for transmission to Washington six weeks earlier, Roosevelt had not consulted Chiang Kai-shek. Now, he sought to tone down the Soviet position by suggesting that the railway could be operated by a joint commission with the Chinese. As though it nagged at him, he referred three times to his lack of consultation with the Chinese, at one point giving the explanation that 'anything said to them was known to the whole world in twenty-four hours'. Secrecy was considered vital because of the possibility that, if word leaked out, Japan might attack Siberia before the Soviet Union had been able to move troops to Asia.

The two men then talked briefly about trusteeships for Korea and Indochina – the Indochinese, Roosevelt remarked, were 'of small stature and . . . not warlike'. Turning back to China, Stalin said he thought the Nationalists and Communists should get together under Chiang. Then they went into the plenary session to resume the discussion of Poland.

'This is the crucial point of the conference,' Churchill said.[18]

Molotov argued that the way ahead was enlargement, not a new government. Creating a presidential committee, as the Americans suggested, might cause problems since a national council already existed. He, Clark Kerr and Harriman could meet Poles in Moscow, but he was not sure about inviting Mikołajczyk on the evidence of the autumn talks with him.

'The whole world is waiting for a settlement, and if we separate still recognising different Polish governments the whole world will see that fundamental differences between us still exist,' Churchill declared. 'The consequences will be most lamentable, and will stamp our meeting with the seal of failure.'

The British understood that the Lublin group did not 'commend itself' to the majority of Poles, he added, so 'we cannot feel that it would be accepted abroad as representing them'. Marshalling his arguments, he said that brushing aside the London government would bring world protests and virtually united opposition of Poles abroad. Some 150,000 Poles had fought with the Allies 'very bravely', and were still doing so.

He acknowledged that he had no way of knowing what was going on inside Poland, but, if he fell in with what the Lublin group reported, his government would be charged in Parliament with 'having altogether forsaken the cause of Poland'. The ensuing debates would be most painful and embarrassing to Allied unity. Molotov's proposals did not go nearly far enough. Only after a free general election with universal suffrage would Britain be able to 'salute the Government that emerges without regard to the Polish Committee in London'. In his memoirs, he wrote that the President supported him; but the US record has Roosevelt saying merely that they all agreed on the need for free elections, and that the only problem was how Poland was to be governed in the interval.

While resonant and well-argued, Churchill's intervention was water off the dictator's back. Stalin responded with an unusually lengthy speech in which he threw out assertions without evidence, dismissed contrary views out of hand, and ended with a restatement of his basic position.

He did not see why the British and Americans could not send their people to judge the situation on the ground. The Lublin group might not be geniuses, but its leaders were popular, having not fled during the war. The Red Army's liberation made Poles more friendly towards Russia, but the London politicians had not participated in the national celebrations. He reiterated a favourite gambit in asking how the provisional government differed from de Gaulle, who was, he said, in fact less popular. Molotov was right. The provisional government should be reconstructed. That was all.

Moving off to one side, Roosevelt asked how long it would take to hold elections. A month if there was no catastrophe at the front, was the Soviet reply. At which, the President suggested referring the matter to the foreign ministers. There followed a brief excursion through Yugoslavia, where an accord had been worked out between Tito and the British-backed regent. Stalin raised Greece, as if to remind Churchill of his compliance there. The Prime Minister said he was 'very much obliged to Marshal Stalin for not having taken too great an interest in Greek affairs'. Then the session ended.

Churchill was 'puzzled and distressed', Moran recorded in his diary that day. 'The President no longer seems to the P.M. to take an intelligent interest in the war; often he does not seem even to read the papers the P.M. gives him. Sometimes it appears as if he has no thought-out recipe for anything beyond his troubles with Congress.' With a doctor's eye, Moran added in his diary that Roosevelt was 'a very sick man. He has all the symptoms of hardening of the arteries of the brain in an advanced stage, so that I give him only a few months to live.'[19]

The interpreter Birse recalled that, at the opening session, the President appeared to be far away from the proceedings, and that Stettinius and Byrnes seemed to be prompting him. The ever-dismissive Cadogan found Roosevelt 'very woolly and wobbly'. 'I got the impression that most of the time he really hardly knew what was going on,' the diplomat wrote to Halifax. When the President was in the chair, he added, he made hardly any effort to guide the discussion, but sat silent 'or, if he made any intervention, it was generally completely irrelevant'.

On the night of 8 February, Stalin gave a dinner at his Tsarist palace. He was 'in an excellent humor, and even in high spirits,' the US record noted. Forty-five toasts were drunk. Brooke found the dictator 'full of fun and good humour'. Sarah Churchill wrote to her mother that 'The "Bear" was in terrific form and it was very friendly and gay.' Kathy Harriman excelled herself by replying in Russian to a toast to the three women, but the food was too much for them – they could only toy with the suckling pig.[20]

Introduced to Beria before the meal, Sarah Churchill used one of five Russian phrases she had learned to ask if she could have a hot-water bottle.

'I cannot believe that you need one!' the lascivious killer replied. 'Surely there is enough fire in you!'

At dinner, Sarah found herself seated next to Vyshinsky. She tried out her hot-water bottle line on him. 'Why?' he replied. 'Are you ill?' With difficulty, she explained that it had been a joke.

Gesturing towards Beria, Roosevelt asked 'Who's that in the pince-nez?' Stalin replied: 'Ah, that one, that's our Himmler.' The squat, balding secret police chief smiled, showing yellow teeth inside his flabby lips. Roosevelt appeared discomforted, – he did not wish to be reminded of his ally's murderous ways.

Kathy Harriman found the secret police chief 'little and fat with thick lenses, which give him a sinister look, but quite genial'. When Clark Kerr raised his glass to Beria as 'the man who looks after our bodies', Churchill swiftly admonished him. 'None of that,' he said. 'Be careful, Archie, be careful.' This did not stop Clark Kerr and the police boss embarking on a long conversation about the sex life of fish.

When it was his turn to toast Stalin, Churchill praised the Soviet leader as a statesman and conqueror, and added: 'I walk through this world with greater courage and hope when I find myself in a relation of friendship and intimacy with this great man.' In response, the Soviet leader called Churchill 'the most courageous of all Prime Ministers in the world' for having carried on the fight against Hitler alone. He knew, he added, of few examples where the courage of one man had been so important to the history of the world. Stalin evidently felt no shame about evoking a period when he had been allied with Hitler. He toasted Roosevelt as the man who brought a country that was not seriously threatened into the war, paying tribute to the 'remarkable and vital achievement' of Lend-Lease. To which, the President reached out to one of his favourite notions, that they were like a family. Stalin said the real test would be to keep post-war unity. Churchill compared the three of them to men standing on the crest of a hill looking at the prospect of overcoming 'poverty, confusion, chaos and oppression'.

'I am talking as an old man,' Stalin said. 'That is why I am talking so much. But I want to drink to our alliance, that it should not lose its character of intimacy, of its free expression of views. In the history of diplomacy I know of no such close alliance of three great powers as this, when allies had the opportunity of so frankly expressing their views.'

'In an alliance the allies should not deceive each other,' he went on. 'Perhaps that is naive? Experienced diplomats may say, "Why should I not deceive my ally?" But, as a naive man, I think it best not to deceive my ally even if he is a fool. Possibly our alliance is so firm just because we do not deceive each other; or is it because it is not so easy to deceive each other? I propose a toast to the firmness of the Three-Power Alliance. May it be strong and stable; may we be as frank as possible.'

VIII

9 February

When the Foreign Ministers met at noon the next day, Stettinius withdrew the US proposal to set up a committee for Poland. He stressed the domestic debate in America about the global organisation, and said the Polish question was important in this respect. He read out a note which moved towards the Soviet position by proposing 'that the present Polish Provisional Government be reorganized into a fully representative government based on all democratic forces in Poland and including democratic leaders from Poland abroad.'[21]

Eden objected that the lack of support for Lublin meant a new start should be made. The presence of Mikołajczyk would, he added, do more than anything to give a government authority, and convince the British people of its representative character. If the election was controlled by Lublin, British opinion would not see it as free. Stettinius said he backed the British in this respect, then shifted his opening position to argue that it would be preferable to start with an entirely new government. No agreement would be possible if the Soviet reference to the 'existing Polish Government' was kept, he added. Roosevelt and Churchill, meanwhile, were discussing the United Nations over a lunch arranged by Hopkins. Byrnes conjured with the idea of seats for Hawaii, Puerto Rico and Alaska. When it was put to him, Stalin said he could see the point. But nothing was decided.

At 4 p.m., Stalin and Roosevelt went into the courtyard of the Livadia, which had been covered with carpets. Three chairs were set up by the well in the centre. Churchill walked out to join them, wearing a Russian fur hat that raised smiles from the other two.

'How do you want to handle this, Robert?' the President asked Hopkins's photographer son.[22]

The young man suggested the Foreign Ministers stand behind each of the principals, which they did. His father was too ill to come down.

The most frequently used shot shows Roosevelt wearing his cape and looking slack-jawed, though others depict him appearing more alert. Stalin sits to his left, self-contained in his patched greatcoat and military cap. Churchill, dumpy in a thick coat, either stares ahead or looks round at Stettinius. In some shots, the Secretary of State, Eden, Molotov, Clark Kerr and Harriman stand behind the leaders; in others, the background is made up of military men, with Brooke and Marshall modestly at the rear. After fifteen minutes, they all headed for the ballroom. On the way, Robert Hopkins snapped the Soviet leaders under the arcade running round the courtyard.

Stalin, who had met him at Teheran, beckoned to the young man to come closer.

What were his plans? he asked.

He would like to be the first American photographer in Berlin, Robert replied. But US forces were still far from the city.

How would he like to be attached to the Red Army? Stalin inquired.

Could Stalin arrange that? Robert inquired.

'You take care of it from your end, and I'll take care of it from ours,' came the response.

After shaking hands, Robert hurried into the palace where he met Marshall. Could he be seconded to the Red Army? he asked. Yes, that could be arranged.

But when he got to his father's bedroom and told him the news, Hopkins vetoed it. Even if he did get to the battlezone, his son would not be allowed to take pictures, he predicted. And even if he did manage to do that, he would never be able to transmit the result. 'You go into Berlin with the American army,' his father ruled.

Robert went to tell Stalin. The dictator shrugged.

Molotov began the two and a half hour plenary session by giving out proposed new wording on Poland. But proceedings were then temporarily derailed when Stettinius read a general report on the deliberations of the Foreign Ministers which touched on territorial trusteeships under the United Nations. Jumping to his feet and speaking so fast that Hopkins, for one, could hardly follow what he was saying, Churchill objected that he had not been consulted, and did not agree with a single word of the draft. He would not consent to forty or fifty nations 'thrusting interfering fingers' into the Empire.[23]

Stalin rose to walk up and down the room, beaming and applauding. Roosevelt looked embarrassed. Every scrap of territory over which the British flag flew was immune from interference, Churchill insisted. No British representative would go to a conference where his country would have to defend itself. 'Never. Never. Never,' he growled as he sat down. Stettinius said the draft was not intended to refer to the British Empire, but to areas taken from enemy control. In which case, Churchill replied, it would be better to say this. How would Stalin feel if it was suggested that the Crimea should be internationalised as a summer resort? The Soviet leader said he would be glad to dedicate it to summit meetings.

Later in the afternoon, the subject came up again in a discussion on liberated areas. Churchill insisted that the Atlantic Charter should not apply to the Empire. He had, he remarked, told the Commons this, and had given Wendell Willkie a copy of his speech.

'Was that what killed him?' Roosevelt asked.

Returning to Poland, Molotov produced new wording that the 'present

Provisional Government should be reorganized on a wider democratic basis with the inclusion of democratic leaders from Poland itself and from those living abroad.' This, Roosevelt said, meant they were very near agreement. Churchill pleaded that observers should be allowed to provide information on conditions in the country. He would welcome Soviet observers in Greece, he added. To avoid any quid pro quo, Stalin replied that he had complete confidence in British policy there.

'I must be able to tell the House of Commons that the elections will be free and that there will be effective guarantees that they are freely and fairly carried out,' Churchill insisted. Would Mikołajczyk be allowed to return? The Polish politician belonged to a non-fascist party, so he could take part in the election, Stalin replied.

According to the US record, Churchill said, 'I do not care much about Poles myself.' What concerned him was what he could tell Parliament.

'There are some very good people among the Poles,' Stalin remarked. They were good fighters, and had some good scientists and musicians, 'but they fight among themselves, too'.

Roosevelt brought up his need to assure voters of Polish extraction in America that the poll would be freely conducted.

'I want this election in Poland to be the first beyond criticism,' he said. 'It should be like Caesar's wife. I did not know her but they say she was pure.'

'They said that about her,' Stalin interjected, 'but in fact she had her sins.'

'I don't want the Poles to be able to question the Polish elections,' Roosevelt continued. 'The matter is not only one of principles but of good politics.'

IX

10 February

After lunch the next day Molotov handed Harriman an English translation of Stalin's conditions for entering the Pacific war.[24] The document provided for 'possession' of Dairen and the other north-eastern harbour of Port Arthur and for sole Soviet operation of the Manchurian railway.

The ambassador said he believed Roosevelt would want to change 'possession' to 'lease' and insert a reference to the harbours becoming free ports under international control. As for the railway, there should be a reference to it being run by a Chinese–Soviet commission. In addition, Harriman said he felt sure the President would not reach a final agreement until he had got Chiang's accord. Molotov agreed to the first two points, but took some time to grasp the third.

Returning to the Livadia, Harriman showed the document with his amendments to Roosevelt, who approved it after adding a sentence reading: 'It is understood that the agreement concerning the ports and railways referred to above requires the concurrence of Generalissimo Chiang Kai-shek.' At 4.30, Roosevelt received Stalin for fifteen minutes to confirm the secret accord, under which the USSR undertook to enter the war in their Far East two or three months after the defeat of Germany in return for recognition of continuing control of Outer Mongolia, the return of islands, the concessions in Manchuria with joint Soviet–Chinese operation of the railway, internationalisation of Dairen, and a naval base at Port Arthur. The Kremlin was also to sign a treaty with Chiang Kai-shek, recognising him as head of the government and China's sovereignty over Manchuria.

When Stalin told Churchill of his demands in the Far East, the Prime Minister welcomed the presence of Soviet ships in the Pacific, and favoured restoring Tsarist-era rights. But, on being shown the US–Soviet document on the last day of the conference, Eden regarded it as 'discreditable'. Backed by Cadogan, he argued that Churchill should not add his signature. The Prime Minister insisted, in the interests of his country's presence in the Far East. In his memoirs, he calls it a 'remote and secondary' matter which did not merit an argument with Roosevelt. A note in Hopkins's files records that 'there appear to be elements among the British who, out of imperial considerations, desire a weak and possibly disunited China in the post-war period.'

Though Roosevelt had promised to get his agreement, Chiang Kai-shek was not formally told for four months. 'I feel more than simply hurt and sad,' the Generalissimo wrote in his diary when finally informed. 'The Chinese people have . . . been placed in an unparalleled and dangerous predicament.'

Later on the afternoon of 10 February, it was time to return to Poland at a three-hour plenary. Eden read a new draft from the Foreign Ministers, calling for the Provisional Government to be reorganized on a broader democratic basis. Molotov and the ambassadors in Moscow would consult groups from inside and outside Poland about free, unfettered elections with universal suffrage and a secret ballot. When a new government was chosen, the three Allies would recognise it.[25]

The draft made no mention of frontiers, and Churchill returned to his theme of limiting Poland's expansion to the west. He had received a cable from the War Cabinet saying that the size of the population transfer under the borders proposed by Stalin would be too big to handle. Roosevelt said he did not have the right to commit on this point. That must be done by the Senate. But something should be said about the Curzon Line in the east, Molotov interjected, though they need not mention the west. How about a statement that Poland would get compensation in the west, but that this had to be discussed with the new government in Warsaw, Churchill suggested. Very good, Molotov concurred.

Later, the Soviets proposed wording referring to the return to Poland of its ancient frontier of East Prussia and the Oder.

'How long ago had those lands been Polish?' Roosevelt asked.

'Very long ago,' Molotov replied.

'Perhaps you want us back,' Roosevelt said to Churchill with a laugh.

'You might be as indigestible for us as it might be for the Poles if they took too much German territory,' the Prime Minister responded. Stalin accepted a British draft stating that Poland 'must receive substantial accessions of territory in the North and West' but that final delimitation should await a post-war peace conference.

When the talk turned to Germany, Roosevelt said he had changed his mind about the Control Commission – he now agreed with Churchill that France should be a member since it would have an occupation zone. He had already told Stalin this through Harriman. Playing the game, the Soviet leader raised his arms above his head and said '*Sdaiyous*' – 'I surrender'. Roosevelt took this as evidence of his influence with the dictator.

The Soviet leader then showed a rare burst of fury when the matter of German reparations came up, and Churchill expressed British reservations about the Soviet proposals. A message from the War Cabinet told him to avoid specific figures, which should be left for a commission that would consider the matter in Moscow. Roosevelt chipped in to say that if figures were mentioned, the American people would believe cash was involved.

This was all too much for the leader of the country which had suffered most at the hands of Hitler. Rising to his feet, Stalin spoke, Hopkins noted, as if his words burnt his mouth. He gripped the back of his chair so tightly that his knuckles turned white.

If Britain did not want the USSR to get reparations, it should say so openly, he said. The price for war should be $20 billion, with Moscow getting half.

Churchill read out the message from London that this would be beyond Germany's ability to pay. 'We bring our figures before the Commission and you bring yours,' Stalin responded. Hopkins passed Roosevelt a note: 'The Russians have given in so much at this conference that I don't think we should let them down. Let the British disagree if they want to – and continue their disagreement at Moscow. Simply say it is all referred to the Reparations Commission with the minute to show the British disagree about any mention of the 10 billion.' This was adopted.

Then Roosevelt lobbed in the information that he had to leave by 3 p.m. the following afternoon for meetings in Egypt with King Farouk, Emperor Haile Selassie of Ethiopia and King Ibn Saud of Saudi Arabia.

'Franklin, you cannot go,' Churchill objected. 'We have within reach a very great prize.'

'Winston, I have made commitments and must depart tomorrow as planned,' Roosevelt replied.

Roosevelt's news worried Churchill. He feared that the President was seeking to make inroads into Britain's position in the Middle East. When he asked Hopkins what it was all about, the aide said he had no idea – he thought it was probably 'a lot of horseplay' involving meetings with exotic rulers in robes. But Churchill promptly sent messages to the three monarchs to arrange meetings for himself.

Before the banquet that night, Soviet soldiers arrived at the British mansion to search behind the walls, under the tables and in the garden.[26]

During the flow of toasts Churchill assured Stalin that Britain was his good friend. 'There was a time when the Marshal was not so kindly towards us, and I remember that I said a few rude things about him, but our common dangers and common loyalties have wiped all that out,' he continued. 'The fire of war has burnt up the misunderstandings of the past. We feel we have a friend whom we can trust, and I hope he will continue to feel the same about us. I pray that he may live to see his beloved Russia not only glorious in war but also happy in peace.'

There was an awkward moment when Stalin proposed to drink to the health of George VI but added that he was against kings. Churchill intervened to suggest that the toasts should be to the 'heads of State'. On a lighter note, Churchill raised his glass to the translators with a cry of 'Interpreters of the world unite! You have nothing to lose but your audience.' Stalin was greatly amused.

After dinner, Churchill took the other two to his travelling map room. The German town of Cleves had fallen. The Prime Minister spoke about the princess from there who had been married to Henry VIII. Then he sang a First World War song, 'When We've Wound up the Watch of the Rhine'. Stalin broke this up by suggesting that Britain might be ready to make an armistice with the Germans before the Russians did. Churchill looked hurt. He went into a corner to sing a few lines of the song 'Keep Right on to the End of the Road'. When Stalin looked puzzled, Roosevelt instructed Pavlov: 'Tell your chief that singing by the Prime Minister is Britain's secret weapon.'

Returning to the dining room, they discussed the British general election. Unaware of the extent to which Churchill's concentration on the war had put him out of touch with opinion and of the way the Labour Party represented the future, Stalin said he was sure the Prime Minister would win. Voters would see that 'they needed a leader and who could be a better leader than he who had won the victory?' When Churchill pointed out that he was the leader of one of two competing parties, the dictator replied, with deep conviction, 'One party is much better.'

Speaking to Stalin, Roosevelt, who looked very tired, asked him if he backed Zionism. In principle, the Georgian replied warily, but he recognised the difficulties of the issue. A Soviet attempt to establish a Jewish home had failed because the inhabitants scattered elsewhere, he went on. When he asked Roosevelt what gift he would offer the Saudi monarch when they met, the President replied with a grin that he might give the six million Jews in the United States. According to Bohlen's account, Stalin called Jews 'middlemen, profiteers and parasites'.

When Stalin left, Churchill called for three cheers from members of the British party in the hall. The response was a round of hip, hip, hoorays.

*

X

11 February

At breakfast the next morning, Churchill told Moran that Roosevelt was 'behaving very badly. He won't take any interest in what we are trying to do.'[27]

The doctor replied that the President seemed to have lost his grip. The Prime Minister agreed.

At noon, the Big Three met for fifty minutes, and went on to lunch in the Tsar's billiard room. They agreed on the communiqué which, as Churchill noted, left 'many grave issues' unsettled. Issued the following day, it set out the Allies' 'inflexible purpose to destroy German militarism and Nazism and to ensure that Germany will never again be able to disturb the peace of the world.' Unconditional surrender would be imposed. Germany would be disarmed; its General Staff would be broken up; all industry that could be used for military purposes would be removed or destroyed; war criminals would swiftly be brought to justice; reparations in kind would be exacted. The Allies would each take an occupation zone, plus one for France. 'It is not our purpose to destroy the people of Germany, but only when Nazism and Militarism have been extirpated will there be hope for a decent life for Germans, and a place for them in the comity of nations,' the first section of the document concluded.[28]

A Rooseveltian-inspired Declaration on Liberated Europe pledged to help countries freed from the Nazis to solve their pressing political and economic problems by democratic means. Stalin had sought to insert a sentence referring to helping 'those people in these countries who took an active part in the struggle against German occupation'. The US rejected this, fearing it could be used to advance pro-Soviet groups. The dictator accepted the original draft.

Evoking the Atlantic Charter, the communiqué stated that the establishment of order in Europe and the rebuilding of national life must be based on 'the right of all peoples to choose their form of government and on the restoration of sovereign rights and self-government'. Molotov warned Stalin that this amounted to interference in national affairs, but his master disregarded him. Harriman thought Stalin believed assurances by national Communists in Europe that they would win free elections.

The section on Poland affirmed the well-rehearsed desire to see the country strong, free, independent and democratic. 'As a result of our discussions we have agreed on the conditions in which a new Polish Provisional Government of National Unity may be formed in such a manner as to command recognition by the three major Powers,' it went on. The communiqué talked of reorganising the existing government on a broader basis after Molotov and the ambassadors had consulted Polish groups. Elections would be held as soon as possible; all democratic, anti-Nazi parties could participate. The eastern frontier would follow the Curzon Line with some small digressions. Warsaw would get 'substantial accessions of territory in the north and west' to be fixed by a peace conference.

Another section of the statement set 25 April as the date for the United Nations meeting to open in San Francisco. The Yugoslavs were urged to form a government of Communists and non-Communists – this was done, but the non-Communist regent lasted only until March when Tito took over. There was also agreement for the return of freed prisoners of war taken by the enemy, which gratified the British and Americans, but led to the deaths of thousands of those the Kremlin regarded as traitors for having been captured by the Nazis.

'We will meet again soon, in Berlin,' Roosevelt told Stalin as the last lunch ended at 3.45. After the President handed over medals for Red Army officers, the Soviets presented the visitors with vodka, wine, champagne, caviar, butter, oranges and tangerines. The British interpreter Birse gave his Soviet opposite number a complete set of the works of Dickens, which brought a menacing remark from Stalin about how close Pavlov was getting to the ally. The Americans were planning to give cigarettes to the tall man who stood behind the Soviet leader at meals dressed as a waiter, but then discovered that he was a major general in the NKVD.[29]

At 3.55, Stalin drove off to board his train for Moscow. Five minutes later, Roosevelt began the road journey to the port of Sebastopol, where a US warship waited for him. Turning to Eden after bidding farewell to the other two leaders, Churchill muttered that 'the only bond of the victors is their common hate'.[30]

Averell and Kathy Harriman accompanied the President on the three-hour trip along eighty miles of mountain roads past the scene of the Charge of the Light Brigade in the Crimean War. Sebastopol was virtually levelled except for a few walls standing up like billboards. Spotlights illuminated rebuilding work at night. The waiting American warship was overheated, and Roosevelt had a bad night. But the official log recorded that the Americans greatly appreciated the steak dinner they were served on the warship after eight days of Russian fare. In the morning, seen off by Molotov, Roosevelt flew out to meet the three kings in Egypt. As the plane took off, Harriman waved goodbye – it was the last time he saw the President.

Churchill felt lonely when he and Sarah were driven back to their mansion. 'Why do we stay here?' he asked. 'Why don't we go tonight? I see no reason to stay here a minute longer – we're off!'

Jumping out of the car, he hurried inside to tell his staff he was leaving in fifty minutes. After a stunned silence, everyone went into action. Trunks and gifts from the Russians filled the hall. Then the Prime Minister changed his mind; they would stay. Then he changed it again; they would go. 'They can't do this to me,' his butler, Sawyers, complained, tears in his eyes. Churchill walked from room to room, genial and sprightly like a boy let out of school, his homework done, Sarah recorded. 'Come on, come on!' he called. At 5.30 the motorcade pulled out.

Reaching Sebastopol, the British went aboard a former Cunard liner, the *Franconia*, where they were joined by Brooke and the Chiefs of Staff. A meal of dressed crab, roast beef, apple pie and gorgonzola, washed down with Liebfraumilch and port was particularly well received. Then they went to inspect the Crimea battlefields. At dinner, Churchill ranted about how he was saving Greece from Communism, and rambled on about British politics and the Boer War. The next morning, after breakfast in bed of fried fish, bacon, oranges, marmalade and coffee, he decided to fly to Athens where he harangued a crowd of 50,000 in the main square, calling for national unity, before following Roosevelt to Egypt.

The Yalta Conference would come to be demonised, particularly by the uninvited French, as the moment when the Big Three cynically carved up Europe, and so laid the foundation for the Cold War. It would be a key item on the McCarthyite charge sheet against Roosevelt, and lead to denunciations of secret betrayals by Republicans. Half a century later, George W. Bush declared in Warsaw: 'No more Munichs; no more Yaltas.' In fact, the division of Europe was set well before the meeting by the Black

Sea. Teheran had sown the seeds. Then had come Warsaw, Greece and Romania, the percentages proposal and the Red Army advance through eastern and central Europe. The reality on the ground formed an inescapable backdrop to the Crimean deliberations. On paper, the West salvaged something on the key issue of Poland by getting agreement to the enlargement of the government – but there was no way of implementing this if Stalin decided otherwise. The one place where the summit did see a cynical trade-off of another nation's interests concerned China, but that worried few people until after the Communists gained power there in 1949 when Yalta could be blamed, in part, for the loss of the Fourth Policeman.[31]

Each of the parties had reasons to feel content, however illusory this would prove for the West. Bohlen recalled that, at the end of the summit, 'although there was a sense of frustration and some bitterness in regard to Poland, the general mood was one of satisfaction'. The agreements, he added, 'seemed to us to be realistic compromises between the various positions of each country'. 'I think the Conference has been quite successful,' Cadogan wrote to his wife. 'I hope the world will be impressed.'

Roosevelt had his accord on the global body and a firm commitment on the Soviet entry into the war against Japan. Though de Gaulle's pique ruled out any gratitude, Churchill had got confirmation that France would have an occupation zone in Germany and membership of the Control Commission. He had also, in a negative way, steered the summit clear of any embarrassing pledges that would chip away at the Empire.

Hopkins's biographer Robert Sherwood described the mindset of Roosevelt and his adviser as 'one of supreme exultation'. 'We really believed in our hearts that this was the dawn of the new day we had all been praying for and talking about for so many years,' the aide would tell him. 'We were absolutely certain that we had won the first great victory of the peace ... The Russians had proved that they could be reasonable and farseeing and there wasn't any doubt in the minds of the President or any of us that we could live with them and get along with them peacefully for as far into the future as any of us could imagine.'

Churchill shared this personal faith in Stalin. During the summit, he remarked to Moran that the next war would be an ideological one. 'Between whom?' the doctor asked. Churchill shrugged. 'I do not think that Russia will do anything while Stalin is alive,' he said. 'I don't think he is unfriendly to us.' Chamberlain had been wrong to trust Hitler, he reflected, but he did not think he was wrong to trust Stalin.

If the Western leaders went home in contented frame of mind, Stalin and Molotov had more reason for celebration. Whatever the form of words on Poland, the Soviet grip on the country had not been compromised. The USSR had obtained a big swathe of territory and a deep security zone west of its new frontier, much more than it had obtained under the treaty with Hitler. It would have a free hand from the Baltic to the Adriatic. The administration in Warsaw would clearly be based on the Lublin group, and other governments in countries liberated in eastern and central Europe would be of Moscow's choosing. The West had not insisted on joint supervision of elections. Nor had Stalin made any commitment as to how many non-Communists would join such governments or what posts they might fill.

The harsh Soviet reparation terms for Germany would be on the table when the commission met in Moscow. In the Far East, Stalin had got what he wanted. In Yugoslavia, the coalition government was only a brief stepping stone in Tito's acquisition of power. The Declaration on Europe might provide a platform from which critics could cast moral opprobrium at the Kremlin, but mere words would never hurt Stalin. The agreement on voting in the United Nations ensured that the world body would not be able to act against Moscow. Thus, while it was not the moment at which Europe was split, as critics claimed, Yalta did consolidate the power of the man whose policies, more than anything else, would bring about that division.

Might the two Western leaders have done more? Only by taking risks which would have seemed to them to outweigh the benefits, and which would have destroyed Roosevelt's aims.

They could have dug in their heels on Poland and sat it out in Yalta till the Lublin Committee and other Polish groups were summoned – but that might never have come to pass. They could have rejected Soviet demand for additional United Nations seats, but that would have put the President's pet project at risk. They could have insisted that Moscow's scale of reparations would be counter-productive, but Stalin had shown how sensitive the subject was for him. Roosevelt could have avoided giving Stalin territorial concessions in China, but Marshall and his colleagues were intent on getting an assurance of Moscow's entry into the Pacific war.

Above all, confronting Stalin would have brought the twin dangers that Allied unity would be shattered just as Germany was being beaten and that a disillusioned American public would turn its back on the world again. George Kennan was right to point out that Europe was already divided and that the West could not influence what happened in Moscow's sphere. But his conclusion – that it should not bargain with the Kremlin – was unacceptable after three years of alliance. The dominant faction in Washington believed that the war in Europe could only be won in accord with Moscow. Since military victory was the paramount consideration, the necessary price had to be paid for that alliance. Looking farther ahead, Roosevelt saw the construction of an orderly relationship with Moscow as the key to the post-war world order. Even if Churchill had been tempted to be tougher, Britain was exhausted by war. A fresh confrontation would not have won support at the coming election.

Roosevelt's health has often been invoked as a reason why the West did not play a stronger game at Yalta. The US leader did undoubtedly become extremely tired at times and ramble at others, but there is little evidence to show that he was not mentally alert when it mattered. His biographer Conrad Black argues convincingly against placing too much weight on the health argument and, in particular, on Halifax's assertion that Hopkins told him the President did not follow more than half of what was said at the summit.

Roosevelt's behaviour was the culmination of the approach he had pursued throughout the war, and of the way he did business. At Yalta, he thought he had found the kind of understanding with Stalin he had forged so often at home. Two weeks after the summit ended, he wrote to the Soviet leader that it would 'hasten victory and the establishment of a firm foundation for a lasting peace'. Their joint military effort would 'assure the speedy attainment of our common goal – a peaceful world based upon mutual understanding and cooperation.' There is no reason to doubt that he believed this, or, at least, believed that this was attainable.

To admit the true nature of Uncle Joe and his regime would have been to admit the missing trump in the President's hand, the lack of troops in eastern Europe to confront the 10 million-strong Soviet forces – the Red Army reached Budapest two days after the end of the summit. Stalin might agree to verbal compromises and appear to be a dictator with whom one could do business, but he had no motivation to give way when his core interests were concerned. His position was strengthened by the domestic political factors Roosevelt and Churchill had to keep in mind – even if they had wished to put up a stronger front, voters were counting the days to the end of the war and generally regarded the USSR as a heroic power. With little time left to realise his dream of bringing a new deal to the world, Roosevelt knew he had to settle for agreements that fell short of perfection. When Leahy reflected that the section of the communiqué on Poland was 'so elastic that the Russians can stretch it all the way from Yalta to Washington without ever technically breaking it', the President replied: 'Bill, I know it. But it's the best I can do for Poland at this time.' Later, after reporting to Congress on the summit, he similarly remarked to the New Deal veteran Adolph Berle: 'I didn't say the result was good. I said it was the best I could do.'

A Russian story had Stalin going hunting with the other two leaders. When they killed a bear, Churchill proposed taking the skin, and leaving the meat for Stalin and Roosevelt.[32]

'No, I'll take the skin. Let Churchill and Stalin divide the meat,' Roosevelt said.

When Stalin remained silent, the other two asked what he suggested.

'The bear belongs to me – after all I killed it,' he replied.

21

Death at the Springs

'Be careful.'

ROOSEVELT

ROOSEVELT AND THREE AMERICAN ADMIRALS stared out from the cruiser *Quincy* across the Great Bitter Lake on the Suez Canal as the destroyer USS *Murphy* sailed into view. On the deck sat King Ibn Saud on a great throne guarded by Nubians bearing drawn sabres. The sixty-eight-year-old monarch, who dyed his beard black, had ruled the desert kingdom since 1927. The war had increased the interest of the United States in its oil reserves; though its position on supply routes to the Pacific was cited when Roosevelt had declared it eligible for Lend-Lease in 1943. The following year, he told Churchill he was disturbed by 'rumours that the British wish to horn in on Arabian oil reserves'. For his part, the Prime Minister was worried that his country might be 'hustled' out of its oil interests in the region; Roosevelt assured him that America was not 'making sheep's eyes at your oil fields in Iraq and Iran'. Anglo-American oil talks in Washington then worked out an agreement that gave US firms the leading role in the kingdom – by 1946 Aramco was lifting a hundred times as much crude as before the war.[1]

With the King on the *Murphy* were his astrologer, a coffee server, and what the US record described as 'nine miscellaneous slaves, cooks, porters and scullions'. A sheep was slaughtered as the destroyer crossed the lake, the monarch sleeping in an improvised tent on deck.

Roosevelt, who had met the rulers of Egypt and Ethiopia earlier, treated the King with great respect. Considering it impolite to smoke in royal company, the President stopped the lift taking him down to lunch to give himself time to have two cigarettes before the meal. When the visitor admired his wheelchair, the American leader handed over a spare one he had with him, and also offered a gift of a plane with an American crew. (Churchill's gift was a £6,000 Rolls-Royce. His meal with Ibn Saud produced one of his celebrated remarks about alcohol when he said that, if Islam imposed prohibition, his own religion prescribed an absolute sacred rote of drinking before, during and after meals and in the intervals between them.)

At his lunch with the monarch, Roosevelt said he hoped Arab countries would accept 10,000 Jews from eastern Europe and Germany. Ibn Saud responded with a long speech about the trouble caused by emigration of European Jews, who were technically and culturally more advanced than Arabs. When Roosevelt mentioned their suffering, the ruler said he did not see why Arabs should expiate the sins of Hitler. Arabs, he added, 'would choose to die rather than yield their land to Jews'. The reason the newcomers made the desert bloom was the funds they received from the United States and Europe. If the Arabs had been helped in that way, they would have done as well. Roosevelt persisted, but each time he raised the issue, the opposition grew more determined.

The President noted that he could not stop Zionist press articles, speeches and legislative resolutions. But he said he would never make a move hostile to the Arabs. After lunch, the two men took coffee on the deck, a uniformed interpreter kneeling before them. The Saudis agreed to let the Americans have a base on their territory as part of the supply chain to the Far East. Impressed, Roosevelt told Congress that he had learned more in five minutes conversation with Ibn Saud than he could have done from three dozen letters. But the monarch was disappointed when, on his return to Washington, Roosevelt assured Jewish leaders he still supported Zionism. Writing to Daisy Suckley, he described the shipboard encounter as 'a scream', adding: 'All goes well but I still need sleep.'

On 5 February, he had lunch with Churchill on the *Quincy*. The Prime Minister noted that the President looked 'placid and frail'. 'I felt he had a slender contact with life,' he wrote. 'I was not to see him again. We bade affectionate farewells.'[2]

On his homeward trip, Roosevelt encountered irritation from a familiar quarter when de Gaulle turned down a meeting they had scheduled for Algiers because of his umbrage at Yalta. Furious, Roosevelt dictated a terse reply that attacked France as well as its leader. The sick Hopkins sent Bohlen to reason with the President.

Roosevelt insisted that the United States had been insulted, and that a response had to be made. Bohlen said he agreed that de Gaulle was 'one of the biggest sons of bitches who ever straddled a pot'. The phrase amused Roosevelt who told him to go and cook up a new draft with Hopkins, which they duly did in diplomatic language.

The journey was marked with mortality. Roosevelt's long-time White House aide, 'Pa' Watson, had a stroke and died. Hopkins was too ill to make the sea voyage, and went to the villa in Marrakech used by Roosevelt and Churchill to rest before flying home in the 'Sacred Cow'. His parting from the President was not amiable – Roosevelt wanted his company on the voyage. As with Churchill, it was the last time they would see one another.[3]

When he got home, Roosevelt was very weary indeed, his hands shaking, his eyes sometimes vague. Reporting to Congress on the summit, he said he had returned to Washington 'refreshed and inspired' and denied that he had suffered any ill-health at Yalta. That was far from the truth. Robert Sherwood found him in worse condition than ever – 'unnaturally quiet, and even querulous'. The poet Archibald MacLeish, who was working at the State Department, detected 'death in his eyes'. Churchill continued to send messages to the White House as if all was as before, but recalled 'I was no longer being fully heard by him'.[4]

Roosevelt told Frances Perkins that, when he left the White House, he would make a visit to Britain; then he and Eleanor would go to the Middle East to mount the equivalent of the New Deal Tennessee Valley Authority to bring irrigation and greater prosperity. 'We could do wonders,' he mused, leaning back in his chair. There was plenty to be done at home, she said.[5]

'Well, I can't be President for ever,' Roosevelt replied.

Reporting on Yalta to Congress on 2 March, he sat for the first time for such a speech, explaining what a relief it was not to have ten pounds of steel on his legs to stand up. Ad-libbing much of the speech, he revealed little of the substance of the summit. He hoped for an end to unilateral action on the international stage, exclusive alliances and spheres of influence, balances of power 'and all the other expedients which have been tried for centuries and have always failed'. 'It has been a long journey,' he went on. 'I hope you will agree that it was a fruitful one.'

As he spoke, American bombers were attacking Tokyo, and US forces were engaged in the six-week battle for the island of Iwo Jima, which killed 7,700 Americans and more than twice as many Japanese. In Germany, US troops reached the Rhine at the town of Remagen. Visiting the area at the time, Churchill declined an offer of the use of a lavatory before being driven to the front. Once he arrived, he undid his fly buttons and urinated, telling the photographers: 'This is one of the operations connected with this great war which must not be reproduced graphically.' 'I shall never forget the childish grin of intense satisfaction that spread over his face as he looked down at the critical moment,' Brooke recalled.

To the north, Montgomery's troops advanced on Bremen, and the concentration camps at Belsen and Buchenwald were discovered. In Italy, Alexander successfully launched his delayed offensive. The Red Army reached both the Baltic and Vienna. Goebbels warned the Germans that, if they stopped fighting, 'an iron curtain would fall over this enormous territory controlled by the Soviet Union, behind which nations would be slaughtered.'[6]

Despite this good military news, the Yalta aura quickly dissipated. In Romania, Vyshinsky showed how little the Declaration on Europe counted – and what he had meant by telling Bohlen that people should do as they were told. When King Michael resisted his demands to appoint a government chosen by Moscow, Vyshinsky gave him 'two hours and five minutes' to change the administration, banged his fist on the table and slammed the door as he stalked from the room. Soviet tanks took up positions in the streets of Bucharest. On 6 March, the administration Stalin wanted was installed. This was *bad*, Cadogan noted in his diary.[7]

Harriman protested on behalf of Washington in the name of the Atlantic Charter and the Yalta Declaration on Europe, but Molotov brushed this aside. Roosevelt told Churchill Romania was not a good place for a test case given its strategic importance for the USSR. Eden insisted on giving the deposed Prime Minister asylum in the British Embassy, but

Churchill felt that his percentages plan and Stalin's non-interference in Greece meant he could not protest too vigorously. Nor did he want the Kremlin to take offence and upset the negotiations on Poland in Moscow. He favoured British disengagement from Yugoslavia, leaving it to the Soviet Union, and concentrating rather on preventing the powerful Italian Communist Party from gaining power.

There were also domestic political flurries. Labour members of the War Cabinet, Ernest Bevin in particular, were looking to the coming general election and asserting their party roots. At a Cabinet meeting on 22 March, Churchill talked of the danger of the government breaking up before Germany was beaten. Across the ocean, there was a fuss when a briefing to congressional leaders led to a leak of the Soviet call for three seats in the new global body. This gave rise to speculation about secret deals at Yalta. What else was being hidden? Roosevelt's critics demanded.

But it was Poland that was the key test. Meeting Harriman and Clark Kerr, Molotov said the Yalta accord meant the addition of only one or two non-Communist ministers with the Lublin group determining who would be in the government.[8]

When the Western ambassadors submitted eight names for ministerial posts in Warsaw, the Kremlin rejected seven, declaring Mikołajczyk unacceptable. Churchill sent Roosevelt a four-page list of murders, arrests and deportations in Poland. He proposed that they protest to Stalin, but the President declined. He feared the shadow that a major rupture over Poland would throw on the forthcoming United Nations conference in San Francisco. Instead, he suggested a truce under which the London Poles would stop armed attacks on the Red Army and the Lublin group. Talks should be continued through the ambassadors, he added.

'I feel that our personal intervention would best be withheld until every other possibility of bringing the Soviet Government into line has been exhausted,' he told the Prime Minister. Churchill agreed, though 'with much reluctance', as he recalled in his memoirs. Committed to inform Parliament about Poland, he feared having 'to make it clear that we are in the presence of a great failure and an utter breakdown of what was settled at Yalta'. If Molotov got away with blocking consultations on the new government in Warsaw, 'he will know that we will put up with anything', he warned the President.

That produced a lengthy reply from Washington, which Churchill reckoned had been brewed by the State Department for Roosevelt to sign, expressing concern at any suggestion of transatlantic divergences. Roosevelt said he could not agree that the Yalta process had broken down so long as the ambassadors went on talking. In his response, Churchill wrote: 'There is no doubt in my mind that the Soviets fear very much our seeing what is going on in Poland.' Surmising that others were writing Roosevelt's messages for him, he sent a personal cable recalling their work together during the war – their friendship was 'the rock on which I build for the future of the world'.

By the end of March, the British were near breaking point – a phrase Harriman also used in a cable to Washington. Public and parliamentary concern was sharpened by the disappearance of sixteen non-Communist Polish figures who had gone to Moscow. A note from Eden to Churchill suggested that he should cut his messages to Stalin to a minimum since 'the Russians are behaving so badly' – the Foreign Secretary crossed out the adverb on the typescript and replaced it with 'abominably'. He believed Molotov sought 'to drag the whole business out while his stooges consolidate their powers'. 'Is it of any value to go to San Francisco in these conditions?' he asked. 'How can we lay the foundation for any New World Order when Anglo-American relations with Russia are so completely lacking in confidence?' Apart from anything else, the danger loomed that Poland could become a destructive election issue, suggesting disturbing parallels with the way Chamberlain had written off Czechoslovakia.

Still Roosevelt could not bring himself to admit the effect of the fundamental differences between the Western and Soviet systems. He squirmed when asked by reporters how the Yalta decisions conformed with the Atlantic Charter, at one point calling the 1941 accord 'some scraps of paper', virtually denying that it existed and portraying it more as an aspiration akin to the Ten Commandments. He could not give up on his hope of keeping the alliance together for the post-war world. On his return from Yalta, he had speculated that, during Stalin's early religious training, 'something entered into his nature of the way in which a Christian gentleman should behave'.[9]

Washington and London knew that, if the Moscow talks collapsed, they would lose their last hope of influencing developments in Warsaw. 'The Polish question is, and must remain, one of the utmost consequence, for upon its satisfactory solution rests a great part of our hope and belief in the possibility of a real and cordial understanding between the Soviet people and our own,' Clark Kerr wrote to the Foreign Office.

Yet Stalin was upping the game by the week. He insisted that the Lublin group alone should represent Poland at San Francisco, and, when this was refused, said Molotov would not attend the UN conference. In hospital with pneumonia and a low blood count, Hopkins found the Soviet attitude 'bewildering'. In London Cadogan agonised that 'our foreign policy seems a sad wreck'. In Moscow, Harriman attributed the stiff line to Stalin's realisation that the Lublin group would lose a free election, while a democratic leader such as Mikołajczyk would rally voters.[10]

Eden drafted a message to tell Molotov Britain was withdrawing from the Moscow talks. 'We should not accept to continue in a Commission that has become a farce,' he wrote in a covering note to Churchill. 'It is in the interests of future relations between the Russians, the Americans and ourselves that we should speak plainly. I hope the Americans will also take this view.'[11]

'Surely we must not be manoeuvred into becoming parties to imposing on Poland – and on how much of Eastern Europe – the Russian version of democracy?' Churchill cabled the President on 27 March. Roosevelt replied that he had been watching 'with anxiety and concern the development of the Soviet attitude'. But he wished to address Stalin directly.

'I cannot conceal from you the concern with which I view the development of events of mutual interest since our fruitful meeting at Yalta,' his lengthy message to the Kremlin on 29 March began. He drew attention to what had happened in Romania, saying he did not understand why no account had been taken of the Declaration on Europe agreed at the summit. Blaming the lack of progress on Poland on the way Moscow was interpreting the Yalta decisions, he proposed a truce and the admission of observers. Otherwise Allied unity would be at risk. Stalin should not underestimate the strength of US public opinion, he warned.

Two days later, Churchill followed up with a cable taking the Soviets to task on everything from the veto Molotov claimed for Lublin to the refusal to admit observers. A week later, Stalin, who had just received Clementine Churchill on a visit to Moscow, replied that a dead end had been reached. At Yalta, there had been agreement to use the Lublin Committee as a nucleus for government, but Clark Kerr and Harriman were trying to abolish it and create a new administration, he charged. Only Poles friendly to Moscow who accepted the Yalta decisions and the Curzon line could take part in the process.

In a separate message to Churchill, Stalin repeated that observers would be seen as an insult, and Lublin must be the first to be consulted. 'I think that if the above observations are taken into account an agreed decision on the Polish question could be arrived at in a short time,' he said. Churchill thought the reply offered some hope. Only now did he start to inform the London Poles what had gone on at the summit in the Crimea. Mikołajczyk told a London newspaper his suggestions had not been taken into account, and proposed a round-table of Polish resistance groups. His successors in the London government called Yalta 'a contradiction to the elementary principles binding the Allies [which] constitutes a violation of the letter and spirit of the Atlantic Charter and of the rights of every nation to defend its own interests.'

As Roosevelt came closer to Churchill on Poland, a major difference opened up on military strategy. A running battle had broken out between the assertive, individualistic Montgomery and Eisenhower, the team player dedicated to advance on a broad front. Brooke still despaired of Eisenhower as a strategist. Churchill's growing concern was that, 'Soviet Russia had become a mortal danger to the free world'. He believed a new front should be created as far east as possible to stem Moscow's onward sweep and race to Berlin. But the Red Army was only thirty-five miles from the city while the Anglo-American forces were more than 200 miles away. Getting there ahead of the Soviets would require an enormous effort and a radical change in strategy. This could entail 100,000 additional casualties, the Americans warned.[12]

Eisenhower believed that going for the German capital would be seen as an enormous slap in the face by the Soviet Union after all its losses fighting Hitler. The division of Berlin between the Allies had been agreed, and if Western troops did manage to reach the capital, they would have to withdraw subsequently since the city was not in their zones. So the Supreme Commander proposed to order his troops to head for the Elbe, further south, to link up with the Red Army there. On 28 March, he cabled Stalin informing him of this. Naturally, the dictator agreed. 'Berlin has lost its former strategic importance,' he wrote, even as he set two Soviet marshals to compete to get to the city first.

Churchill was annoyed. Not only had Eisenhower taken no account of his strategic ideas, he had also acted without having informed his British subordinates, and told Downing Street only after getting Stalin's agreement. Though Marshall and his colleagues argued that Eisenhower was acting from operational necessity, Churchill did not give up. He sent a note to the Supreme Commander calling for an advance pitched further east, adding that he did not consider Berlin had lost its military and political significance – the idea that taking Dresden and connecting with the Russians there would be a greater gain 'does not commend itself to me', he wrote.

Eisenhower was polite, but unyielding. So Churchill moved up a rung with an eight-point message to Roosevelt, warning that, if the Red Army took Berlin, the Soviet Union would appear as the overwhelming contributor to victory, with grave implications for the future. The President's reply, drafted by Marshall, again backed Eisenhower. The important thing, the Americans stressed, was to ensure that German forces were completely broken up and destroyed in their separate parts. Churchill had to accept defeat.

This last strategic dispute came amidst the rawest exchange between Roosevelt and Stalin as the dictator accused Washington of seeking a secret peace with the Germans. The row sprang from an approach in February by German commanders in Italy to Allen Dulles, the OSS chief in the Swiss capital of Berne. Discussions followed at which the Americans insisted on unconditional surrender, but did not close the door to further contacts.[13]

Roosevelt informed Stalin. He and Churchill said Soviet officers would be welcome at any subsequent talks but first, the Americans wanted to establish the Germans' credentials – there were fears that the Nazis might shy away if Russians were present at preliminary talks. Churchill says in his account that it proved impossible for the Soviet representatives to get to Berne in time. The negotiations dropped away, but the episode revived old Soviet suspicions about the West being ready for an accord to leave Hitler free to throw all his forces into the battle against the Red Army.

A letter from Molotov inveighed against the 'entirely inexplicable and incomprehensible' attitude in allegedly not facilitating Soviet participation in the Berne contacts. On 3 April, Stalin wrote to the President that his military colleagues had no doubt that negotiations had led to an agreement by which the German command in Italy let Allied forces advance. That was why Alexander was doing so well. Germany was now no longer at war with Britain and America, only with Russia, the dictator went on. As if that was not enough, he ended by reading Roosevelt a homily about the 'momentary advantage . . . fading before the principal advantage of the preservation and strengthening of the trust among the Allies.'

The President grew furious as he read this, sitting at his desk, his eyes flashing, his face flushed. Harriman wrote that it 'jarred Roosevelt into recognizing that the postwar period was going to be far less pleasant than he had imagined. The President was deeply hurt. It made him realize what we were up against.'

'We can't do business with Stalin,' Roosevelt told a lunch guest. 'He has broken every one of the promises he made at Yalta.'

But the Kremlin was true to its word as regards Japan. On 5 April, Molotov called in Tokyo's ambassador to denounce the neutrality pact between the two nations. The news was given out on Soviet radio that night. A troop build-up began in the Far East which would unleash a million men across the border with Siberia four months later.

This did not assuage Roosevelt's anger at Stalin's accusations. He replied that he had received the Soviet leader's message with astonishment. He denied any deal, and recalled that he had said Red Army officers would be welcome if talks were held. 'I must continue to assume that you have the same high confidence in my truthfulness and reliability that I have always had in yours,' he added, attributing the stories Stalin had put to him to German disinformation. 'Frankly, I cannot avoid a feeling of bitter resentment toward your informers, whoever they are, for such vile misrepresentation of my actions or those of my trusted subordinates.'

Churchill associated himself with this. Stalin was unabashed. He told Roosevelt that the Russians would never have denied the West access to any contacts it might have with the Germans, but that this was what had happened in Berne. He contrasted the hard fighting in the East to the German surrender of towns on the Western front. His informants were 'extremely honest and modest people who discharge their duties conscientiously', he added. For Churchill, Stalin saved a special reproach. He wrote that his messages were personal and strictly confidential. But if 'you are going to regard every frank statement of mine as offensive, it will make this kind of communication very difficult.'

*

Roosevelt's command of business in Washington was growing ever more fragile. He signed a document on post-war Germany put forward by a State Department official who favoured a soft approach, and then reversed course after pressure from Morgenthau, telling Stimson afterwards: 'I have no idea what I signed.' On Poland, Leahy's advocacy of a calm approach provoked Churchill to warn of a second Romania, with Britain and the United States losing any influence.[14]

Anna and John Boettinger tried to act as a White House praetorian guard, keeping at bay those they did not approve of. Infuriated by presidential indecision and back-tracking, Stimson wrote in his diary. 'Never has anything I have witnessed in the last four years shown such instances of the bad effects of our chaotic administration and its utter failure to treat matters in a well organized way.' Leaving a White House meeting to appoint him to run the US zone in Germany, General Lucius Clay told James Byrnes: 'We've been talking to a dying man.'

After a Cabinet session on 23 March, Roosevelt collapsed. 'He really sank down and couldn't stand up,' Frances Perkins recalled.

Resting at his cottage at the treatment centre of Warm Springs, he dictated drafts of the address he would give two days later on Jefferson Day, and of his speech to the inaugural United Nations conference. In the first, he declared that the aim was 'an end to the beginnings of all wars'. Echoing his remark about the only thing America had to fear in the Great Depression was fear itself, he went on: 'I say: The only limit to our realization of tomorrow will be our doubts of today. Let us move forward with strong and active faith.' He also drafted a message to Churchill on 11 April turning down his suggestion of a fresh démarche to Moscow. The wording, style and sentiments were redolent of the basic Rooseveltian approach. 'I would minimise the general Soviet problem as much as possible, because these problems . . . seem to arise every day, and most of them straighten out, as in the case of the Berne meeting,' he wrote. 'We must be firm, however, and our course thus far is correct.'

A cable for Stalin was in similar vein. The Berne incident appeared to have 'faded into the past', it said. 'There must not, in any event, be mutual mistrust and minor misunderstandings of this character should not arise in the future.' They were the last messages he wrote to the other two Allied leaders.

At Warm Springs, Roosevelt was joined by Lucy Rutherfurd, Margaret

Suckley, Polly Delano, another cousin, and an Amazonian painter of Russian extraction who was doing his portrait. When Morgenthau visited, he talked of the speech he would make at San Francisco. The Treasury Secretary spoke at length about Germany, and the President made his remark that he was 'hundred per cent' behind him. When Morgenthau left, Roosevelt seemed happy.

The next day, 12 April, he woke with a headache and stiff neck. Putting on a grey, double-breasted suit and crimson tie, he worked on his UN speech. The scene in the cottage was thoroughly domestic. Rutherfurd sat on a sofa, alongside Suckley, who crocheted. Polly Delano arranged the flowers. As she worked her watercolour, the painter asked Roosevelt if he liked Stalin; he said he did, but thought the Soviet leader had poisoned his wife. The war might end 'at any time', he added.

At 1.15, Roosevelt's head slumped forward. It seemed as if he was searching for something. Daisy asked if he was looking for his cigarettes. Putting his hand to his skull, he said in a low but distinct voice, 'I have a terrific pain in the back of my head.'

Lucy and Polly tilted his chair back, while Daisy telephoned for the doctor. Two staff carried the President to his adjoining bedroom. As they did so, Polly understood him to say, semi-conscious, 'Be careful.'

Daisy held his hand. Lucy waved camphor under his nostrils. Polly fanned him. Two or three times he rolled his head from side to side, but there was no recognition in his eyes. Dr Bruenn arrived to administer an injection. His patient had suffered a cerebral haemorrhage. His breathing was loud. Even adrenaline direct into the heart failed to revive him. At 3.55 p.m. Franklin Roosevelt died. His name headed the list of American war dead the next day.

On 13 April, the body was taken by train in a flag-draped coffin 800 miles to Washington. The coffin was raised so it could be seen from outside. At night, it was illuminated. Eleanor, who had arrived in Warm Springs on the night of the 12th, looked out of the window of her compartment at the crowds along the way – 2 million people are estimated to have stood in homage. Roosevelt's admirers wept across the nation; even his long-standing opponents paid tribute to the man who had headed the nation for a dozen years, pulled it out of depression and led it to the brink of victory in the greatest war it ever fought.

Harry Truman and the Cabinet waited at the Union Station, from where the coffin was taken to the White House on a horse-drawn carriage, a riderless horse following with stirrups reversed in the traditional symbol of a fallen warrior. In the presidential mansion, Eleanor asked for the coffin to be opened so that she could spend a few minutes alone with her husband. She slipped a gold band from one of her fingers to put it on one of his.

The White House funeral was held at 4 p.m. on 14 April. Harry Hopkins, who had flown in from the Mayo Clinic in Minnesota, sat on a small chair, weeping uncontrollably through the short, simple service. The aide looked 'like death, the skin of his face a dreadful cold white with apparently no flesh left underneath it,' Robert Sherwood recalled. 'I believed that he now had nothing left to live for, that his life had ended with Roosevelt's.' In a telephone conversation with Sherwood he had reflected: 'You and I have got something great that we can take with us for the rest of our lives . . . we know it's true what so many people believed about him and what made them love him. The President never let them down . . . In the big things – all the things that were of real, permanent importance – he never let the people down.' Later in the day, Hopkins seemed to revive as he talked of working on. Since Roosevelt was no longer there, he told Sherwood, 'we've got to find a way to do things ourselves.'

That night, the body was taken by train to Hyde Park. Anna recalled looking out of the window of her carriage at 'little children, fathers, grandparents. They were all there . . . at all hours during that long night.'

At the estate, the coffin was lowered into a grave in the garden. A bugler played 'Taps', Cadets from West Point fired three rifle volleys; Fala barked after each.

In Moscow, Harriman telephoned Molotov with the news in the middle of the night. Coming to the embassy at 3 a.m., the Foreign Minister seemed deeply moved and disturbed. He spoke of Stalin's respect for Roosevelt, and said Moscow would have confidence in Truman because he had been selected by the late leader.[15]

The following night, Harriman called at the Kremlin. Stalin held his hand for thirty seconds in silence before they sat down. The dictator said he did not believe there would be any change in US policy. Not in areas where Roosevelt had made his plans clear, Harriman replied. But, he went on, his successor would not have the same prestige.

'President Roosevelt has died but his cause must live on,' Stalin broke in. 'We shall support President Truman with all our forces and all our will.'

Harriman then moved on to his main purpose. The most effective way for Moscow to show its desire for continued cooperation would be for Molotov to visit the United States, meet Truman and attend the San Francisco conference. Stalin agreed.

In Chungking, Chiang Kai-shek noted that 'Roosevelt had at times shown a tendency to appease the Communists. But he set a limit to that . . . After his death, I am afraid that the British will exert a greater influence on Anglo-American policy. As to Sino-Soviet relations, we should all the more be vigilant.' In Paris, de Gaulle declared a week of national mourning, and sent Truman a message which spoke of the 'imperishable message' Roosevelt had left. In Berlin, Hitler said that 'fate has removed the greatest war criminal of all time'. Goebbels called for champagne, declaring that the stars foretold a turn in the fortunes of war. Tokyo Radio, on the other hand, spoke of 'the passing of a great man'.[16]

Addressing Parliament, the nation and the Empire, Churchill hailed 'the greatest American friend we have ever known, and the greatest champion of freedom who has ever brought help and comfort from the New World to the Old.' The news of Roosevelt's death had reduced him to tears in the night, and he immediately made arrangements to fly to Washington. Then he decided he could not leave London at 'this most critical and difficult moment'. Too many ministers were out of the country for him to go, too, he argued. This was nonsense. His real motivation remains unclear. He may have feared breaking down in public at the funeral, or that the long flight and the emotion would bring on one of his recurrent attacks of depression. In his place, Eden made the trip while Gromyko represented the Soviet Union.

The new President was an unlikely heir to the Roosevelt heritage. A haberdasher by trade, he had risen through the machine politics of Kansas City boss Tom Pendergast to win election to the Senate where he joined a convivial group of whisky-drinking, poker-playing legislators. 'I felt like the moon, the stars and all the other planets had fallen on me,' he said of becoming President. A month off his sixty-first birthday when he moved into the White House, the short, brisk Truman was totally inexperienced as far as the rest of the world was concerned – he had served in France in the First World War but had not been abroad since. Roosevelt had told him nothing about Yalta or his dealings with the Allies – or the atom bomb.

The day after the White House funeral, Truman spent two hours with Hopkins. Pale and thinner than ever, the aide passed on his views of the other two Allied leaders. Stalin, he said, was a 'forthright, rough, tough Russian . . . a Russian partisan through and through, thinking always first of Russia.' But one could have a frank conversation with him. The aide urged Truman to work closely with Churchill. Above all, he thought Roosevelt's policies must be continued. As the meeting drew to a close, Hopkins said he was going to resign. Truman urged him to stay if his health permitted. The aide said he would think it over.

As he read through secret documents in the Map Room, for the first time, Truman was startled by the hostile character of Stalin's messages. The day after taking office, he cabled Churchill that Poland was a 'pressing and dangerous problem'. Meetings in Washington produced tough talk, particularly from Harriman. It was as if Roosevelt's death had removed inhibitions about speaking frankly.

James Forrestal, the Secretary of the Navy, warned of an ideological war with the USSR. Truman said that any treaty binding America to the new world organisation would fail unless Moscow kept its word on Poland. Agreements with the USSR had been a one-way street, he added; that could not continue. Stimson worried they might be heading into uncharted waters.

Meeting Molotov on 22 April, as the Red Army began to fight its way through the suburbs of Berlin, Truman said he stood by the deal Roosevelt had promised at Yalta for Moscow entering the war against Japan. But he added that the United States had gone as far as it could on Poland. He emphasised the importance of US public opinion, and said Washington was getting tired of waiting for Moscow to carry out its undertakings to allow free elections in eastern Europe. Molotov repeated Soviet complaints about non-Communist Poles attacking the Red Army. Truman responded that he was not interested in propaganda. 'An agreement had been reached on Poland and it only remains for Marshal Stalin to carry it out in accordance with his word,' he went on, his voice rising.[17]

'I have never been talked to like that in my life,' Molotov objected.

'Carry out your agreement, and you won't get talked to like that,' Truman replied.

When the Foreign Minister tried to turn the talk back to the Far East, Truman broke in to say: 'That will be all, Mr Molotov, I would appreciate it if you would transmit my views to Marshal Stalin.' Molotov told Stalin Roosevelt's policies were being abandoned. Two days later, in a message to Churchill, the Soviet leader accused Britain and America of working together 'to put the Government of the USSR in an intolerable position by attempting to dictate their demands to it'. The following day, Truman spoke by telephone to the Prime Minister about an approach for peace to the Western Allies by Heinrich Himmler. While Churchill expressed concern that the SS chief might also be trying to cut a deal with Stalin, the President insisted that surrender must be to all three powers together. Absolutely sound, the Soviet leader replied when told of this. That day, Truman was briefed for the first time on the atom bomb. Three days later, US and Red Army troops met in Germany, inside the Soviet occupation zone. In keeping with their agreements, the Americans pulled back after the celebrations.

22

Journey's End

POTSDAM
17 JULY–2 AUGUST 1945

'The Soviet Union always honours its word, except in case of extreme necessity'

STALIN

AT 5 P.M. ON 17 JULY 1945, using separate doors, Churchill, Stalin and Truman entered the conference room at the mock-Tudor Cecilienhof Palace in the Soviet zone near Babelsberg outside Berlin for the last summit of the alliance. They sat round a circular table covered with a burgundy-coloured cloth on wooden armchairs upholstered in red plush. In front of them, the lawn of the 176-room building sloped down to a lake from which swarms of mosquitoes buzzed in through the unscreened windows. The Red Army had planted a huge star of red geraniums in the garden. The security consisted mainly of green-hatted Soviet frontier guards from Central Asia, though there were also women traffic police whose smart uniforms, Andrei Gromyko said, caused Churchill to drop cigar ash all over his suit.

The delegations were lodged in solid villas round the lake and in woods. While the German capital had been devastated by the last stage of the war, Babelsberg had escaped relatively unscathed. Many houses still had grand pianos.

In the ten weeks since Hitler's suicide and the surrender of the Reich, relations between the Big Three remained bumpy. At the San Francisco conference, the Soviets were insisting that, on top of their veto on UN action, the big powers must be able to prevent even verbal complaints being raised against them. Churchill wanted the West to take a stronger line with Stalin. As the British general election drew near, he knew the danger of being seen to have reneged on the principles for which the war was fought. He wrote to the Kremlin of meeting 'a stone wall upon matters which we sincerely believed were settled in a spirit of friendly comradeship in the Crimea.'

In a twelve-point 'outpouring of my heart' to Stalin in the spring, he went through the differences between London and Moscow over Poland and in Yugoslavia where 'Tito has become a complete dictator [and] proclaimed that his prime loyalties are to the Soviet Union'. A division between Communist states and the English-speaking nations would 'tear the world to pieces,' he warned. 'Do not, I beg you, my friend, Stalin, under-rate the divergencies which are opening up about matters which you may think are small to us but which are symbolic to the way the English-speaking democracies look at life.' At the same time, he asked the British Joint Planning Staff to prepare a paper on a possible 'total war' with the Soviet Union. The object of 'Operation Unthinkable' would be 'to impose upon Russia the will of the United States and British Empire' and to achieve 'a square deal for Poland.' Hostilities would start on 1 July. The British Chiefs of Staff rejected the idea as militarily unfeasible.[1]

Writing to Truman, Churchill changed his metaphor to warn of 'an iron curtain' being drawn down along the Soviet front line. He expressed his fears that the Soviet leader might 'play for time in order to remain all-powerful in Europe when our forces have melted'. To Eisenhower, he showed concern at the destruction of German aircraft since 'we may have great need of these some day'. In a note to Eden, he highlighted the danger that withdrawal of US troops would lead to domestic pressure in Britain for demobilisation while the Red Army maintained hundreds of divisions from the Baltic to the Adriatic.[2]

The tone in Washington was changing, as presaged by Truman's remarks to Molotov. Lend-Lease to the USSR was cut off four days after the surrender of Germany on 8 May, a decision that Stalin branded 'unfortunate and even brutal' and which was swiftly reversed and blamed on a bureaucratic misunderstanding. Washington did not want to give Stalin a reason to renege on his undertaking to enter the war against Japan so the programme continued until September 1945.

Though Stalin raised the matter later in the year, nothing came of the scheme for a reconstruction loan for the USSR. When Moscow proposed that the Big Three recognise the regimes in other countries under its influence, the President replied that in Romania, Hungary and Bulgaria he had been 'disturbed to find governments that do not accord to all the democratic elements of the people the rights of free expression'.[3]

But Truman also had a shock in store for Churchill. On 26 May, a presidential envoy went to Chequers for a conversation that lasted from 11 p.m. until 4.30 a.m. Truman could hardly have picked a worse envoy – the pro-Soviet, anti-British former ambassador to Moscow, Joseph Davies. The choice had been urged on him by the outgoing White House spokesman, Steve Early, who was going to a job with a company of which Davies was a director. Churchill's warnings of the spread of Soviet power put him in the same camp as Hitler, Davies said. Eden summed him up as 'the born appeaser [who] would gladly give Russia all Europe, except perhaps us, so that America might not be embroiled'.[4]

Davies said the President wanted a bilateral meeting with Stalin before they were joined by Churchill for a trilateral summit. The Prime Minister feared a bilateral deal – and could only resent the way Truman made his priorities so clear. Unless the three men met simultaneously and on equal terms, he warned Truman, he would not attend a summit. In a long despatch to the White House on 27 May, he pointed out that the Soviets were using 'to the full the methods of police government, which they are applying in every State which has fallen victims to their liberating arms.' 'The Prime Minister cannot readily bring himself to accept the idea that the position of the United States is that Britain and Soviet Russia are just two foreign powers, six of one and half a dozen of the other, with whom the troubles of the late war have to be adjusted,' he went on. 'The great causes and principles for which Britain and the United States have suffered and triumphed are not mere matters of the balance of power. They in fact involve the salvation of the world.'

Like Churchill, Truman was facing growing concern in America about events since Yalta, though some opinion-formers and military chiefs still believed cooperation with Moscow was essential – the leading commentator Walter Lippmann stalked out of a briefing by Harriman when the ambassador criticised Moscow. To try to clear the air, Truman sent Hopkins to Moscow to meet Stalin. The aide was lying emaciated in bed at his Georgetown home when Harriman and Bohlen called to tell him of the mission. The new President said he wanted 'a fair understanding' with the

Kremlin but 'intended to have a way of carrying out the agreements purported to have been made at Yalta. The aid should make clear to Stalin 'that we never made commitments which we did not expect to carry out to the letter and we intended to see that he did.' To make his point, Hopkins could use diplomacy, a baseball bat or anything else he considered appropriate. Louise accompanied her husband to look after him, and was a hit with Soviet generals, being forced, however, by US regulations to turn down nearly all the many gifts she was offered.[5]

Accompanied by Harriman and Bohlen, Hopkins had six sessions with Stalin over ten days. He began by explaining that Truman would find it hard to continue cooperation without the support of public opinion. Going to the root of the matter, he ascribed popular concern to 'a sense of bewilderment at our inability to solve the Polish question'.

Stalin was courteous – he told Bohlen once that Hopkins was the first American to whom he had spoken 'from the soul'. But, below the relaxed, informal nature of the discussions, he stood firm, deploying the debating skills he had shown at Teheran and Yalta. At one point, he said that the Soviet Union always honoured its word, and then, lowering his voice, added 'except in case of extreme necessity'.

The interpreter Pavlov did not immediately translate these last words.

'I believe there is a little more,' Bohlen said. Pavlov mumbled the qualification.

Stalin reeled off a list of complaints – at the admission of Argentina to the United Nations although it had never declared war on Germany; at the temporary halt to Lend-Lease; at the suggestion that France should join the Reparations Commission; and at the prospect the USSR might not get a third of the German fleet. Hopkins produced answers, but the key discussions on Poland were long and tortuous, continuing till the last session on 6 June.

Hopkins said the issue was 'a symbol of our ability to work out problems with the Soviet Union'. He set out the freedoms which Americans thought necessary – if Stalin accepted these, agreement could be reached. 'These principles are well known and would find no objection on the part of the Soviet government,' Stalin replied. But they could only be applied in peacetime, and then with certain limitations. Hopkins hoped an accord was in sight, but, Stalin's provisos meant he had not committed himself. In any case, as always, the West had no means of holding him to any word he gave.

When it came to the composition of the Warsaw administration, Stalin said four or five of the eighteen to twenty ministries might go to figures nominated by the United States and Britain. Mikołajczyk could take part in talks on a new government together with two other London Poles and five non-Communists. When Hopkins raised the issue of the sixteen non-Communist figures who had been arrested after being invited to Moscow, Stalin stonewalled, saying they had shot Red Army men in the back while their country was being liberated. So they would have to stand trial – had not the Allies arrested saboteurs? Hopkins sent a message to Churchill saying he was 'doing everything under heaven to get these people out of jug', but adding that the more important objective was to have Mikołajczyk and other non-Communist Poles in Moscow for talks.

The aide scored a significant success when he raised the matter of Soviet insistence that the great powers should be able to veto even discussion of their conduct at the United Nations. 'What is this all about, Molotov?' Stalin asked. The Foreign Minister said big countries should have this right from the start of any discussion. 'That's nonsense,' Stalin replied. Gromyko in San Francisco was told to give way, thus enabling the Charter of the United Nations to be adopted. The global body Roosevelt had dreamed of had finally come into being, but despite Stalin's concession, the big nations as permanent members of the Security Council would be in charge. If that had been Moscow's essential condition, it had also been a consistent theme of Roosevelt's thinking; he had never seen the organisation as truly democratic, or thought that smaller nations should be able to overrule the great powers.

Hopkins also got a firm date for Soviet entry into the war in the Far East – 8 August – so long as the conditions agreed at Yalta were confirmed. Stalin said he saw the United States playing the major role in China after the war since the USSR would be so occupied with its own reconstruction. His main, unstated, aim was to keep the vast country as a weak neighbour, which was more likely to be achieved by perpetuating the highly flawed Nationalist regime than by putting the Communists in power.

On the night of 1 June, Stalin gave the last Kremlin banquet for visiting allies. By the standards of previous occasions, it was restrained. There were forty guests, and the vodka bottles were removed early on. After the meal, Hopkins again raised the question of the sixteen Poles. Stalin would not give ground. The American let the matter drop. Fourteen of them were imprisoned; some of them died in detention while others were later re-arrested after being released – or fled to the West.

Harriman reported that 'Harry did a first-rate job.' But he felt that Stalin was probably left bewildered by the way the Americans insisted on focusing on what he must have seen as a lost cause for them. 'I am afraid that Stalin does not and never will understand our interest in a free Poland as a matter of principle,' Harriman wrote to Washington. 'He is a realist in all his actions, and it is hard for him to appreciate our faith in abstract principles.'

Reckoning they had got all they could expect, Truman and Churchill recognised the Provisional Government in Warsaw at the beginning of July after the addition of non-Communist members. The fate of the sixteen Poles had made Mikołajczyk wary of going to Moscow for talks on a coalition government, but Churchill persuaded him, saying: 'You have put your foot in an open door, and should not miss this opportunity.' Closely watched by Clark Kerr and Harriman, the initial contacts with the Lublin leaders went well, and Mikołajczyk became Vice Premier and Agriculture Minister in the new administration in Warsaw. But the Soviet-backed group, and, through it, Moscow, kept hold of the levers of power in the police and the army. The State Department later identified the Lublin Committee chief as a Communist agent of two decades standing.[6]

In his memoirs, Churchill wrote that it was difficult to see what more could have been done, but also acknowledged: 'We were still as far as ever from any real and fair attempts to obtain the will of the Polish nation by free elections.' Leaving Moscow for Warsaw, Mikołajczyk told Harriman of his grave doubts about the chances of success. 'I may never see you again,' he said. He ended up in exile in the United States.[7]

Hopkins flew home via Berlin, where his wife was photographed arm-in-arm with Red Army officers, surrounded by other grinning Russians and her husband, who looks equally happy. The aide lunched with Marshal Zhukov and Vyshinsky, who was running political affairs in the Soviet zone. When the former prosecutor spoke hopefully of Allied cooperation, Hopkins sipped his coffee and then replied, sighing: 'It's a pity President Roosevelt didn't live to see these days. It was easier with him.'[8]

Talking to Bohlen on the flight home, Hopkins voiced doubts about the possibility of real cooperation with Moscow, saying differences over the issue of freedom boded ill. But he still saw preventing a revival of German militarism as the first priority. On his return to America, he resigned from government service, turning down an offer from Truman to join the forthcoming summit. 'I am sure my decision is the right one because I have every chance of getting well now,' he wrote to Harriman. 'I have taken a job in New York as Impartial Chairman of the Ladies Cloak and Suit Industry . . . they are paying me a reasonably good salary and the work is not going to be too hard. Then I am going to get busy writing a book so, all in all, I will have plenty to do.' He was given an honorary degree by Oxford, and awarded a Distinguished Service Medal by Truman for the 'outstanding value' of his 'piercing understanding of the tremendous problems incident to the vast military operations throughout the world' as well as his 'selfless, courageous, and objective contribution to the war effort'. He spent the summer in Maine, telling Bohlen that everything should be done to foster relations between Washington, Moscow and London. Then he went back into hospital.

On the voyage across the Atlantic on the *Augusta*, the heavy cruiser used by Roosevelt at Placentia Bay, Truman was given extensive briefings, played poker and one day queued for food with an aluminium tray in the mess hall. Aides found him very businesslike, free from Rooseveltian ramblings, though he wrote to his wife: 'How I hate this trip! But I have to make it.'[9]

Docking in Antwerp, he was driven to Brussels from where he flew to Berlin in the 'Sacred Cow'. He was lodged in a three-storey stucco house by Lake Griebnitz which was immediately nicknamed 'The Little White House' – the road on which it stood had been known as the Street of the Brownshirts, and was subsequently renamed Karl Marx Strasse. Though it had been done up, Truman found the building gloomy and the Presidential Log recorded that the bathroom facilities were wholly inadequate.

As Truman slept that night, the technicians at the test site in Alamogordo, New Mexico, made the final check on an atomic device set on top of a tower. Three days earlier, the Emperor of Japan had instructed that peace feelers should be put out in Moscow, but also warned that, if the United States and Britain insisted on unconditional surrender, it would be necessary to fight to the bitter end.

Truman's main companion for the summit was James Byrnes, the new Secretary of State and veteran of Yalta, who might well have thought he should have been in Truman's place. Described by *Time* magazine as 'the politicians' politician', the small, wiry South Carolinian had fancied himself as Roosevelt's running mate in 1944 – Truman had been due to nominate him at the convention. But he aroused strong opposition on the left of the Democratic Party and was not likely to attract black voters.

Once in the White House, Truman sought to build bridges by naming Byrnes to replace Stettinius. Since there was no vice president, this made the Secretary of State next in line for the succession. Byrnes was highly self-confident. He had no experience of foreign affairs, but he and the President were on the same wavelength.

Truman was also accompanied by Harriman and Bohlen. But he was free of the influence of Morgenthau whose resignation from the Cabinet he had contrived shortly before he left Washington. According to an account cited by the historian Michael Beschloss, Truman told Stimson, 'Don't worry, neither Morgenthau nor Baruch, nor any of the Jew boys will be going to Potsdam.'

Churchill had flown to Berlin from a holiday in France, where he had taken up painting again. He invited Attlee to accompany him. He was put up two blocks away from Truman in a stone house with chandeliers and dirty French windows. Arriving in the evening of 15 July, the Prime Minister flopped into a garden chair between two big tubs of hydrangeas. He seemed, Moran recorded, too weary to move. Drinking a whisky and soda, he stared silently at the lake, where the Russians were said to have drowned wounded German prisoners. A soldier came out of the wood opposite, looked around and disappeared. As night fell, a rifle shot sounded from the wood.[10]

The 16th and 17th of July saw a series of bilateral meetings. Cadogan recorded that Churchill was delighted by Truman, noting his 'precise, sparkling manner', 'immense determination' and firmness. The American formed an instant liking for the older man. Still, when Churchill said Britain would like to contribute forces against Japan, he was reserved. He wanted the Far East to be an American show, and to keep his freedom of action in deciding whether to use the atom bomb.[11]

Meeting Churchill the next day, Stalin told him of the Japanese peace feeler which, he said, showed that Tokyo was very frightened. There was some chat about the disciplined nature of the Germans – 'like sheep', the Georgian observed. Stalin remarked that he had taken to smoking cigars. Churchill replied that if a photograph of the Georgian smoking one could be flashed round the world 'it would cause an immense sensation' by appearing to show his influence on the Soviet leader. More seriously, Churchill ended by saying he particularly welcomed the USSR as a great naval power, a statement he would come to regret as the Kremlin pressed for a big chunk of the German fleet.

At noon on 17 July, Stalin drove from his house to meet Truman. He had been the last of the leaders to arrive, travelling in an ornate Tsarist train taken out of a museum for his use. While waiting for him, the other leaders had visited the ruins of Hitler's Berlin.

Stalin was lodged in a mansion which had once belonged to Ludendorff, the First World War commander, with fifteen rooms, a veranda and specially installed electricity, heating and telephone systems. As usual, he was surrounded by extremely heavy security, including seven NKVD regiments and 900 bodyguards. Though this was kept secret, he had suffered a slight heart attack before leaving Moscow.[12]

Truman was working at his desk when he looked up to see Stalin in the doorway. In keeping with his recent promotion to the rank of Generalissimo, he wore a white uniform tunic with red epaulettes. Truman was struck by his directness and politeness. He noted that they were the same height, but that Stalin tried to position himself one step higher when photographs were taken of them standing together on the steps of the Cecilienhof Palace.

Not knowing of the Truman–Churchill exchange the previous day, Stalin lost little time in trying a touch of splittist tactics, observing that Britain was not ready to play its role against Japan but that the USSR was ready to come into the war in the Pacific in the middle of August. In reply, Truman said the Yalta agreement on concessions in China would be kept.

Would Stalin stay for lunch? Truman asked.

No, he could not, the dictator replied.

'You could if you wanted to,' the President said.

So he did. Table talk was inconsequential. Stalin complemented Truman on the Californian wine. Afterwards, the leaders and their Foreign Ministers went out on to the balcony where they were photographed. Then they parted. 'I can deal with Stalin,' Truman decided. 'He is honest, but smart as hell.' He likened him to his mentor in Kansas City, Tom Pendergast. While they had been meeting, a message had arrived from New Mexico: 'Babi satisfactorily born.' America had become a nuclear power.

Truman followed the Roosevelt precedent by taking the chai Cecilienhof. It was his chance to show he was his own man a highest level. He and Byrnes might not be cosmopolitans summitry behind them, but the way they sidelined Harriman and Bohlen demonstrated that they were intent on setting a new path.[13]

Truman wrote to his mother that he found the job nerve-wracking – 'Churchill talks all the time and Stalin just grunts but you know what he means.' At the longest of the Allied summits, he would become increasingly impatient with both British verbosity and Soviet intransigence and, as his confidence grew, would feel able to suggest that, if they were getting nowhere, the participants should go home.

Churchill was in poor form, tired, suffering from indigestion and dogged by his country's parlous economic position, telling Truman that Britain was coming out of the war as the greatest debtor nation on earth. A paper from Keynes pointed out that foreign aid had enabled Britain to overspend its income during the war years by some £2 billion a year; if the aid ended, it would be bankrupt. The Prime Minister also had to confront the looming election which he likened to a 'vulture of uncertainty'. His campaign focused on him as the great war leader, and he had been greeted by cheering crowds. But, as Eden noted, 'in truth they were only saying "Thank you. You have led us superbly. We shall always be grateful to you."' As Roosevelt had predicted, once the war was won, Churchill became a figure from the past.

The Prime Minister looked disgruntled as he sat with the other two leaders in wicker chairs for the first group photograph. Eden, who had suffered a huge blow with news of the death of his son in action, found Churchill under Stalin's spell as he repeated: 'I like that man.' Over dinner on 17 July, the Foreign Secretary urged his leader 'not to give up our few cards without return', and wrote a memorandum describing Soviet policy ᵃs 'aggrandisement'. Moscow's intentions, he concluded, were becoming ⸺ʳ as they become more brazen every day'.

⸻ ḫill was not convinced. Though he could see the Iron Curtain
⸻ ḫe need for western Europe to be strengthened, he still
⸻ blishing man-to-man contact with the dictator to
⸻ recorded him as saying: 'Stalin gave me his
⸻ lections in countries set free by his armies.
⸻ t see why. We must listen to these Russians,
⸻ men, and nearly half of them were killed or
⸻ ḫe was saying that the Soviets 'talk about the
⸻ edom and justice and that sort of thing, but

prominent people are removed and not seen again.' Later, he told Moran: 'I shall ask Stalin, does he want the whole world?'[14]

Cadogan noted in his diary that Churchill did not read his paperwork, and 'butts in on every occasion and talks the most irrelevant rubbish'. His humour was not improved when a storm destroyed the water main by the British villas, depriving him of his bath – other problems with the water supply caused outbreaks of diarrhoea during the summit. In contrast, the Foreign Office mandarin found Truman 'most quick and businesslike' – 'I don't want to discuss, I want to decide,' the President remarked at one point, in words very similar to Stalin's at Yalta. The Soviet leader, meanwhile, watched the way the discussions were going, giving no ground but seeming relaxed, and, at times, amused as he doodled on the pad in front of him.[15]

Reading from his script at the opening session, Truman listed subjects for the agenda, starting with the proposed establishment of a five-nation Council of Foreign Ministers. This provoked objections from Stalin. France's war record did not justify a place, he said. Why should China have any say in European matters?

Unabashed, Truman seized on one of the most sensitive issues between the Allies – the holding of free and fair elections in Europe. In particular, he mentioned Romania and Bulgaria. Then he suggested that policy towards Italy should be revised to enable the new government in Rome to join the United Nations. This time it was Churchill who objected, before Stalin chipped in to say that Italy should not get any preferential treatment not offered to Germany's former allies in eastern Europe.

Sensing he was out of tune, Truman noted that he had taken the place of 'a man who was really irreplaceable'. He only hoped to be able to inherit some of the friendship and goodwill Roosevelt had enjoyed. That brought an outpouring of warmth from Churchill, with which Stalin associated himself.

The Prime Minister said they should add Poland to the agenda. Overriding interruptions from Churchill, Stalin laid out his list of subjects – the German merchant fleet and navy, reparations, trusteeships for the Soviet Union, relations with former Axis allies, the removal of the Franco regime in Spain, the futures of Tangiers, Syria and Lebanon, Poland's western frontier and 'the liquidation of the [Polish] London government'.

There was then a discussion about the Council of Foreign Ministers. Would it prepare questions for a peace conference? Stalin asked. Yes, Truman replied. In fact, the administration was leery of anything that might come to resemble Versailles in 1919. But it might be useful to discuss the idea to try to hold Stalin to his engagements.

The session ended in good humour as the delegations went into an adjoining room for champagne and caviar. Stimson had been handed a cable saying that 'the little boy' – the atom bomb to be used against Japan – would be 'as husky as his brother' – the one already tested. The decoder thought the seventy-seven-year-old Secretary of War had become a father. Stimson wanted to give Japan a last warning before using the weapon. Truman and Byrnes did not agree. As the President stuck to the doctrine of unconditional surrender, the use of the bomb became more probable, day by day.

The tradition of summit dinners was maintained with each of the Big Three playing host in turn. Truman brought in a pianist and violinist for his occasion. Stalin doubled the number of musicians for his banquet. Truman wrote to his mother that the evening was 'a wow. Started with caviar and vodka and wound up with watermelon and champagne, with smoked fish, fresh fish, venison, chicken, duck, and all sorts of vegetables in between. There was a toast every five minutes . . . I ate very little and drank less, but it was a colourful and enjoyable occasion.' Truman remarked that the Soviet musicians had dirty faces and that the two women violinists were 'rather fat'. Himself an accomplished pianist, he rebuffed suggestions from the unmusical Churchill they should leave, reducing the Prime Minister to sulking as he drank brandy and puffed on his cigar. As the party ended, he muttered to Leahy that he would 'get even' with the other two for all the music they had inflicted on him.[16]

He did this on 23 July by bringing in the whole of an RAF band for his dinner. It played so loudly that Stalin got up to ask for some quiet tunes. Churchill raised his glass to 'Stalin the Great' and the Soviet leader drank to a joint war against Japan. Truman said he was a timid man who had been overwhelmed to have been made chairman of the summit. 'Modesty such as the President's is a great source of strength and a real indication of character,' Stalin responded.

The Soviet leader went round the table asking others to sign his menu card. Truman and Churchill followed suit. So did the diplomats, and officials and military men. After midnight, the band played the three national anthems and the last convivial occasion of the alliance ended at 1.30 a.m. – late for Truman who liked to be in bed by 10.30.

*

At a tête-à-tête conversation with Churchill, Stalin predicted that the Conservatives would win a majority of eighty in the election. When the Prime Minister said he was not sure of the votes of servicemen, the dictator replied that an army preferred a strong government, and so would vote for the Tories. He stated blandly that he wanted to see countries liberated by the Red Army becoming strong, independent, sovereign states. 'Sovietization' should not take place. Free elections should be held open to all parties except Fascists. When Churchill repeated his complaints about Yugoslavia, Stalin said the USSR had no interests there, and often did not know what Tito was doing. He was 'hurt' by American criticism over Romania – harking back to the percentages agreement, he pointed out that he was not meddling in Greek affairs.

Taking a map, Churchill drew a line through Europe, naming capitals in Soviet hands. It looked, he added, as though the USSR was rolling westwards. On the contrary, Stalin replied, he was pulling forces back – two million would be demobilised within four months.

Churchill returned to the subject during the plenary session on 24 July, drawing attention to the way eastern Europe was being closed off under Moscow's domination. 'An iron fence' was being erected, he said. 'Fairy tales!' Stalin growled.

At the end of that session, Truman walked round the circular table. Having been told what he was going to do, Churchill watched closely. The President casually mentioned to the dictator that 'we have a new weapon of unusual destructive force'.[17]

Stalin showed no special interest, Truman recalled. His face remained expressionless. He just said he was glad to hear the news, and hoped America would make 'good use of it against the Japanese'.

Churchill, who described the test as 'the Second Coming', felt that Stalin had no idea of the significance of what he had been told. As he and Truman left, the Prime Minister asked the President: 'How did it go?' 'He never asked a question,' Truman replied. Byrnes hoped that the information about the bomb might give Washington leverage with Moscow, and help keep the Red Army out of Manchuria.

The calm was deceptive. Stalin had known about the Manhattan Project for some months. Based on information from Soviet agents, Beria had informed him of the explosion in New Mexico. They had decided that, if Truman broke the news, the dictator should pretend not to understand. That night, Stalin told Molotov, who was in charge of the atomic programme, of the conversation with Truman. The Foreign Minister ordered work to be speeded up, but Stalin judged that he was not getting adequate results and switched responsibility for the project was soon entrusted to Beria as the ultimate weapon was dropped on Hiroshima while the President sailed home.

On the morning of 25 July, Truman stood, his arms crossed over his chest, to grasp the hands of the Soviet and British leaders for photographs. He smiled at Stalin, who seemed set in stone in his white tunic. Churchill looked all too human, his uniform rumpled, his face pink.[18]

The plenary session that day wandered over familiar subjects such as Germany and Poland. Truman intervened to remind the others that treaties had to be approved by the Senate. So anything he said did not 'preclude my coming back and informing you when I find that political sentiment at home on a proposition is such that I cannot continue to press its acceptance without endangering our common interests in the peace'. It was a constitutional point Roosevelt had brought up, but the directness of Truman's statement made it a warning.

Welcoming his directness, Churchill told Moran: 'If only this had happened at Yalta. It is too late now.' He flew to Britain in the afternoon to await the election result.

'I hope to be back,' he said as he left.

'Judging from the expression on Mr Attlee's face, I do not think he looks forward avidly to taking over your authority,' Stalin replied.

But the previous night, Churchill had dreamed of lying dead in an empty room under a white sheet, his feet protruding. 'Perhaps this is the end,' he told his doctor.

Though voting had taken place three weeks earlier, the declaration was delayed to allow for ballots from servicemen abroad to be counted. Churchill recorded that he went to bed that night 'in the belief that the British people would wish me to continue with my work'. Just before dawn, he woke with a stab of almost physical pain. After which, 'a hitherto subconscious conviction that we were beaten broke forth and dominated my mind.'

He went back to sleep, waking at 9 a.m. Going to the Map Room, he saw the unfavourable results coming. By lunchtime on 26 July, it was clear that Labour had won. The voters had determined that the bulldog of 1940 was, as Roosevelt had forecast, not the man to lead them in peacetime, and had given their belated verdict on pre-war Conservative rule. Clementine said defeat might be a blessing in disguise. 'At the moment,' her husband replied, 'it seems quite effectively disguised.'

Clement Attlee, the pipe-smoking socialist, could not have been more of a contrast to his predecessor. Methodical and personally modest – he had been driven round the country during the election campaign by his wife in their family car – Attlee's demeanour made him easy to underestimate. Cadogan noted in his diary that the new Prime Minister 'recedes into the background by his own insignificance'. He had been part of the British delegation from the start of the summit. Though he had said little, he knew what had gone on, and his self-effacing style hid a lot of steel.

The dominant figure in the British team was Ernest Bevin, the new Foreign Secretary, a proletarian mastiff in place of a Tory bulldog. The burly, hard-drinking former trade union boss did not hide his suspicions of the Soviet Union, repeatedly confronting Stalin and Molotov. He had learned the way Communists operated during his years in the labour movement. But his blunt manner did not go down well with the Americans at first, and the Potsdam meeting continued to get nowhere as each side trotted out familiar arguments and counter-arguments.[19]

The Soviets pressed for a definite figure for German reparations, though they scaled down the original $20 billion. The Americans insisted that no figure could be agreed, and the British worried about the effect on the Ruhr, which lay in their occupation zone.

Stalin and Molotov insisted on the western Neisse as Poland's border. A Polish delegation arrived, much to the annoyance of the French who felt that they should be present, too. The Lublin Committee sat up over sandwiches and whisky till 1.30 a.m. with the British. Mikołajczyk handed Harriman a note saying proper elections were impossible so long as the Red Army and NKVD remained in Poland.

Byrnes evolved a package deal, linking German reparations and Poland's western frontier. He pointed out that moving the border as Moscow wanted would make payment of reparations difficult since the areas acquired by Warsaw contained raw materials needed in Germany. In addition, the Soviets had already removed large amounts of German plant. Setting a sum for payment as the USSR wished would mean

Washington would have to put money into Germany to enable it to satisfy Moscow. That the United States would not do.

Stalin pleaded a cold and sent Molotov in his place to a bilateral session with Truman. The Foreign Minister agreed to an American proposal that, instead of a set sum, each occupying power would take what it chose in the way of reparations from its sector, thus, in effect, dividing Germany into four zones, each under the command of a military governor who would decide policy on the spot. This was not dismemberment as originally envisaged, but provided a clear West–East split, with potential for each zone to evolve in different ways.

In addition to what it chose to take from the east, the USSR was to receive 10 per cent of assets from the western areas, plus another 25 per cent in return for supplying food – which never happened. When the British were brought in, Bevin objected, noting that Moscow would get more than the 50 per cent of reparations it had requested. But Britain's opposition carried less weight than it might once have done.

On Poland, Byrnes–Truman scheme proposed to recognise the western Neisse frontier as the de facto line pending a peace conference. On recognition of the Communist-dominated governments in Romania, Hungary and Bulgaria, the Secretary of State came up with another formula designed to get round British objections. The Big Three powers would examine the question of establishing relations with such regimes 'to the extent possible'.

Bevin was not happy. He suggested that reparations should be put on one side, and that the meeting should concentrate on Poland. This was not at all what Byrnes had in mind. With long experience of stitching together packages in the Senate, he insisted that the proposals stood or fell as a whole. If America was to give way on Poland, he wanted to be sure of agreement on reparations. In place of the cloudy wording of Teheran and Yalta, the new administration wanted a clear deal. To hammer in his point, Byrnes told Molotov that he and Truman were preparing to go home, and would leave with agreement on all counts or no agreement at all.

Recovered from his diplomatic illness, Stalin turned up at the next plenary on 31 July, and went along with the American scheme for zonal reparations, with special allocations for the Soviet Union. Inconclusive discussions followed on such matters as the German navy and Truman's scheme to internationalise waterways running between countries. Then, at a night session on 1 August, the other key points in Byrnes's package were sewn up. Diplomatic recognition of the new regimes in eastern Europe was watered down to a statement that peace treaties should be concluded with those countries, as well as with Finland. The final definition of Poland's western border should await a peace conference. Pending that, former German territories up to the western Neisse and East Prussia, except for areas taken by the USSR by the sea, 'shall be under the administration of the Polish state'.

'The Conference can, I believe, be considered a success,' Stalin said finally. At which, after thanks to the Foreign Ministers, Truman declared the summit closed. As he bade farewell and left for home, he said he hoped the next meeting would be in Washington. 'God willing,' Stalin replied. Though they both would lead their countries into the 1950s, they would not meet again.

The personalities at the top of the wartime alliance had always been vital, their relationships crucial. Now, Roosevelt was dead. Churchill was out of office, succeeded by a Labour government ready to take a tough line with Moscow while greatly broadening the welfare state, implementing nationalisations and achieving Roosevelt's goal of granting independence to India. For Eden, the shock was brought home when Japan surrendered on 14 August. He was dining with Churchill at Claridge's Hotel. After the meal, they listened to Attlee giving the news on the BBC. Then 'there was a silence. Mr Churchill had not been asked to say any word to the nation. We went home. Journey's End.' The British had got into their 'glorious struggle . . . in one muddle and have come out of it in another,' Churchill wrote.

After the defeat of Japan, America cut off Lend-Lease to Britain. Cadogan laid aside his customary disdain to note in his diary: 'The problems ahead of us are manifold and awful. But I've lived through England's great hour, and if I can see no falling away from that, I shall die happy.'[20]

In Washington, the cast changed, too. Morgenthau was gone. Two months after Potsdam, Stimson resigned. Having felt snubbed by Truman and Byrnes, Harriman left the embassy in Moscow. Hopkins's life was drawing to a close as his liver disintegrated. He had a stand with a bottle of blood plasma rigged up by his bed so that he could insert the needle himself. But his stomach would not take food, and he sometimes woke up soiled by diarrhoea. He could still hit his habitual wry note, writing to Churchill that his cirrhosis was 'not due, I regret to say, from taking too much alcohol'. That letter, on 22 January 1945, was his last. As his body turned to skin and bone and his gaze became vacant, the carpenter of the alliance slipped away. 'You can't beat destiny,' he told his valet. On 29 January, his wife left his bedside to cable friends with news of his condition. When she returned, Harry Hopkins was dead. He was just fifty-five.

Reporting to the American people on his return from Europe, Truman noted that: 'Nearly every international agreement has in it an element of compromise.' He had let Poland go. Though a referendum in 1946 gave strong support to Mikołajczyk's party, a mixture of fraud and harrassment earned the Communists a large majority when a general election was held the following year; Moscow's control became complete as opposition leaders fled the country. Germany was divided into zones dominated by the Soviets and the West, which would go their separate ways for the next half-century.

The Cold War had taken shape during the hot war. Potsdam opened the age of atomic anxiety as the world split in two – a division to become even greater when Chiang Kai-shek lost power to Mao at the end of 1949. The accidental alliance was over; as Churchill remarked in a speech to the Commons in 1944 the marvel was that it had survived. With victory, divergences of ideology, geography and national cultures that had been submerged by common need rose to the surface.

The threat they faced had convinced three strong and very different leaders of the absolute importance of cooperation, however strained it might become. Though there were many side roads, many moments of indecision, many episodes when linguistic gloss overlaid reality, they knew two things – they had to defeat the evil enemy and, to do so, they had to remain in alliance.

Each played his role to the utmost. First into the pit, Churchill used all his powers of rhetoric and emotion to court Roosevelt, but was also ready to cut territorial percentages with Stalin; he warded America off from a potentially disastrous invasion of France in 1942, and identified the danger of Soviet power in Europe.

Forced into war ahead of his planning, Stalin saw his country take huge losses, but knew more clearly than either of the other two leaders what he wanted, using his army to get it and constructing a national security empire stretching to the middle of Europe. 'In politics,' he observed at Potsdam, 'one should be guided by the calculation of forces.'

Always the most sensitive to domestic opinion, Roosevelt moved his country from isolationism to internationalism and created an organisation which was meant to keep the peace. But he left no road map and, having decided from the start not to confront Stalin, could do nothing to turn words into action in the half of Europe taken by the Red Army. Had he lived, he might have produced a joker, on the evidence of his performance, one must doubt it.

With Roosevelt dead and Churchill out of office, only the dictator with his clear priorities remained in power – for another eight years. The alliance had rid the world of Nazism and its Japanese equivalent. But this could only be done in a way that would move the world to nearly fifty years of cold confrontation. The alliance had been for war, not peace. It ended by dividing the globe more sharply and on a broader scale than ever before. Europe was more clearly organised, and less prone to war, each of its nations living within clearly defined boundaries overseen by two superpowers under the umbrella of the nuclear stand-off.

Western Europe thrived under the shield of Pax Americana while the eastern half of the continent was confined in the Soviet Empire. The outcome of the alliance was not one that could be openly admitted, particularly not in the West. There would be major conflicts, especially in Asia, which would take millions more lives and cause great destruction. But, in Europe, neither side could risk a fresh war on the scale of the one they had just won. When that stand-off ended, the continent could move into a new era of peaceful cooperation.

Sixty years on, Roosevelt might grin at the triumph of the American capitalism he had rescued; Churchill might growl at the loss of Empire but not be too unhappy at the way his country had followed his lead in continuing to punch above its weight – and glory in the way American presidents evoke him as a heroic role model; Stalin would have deplored the break-up of the Soviet Union, but, no doubt, made a sardonic observation about the new authoritarianism in the Kremlin.

The Big Three now belong to history, as does the 45-year confrontation for which their alliance paved the way. As has so often been the case with such alliances, theirs was forced on them by enemies. Once those foes had been defeated, the tripartite structure fell apart, though, to this day, British prime ministers hail the 'special relationship' conjured up by Churchill during the conflict and enshrined in memoirs.

Still, without the success of the Big Three in maintaining their coalition for four years, the world would have become an unrecognisable place. No

Cold War, no hot wars in Korea and Vietnam, no United Nations, no European Union, no international monetary and financial organisations, no Communist China, no end to the Holocaust, no state of Israel.

The prospect would have been of an America standing on its own, wielding great political, economic and military force but torn between global empire and a return to atomic-tipped isolationism as it pursued the endless task of trying to make its interests and values rhyme – would Truman have unleashed atomic warfare in Europe, too? Alone against the Axis in Europe, Britain could hardly have survived as much of a medium-sized power – the idea that it might have stood aside from the war and held on to the Empire makes no sense given the strain on its economy, the Fuhrer's intentions, Japan's advance in Asia, German naval power, rising nationalism in India and the threat to the Suez Canal. Even if its space saved it from the Wehrmacht's advance, the Soviet Union would have found resistance much harder, and might well have reached the second pact with Berlin, which Stalin wanted to pursue in 1941. That would have enabled the Third Reich to survive and maintain its dominion in Europe. The oil of the Middle East would have been up for grabs. Japan could still have been forced to surrender by America's atomic bombs, but the Far East would have become either a theatre of anarchy or a long-term US protectorate, with Washington endlessly in two minds about which side to back in China.[31]

In banishing such what-ifs of history, the Big Three played the most important role of any group of leaders in the twentieth century. Their fractured but necessary partnership showed the strains and challenges involved in constructing and maintaining such a coalition of global partners, the need for subtle judgments and diplomacy, and for recognition of the fundamentals of world politics. As Churchill's remark at the very start of this book demonstrates, all three knew the primacy of alliance in achieving the common objective they had set – or been forced to set by their adversaries. For Britain, the alliance was the lifeline. For the Soviet Union, it was the avenue to super-power status. For America, it represented the recognition that, however great its power and whatever unacceptable accommodations were involved, the United States could not walk alone in seeking over-arching objectives reaching far beyond its narrow national interests. Those considerations are as valid today as they were between 1941 and 1945.

SOURCE NOTES

FRUS – Foreign Relations of the United States collections
WSC – Churchill War Memoirs
CAB, PREM archives from Public Record Office, London
FO – Foreign Office archive
FDR library papers from Hyde Park Library
Roosevelt–Churchill correspondence from Loewenheim et al., and Kimball
Stalin–Churchill–Roosevelt correspondence from Progress Publishing House, Moscow
Stalin–Roosevelt correspondence also from Butler
NYT – *New York Times*
ER – Elliott Roosevelt

PROLOGUE

1 Letter from his wife to Churchill 23 Nov 1943 in Churchill Museum, Cabinet War Rooms, London
2 dinner, FDR Library, Hopkins papers, Box 332; WSC, Vol. V, pp. 329–30; Bohlen, pp. 147–8; Harriman, pp. 273–4; Moran, p. 140; ER, *As He Saw It*, pp. 186–191, *Destiny*, p. 357; Gillies, p. 155; FRUS, Teheran, p. 837; Berezhkov, *History*, pp. 289–92
3 Holmes, p. 267
4 Beria, p. 94; Gillies, p. 155; Bohlen, p. 148; Sainsbury, p. 248; Churchill, Wheeler-Bennett, p. 96, from BBC interview with Lady Bonham-Carter, 13 April 1967

1: BUFFALO, BEAR AND DONKEY

1 FDR address to Congress, 1 March 1945
2 Montefiore, *Stalin*, p. 358
3 Jackson, p. 110
4 Hobsbawm, pp. 45, 48, 50
5 Andrew and Mitrokhin, p. 717
6 Dalleck, p. 420
7 Reynolds, *Command*, p. 414; FRUS, Teheran, pp. 862–3
8 James Roosevelt, *Parents*, p. 203
9 ER, *Destiny*, p. 345
10 Christopher Harmon essay, 'Churchill as Coalition War Leader', Churchill Center 1999. http://www.winstonchurchill.org/i4a/pages/index.cfm?pageid=681
11 Wallace diary, 22 May 1943
12 Jonathan Sikorsky, 'From British Cassandra to American Hero', in Finest Hour series, Churchill Center
13 For brushes with death, see Hickman. Also, for this and next para, Ismay, p. 344; Perkins, p. 307
14 Clementine Churchill, letters in Churchill Museum, London
15 Reynolds, *War Person*, p. 268; Berlin, 'Winston Churchill in 1940'
16 Holmes, p. 295
17 Jacob, Wheeler Bennett, pp. 199–201
18 FRUS, 1940, Vol. I, p. 116; Welles, Meacham, p. 51; Black, p. 91
19 Perkins, p. 308
20 *New Yorker*, 8 and 15 August 2005
21 receiver, Burnham, p. 264
22 Black, p. 995; Alanbrooke, pp. 403–4; Kimball, *Juggler*, p. 14; Eisenhower, Beschloss, p. 29; Cadogan, pp. 577–8; Sherwood, pp. 10, 73; Einstein, *Morgenthau*, p. 244
23 Dutton, p. 153
24 Bohlen, p. 210
25 Parrish, p. 282; Davis, pp. 211–2; Beschloss, p. 219; Stilwell, pp. 260–1; Kimball, *Juggler*, p. 199; Morgan, p. 550
26 US view of Stalin, see Kennan, p. 279; Sherwood, p. 34; Harriman, pp. 81, 536; Schlesinger, introduction to Butler; James Roosevelt, *Parents*, p. 203; Kershaw, p. 516
27 Chuev, p. 50
28 Berezhkov, *At Stalin's Side*, p. 203; Gillies, p. 125; Djilas, pp. 59–60
29 Stilwell, p. 259
30 Montefiore, p. 443; Butler, p. 23; *Modern Monthly*, December 1934
31 Bohlen, p. 211; Montefiore, p. 426; Butler, p. 328; *NYT*, 13 April 1946
32 Black, p. 865; Beria, p. 95; Cadogan, p. 578; Kissinger, p. 401; Kennan, http://edition.cnn.com/SPECIALS/cold.war/episodes/01/interviews/kennan/; Dalleck, p. 521
33 Morton, p. 16

34 Desk at Hyde Park museum; Alanbrooke, pp. 403–4; Black, p. 596

35 Jenkins, p. 651; Colville, *Fringes*, p. 417

36 War Cabinet Rooms and Churchill Museum

37 Ismay, pp. 174–5; James Roosevelt, *Parents*, p. 204; Hassett, pp. 169–71

38 Perkins, p. 84 and Columbia Oral History, p. 348; Black, p. 970; Meacham, p. 261

39 McIntire, pp. 9, 132; WSC, Vol. IV, p. 338

40 Harvey, p. 239

41 Hopkins, Sherwood, p. 113; Stalin, Chuev, pp. 17–8

42 drinking, Cadogan, pp. 402, 555, 570; Fort, p. 280; Alanbrooke, p. 390; Jacob, pp. 182–3

43 Montefiore on-line interview, Random House; Jenkins, p. 448

44 Black, p. 902

45 Anna Roosevelt, Columbia Oral History, p. 26

46 Ward, p. 323

47 Anna Roosevelt Halstead in Columbia Oral History; Burns, *Soldier*, p. 61; James Roosevelt, *Parents*, pp. 101–2

48 Churchill, Moran, p. 247

49 Letter to Robert Hannegan on display at Hyde Park Museum

50 Moran, p. 57; WSC, Vol. IV, p. 437; Cadogan, p. 472

51 Alanbrooke, p. 417

52 Churchill, *News of the World*, 15 May 1938; Hale, p. 288; Chamberlain, R.W. Johnson, *London Review of Books*, 17 Aug 2006

53 Kimball, *Juggler*, p. 49; Halifax, Charmley, *Alliance*, p. 51

54 WSC, Vol. III, p. 673

55 Roosevelt, Dalleck, p. 324; Stimson, Hodgson, pp. 267–8; Murrow, CBS, 4 September 1946

56 Perkins, p. 72; R.W. Johnson, *London Review of Books*, 17 Aug 2006

57 Roosevelt and USSR, Kimball, *Juggler*, Ch. 2, pp. 39–41, 198–9; dictatorship, ibid, p. 216; Edmonds, p. 186; FRUS, 1942, Vol. III, p. 460; Bohlen, pp. 210–11; Arthur Schlesinger in Introduction to Butler. See also Aileen Kelly, 'A Great Russian Prophet'

2: THE FIRST SUMMIT

1 distraction, Burns, *Soldier*, p. 143; *NYT*, 9 September 1941

2 Sherwood, p. 293; Parrish, p. 186; Stimson diary, 30 June 1941; Burns, *Soldier*, p. 143; Black, p. 631

3 Early correspondence is dealt with fully in Gilbert, *America*, Ch. 18

4 Gilbert, *America*, pp. 189, 206

5 Vandenberg, Kissinger, p. 385; see analysis in Kissinger, pp. 371–2

6 Kissinger, p. 368; George VI, Black, p. 634; Morison, p. 29; Charmley, *Alliance*, p. 18

7 Letter of 22 August 1941, Hopkins papers, FDR Library, Group 24, Box 135

8 Fenby, p. 304; Hopkins papers, FDR Library, Group 24, Box 135

9 navy, Eisenhower, p. 3; Morgan, p. 598
10 FDR Safe File, Box 1, FDR and Princess, James Roosevelt, *Parents*, p. 109
11 FDR Safe File, Box 1
12 Burns, *Soldier*, p. 124; Parrish, p. 183
13 FDR Safe File, Box 1; fish, Parrish, p. 187
14 FDR account in Safe File Boxes marked 'for historical purposes and possible use in preparing a magazine article'; cousin, Ward, p. 140
15 FRUS, 1940, Vol. I, pp. 28–116
16 Morton, pp. 57–8; Bartholomew, p. 188
17 Reynolds, *History*, p. 414
18 $13 billion, Bercuson and Herwig, pp. 30–32
19 PREM 4/17/1; FRUS, 1940, Vol. III, p. 67; Dalton, Thorne, p. 121; Black, p. 622; Gilbert, *America*, p. 218; Charmley, pp. 21–3
20 Keynes mission, Skidelsky, Ch. 4; gangsters, Black, p. 622
21 Kimball, *Churchill and Roosevelt*, pp. 177–85; Davis, pp. 177–9
22 This and following, McJimsey, p. 129; Davies, Sherwood, pp. 35, 49; Goddard, Ward, p. 157
23 Moran, p. 224
24 Lippmann, *Today and Tomorrow* column 31 January 1946
25 Bohlen, pp. 168, 135; Sherwood, pp. 4, 751
26 Moran, p. 126; Kimball, *Forged*, pp. 77–8
27 Kimball, *Forged*, pp. 77, 216
28 Moran, pp. 5–6; Jenkins, p. 650; Sherwood, p. 266
29 Letter in the War Cabinet Rooms, London
30 This and following section on preparations for Hopkins trip, Maisky, pp. 177–182
31 Stalin, *Correspondence*, Vol. I, pp. 14–17; WSC, Vol. III, pp. 342–7
32 Maisky, p. 33
33 FDR Safe Files, Box 3, http://www.fdrlibrary.marist.edu/psf/box3/a3 2f01.htlm :
34 FDR Safe Files, Box 4, http://www.fdrlibrary.marist.edu/psf/box3/a32d01.html; Dalleck, p. vii
35 Harriman, p. 73; Stalin, *Correspondence*, Vol. I, p. 16
36 Hopkins, FRUS, 1941, Vol. I, pp. 802–3; Berezhkov, *History*, pp. 126–130; Sherwood, Ch. XV
37 Sherwood, p. 104
38 Kimball, *Juggler*, pp. 187–8; Sherwood, pp. 3, 46, 344–5
39 Kimball, *Juggler*, p. 35
40 FRUS, 1941, Vol. I, pp. 813–4
41 FRUS, 1941, Vol. I, p. 813
42 FRUS, 1941, Vol. I, p. 344
43 FDR Safe Files, Box 3, Hopkins file; FRUS, 1941, Vol. I, p. 814
44 ER, *As*, p. 22
45 FRUS, 1941, Vol. I, pp. 637–8
46 Hopkins's flight, McJimsey, p. 188; Sherwood, p. 348
47 Morton, p. 38; Sherwood, pp. 348–9

48 Morton, pp. 43, 62; Cadogan, pp. 396–7
49 Morton, pp. 91–2, 105, 88–9; Wedemeyer, p. 118
50 Jenkins, p. 663; FDR Safe File, http://www.fdrlibrary.marist.edu/psf/box1/a07 io1.html
51 CAB 66/18, pp. 109–10
52 Wilson, pp. 87, 120; Lindemann, McIntire, p. 135; de Groot, p. 27; politicians, de Groot, p. 28; Edmonds, pp. 394–8
53 Wilson, p. 100
54 Wilson, pp. 103–4
55 Pawle, p. 128
56 CAB 66/18, pp. 108, 115; McIntire, p. 133
57 FDR Safe Files, http://www.fdrlibrary.marist.edu/psf/box1/a07h01.html; FDR Library, ABCD 1941, Box 1 PSF
58 Cadogan, p. 398; Thompson, p. 235
59 FDR Library, ABCD 1941, Box 1 PSF; Morton, pp. 104–6; Harriman, p. 75
60 Jacob diary, 19 July 1941, quoted in Edmonds, p. 224
61 Danchev, *Specialness*, p. 71; Alanbrooke diary, 3 February 1942
62 Alanbrooke, p. 226; Wilson, pp. 126–131 has accounts of talks, and pen portraits; Harriman, p. 185; Ismay, p. 253; Parrish, p. 283
63 Wilson, p. 130
64 Parrish, p. 470; Holmes, p. 244; for Dill, see Danchev, *Specialness*, Ch. 5
65 Parrish, p. 454
66 Wilson, p. 145 et seq contains summary of discussions; Loewenheim, pp. 386–9
67 Holmes, p. 210
68 ER, *As*, p. 44
69 Berle, p. 406; Beschloss, pp. 18–19
70 Thompson, p. 271; Freidel, p. 474
71 WSC, Vol. II, p. 395
72 Berle, p. 372; Loewenheim, Doc. 66, pp. 149–51; FDR Library, ABCD 1941, Box 1 PSF
73 Avalon, p. 28
74 Empire, from quotation at Churchill Museum, London
75 Kimball, *Forged*, pp. 101, 29–31
76 ER, pp. 35–7; Wilson, pp. 189–90
77 Avalon, pp. 39–45
78 Avalon, p. 31
79 Draft reproduced in WSC, Vol. II, p. 395
80 Cadogan, p. 402
81 Loewenheim, p. 71
82 FDR Library, ABCD 1941, Box 1, PSF
83 poll, Edmonds, p. 223; Taft, James Patterson, *Mr Republican*, p. 247; FDR, Freidel, p. 394; *NYT*, 15 August 1941; Burns, *Soldier*, p. 131
84 Ward, p. 142; Hale, p. 135

85 Randolph, Charmley, *Glory*, p. 462; Hopkins, FDR Library, ABCD 1941, Box 1 PSF
86 CAB 66/18, p. 113; Morton, p. 95; Beaverbrook, Sherwood, p. 368

3: UNCLE JOE

 1 FRUS, 1941, Vol. I, pp. 822–3; FDR Safe File, Box 1
 2 FDR Safe File, Box 1; Report, Sherwood, pp. 419, 421; draftees, Friedlin, p. 365
 3 Kimball, Churchill Center review of Carlton, *Churchill and the Soviet Union*, makes this point.
 4 David Carlton talk at Christ Church conference, 3 September 2004; Dill, Pawle, p. 122; mission, FRUS 1941, Vol. I, p. 177; *Jacob*, p. 89; WSC, Vol. III, pp. 340, 426, 353
 5 WSC, Vol. III, pp. 405–6.
 6 This and following, ibid, pp. 406–7, 420, 409; Harriman, pp. 81–2; Feis, p. 15
 7 Chuev, pp. 45–6; Butler, p. 179
 8 Danchev, *Specialness*, pp. 55–7
 9 WSC, Vol. III, pp. 402–3
10 Moran, p. 26; Soames, p. 464; Letter, PREM 401/7, p. 175
11 WSC, Vol III, p. 414
12 PREM 401/7, p. 175; Pamela, Bedell Smith, pp. 83–7; ambassador, Gillies, p. 132; Litvinov, Harriman, pp. 362–3
13 soap, CAB 120/37; Churchill, CAB 120/38
14 Ismay, p. 231
15 PRO, BBK/D/96/98/99/100P; Montefiore, p. 344; Harriman, pp. 87–8; Ross, Document 3; CAB 120/39
16 Letter, PREM 401/7, p. 1
17 Beaverbrook, CAB 120/39
18 Harriman, p. 89
19 FDR Safe File, Box 3, http://www.fdrlibrary.marist.edu/psf/box3/a32h01.html, http://www.fdrlibrary.marist.edu/psf/box3/a32g01.html
20 Harriman, p. 90
21 FRUS, 1941, Vol. I, pp. 851, 844, CAB 120/39
22 Harriman, p. 90
23 Harriman, pp. 91–4; Deane, p. 49; Beaverbrook, CAB 120/39
24 nationalist, Ciechanowski, p. 74
25 Ismay, pp. 230–1
26 Harriman, p. 102
27 dinner, Harriman, pp. 98–9; Montefiore, pp. 344–5; Ismay, p. 244
28 Harriman, pp. 100–1
29 Montefiore, p. 345; Roads to Moscow at http://www.alstewart.com/history/roadstom.htm
30 Churchill, CAB 120/38; Hurry, photograph in Sherwood opposite, p. 400; Butler, p. 48
31 Stalin, *Correspondence*, Vol. II, p. 14; FDR Safe File, Box 5; FRUS, 1941, Vol. I, p.

854; Hopkins, PREM 401/7, p. 1974; Truman, Beschloss, p. 229; Burns, *Soldier*, p. 152; Sherwood, pp. 400–1

32 Maisky, pp. 198–203

33 This and following FO 371/29471/N6540; WSC, Vol. III, pp. 469–73

34 PREM 3/402–3

35 Wilson, p. 8

36 Reynolds, *History*, pp. 156–7; Sherwood, p. 384; Mussolini, Ciano, p. 391

37 US–Japan negotiations are summarised in Burns, *Soldier*, pp. 154–60. Sherwood, Ch. 19, has a contemporary account. Tokyo message, WSC, Vol. III, p. 533; Hopkins, Lash, p. 476

38 Carlton, *Eden*, pp. 188–9 for analysis of British position

39 Friedel, p. 398

4: WORLD WAR

1 Friedel, p. 402

2 Burns, *Soldier*, p. 161

3 Burns, *Soldier*, p. 165

4 McJimsey, p. 209

5 WSC, Vol. III, pp. 537–8

6 Carlton, *Eden*, p. 190; Harriman, pp. 111–2; WSC, Vol. III, p. 540; Burns, *Soldier*, pp. 163–4; Reynolds, *History*, p. 264

7 Black, p. 686; Stalin, *Correspondence*, Vol. II, p. 17; Berezhkov, *History*, pp. 261,158, 263; Kimball, *Forged*, p. 135; Montefiore, p. 349

8 Kersaudy, *Roosevelt*, p. 97; Rosos, p. 58

9 Parker, p. 131, for Germany economy, see Tooze, pp. XXIV-V & ch. 9

10 Hitler, Kershaw, p. 448; ambassador, Fest, p. 655; Hirohito, Morgan, p. 619

11 Kershaw, pp. 445–6, 401; WSC, FDR, Speer, pp. 306–7; telephones, Kennan, p. 135

12 Kershaw, pp. 490, 456; Bullock, p. 672; Wilson, p. 255; Black, pp. 505–6;

13 Ribbentrop, Boyd, pp. 35–6; Ciano, *Diary*, pp. 405, 407

14 Mussolini, *NYT*, 12 December 1941; Ciano, p. 408

15 Berezhkov, *History*, p. 161

16 Hitler speech, BBC monitoring, 11 December 1941

17 *NYT*, 12 December 1941

18 Kennan, pp. 135–7

19 Berezhkov, *History*, p. 162; London *Times*, 13 December 1941

20 Loewenheim, p. 22; Kimball, *Forged*, p. 122; Gilbert, *Churchill*, pp. 1274, 1611; harem, Alanbrooke, p. 209

21 *NYT*, 12 December 1941

22 Press round-up, *NYT*, 12 December 1941; troop numbers, London *Times*, 12 December 1941

5: FOUR MEN TALKING

1 WSC, Vol. III, p. 540
2 WSC, Vol. III, pp. 556, 560; Soames, p. 459; Moran, pp. 7, 9; Alanbrooke, p. 211; Harriman, p. 113
3 WSC, Vol. III, pp. 469, 551; Stalin, *Correspondence*, Vol. 1, p. 32
4 Soames, p. 461; Cherwell, Fort, p. 256. This and next paras, WSC, Vol. III, pp. 581–3
5 FRUS, Teheran, p. 481
6 WSC, Vol. III, p. 571
7 Avon, *Reckoning*, Book 3, Chapter 2; Cadogan, p. 286; Harvey, pp. 71–2; Alanbrooke, pp. 206–7.
8 FDR, Ward, p. 207; Molotov, Chuev, p. 50; Hopkins, McJimsey, p. 149; Cadogan, p. 345
9 Dutton, pp. 182–5; Harvey, pp. 17–18, 77; WSC, Vol. I, p. 190
10 CAB 66/20, p. 288
11 Cadogan, p. 287; Harvey, pp. 72–3
12 Cadogan, p. 240
13 Avon, pp. 289, 292; Cadogan, p. 422
14 Eden in WSC, Vol. III, pp. 558–9; Cadogan, p. 422; Harvey, pp. 74–5
15 Avon, p. 293; Maisky, p. 231; Cadogan, p. 422; FRUS, 1942, Soviet Union, pp. 494–503
16 Avon, pp. 291, 289
17 Harvey, pp. 75–6
18 Wilson, p. 37
19 Hull, FRUS, 1941, Vol. 1, pp. 194–5; US reaction, WSC, Vol. IV, p. 293 et seq
20 Kimball, *Forged*, p. 167
21 Carlton, *Eden*, p. 192; Avon, pp. 319–20
22 Avon, p. 302; Maisky, p. 236
23 dinner, Cadogan, pp. 422–3; Harvey, pp. 78–9
24 message, Avon, p. 303; Harvey, pp. 80–1; Cadogan, p. 423
25 Bercuson and Herwig, p. 120
26 Bercuson and Herwig, p. 125
27 A reconstruction can be seen in the Roosevelt Museum, Hyde Park
28 Sherwood, p. 446; Patrick Kinna, Gilbert, *America*, p. 249
29 Tuttle, p. 268; Moran, p. 21; Sherwood, p. 484; Soames, p. 460
30 FRUS, 1942, Vol. II, pp. 6, 19
31 Attlee, p. 123; Harriman, p. 117; Pogue, pp. 263–4
32 Pogue, pp. 265–6; Tuttle, p. 131
33 Stimson diary, 25 December 1941; Loewenheim, p. 23; McJimsey, p. 213
34 Kersaudy, *Churchill*, p. 177; FRUS, 1942, Vol. II, p. 119
35 Kersaudy, p. 101 et seq; Tuttle, pp. 131–2; FRUS, 1942, Vol. II, p. 33
36 WSC, Vol. III, pp. 593–4; Bercuson and Herwig, pp. 155–7
37 Moran, pp. 14–15
38 Moran, p. 15

39 *Time*, 5 January 1942; *NYT*, 27 December 1941; *Life*, 5 January 1942; for US media and WSC, see Jonathan Sikorsky, *From British Cassandra to American Hero* in Finest Hour series, Churchill Center

40 Moran, pp. 17–18

41 muscle strain, Gilbert, *America*, p. 250

42 Moran, p. 12

43 WSC, Vol. III, p. 603

44 Carlton, pp. 192–3

45 Martin, in Wheeler-Bennett pp. 104–5

46 Thompson, *Beside the Bulldog*, pp. 104–5

47 Moran, pp. 22–3; WSC, Vol. III, p. 624

48 Moran, pp. 21–2; Pogue, pp. 286–8; Morgan, p. 63

49 Meacham, p. 165.

6: UNDECIDED

1 Lamb, p. 176; Harvey, pp. 86, 94; Thorpe, p. 271

2 Attlee, *Observer*, 5 May 1944; Beaverbrook, WSC, Vol. IV, pp. 66, 384; Soames, p. 464; Hopkins Papers, FDR Library, Box 136: Cadogan, pp. 444, 452

3 This and following, Cadogan, p. 443; Soames in Lamb, p. 176; Kimball, *Correspondence*, Vol. I, pp. 381, 393; WSC, Vol. IV, p. 94

4 Cadogan, pp. 577–8; Charmley, *Alliance*, p. 33

5 FRUS, 1942, Vol. I, pp. 518–9; Harvey, p. 102

6 Berle, p. 403

7 *Financial Times* Magazine, 20 August 2005

8 Harriman, p. 268; Andrews and Mitrokhin, pp. 147, 784

9 FDR-Morgenthau, Butler, p. 63

10 Feis, p. 59

11 Cadogan, pp. 437, 443; Feis, p. 59

12 Harvey, p. 105; WSC, Vol. IV, pp. 293–4

13 Harvey, p. 109

14 Berle memo, FRUS, 1942, Vol. I, p. 519

15 FRUS, 1942, Vol. I, p. 538

16 Hull, p. 1172; Harvey, pp. 109, 117

17 FRUS, 1942, Vol. III, pp. 5, 29, 534–7; Kimball, *Forged*, pp. 201, 268, 334

18 Kimball, *Correspondence*, Vol. I, p. 421

19 Parrish, pp. 255–6; McJimsey, pp. 242–3; Feis, p. 40; Parker, p. 119

20 WSC, Vol. IV, pp. 280–1

21 Chargé, Kitchen, p. 101; Ismay, p. 226

22 Alanbrooke, p. 712

23 Powell, p. 53; Alanbrooke, p. 474; Moran, p. 53

24 This and next paras, Alanbrooke, pp. 199–200, 340, 203, 170, 100; John Kennedy, p. 104; Fraser, p. 295

25 Fraser, p. 295

26 Hopkins papers, FDR Library, Box 136; Sherwood, pp. 521, 632, 520; Kissinger, p. 401
27 Hopkins papers, FDR Library, Box 154, message of 12 April 1942
28 WSC, Vol. IV, pp. 281–2
29 Ismay, pp. 249, 252
30 Alanbrooke, pp. 246, 247, 249
31 WSC, Vol. IV, pp. 283–6, 290, 318, 309; Moran, p. 35
32 Alanbrooke, p. 249

7: THE COMMISSAR CALLS

1 visit, Avon, *Reckoning*, pp. 327–9; Chuev, p. 48; Berezhkov, *At Stalin's Side*, p. 341
2 Chuev, pp. xv, 8; Berezhkov, *At Stalin's Side*, pp. 342–3
3 Harriman, p. 94; subordinates, Berezhkov, *At Stalin's Side*, pp. 211, 222
4 FRUS, 1942, Vol. I, pp. 437–8
5 FO 800/300/23–24; FO 800/300/9; Gillies, p. 125
6 Cadogan, p. 450
7 Chuev, pp. 47, 199; WSC, Vol. IV, p. 301; Cadogan, p. 456
8 Berezhkov, *At Stalin's Side*, p. 293; L. V. Pozdeeva, *Vesti Ru*, 8 January 2005; Eden's account of Molotov visit, *Reckoning*, pp. 453–4
9 talks, WSC, Vol. IV, pp. 297–300; Avon, p. 328; Cadogan, pp. 297–300
10 FRUS, 1942, Vol. III, pp. 552–3; Hull, *Memoirs*, p. 1172
11 FRUS, 1942, Vol. III, p. 560
12 Avon, p. 329
13 Cadogan, p. 453; Alanbrooke, p. 260
14 WSC, Vol. IV, pp. 303–4; Harvey, p. 130
15 Ward, p. 159
16 Molotov talks, FRUS, 1942, Vol. II, pp. 566–83; Hopkins papers, FDR Library, Box 136; Sherwood, pp. 561–70
17 Sherwood, pp. 561–3; FRUS, 1942, Vol. III, p. 569
18 FRUS, 1942, Vol. III, p. 570
19 Chuev, p. 200
20 Kershaw, Hitler, pp. 517–18
21 Sherwood, p. 565
22 Parrish, p. 236
23 Sherwood, p. 578
24 WSC, Vol. IV, pp. 304–5; Chuev, pp. 46–7
25 WSC, Vol. IV, p. 305; Reynolds, *History*, p. 323; Avon, p. 320
26 landing craft, Alanbrooke, p. 261
27 WSC, Vol. IV, p. 323

8: TORCH SONG

1 Moran, p. 37; Alanbrooke, pp. 266–7
2 WSC, Vol. IV, p. 338
3 WSC, Vol. IV, pp. 338–9
4 James Roosevelt, *Parents*, p. 206
5 Edmonds, pp. 399–400; Reynolds, *History*, pp. 333–5
6 Kimball, *Correspondence*, Vol. I, p. 515
7 Hopkins, London *Times*, 22 June 1942; Stimson, Hodgson, p. 267
8 WSC, Vol. IV, p. 347
9 Alanbrooke, p. 271, photograph FRUS, Washington Conferences; Parrish, p. 288
10 Alanbrooke, p. 271; Moran, p. 165
11 WSC, Vol. IV, pp. 344–5
12 Wedemeyer, pp. 164–5
13 This and following, WSC, Vol. IV, pp. 343–4; Ismay, pp. 254–5; Parrish, pp. 286–7
14 Parrish, p. 287
15 Ismay, p. 257
16 Danchev, *Specialness*, p. 25; Harvey, p. 165
17 Danchev, *Specialness*, p. 35; Sherwood, p. 590
18 This and following, Parrish, p. 569; Hopkins papers, FDR Library, Box 136; Sherwood, p. 569; Ward, p. 151; Sherwood, pp. 602–3
19 Sherwood, p. 606
20 This and following, Sherwood, pp. 603–4
21 Parrish, p. 292
22 Sherwood, p. 607
23 Sherwood, p. 607; McJimsey, pp. 282–3
24 Parrish, p. 292; Alanbrooke, pp. 282–5; Parrish, p. 295
25 Hodgson, p. 268
26 FDR Safe Files, Box 3
27 This and following, Sherwood, pp. 610–11
28 Parrish, pp. 295–7
29 WSC, Vol. IV, p. 404; McJimsey, p. 254; ER, *Destiny*, p. 317
30 Sherwood, pp. 612, 753; Parrish, p. 289
31 ER, *Destiny*, pp. 317–8
32 Parrish, p. 297
33 Holmes, pp. 292–3
34 This and following, Maisky, pp. 292–3
35 Leahy, p. 122
36 Kimball, *Correspondence*, Vol. I, p. 545
37 WSC, Vol. IV, p. 425; Moran, p. 48

9: MIDNIGHT IN MOSCOW

1 WCS, Vol. IV, p. 428; Harriman, p. 152; *Vesti Ru*, 8 January 2005
2 FO 800/300

3 Berezhkov, *History*, p. 193; Moran, p. 54; WSC, Vol. IV, p. 472

4 This and following, Moran, p. 54; WSC, Vol. IV, p. 429

5 Clark Kerr, Birse, p. 135

6 Berezhkov, *At Stalin's Side*, p. 293

7 This and following, Berezhkov, *At Stalin's Side*, pp. 294–5, *History*, pp. 194–6; WSC, Vol. IV, pp. 429–35; Moran, pp. 54–6; CAB 127/23; Document 29 in Churchill and Stalin papers; Harriman, pp. 152–67; older and greyer, Harriman, p. 152

8 FRUS, 1942, pp. 618–20

9 Berezhkov, *History*, p. 194; FO 800/300/50

10 Reynolds, *History*, p. 322

11 Wedemeyer, pp. 120, 134

12 Berezhkov, *History*, p. 196

13 Moran, p. 56; WSC, Vol. IV, p. 435

14 Cadogan, p. 471

15 Alanbrooke, p. 300

16 Gillies, pp. 131–2

17 This and following, CAB 127/23; WSC, Vol. IV, pp. 437–42

18 Cadogan, p. 471

19 Alanbrooke, pp. 299–300

20 WSC, Vol. IV, p. 400

21 Harriman, pp. 159, 181

22 Gillies, p. 133; FO 800/300

23 FO 800/300; Alanbrooke, p. 303; Montefiore, p. 371; FRUS, 1942, p. 452; Reed, Intelligence Officers, FO 800/300; dinner, WSC, Vol. IV, pp. 442–4; Alanbrooke, pp. 301–3; Moran, pp. 57–60; Cadogan, p. 472

24 cigar, Hickman, p. 145

25 Moran, pp. 60–1

26 L.V. Pozdeeva, *Vesti Ru*, 8 January 2005

27 Clark Kerr journal, FO 800/300; Reed letter, idem; cock-teasing, Gillies, p. 300

28 This and following account, WSC, Vol. IV, pp. 445–9; Berezhkov, *At Stalin's Side*, pp. 298–302; Cadogan, pp. 373–4; Birse, pp. 98–104; Moran, pp. 62–5; Montefiore, p. 372

29 Birse, pp. 100–1

30 Harriman, p. 16

31 WSC, Vol. IV, p. 447; Chuev, pp. 200–1

32 dacha, FO 800/300; Cadogan, p. 473

33 Cadogan, p. 474

34 Moran, p. 64

35 FO 800/300

36 This and following Cadogan, p. 474; Harriman, p. 152; WSC, Vol. IV, p. 450

37 Andrew and Mitrokhin, p. 157

10: AS TIME GOES BY

1 WSC, Vol. IV, pp. 472, 482, 486–7; Hopkins papers, FDR Library, Box 136

2 Williams, pp. 3, 80, 383–5

3 The Roosevelt–de Gaulle relationship is covered in Kersaudy, *Roosevelt*, FDR view, Loewenheim, pp. 344–5

4 ER, *Destiny*, pp. 320–1

5 Kershaw, Vol. II, p. 539

6 FRUS, 1942, Vol. III, pp. 467, 478–9; Stalin, *Correspondence*, Vol. I, p. 70; *Mezhdunarodnaya Zhizn*, No 2, 2003, 'Sovetsko–Amerikanskie otnosheniya vo vremya Velikoi Otechestvennoi Voiny. 1941–1945' (Soviet–American Relations during the Great Patriotic War. 1941–1945) Vol. 1, Moscow, 1984

7 Gillies, pp. 137–8

8 FRUS, 1942, Vol. II, pp. 656–8; Butler, p. 94

9 Stalin, *correspondence*, Vol. II, pp. 42–5; FRUS, 1942, Vol. III, pp. 461, 464–7, 662–4, 666, 472; WSC, Vol. IV, pp. 519–22; FRUS, Casablanca, p. 490.

10 Gillies, p. 141 quoting Hugh Dalton; V.I. Trubnikov, *Mezhdunarodnaya Zhizn*, No. 2, 2003, AVP RF Fo59 Op. 1, P. 374 D.2543 L.38–43; *Istoriya vneshnei politiki SSSR* (History of Foreign Politics of the USSR), Vol. 1, Moscow, 1986, pp. 42–5.

11 FRUS, 1942, Vol. II, p. 448; Butler, pp. 101, 104–5, 107–9

12 FRUS, Casablanca, pp. 505–6

13 Harriman, pp. 179–80

14 WSC, Vol. IV, pp. 604–5; Moran, pp. 78–9

15 Harriman, p. 180

16 Sherwood, pp. 571–2; ER, *Destiny*, p. 330; Ward, pp. 197–8, Moran, p. 79

17 This and following, Sherwood, p. 673; p. 359; ER, *As*, pp. 67–8; Harriman, p. 179; Macmillan, pp. 7–9

18 Summit Hopkins, Soames, p. 473; Conference, WSC, Vol. IV, Ch. 38; FRUS, Casablanca, pp. 500 et seq; Kimball, *Juggler*, Ch. IV; Kersaudy, *Roosevelt*, Ch. 6; Moran, Ch. 10; Alanbrooke, pp. 357–69; de Gaulle, *Mémoires*, Vol. l'Unité; Harriman, pp. 177–92; Codenames, FRUS, *Casablanca*, pp. 504–5

19 Soames, p. 476

20 Macmillan, pp. 7–9; Soames, pp. 473, 475; Cadogan, p. 207

21 Macmillan, p. 4

22 Alanbrooke, pp. 73–5

23 This and following, FRUS, Casablanca, pp. 619–2, 587–94

24 FRUS, Casablanca, p. 594; Harriman, p. 160

25 King, Larabee, p. 173; China, Fenby, pp. 384–5, 387–93; Wedemeyer, p. 135; China, FDR Library, Hopkins papers, Group 24, Box 135; Gardner Cowles, *Mike Looks Back*, Annenberg Library, pp. 88–9

26 This and next para, Parker, pp. 124–5; Wedemeyer, p. 192

27 Wedemeyer, Ch. XIV, gives his view of how the British out-manoeuvred the Americans at the summit.

28 French, Moran, p. 81; ER, *As He Saw It*, pp. 68–9, *Destiny*, p. 327 et seq

29 This and next para, FRUS, Casablanca, pp. 73–5

30 FO 954/8; Kersaudy, *Churchill*, p. 504
31 de Gaulle, *l'Unité*, pp. 643–6
32 Ward, p.199
33 WSC, Vol. IV, p. 610; Cadogan, p. 505
34 Kersaudy, *Roosevelt*, p. 227
35 ER, *As He Saw It*, pp. 107–8
36 Ward, p. 199; FRUS, Casablanca, p. 525
37 This and following, ER, *As He Saw It*, pp. 57–8
38 French–US–British exchanges at Casablanca, de Gaulle, *l'Unité*, pp. 78–85; Kersaudy, *Roosevelt*, pp. 231–46; FRUS, Casablanca, pp. 694–6; ER, *Destiny*, pp. 112–4; Sherwood, pp. 677, 685–6, 688, 693; Moran, pp. 80–1; Macmillan, p. 250
39 Unconditional surrender, Feis, p. 108; Harriman, pp. 189–90; ER, *As He Saw It*, p. 117; FRUS, Casablanca, pp. 505–6; 726–31; WSC, Vol. IV, pp. 613–16; Harriman, pp. 188–90; Jackson, p. 109; Beschloss, pp. 33–4; Liddell Hart, *Listener*, 9 August 1951; Reynolds, *History*, p. 353; Kershaw, *Hitler*, p. 577; Beria, p. 106; Bohlen, p. 191; Kimball, *Forged*, pp. 188–9
40 Sherwood, p. 694; Harriman, p. 191; Moran, p. 82; WSC, Vol. IV, pp. 621–2; Soames, p. 476; Pendar, pp. 148–51

11: STORMY WEATHER

1 Pendar, p. 151
2 WSC, Vol. IV, pp. 636–7
3 Moran, p. 88
4 Cadogan, p. 512; Harvey, p. 214
5 Sherwood, p. 703
6 Butler, pp. 117–18
7 Standley, FRUS, 1943, Vol. III, p. 521
8 FRUS, 1943, Vol. I, pp. 695–7; WSC, Vol. IV, pp. 671–3; Hull, p. 1265
9 Katyn, Stalin, *Correspondence*, Vol. I, p. 112, pp. 120–30, Vol. II, pp. 60–2; WSC, Vol. IV, pp. 675–8 et seq; Cadogan, pp. 521, 524–6; Butler, p. 126; Woodward, p. 205
10 Eden visit, Avon, pp. 367, 371–381; Sherwood, pp. 709–12, 717–21; Cadogan, pp. 517, 519; Harvey, pp. 229–32, 238; Communisation, Reynolds, *History*, p. 417
11 WSC, Vol. IV, p. 700
12 Alanbrooke, p. 401
13 Trident, Hopkins papers, FDR Library, Box 329; FRUS, 1943, Vol. I; WSC, Vol. IV, pp. 710–7; Sherwood, p. 729; Harvey, pp. 276–9; Moran, p. 96; FDR Map Room, Box 43
14 Alanbrooke, p. 405
15 Chiefs of Staff and following, FRUS, Washington & Quebec, p. 44 et seq; WSC, Vol. IV, p. 724; Moran, pp. 97–8; Parrish, p. 350; Meacham, p. 211
16 visit, Fenby, pp. 394–7
17 WSC, Vol. IV, pp. 712–14, 716–17
18 This and next para, Meacham, p. 225; photograph of FDR & WSC, Loewenheim, after p. 399; WSC, Vol. IV, pp. 710–12; Sherwood, p. 729

19 Stalin explanation, Dimitrov, p. 275; FRUS, 1943, Vol. III, pp. 532–7
20 WSC, Vol. V, pp. 155–7; Harvey, pp. 276–9; Stilwell, pp. 204–5
21 Moran, pp. 97–8
22 Davies visit, FRUS, 1943, Vol. III, p. 653; Burns, *Soldier*, p. 368; Elizabeth
    MacLean, *Diplomatic History*, Winter 1980; Sherwood, p. 737; Maisky, p. 363;
    Kimball, *Correspondence*, Vol. II, pp. 278, 284–4; Stalin, *Correspondence*, pp. 63–6
23 Ward, p. 229
24 Bix, *Hirohito*, p. 464
25 Quadrant, WSC, Vol. V, pp. 34–7, 42 et seq; FRUS, 1943, Vol. III, Quebec;
    Harriman, p. 549; Gillies, pp. 144–5; Moran, p. 102; Loewenheim, pp. 341,
    347–8; Sherwood, pp. 748–9; PREM 3/333/5; Alanbrooke, pp. 420–49, 445–6;
    Edmonds, pp. 487–9; Ward, p. 229; Bix, p. 464; Hull, pp. 748–9; Perkins,
    Columbia Oral History
26 Alanbrooke, pp. 420, 427, 429, 441; WSC, Vol. V, p. 76
27 Harriman, p. 225; Cadogan, p. 554

12: RUSSIAN OVERTURE

1 FDR–WSC–JS– Eden–Hull exchanges, FRUS, 1943, Vol. 1, pp. 513–4, 521 et seq,
   539, 541; WSC, Vol. V, pp. 83–4, 115, 237–41, 248; Cadogan, pp. 559, 568;
   Stalin, *Correspondence*, pp. 171–2
2 meeting, FRUS, 1943, Vol. I; Hull, *Memoirs*, Vol. II, Chs 92–94; Avon, p. 407;
   Birse, pp. 137–42; Bohlen, p. 127; WSC, Vol. V, pp. 252, 254–9; FDR Library,
   Map Room papers, Box 17; Harriman, pp. 236–7, 242–5
3 Berezhkov, *At Stalin's Side*, pp. 263–4
4 This and following, WSC, Vol. V, pp. 254–61; FDR Library, Map Room papers,
   Box 17; Harvey, pp. 309–10, 312–16; Loewenheim, pp. 386–9; PREM 3/172/5,
   pp. 255–6; Avon, p. 415; Ismay, p. 326; Seaton, p. 197; Reynolds, p. 382
5 Harriman, p. 255; Gillies, pp. 151–2; FO 800.301/250; FDR Library, Map Room
   Box 170
6 FRUS, 1943, Vol. III, p. 595; Beria, p. 92
7 Exchanges on summit, Stalin, *Correspondence*, Vol. I, pp. 149–50, 157, 163, 176, Vol.
   II, pp. 99–111; Bohlen, p. 132; Harriman, pp. 241, 251; FRUS, Teheran, pp. 70–1

13: PYRAMID

1 This and following on FDR trip, FRUS, Cairo and Teheran p. 274 et seq;
   Beschloss, pp. 22–3; Sherwood, pp. 762–3; Parrish, pp. 371, 374–5, 377–84
2 FDR Library, Map Room file, Box 17; Parrish, p. 380; Sherwood, pp. 768–70
3 WSC letter to Clementine, 21 February 1936, in Churchill Museum, London
4 Moran, p. 125; Clementine letter, Soames, p. 486, original in Churchill Museum
   London
5 WSC, Vol. V, pp. 291–4; Reynolds, *Command*, pp. 382–3
6 Alanbrooke, pp. 472–5

7 messages, FDR Library, Map Room, Boxes 170 and 17; Loewenheim, pp. 393, 391, 386–7; Sherwood, pp. 748–9; Black, p. 853; Gilbert, *America*, p. 284; FRUS, Cairo, pp. 1–2, 47–50, 78–8, 1350, 82; WSC, Vol. V, pp. 279–80, 284; Sainsbury, *Turning Point*, pp. 129–30

8 Harriman, p. 259; WSC, Vol. V, p. 290

9 Alanbrooke, p. 475; Parrish, pp. 384, 392

10 US Joints Chief of Staff paper to FDR, 17 November 1943, FDR Library; Alanbrooke, p. 474; Cadogan, pp. 577–8; Avon, pp. 425–6; Cadogan, pp. 577–8; FRUS, Cairo, p. 352

11 Parrish, p. 390

12 Moran, pp. 131–2; Harriman, p. 258

13 This and next paras, FDR Library, Map Room papers, Box 17; WSC, Vol. V, p. 290; Alanbrooke, pp. 473, 481; Sherwood, p. 772; Parrish, p. 387; ER, *As*, pp. 144, 147; Stilwell, p. 245; FRUS, Cairo, pp. 331–3, 343; Hickman, p. 168; Cadogan, p. 571; Moran, p.131

14 Chinese, Fenby, pp. 403–7; Alanbrooke, pp. 470, 477–8; letter of 26 November 1943, Churchill Museum and in Soames, p. 487; Moran, p. 130, Cadogan, p. 577; FRUS, Cairo, pp. 323–5, 366, 748, 448–9; FRUS, 1944, Vol. VI, p. 299; Hull, p. 1317; Sainsbury, *Turning Point*, p. 216; WSC, Vol. V, p. 290

15 This and following, WSC, Vol. V, p. 289; Alanbrooke, pp. 479–80; Stilwell, pp. 245–6

16 pyramids, Thanksgiving, Meacham, pp. 246–8; FRUS, Cairo, pp. 205–6, 298–9, 300; Sarah Churchill, *Dancing*, p. 71; WSC, Vol. V, p. 301

17 FRUS, Cairo, p. 300; Moran, p. 132

14: OVER THE RAINBOW

1 Teheran record, FDR Library, Hopkins papers, Box 332; British papers, CAB 120/113, CAB 80/77, PREM 3/136/10; FRUS, Teheran Conference; Avalon Project, w.yale.edu/lawweb/avalon/wwii/tehran.htm; Beria, p. 92; Bohlen, p. 139 et seq, Alanbrooke, Ismay, Cadogan, Moran, Sherwood, Hopkins papers; Salisbury, *Turning Point*, Ch. 8; Bohlen, Ch. 9; WSC, Vol. V, Chs 19–22; Parrish, Ch. 17; Avon, pp. 426–9, Harriman, Ch. 12; Reynolds, *Command*, pp. 382–8, 414–18; Berezhkov, *History*, pp. 238–241; Edmonds, Chs 1, 13, 14; Feis, Chs 25–8; http://www.history.upenn.edu/phr/archives/97/sanchez.html

2 Beria, p. 92; Bohlen, p. 139; Cadogan, p. 580; Montefiore, pp. 412–13; Parrish, p. 396; Berezhkov, *History*, p. 238

3 Parrish, p. 396

4 FRUS, Teheran, p. 872

5 Churchill, FRUS, Teheran, pp. 631–2; WSC to Clementine, 21 & 26 November 1943 in Soames pp. 485, 487; Cadogan, pp. 579, 582; Moran, pp. 134–5; Reynolds, *Command*, pp. 414–16; Bohlen, p. 146; Harriman, p. 265

6 Stalin, Harriman, p. 266; Seaton, pp. 197–8; Beria, p. 93; Montefiore, p. 411; Parrish, p. 413; Birse, p. 154

7 Moran, p. 133; WSC, Vol. V, pp. 301–2

8 move, quarters, Harriman, pp. 262–4; Parrish, pp. 394–5; FDR Library, Map Room papers, Box 170; Hopkins papers, Box 332; FRUS, Teheran, pp. 463–4; WSC, Vol. V, p. 303; Gillies, pp. 153–4; Konstantin Syomin, *Vesti Ru*; Montefiore, pp. 412–3; Perkins, p. 69; Bohlen, p. 148; Cadogan, p. 587; Berezhkov, *History*, pp. 252–9; Parrish, p. 410

9 Beria, p.93

10 session, FDR Library, Hopkins papers, Box 332; FRUS, Teheran, pp. 497–508; Soviet Archive, Teheran, pp. 7–16; WSC, Vol. V, pp. 306–16; Bohlen, pp. 141–2; Birse, pp. 154–6; Alanbrooke, p. 483; Harriman, pp. 266–7

11 dinner, FDR Library, Hopkins papers, Box 332; FRUS, Teheran, pp. 509–14; WSC, Vol. V, pp. 317–20; but makes no mention of FDR illness; Harriman, pp. 268–9; Bohlen, pp. 143–4; Parrish, p. 402; Ward, p. 299; Bohlen, pp. 143–4; Avon, p. 427; ER, *As*, p. 177; Moran, p. 135

12 talk, PREM 3/136/8; WSC, Vol. V, pp. 317–20

13 FRUS, Teheran, pp. 516–28; Alanbrooke, pp. 485, 488

14 meeting, FDR Library, Hopkins papers, Box 332; Bohlen, p. 144; ER, *As*, p. 179; FRUS, Teheran, pp. 618–9; Kissinger, p. 409; Berezhkov, *History*, p. 294; Schlesinger, in introduction to Butler

15 Birse, pp. 159–60; WSC, Vol. V, p. 321; Perkins, p. 71; Montefiore, pp. 414–15, quoting the interpreter Hugh Lunghi who declined to be interviewed for this book, but who gives his account on http://www2.gwu.edu/~nsarchiv/coldwar/interviews/episode-1/lunghi1.html

16 FDR Library, Hopkins papers, Box 332; FRUS, Teheran, p. 541 et seq; Soviet Archive, Teheran, pp. 25–37; WSC, Vol. V, pp. 322–9; Bohlen, pp. 145–6; Harriman, pp. 271–2; Parrish, p. 407; Berezhkov, *History*, p. 281; Montefiore, p. 415

17 WSC, FDR, Moran, p. 142; ER, *As*, pp. 183–4

18 dinner, Bohlen, p. 147; FRUS, Teheran, p. 837; Moran, pp. 140, 142; Meacham, p. 261; FDR Library, Hopkins papers, Box 332

19 Bohlen, p. 148

20 Moran, pp. 139–141

21 WSC, Vol V, pp. 331–6; Birse, p. 159

22 Paper, lunch, FRUS, Teheran, p. 564; Alanbrooke, p. 486; Moran, p. 142

23 FDR Library, Hopkins papers, Box 332; Moran, p. 142 WSC, Vol. XX

24 Dinner, WSC, Vol. V, pp. 339–41; Bohlen, 149–50; Moran, pp. 143–4; Brooke, pp. 476–9; Harriman, pp. 276–8; Edmonds, p. 29; pp. 412–3; Sarah Churchill, pp. 70–1; Sainsbury, p. 226; Gillies, pp. 155–6; ER, *As*, p. 191

25 Moran, p. 144

26 Perkins, pp. 70–1

27 PREM 3/136/8; FRUS, pp. 602–4; Soviet Archive, pp. 44–50; Bohlen, pp. 151–2; WSC, Vol. V, pp. 354–7; Harriman, pp. 280–2; *As*, p. 198

28 Avon, Reckoning, p. 427; FRUS, Teheran, pp. 594–5, Bohlen, p. 152, Harriman, pp. 278–9

29 Harriman, p. 367

30 Last plenary, FRUS, Teheran, pp. 596 et seq; Bohlen, pp. 151–3; WSC, Vol. V, pp. 348–57; Harriman, pp. 278–82; Reynolds, *Command*, p. 417

31 WSC, Vol. V, p. 838; Berezhkov, History, pp. 177, 194, FRUS, Teheran, pp. 471–2, 490; ER, *As*, p. 177

32 WSC, JS, FRUS, Yalta, p. 5; Hickman, p. 174; Montefiore, p. 307

33 This and next two paras: Harriman, pp. 418, 284; Sherwood, p. 803; Berezhkov, *History*, pp. 307–8; Bohlen, pp. 152–3

15: ILL WIND

1 FRUS, Teheran, pp. 796–7, 803–4; FDR Library, Hopkins papers, Box 332

2 Davies, pp. 279–81; Stilwell, pp. 251–2, 321–2; FRUS, 1944, Vol. IV, pp. 312–3, 319–26, 334–6 has US accounts of the plot making clear to Washington the degree of discontent with the Chiang regime.

3 Chiang, Fenby, p. 416

4 Parrish, pp. 415–7; Eisenhower, *Crusade*, p. 227; Reynolds, *History*, p. 386; Sherwood, p. 807

5 FDR, WSC and following, FRUS, Teheran, pp. 817, 660, 822–4, 658, 820; Avon, p. 429; Macmillan, *Diaries*, p. 318; WSC, Vol. V, p. 371; Harvey, pp. 324–5; Eisenhower, *Crusade*, p. 229; d'Este, p. 467; Reynolds, *History*, p. 387; Harriman, p. 285; Berezhkov, pp. 311–2; Alanbrooke, p. 492

6 WSC illness, Moran pp. 144–8; Alanbrooke, pp. 493–4, 490–1; Macmillan, pp. 321–2, 327, 333–4, 338–9; WSC, Vol. V, pp. 373–4; Soames, pp. 461–2; Churchill, *Tapestry*, pp. 461; Loewenheim, pp. 398, 484; Harvey, p. 323. For the penicillin report, I am indebted to Michael Barratt Brown.

7 Anzio, WSC, Vol. V, pp. 377–9, 386–7, 389–90; Loewenheim, p. 399

8 Moran, p.157

9 WSC, Vol. V, pp. 399–401

10 Loewenheim, pp. 412–3, 416–17; FRUS, Teheran, pp. 871, 878, 597; Black, p. 895; WSC, Vol. V, p. 398; Reynolds, *History*, p. 387

11 Macmillan, p. 361; Gilbert, *America*, p. 292; WSC, Vol. V, p. 407

12 Marshall, FDR, Parrish, pp. 421–3; Sherwood, p. 804; Morgan, p. 708; Harriman, p. 294

13 Parrish, pp. 424–6

14 Sherwood, pp. 804–6, 6–8; McJimsey, pp. 313, 332–3; Parrish, pp. 437–9; WSC, Vol. IV, p. 806; Gilbert, *America*, p. 293

15 FRUS, 1943, Vol. IV, pp. 824, 1044, 873–4, 703–4; 1944, Vol. III, pp. 1036, 1046–7, 1054, 1056, 1078–9, 1089, Moscow Conference volume, pp. 273–4, Yalta volume, pp. 107–8; FO 371/3/37031, p. 216; Hull, p. 1282; Harriman, pp. 295–6, 298–9, 302; Black, p. 922; Beschloss, p. 150

16 WSC–FDR, Europe, WSC, Vol. V, Ch. XXVII, pp. 454, 467–8; Wedemeyer, p. 231; Sherwood, pp. 812–3; Kimball, *Correspondence*, Vol. II, pp. 145, 767; Loewenheim, pp. 501, 493–5, 459, 493–6, 482, 432, 450; WSC, Vol. V, Ch. XXVI gives his account of policy towards Yugoslavia; FRUS, 1944, Vol. III, p. 6; Vol. II,

pp. 1–2, 4, 11, 61; Avon, pp. 425, 443; Feis, p. 340; Gilbert, *America*, pp. 294–5; Harriman, p. 353

17 FDR health, Parrish, pp. 418–9, 435, 428–9; Morgan, pp. 710–11; Ward, p. 291; Post and Robins, pp. 27–30

18 Poland, Mikołajczyk, p. 56; *Jacob*, p. 91; Loewenheim, pp. 420, 422, 430, 444, 474, 476, 478–80; Gillies, pp. 157–8; Stalin, *Correspondence*, Vol. 1, pp. 212–3; Harriman, p. 290

19 FDR, Morgan, pp. 510–11; press conference, 6 May 1944; Sherwood, pp. 6–8

20 This and following, Stalin, *Correspondence*, Vol. 1, pp. 140–1; Loewenheim, p. 495; Harriman, p. 311; RUS, 1944, Vol. VI, p. 331; Gilbert, *America*, pp. 298–9; WSC, Vol. V, pp. 539–40

16: TRIUMPH AND TRAGEDY

1 Eisenhower, WSC, FDR, JS, d'Este, pp. 527–8; Pawle, p. 302; Loewenheim, pp. 503–4; Parrish, p. 448; Black, pp. 943–4; Stalin, *Correspondence*, Vol. I, pp. 224–6

2 Theodore, Black, pp. 904, 911; Sherwood, p. 807

3 WSC, Vol. VI, pp. 10–11; Holmes, p. 268

4 Stalin, *Correspondence*, Vol. I, pp. 232, 235–6; Holmes, pp. 311–2; Hull, Vol. II, pp. 1451–3

5 Stavrakis, pp. 9–10, 13–15, 17–18, 25–8

6 de Gaulle–FDR, Kersaudy, pp. 362–4, 451–22; de Gaulle, *Mémoires de Guerre*, Vol. II, p. 573 et seq; Black, pp. 940, 964; Aglion, pp. 168, 181, 179, 173 et seq. Churchill's memoirs omit this.

7 Cadogan, pp. 673, 677; Dimitrov, 4 March 1944; WSC, Vol. VI, Ch. 4; Soames, pp. 300–1; Loewenheim, pp. 542–4, 547–9, 553; Sherwood, p. 810; Parrish, pp. 449–50; Moran, pp. 165, 161

8 This and following, Soames, p. 501; Sherwood, p. 812; Loewenheim, pp. 546–8

9 FRUS, Yalta, pp. 3–4; Stalin, *Correspondence*, Vol. II, pp. 150–1

10 messages, Loewenheim, p. 504

11 collapse, trip, speech, Dewey, Black, pp. 954–5, 949–50, 1001; Morgan, pp. 731, 777; Parrish, pp. 455–7; Bishop, p. 196

12 Schlesinger, in Butler, pp. 33–4; Cadogan, pp. 655–62; Loewenheim, p. 553; FRUS, 1944, Vol. IV, pp. 991–3

13 Mikołajczyk, pp. 65–7

14 Stalin, *Correspondence*, Vol. II, pp. 148, 152; Loewenheim, pp. 556, 554, 553–4; *Documents of Polish–Soviet Relations* (London, 1956) Vol. II, document no. 164–5; Davies, *Rising*, pp. 206–9

15 Moscow, Warsaw, messages, Davies, *Rising*, pp. 272–5, 268, 315–6, 320–1, 342; Stalin, *Correspondence*, Vol. II, pp. 154, 156–7; Polish–Soviet relations, Vol. II, Document 202; Loewenheim, pp. 563–4, 558, 564, 566–8, 571, 572–3; Harriman, pp. 339–42, 347–9, 344; McJimsey, p. 356; FDR Library, Hopkins papers, Box 10, Map Room, Box 20; WSC, Vol. VI, p. 143; Wheeler-Bennett, p. 92

17: THE PLAN

1 only Jew, Beschloss, p. 49

2 Craig makes the case for White acting from idealism; Ted Morgan review of his book in the *Washington Post* (2004) takes issue.

3 This and following on Morgenthau, Jews, Morgenthau, p. 211; Black, pp. 814–5, 927; Smith, pp. 309, 313; Beschloss, pp. 38, 42, 51, 56–7, 59, 66–7; Morgan, p. 711; Alan Ryan, *New York Review of Books*, 3 November 2005

4 visit, Rees, pp. 267–8; FRUS, 1944, Vol. III, pp. 70–5; WSC, Vol. VI, p. 137; Morgenthau, pp. 361, 370; McJimsey, p. 342; Beschloss, pp. 75, 78–9

5 Cabinet in-fighting, Morgenthau, pp. 313, 370–1, 362, 368, 352–3, 359, 371–6, 370–1; Stimson, pp. 568–83; Sherwood, pp. 813–19; Hull, Vol. II, pp. 1601–22; FRUS, Teheran, p. 881; Loewenheim, p. 411; Beschloss, pp. 80–1, 99–101, 108–9; Rees; pp. 253, 106–17; Cadogan, p. 660; Morgenthau's own exposition of his views in his book, *Germany is our Problem* (New York, 1947)

6 plan, Morgenthau, pp. 376–8

7 meeting, Beschloss, pp. 117–8

8 summit, Gilbert, *Churchill*, pp. 961–7; Alanbrooke, p. 592; Beschloss, p. 121; Ward, pp. 326–9; Morgenthau, p. 367; Colville, *Footprints*, pp. 164–5; Moran, pp. 179, 176; FDR Library, Map Room, Box 169; Alanbrooke, p. 588 et seq

9 FRUS, 1944, Vol. II, pp.70–75; WSC, Vol. VI, p. 137

10 discussion and plan, Rees, pp. 287, 273; FRUS, Vol. III, pp. 57–9, 65, Yalta, p. 134; NY Post, 24–29 November 1947; Fort, p. 282 et seq; Dimitrov, p. 363; Moran, pp. 178–9; WSC, Vol. VI, pp. 138–9; Avon, p. 476; Morgenthau, pp. 385–6; Black, p. 988

11 rest of conference, Kennan, p. 171; Cadogan, p. 664 et seq; Fenby, pp. 425–31; Morgan, p. 733

12 Edmonds, Ch. 16, p. 405 and Appendix; PREM 3/139/8A–6698; WSC, Vol. VI, p. 242; FRUS, 1944, Vol. II, pp. 1026–30; Black, p. 997

13 discussions, Morgenthau, pp. 387–8; FRUS, Yalta, pp. 134–41, 142, 155; Beschloss, pp. 135–9; Rees, p. 276

14 press war, FDR, Beschloss, pp. 162–5, 143–9; Rees, pp. 274, 282, 285; Beria, p. 106; Isaacson and Thomas, p. 238; Morgenthau, p. 389

15 fall-out, FDR, Hopkins, Stimson, Bundy, p. 581; Cadogan, p. 666; Bohlen, p. 166; McJimsey, pp. 346–8, 354; FRUS, Yalta, pp. 437, 163–5, 173; 1945, Vol. II, p. 79; Beschloss, pp. 156, 158–60, 168–9; Morgenthau, p. 403

18: PERCENTAGE POINTS

1 meeting, WSC, Vol. VI, pp. 198–9; Berezhkov, *History*, pp. 369–72; Reynolds, *History*, p. 458; Cadogan, pp. 668, 671; FRUS, 1944, Vol. IV, p. 1004; Moran, pp. 193–4; Harriman, p. 354; PRO, PREM3/66/7, FO 800/302

2 This section, Soames, p. 505; WSC, Vol. VI, pp. 199–201; CAB 120/164 – the message is wrongly dated 11 September; Moran, p. 203; Berezhkov, *History*, pp. 369–71; Avon, pp. 482–3; Harvey, p. 359

3 letter, Harriman, FRUS, 1944, Vol. IV, p. 1011; WSC, Vol. VI, pp. 201–3; Reynolds, *History*, p. 460; Harriman, pp. 357–8

4 WSC, Cadogan, pp. 668, 671; FRUS, 1944, Vol. IV, p. 1004; Moran, pp. 193–4

5 Hopkins message, Harriman, p. 354

6 Stalin, *Correspondence*, Vol. 1, p. 163; FRUS, Yalta, p. 6

7 Polish meetings, Soames, p. 505; Mikołajczyk, pp. 104–8; WSC, Vol. VI, pp. 204–5; FRUS, Yalta, pp. 202–5; Harriman, p. 359; Avon, pp. 486–7; Harvey, pp. 360–1; Moran, p. 200

8 talks, WSC, Vol. VI, p. 207; Harvey, p. 362; Avon, p. 487; Gillies, p. 162; CAB 120/166; WSC, Vol. VI, pp. 208–11; FO 371/43307/N6567; Mikolajczyk, p. 111

9 dinner, Birse, pp. 173–5; CAB 120/164; WSC, Vol. VI, pp. 200, 205–6; Avon, pp. 483–5, 487; FRUS, 1944, Vol. IV, pp. 1012–15; Harvey, p. 380; Moran, p. 201; Harriman, pp. 362–4

10 dinner, Moran, pp. 204–5; Avon, p. 487; WSC, Vol. VI, p. 209; Berezhkov, p. 313; FO 371/43307/M6567; Montefiore, p. 422

19: RED BLUES

1 FDR, Bishop, pp. 197, 201; Burns, *Soldier*, p. 533; Harriman, pp. 371–2; Black, pp. 933, 1035; Goodwin, p. 570

2 This and next two paras Pravda, FO 371/43307/N6567; Cadogan, pp. 677, 683; Mikołajczyk, pp. 113–19; FRUS, Yalta, pp. 210, 221–5; Harriman, p. 369; Kennan, pp. 211, 109; Bishop, p. 204; Stalin, *Correspondence*, Vol. I, pp. 279, 282, 289–93; FRUS, Yalta, pp. 221–5

3 Reflecting its importance to him, Churchill devotes two chapters, totalling 36 pages, to Greece in his memoirs, WSC, Vol. VI, pp. 247–83; Avon, pp. 501–3; Stavrakis, pp. 33–5, 38–9, 41–2; O'Balance, pp. 89–104; Dimitrov, p. 345; FRUS, Yalta, pp. 435–6; Loewenheim, pp. 628–9; ER, *As*, p. 222

4 This and next four paras, FRUS, Yalta, pp. 440, 93–101, 102, 450, 447; Kennan, p. 249; Harriman, p. 382

5 de Gaulle, FRUS, Yalta, pp. 292, 300, 296–7, 450; Loewenheim, pp. 621, 625; Stalin, *Correspondence*, Vol. I, pp. 277–8, 280–2, 284, Vol. II, pp. 170–2; Kersaudy, *Churchill*, p. 411; Harriman, pp. 375–8; Bishop, p. 204; Bohlen, p. 170

6 JS, Europe, FRUS, Yalta, pp. 221–3, 224–5; WSC, Vol. VI, p. 294; Reynolds, *History*, p. 461; Dimitrov, pp. 342–3; Stalin, *Correspondence*, Vol. I, p. 281

7 FRUS, Yalta, pp. 286–8; Harriman, p. 373; Bohlen, p. 169; Harriman interview, http://www.trumanlibrary.org/oralhist/harriman.htmOral, p. 8

8 China, FRUS, Yalta, pp. 346, 349; Fenby, pp. 445–6; FRUS, Yalta, pp. 378–9

9 This section, FRUS, Yalta, pp. 58–9, 63–4, 66, 85, 39–40, 26, 30–1, Stalin, *Correspondence*, Vol. II, pp. 73–4, 178–9, 177, 169, Vol. I, pp. 288, 294, 303, Vol. II, pp. 177, 168–70

20: YALTA

1 FDR, trip, FRUS, Yalta, p. 459; Bohlen, p. 171; WSC, Vol. VI, p. 299; Avon, pp. 511–12; Black, p. 1039, Perkins, Columbia Oral History, pp. 280, 284–5; Beschloss, pp. 210, 179; Bohlen, p. 172; Harriman, pp. 390, 389; Ward, p. 390; Sherwood, p. 845; Anna Roosevelt, Columbia Oral History, p. 43

2 WSC, Sarah Churchill, *Dancing*, pp. 72–3; Moran, p. 217; Soames, pp. 511–13

3 Malta meetings, FRUS, Yalta, photograph after p. 546, pp. 469, 480, 499–500, 462, 546; Moran, p. 218; WSC, Vol. VI, pp. 295, 296, 299–300; Avon, pp. 510, 512; Loewenheim, pp. 647, 644; Stettinius, pp. 74–5; Ward, p. 393; Bohlen, pp. 172, 177; Harriman, p. 390

4 arrival, journeys, WSC, Vol. VI, pp. 300–1; Bohlen, p. 173; Hopkins, *American Heritage*; Beria, p. 104; Moran, p. 218; Sarah Churchill, *Dancing*, p. 74

5 Yalta, quarters, hospitality, security, Anna Roosevelt, Columbia Oral History, p. 44; Bohlen, p. 174; Hopkins, *American Heritage*; WSC, Vol. VI, pp. 302–3; Beschloss, pp. 178–9; Cadogan, p. 706; Sarah Churchill, *Dancing*, p. 75; Beria, p. 104

6 affair, Goodwin, p. 579

7 Yalta records, US, FRUS, Yalta volume, British, CAB 120/170, PREM 4/78/1; Soviet, SSNMK, Vol. VI, Documents on Teheran and Yalta Conferences (Moscow); WSC, Vol. VI, Chs XXI–XXIII; Bohlen, p. 180; Harriman, pp. 393–5

8 meeting, FRUS, Yalta, pp. 570–3; Hopkins, *American Heritage*; WSC, Vol. VI, p. 303; FRUS, Yalta, pp. 572–3; Harriman, p. 394; Beschloss, pp. 179–80

9 meeting, FRUS, Yalta, pp. 573–88; WSC, Vol. VI, pp. 304–5; Harriman, pp. 394–5; Gilbert, *Second World War*, p. 638

10 dinner, FRUS, Yalta, pp. 553, 589–91; Harriman, p. 395; Bohlen, pp. 181–2; Avon, pp. 512–3. The occasion does not figure in Churchill's memoirs.

11 session, procedures, Literaturnaya Gazeta, 24 January 1968; V.Ya. Sipols, I.A. Chelyshev *Krymskaya konferentsiya, 1945* (Crimean Conference, 1945), Moscow, 1984; FRUS, Yalta, pp. 611–33, 608–9; WSC, Vol. VI, pp. 304–8; FRUS, Yalta, p. 611; WSC, Vol. VI, p. 305; Moran, p. 226; Black, p. 1076; Bohlen, pp. 178–9; Cadogan, pp. 704–5; Harriman, p. 392; Beria, pp. 103–4; Andrews and Miktrokin, pp. 175–6; Birse, p. 179

12 plenary, FRUS, Yalta, pp. 611–33; WSC, Vol. VI, pp. 308–12; Bohlen, pp. 182–3; Avon, p. 151; Harriman, pp. 401–4

13 Sarah Churchill, *Dancing*, entry for 6 February 1945

14 plenary, FRUS, pp. 660–82; WSC, Vol. VI gathers discussions on Poland together in Ch. XXII as does Harriman, pp. 405–15; Hopkins, Moran, p. 226; Bohlen, p. 188; Cadogan, pp. 717, 706

15 FRUS, Yalta, pp. 726–8; Avon, p. 517

16 session, FRUS, Yalta, pp. 708–26, 729; WSC, Vol. VI, pp. 325–7, 312–15; Bohlen, pp. 194–5; Moran, p. 223; Harriman, pp. 412–3; Clemens, p. 278 stresses the problem of the attitude of the London Poles

17 FDR-JS, FRUS, Yalta, pp. 766–71; Bohlen, pp. 196–7; Harriman, pp. 397–8

18 plenary, FRUS, Yalta, pp. 771–82; WSC, Vol. VI, pp. 328–34

19 WSC, Moran, p. 226; Birse, p. 183; Cadogan, pp. 717, 706

20 dinner, FRUS, Yalta, pp. 797–9; WSC, Vol. VI, pp. 315–8; Sarah Churchill, *Dancing*, pp. 71–2; Harriman, p. 416; Clark Kerr, Gillies, p. 165

21 Foreign Minister, FRUS, Yalta, pp. 802–11; Harriman, p. 409

22 photograph, Robert Hopkins, *American Heritage*

23 rest of plenary, FRUS, Yalta, pp. 841–57; Moran, p. 228; Stalin, Avon, p. 514

24 JS, China, FRUS, Yalta, pp. 894–7, 984; WSC, Vol. VI, p. 337; Avon, pp. 513–14; FDR Library, Hopkins papers, pre-Yalta Box; Moran, p. 230; Harriman, pp. 339–40; Fenby, p. 450

25 plenary, FRUS, Yalta, pp. 897–918; Bohlen, p. 185; Sherwood, pp. 859–60, 871; Moran, pp. 229–30; Anna Roosevelt, Columbia Oral History, p. 46

26 dinner, WSC, Vol. VI, pp. 342–4; Birse, p. 185; Meacham, p. 320; Bohlen, p. 203

27 Moran, p. 230

28 communiqué, FRUS, Yalta, pp. 968–83; signing, Harriman, p. 417; JS, Bohlen, p. 193; Harriman, p. 414

29 FRUS, Yalta, p. 558; Beschloss, p. 188

30 hate, Gilbert, *Victory*, p. 1196

31 WSC, Sarah Churchill, *Dancing*, p. 77; WSC, Vol. VI, pp. 345–8; Moran, p. 231; Cadogan, p. 710

32 Yalta evaluation, Clemens, p. 280; Bohlen, pp. 200, 175; Cadogan, p. 709; Sherwood, pp. 869–70; Moran, pp. 225, 227; WSC, Vol. VI, pp. 350–1; Harriman, pp. 412–5; Black, pp. 1075, 1081; FDR Library, Map Room, Boxes 170–2; Berle, p. 471

21: DEATH AT THE SPRINGS

1 FDR, Saud, oil, PREM 3.332/6, Stoff, pp. 59, 148, 177; Bohlen, pp. 202–4; Sherwood, p. 872; coffee, photographs on show at Hyde Park; Ward, p. 396; Yergin, pp. 404–5

2 WSC, Vol. VI, p. 348; Soames, p. 518

3 Bohlen, pp. 204–5

4 FDR to Congress, 1 March 1945, MacLeish, Beschloss, p. 190; Sherwood, p. 808; WSC, Vol. VI, p. 368

5 Anna Roosevelt, Columbia Oral History, p. 45; Perkins, pp. 73–4; Columbia Oral History, p. 762

6 *Das Reich*, 23 February 1945

7 This and next para, Avon, p. 523; WSC, Vol. VI, pp. 368–9, Harriman, pp. 424–6; Cadogan, p. 721

8 Poland, Harriman, pp. 412–13, 426–31; Gillies, pp. 165–66; Cadogan, pp. 718–19; WSC, Vol. VI, pp. 372–9; Avon, pp. 525–61; Gardner, pp. 247–8

9 Christian gentleman, Dalleck, p. 521

10 Sherwood, p. 880; Cadogan, p. 719; Harriman, p. 445

11 messages, Avon, p. 526 ; WSC, Vol. VI, Appendix C, pp. 382–4; Harriman, p. 431; Gardner, pp. 245–6

12 WSC, Vol. VI deals with the strategic debate in Ch. XXVII; Ambrose, *Eisenhower*, pp. 394–7, 401; Gilbert, *America*, pp. 337–9; Beschloss, p. 204; Harriman, pp.

434–52, Episode, WSC, Vol. VI, pp. 387–8; Bohlen, pp. 208–9; Beschloss, pp. 205–6; Harriman, pp. 432–4

13 WSC, Vol. VI, pp. 392–8; Bohlen, pp. 208–9; Harriman, p. 438; CAB 120/859; Harriman, p. 444

14 FDR end, Beschloss, pp. 193–4, 197, 200, 202, 211–2, 214; Perkins, Columbia Oral History, pp. 758–9; Kimball, *Correspondence*, Vol. 3, p. 630; WSC, Vol. VI, p. 398; Black, pp. 1109–11, 1114–5; Sherwood, pp. 880–1; Bohlen, p. 209; Goodwin, p. 615

15 Soviets, Harriman, pp. 441–3, 445–52; FRUS, 1945, Vol. V, pp. 231–4; Gardner, pp. 255–7

16 Chiang, Fenby p. 450; de Gaulle, Kersaudy, *Roosevelt*, pp. 479–80

17 Molotov, Truman, pp. 78–82; Bohlen, p. 213; Gardner, pp. 327–8; Harriman, pp. 453–4

22: JOURNEY'S END

1 PREM 3/356/12

2 WSC, Vol. VI, pp. 498–9; Harriman, p. 461

3 Mee, p. 66

4 WSC, Vol. VI, pp. 502–5; Harriman, p. 463; Bohlen, pp. 215–6; Avon, p. 539; Gilbert, *America*, p. 355

5 Hopkins mission, FRUS, 1945, Vol. V, p. 334; Harriman, pp. 463–75; Bohlen, pp. 217–222, 244, 219; Mee, pp. 60–5; WSC, Vol. VI, pp. 505–7

6 Harriman, pp. 480–2

7 WSC, Vol. VI, pp. 506–7

8 Hopkins, Harriman, p. 470

9 trip, Truman diary, 7 July 1945; Beschloss, pp. 253–4, 245; PREM 3.430/7; Mee, p. 6; Harriman, p. 488

10 Moran, pp. 267–8

11 WSC, Vol. VI, p. 545; Cadogan, p. 763, 74–7; Mee, p. 74; PREM 3/430/7

12 Truman diary, 17 July 1945; Beschloss, p. 256; Mee, pp. 90–4; Gardner, p. 215

13 session, FRUS, Berlin, Vol. II, pp. 52–63; Mee, pp. 95–108; Beschloss, pp. 256–7; WSC, Vol. VI, pp. 561–2; Bohlen, p. 229

14 Moran, pp. 275–6, 279

15 Avon, pp. 545–7; Cadogan, p. 765; Beschloss, p. 256; Mee, p. 103

16 dinners, 3 Mee, pp. 165–6, 173–5; PREM 3/430/6

17 Mee, pp. 221–3; WSC, pp. 581–2; Moran, p. 280; de Groot, pp. 130–1

18 Mee, p. 228; Moran, p. 285; WSC, Vol. VI, p. 583

19 Harriman, p. 482; Potsdam Declaration, Section IX; Moran, p. 285; Cadogan, pp. 774, 782; Avon p. 555

20 Cadogan, p. 778

21 Rhyme, George Packer, *New Yorker*, 10–17 July 2006

BIBLIOGRAPHY

PRINCIPAL ARCHIVE SOURCES

Avalon Project, Yale University, documents on Placentia Bay, Teheran, Yalta
  conferences
Columbia University Oral History Archive, New York
Churchill Archives, Cambridge
Foreign Office, London
Foreign Relations of the United States, Volumes for 1939–45 and special volumes
  on Washington Conferences, 1942, Casablanca, 1943, Washington and Quebec,
  1943, Teheran, 1944, Yalta, 1945 (Washington: US Government Printing Office)
Foreign & Commonwealth Office, Churchill and Stalin (London FCO, 2002)
Public Records Office, London (particularly CAB, PREM files)
Ministry of Foreign Affairs of the USSR, Stalin's correspondence with Roosevelt
  and Churchill
Roosevelt Library, Hyde Park, New York, Roosevelt Safe Files
Soviet Archives on Teheran and Yalta

BOOKS

Acheson, Dean, *Present at the Creation* (London: Hamish Hamilton, 1970)
Adams, Henry, *Harry Hopkins* (New York: Putnam, 1977)
Addison, Paul, *Churchill* (Oxford University Press, 2005)
Aglion, Raoul, *Roosevelt and de Gaulle* (New York: Free Press, 1988)
Alanbrooke, Lord, *War Diaries*, ed. Alex Danchev and Daniel Todman (London:
  Weidenfeld and Nicolson, 2001)

Andrew, Christopher and Mitrokhin, Vasili, *The Mitrokhin Archive* (London: Allen Lane, 1999)

Attlee, Clement, *As it Happened* (London: Heinemann, 1954)

Avon, Earl, (Anthony Eden) *Memoirs, Vol. II, The Reckoning* (London: Cassell, 1965)

Banac, Ivo (ed.) *Diary of Georgi Dimitrov* (New Haven: Yale University Press, 2003)

Bedell Smith, Sally, *Reflected Glory* (New York: Simon & Schuster, 1996)

Beevor, Anthony, *Stalingrad* (London: Viking, 1998)

Bercuson, David and Herwig, Holger, *One Christmas in Washington* (Woodstock: Overview Press, 2005)

Berezhkov, Valentin, *History in the Making* (Moscow: Progress Publishing, 1983)

—— *At Stalin's Side* (New York: Birch Lane Press, 1994)

Beria, Sergio, *My Father* (London: Duckworth, 1999)

Berle, Beatrice and Jacobs, Travis (eds) *Navigating the Rapids 1918–71, From the Papers of Adolf A. Berle* (New York: Harcourt, Brace, Jovanovich, 1973)

Berlin, Sir Isiah, 'Winston Churchill in 1940', in *Personal Impressions* (Oxford University Press, 1982)

Berthon, Simon, *Warlords* (London: Politico's, 2005)

Beschloss, Michael, *The Conquerors* (New York: Simon & Schuster, 2002)

Birse, Arthur, *Memoirs of an Interpreter* (London: Michael Joseph, 1967)

Bishop, Jim, *FDR's Last Year* (London: Hart-Davis, 1975)

Bix, Herbert, *Hirohito* (London: Duckworth, 2000)

Black, Conrad, *Franklin Delano Roosevelt, Champion of Freedom* (London: Weidenfeld and Nicolson, 2003)

Blum, John Morton, *From the Morgenthau Diaries* (Boston: Houghton, Mifflin, 1959–65)

Bohlen, Charles, *Witness to History* (New York: Norton, 1973)

Boyd, Carl, *Hitler's Japanese Confidant* (Lawrence: University of Kansas, 1993)

Bromage, Bernard, *Molotov* (London: Peter Owen, 1956)

Bruce, George, *Second Front Now!* (London: MacDonald and Jane's, 1979)

Bullard, Reader, *Letters from Teheran* (London: I.B.Tauris, 1991)

Bullock, Alan, *Hitler and Stalin* (London: Fontana, 1998)

Burleigh, Michael, *The Third Reich* (London: Pan, 2001)

Burnham, James, *The Managerial Revolution*, (Westport, Greenwood Press, 1972)

Burns, James McGregor, *Roosevelt, the Lion and the Fox* (New York: Harcourt Brace, 1956)

—— *Leadership* (New York: Harcourt, Brace, Jovanovich, 1970)

—— *Roosevelt, The Soldier of Freedom* (New York: Harper & Row, 1978)

Butler, Susan, *My Dear Mr Stalin* (Yale University Press, 2006)

Cadogan, Alexander, *Diaries* (London: Cassell, 1971)

Calvocoressi, Peter, Wint, Guy and Pritchard, John, *Total War* (New York: Pantheon, 1989)

Carlton, David, *Anthony Eden* (London: Allen Lane, 1981)

—— *Churchill and the Soviet Union* (Manchester University Press, 1999)

Chace, James, *Acheson* (New York: Simon & Schuster, 1998)

Charmley, John, *Churchill, the End of Glory* (New York: Harcourt, Brace, 1991)
—— *Churchill's Grand Alliance* (Hodder & Stoughton, 1995)
Chuev, Felix, *Molotov Remembers* (Chicago: Ivan R. Dee, 1993)
Churchill, Sarah, *Keep on Dancing* (London: Weidenfeld, 1981)
—— *A Thread in the Tapestry* (London: Sphere, 1968)
Churchill, Winston, *The Second World War* (London: Cassell, 6 Vols: 1948, 1949, 1950, 1951, 1952, 1954)
—— *A Thread in the Tapestry* (London: Deutsch, 1967)
Ciano, Count, *Dairies* (ed. Malcolm Muggeridge) (London: Heinemann, 1947)
Ciechanowski, Jan, *Defeat in Victory* (London: Gollancz, 1948)
Clemens, Diane Shaver, *Yalta* (Oxford University Press, 1970)
Close, David, *The Origins of the Greek Civil War* (London: Longman, 1995)
Colville, John, *Footprints in Times* (London: Collins, 1976)
—— *The Fringes of Power* (London: Hodder and Stoughton, 1985)
Craig, R. Bruce, *Treasonable Doubt* (University of Kansas, 2004)
Dallas, Gregor, *Poisoned Peace* (London: John Murray, 2005)
Dalleck, Robert, *Franklin D. Roosevelt and American Foreign Policy 1932–45* (New York: OUP, 1979)
Danchev, Alex, *Very Special Relationship* (London: Brassey's, 1986)
—— *On Specialness* (London: Macmillan, 1998)
Davies, John Paton, *Dragon by the Tail* (London: Robson Books, 1974)
Davies, Norman, *Rising '44, The Battle for Warsaw* (London: Pan, 2004)
—— *God's Playground* (Oxford University Press, 2005)
Davis, Kenneth, *FDR, The War President* (New York: Random House, 2000)
Deane, John, *Strange Alliance* (Viking: New York, 1950)
de Gaulle, Charles, *Mémoires de Guerre*, 3 Vols (Paris: Plon, 1970)
de Groot, Gerard, *The Bomb* (London: Jonathan Cape, 2004)
d'Este, Carlo, *Eisenhower* (London: Weidenfeld & Nicolson, 2003)
Djilas, Milovan, *Conversations with Stalin* (London: Hart-Davis, 1962)
Duff Cooper, Alfred, *Diaries* (London: Weidenfeld & Nicolson, 2005)
Dutton, David, *Anthony Eden* (London: Arnold, 1997)
Eade, Charles, *The War Speeches of the Rt. Hon Winston Churchill* (London: Hutchinson, 1965)
Edmonds, Robin, *The Big Three* (London: Penguin, 1991)
Eisenhower, Dwight, *Crusade in Europe* (New York: da Capo, 1997)
Ferrell, Robert, *The Dying President* (Columbia: University of Missouri Press, 1998)
Feis, Herbert, *Churchill, Roosevelt, Stalin* (Princeton University Press, 1957)
Fenby, Jonathan, *Generalissimo: Chiang Kai-shek and the China He Lost* (London: Free Press, 2003)
Fest, Joachim, *Hitler* (London: Weidenfeld and Nicolson, 1973)
Flynn, John, *The Roosevelt Myth* (New York: Devin-Adair, 1948)
Fort, Adrian, *Prof* (London: Pimlico, 2004)
Fraser, David, *Alanbrooke* (London: Collins, 1982)
Friedel, Frank, *Franklin D. Roosevelt* (Boston: Little, Brown, 1990)

Gaddis, John Lewis, *The Cold War* (London: Allen Lane, 2006)

Gardner, Lloyd, *Spheres of Influence* (London: John Murray, 1993)

Gellman, Irwin, *Secret Affairs: Franklin Roosevelt, Cordell Hull and Sumner Welles* (Baltimore: John Hopkins Press, 1995)

Gilbert, Martin, *Winston S. Churchill, Vol. VI, Finest Hour* (London: Minerva, 1989)

—— *Winston S. Churchill, Vol. VII, Road to Victory* (London: Heinemann, 1986)

—— *Second World War* (London: Fontana, 1990)

—— *Churchill, A Life* (London: Pimlico, 2000)

—— *The Churchill War Papers* (New York: Norton, 2001)

—— *Continue to Pester, Nag and Bite, Churchill's War Leadership* (London: Pimlico, 2005)

—— *Churchill and America* (London: Free Press, 2005)

Gillies, Donald, *Radical Diplomat, The Life of Archibald Clark Kerr* (London: I.B. Taurus, 1999)

Goodwin, Doris Stearns, *No Ordinary Time: Franklin and Eleanor Roosevelt, The Home Front in World War II* (New York: Simon & Schuster, 1994)

Gorodetsky, Gabriel, *Grand Delusion* (New Haven: Yale University Press, 1999)

Grayling, A.C., *Among the Dead Cities* (London: Bloomsbury, 2006)

Halle, Kay, *Winston Churchill on America and Britain* (New York: Walker, 1970)

Harriman, Averell, *Special Envoy* (New York: Random House, 1975)

Harrod, Roy, *The Prof* (London: Macmillan, 1959)

Harvey, John, *War Diaries of Oliver Harvey, Vol. II* (London: Collins, 1978)

Hassett, William, *Off The Record with F.D.R.* (London: George Allen & Unwin, 1960)

Hickman, Tom, *Churchill's Bodyguard* (London: Headline, 2005)

Hildebrand, Robert, *Dumbarton Oaks* (Chapel Hill: University of North Carolina Press, 1990)

Hitchens, Christopher, *Blood, Class and Nostalgia* (New York: Nation Books, 2004)

Hobsbawm, Eric, *Age of Extremes* (London: Michael Joseph, 1994)

Hodgson, Godfrey, *The Colonel* (New York: Knopf, 1990)

Hoehling, A.H., *America's Road to War* (London: Abelard-Schuman, 1970)

Holland, James, *Together We Stand* (London: HarperCollins, 2005)

Holmes, Richard, *In The Footsteps of Churchill* (London: BBC Books, 2005)

Hopkins, Robert, *American Heritage*, June/July 2005

Hough, Richard, *Former Naval Person* (London: Weidenfeld & Nicolson, 1985)

Hull, Cordell, *Memoirs, Vol. 2* (London: Hodder & Stoughton, 1948)

Isaacson, Walter and Thomas, Evan, *The Wise Men* (London: Faber, 1986)

Ismay, Hastings, *Memoirs of Lord Ismay* (London: Heinemann, 1960)

Jacob, Ian, *Action This Day*

Jackson Robert, H., *That Man: An Insider's Portrait of Franklin D. Roosevelt* (Oxford University Press, 2003)

Jenkins, Roy, *Churchill* (London: Pan, 2002)

—— *Roosevelt* (London: Pan, 2005)

Kelly, Aileen, 'A Great Russian Prophet', *New York Review of Books*, 3 Nov 2005

Kennan, George, *Memoirs* (London: Hutchinson, 1968)

Kennedy, John, *The Business of War* (London: Hutchinson, 1957)

Kersaudy, François, *De Gaulle et Churchill* (Paris: Tempus, 2003)

—— *De Gaulle et Roosevelt* (Paris: Perrin, 2004)

Kershaw, Ian, *Hitler, Nemesis, 1936–45* (London: Penguin, 2001)

Kimball, Warrren, *The Juggler* (Princeton University Press, 1991)

—— *Forged in War* (London: HarperCollins, 1997)

—— *Churchill and Roosevelt, The Complete Correspondence, 3 Vols* (Princeton University Press, 1984)

—— *Churchill and the Americans, the Americans and Churchill* (Washington: Churchill Center, www.winstonchurchill.org/i4a/pages/index.cfm?pageid=612)

King, Ernest and Whitehall, William, *Fleet Admiral King* (New York: Da Capo Press, 1976)

Kissinger, Henry, *Diplomacy* (New York: Simon & Schuster, 1994)

Kitchen, Martin, *British Policy towards the Soviet Union during the Second World War* (Basingstoke: Macmillan, 1986)

Lacqueur, Walter (ed.), *The Second World War* (London: Sage, 1982)

Larrabee, Eric, *Commander in Chief* (London: Andre Deutsch, 1987)

Lash, Joseph, *Roosevelt & Churchill* (London: Andre Deutsch, 1977)

Lawlor, Sheila, *Churchill and the Politics of War* (Cambridge University Press, 1994)

Leahy, William, *I Was There* (New York: Arno, 1979)

Loewenheim, Francis, Langley and Harold, Jonas, Manfred (eds) *Roosevelt and Churchill, Their Secret Wartime Correspondence* (London: Barrie & Jenkins, 1975)

MacIntyre, Donald, *The Naval War Against Hitler* (London: Batsford, 1971)

Macmillan, Harold, *The Blast of War* (London: Macmillan, 1967)

—— Harold, *War Dairies* (London: Macmillan, 1984)

Maisky, Ivan, *Memoirs of a Soviet Ambassador* (New York: Scribner, 1967)

Malliarakis, Jean Gilles, *Yalta de la Naissance des Blocs* (Paris: Editions Albatross, 1982)

McIntire, Ross T., *Twelve Years with Roosevelt* (London: Putnam, 1948)

McJimsey, George, *Harry Hopkins* (Cambridge: Harvard University Press, 1987)

Mee, Charles, *Meeting at Potsdam* (London: Andre Deutsch, 1975)

Mikołajczyk, Stanislav, *The Pattern of Soviet Domination* (London: Sampson, Low, Marston, 1948)

Ministry of Foreign Affairs of the USSR, *Stalin's Correspondence with Churchill, Attlee, Roosevelt and Truman* (Moscow: Foreign Languages Publishing House, 1957)

Montefiore, Simon Sebag, *Stalin* (London: Weidenfeld & Nicolson, 2003)

Moran, Lord, *Winston Churchill, The Struggle for Survival* (London: Constable, 1966)

Morgan, Ted, *FDR* (New York: Simon & Schuster, 1985)

Morgenthau, Henry III, *Mostly Morgenthaus* (New York: Ticknor & Fields, 1991)

Morison, Samuel Eliot, *The Two-Ocean War* (Boston: Little, Brown, 1963)

Morton, H.V., *Atlantic Meeting* (London: Methuen, 1943)

Murphy, David, *What Stalin Knew* (Yale University Press, 2005)

Nicolson, Harold, *The War Years* (New York: Athenaeum, 1967)

O'Balance, Edgar, *The Greek Civil War* (London: Faber, 1966)

Parker, R.A.C., *Struggle for Survival* (Oxford University Press, 1989)

Parrish, Thomas, *Roosevelt and Marshall* (New York: William Morrow, 1989)

Pawle, Gerald, *The War & Colonel Warden* (London: Harrap, 1963)

Pender, Kenneth, *Adventure in Diplomacy* (London: Cassell, 1966)

Perkins, Frances, *The Roosevelt I Knew* (London: Hammond, Hammond, 1947)

Peters, Charles, *Five Days in Philadelphia* (London: Public Affairs, 2005)

Pogue, Forrest, *George C. Marshall; Organizer of Victory 1953–5* (New York: Viking, 1973)

Post, Jerrold and Robins, Robert, *When Illness Strikes the Leader* (Yale University Press, 1991)

Powell, Anthony, *The Military Philosophers* (University of Chicago Press, 1995)

Ranelagh, John, *CIA* (London: BBC Books, 1992)

Rees, David, *Harry Dexter White* (London: Macmillan, 1974)

Reynolds, David, Kimball, Warren F., and Chubarian, A.O. (eds) *Allies at War* (London: Macmillan, 1994)

Reynolds, David, *In Command of History* (London: Allen Lane, 2004)

—— *From Munich to Pearl Harbour* (New York: Ivan Deem, 2002)

—— *From World War to Cold War* (Oxford University Press, 2006)

Rhodes James, Robert, *Anthony Eden* (London: Weidenfeld and Nicolson, 1986)

Roberts, Andrew, *The Holy Fox* (London: Weidenfeld & Nicolson, 1991)

Roosevelt, Eleanor, *This I Remember* (New York: Greenwood Press, 1975)

Roosevelt, Elliott, *As He Saw It* (New York: Duell, Sloan and Pearce, 1946)

Roosevelt, Elliott, and Brough, James, *A Rendezvous with Destiny* (London: W.H. Allen, 1977)

Roosevelt, James and Shalett, Sidney, *Affectionately FDR* (London: Harrap, 1960)

Roosevelt, James and Libby, Bill, *My Parents, A Differing View* (London: WH Allen, 1977)

Rosenman, Samuel, *Working with Roosevelt* (New York: Harper and Brothers, 1952)

Rosos, Mario, *Roosevelt and the French* (New York: Preager 1993)

Ross, Graham, *The Foreign Office and the Kremlin* (Cambridge: University Press, 1984)

Sainsbury, Keith, *The Turning Point, The Moscow, Cairo and Teheran Conferences* (Oxford University Press, 1985)

—— *Churchill and Roosevelt at War* (London: Macmillan, 1994)

Schlesinger, Arthur M., *The Age of Roosevelt* (Boston: Houghton Mifflin, 1957–60)

Schlesinger, Stephen, *Act of Creation, The Founding of the United Nations* (Boulder: Westview Press, 2003)

Seaton, Albert, *Stalin as Warlord* (London: Batsford, 1976)

Sherwood, Robert, *Roosevelt and Hopkins* (New York: Harpers, 1948)

Skidelsky, Robert, *John Maynard Keynes*, Vol. III (London: Macmillan, 2001)

Smith, Neil, *American Empire* (Berkely: University of California Press, 2003)

Snell, John, *The Meaning of Yalta* (Baton Rouge: Louisiana State University Press, 1956)

Soames, Mary, *Speaking for Themselves* (New York: Doubleday, 1998)

Soviet Archive, *The Teheran, Yalta and Potsdam Conferences* (Moscow: Progress Publishers, 1969)

Speer, Albert, *Inside the Third Reich* (London: Weidenfeld & Nicolson, 1970)

Stafford, David, *Roosevelt and Churchill, Men of Secrets* (London: Little, Brown, 1999)

Stalin, Joseph, *Correspondence with Churchill, Attlee, Roosevelt and Truman*, 2 Vols, (London: Lawrence & Wishart, 1958)

Standley, William and Ageton, Arthur, *Admiral Ambassador to Russia* (New York: Regnery, 1955)

Stavrakis, Peter, *Moscow and Greek Communism, 1944–49* (Ithica: Cornell University Press, 1989)

Stettinius, Edward, *Roosevelt and the Russians* (London: Cape, 1950)

—— *Diaries* (New York: New Directions, 1975)

Stevenson, William, *A Man Called Intrepid* (London: Macmillan, 1976)

Stilwell, Joseph, *The Stilwell Papers* (ed. T White) (New York: Shocken Books, 1972)

Stimson, Henry and Bundy, McGeorge, *On Active Service in Peace and War* (New York: Harper, 1948)

Stoff, Michael, *Oil, War and American Security* (New Haven: Yale University Press, 1980)

Stoler, Mark, *Allies & Adversaries* (Chapel Hill: University of North Carolina Press, 2000)

Taubman, William, *Krushchev* (London: Free Press, 2003)

Teheran, Yalta and Potsdam Conference, documents (Moscow: Progress Publishers, 1969)

Thompson, Walter, *Beside the Bulldog, The Intimate Memoirs of Churchill's Bodyguard* (London: Apollo Publishing, 2003)

Thorne, Christopher, *Allies of a Kind* (London: Hamish Hamilton, 1978)

Tooze, Adam, *The Wages of Destruction* (London: Allen Lane, 2006)

Truman, Harry, *Year of Decisions* (New York: Doubleday, 1955)

Tully, Grace, *FDR, My Boss* (New York: Scribner, 1949)

Tuttle, Dwight William, *Harry L. Hopkins and Anglo-American-Soviet Relations, 1941–45* (New York: Garland Publishing, 1983)

Ulam, Adam, *Stalin* (New York: Viking, 1973)

Volkogonov, D.A., *Stalin, Triumph and Tragedy* (London: Weidenfeld & Nicolson, 1991)

Ward, Geoffrey, *Closest Companion* (Boston: Houghton Mifflin, 1995)

Wedemeyer, Albert, *Wedemeyer Reports!* (New York: Henry Holt, 1958)

Weiss, Steve, *Allies in Conflict* (Basingstoke: Macmillan, 1996)

Welles, Sumner, *Where Are We Heading?* (New York: Greenwood Press, 1974)

Williams, Charles, *Pétain* (London: Little, Brown, 2005)

Wilson, Theodore, *The First Summit* (London: Macdonald, 1970)

Wingate, Robert, *Lord Ismay* (London: Hutchinson, 1970)

Wheeler-Bennett, John (ed.) *Action This Day* (London: Macmillan, 1968)

Woodward, Llewellyn, *British Foreign Policy in the Second World War* (London: Stationery Office, 1976)

Yergin, Daniel, *The Prize* (New York: Simon & Schuster, 1991)

INDEX

Advisory Commission for Europe, 207
Afrika Corps, 86
Albania, 345
Alexander, Harold, 138, 167, 197, 203, 338
Allied Control Commission, 278
Amery, Leo, 104
Anzio (Italian operation), 270, 275, 277, 282
Arcadia summit (Washington) (1941/42), 85–7, 94–102, 103, 111
Argentina, 404
Argonaut summit (1942) (Washington), 128–30
Arnhem, 310
Arnold, General Henry, 53
Atlantic Charter, 56–62, 88, 90, 91, 97, 105–6, 109, 207
atom bomb, 127, 158, 182, 197–8, 315–16, 400, 412, 413–14
Attlee, Clement, 11, 30, 60, 104, 193, 415

Auchinleck, Claude, 138
Augusta, 36
Austria, 259, 346

B-29 Superfortress, 6
Badoglio, Marshal, 278
Bagration operation, 293
Balkans, 199, 324
Baltic States, 90, 91, 92, 105, 109, 120, 207, 258, 345
Barbarossa operation, 293
Baruch, Bernard, 282
Beaverbrook, Lord, 10, 50, 101–2; background, 68; and Placentia Bay summit, 57, 61, 63; resignation, 104; and US/British mission to Moscow (1941), 67–72
Beneš, Eduard 271
Berezhkov, Valentin, 140, 323–4
Beria, Lavrenty, 36, 66, 230
Beria, Sergio, 232–3, 261
Berle, Adolf, 106, 107, 162
Berlin: division of, 392–3

Berlin, Isaiah, 12
Bessarabia, 105
Bevin, Ernest, 104, 255, 389, 415,
    416
Birse, Arthur, 152, 206, 233, 331, 379
Black, Conrad, 14, 383
Boettinger, Anna (Roosevelt's
    daughter), 280, 319, 350, 355,
    395, 397
Boettinger, John, 251, 395
Bohlen, Charles 'Chip', 1, 14, 29, 40,
    178, 206, 229, 320, 381
Bohr, Niels, 315–16
Bretton Woods conference (1944),
    303, 305, 347
Britain: impact of war on, 6; post-war
    financial arrangements, 311–12;
    propaganda campaign to get US
    into war, 34; US help before
    entering war, 32–3, 35, 38; see
    also Churchill, Winston
British Empire, 8, 10, 186–7, 372
British Security Coordination (BSC),
    34
Brooke, Alan, 26–7, 53, 86, 121, 128,
    134, 168, 188, 189, 198, 220,
    310–11; background and
    character, 112–13; and
    Churchill, 12, 113; and cross-
    channel invasion plan, 115, 116,
    167; and Teheran conference,
    241, 242, 253, 254
Bruenn, Dr Howard G., 279–80
Bulgaria, 323, 324, 345, 403, 411
Bullitt, William, 56
Burma, 115, 168, 169, 199, 220, 222,
    223, 249; cancellation of landing
    in, 263, 265, 268, 314–15
Bush, George W., 380
Byrnes, James, 407–8, 410, 415, 416

Cadogan, Alexander, 22, 50, 56, 88,
    104, 110, 148, 149, 219, 292, 369
Cairo summit: (first) (1943), 213–25;

249; (second) (1943), 263–8
Casablanca summit (1943), 164–78
Chamberlain, Neville, 27, 88
Chiang Kai-shek, 6, 80, 96, 115, 168,
    191, 249, 315, 347, 367, 374,
    398, 418; and Burma, 220, 264,
    265, 314–15; and Cairo summit,
    217, 219, 221–3; and war with
    Japan, 76
Chiang Kai-shek, Madame, 35, 168,
    190–1, 221–2, 223
Chicago Tribune, 34
Childs, Marquis, 40
China, 209, 235, 264–5, 347, 367,
    405; agreements between
    Roosevelt and Chiang at Cairo
    summit, 222–3; relations with
    US, 35–6; source of discord
    between Roosevelt and
    Churchill, 7–8, 217–18;
    territorial concessions given to
    Stalin at Yalta, 366–7, 374, 381,
    382; war with Japan, 35, 76, 315;
    see also Chiang Kai-shek
Churchill, Clementine, 24, 68, 86
Churchill, Mary, 104
Churchill, Pamela, 68
Churchill, Randolph, 68, 166, 251,
    278
Churchill, Sarah, 78, 214, 224, 245,
    251, 269, 351, 355–6, 369
Churchill, Winston, 418; and
    American media, 96, 99–100;
    appearance, 17; belief in own
    indestructibility, 11; and Brooke,
    113; character and attributes, 10,
    11–12, 150; and China, 7–8;
    concern about Soviet power, 8;
    confidants, 10; criticism of,
    103–4; and de Gaulle, 143,
    160–1, 172, 174, 193, 218, 271;
    and death of Roosevelt,
    398; differences between
    Roosevelt, Stalin and 18–30;

and domestic politics, 10–11,
27–8, 389, 410; and drinking,
22, 94–5; and Eden, 88, 104;
family, 22–3; and frontier issue,
109, 110; and Greece, 286,
338–40, 341–2; health problems,
2, 26–7, 100, 182, 214–15,
268–9, 280, 310; and imperial
issue, 57–60, 110–11; and Italian
operation, 270; loses election
(1945), 410, 414–15; marriage,
24; and North Africa, 129, 134;
and Overlord, 209, 210, 215,
237, 245, 246, 249–50, 270,
277–8, 282–3, 284; and Pearl
Harbor attack, 79; percentages
proposal to Stalin, 323–5, 381,
413; and Polish issue, 281, 294,
326, 327, 328–30, 363–4, 367–8,
372, 375, 389–90, 406; political
career, 9, 12; popularity, 162;
and post-war Germany, 256–7,
312–13, 361; post-war vision,
181–2, 187, 192, 243;
recreational pursuits and tastes,
21–2; relationship with
Roosevelt, 2, 8, 12–13, 95, 127,
179, 192, 216, 219, 224–5, 289,
316–17; relationship with Stalin,
1, 2–4, 12–13, 73–5, 146,
149–50, 152–3, 155, 179, 204,
216, 224–5, 316–17, 325–6, 335,
369–70, 410; relationship with
Truman, 408; residences, 25;
role played in Alliance, 418; and
Roundup-Sledgehammer plan,
115–16; and second front issue,
66, 112, 124–5, 127–8, 141–2;
and smoking, 26; style, 19, 20;
and Torch operation, 143, 159;
view of Americans, 28, 38; view
of Communism, 65, 325; view of
Soviet Union, 325; war strategy,
86–7; and Warsaw rising,

299–300; wartime performance,
10; working methods, 19–20
SUMMITS/CONFERENCES:
Arcadia (1941–2), 85–7,
94–102, 103, 111; Argonaut
(Washington) (1942), 128–30;
Cairo (first) (1943), 213–25;
Cairo (second) (1943), 263–8;
Casablanca (1943), 164–78;
Hyde Park (1942), 126–8;
Molotov talks (1942), 119–20,
124–5; Placentia Bay (1941) *see*
Placentia Bay summit; and
Potsdam 407–17; Quebec
(1943), 197–200; Quebec
(1944), 310–15, 317; with Stalin
(Moscow) (1942), 138–57; with
Stalin (Tolstoy) (1944), 322–35;
Teheran *see* Teheran
conference; Washington
(Trident) (1943), 187–94; and
Yalta *see* Yalta Conference
Clark Kerr, Archibald, 4, 17, 118,
140, 144, 147, 150–2, 155, 163,
183, 206, 211, 252, 281, 369
Cold War, 348, 418
Colville, John, 341
Combined Development Trust, 315
Comintern, 193
Cooper, Duff, 271
Corsica, 205
Coughlin, Father, 34
Council of Foreign Ministers, 411,
411–12
Cripps, Stafford, 66, 69, 71, 104,
105, 162
Cunningham, Admiral Andrew, 201
Curie, Lauchlin, 107
Curtin, John, 58

Darlan, Admiral François, 159–60,
161; assassination of, 169
Davies, John Paton, 263
Davies, Joseph, 194, 403

Davies, Norman, 295
de Gaulle, Charles, 6, 98, 182, 198,
    387; background, 160; and
    Churchill, 143, 160–1, 172, 174,
    193, 218, 271; and Giraud, 160,
    170, 174–6, 193; meeting with
    Roosevelt/Churchill at
    Casablanca, 171, 172–4; and
    Overlord, 287–8; and Pearl
    Harbor attack, 79–80; policy, 343;
    returns to France as leader,
    288–9; and Roosevelt, 161, 170–1,
    172–3, 288, 387, 398; Stalin's view
    of, 227–8; talks with Stalin, 344–5
Deane, General John, 206, 343
Declaration of Liberated Europe,
    378, 382, 388, 391
Dewey, Thomas, 292
Dietrich, Otto, 72
Dill, Field Marshal John, 54, 86
Djilas, Milovan, 17
Donovan, William, 218, 346
Driberg, Tom, 131
Dulles, Allen, 393
Dumbarton Oaks talks (1944),
    292–3, 347

Early, Steve, 403
eastern Europe: Moscow domination
    of, 413
Eden, Anthony, 14, 15–16, 28, 38,
    75, 101, 278; background and
    character, 87–8; and Churchill,
    88, 104; and Foreign Ministers
    meeting (Moscow) (1943), 206,
    207, 208; and frontier issue, 108,
    109, 119; meeting with Roosevelt
    (1943), 185–6; meeting with
    Stalin (1943), 207; and Molotov
    talks (1942), 120, 121; and
    percentages proposal, 323–4;
    and Polish issue, 294; and post-
    war Germany, 313–14; and
    Potsdam conference, 410; and

Quebec conference, 310; and
    Soviet territorial demands issue,
    105; and Teheran conference,
    238; visit to Moscow (1941),
    87–94; and Yalta, 352, 371, 374
Einstein, Albert, 14
Eisenhower, Dwight, 12, 14, 54, 111,
    133, 134, 161, 174, 178, 197,
    271, 352, 392–3; appointed
    commander of Overlord, 266,
    267, 284
El Alamein, 158, 162
Emmanuel, King Victor, 278
'Europe First' strategy, 96, 132
European Advisory Commission
    (EAC), 278, 343
European Commission, 211, 219

Farouk, King, 376
Final Solution, 303
financial system, post-war 110, 267,
    303, 347 *see also* Bretton Woods
    conference
Finland, 90, 105, 119, 345
First World War, 55
Ford, Henry, 33
Foreign Ministers meeting (Moscow)
    (1943), 205–11
Forrestal, James, 399
France, 343, 346; Anvil landing (later
    Dragoon), 289, 290; invasion of
    see Overlord; occupation zone in
    Germany, 357–8, 361–2, 375,
    381; return of de Gaulle, 288–9;
    second front issue and plans for
    invasion, 103, 111–12, 119, 123,
    124, 198; treaty with Soviet
    Union (1944), 344–5; Vichy,
    159–60, 161, 162, 169, 173–4;
    see also de Gaulle, Charles
Frankfurter, Justice Felix, 62, 316
Free French, 97, 98, 160, 161,
    170–1, 173, 218, 227, 277–8
French Committee of National

Liberation, 198
frontier issue, 101, 103, 105, 107–10,
    111, 118, 119, 119–20, 122,
    185–6, 207–8

George VI, King, 35
Germany: Allied forces offensive, 388;
    offensive in Soviet Union, 44–5,
    55, 64–5, 80, 137, 158, 235
Germany, post-war, 238–9, 306–9, 334;
    Anglo-American differences over
    future occupation of, 278; and
    Morgenthau Plan, 308–9, 312–14,
    318–21, 335, 362; occupation
    zones, 360–1, 378, 418; and
    Potsdam, 416; reparations issue,
    362, 375–6, 382, 415, 416–17;
    and Ruhr, 306, 308, 309, 313;
    Teheran discussions, 238–40, 243,
    256–7; US departmental rivalries,
    306–8; Yalta discussions, 360–2,
    375–6, 378
Giraud, General Henri, 159–60,
    169–70, 172, 174–6, 182, 198
Gloucester, Duke of, 131
Goddard, Paulette, 39
Goebbels, Josef, 81, 388, 398
Göring, Hermann Wilhelm, 82
Goussev, Fedor Tarasovich, 200
Greece, 281, 286, 322, 341–2, 352,
    368; attempt by Communists to
    seize power and defeat
    (1944/45), 338–40
Gromyko, Andrei, 200, 277, 292, 347

Halifax, Lord, 28, 34, 106, 107
Harriman, Averell, 10, 37, 139, 143,
    147, 273, 276, 417; background,
    68; leaves embassy in Moscow,
    417; and Roosevelt, 20–1;
    US/British mission to Moscow
    (1941), 68–72, 118; view of
    Stalin, 16; and Yalta, 373–4
Harriman, Kathy, 369, 379

Harvey, Oliver, 28, 92, 109, 206
Henderson, Loy, 216–17
Herbert, A.P., 112
Himmler, Heinrich, 400
Hirohito, Emperor, 6, 80
Hiss, Alger, 107
Hitler, Adolf, 6, 16, 62, 80–3, 123,
    137, 162, 239, 291, 398
Hobsbawm, Eric, 6
Holmes, Richard, 136
Holocaust, 303, 304
Hong Kong, 222–3, 264
Hopkins, Harry, 39–48, 106, 219,
    289, 307, 316, 341, 387;
    attributes, 40; awards, 407;
    background, 39; and Churchill,
    41–2; and death of son, 274;
    deterioration in health and
    death, 417–18; health
    problems, 40, 113–14, 273;
    meeting with Stalin (1945),
    403–6; mission to Moscow and
    meeting of Stalin (1941), 43–7;
    and Molotov talks, 122, 124;
    and North Africa, 135; personal
    life and marriage, 135–6, 273;
    and Placentia Bay summit, 39,
    56; relations with Russians,
    106–7; resignation from
    government service, 406–7;
    return to favour, 320; and
    Roosevelt, 10, 39–40, 252,
    316–17; and Roosevelt's
    funeral, 397; and Stalin, 16,
    234; stomach operation, 273,
    275; and Teheran conference,
    2, 4, 232, 234, 252; and
    Truman, 399; visits to Britain,
    41–2, 113–14, 132, 133–4;
    wartime performance, 40; and
    Yalta, 360
Hopkins, Louise (wife), 135
Hopkins, Robert (son), 274, 371–2
Hopkins, Stephen (son), 274

Hull, Cordell, 56, 57, 60, 92, 97, 106, 123, 204, 292, 293, 317; background, 205; and Foreign Ministers meeting in Moscow (1943), 206, 208–9; and Jewish question, 304; and post-war Germany, 307, 309; resignation, 320
Hungary, 323, 324, 403
Hurley, Patrick, 163, 347
Hyde Park meeting (1942), 126–8

Ibn Saud, King, 376, 385–6
Ickes, Harold, 32
imperial issue, 57–60, 110–11, 228
India, 228
Indochina, 228, 367
Inonu, Ismet, 267
International Bank for Reconstruction and Development (later World Bank), 303
International Monetary Fund, 303
Iran, 260
Ismay, Hastings 'Pug', 11, 69, 71, 113, 128
Italy, 188, 189, 200, 205–6, 236, 388, 411; Anzio landing, 270, 275, 277, 282; government of, 278; overthrowing of Mussolini, 197; reduction of US forces due to Anvil landing in France, 289–90

Jackson, Robert, 6, 177
Jacob, Ian, 53
Japan, 6, 55, 62, 76, 97, 168, 366; attack on Pearl Harbor, 78–80; decision by Stalin to enter Pacific war, 366–7, 373–4, 394, 402, 405; and Pacific war, 197, 235, 366, 388; and Soviet Union, 7, 47, 209; surrender of, 417; taking of Singapore, 103; US declaration of war against, 78; war against China, 35, 76, 315

Jews, 6, 169, 185, 303–4, 386

Kagonovich, Lazar, 331
Katyn massacre, 184, 276
Kennan, George, 16, 18, 337, 338, 342, 383
Keynes, John Maynard, 38, 110, 303, 311
Khrushchev, Nikita, 26
Kimball, Warren, 13, 57
King, Admiral Ernest, 53, 122, 132, 134, 166–7, 189, 220, 291, 341, 355
Kissinger, Henry, 35
Koiso, General Kuniaki, 291
Krock, Arthur, 318
Kurile Islands, 366

Laval, Pierre, 159, 161
Le Hand, Marguerite 'Missy', 15, 23, 31–2
League of Nations, 362
Leahy, Admiral, 262, 277, 288
Leathers, Lord, 166
Lend-Lease, 32, 38, 55, 60, 276, 305, 311, 312, 317, 370, 402, 404, 417
Leros, 229
Libya, 130
Liddell Hart, Basil, 178
Lindberg, Charles, 33
Lindemann, Professor, 38, 50
Lippmann, Walter, 40, 403
Litvinov, 69, 70, 73, 98, 121, 122, 163, 200, 206, 208
London Poles, 184–5, 186, 208, 257, 259, 271, 275, 281, 293–5, 296–7, 326–7, 363, 367, 389
Long, Breckinridge, 304
Lublin Committee, 193, 294, 295, 296, 297, 301, 326–7, 330, 344, 345, 352, 363, 367, 368, 370–1, 391, 406, 415

MacArthur, Douglas, 105, 291, 336

McCloy, John, 283, 305
McIntire, Ross, 279, 280, 336
Macmillan, Harold, 160, 165
Maisky, Ivan, 42, 43, 44, 74, 89, 92, 120, 137, 195, 200
Manchuria, 347, 366, 374
Manhattan Project, 158, 413
Mao Zedong, 6, 347, 418
Marshall, George, 53–4, 219–20; comments on strikes, 272; invasion of France issue, 55, 115, 129, 135, 188, 189, 190; and North Africa, 131, 132–3; and Overlord, 220, 241, 265–6, 267; and Pacific war, 131–2, 190; put in overall military charge, 203; rise of, 96; view of Stalin, 229; and Yalta, 355
Marshall Islands, 169
Merrill, Frank, 199
'Merrill's Marauders', 265
Midway, Battle of, 131–2
Mikołajczyk, Stanislaw, 293, 294, 295, 296, 300, 326–8, 333–4, 338, 371, 392, 406
Mitrokhin, Vasili, 106, 107
Moldavia, 105
Molotov, Vyacheslav, 4, 10, 18, 65, 67, 155, 298; background and character, 117–18; and Churchill's visit to Moscow (1942), 139; and Foreign Ministers meeting (1943), 206, 210; and Hitler, 123; and post-war arrangement discussions, 323–4; and Teheran summit, 230; and Truman, 399–400; visit to Washington (1942), 121–4; visits Britain and talks with Churchill (1942), 117–21, 124–5; and Warsaw Rising, 298; and Yalta conference, 365, 367, 372, 375
Monnet, Jean, 170

Montgomery, Bernard, 138–9, 158, 162, 267, 285, 310, 392
Moran, Lord (was Wilson), 100, 139, 165, 220, 238, 248, 310, 330, 368
Morgenthau, Henry, 14, 302–3, 305, 306–7, 308, 311, 312, 317, 318, 319–21, 395, 417
Morgenthau Plan, 308–9, 312–14, 318–21, 335, 362
Morrison, Herbert, 162
Moscow: joint aid mission to (1941), 64, 67–72; meeting between Stalin and Churchill (1942), 138–57
Mosley, Oswald, 255
Mountbatten, Admiral Lord Louis, 127, 199
Murphy, Robert, 182
Murrow, Edward, 11, 78
Mussolini, Benito, 6, 37, 76, 82, 197

Neutrality Acts, 32, 75
New Guinea, 169
Noguès, General, 169
North Africa, 95, 96, 103, 173; Allied attack on, 161–2; Churchill's call for invasion of and US agreement, 96, 102, 129, 131, 133, 134–5; Jews in, 169; *see also* Torch operation
Northern Sumatra, 199

Orwell, George, 287
Oumansky, Constantin, 71
Overlord, 215, 236, 282–3; advance, 285; British-US rows over, 220–1; and Churchill, 209, 210, 215, 237, 245, 246, 249–50, 270, 277–8, 282–3, 284; command of, 265–6; and de Gaulle, 287–8; debates over timing of, 199, 209–10, 235, 271–2;

Overlord – *continued*
discussions of at Teheran, 236–7, 241, 245–6, 247, 249–50; Eisenhower appointed commander, 266, 267; launching of, 284–5; and Stalin, 236–7, 245–6, 249–50

Pacific war, 131–2, 134, 163, 182–3, 188, 235, 275, 310, 336, 388; Soviet entry into and Stalin's conditions, 366–7, 373–4, 381, 394, 402, 405
Papandreou, George, 339
Partsalides, 339
Pasvolsky, Leo, 292, 347
Patton, George, 54
Pavlov (interpreter), 253
Pearl Harbor: attack on (1941), 7, 8, 13, 78
Pendergast, Tom, 409
Perkins, Frances, 13, 29, 350
Pétain, Marshal, 159, 160
Philippines, 96, 97
Placentia Bay summit (1941), 37–63, 75; differences of intention and policy, 50; disagreements over imperial issue, 57–60; groundwork for, 39–48; impressions made, 52–3; lack of commitment of US delegation, 53, 63; negotiating Atlantic Charter, 56–61; religious service, 51–2; US and British delegations, 53–4
Poland, 90, 92, 185–6, 208, 258, 293–7, 389–92, 399, 404–5, 406; arrest of sixteen non-Communist figures, 389, 405, 406; discussions at Teheran conference, 240–1, 257, 258, 259, 328, 329; discussions at Yalta, 363–4, 365–6, 367–8, 370–1, 372–3, 374–5, 379, 381, 382, 384, 389, 391;

discussions with Mikołajczyk, 326–30; election issue, 373, 375, 379, 418; expansion of territory after border changes, 345; frontier issue and Curzon Line, 119, 120, 240, 257, 259, 281, 293, 327–30, 333, 337, 366, 375, 379, 415, 416, 417; government issue, 275, 281, 294–5, 337–8, 352, 370–1, 372–3, 375, 379, 389, 391–2, 406; and Lublin Committee *see* Lublin Committee; and Potsdam, 415, 416, 417; proclaiming of Lublin Committee as provisional government, 345; Warsaw Rising, 295, 296, 297–301, 326, 331, 337; *see also* London Poles
Polish Committee of National Liberation *see* Lublin Committee
Portal, Charles, 53, 189
Potomac, 36
Potsdam conference (1945), 401, 407–17, 418
Pound, Admiral Dudley, 53, 189, 201
Powell, Anthony, 112–13
PQ-17 Arctic Convoy, 154
Prince of Wales, 86
Purvis, Arthur, 50

Quebec summits: (1943), 197–200; (1944), 310–15, 317

Red Army, 17, 64, 65, 117, 205, 280, 293, 358
Reed, John, 147
Reynolds, David, 127, 215
Rhodes, 203, 206, 220
Ribbentrop, Joachim von, 123, 155, 162
Rokossovsky, 296, 297
Romania, 90, 119, 281, 286, 297, 322, 345, 388, 391, 403, 411, 413
Rommel, Erwin, 103, 130, 137
Roosevelt, Anna *see* Boettinger, Anna

Roosevelt, Eleanor, 23, 24, 396
Roosevelt, Elliott, 3, 9, 23, 37, 47, 49, 51, 58, 59, 60, 170, 172, 174–8, 219, 224, 227–8, 242, 246, 251, 261, 266, 336, 341
Roosevelt, Franklin D., 1, 418–19; accused by Stalin of seeking a secret peace with Germany, 393–4; affair with Lucy Mercer, 23; anti-imperialism, 8, 15, 57, 58–60, 172, 219, 228; approach to war, 15; and Burma offensive, 263, 314–15; and Chiang Kai-shek/China, 168, 191, 219, 222, 223, 264–5, 314–15; coldness of, 15; confidantes, 10; confined to wheelchair, 9; and de Gaulle, 161, 170–1, 172–3, 288, 387, 398; death and funeral, 396–8; and death of mother, 31; differences between Churchill, Stalin and 18–30; and domestic politics, 13, 27, 272, 273, 290–1, 291; entering of US into war issue, 32–6, 62, 75; family, 22, 23; family residence, 24–5; and frontier issue, 108, 109–10, 111, 185–6; health problems, 2, 26, 31, 181, 194, 273, 279–80, 282, 291–2, 310, 336–7, 350, 368, 387, 395; humour of, 20–1; and Japan, 76; and Jews, 303–5, 386; marriage, 23–4; meeting with King Ibn Saud, 385–6; and North Africa, 131, 135, 136; not wanting US involvement in reconstituting West European countries after war, 278–9, 346, 358; and Overlord, 237, 245, 284–5; personality, 13–15; physical deterioration, 350; and Polish issue, 293, 328, 337–8, 345, 363–4, 368, 373, 389, 391; political career, 9; and post-polio syndrome, 279–80; and post-war Germany, 256–7, 307–8, 308, 314, 319–20, 321, 360, 375–6; post-war world vision, 250; and presidential election (1944), 258, 292, 320, 336; recreational activities, 21, 25–6; relationship with Churchill, 2, 8, 12–13, 95, 127, 179, 192, 216, 219, 224–5, 289, 316–17; relationship with Stalin, 2, 8, 17–18, 106, 111, 194–6, 216, 255–6, 276, 346, 383, 393–4; and second front issue, 111–12, 159; and smoking, 26, 282; and Stalin's entry into Pacific war, 366–7; and Torch, 159, 162; and unconditional surrender statement, 176–8; and United Nations, 186, 243, 259, 292–3, 362–3; view of Russians, 29; and Vichy France, 159–60, 161, 162, 169, 173–4; view of Stalin, 246; and Warsaw Rising, 299, 300; working methods and style, 19
  SUMMITS/CONFERENCES:
    Arcadia (1941–2), 85–7, 94–102, 103, 111; Cairo (first) (1943), 213–25; Cairo (second) (1943), 263–8; Casablanca (1943), 164–71; Hyde Park (1942) 126–8; Placentia Bay *see* Placentia Bay; Quebec (1943), 197–200; Quebec (1944), 310–15; and Teheran *see* Teheran conference; Washington (1943), 187–92; and Yalta *see* Yalta conference
Roosevelt, James, 16, 24
Roosevelt Jr, Franklin, 37
Roosevelt Jr, Theodore, 285
Roundhammer, 190
Roundup, 114–16, 167

Rutherfurd, Lucy (née Mercer), 23, 282

St Pierre islands, 97
San Francisco conference (1945), 398, 401–2
Saudi Arabia, 386–7
Scandinavia, 154
Schlesinger, Arthur, 243
second front issue, 66–7, 103, 111–12, 119, 122–3, 124–5, 127–8, 141, 143, 145, 147, 167, 188, 195; see also Overlord; Roundup; Sledgehammer
Second World War, 5–6; death toll, 5; impact of, 5–6; progress of, 86, 101, 103, 131, 158, 197, 203, 205, 295, 310, 342, 388
Selassie, Haile, 52, 376
Shaposhnikov, Marshal, 138
Sherwood, Robert, 14, 75, 381, 387, 397
Sicily, 167, 184, 188; invasion of, 189, 197, 201
Sikorski, General, 121, 184, 293
Singapore, 96, 101, 103
Sledgehammer, 114–16, 127, 129, 131, 132, 134, 136, 190
Snow, C.P., 22
Sorge, Richard, 47
Soviet Union, 42–3; British/US aid and armaments to, 42–3, 64, 65, 67, 72–3, 163, 276; dissolution of Comintern, 193; entry into Pacific war, 366–7, 373–4, 381, 394, 402, 405; German offensive, 44–5, 55, 64–5, 80, 137, 158, 235; importance of survival to Britain/US, 65; and Lend-Lease, 276–7, 402; pact with Hitler (1939), 65, 72, 155; post-war reconstruction and US, 276–7; post-war territorial demands, 89–90, 101, 103, 105;
relations with Britain, 73–4, 118; taking over of states, 342–3, 345; see also Stalin, Josef
Stalin, Josef, 207, 418; accuses Roosevelt of seeking a secret peace with Germany, 393–4; appearance, 17; and atom bomb, 413–14; background, 15, 17; and China, 217–18, 405; and collectivisation, 154; conditions for entering Pacific war, 366–7, 373–4, 402; confidantes, 10; and death of Roosevelt, 397–8; family, 22, 23; fear of Germany, 239–40, 243; and Greece, 368; health problems, 26; and Japan, 7, 209; and Jews, 377; and London Poles, 184–5, 281; meeting with Churchill (1942), 138–57; meeting with Eden (1941), 89–94; meeting with US/British envoys to discuss aid (1941), 69–71; meetings with Hopkins, 45–7, 403–6; and Overlord, 236–7, 245–6, 249–50, 285; pact with Germany (1939), 65, 72, 155; and Pearl Harbor attack, 79; personality and style, 15–26, 19, 20, 45; and Polish issue, 259, 294, 295–6, 297, 327, 328, 334, 345, 363, 368, 373, 375, 382, 391, 392, 404–5; political career, 9; and politics, 28; and post-war arrangements issue, 89–92, 334; and post-war Germany, 256–7, 334, 361, 362, 375–6, 416; and Potsdam see Potsdam conference; purges, 9, 10, 15; recreational pursuits and tastes, 21, 26; relationship with Churchill, 1, 2–4, 12–13, 17–18, 73–5, 146, 149–50, 152–3, 155, 179, 204, 216, 224–5, 316–17, 325–6, 335, 369–70, 410; relationship

with Roosevelt, 2, 8, 17–18, 106, 111, 194–6, 216, 255–6, 276, 346, 383, 393–4; residences, 25; and second front issue, 66–7, 136–7, 141–2, 145, 147, 183, 195; sense of humour, 335; and smoking, 26, 408; summit with Churchill (Tolstoy) (1944), 322–6; talks with de Gaulle, 344–5; and Teheran *see* Teheran conference; *Time* Man of the Year, 180; and Torch, 143, 152, 156; and United Nations, 362–3, 405; view of Churchill, 17–18; view of de Gaulle, 227–8; view of Roosevelt, 17–18; and Warsaw Rising, 297, 299, 301, 331; working methods, 19, 20; and Yalta *see* Yalta conference

Stalin, Svetlana, 23, 153

Stalingrad, Battle of, 164, 180

Standley, Rear Admiral William, 73, 183

Stark, Harold, 53, 55

Steinhardt, Laurence, 45, 46, 69

Stettinius, Edward, 101, 292, 320, 340, 348, 352, 371

Stilwell, Joseph, 15, 115, 168, 191–2, 263, 265, 315

Stimson, Henry, 14, 29, 44, 97, 128, 134, 198, 306–7, 308, 309, 317–18, 395, 417

Strang, William, 206

Suckley, Margaret, 23, 25, 126, 350

Teheran conference (1943), 1–4, 7, 16, 67, 218, 226–62, 272, 306, 381; arrival of Big Three, 230–1; Chiefs of Staff meeting, 241–2; Churchill's birthday celebrations, 250–4; compound staying at, 231–2; discussions on Poland, 240–1, 257, 258, 259, 328, 329; discussions on post-war

arrangements, 247; discussions on post-war Germany, 238–40, 243, 256–7; goading of Churchill by Roosevelt to win over Stalin, 3–4, 255–6, 359; group photographs, 244–5; isolation felt by Churchill, 238, 256; meetings between Stalin and Roosevelt, 226–8, 242–3, 249, 258–9; and Overlord, 236–7, 241, 245–6, 247, 249–50; talks between Stalin and Churchill, 239–41

Thompson, Walter, 101, 139

Thorez, Maurice, 346

Three Demands, 168

Tito, Marshal, 278, 289, 324, 332, 338, 345, 368, 379, 382, 402, 413

Tobruk disaster, 130, 131, 187

Togliatti, Palmiero, 278, 289, 346

Tojo, General, 6, 35

Tolstoy summit (Moscow) (1944), 322–35

Toose, Adam, 80

Torch operation, 136, 143, 152, 156, 158–9, 161–2, 169

Trident *see* Washington summit

Trotsky, Leon, 9

Truman, Harry, 30, 73, 291, 397, 398–9, 403–4, 418; background, 398–9; first meeting with Stalin, 409; and Polish issue, 399; and Potsdam *see* Potsdam conference; relationship with Churchill, 408

Truman Doctrine, 340

trusteeships, 228

'Tube Alloys', 127

Tully, Grace, 194

Tunisia, 187–8

Turkey, 169, 181, 236, 267

Ukraine, 72, 227

unconditional surrender doctrine, 176–8, 238–9, 393, 412

United Nation Pact, 97–8

United Nations, 60, 336, 353, 362; discussions at Yalta, 371, 372, 379; Roosevelt's vision and proposal for, 186, 243, 259; and San Francisco conference, 401–2; seats on, 292–3; voting system and veto, 293, 314, 347–8, 364–5, 382, 405

United Nations Declaration (1942), 365

United States: aid to Soviet Union, 64, 73, 163, 276; declaration of on war by Hitler, 82–4; declaration of war on Japan, 78; entering of war issue and opposition, 32–6, 62, 75; help given to Britain before entering war, 32–3, 35; military strength, 35–6; Pearl Harbor attack (1941), 7, 8, 13, 78; relations with China, 35; see also Roosevelt, Franklin D.; Truman, Harry

Vandenberg, Senator Arthur, 34

Vichy France, 159–60, 161, 162, 169, 173–4

Viénot, Pierre, 287

Voroshilov, Marshal, 93, 140, 148, 230, 241

Vyshinsky, Andrei, 2, 206, 218, 298, 331, 358, 388, 406

Wallace, Henry, 28

Wallonia, 186

War Cabinet, 104, 110, 119

Warsaw Rising, 295, 296, 297–301, 326, 331, 337

Washington summit (Trident) (1943), 187–92, 194

Wavell, General Archibald, 74, 96

Wedemeyer, Albert, 129, 315

Welles, Sumner, 12, 29, 37, 56, 58, 105–6, 107, 111, 204–5

Wells, H.G., 18

White, Harry Dexter, 107, 110, 205–6, 302–3, 305, 308–9

Willkie, Wendell, 33, 42, 162–3, 168, 191

Wilson, Charles see Moran, Lord

Wilson, Edmund, 29

Wilson, Theodore, 53

Wilson, Woodrow, 57

Winant, John, 43, 78, 120, 278

Windsor, Duke of, 316

Wingate, Orde, 199

Yalta conference (1945), 7, 348, 349–84, 387–8; aims of leaders, 353; communiqué issued, 378–9; demonisation of, 380–1; discussions on Pacific War, 366–7; discussions on Poland, 363–4, 365–6, 367–8, 370–1, 372–3, 374–5, 379, 381, 382, 384, 389, 391; discussions on post-war Germany, 360–2; 375–6, 378; discussions on United Nations, 362–3, 371, 372, 379; journey to, 349–55; meetings between Roosevelt and Stalin, 357; photographs taken, 371; residences stayed in, 355–6; Roosevelt's health and behaviour, 368–9, 378, 383; and Soviet entry into Pacific war and trade-off of interests in China, 366–7, 373–4, 381

Yugoslavia, 242, 278, 324, 332, 338, 345, 368, 379, 382, 389, 402, 413

Zhukov, Marshal, 297, 406